107

NOTABLE AMERICAN NOVELISTS

REVISED EDITION

MAGILL'S CHOICE

NOTABLE AMERICAN NOVELISTS

REVISED EDITION

Volume 2
John Gardner — Flannery O'Connor
505 – 1014

edited by
CARL ROLLYSON
BARUCH COLLEGE, CITY UNIVERSITY OF NEW YORK

SALEM PRESS, INC.

Pasadena, California   Hackensack, New Jersey

Some essays in these volumes originally appeared in *Critical Survey of
Long Fiction, Revised Edition,* 2000. New material has been added.

∞ The paper used in these volumes conforms to the American National Standard for Permanence of Paper for Printed Library Materials,
Z39.48-1992 (R1997).

Library of Congress Cataloging-in-Publication Data

Notable American novelists / edited by Carl Rollyson.
   p. cm. — (Magill's choice)
   Includes bibliographical references and index.
   ISBN 978-1-58765-393-3 (set : alk. paper) — ISBN 978-1-58765-394-0
(vol. 1 : alk. paper) — ISBN 978-1-58765-395-7 (vol. 2 : alk. paper) —
ISBN 978-1-58765-396-4 (vol. 3 : alk. paper) 1. Novelists, American—
Biography—Dictionaries. 2. American fiction—Bio-bibliography—Dic-
tionaries. 3. American fiction—Dictionaries. I. Rollyson, Carl E. (Carl
Edmund)

PS371.N68 2007
813.009'0003—dc22
[B]

2007018542

First printing

PRINTED IN CANADA

Contents—Volume 2

Complete List of Contents

Contents—Volume 1

Contents—Volume 2

Contents—Volume 3

Complete List of Contents

NOTABLE AMERICAN NOVELISTS

NOVELISTS

REVISED EDITION

John Gardner

Born: Batavia, New York; July 21, 1933
Died: Susquehanna, Pennsylvania; September 14, 1982

Principal long fiction • *The Resurrection*, 1966; *The Wreckage of Agathon*, 1970; *Grendel*, 1971; *The Sunlight Dialogues*, 1972; *Nickel Mountain: A Pastoral Novel*, 1973; *October Light*, 1976; *In the Suicide Mountains*, 1977; *Freddy's Book*, 1980; *Mickelsson's Ghosts*, 1982; *"Stillness" and "Shadows,"* 1986 (with Nicholas Delbanco).

Other literary forms • As a writer, John Gardner was as versatile as he was prolific. In addition to his novels, he published an epic poem (*Jason and Medeia*, 1973), two collections of short stories, four books for children, poetry, and reviews. During the early 1960's, when Gardner was a struggling assistant professor with a growing backlog of unpublished fiction and rejection slips, he turned to more academic pursuits. Although some of this work is distinctly scholarly in nature, much of it is directed at a less specialized audience and is designed to make the literature more accessible and more understandable to the general reader or undergraduate student: thus Gardner's translations, or modernized versions, of medieval poetry, a textbook-anthology of fiction, a popular biography of Geoffrey Chaucer, his controversial attack on the contemporary arts and criticism, *On Moral Fiction* (published in 1978 but, like his Chaucer books, begun more than ten years earlier), and a book of advice for young writers, *The Art of Fiction* (1984). Gardner also wrote a number of plays for National Public Radio's "Earplay" series and several opera librettos (one of which, *Rumpelstiltskin*, 1979, was professionally staged by the Opera Company of Philadelphia).

Achievements • At a time when the line between popular and innovative fiction was often considered, in critic Raymond Federman's word, "uncrossable," Gardner managed to make his mark in both camps. Although his first novel, *The Resurrection*, was indifferently received, his second, *The Wreckage of Agathon*, which deals with law and order in ancient Sparta, gained a small following as a result of its relevance to the Vietnam war and the Nixon administration. *Grendel*, a parodic retelling of *Beowulf* (c. 1000) from the monster's point of view, was widely praised and in its paperback edition became as popular as *The Catcher in the Rye* (J. D. Salinger, 1951) was during the 1950's. Its success established Gardner's reputation as both an entertaining storyteller and an innovative parodist, a view that was confirmed by the publication of *The King's Indian: Stories and Tales* in 1974. His next three novels all became best-sellers: *The Sunlight Dialogues, Nickel Mountain*, and *October Light*, which won the 1977 National Book Critics Circle Award for fiction. Among his other awards and honors were a Woodrow Wilson Fellowship (1955), a Danforth Fellowship (1970-1973), an award from the National Endowment for the Arts (1972), a Guggenheim Fellowship (1973-1974), an American Academy of Arts and Letters prize for fiction (1975), the Armstrong Prize for his radio play, *The Temptation Game* (1977), and the 1978 Lamport Foundation award for his essay "Moral Fiction."

Upon the publication of the full text of *On Moral Fiction* in 1978, Gardner became a center of literary attention. His plainspoken criticism of fashionable pessimism in the contemporary arts and his generally negative remarks concerning individual writers led to an appearance on *The Dick Cavett Show* in May, 1978, a cover story in *The New York Times Magazine* in August, 1979, a special issue of the journal *Fiction International* devoted to the question of "moral" art, as well as the censure of those who saw Gardner as a reactionary and the praise of others who quickly adopted him as a spokesman for a more traditional approach to fiction.

Biography • John Champlin Gardner, Jr., was born on July 21, 1933, in the western New York community of Batavia, the setting of *The Resurrection, The Sunlight Dialogues*, and a number of short stories. Strongly influenced by his father, a farmer and lay preacher, and his mother, an English teacher, Gardner, nicknamed Bud (Welsh for poet), began writing stories when he was eight years old and reading his work aloud to the family in the evening. The death of his younger brother, Gilbert, in a farm accident on April 4, 1945, seems to have been the most formative event in Gardner's life. He felt responsible for his brother's death, which he fictionalized in the story "Redemption" (1977), and as a result became deeply introspective. His mother suggested that Gilbert's death may also account for her son's remarkable energy and productivity, as if he wished to live both his own life and his brother's. During his high school years, Gardner commuted to the Eastman School of Music in nearby Rochester, where he took French horn lessons. He attended DePauw University for two years, majoring in chemistry, and then, following his marriage to Joan Patterson, a cousin, on June 6, 1953, transferred to Washington University, where, under the tutelage of Jarvis Thurston, he began writing *Nickel Mountain*. From 1955 to 1958, Gardner attended the University of Iowa; at first he studied at the Writers Workshop (his master's thesis and doctoral dissertation were both creative rather than scholarly: one a collection of stories, the other a novel, *The Old Men*) but later switched to the study of Anglo-Saxon and medieval literature under the guidance of John C. McGalliard.

Following his study at Iowa, Gardner held faculty appointments at various colleges and universities: Oberlin College (1958-1959); Chico State University (1959-1962), where he coedited *MSS* and the student literary review *Selection*; San Francisco State University, where he translated the alliterative *Morte d'Arthure* and the works of the Gawain-Poet and began writing *The Resurrection, The Sunlight Dialogues*, and a study of Chaucer; Southern Illinois University (1965-1976), including visiting professorships at the University of Detroit (1970), Northwestern University (1973), and Bennington College (1975-1976), a sabbatical in England (1971), and a month-long tour of Japan for the United States Information Service (September-October, 1974); Skidmore and Williams Colleges (1977); George Mason University (1977-1978); and, from 1978 until his death, the State University of New York at Binghamton, where he directed the writing program.

Especially significant in Gardner's biography is the period from 1976 through 1978, when *October Light* won popular and critical acclaim. During that time, Gardner lectured on moral fiction at campuses across the country, and his opera *Rumpelstiltskin* premiered in Lexington, Kentucky. Then Gardner's life took a darker turn: the breakup of his first marriage; a plagiarism charge leveled against him for his Chaucer biography, a charge that for some reason made its way into the pages of *Newsweek* magazine; a successful operation for intestinal cancer; and the uproar over *On Moral Fiction*, as well as the often hostile reviews of *Freddy's Book* and *Mickelsson's Ghosts*. Until their amicable divorce in 1982, Gardner lived with his second wife, the poet L. M. (Liz) Rosenberg, in Susquehanna, Pennsylvania, where he became active in the Lau-

rel Street Theatre both as an actor
and as a writer. He died in a motorcycle accident on September 14, 1982,
a few days before he was to marry
Susan Thornton of Rochester, New
York. At the time of his death, Gardner had been working (as was his
habit) on a variety of projects: operas,
radio plays, a revival of his literary
journal *MSS*, a television talk show on
the arts, a book of advice for young
writers (*The Art of Fiction*), a translation of *Gilgamesh* (a poem that figures prominently in *The Sunlight Dialogues*), and the novel *Shadows*.

©Joel Gardner

Analysis • John Gardner is a difficult
writer to classify. He was alternately
a realist and a fabulist, a novelist of
ideas and a writer who maintained
that characters and human situations
are always more important than
philosophy. He was, as well, an academically inclined New Novelist
whose work is formally innovative, sty-
listically extravagant, openly parodic, and highly allusive; yet, at the same time, he was
an accessible, popular storyteller, one whom some critics, in the wake of *On Moral Fiction*, have labeled a reactionary traditionalist. It is perhaps best to think of Gardner
not as a writer who belongs to any one school but instead as a writer who, in terms of
style, subject, and moral vision, mediates between the various extremes of innovation and tradition, freedom and order, individual and society. He employed the
metafictionist's narrative tricks, for example, not to show that fiction—and, by extension, life—is mere artifice, meaningless play, but to put those tricks to some higher
purpose. His fiction raises a familiar but still urgent question: How is humankind to
act in a seemingly inhospitable world where chance and uncertainty appear to have
rendered all traditional values worthless?

As different as his characters are in most outward aspects, they are similar in one
important way: They are idealists who feel betrayed when their inherited vision of
harmony and purpose crumbles beneath the weight of modern incoherence. After
being betrayed, they abandon their childlike ideals and embrace the existentialist
position that Gardner deplores for its rationalist assumptions and pessimistic moral
relativism. His antidote to the modern malaise in general and Jean-Paul Sartre's
"nausea" in particular is a twentieth century version of the heroic ideal: common
heroes—fathers and husbands, farmers and professors, for example—who intuitively understand that whatever the odds against them, they must act as if they can
protect those whom they love. Instead of pure and powerful knights dedicated to a
holy quest, Gardner's heroes are confused, sometimes ridiculous figures who learn
to overcome their feelings of betrayal and find their strength in love, memory, and
forgiveness. Choosing to act responsibly, they achieve a certain measure of human

dignity. In effect, the choice these characters face is a simple one: either to affirm "the buzzing blooming confusion" of life, as Gardner, quoting William James, calls it, or to deny it. Whereas the existentialist finds in that confusion meaningless abundance and historical discontinuity, Gardner posits meaningful variety and an interconnectedness that assumes value and makes the individual a part of, not apart from, the human and natural worlds in which he or she lives.

To find, or imagine, these connections is the role Gardner assigns to the artist. This view, propounded at length in *On Moral Fiction*, clearly puts Gardner at odds with other contemporary writers of innovative fiction who, he claims, too readily and uncritically accept the views of Sartre, Sigmund Freud, Ludwig Wittgenstein, and other twentieth century pessimists. Art, Gardner maintains, ought not merely to reflect life as it is but also should portray life as it should be. This does not mean that Gardner approves of simple-minded affirmations, for he carefully distinguishes "true" artists from those who simplify complex moral issues, as well as from those who, like William H. Gass, sidestep such issues entirely by creating "linguistic sculpture" in which only the "surface texture" is important.

Believing that art does indeed affect life and accepting Percy Bysshe Shelley's conception of the artist as legislator for all humankind, Gardner calls for a moral fiction that provides "valid models for imitation, eternal verities worth keeping in mind, and a benevolent vision of the possible" that will cause the reader to feel uneasy about his or her failings and limitations and stimulate him or her to act virtuously. Moral fiction, however, is not didactic; rather, it involves a search for truth. The author "gropes" for meaning in the act of writing and revising his story; then, by creating suspense, he devises for the reader a parallel experience. The meaning that author and reader discover in Gardner's work emphasizes the importance of rejecting existential isolation and accepting one's place in the human community, the "common herd" as Gardner calls it in one story. This meaning is not so much rational and intellectual as intuitive and emotional, less a specific message than a feeling—as is entirely appropriate in the case of a writer who defines fiction as "an enormously complex language."

Despite their very different settings—modern Batavia, New York, and ancient Sparta—Gardner's first two published novels, *The Resurrection* and *The Wreckage of Agathon*, share a number of common features—main characters who are professional philosophers, for example—and also share one fault: Both are overrich in the sense that they include too many undeveloped points that seem to lead nowhere and only tend to clutter the narrative.

The Resurrection • *The Resurrection* is a fairly straightforward, realistic novel about the ways in which its main character, James Chandler, confronts the fact of death. His disease, leukemia, involves the mindless proliferation of lymph cells and so reflects the universe itself, which may be, as Chandler speculates, similarly chaotic and purposeless. Philosophy does not at first provide Chandler with a Boethian consolation because he, as a distinctly modern man, suspects that philosophy may be nothing more than a meaningless technique, a self-enclosed game. The novel thus raises the question of the purpose of philosophy, art, literature, and even medicine. Chandler's mother knows that the job of philosophers is to help people like her understand what their experiences and their world mean. Meaning, however, is precisely what contemporary philosophy generally denies and what Chandler wisely struggles to find. His breakthrough occurs when he realizes Immanuel Kant's fundamental error, the failure to see that moral and aesthetic affirmations are interconnected and need not—or should not—necessitate that the individual who makes the affirmation be entirely disinterested; that is, the affirmation may have—or should have—some practical application, some usefulness.

Sharing this knowledge becomes rather difficult for Chandler. His sympathetic and loving wife, Marie, is too practical-minded to understand him. Nineteen-year-old Viola Stacey, who, torn between cynicism and her childlike "hunger for absolute goodness," falls in love with Chandler, misinterprets his writing as an escape from reality precipitated by his intense physical suffering. More interesting is John Horne, who, like Chandler, is a terminal patient. According to Horne, a believer in legal technique, love is illusion and humanity is composed of clowns who act with no reason for their behavior. Like Viola, he assumes that art is an escape from life, or an "atonement" for one's failures and mistakes. Although he is interested in philosophy and acquainted with Chandler's published works, his endless prattling precludes Chandler's sharing the discovery with him. However, Chandler does finally, if indirectly, communicate his vision. By putting it to some practical use (he dies trying to help Viola), Chandler finds what Horne never does: something or someone worth dying for, some vision worth affirming. "It was not the beauty of the world one must affirm," he suddenly understands, "but *the world*, the buzzing blooming confusion itself." Understanding that life is what drives humanity to art and philosophy, to fashion a life for oneself and others that is ennobling and useful (realistically idealistic, Gardner seems to suggest), Chandler fights down his physical and philosophical nausea. His vision worth perpetuating, he lives on—is resurrected—in the memories of those whom he loved, and thus for whom he died.

The Wreckage of Agathon • Early in *The Resurrection*, Gardner quotes the British philosopher R. G. Collingwood: "History is a process . . . in which the things that are destroyed are brought into existence. Only it is easier to see their destruction than to see their construction, because it does not take long." Like Gardner, James Chandler in *The Resurrection* affirms Collingwood's optimistic position, a position which the title character of *The Wreckage of Agathon* unwisely rejects. Insofar as he stands in opposition to the law-and-order society established in Sparta by the tyrant Lykourgus, the seer Agathon is an appealing figure. No system built solely upon reason, least of all one as inflexible as Sparta's, is adequate to the variety and complexity of life, Gardner implies, but this does not mean that the only alternative is the nihilism espoused by Agathon, who had "spent so much time seeing through men's lies he'd forgotten what plain truth looked like." Having once been a lover of truth and beauty, Agathon ("the good") now mocks them; choosing to embody "the absolute idea of *No*," he is the one who sees the wreckage that was, is, and will be, the one who dismisses all art and ideals as mere illusions.

Whereas Chandler learns to put his philosophy to some use, Agathon comes to value his ideas more highly than people. Unlike Chandler, who eventually accepts death, mutability, and human limitations and in this way transcends them, Agathon refuses to see wreckage as being part of life; for him it is the ultimate fact. The cause of Agathon's pessimism is not cosmic but personal; it is the result of his repeated betrayals of his friends, his wife, and his lover. This is the knowledge that haunts Agathon, however much he tries to hide it behind his leering clown's mask, leading him to believe that to be alive is necessarily to be a threat to others. Although he dies of the plague, Agathon's real sickness is of the soul: the inability to believe in love and human dignity as actual possibilities. The fact that they are real is clearly shown in the characters of his friend Dorkis, leader of the Helot revolt, and his young disciple Demodokos, whose prison journal alternates with Agathon's (together they make up Gardner's novel). Demodokos, the "Peeker" to Agathon's "Seer," represents that childlike faith and goodness of heart that the disillusioned Seer has renounced. Patient, understanding (if not completely comprehending), and above all committed to others, the Peeker is the one who, for all his naïveté, or perhaps because of it, serves as Gardner's hero.

Grendel • Agathon reappears in Gardner's next novel as the perversely likable narrator of *Grendel*, a retelling of *Beowulf* from the monster's distinctly modern point of view. In his 1970 essay, "Fulgentius's *Expositio Vergiliana Continentia*," Gardner argues that the *Beowulf* poet used his three monsters as perversions of those virtues affirmed by Vergil in the *Aeneid* (c. 29-19 B.C.E.): valor, wisdom, and goodness (the proper use of things). Specifically, Grendel represents perverted wisdom; in Gardner's novel, he is the one who mistakenly chooses to believe in what he rationally knows and to reject what he intuitively feels. In both the epic and the novel, Grendel is an isolate, a cosmic outlaw, but Gardner's monster is less a hulking beast than a shaggy Holden Caulfield (*The Catcher in the Rye*), a disillusioned and therefore cynical adolescent. Not simply a creature cursed by God, he is a detached Sartrean observer, a relativist for whom "balance" can be both "everything" and "nothing," and a comic ironist trapped within his own mocking point of view. For him the world is a meaningless accident, "wreckage." Although he finds the indignity of the men he observes humorous, he is less tolerant of the factitious patterns they use to make sense of their existence.

Grendel makes his chief mistake when, having become dissatisfied with what is, he goes to the Dragon for advice and guidance. The Dragon is a bored and weary existentialist who espouses the philosophy of Sartre's *L'Être et le néant*, 1943 (*Being and Nothingness*, 1956). He tells the confused and terrified Grendel that values are merely things, all of which are worthless, and counsels fatalistic passivity in the face of a fragmented, purposeless world. Although Grendel becomes infected by the Dragon's nihilism, he still feels attracted to King Hrothgar's court poet, the Shaper, whose songs he believes are lies. Unlike the Dragon, who is the ultimate realist and materialist, the Shaper is a visionary who sings of the "projected possible" and an alchemist who transforms the base ore of barbarism into the gold of civilization. His songs bespeak hopefulness and, by means of what the Dragon scornfully terms the "gluey whine of connectedness," a dream of order. Moreover, his singing works: The Shaper's words first envision Hrothgar's splendid meadhall and then inspire the men to build it.

Grendel's ambivalence toward the Shaper also marks his attitude toward Wealtheow, the wife bestowed on Hrothgar by her brother in order to save his tribe from the king's army. Whereas Grendel gloats over man's indignity, Wealtheow, whose name means "holy servant of the common good," has the power to absolve it. She brings to Hrothgar's kingdom the illusion of timeless peace, an illusion that, like the Shaper's words, works. Although her "monstrous trick against reason" enrages Grendel, he too is affected by it, temporarily discontinuing his attacks and choosing not to commit "the ultimate act of nihilism," murdering the queen.

The Shaper (art), the queen (peace and love), and the hero Beowulf represent those values "beyond what's possible" that make human existence worthwhile. Interestingly, Gardner's Beowulf is, like Grendel, an isolate, and, in his fight with the monster, appears as a dragon—not Grendel's adviser but the celestial dragon that figures chiefly in Eastern religions. Where Grendel sees accident and waste, the hero finds purpose and regeneration. During their struggle, Beowulf forces Grendel to "sing walls," that is, to forgo his mocking cynicism and to take on the role of Shaper, the one who by his art shapes reality (what is) into an illusion or vision of what can or should be. Thus, Grendel is not simply defeated; he is transformed—his death a ritual dismemberment, a symbolic initiation and rebirth.

Although the novel affirms the heroic ideal, it nevertheless acknowledges the tragic view that informs its Anglo-Saxon source. The meadhall the Shaper sings into existence, to which the queen brings peace, and that Beowulf saves, is a symbol of what virtuous man can achieve, but it is also tangible evidence that art, love, and heroic action can defeat chaos for a limited time only and that, finally, the Dragon is right: "Things fade." Against this tragic awareness, to which the Dragon and Grendel passively acquiesce, Gardner posits the creative possibilities of human endeavor, especially art. It is, after all, as much the action (plot) of *Beowulf* as Beowulf's heroic act that defeats Gardner's Grendel and the monstrous values he represents. Gardner's alternative to Grendel's mindless universe and brute mechanics is implied in the novel's very structure. Its twelve chapters suggest not only Grendel's twelve-year war against Hrothgar and the twelve books of literary epics but also the symbol of universal harmony, the zodiac (each chapter of the novel is keyed to an astrological sign). *Grendel*, therefore, is not a postmodern parody of *Beowulf*; rather, it is a work in which parody is used to test the values presented in *Beowulf* (and its other sources: William Shakespeare, William Blake, John Milton, Samuel Beckett, Georges Sorel, Sartre, and others) to discover their usefulness in the modern world.

The Sunlight Dialogues • Like *Grendel, The Sunlight Dialogues* (which was written earlier) depends in part on Gardner's skillful interlacing of his literary sources: *Gilgamesh*, Sir Thomas Malory's *Le Morte d'Arthur* (1485), Dante, Herman Melville's *Moby Dick* (1851), William Faulkner, and A. Leo Oppenheim's *Ancient Mesopotamia: Portrait of a Dead Civilization* (1977). It appears to be, at first glance, part family chronicle, part mystery story, but beneath the surface realism, the reader finds elements of fantasy and myth. By an elaborate system of plots and subplots, each echoing the others, Gardner weaves together his eighty-odd characters into a densely textured whole that contrasts with his characters' sense of social and spiritual fragmentation. The main characters appear as isolates—the marked children of Cain—and as prisoners trapped in cells of their own making. Some blindly strike out for absolute personal freedom (Millie Hodge, for example), while others passively accept the small measure of freedom to be had in the cage of their limitations (Millie's ex-husband, Will Hodge, Sr.). As adults living in a world "decayed to ambiguity," they are like one character's young daughter whose toys frustrate her "to tears of wrath." Their frustration leads not to tantrums but to cynical denial of all hope, all ideals, and all connections between self and other.

The modern condition is illustrated in the fate of the Hodge clan. Just as their farm, Stony Hill, is said to symbolize "virtues no longer found," the late congressman represents the unity and sense of idealistic purpose missing in the Batavia of 1966. His qualities now appear in fragmented and diluted form in his five children: Will, Sr., a lawyer and toggler who can repair but not build; Ben, the weak-willed visionary; Art, Jr., the tinkerer; Ruth, the organizer; and Taggert, who inherits his father's genius, purity of heart, and pride, but not his luck. The failure of the congressman's harmonious vision leads to the moral relativism of the Sunlight Man on one hand and the reductive law-and-order morality of Batavia's chief of police, Fred Clumly, on the other.

The Sunlight Man is the congressman's youngest child, the angelic Tag, transmogrified by misfortune into a forty-year-old devil. Badly disfigured by the fire that kills his two sons, he returns to his hometown in the shape of a Melvillean monomaniac. Having searched for love and truth but having found only betrayal and illusion, he claims that love and truth do not exist; having failed to heal his psychotic wife or protect his sons, he proclaims all actions absurd. His magic tricks are cynical jokes intended to expose all meanings as self-delusions. His four dialogues with the police chief serve the same purpose: to disillusion Clumly, representative of the Judeo-Christian culture. Taking the Babylonian position, the Sunlight Man propounds the complete separation of spirit and matter, the feebleness and inconsequentiality of the individual human life, and the futility of the desire for fame and immortality. Personal responsibility, he says, means nothing more than remaining free to act out one's fated part. Although his dialogues are in fact monologues, it is significant that the Sunlight Man feels it necessary to make any gesture at all toward Clumly and that he finds some relief once he has made it. Similarly, his magic not only evidences his nihilism but also serves to mask the fact that despite his monstrous appearance and philosophy, he is still human enough—vulnerable enough—to feel the need for fellowship and love.

It is this need that Clumly eventually comes to understand. Powerless to stop either the local or the national epidemic of senseless crimes and bewildered by a world that appears to be changing for the worse, the sixty-four-year-old police chief at first seizes upon the Sunlight Man as the embodiment of evil in the modern world. Slowly the molelike, ever-hungry Clumly abandons this Manichaean notion and begins to search for the complicated truth. Clumly strikes through the pasteboard mask and, unlike Melville's Ahab, or the Sunlight Man who is made in his image, finds not the abyss but Taggert Hodge.

Throughout the novel, Clumly feels a strong sense of personal responsibility for his town and all its citizens, but, at the same time, he finds no clear answer to his repeated question, "What's a man to do?" He understands that there is something wrong with the Sunlight Man's philosophy but is not able to articulate what it is; he realizes that in separating the world into actual and ideal, the Sunlight Man has limited the choices too narrowly, but he has no idea what the other choices might be. The conflict between head and heart affects Clumly profoundly and eventually costs him his job. Only at this point can he meet Taggert Hodge as "Fred Clumly, merely mortal." In the novel's final chapter, Clumly, speaking before a local audience, abandons the text of his hackneyed speech on "Law and Order" and delivers instead an impromptu and inspired sermon, or eulogy (Taggert having been killed by a policeman) that transforms the Sunlight Man into "one of our number." Ascending to a healing vision of pure sunlight, Clumly, "shocked to wisdom," spreads the gospel according to Gardner: Man must try to do the best he possibly can; "that's the whole thing."

Nickel Mountain • Although not published until 1973, *Nickel Mountain* was begun nearly twenty years earlier while Gardner was an undergraduate at Washington University. The fact that parts of the novel originally appeared as self-contained short stories is evident in the work's episodic structure and unnecessary repetition of background material. Nevertheless, *Nickel Mountain* is one of Gardner's finest achievements, especially in the handling of characters and setting.

The novel's chief figure is the enormously fat, middle-aged bachelor Henry Soames, owner of a diner somewhere in the Catskill Mountains. Alternately sentimental and violent, Henry is a kind of inarticulate poet or priest whose hunger is not for the food he eats but for the love he has never experienced. Similarly, his Stop Off is less a run-down diner than a communal meeting place, a church where the light ("altar lamp") is always on and misfits are always welcome. Willard Freund and Callie Wells, for example, see in Henry the loving father neither has had. Longing to escape their loveless families and fulfill their adolescent dreams, they find shelter at the diner. Willard, however, chooses to follow his father's advice rather than act responsibly toward Callie, whom he has impregnated—a choice that, perversely, confirms Willard in his cynicism and colors his view of human nature. Betrayal comes early to sixteen-year-old Callie (Calliope: the muse of epic poetry) and, as with Willard, leaves its mark. When Henry fumblingly proposes marriage, she interprets her acceptance as an entirely selfish choice. Gardner's description of the wedding, however, shows that, whatever Callie's motivation, the ceremony serves as a communal celebration of those values she and Henry unconsciously affirm and Willard mistakenly denies.

Henry's charity looms as large in the novel as his bulk and seems to extend to everyone but himself. When Simon Bale, a belligerently self-righteous Jehovah's Witness, loses his wife and his home, Henry naturally takes him in, but when Henry accidentally causes Bale to fall to his death, he turns suicidal. Henry's suicide attempt takes a rather comical form—overeating—but his predicament is nevertheless serious. To accept Simon Bale's death as an accident, Henry believes, would be to admit that chance governs the universe and to forfeit all possibility of human dignity. This either/or approach precludes Henry's understanding of one fundamental point: that man is neither hero nor clown, savior nor devil, but a mixture of both; the best he can do is to hope and to act on the strength of that hope.

Henry's friend George Loomis understands Henry's predicament and understands too the flaw in his reasoning, but George is unable to act on this knowledge when he accidentally kills the Goat Lady. As foul-smelling as her goats and even more comically grotesque in appearance than Henry Soames, the Goat Lady passes through the area on her pilgrim's progress in search of her son, Buddy Blatt. Because the drought-stricken farmers turn this mindless creature into a symbol of hopefulness, George's lie—that he knows she is still alive and searching—keeps their illusion and hopes alive; in a sense, he saves his friends from despair, or so Callie believes. From Gardner's perspective, however, George's failure to explain what actually happened and to confess his guilt signals his having lost his place in the human community. The fact that George has always been in danger of losing his humanity, and thus becoming a Grendel, is evident in the way he is described: an ankle smashed during the Korean War, a heart broken by a sixteen-year-old prostitute, an arm torn off by a corn binder, and his lonely existence in a house much too large for one man up on Crow Mountain.

In a key scene, George leaves the Soameses and returns to his house, where, having heard about a recent murder on nearby Nickel Mountain, he becomes terrified, expecting to find murderous thieves looting his "things." Only after he has crawled through the mud, searched the house, and put his rifle down, does he realize his absurdity. More shocking is the knowledge that had Henry Soames acted in precisely the same way, there would have been nothing absurd about it for Henry would have been acting for Callie and their son, Jimmie.

It is true that Henry does appear ridiculous throughout much of *Nickel Mountain*; Gardner's purpose here is not to deny his dignity but to qualify it, to make human dignity a realizable ideal in a fictional world where the prevailing mood is one of comic reconciliation rather than existential despair. Against George Loomis's isolation and love of things, the novel counsels responsibility and charitable love. It is, as its subtitle attests, *A Pastoral Novel*, in which the rural setting is used to affirm the value of community in the face of fragmentation and indifference. Gardner's pastoral simplifies the plight of modern humankind without becoming either simplistic or sentimental. Henry's Nickel Mountain represents freedom and clarity, but it also serves as a reminder of humanity's limitations and mortality. If the Christian virtues of faith, hope, and charity constitute one part of Gardner's approach to life, the other is, as one stoic character puts it, having the nerve to ride life down.

October Light • Gardner has called *Nickel Mountain* his "simplest" novel; *October Light*, also a pastoral of sorts, is a much more complex work—more varied in style and characters, at once funnier and yet more serious than *Nickel Mountain*. Most of *October Light* takes place on Prospect Mountain in Vermont, where seventy-two-year-old James L. Page and his eighty-year-old sister, Sally Abbott, are locked in "a battle of the bowels." James, the taciturn New England farmer, suffers from constipation as a result of having to eat his own cooking. A bigot, he simplifies right and wrong and rages against the valuelessness of modern life to the point of shotgunning Sally's television and locking her in her bedroom. James, however, is more than merely a comic buffoon; he is also a man burdened with guilt and oppressed by mortality—not only his own approaching end but also the accidental death of a young son, the suicides of his son Richard and his uncle Ira, and the passing away of his wife Ariah in bitter silence. Self-reliant in the worst sense, James is outwardly unemotional (except for his anger), distant from those around him and from his innermost feelings. Only when he realizes the degree to which he is responsible for Richard's death and the part Richard played in accidentally frightening his Uncle Horace (Sally's husband) to death, does James once again take his place in the natural world and the human community.

Sally, meanwhile, a self-appointed spokeswoman for all oppressed minorities, remains locked in her room where, having nothing to eat but apples, she suffers from loose bowels. A liberal in name if not in fact, she thinks of her stubborn refusal to leave her room as a protest against her tyrannical brother. She is encouraged in her "strike" by the paperback book she reads, *The Smugglers of Lost Souls' Rock*. Constituting nearly 40 percent of the text of *October Light*, this novel-within-a-novel parodies the two kinds of fashionable literature assailed by Gardner in *On Moral Fiction*: the reflexive and the cynically didactic. Although Sally is not an especially discriminating reader, she does understand that *The Smugglers of Lost Souls' Rock* is trash—entertaining perhaps, but certainly not true. As she continues to read, however, the book, which she begins to see as a reflection of her situation, starts to exert its pernicious influence. Slowly Sally adopts its values and point of view as her own: its moral relativism, nihilistic violence, the acceptance of an accidental and therefore purposeless universe, and a casually superficial and irresponsible attitude toward human relationships. The subjects that are so weightlessly and artlessly handled in her paperback novel (suicide, for one) are substantive matters of concern in the "real"

lives of James and Sally; but this is a point that Sally, caring less for the Pages to whom
she is related than for the pages of her novel, does not understand.

In effect, *October Light* successfully dramatizes the argument of *On Moral Fiction*,
that art provides its audience with models and therefore affects human behavior.
Reading *The Smugglers of Lost Souls' Rock* leads Sally to devise and implement a plan to
kill James; when the plan misfires and nearly results in the death of her niece, Sally,
like the characters in her book, feels neither responsibility nor remorse. James is similarly affected by the violence he sees on television and, more particularly, by his Uncle Ira, who appears to have been more a monster than a man and certainly a poor
model for James to pattern his own life after. The more James and Sally become like
characters in what Gardner calls trivial or immoral fiction, playing out their inflexi-
ble parts as victimized woman locked in a tower or rugged New England farmer, the
greater the danger that they will lose their humanity and become either caricatures
or monsters. One such caricature in *The Smugglers of Lost Souls' Rock* dismisses all fiction, claiming that the trashiest "is all true" and "the noblest is all illusion." In their
wiser moments, Sally and James know better; they understand that art is humanity's
chief weapon in the battle against chaos and death (what James calls "gravity") and
that the true artist is the one who paints "as if his pictures might check the decay—
decay that . . . people hadn't yet glimpsed."

As in *Nickel Mountain*, Gardner's affirmation avoids sentimentality. Acknowledging the fact of death, acknowledging how easily the agreements that bind people
together can be broken, he exposes the fragility of human existence. What makes his
characters' lives even more difficult is the way in which their knowledge is, except for
brief flashes of understanding, severely limited. Instead of the easy generalizations of
trivial fiction, Gardner offers the complex and interrelated mysteries of Horace's
death and Richard's suicide. Memory plays an especially important part in the novel;
implying wordless connections between people and times, it is one effective antidote
to Sally's "reasonable anger" and James's having stubbornly locked his heart against
those he once loved. Another binding force is forgiveness—the willingness to forgive
and to be forgiven—which absolves the individual of the intolerable burden of guilt
without freeing him or her of all responsibility. James's son-in-law, Lewis Hicks, for
example, can see all sides of an issue and so takes the one course open to humankind
(as opposed to monsters): forgiving everyone. Lewis is the dutiful, ever-present
handyman who stands ready to shore up everyone else's ruins, understanding them
to be his own as well. Significantly, it is Lewis who first sees the October light that,
while a sign of winter and therefore a reminder of death, has the power to transform
the everyday world into a vision of radiant, magical beauty, a reminder of that life
that is yet to be lived.

Freddy's Book • Many reviewers regarded *Freddy's Book* as one of the least satisfying of
Gardner's novels; certainly it is the most perplexing. Like *October Light*, it comprises
two distinct stories, but in *Freddy's Book* the two are not interwoven (Gardner thought
October Light was flawed for just that reason). The first part of *Freddy's Book* is sixty-four
pages long and concerns Professor Jack Winesap's visit to Madison, Wisconsin, where
he delivers a lecture on "The Psycho-Politics of the Late Welsh Fairy Tale: Fee, Fie,
Foe—Revolution." Winesap, a psychohistorian, is a gregarious and sympathetic fellow who appears to accept the relativism and triviality of his age until his meeting
with the Agaards makes plain to him the limitations of his easygoing rationalism.

Professor Sven Agaard is a self-righteous dogmatist; his son Freddy, the victim of a genetic disorder, is another in Gardner's long line of misfits: a sickly looking eight-foot monster dripping baby fat. The manuscript Freddy delivers to Winesap at midnight (*Freddy's Book*) constitutes the 180-page second part of Gardner's novel. Freddy's tale of sixteenth century Sweden, titled "King Gustav and the Devil," is a dreadful bore—at least at first. Then the story begins to improve; the style becomes more controlled, the plot more compelling and more complex as Freddy begins to use his fiction writing to explore the possibilities inherent in his story and, analogously, to explore alternatives to his own various confinements.

Many reviewers were puzzled by Gardner's decision to use the ending of Freddy's tale to conclude the larger novel, which, they felt, seemed broken in two. This narrative strategy is both understandable and effective once it is considered in the context of Gardner's "debate on fiction" with his friend, the novelist and critic William Gass. Gass contends that fiction is a self-enclosed and self-referential art object that does not point outside itself toward the world of men but back into "the world within the word." Gardner, on the other hand, maintains that fiction does extend beyond the page into the reader's real world, affecting the reader in various and usually indirect ways. In *Freddy's Book*, Gardner makes the reader think about what effect Freddy's manuscript has had on its midnight reader, Winesap.

Freddy's Book shares with *Grendel*, *The Sunlight Dialogues*, *Nickel Mountain*, and *October Light* the qualities that have made Gardner a significant as well as a popular modern American novelist: the blend of realism and fantasy, narrative game-playing and serious purpose, and the interest in character that implies Gardner's interest in humankind. The reader finds characters such as Winesap and Freddy compelling because Gardner draws them honestly, and he draws them honestly because, in part, each represents a side of his own personality. He is as much Grendel as he is the Shaper, as much the anarchic Sunlight Man as the law-and-order police chief Clumly. Gardner sympathizes with those who show the world as it is, but ultimately he rejects their realism in favor of those heroes—poets, farmers, and others—who choose to do what they can to transform the world into their vision of what it should be, those who, like Gardner, affirm the Shaper's "as if."

Mickelsson's Ghosts • In the case of Peter J. Mickelsson, protagonist of Gardner's ninth and last novel, *Mickelsson's Ghosts*, the similarity between author and character is especially close: Both are middle-aged, teach at the State University of New York at Binghamton, own farmhouses in Susquehanna, Pennsylvania, have two college-age children, marriages that end badly, difficulties with the Internal Revenue Service, and both find that their careers, like the rest of their lives, are in a state of decline. The very texture of the novel's 103-word opening sentence makes clear that "something, somewhere had gone wrong with (Mickelsson's) fix on reality." According to several influential reviewers, it was not only Mickelsson who had lost his fix; in the pages of *Esquire* and *Saturday Review*, for example, Gardner was venomously attacked for his carelessness, boring and pretentious pedantry, implausible language, and failure to resolve or even make sense of his numerous plots: love, ghost, murder, academic life, philosophy, marital stress, sex, environmental issues, and Mormonism. Whether these attacks were directed more against the author of *On Moral Fiction* than the author of *Mickelsson's Ghosts*, as Gardner believed, can only be conjectured. What is certain is that these reviews disturbed Gardner so deeply that for a time he considered giving up novel-writing altogether. Moreover, the hostility shown by reviewers James Wolcott, Robert K. Harris, and others is out of proportion to the novel's actual defects (in particular, the unconvincing last scene and Gardner's ill-advised attempts to deal openly with sex). Rather than being a "whopping piece of academic bull sling-ing" (Wolcott), *Mickelsson's Ghosts* is clearly Gardner's most ambitious work since *The Sunlight Dialogues*, the novel it most resembles both in scope and narrative power.

Mickelsson (who Gardner says is based on his friend, the poet James Dickey) is in most respects a familiar Gardner protagonist. Just as the novel follows no single course but instead branches out in many seemingly unrelated directions, so too is Mickelsson a man torn apart by his own inner conflicts. He fondly recalls the certain-ties and ideals of his past, yet at the same time he finds it easier to live in the present by adopting the cynical, existentially free position he abhors. Finding himself in a world that is at best trivial and at worst self-destructive, Mickelsson recoils from all sense of responsibility and from all human relationships (except the most sordid with a teenage prostitute). Having been betrayed by his wife, he himself becomes a betrayer. Mickelsson is, however, too much the good man, the man desirous of good-ness and truth, unwilling to accept any rift between mind and body, thought and deed, to rest easy in his fallen state. Thus Mickelsson's many ghosts: those of the for-mer owners of his farmhouse, the murderous Spragues; those from his past (wife, children, psychiatrist); the philosophical ghosts of Martin Luther, Friedrich Nietz-sche, Wittgenstein, and others; and most important, the ghost of his better self.

By restoring his farmhouse, Mickelsson is in effect attempting his own moral res-toration project. Before he can be freed of his ghosts, however, Mickelsson must first feel the need to confess his guilt (he is, among other things, responsible for a man's death)—to confess his guilt rather than to internalize it out of shame (as George Loomis does in *Nickel Mountain*) or to wallow in it as if values did not exist. Only then, through forgiveness, can he enjoy the saving grace of human community. Within the novel's murder-mystery plot, Mickelsson escapes from the murderous design of a fa-natical colleague, Professor Lawler, a self-appointed avenging angel, only after mak-ing his act of faith in the form of a wholly irrational "psychic cry for help." Acknowl-edging his dependency on others and, later, accepting his place within the human community, Mickelsson becomes whole again. More than a novel about one man's re-demption, *Mickelsson's Ghosts* is an exploration of the way in which the modern-world individual can truly find himself—the self that he longs to be—and that discovery can only occur, Gardner believes, in the context of the individual's commitment to others and of their commitment to him.

"Stillness" and "Shadows" • The posthumously published book *"Stillness" and "Shadows"* was drawn from the University of Rochester's extensive collection of the author's papers. *Stillness* appears as Gardner wrote it in the mid-1970's, in the form of a complete but unrevised draft that Gardner apparently never intended for publica-tion, though he did mine it for two of his finest short stories, "Stillness" and "Re-demption." Written as psychotherapy in an effort to save his failing first marriage, it is Gardner's most intimate and autobiographically revealing work. The main charac-ters appear as thinly disguised versions of John and Joan Gardner. Martin Orrick, who Gardner nicknamed Buddy, is a professor and novelist; he is stubborn, opinion-ated, unfaithful, and often drunk. Joan, his wife and cousin, is a musician who has given up her career in order to allow her husband to pursue his. Although she has reason to complain, she, too, has faults and must share responsibility for their mari-tal difficulties. Both are, however, redeemed, in a sense, in that, as critical as they may be of each other outwardly, each is inwardly critical of himself or herself. The breakup of their marriage is handled with an intensity and sensitivity unusual in Gardner's fiction but not without the typically Gardnerian concern for seeing an isolated fact of domestic life as a sign of the universal decay that the novel's improbable happy ending serves only, ironically, to underscore.

Stillness evidences considerable promise; *Shadows,* on the other hand, suggests a certain pretentiousness on Gardner's part, given his remarks to interviewers on this work in progress. The published novel is nothing more than a patchwork toggled together by fellow novelist Nicholas Delbanco from the author's voluminous notes and drafts. Set in Carbondale, Illinois, the novel concerns Gardner's seriocomic, hardboiled detective Gerald Craine, as he tries to find a murderer and protect a young Jewish student, Ellen Glass, who has come to him for help. Craine's search for the murderer becomes a search for truth. Delbanco's text makes clear what was to have been the novel's thematic center, Craine's discovery that he cannot protect Ellen, whom he has come to love. The published work, however, does not support Gardner's claim that *Shadows* would be his most experimental work in terms of technique as well as his most conservative in terms of values. That claim is nevertheless important, for much of Gardner's greatness as a novelist derives from the unresolved dialogue between the values he sought to affirm and the often postmodern ways he employed to test and often undermine those values.

Robert A. Morace

Other major works

SHORT FICTION: *The King's Indian: Stories and Tales,* 1974; *The Art of Living, and Other Stories,* 1981.

PLAYS: *The Temptation Game,* pr. 1977 (radio play); *Death and the Maiden,* pb. 1979; *Frankenstein,* pb. 1979 (libretto); *Rumpelstiltskin,* pb. 1979 (libretto); *William Wilson,* pb. 1979 (libretto).

POETRY: *Jason and Medeia,* 1973; *Poems,* 1978.

NONFICTION: *The Construction of the Wakefield Cycle,* 1974; *The Construction of Christian Poetry in Old English,* 1975; *The Life and Times of Chaucer,* 1977; *The Poetry of Chaucer,* 1977; *On Moral Fiction,* 1978; *The Art of Fiction: Notes on Craft for Young Writers,* 1984; *On Writers and Writing,* 1994 (Stewart O'Nan, editor); *Lies! Lies! Lies! A College Journal of John Gardner,* 1999.

CHILDREN'S LITERATURE: *Dragon, Dragon, and Other Tales,* 1975; *Gudgekin the Thistle Girl, and Other Tales,* 1976; *A Child's Bestiary,* 1977; *The King of the Hummingbirds, and Other Tales,* 1977.

TRANSLATIONS: *Gilgamesh,* 1984 (with John Maier).

EDITED TEXTS: *The Forms of Fiction,* 1962 (with Lennis Dunlap); *The Complete Works of the Gawain-Poet,* 1965; *Papers on the Art and Age of Geoffrey Chaucer,* 1967 (with Nicholas Joost); *The Alliterative "Morte d'Arthure," "The Owl and the Nightingale," and Five Other Middle English Poems,* 1971.

Bibliography

Cowart, David. *Arches and Light: The Fiction of John Gardner.* Carbondale: Southern Illinois University Press, 1983. Like so many Gardner critics, Cowart is too willing to take Gardner at his (moral fiction) word. Cowart is, however, an intelligent and astute reader. He devotes separate chapters to *The King's Indian,* the children's stories, and *The Art of Living and Other Stories.*

Gardner, John. *Conversations with John Gardner.* Edited by Allan Chavkin. Jackson: University Press of Mississippi, 1990. Although the nineteen interviews collected here represent only a fraction of the number that the loquacious Gardner gave, they are among the most important and are nicely complemented by Chavkin's analysis of the larger Gardner in his introduction.

Henderson, Jeff, ed. *Thor's Hammer: Essays on John Gardner.* Conway: University of Central Arkansas Press, 1985. Of the fifteen original essays collected here, two will be of special interest to students of the short fiction: John Howell's excellent and groundbreaking essay on "Redemption" and Robert A. Morace's overview of Gardner's critical reception.

Howell, John M. *Understanding John Gardner.* Columbia: University of South Carolina Press, 1993. Provides a thorough discussion of the history and criticism of Gardner.

McWilliams, Dean. *John Gardner.* Boston: Twayne, 1990. McWilliams includes little biographical material and does not try to be at all comprehensive, yet he has an interesting and certainly original thesis: that Gardner's fiction may be more fruitfully approached via Mikhail Bakhtin's theory of dialogism than via *On Moral Fiction.* However, the chapters (on the novels and *Jason and Medeia*) tend to be rather introductory in approach and only rarely dialogical in focus.

Morace, Robert A. *John Gardner: An Annotated Secondary Bibliography.* New York: Garland, 1984. Morace lists and annotates in detail all known speeches and interviews with Gardner and reviews and criticism of his work.

Morace, Robert A., and Kathryn Van Spanckeren, eds. *John Gardner: Critical Perspectives.* Carbondale: Southern Illinois University Press, 1982. This first book devoted to criticism of Gardner's work includes a discussion of "Vlemk the Box-Painter" (in Morace's introduction), separate essays on *The King's Indian* and the children's stories, and Gardner's afterword.

Morris, Gregory L. *A World of Order and Light: The Fiction of John Gardner.* Athens: University of Georgia Press, 1984. In his chapters on *The King's Indian* and *The Art of Living, and Other Stories,* Morris, like David Cowart, stays within the framework that Gardner himself established; unlike Cowart, however, Morris contends that moral art is a process by which order is discovered, not (as Cowart believes) made.

Silesky, Barry. *John Gardner: Literary Outlaw.* Chapel Hill, N.C.: Algonquin Books, 2004. Fascinating study of the forces that drove Gardner's remarkable literary career.

Thornton, Susan. *On Broken Glass: Loving and Losing John Gardner.* New York: Carroll & Graf, 2000. Passionate memoir of Gardner by the woman he was only a few days away from making his third wife when his life was suddenly ended by a motorcycle accident.

Winther, Per. *The Art of John Gardner: Instruction and Exploration.* Albany: State University of New York Press, 1992. Explores the philosophy and technique of Gardner.

Yardley, Jonathan. "The Moral of the Story." *The Washington Post,* April 17, 1994, p. X3. A review of Gardner's *On Writers and Writing,* a collection of his reviews and literary essays. Discusses Gardner's controversial insistence on fiction that was moral and affirmative and his distaste for fiction that celebrated technique for its own sake or for the sake of the author's personal amusement.

Ellen Glasgow

Born: Richmond, Virginia; April 22, 1873
Died: Richmond, Virginia; November 21, 1945

Principal long fiction • *The Descendant*, 1897; *Phases of an Inferior Planet*, 1898; *The Voice of the People*, 1900; *The Battle-Ground*, 1902; *The Deliverance*, 1904; *The Wheel of Life*, 1906; *The Ancient Law*, 1908; *The Romance of a Plain Man*, 1909; *The Miller of Old Church*, 1911; *Virginia*, 1913; *Life and Gabriella*, 1916; *The Builders*, 1919; *One Man in His Time*, 1922; *Barren Ground*, 1925; *The Romantic Comedians*, 1926; *They Stooped to Folly*, 1929; *The Sheltered Life*, 1932; *Vein of Iron*, 1935; *In This Our Life*, 1941.

Other literary forms • In addition to nineteen novels, Ellen Glasgow wrote a book of short stories, *The Shadowy Third, and Other Stories* (1923); a book of poems, *The Freeman, and Other Poems* (1902); a book on her views of fiction-writing (concerned primarily with her own works), *A Certain Measure: An Interpretation of Prose Fiction* (1943); and an autobiography, *The Woman Within* (1954). She also wrote a number of articles on fiction for various periodicals and magazines. Her letters were published in 1958.

Achievements • Although Glasgow never believed that she had received the critical acclaim she deserved, or at least desired, she nevertheless played an important part in the development of southern letters. A significant figure in the so-called southern Renascence, she provided in her novels a new picture of the South, a region reluctantly ushered into the modern world. Against a sentimentalized view of the Old South, Glasgow advocated an acceptance of the inevitability of change.

Prior to 1925, Glasgow's critical reception was mixed—more positive than negative, but nothing that would mark her as a writer of the first rank. With *Barren Ground*, however, Glasgow's reputation began to grow with both critics and readers. That novel made the 1925 *Review of Review*'s list of twenty-five outstanding novels of the year. Represented also on the list for 1925 were Sinclair Lewis's *Arrowsmith*, Edith Wharton's *The Mother's Recompense*, Willa Cather's *The Professor's House*, and Sherwood Anderson's *Dark Laughter*. Glasgow's *The Sheltered Life* was a best-seller and greatly enhanced her reputation. *Vein of Iron* and *In This Our Life*, which received the Pulitzer Prize in 1942, helped to ensure her position as a writer of major significance.

> "The chief end of the novel, as indeed of all literature," Glasgow wrote, is "to increase our understanding of life and heighten our consciousness." To this end she directed her artistic skills, writing with care and precision, for, as she also said, "The true novel . . . is, like poetry, an act of birth, not a device or invention."

Biography • Born in Richmond, Virginia, in 1873, Ellen Glasgow came from a combination of stern Scotch-Irish pioneers on her father's side and Tidewater, Virginia, aristocratic stock on her mother's side. Francis Glasgow was an ironworks executive, an occupation well suited to his Puritan temperament and character. Ellen Glasgow had little positive to say about her father. Her mother, on the other hand, was a cultivated, gracious, and humane woman. These divergent influences provided the crucible from which Glasgow's writings were to emerge.

The next to the youngest in a family of four sons and six daughters, Glasgow experienced a more-or-less lonely childhood, with Rebe, her younger sister, and Mammy Lizzie Jones, her black nurse, providing her only companionship. Because of fragile health and a nervous temperament that precluded adjustment to formal schooling, her isolation was increased, and most of her education came from her father's extensive library.

As a child, Glasgow admired the novels of Charles Dickens, Henry Fielding, and Jane Austen. From Dickens, she gained reinforcement for her already strong aversion to cruelty, and from the latter two, she learned that only honest writing can endure. Lesser novelists, she felt, lacked "the creative passion and the courage to offend, which is the essential note of great fiction."

Library of Congress

Glasgow grew up in that period following the Civil War when, as she described it, the "prosperous and pleasure-loving" agrarians of the antebellum years were struggling for existence amid "the dark furies of Reconstruction." It was a conservative, even reactionary, time when, according to Glasgow, "being a rebel, even an intellectual one, was less exciting and more uncomfortable than it is nowadays." Rejecting the harsh Calvinism of her father and the bloodless social graces of Richmond society, she retreated even further into a life of the mind. Glasgow's growing sense of alienation and rebelliousness has been seen by critics as the wellspring of her literary vision.

By 1890, just one year after her hearing had begun to fade, Glasgow had produced some four hundred pages of a novel, *Sharp Realities* (unpublished). Putting that effort aside, she began writing *The Descendant* in 1891. Two years later, however, upon the death of her mother, with whom she had great affinity, she destroyed a good part of what she had written. Another two years passed before she returned to the novel and completed it. The following year, she made the first of numerous trips to Europe.

With the publication (anonymously) of *The Descendant* in 1897, Glasgow was launched on her prolific career, a career that saw novels appearing every two years or so. Writing became and remained her role in life, and she was ever mindful of the growth of her literary reputation, changing publishers when she felt it to her advantage and making sure that critics were fully aware of her books.

Presumably while on a trip to Europe in 1899, Glasgow fell in love with a married man, to whom she refers in her autobiography *The Woman Within* as Gerald B_____. A mystery man, Gerald B_____ was described by Glasgow as an older man with a wife and children, a Wall Street man. There is some evidence, however, indicating that Gerald B_____ was a physician. Another serious love affair was with Henry Watkins Anderson, a Richmond lawyer. He and Glasgow met in 1915 and were engaged in 1917. In July of the next year, Glasgow attempted suicide when she learned that Anderson, who was working with the Red Cross in the Balkan States, was attracted to Queen Marie of Romania. This turbulent love affair between Glasgow and Anderson was tacitly broken about 1920. In two novels, *The Builders* and *One Man in His Time*, Glasgow incorporated aspects of her relationship with Anderson.

As Glasgow began receiving the critical recognition for which she longed, her health began to fail. A heart condition worsened, and she died on November 21, 1945, in Richmond, Virginia.

Analysis • Turning away from a romanticized view of her own Virginia, Ellen Glasgow became a part of the revolt against the elegiac tradition of southern letters. Although she rejected romance, she did not turn to realism; rather, she saw herself as a "verist": "The whole truth," she said, "must embrace the interior world as well as external appearances." In this sense, she strove for what she called "blood and irony"— blood because the South had grown thin and pale and was existing on borrowed ideas, copying rather than creating; and irony because it is the surest antidote to sentimental decay. Certain that life in the South was not as it had been pictured by previous writers, she produced a series of novels that recorded the social history of Virginia through three generations, picturing sympathetically the social and industrial revolution that was transforming the romantic South.

A central theme in this record is that of change—change brought about by the conflict between the declining agrarian regime and the rising industrial system. Arguing that such change must be accepted and even welcomed, Glasgow observed,

> For thirty years I have had a part in the American literary scene, either as a laborer in the vineyard or as a raven croaking on a bust of Pallas. In all these years I have found that the only permanent law in art, as in the social order, is the law of change.

In pursuing the theme of change, however, Glasgow was careful not to go to the extreme in her presentation of deterioration, feeling that "the literature that crawls too long in the mire will lose at last the power of standing erect." In this respect, her works, unlike those of William Faulkner or Erskine Caldwell, lack shocking or sensational detail and maintain an almost Victorian sense of decorum. For example, when Dorinda in *Barren Ground* goes to the city, she is first approached by a fascinating lady clad in black who wants her to enter into a disreputable house. She is then rescued by a kindly doctor who gives her money to go back to Virginia and establish a dairy farm. This tendency toward propriety found in Glasgow's writing is explained in her plea to the novelist of the southern gothic school:

> All I ask him to do is to deal as honestly with living tissues as he now deals with decay, to remind himself that the colors of putrescence have no greater validity for our age, or for any age, than . . . the cardinal virtues.

The theme of change gives a mythic quality to Glasgow's work. It is that quality that Henry Canby refers to when he says that Glasgow sees her world as always a departing and a becoming. Her instrument for this cutting away is her sense for tender and ironic tragedy, a tragedy that is, in the words of Canby, "a tragedy of frustration—the waste of life through maladjustment of man to his environment and environment to its men."

Often, too, Glasgow's works picture nobility cramped by prejudice, or beauty gone wrong through an inability to adjust to the real, or a good philosophy without premises in existing experience. A good example of the latter theme can be found in the character of John Fincastle in *Vein of Iron*. A man of deep thought, he is considered "as a dangerous skeptic, or as a man of simple faith, who believed that God is essence, not energy, and that blessedness, or the life of the spirit, is the only reality." Fincastle is a part of the constant change in the world, but he himself does not fully realize the implications of the dynamic society in which he lives. He sees nothing of any potential value in the machine age and is unable to reconcile his own philosophy to the reality of the times.

Although all of Glasgow's works contain a note of pessimism, there is also present a note of optimism. More often than not, this hope comes after a protagonist's contact with city life. Dorinda, for example, returns to Pedlar's Mill after her stay in the city, to start a successful farm and gain revenge from Jason. Then, too, there is Ada in *Vein of Iron*, who, with her cynical husband, returns to the manse that was once her home and, strengthened by the recovery of "that lost certainty of a continuing tradition," looks forward to a new beginning.

Perhaps, when compared with Faulkner or Thomas Wolfe, the theme of change, as treated by Glasgow, may seem somewhat sentimental; there is, however, a refreshing and heartening chord in her work that lends credence to the idea that the world is not destined to be one great naturalistic garbage can but may perhaps be fertile enough for an occasional bed of flowers. At any rate, as Glasgow phrased it, "the true revolution may end in a ditch or in the shambles, but it must begin in the stars."

Virginia • In *Virginia*, her first acknowledged masterpiece, Glasgow focuses on the southern woman. "As an emblem," she writes of the southern woman in *The Deliverance*, "she followed closely the mid-Victorian ideal, and though her sort was found everywhere in the Western world, it was in Virginia that she seemed to attain her finest and latest flowering." It would follow, then, that if southern women attained their "finest and latest flowering" in Virginia, that also is where they would be most affected by the winds of social change that were sweeping over the South in the late nineteenth and early twentieth centuries. Bred and reared to tradition, they faced a new order that was both challenging and perplexing. Although some held firmly to the pedestal on which they had been placed, others leaped from it and immersed themselves in the new world.

Virginia Pendleton, the heroine of *Virginia*, is, like her mother, the ideal southern woman, the image of propriety and gentility. "Whenever I attempt to recall the actual writing of Virginia," Glasgow says in *A Certain Measure*,

> and to recapture the mold in which the book was conceived, I find myself moving again in an imaginary world which was then more real to me than the world which I inhabited. I could not separate Virginia from her background, because she was an integral part of it, and it shared her validity. What she was, that background and atmosphere had helped to make her, and she, in turn, had intensified the life of the picture.

In Dinwiddie, Virginia, during the nineteenth century, Virginia has been reared as "the perfect flower of the Victorian ideal" and "logical result of an inordinate sense of duty, the crowning achievement of the code of beautiful behavior and the Episcopal Church." She has been taught that duty, devotion, and sacrifice are the lot of women and that husband and family must come before all else.

Virginia, educated at Miss Priscilla Battle's finishing school, the Dinwiddie Academy for Young Ladies, is indeed "finished," at least as far as any real purpose in life is concerned. The basis of her education was simply that "the less a girl knew about life, the better prepared she would be to contend with it." Thinking him an excellent choice for a husband, she marries Oliver Treadwell, son of an industrialist, and, bearing him three children, settles down to family life. Oliver, like his father, who had dominated Oliver's mother, exercises this same control over Virginia. A would-be dramatist, Oliver is unsuccessful as a serious playwright, but he does receive some financial return by writing claptrap for the New York stage. Although Virginia has become middle-aged and worn, Oliver has maintained the look of youth. Finding no understanding from Virginia, who is not equipped to give him any, he deserts her for Margaret Oldcastle, an actor. Not knowing how to fight for her husband's love, Virginia is left with her two daughters, whose independence and aggressiveness she cannot understand, and her devoted son, Harry. The purpose in life for which she and so many other southern women had been prepared is gone. "Nothing but constancy was left to her," says Glasgow, "and constancy, when it has outlived its usefulness, is as barren as fortitude."

Virginia, in her minor tragedy, represents the ideal woman as victim of change, a change for which she has not been prepared and for which there is no effective antidote. One detects at least a small tear shed by Glasgow for the Virginias of the world. Once seen as ornaments of civilization and as restraints upon the more coarse natures of men, they now must replace self-sacrifice with an assertiveness that will be more in keeping with the changing social order. In that sense, Virginia points forward to *Barren Ground.*

Barren Ground • *Barren Ground* marks Glasgow's emergence not only from a period of despondency regarding her social life but also as a novelist who has moved without question from apprentice to master. Certainly her finest work to that time, *Barren Ground* was to Glasgow the best of all her novels. One of her country novels, it deals with that class of people often referred to as "poor whites." Glasgow herself refutes this appelation, preferring instead to call them "good people," a label that distinguishes them from the aristocratic "good families." Lineal descendants of the English yeoman farmer, these people were the ones who pushed the frontier westward. In this novel, they stand as a "buffer class between the opulent gentry and the hired labourers."

Dorinda Oakley, the heroine, is the offspring of a union of opposites: her father, Joshua, a landless man whose industry and good nature do not compensate for his ineffectuality; and her mother, Eudora, the daughter of a Presbyterian minister, with a religious mania of her own. This background, says Glasgow, has kept Dorinda's heart "in arms against life." More important, however, she has also inherited a kinship with the earth. This kinship enables her to make something positive out of "barren ground."

Dorinda falls in love with Jason Greylock, a young doctor, seeing in him the promise of something more than the grinding poverty she has known. They plan to marry, but Jason cannot go against his father's wishes, and he marries Geneva Ellgood instead. Pregnant by Jason, Dorinda flees to New York, where, after being struck by a taxi, she loses the baby. She works as a nurse for a Dr. Faraday until she learns that her father is dying. She returns home with enough money borrowed from Faraday to start a dairy farm. Back on the land, she becomes a tough-minded spinster and makes a success of the farm. Although she marries Nathan Pedlar, a storekeeper, she remains the head of the family. After his death in a train wreck, she is again alone, but happy, rearing Nathan's child by a previous marriage and managing the farm. Jason, in the meantime, has lost his wife by suicide and is forced to sell his farm to Dorinda. Because he is ill and an alcoholic, she unwillingly provides him with food and shelter. After a few months, he dies, and once more she is alone. When a local farmer asks Dorinda to marry him, she responds, "I am thankful to have finished with all that."

A tragic figure of sorts, Dorinda sees herself trapped by fate, "a straw in the wind, a leaf on a stream." Even so, she is not content to be simply a passive victim of that fate. Unlike Jason, who through his inherited weakness, succumbs to the forces that beset him, Dorinda looks upon the land as a symbol of that fate against which she must struggle. Hardened by adversity and with a deep instinct for survival, she refuses to surrender.

Although Dorinda's life may be compared to barren ground because it has been emotionally unfulfilled, it nevertheless is a successful life in that she does master herself and in turn masters the land. Just as the broom sedge must be burned off the land, so must romantic emotions be purged from Dorinda's soul. In giving her life to the land, she, in a sense, gains it back—and is thus, ironically, both victim and victor.

The Romantic Comedians • Following *Barren Ground*, Glasgow turned to the novel of manners with *The Romantic Comedians*. The first of a trilogy—the subsequent works being *They Stooped to Folly* and *The Sheltered Life*—this novel has been regarded by some critics as Glasgow's finest. After *Barren Ground*, Glasgow comments, a novel "which for three years had steeped my mind in the tragic life, the comic spirit, always restless when it is confined, began struggling against the bars of its cage." Because she never before had turned her hand to comedy of manners, *The Romantic Comedians* was written in the nature of an experiment.

The novel exhibits a high spirit of comedy with tragic overtones. "Tragedy and comedy were blood brothers" in Glasgow's image-making faculty, she writes, "but they were at war with each other, and had steadily refused to be reconciled." In *The Romantic Comedians*, says Blair Rouse, "we see people and their actions as participants in the follies of the comic genre; but we see, too, that a very slight shift of emphasis may reveal a tragic mask upon the actors."

Judge Gamaliel Bland Honeywell, the protagonist, "is a collective portrait of several Virginians of an older school," says Glasgow, "who are still unafraid to call themselves gentlemen." Living in Queenborough (Richmond, Virginia), he seeks female companionship after his wife of thirty-six years dies. At the age of sixty-five, he is expected to marry a former sweetheart, Amanda Lightfoot. Disdaining such expected decorum, however, he falls in love with and marries Annabelle Upchurch, a young cousin of his wife. Annabelle marries him not so much for love, but rather, to heal the pain of being jilted by Angus Blount. As one might suspect in such a marriage, Annabelle is soon looking for greener pastures, finding them in Delaney Birdsong, with whom she goes to New York. Unable to win her back, the Judge, ill and disillusioned, believes that life holds nothing more for him. With the coming of spring, however, he looks upon his attractive young nurse and muses, "Spring is here, and I am feeling almost as young as I felt last year."

Judge Honeywell, like many of Glasgow's women, is of another tradition. More than age separates him from Annabelle. Although he is the target of some satiric jibes in the book and one finds it difficult to find much sincerity in him, he is, nevertheless, a victim of the same kind of romantic claptrap that dooms other Glasgow characters.

A refreshing book when contrasted with Glasgow's previous efforts, *The Romantic Comedians* displays the author's humanity as well as her humor. Although she makes the reader laugh at the actions of the Judge and the other characters of the novel, she never lets them become completely ridiculous. Whatever else the Judge is, for example, he is a human being—and no one recognizes that more than Glasgow.

The Sheltered Life • In *The Sheltered Life,* the last novel of her trilogy on manners, Glasgow employs two points of view—that of youth and that of age, in this case a young girl and an old man. Against the background of a "shallow and aimless society of happiness hunters," she presents more characters of Queenborough as they are revealed through the mind and emotions of Jenny Blair and her grandfather, General David Archbald.

Glasgow intended General Archbald as the central character in the novel—a character who "represents the tragedy, wherever it appears, of the civilized man in a world that is not civilized." General Archbald sees before him a changing world, a world that is passing him by. Thus, he holds to the social traditions of the nineteenth century, which have provided little shelter for him. He was never a man for his time. A sensitive person who had wanted to be a poet, he was ridiculed in his earlier years. Poetry had been his one love in life; it was lost before it could be realized. He married his wife only because of an accidental, overnight sleigh ride that, in tradition-bound Queenborough, demanded marriage to save appearances. A compassionate man, he gives up his desire to marry again after his wife dies in order not to disrupt the lives of his son's widow and her daughter Jenny.

Jenny, too, unknowingly is caught in the patterned existence of the Archbald heritage. A willful girl, she has been sheltered from the real world by culture and tradition and can see things only in terms of her own desires. At the age of eighteen, she falls in love with an older married man, George Birdsong. George's wife, Eva, eventually finds them in each other's arms. Jenny flees the scene, only to learn later that Eva has killed George.

Eva Birdsong is another perfect image of southern womanhood, beautiful and protected all her life. A celebrated belle prior to her marriage to George, she has striven to achieve a perfect marriage. Without children, she and George are thrown upon each other. Over the years, George has been a bit of a roué, seeking pleasure where he could find it. In the end, Eva is left with the realization that what women "value most is something that doesn't exist."

When Jenny realizes what she has done, she flies to the General's understanding and sheltering arms, crying, "Oh, Grandfather, I didn't mean anything. . . . I didn't mean anything in the world." Ironically enough, she is right: She did not mean anything.

The Sheltered Life is more a tragicomedy than simply a comedy of manners. It is also, perhaps, Glasgow's best work, the novel toward which its predecessors were pointed. Symbol, style, characterization, and rhythm all combine to make *The Sheltered Life* a poignant and penetrating illustration of the futility of clinging to a tradition that has lost its essential meaning.

Glasgow's goal in all of her writing is perhaps stated best in *A Certain Measure,* when she says in reference to her last novel, *In This Our Life,* that she was trying to show "the tragedy of a social system that lives, grows, and prospers by material standards alone." One can sense in such a statement a conservative regard for tradition; even though Glasgow and many of her characters struggled against a shallow romanticism, a yearning for a genuine tradition was never far from her own artistic vision. The land seems to be the single sustaining factor in all of Glasgow's novels—it was the land that gave rise to and nourished the so-called southern tradition and that provides the "living pulse of endurance" to so many of her characters.

Wilton Eckley

Other major works

SHORT FICTION: *The Shadowy Third, and Other Stories,* 1923; *The Collected Stories of Ellen Glasgow,* 1963.

POETRY: *The Freeman, and Other Poems,* 1902.

NONFICTION: *A Certain Measure: An Interpretation of Prose Fiction,* 1943; *The Woman Within,* 1954; *Letters of Ellen Glasgow,* 1958; *The Battle-Ground,* 2000 (Pamela R. Matthews, editor); *Perfect Companionship: Ellen Glasgow's Selected Correspondence with Women,* 2005.

Bibliography

Glasgow, Ellen. *The Woman Within.* New York: Harcourt, Brace, 1954. Glasgow's autobiography is one of the best sources for the philosophy behind her fiction. This volume is more of a literary autobiography than a personal one, indicating shifts of perceptions, understanding, and attitude. It was published posthumously.

Godbold, E. Stanly, Jr. *Ellen Glasgow and the Woman Within.* Baton Rouge: Louisiana State University Press, 1972. A literary biography, interesting mainly as an example of prefeminist interpretation of Glasgow's work.

Goodman, Susan. *Ellen Glasgow.* Baltimore: Johns Hopkins University Press, 1998. A biography that focuses on showing Glasgow's significance as a southern author at the turn of the twentieth century; discusses the gap between her reception by her contemporaries and her later reception.

McDowell, Frederick P. W. *Ellen Glasgow and the Ironic Art of Fiction.* Madison: University of Wisconsin Press, 1960. Interesting and penetrating analysis of Glasgow's oeuvre mostly in terms of style, irony, and wit. Extensive bibliography.

Matthews, Pamela R. *Ellen Glasgow and a Woman's Traditions.* Charlottesville: University Press of Virginia, 1994. Discusses Glasgow's feminism and her place as a twentieth century southern female author. Includes bibliographical references and an index.

The Mississippi Quarterly 49 (Spring, 1996). A special issue on Glasgow with essays on her short stories that discuss her focus on struggling underprivileged farmers, her modernity, the effect of Henry Watkins Anderson on her work, and her use of clothing imagery.

Rouse, Blair. *Ellen Glasgow.* New York: Twayne, 1962. Presents facts, analyses, and interpretations of Glasgow's life, the nature and purposes of her writing, the scope of her work, and her attainment as an artist in fiction; the author is a southerner who was one of the first contemporary critics to appreciate Glasgow. Annotated bibliography.

_____. Introduction to *Letters of Ellen Glasgow.* Compiled and edited by Blair Rouse. New York: Harcourt, Brace, 1958. The introduction to this volume sketches Ellen Glasgow's achievement in relation to her letters and other autobiographical writings. Rouse also provides commentary on the letters.

Scura, Dorothy M., ed. *Ellen Glasgow: New Perspectives.* Knoxville: University of Tennessee Press, 1995. Detailed essays on Glasgow's major novels and themes, two essays on her autobiographies, and two essays on her poetry and short stories. Includes a helpful overview in the introduction and a bibliography.

Taylor, Welford Dunaway, and George C. Longest, eds. *Regarding Ellen Glasgow: Essays for Contemporary Readers.* Richmond: Library of Virginia, 2001. Collection of critical essays on Glasgow's writings.

Wagner, Linda W. *Ellen Glasgow: Beyond Convention.* Austin: University of Texas Press, 1982. An excellent, penetrating analysis of all Glasgow's work, placing it in the context of her time and place, as well as in relation to later work by American authors.

John Grisham

Born: Jonesboro, Arkansas; February 8, 1955

Principal long fiction • *A Time to Kill*, 1989; *The Firm*, 1991; *The Pelican Brief*, 1992; *The Client*, 1993; *The Chamber*, 1994; *The Rainmaker*, 1995; *The Runaway Jury*, 1996; *The Partner*, 1997; *The Street Lawyer*, 1998; *The Testament*, 1999; *The Brethren*, 2000; *A Painted House*, 2001; *Skipping Christmas*, 2001; *The Summons*, 2002; *Bleachers*, 2003; *The King of Torts*, 2003; *The Last Juror*, 2004; *The Broker*, 2005.

Other literary forms • Long known only for his novels, John Grisham published his first nonfiction book, *The Innocent Man: Murder and Injustice in a Small Town*, in 2006. Drawing on his legal training, he used this book to reconstruct the case history of Ron Williamson, a one-time major league baseball prospect who was falsely convicted of murder and rape in Oklahoma in 1988 and kept on death row until he was exonerated in 1999.

Achievements • John Grisham joined novelist-lawyer Scott F. Turow in establishing and popularizing the genre of legal fiction. Grisham is one of a small group of American novelists whose books are termed "blockbuster" novels; so popular is his fiction that his books are almost guaranteed to lead the best-seller lists from the moment they are published. *Publishers Weekly* called Grisham the "best-selling novelist of the 1990's." Most of his novels have been made into films, from *The Firm* in 1993 to *Christmas with the Kranks* (adapted from *Skipping Christmas*) in 2004.

Biography • The second of five children, John Grisham was born and raised in the South. His father was a construction worker, so his family moved frequently during his childhood. He lived in Arkansas, Louisiana, and Mississippi while he was growing up. Whenever his family moved to a new town, his mother saw that the children received library cards as soon as possible, because, as Grisham said, his mother encouraged reading over watching television. He attended high school in Southaven, Mississippi, a small town outside Memphis. He has said that his writing ability grew out of his involvement in a family of readers and storytellers.

Grisham wanted to play professional baseball, and he spent his early college years largely ignoring his studies and concentrating on sports. When he determined that a baseball career was not likely to happen, he turned to accounting as a major, graduating from Mississippi State University in 1977 with a bachelor's degree. He attended law school at the University of Mississippi, where he received his law degree in 1981. During that year he married Renee Jones, with whom he would have two children. They would reside in Charlottesville, Virginia, with Grisham writing six months of the year and coaching his son's Little League baseball team the other six months.

From 1981 to 1991, Grisham practiced law in Southaven. He also served in the Mississippi House of Representatives from 1984 to 1990. Although Grisham was a moderately successful lawyer, he said that he found himself becoming rather cynical toward the legal profession, and thus he became increasingly interested in literature and in writing. He wrote his first novel, *A Time to Kill*, in longhand, rising every morn-

Courtesy, Doubleday & Co.

ing at 5:00 A.M. and writing for one to two hours each day; he took three years to write his first book. Eventually it was published by a small press, and Grisham personally visited bookstores in numerous locales to try to augment its sales. In spite of his efforts, the book initially sold only about five thousand copies.

The phenomenal success of his writing began with his second novel, *The Firm. The Firm* was a major bestseller, and it was made into a film, the first of many of Grisham's novels to become motion pictures. All of Grisham's novels since *The Firm* have also reached the top of the bestseller lists, and most of them have been adapted to the screen. During an interview on a radio program in 2006, Grisham admitted that it takes him only six months to write a novel.

Analysis • Grisham writes legal thrillers, a type of novel that has virtually become a genre of its own in recent years. Grisham credits writer Scott F. Turow's *Presumed Innocent* (1987) for beginning the trend, but his own novels have served to define that trend. If, as conventional wisdom holds, Americans do not like lawyers, they have shown that they certainly do like books about lawyers. The reading public has purchased vast numbers of Grisham's books and those of other writers of fiction dealing with the legal profession.

With *The Firm*, Grisham began a pattern (some critics call it a formula) that he used, with variations, in most of his succeeding books. His plots usually center around protagonists who are young and in some way vulnerable, who are placed in extraordinary circumstances. They find themselves fighting against overwhelming odds in situations in which they should not be able to prevail. Ultimately they may win out over antagonists of apparently superior strength: the U.S. government, the Mafia, giant insurance companies. However, Grisham cannot be counted on to give his readers a standard happy ending.

Some critics have faulted Grisham for shallow character development and for implausible plots; other critics point out, however, that popular fiction is virtually defined by such plots. Grisham himself said that he writes "to grab readers. This isn't serious literature." Still, some of Grisham's books are set apart from other action thrillers by his genuine interest in, and engrossing presentation of, social concerns affecting modern readers.

Grisham's books are based in the legal profession that he pursued for many years and are usually set in the South, where he grew up and with which he is deeply familiar. Readers curious about the internal functioning of the legal world undoubtedly find his books satisfying in their detailed outlining of the way the law works in actual practice. Readers familiar with southern settings find few false notes in Grisham's descriptions of his settings in Mississippi, Louisiana, and Tennessee.

A Time to Kill • *A Time to Kill*, set in Mississippi, begins with the brutal rape of a young black girl by two white men. The child survives, and the men are arrested, but before they can be tried the girl's father shoots them both. The question of his guilt is not at issue; he has committed the killings in public, in full view of numerous witnesses. The plot centers on whether the jury can be persuaded to release a man who has acted to avenge a terrible crime inflicted on his family. Because the killer is black and the victims white, the racial implications are obvious. The book considers the uneasy nature of race relations in modern Mississippi, and it spares neither black nor white southerners in its look at the manipulations for position and media attention related to a highly publicized trial. Some critics have said that the character development in this novel is richer than in Grisham's subsequent works. The book suffers from faults common to first novels, however; Grisham fails to tie up some of his plot lines in ways that more experienced writers might. After finishing with a character or situation, he tends simply to abandon the person or issue without resolution. Nonetheless, Grisham and some critics consider this his best book.

The Firm • In *The Firm*, Grisham debuted the formula that would propel his books to the top of the best-seller lists. Protagonist Mitch McDeere is graduating third in his Harvard Law School class. He has several job offers, but the best is from a firm in Memphis, which offers an outstanding salary, an expensive car, an accessible purchase of an expensive home—all sounding too good to be true. Mitch begins to have questions about the firm almost at once: Why has no one ever quit? What about the two people who died a few years back? The law firm has a dirty secret, which would be deadly for Mitch to find out: The firm works for the Mafia. After Mitch learns this, he must also learn enough to bargain for his life. The plot of *The Firm* is fast-paced and fairly straightforward. It has been called simplistic, but in some ways—concerns of popular fiction aside—it also seems more realistic than some of Grisham's later novels. That is, one might actually imagine the events of this book happening; in some subsequent Grisham books, one would be hard put to believe the occurrence of the events.

The Pelican Brief • Grisham said that he wrote *The Pelican Brief* and *The Client* to prove to his wife that he could create credible female protagonists. Both books are examples of the compelling, if improbable, popular novel. In *The Pelican Brief*, a law student named Darby Shaw writes a legal brief outlining a probable cause for the recent murders of two Supreme Court justices. After she writes the brief, Darby decides it is essentially worthless, but it is picked up and handed to the Justice Department by a law professor, who is also her lover. In fact, Darby has inadvertently discovered the truth of the situation, and from that point on, her life is in jeopardy. The book is exciting and readable but rather hard to believe, qualities shared with his fourth novel, *The Client*. Neither of these books received particularly strong reviews, though they both sold many copies and were made into films.

The Chamber • *The Chamber* represents a departure from Grisham's two preceding novels. Dealing as it does with the imposition of the death penalty, the book is the first of Grisham's novels to take on a social issue. Sam Cayhall is scheduled to be executed for murder by the state of Mississippi. He has been convicted of planting a bomb that resulted in the deaths of two Jewish children, and his guilt is not in question. Cayhall has few redeeming qualities: He is an unrepentant racist and a member of the Ku Klux Klan.

Cayhall's case is taken in the final stage of appeals by young lawyer Adam Hall. He is the grandson of the prisoner, although Cayhall is unaware of this at the beginning of their involvement. Hall realizes that he is facing an uphill fight, but he struggles with the case as if he has a chance to win. The strength of this book lies in the picture it offers the reader of the reality of the death penalty. Grisham does not rail against capital punishment; he simply shows the reader the unattractive truth of it. Even given the horror of Cayhall's crime, one is led to question whether the inhumanity of the death penalty is an appropriate response. The book is flawed by some annoying lapses in editing, but at the time it was published, it received some of Grisham's strongest critical reviews.

The Runaway Jury • This book is based on an initial premise that may be difficult for some readers to accept: By skillful positioning and design, one might arrange to become a member of a given jury. This book offers a fascinating look at the inside functions of a jury and at the incredible resources wealthy corporations can offer to secure verdicts.

In this case, the juror is Nicholas Easter, and the jury is hearing a case against a major tobacco company. When the story begins, the tobacco companies have never lost a lawsuit brought because a smoker died of cancer, and they have no intention of losing this one. The lawyers for the tobacco companies have volumes of information on everyone called for jury selection, billions of dollars for defense, and no scruples. What they do not know, however, is that they are up against a person almost as skillful and knowledgeable as they are. Grisham's inside views of the law are, as always, interesting, and the inside views of the jury as it takes shape and reaches its conclusions are particularly fascinating in this novel.

The Street Lawyer • *The Street Lawyer* represents an interesting departure for Grisham. The book is set in Washington, D.C., rather than in his usual locations further south. Moreover, the story is less a novel than an attempt to raise social consciousness about the plight of the homeless. Grisham has dealt with issues of social interest before, but always in the context of a protagonist fighting large corporations for particular clients: *The Runaway Jury* took on big tobacco companies, and *The Rainmaker* was scathing in its condemnation of practices used by unscrupulous insurance companies. *The Street Lawyer,* however, has a slim plot, with the bulk of the book devoted to the condition of being homeless in America.

In the novel, Michael Brock is a successful young attorney with a large, powerful firm. When a homeless man enters the offices one morning to seek satisfaction for a grievance inflicted by the firm, Michael's life is changed drastically. His search for answers to the man's situation leads him into the world of the homeless and those who fight their battles. It also causes him to steal a file that has the potential to cause problems for his firm.

The firm fights to have Michael arrested for theft; still, Michael has the damning file. The parties are at something of a standoff. The resolution to the conflict gives the book something of a feel-good ending, but Grisham achieves his purpose: The book is bound to make readers think twice about the ways in which government and society in the modern United States deal with the poor.

June Harris

Other major works

NONFICTION: *The Innocent Man: Murder and Injustice in a Small Town*, 2006.

Bibliography

Bearden, Michelle. "John Grisham: In Six Years He's Gone from Rejection Slips to Mega-Sales." *Publishers Weekly* 240 (February, 1993): 70-71. Discussion of Grisham's early career and his rise to best-selling writer.

Cauthen, Cramer R., and Donald G. Alpin III. "The Gift Refused: The Southern Lawyer in *To Kill a Mockingbird, The Client*, and *Cape Fear.*" *Studies in Popular Culture* 19, no. 2 (October, 1996): 257-275. A comparative study of the treatment of the southern lawyer in modern popular fiction.

Duffy, Martha. "Grisham's Law." *Time* 145, no. 19 (May 8, 1995): 87-88. Takes a look at Grisham's life and influence at the time of the publication of *The Rainmaker.*

Goodman, Walter. "Legal Thrillers Obey Laws of Commerce." *The New York Times*, February 29, 2000, Late Edition, p. E1. Goodman discusses Grisham's ability to hold his legion of readers through the analysis of five novels.

Harris, June. "John Grisham." In *Contemporary Novelists*, edited by Susan Brown. Detroit: St. James Press, 1996. Focuses on Grisham's work and its place in contemporary fiction.

Mote, Dave. "John Grisham." In *Contemporary Popular Writers,* edited by Mote. Detroit: St. James Press, 1997. A critical look at Grisham's place among popular writers. Looks at comparative merits of several books.

Frederick Philip Grove

Born: Radomno, Prussia (now Russia); February 14, 1879
Died: Simcoe, Ontario, Canada; August 19, 1948

Principal long fiction • *Settlers of the Marsh*, 1925; *A Search for America*, 1927; *Our Daily Bread*, 1928; *The Yoke of Life*, 1930; *Fruits of the Earth*, 1933; *Two Generations*, 1939; *The Master of the Mill*, 1944; *Consider Her Ways*, 1947.

Other literary forms • Beyond the novel, Frederick Philip Grove has published travel sketches, represented by his first two published books, *Over Prairies Trails* (1922) and *The Turn of the Year* (1923). Actually narrative essays, the pieces detail Grove's weekly horse-and-carriage journeys between distant points of rural Manitoba. His other essays on a variety of topics appeared in Canadian periodicals and in the collection *It Needs to Be Said* (1929), and a much smaller number of short stories collected and edited by Desmond Pacey appeared under the title *Tales from the Margin* (1971).

In Search of Myself (1946), Grove's autobiography, contains a detailed account of his life before he arrived in Canada and of his struggles to achieve recognition as a writer. *Consider Her Ways* (1947), written at the time the autobiography was coming out but conceived much earlier, reflects Grove's long-standing scientific interests, as well as his familiarity with travel literature and with various models of the satiric fable. Grove casts his fable as a narrative communicated to a sympathetic scientist by a tribe of South American ants on an expedition to the north in search of further knowledge about humans. He cleverly satirizes Western civilization not only through the ants' discoveries and observations about the human society they find but also through the behavior of the ants themselves, who engage in the same power struggles and exhibit the same vanity of species they impute to humankind. Although a curiosity in Grove's canon, *Consider Her Ways* displays a tighter structure than most of his more conventional writings as well as many of the same attitudes toward human behavior and history.

Achievements • Grove's fiction constitutes Canada's most distinguished contribution to the literature of frontier realism. His work presents an authentic image of pioneer life, particularly in the central Canadian provinces. As an immigrant to Canada, Grove was able to question the North American pioneering effort in a disturbing and often profound manner and to form a perspective unique among the major English realists. Almost all of his fiction in some way scrutinizes the value system of progress behind the frontier movement in Canada and the United States, with implications reaching far beyond the time in which a work was set or written. His portrayal of social change transcends the limits of most frontier realism, often approaching the resonance of Thomas Hardy or Ivan Turgenev.

Grove's writing, however, is not without flaws. Because he acquired English in a purely academic manner, his prose is too often turgid. Also, his plots often lack a logical development that makes events appear arbitrary. Nevertheless, most of his novels offer a careful delineation of settings and incidents; he also gives his reader many vivid and memorable characters and situations, informed always by a frankness of tone and attitude.

The peculiarly telescoped nature of Canadian literature—whereby the development of basically eighteenth century models into modernism, which occurred more rapidly than in England or the United States—is reflected in the intensity of Grove's writing and vision, an intensity that links him to the later Theodore Dreiser and even to John Steinbeck, and that dramatizes the romantic basis of a realism bent on escaping Romanticism. Grove's fiction, and particularly his three strongest novels—*Settlers of the Marsh, A Search for America,* and *Fruits of the Earth*—thus carries much interest and value for the literary historian, as well as for the general reader.

Biography • Frederick Philip Grove was born Felix Paul Greve on February 14, 1879, in Radomno, Poland—on what was then the border with Prussia. Grove's most effective fictions were a result of these first thirty years of his life. His parents were middle-class citizens of Hamburg, and he attended the University of Bonn for a few years before dropping out for financial reasons and embarking on a career as a freelance writer and translator. Grove may have known André Gide and others in turn-of-the-century Paris literary circles, and he certainly did write and publish poetry, fiction, and even drama in addition to his literary criticism and extensive translation.

Grove's migration to North America, in 1909 or 1910, provided for him a new source of subject matter for his fiction. Whether he rode the rails as an itinerant workman, as he often said, is open to question. Most certainly he could have done so for only a year or two, and not for the much longer period suggested in *In Search of America* and reiterated in the autobiography. One can only speculate about his reasons for coming to America and for adopting so elaborate a disguise—of name, of parentage, even of the year of his birth. Perhaps he wished to transcend his modest social station, or to elude the law or creditors—Grove had spent a year in Bonn prison for fraud—or perhaps to escape a constraining marriage.

In 1912, Grove was hired as a public schoolteacher in rural Haskett, Manitoba, which was the first of several appointments in a rather unhappy career that would last fifteen years. In the summer of 1914, he married Catherine Wiens, a teacher in a school where he had become principal. They had a daughter and a son. The daughter's death in 1927, when she was only eleven, climaxed a string of difficulties besetting Grove during the 1920's, difficulties caused by the backward and often intolerant communities in which he found himself employed, by his own ill temper and inflexibility toward the rural mentality, by overwork and chronic financial hardship, and, perhaps most of all, by the erratic and ultimately unencouraging response of publishers and readers to his books.

During the late 1920's, Grove's fortunes turned somewhat as he became championed by a small but loyal and influential group of Canadian writers and academics. Increasing critical recognition of his work led to two lecture tours in 1928, to a brief career in the publishing business from 1929 to 1931, and to Grove's receiving the prestigious Lorne Pierce Medal of the Royal Society of Canada in 1931. Meanwhile, Grove had left teaching and settled with his wife and son on a small farm near Simcoe, Ontario, where he lived until his death. Although his writing never made him much money, it won him growing acclaim. He was elected to the Royal Society in 1941, received several honorary degrees, and was given a lifetime grant of one hundred dollars per month by the Canadian Writers Foundation in 1944. A stroke that year left him partly paralyzed. He died in 1948 after a lengthy illness.

Analysis • Among Frederick Grove's primary themes, the foremost is the issue of free will. Through his characters, Grove asks how much freedom anyone has in the face of often accidental but usually overwhelming pressures of instinct and environment. Even as he dramatizes the complexity and frustration wrought by such pressures, Grove seems, paradoxically, to celebrate the determination of his heroic figures to act as if such pressures hardly exist. Of almost equal importance to Grove's vision is the more existential question of where in time one ought to situate objectives. Although he can admire the person who plans and looks toward the future, he often exposes the illusions attending such an orientation. His novels also involve themes that develop out of the distinction made between materialism and a more transcendental value system, a distinction that his characters frequently fail to identify. The fact that Grove does not always favor his characters, even as he sympathizes with their search for an authentic New World, suggests the complex viewpoint and dilemma central to much of his writing.

Settlers of the Marsh • After publishing his two books of travel sketches, Grove moved into book-length and explicitly fictional narrative, retaining this critical stance toward the efforts of pioneers to conquer the plains. Although the detailed accounting of nature continues in *Settlers of the Marsh*, Grove's sympathy with nature and his corresponding critique of man-in-nature are found in the novel's characterization and plotting. The pioneering enterprise is questioned through the depiction of Niels Lindstedt, a young Swede who emigrated to escape the perpetual poverty meted him in Europe and to build his own fortune through hard work. Niels outdoes his neighbors and succeeds handsomely: He saves money, clears land, and harvests a bounteous crop. His crowning achievement is the building of a great house, in which he plans to live with Ellen Amundsen. Out of the presumptuousness and naïveté of Niels's scheme, Grove constructs the complications of his novel.

A curiously antiromantic love triangle develops in the novel, which combines elements of Thomas Hardy and D. H. Lawrence with those of Gustave Flaubert. Niels is cast as impressionable and sexually vulnerable, not unlike Hardy's Jude or the young Paul Morel of *Sons and Lovers* (1913). Just as Paul turns to an older, more aggressive woman when the younger woman of his choice rebuffs his sexuality, so Niels falls prey to the seductiveness of Clara Vogel—whose first name significantly matches that of her counterpart in the Lawrence novel. Grove's Clara, unlike Lawrence's and like Arabella in *Jude the Obscure* (1896), knowingly takes advantage of his ignorance and inexperience in sex. The literary triangle is completed in Ellen's aversion to sex despite her affection for Niels; the complex psychology behind her refusal to marry him recalls the different but equally complex reasoning of Lawrence's Miriam and Sue Bridehead.

To a much greater degree than Hardy or Lawrence, Grove limits sympathy with his central character. Although the reader sees the novel's action almost exclusively from Niels's viewpoint, and although Niels's strengths are reported and his intentions are understandable, each of the two women in his life is given a position of equal validity to his, and Niels's inability, or unwillingness, to appreciate that position constitutes a grave weakness. Ellen's sexual problems stem from her having witnessed the brutal subjugation of her mother by her father—who forced sex on his wife when she was ill and pressured her to seek abortions when she was pregnant— and from having promised her mother she would avoid intimacy with a man. Ellen's telling Niels all of this, even as she insists she admires him and desperately needs his friendship, shocked many of the novel's first readers.

Niels cannot bring himself to accept a purely friendly relationship with Ellen, or to wait for her to feel differently about him—although subsequent developments suggest waiting might not have gone unrewarded. Instead, he ignores her plea for friendship and largely avoids her. His assumption that he can control his own sexuality backfires in his going to town in search of pleasure, in his succumbing there to Clara, and in—to her astonishment—his remorsefully insisting that they marry.

Despite Clara's promiscuous past, it is mostly Niels's blindness to the dullness of farm life for a city woman and his refusal to free her that lead to Clara's actively seeking other men and to the climactic discovery scene in which Niels murders her. Just as Clara would not idealize sexuality, neither would she denigrate it, or try to compensate for it, as does Niels. His response to the compelling problems of Ellen and Clara reveal him to be more insensitive and more shackled by sex than either of them. Objections to the final reunion of Niels with a now-willing Ellen reflect readers' uneasiness with Niels's ultimately receiving rewards without acknowledging the legitimacy of the two women's claims against him. Aesthetically pleasing injustice in a more-or-less tragic plot thus gives way to the jarring injustice of a romantic finale.

The problems of the novel's ending are reinforced by Grove's portrayal of prairie women as victims of male stupidity and insensitivity. If Niels's friend Nelson enjoys a happy marriage because, unlike Niels, he pursues a simple, earthy type of women, Nelson is the exception. Otherwise, Grove surrounds Niels with consistently unhappy marriages, where the blame rests mostly on husbands whose wives are burdened with hard work, too many children, and too little sympathy. Grove finds the problem not to be so much marriage itself but specifically marriage between unequals to which the male pioneer aspires and in which the wife becomes simply another beast of burden subordinate to the husband's selfish ambitions. Grove ironically compounds the human toil of such selfishness in the case of Niels, who has a measure of sensitivity not shared by his fellow settlers. Niels mistakenly acts as if this sensitivity translates into completely good behavior. Having sought a land of freedom, Niels increasingly wonders if he is not, in fact, enslaved. Never, though, does he fully put together the puzzle of his failures. Through one of its gentlest members, Grove thus indicts a whole pioneer movement.

A Search for America • *A Search for America* proved to be much less offensive and much more popular to its first readers than *Settlers in the Marsh*; in fact, it became the most popular of Grove's books. Rather than a narrative of constriction, it offers a story of discovery, of an opening up to the positive possibilities of life in America. In Phil Brandon, the narrator and protagonist, Grove presents his true adventurer, who reveals the moral ambiguities of the feverish activity characterizing North America at the turn of the century. Until recently, readers saw the narrative as thinly disguised autobiography; certainly Grove encouraged this notion by inserting parts in *In Search of Myself*. So convincing are many of the novel's scenes and incidents that even now, after the serious inaccuracies in Grove's account of his early years have been exposed, one believes he must have experienced most of the encounters and difficulties Brandon describes.

The literary antecedents of this book are, on one hand, *Walden* (1854) and *Adventures of Huckleberry Finn* (1884), and, on the other, a string of later immigrant narratives, from Jacob Riis's affirmative autobiography, *The Making of an American* (1901), to the fictional and more skeptical *Rise of David Levinsky* (1917) by Abraham Cahan. How much of this immigrant writing Grove himself had read is unknown; Henry David Thoreau and Mark Twain he cites explicitly. To all of these he adds, as the narrative progresses, strains of Thomas Carlyle and Leo Tolstoy: he takes the injunction from *Sartor Resartus* (1835) about increasing the "fraction of Life" by lessening the denominator as the basis for his turnabout in the middle of his "search," and in the final section compares the magnificent hobo Ivan in Leo Tolstoy's *Anna Karénina* (1875-1877).

Phil Brandon is a young man from a wealthy Swedish family whose father's financial crisis drives him to Canada. From Toronto, where he finds work as a waiter, he moves to New York, as a door-to-door book salesman; to the Midwest, as a drifter on the Ohio River; and finally, to the Dakotas, where he works in the great wheat harvest. Although Grove cut his original manuscript in half, the published narrative is frequently rambling and episodic. Nevertheless, it continues to have a legitimate appeal.

The novel features the memorable episodes and characters for which Grove is known, from the cultured young European's encounter with the strange and raw people on his first train trip in the New World, from Montreal to Toronto, to Brandon's being tossed out of a Western town as a radical agitator trying to defend immigrants' property rights. Along the way he meets restaurant employees who cheat in various ways, the rich and the poor on whom publishers try to foist books, a riverman so taciturn Brandon mistakes him for a deaf-mute, a village doctor completely trusting of the down-and-out, a millionaire landowner fascinated by radical political talk, and many other notable figures.

In *Frederick Philip Grove* (1973), Margaret R. Stobie points to the dreamlike quality, as well as the double movement, of Brandon's quest. Grove extends his story beyond the limitations of immigrant initiation by moving Brandon from a geographical to a psychological quest, from seeking an America outside himself to finding those "American" values in himself that lead to a vocation. Although the result for Brandon is the decision to become a teacher aiding the newly arrived immigrants, the meaning of this decision and the shift of objectives preceding it even speaks to readers solidly established in American society. Grove parallels this shift with the development of the distinction between the superficial America—represented in the novel's first two books by the petty fraud of business—and the "real" America promised in book 3, when Brandon travels the countryside by himself, and in book 4, when he reattaches himself to humanity. He becomes convinced that, his misadventures notwithstanding, there are "real Abe Lincolns" out there, worth seeking and worth cultivating.

Grove's narrator-protagonist comes to devalue "culture" in the European sense, as prefabricated and fragile, and to appreciate the need for developing one's personal culture. Grove's affinity with Thoreau and Twain, as well as with Henri Rousseau, shows especially in Brandon's discovery of a new relationship with nature, responding to the commonplace in nature. Nature suggests to Brandon not only the insignificance of the past—which his flight from European artifice may have already taught him—but also the virtual irrelevance of the future, as he learns to concentrate more on his present situation and less on what it might be. Repeatedly, Brandon wonders at the nature of being, at where he is through no effort or intention. The novel's basic optimism is underlined by the possibility for positive unforeseen events, which softens the determinism of much social thinking in the novel. If the European immigrant's experience during the 1890's seems remote today, Grove's warnings about a culture mired in materialism and separated from its roots in nature still have force.

Fruits of the Earth • Continuing the ideological tendencies of Grove's earlier fiction, *Fruits of the Earth* is not only his most satisfying and moving novel but also arguably one of the two or three finest works to come out of the American frontier tradition. Strictly speaking, it does not concern the frontier so much as the painful transition from pioneer to modern life on the prairie. Abe Spaulding represents one answer to Phil Brandon's search for the authentically Lincolnesque American. Grove describes Spaulding's experiences and development from 1900, when he arrives from Ontario to clear a piece of land near a remote Manitoba village, to the 1920's, when—in his fifties and having achieved patriarchal status among his neighbors—he wrestles with the moral dilemmas posed by community growth, related pressures of mass culture, and his own children's coming of age.

Grove divides his novel into two principal sections. The first traces Abe from his start as a young homesteader through his remarkable economic success, which culminates in his building a great house on the site of his beginning. Paralleling this ascent is his rise in the school district and the municipality, where he is respected for his sagacity and honesty and is ultimately elected reeve. Early in the narrative a conflict develops in Abe, by which feelings for his family—to a lesser extent for his wife, who is ill-suited for prairie life, and to a greater extent for his son Charlie, whose sensitivity Abe comes increasingly to value—detract from his sense of external success. Such success is superseded, in Abe's and the reader's minds, by the accidental death of Charlie midway through the novel.

Grove ascribes Spaulding's success largely to the preeminent strengths he brings to the challenge of homesteading. Repeatedly, the secondary characters and events testify to Abe's intelligence and shrewdness, of which his imposing physique is emblematic. He nurses the pioneer ambitions to escape a constricting life, represented by the small family farm he had sold, and to pursue what Grove terms "a clear proposition," unencumbered by complexity. Such a plan rests on the premise that such objectives are inherently good and satisfying, as well as obtainable. Abe soon begins to suspect the fallaciousness of his premise when other values detract from the satisfaction of his success. Grove significantly casts Abe's happiness in the past, so that he rarely experiences it except in memory. His growing property holdings are accompanied by a sense of diminishing economic returns and by a feeling of increasing enslavement by his acquisitions. Even as he builds the magnificent house, Abe feels powerless; house construction, like the prairie itself, is beyond his grasp. Like Hardy and many naturalists, Grove portrays his protagonist in rather unflattering terms against the backdrop of nature. Abe seems never very far ahead of the natural forces he tries to control, and therefore he is unable to enjoy any real repose.

All of these characteristics emerge in the novel's first part. Charlie's death, which coincides with Abe's greatest public triumphs, brings out a latent dissatisfaction with such triumphs. Abe sees in the death an ominous sign of his inability to capture what he has belatedly recognized as more valuable than material or external success. Charlie's death reinforces a depressing sense of fatality, of an irreversible and unmodifiable commitment to decisions made and courses taken many years earlier. Having attended increasingly to Charlie, not only to atone but also to make up time he had believed he was losing, Abe retreats into himself once Charlie is gone.

The second part of the novel, titled "The District," depicts various changes brought on by the postwar era. Against this background and despite his skepticism regarding "progress"—a skepticism explicitly echoed by Grove—Abe allows unscrupulous political enemies to rob him of power and to proceed to transform the district in the modern commercial spirit he despises. The novel's first part centered on the suspense of when and at what price Abe would realize fully the conflict of values in himself; in the second part, Grove turns the issue to whether, having recognized that conflict, Abe will succumb to a paralysis of will.

Abe, however, ultimately chooses to assert whatever limited influence he may have and to take a stand despite his awareness of his power's limits. Grove indicates that Abe's heroism comes from that awareness rather than from the skills that helped him fashion out his estate or the sensitivity brought out in his relationship to Charlie. Having learned that life's "clear propositions" tend to be elusive and fundamentally unsatisfying, Abe in the end rises from psychological and moral torpor to act with genuine courage.

Grove's artistic successes have helped extend frontier realism beyond the dimensions it is usually accorded. Like his more celebrated American counterparts, Grove marked the ambitions, hopes, and disappointments attending pioneer life around the turn of the twentieth century. He also marked the ways in which such universally destructive aspects of human behavior as greed, jealousy, and snobbery found their way into a frontier experience, which had promised escape from them.

Grove's novels came too late to put him in the forefront of frontier realists. Nevertheless, his novels' tardy appearance permitted a perspective of which the other frontier realists were rarely capable. Grove was able to capture not only the futility but also the ultimate immorality of much pioneer venturing. His best fiction records the compromise of simple virtue and pleasure demanded by the misleading complex life on the prairie. This ethical perspective deepens as Grove follows his pioneers beyond World War I and even into the 1930's, where pioneer and modern notions of progress clash openly.

Significantly, Grove shows women and children suffering the consequences of commitments made solely by adult men. Yet, even the hardy pioneers in Grove's world sense the inherent limitations of the economic and social system to which they commit themselves and their families. In depicting their failures, economic and moral, as inevitable, Grove is a pessimist, particularly as he assigns a measure of responsibility to the pioneers themselves. In continuing to insist, however, on the ability of humankind to recognize good and to act on that recognition, Grove avoided naturalistic determinism and offered a measure of hope to the twentieth century.

Bruce K. Martin

Other major works

SHORT FICTION: *Tales from the Margin: The Selected Short Stories of Frederick Philip Grove*, 1971 (Desmond Pacey, editor).

NONFICTION: *Over Prairie Trails*, 1922; *The Turn of the Year*, 1923; *It Needs to Be Said*, 1929; *In Search of Myself*, 1946 (fictionalized autobiography); *The Letters of Frederick Philip Grove*, 1976 (Desmond Pacey, editor); *A Stranger to My Time: Essays By and About Frederick Philip Grove*, 1986.

CHILDREN'S LITERATURE: *The Adventure of Leonard Broadus*, 1983 (in *The Genesis of "The Adventure of Leonard Broadus": A Text and Commentary*).

Bibliography

Hjartarson, Paul, ed. *A Stranger to My Time: Essays by and About Frederick Philip Grove.* Edmonton, Alberta: NeWest Press, 1986. Divided into four sections, each concerned with a Grove persona, the figures of the Other, the Immigrant, Estrangement, and Posterity. Thoroughly updates the evaluation of Grove and his contribution to Canadian literature. Includes an extensive, selected bibliography and an explicit index.

Martens, Klaus. *F. P. Grove in Europe and Canada: Translated Lives.* Translated by Paul Morris. Edmonton: University of Alberta Press, 2001. A biography of Grove that examines his homes and correspondence.

Pacey, Desmond, ed. *Frederick Philip Grove.* Toronto: Ryerson Press, 1970. Encompasses Pacey's introduction, chronologically arranged critical essays by other authors, book review excerpts on Grove's novels, and a bibliography of Grove's entire canon. Reflects Pacey's skill at providing a useful overview.

Spettigue, Douglas O. *Frederick Philip Grove.* Toronto: Copp Clark, 1969. Spettigue, who has done the most to untangle the enigma of Grove's origins, arranges this scholarly, objective book around a consideration of the interdependence between Grove's personality and the themes and heroes of his novels. Notes and a bibliography enhance this important analysis.

Stobie, Margaret R. *Frederick Philip Grove.* New York: Twayne, 1973. Stobie does as much as possible to discover Grove, the man, behind the central theme in his writing: human as social and natural being. Comprises an interwoven analysis of Grove's life and his writing, presenting new insights gleaned from unpublished material and from personal anecdotes of people who knew him. Emphasizes Grove's successes over his failures as a writer. A chronology, a selected bibliography, and an index contribute to the thoroughness of this admiring study.

Stuewe, Paul. "The Case of Frederick Philip Grove." In *Clearing the Ground: English-Canadian Literature After "Survival."* Toronto: Proper Tales Press, 1984. Stuewe bluntly dismisses Grove as an inept writer but acknowledges his nonliterary value as a chronicler of social and historic themes of the late nineteenth and early twentieth centuries.

Sutherland, Ronald, ed. "Thoughts on Five Writers: What Was Frederick Philip Grove?" In *The New Hero: Essays in Comparative Quebec/Canadian Literature.* Toronto: Macmillan, 1977. Sutherland calls this series of interesting linked essays, on the individualistic "new" hero emerging from Canadian literature, "para-literary." The section on Grove reflects Sutherland's fascination with that enigmatic personality and praises his writing as that of a literary naturalist, not a social realist. Includes notes and a thorough bibliography.

Dashiell Hammett

Born: St. Mary's County, Maryland; May 27, 1894
Died: New York, New York; January 10, 1961

Principal long fiction • *$106,000 Blood Money*, 1927 (also known as *Blood Money* and *The Big Knockover*); *Red Harvest*, 1927-1928 (serial; 1929, book); *The Dain Curse*, 1928-1929 (serial; 1929, book); *The Maltese Falcon*, 1929-1930 (serial; 1930, book); *The Glass Key*, 1930 (serial; 1931, book); *The Thin Man*, 1934; *Dead Yellow Women*, 1946; *Hammett Homicides*, 1946; *Complete Novels*, 1999.

Other literary forms • Dashiell Hammett first attracted critical attention as the author of short detective fiction published in *Smart Set* and *Black Mask* magazines as early as 1923. The best of his stories were narratives told in the first person by the nameless "Continental Op," a fat, balding operative working out of the San Francisco office of the Continental Detective Agency. The Continental Op is also the narrator and principal character of Hammett's first two novels, both of which were published in magazines before their appearance in book form. A number of his short stories were anthologized in *The Continental Op* (1945) and, after Hammett's death in 1961, *The Big Knockover* (1966).

Achievements • Together with his contemporary Raymond Chandler (1888-1959), Hammett is credited with defining the form, scope, and tone of the modern detective novel, a distinctly American genre that departs considerably from the earlier tradition inspired by the British. Chandler, although some six years Hammett's senior, did not in fact begin publishing detective fiction until 1933 and readily acknowledged the younger writer's prior claim. Together, both authors have exerted considerable influence upon later exponents of the detective genre, notably on Ross Macdonald, their most distinguished successor. Hammett's work in particular has served also as a stylistic model for many novelists working outside the detective genre, among them Ernest Hemingway and John O'Hara.

Unlike his predecessors in the mystery genre, Hammett adopted a starkly realistic, tough-minded tone in his works, sustaining an atmosphere in which questions outnumber answers and no one is to be trusted. Hammett's reputation ultimately rests on his creation of two characters who embody the moral ambiguities of the modern world: Sam Spade (*The Maltese Falcon*) and Nick Charles (*The Thin Man*). Widely popularized through film adaptations of the novels in which they appear, Spade and Charles are among the most famous American detectives, known even to those with little more than marginal interest in the mystery genre. Tough-minded if occasionally softhearted, both characters may be seen as particularized refinements of Hammett's Continental Op, professional detectives who remain true to their personal code of honor and skeptical with regard to everything and everyone else.

Partially because of declining health, Hammett wrote no novels after the age of forty. His reputation, however, was by that time secure; even in the following century, his five novels would remain landmarks of the genre, a model for future novelists and a formidable standard of comparison.

Biography • Samuel Dashiell Hammett was born in St. Mary's County, Maryland, on May 27, 1894, of an old but modest Roman Catholic family. Leaving high school at the age of fourteen after less than a year of attendance, Hammett worked indifferently at a variety of odd jobs before signing on with the Pinkerton Detective Agency around the age of twenty. At last, it seemed he had found work that he enjoyed and could do well, with a dedication later reflected in the character and behavior of the Continental Op. With time out for service in World War I, from which he was demobilized as a sergeant, Hammett continued to serve Pinkerton with distinction until failing health caused him to consider other options. In 1921, he married Josephine Dolan, a nurse whom he had met during one of his recurring bouts with tuberculosis. The couple moved west to San Francisco, where Hammett returned to work for Pinkerton, only to resign in frustration and disgust after an ironic incident in which his detective talents proved too great for his own good: Assigned by Pinkerton to ship out on an Australian freighter in search of stolen gold believed to be hidden aboard, Hammett managed to find the missing gold in a smokestack during a cursory search just prior to departure and was thus denied the anticipated voyage to Australia.

During such spare time as he could find, Hammett had been trying to prepare himself as a writer; upon leaving Pinkerton, he devoted himself increasingly to writing, eventually leaving his family (which by then included two daughters) and moving to a cheap furnished room where he could live and write. Fearing that he had little time left to live, he wrote at a determined pace; encouraged by his first successes, he gradually developed and refined the writing style that was to make him famous. His first story featuring the Continental Op appeared in October, 1923. Increasingly successful, Hammett soon progressed to the writing of longer stories that were in fact independent sections of novels, eventually published as *Red Harvest* and *The Dain Curse*. Both appeared as hardbound editions in 1929. The following year, Hammett achieved both critical recognition and financial independence with the publication of *The Maltese Falcon,* an unquestionably mature and groundbreaking work that sold at once to the film industry; John Huston's landmark 1941 version of *The Maltese Falcon* was the third Hollywood film to be drawn from Hammett's original novel.

During the year 1930, Hammett made the acquaintance of dramatist Lillian Hellman, eleven years his junior, who was to become the most important and influential woman in his life. Although they never married (each was unhappily married to someone else at the time of their first meeting), Hellman and Hammett remained together in an intense, often turbulent, but intellectually rewarding relationship until Hammett's death some thirty years later at the age of sixty-six. *The Thin Man*, Hammett's next and last published novel (*The Glass Key* having already been written by the time he met Hellman), reflects the author's relationship with Hellman in the portrayal of Nick and Nora Charles, represented in the screen version and its sequels by William Powell and Myrna Loy.

Following the success of *The Thin Man* both as book and as film, Hammett moved to Hollywood, where he worked as a writer and script doctor on a variety of screen projects. He became increasingly involved in leftist politics and toward the end of the Great Depression became a member of the Communist Party. Hammett did not, however, consider his politics an impediment to patriotism; soon after the United States went to war in 1941, he was back in a sergeant's uniform, despite his advanced age and obviously declining health. Attached to the Signal Corps, he served three years in the Aleutian Islands, where his duties included editing a daily newspaper for service personnel. By the end of the war, however, his health was more precarious

Library of Congress

than ever, undermined by years of recurrent tuberculosis and heavy drinking. After an alcoholic crisis in 1948, Hammett forswore drinking for the remainder of his life. At the same time, his political past was coming back to haunt him; like his fictional characters, however, he remained loyal to his convictions and his friends, declining to testify against his fellow associates in the Communist Party and other political organizations. In 1951, Hammett spent five months in various prisons for contempt of court as a result of his refusal to testify; around the same time, government authorities determined that he was several years behind in the payment of his income tax. Unable to find work in Hollywood because of his political views, Hammett was further impoverished by the attachment of his remaining income for the payment of back taxes. Increasingly infirm, Hammett spent his last years in the care and company of Hellman. He died at Lenox Hill Hospital in New York City on January 10, 1961.

Analysis • Unlike most of their predecessors in the genre, Dashiell Hammett's detectives live and work, as did Hammett himself, in a world populated with actual criminals who violate the law for tangible personal gain. Significantly, Hammett did all of his creative writing during the years of Prohibition, when lawlessness was rampant and organized crime was rapidly gaining a foothold in the American social structure. Prohibition indeed functions prominently in all of Hammett's published work as background, as atmosphere, and frequently as subject. In *Red Harvest*, Hammett's first novel, a loose confederacy of bootleggers, thieves, and hired killers has set up what appears to be a substitute government, replacing law and order with values of their own; the resulting Hobbesian chaos clearly reflects, however indirectly, Hammett's own developing political consciousness. There is little place in such a world for genteel detectives cast in the mold of Dorothy Sayers's Lord Peter Wimsey; accordingly, Hammett presents in the Continental Op and his successors the kind of detective who can deal routinely and effectively with hardened criminals. As Raymond Chandler observed, "Hammett gave murder back to the kind of people who commit it for reasons."

Within such an evil environment, the sleuth often becomes as devious and mendacious as those whom he is pursuing, remaining faithful nevertheless to a highly personal code of honor and justice. Sam Spade, perhaps the most intriguing of

Hammett's literary creations, is so well attuned to the criminal mind that he often appears to be a criminal himself; he is known to have been involved romantically with his partner's wife and is thus a likely suspect after the man is murdered. Nevertheless, at the end of *The Maltese Falcon*, he persists in turning over to the authorities the thief and murderess Brigid O'Shaughnessy, despite an acknowledged mutual attraction. Ned Beaumont, the protagonist of *The Glass Key*, remains similarly incorruptible despite outward appearances to the contrary: A detective by temperament, if not by trade, Ned serves as friend and aide to the rising local politician Paul Madvig, involving himself deeply in political deals and trades; still, he persists in revealing a United States senator as the murderer of his own son and insists that the senator stand trial rather than commit suicide. The law of the land, however tarnished, remains a strong value in Hammett's novels, suggesting an abiding need for structure against the threat of anarchy.

With *The Thin Man*, Hammett moved in a new direction. For the first time, humor became a significant element in Hammett's fiction, infusing the novel with a lightness of tone that sets it quite apart from the almost documentary seriousness of *Red Harvest* and *The Glass Key*. Its protagonist, Nick Charles, has retired from the detective trade after his marriage to the rich and pretty Nora, some fifteen years his junior. Released from the need to work, he clearly prefers the carefree life of parties, travel, hotels, and round-the-clock drinking, all the while trading jokes and friendly banter with his attractive wife and other boon companions. Nevertheless, some habits die hard, and unpredicted events soon bring Nick's well-honed detective instincts back into operation. Moving back and forth between speakeasies and his lavish hotel suite, getting shot at by enraged gangsters, Nick urbanely unravels the mystery until, to no one's real surprise, one of his many casual friends stands revealed as the culprit.

It is no secret that Hammett, in his portrayal of the witty Nora and her relationship with Nick, was more than a little influenced by his own developing relationship with Lillian Hellman, who returned the favor in her several volumes of memoirs. Like Nick, Hammett at the time of *The Thin Man* was approaching middle age without the need to work, free at last to indulge his taste for parties and other carefree pursuits. *The Thin Man*, although certainly not planned as Hammett's final novel, is in a sense a fitting valedictory, an exuberant tour de force in which, ironically, the tensions contained in the earlier novels are finally released and perhaps dissipated. An additional irony exists within the book: Nick and Nora Charles may well be Hammett's best-known literary creations, perpetuated by the film version of the novel as well as by several sequels scripted in Hollywood by Hammett himself.

Red Harvest • Hammett's first published novel, *Red Harvest*, originally serialized in *Black Mask*, delivers in ample portion the harsh realism promised in its title. Indeed, the high body count of *Red Harvest* may well have set a kind of record to be met or broken by later efforts in the detective genre. Hammett's intention, however, is not merely to shock the reader; seen in retrospect, *Red Harvest* emerges as a parable of civilization and its possible mutations.

Nowhere in *Red Harvest* are Hammett's intentions more evident than in his choice of location, a mythical western community called Personville, better known as Poisonville. Some fifty years after the lawless days of the Wild West, Personville/ Poisonville has yet to be tamed, even as outlaws have been replaced by gangsters with East Coast accents wearing snap-brim hats instead of Stetsons. The Op, sent to

Personville at the request of one Donald Willsson, makes an appointment with Willson only to discover that he has been murdered before the planned meeting can take place. Undaunted, the Op proceeds to investigate Donald Willsson's murder, plunging deeper and deeper into the town's menacing and malevolent atmosphere. Among the more likely suspects is Willsson's father, Elihu, the town boss, who may well have tried to put a stop to his son's muckraking activities as publisher of the local newspaper. Other suspects, however, are present in abundance, at least until they begin to kill off one another during internecine combat partially masterminded by the Op. The Op, it seems, is particularly skillful in setting the various criminal elements loose upon one another, paving the way for eventual martial law and relative peace, "a sweet-smelling and thornless bed of roses." In the process, however, he frequently faces criminal charges himself; at the same time, the authorities who are pressing the charges may well be as corrupt as the more obvious criminals. In such an environment, the closest thing to a moral imperative is the Op's own case-hardened sense of justice.

The major weakness of *Red Harvest* is a bewildering multiplicity of characters and actions; often, a new character will be introduced and established, only to be killed on the following page. The acts of violence, although symptomatic of social ills and not included for their own sake (as in the work of later hard-boiled mystery writers such as Mickey Spillane), are so numerous as to weary even the least squeamish of readers, although a number of scenes are especially effective; in one, the Op, watching a boxing match that he has helped to "unfix," stands helpless as the unexpected winner falls dead in the ring with a knife at the base of his neck.

The Dain Curse • Later in the same year, 1929, Hammett published *The Dain Curse*, another formerly serialized novel featuring the Op as narrator and main character. Less sophisticated in its presentation than *Red Harvest*, *The Dain Curse* is more severely hampered by a multiplicity of characters and plot twists, all turning around the possibility of a family "curse" brought on by incest. Despite some rather skillful and memorable characterizations, *The Dain Curse* is generally agreed to be Hammett's weakest and least effective novel. Significantly, it is the last of Hammett's novels to feature the Op and the last (until *The Thin Man*, a different sort of novel) to be narrated in the first person.

The Maltese Falcon • Hammett's third novel, *The Maltese Falcon*, narrated dispassionately in the third person, combines the narrative strengths of his earlier works with a far more developed sense of characterization. Its protagonist, Sam Spade, although enough like the Op to be his slightly younger brother, is a more fully realized character caught and portrayed in all his ambiguity. Clearly the "brains" of the Spade and Archer Agency, he is careful to turn over to Miles Archer the case of a young woman client in whose presence he senses trouble. When Archer, blinded by the woman's flattery, goes forth to his death, Spade is hardly surprised, nor does he take many pains to hide his recent affair with the woman who is now Archer's widow. Spade, meanwhile, has grown tired of Iva Archer and her advances. Himself under suspicion for Archer's murder, Spade delves deeper into the case, learning that the young woman has given a number of aliases and cover stories. Her real name, it appears, is Brigid O'Shaughnessy, and it is not long before Spade connects her to a ring of international thieves, each of whom seems to be competing with the others for possession of an ancient and priceless treasure known as the Maltese Falcon. Supposedly, the football-sized sculpted bird, encrusted with precious stones, has been stolen and re-possessed numerous times in the four hundred years of its existence, having surfaced most recently in the hands of a Russian general.

Spade's quest eventually brings him in contact with most of the larcenous principals except for the general himself (who at the end of the novel is found to have substituted a worthless leaden counterfeit for the genuine article). Among the thieves are two particularly memorable characters, interpreted in the John Huston film by Sydney Greenstreet and Peter Lorre, respectively: Casper Gutman, an eloquent, grossly fat manipulator and adventurer, keeps trying to maneuver Spade into his confidence; meanwhile, the other, Joel Cairo, an obvious homosexual and member of the international underworld, repeatedly (and most unsuccessfully) tries to intimidate Spade with a handgun that Spade keeps taking away from him. In 1930, Hammett's frank portrayal of a homosexual was considered daring in the extreme; by 1941, it was possible for Huston to apply such a characterization to Gutman as well, whose homosexuality in the novel is little more than latent. The book, for example, mentions that Gutman is traveling with a grown daughter, but the daughter is never mentioned in the Huston film.

In both novel and film, Spade's character develops considerably as he attempts to deal simultaneously with the matters at hand and with his growing affection for the obviously perfidious Brigid O'Shaughnessy. In Brigid, it seems, Spade has at last met his proper match, a woman whose deviousness and native intelligence compare favorably with his own. In her presence, it is all too easy for Spade to forget the cloying advances of Iva Archer or even the tomboyish charms of his secretary Effie Perine; it is less easy, however, for him to forget the tightening web of circumstantial evidence in which he finds Brigid strongly enmeshed. After the coveted falcon has been revealed as a forgery, Spade confronts Brigid with evidence that she, and not her deceased cohort Floyd Thursby, fired the bullet that killed Miles Archer. For all Archer's weaknesses and Spade's personal contempt for the man, Spade remains true to the code that dictates arrest and prosecution for his partner's murderer. Explaining to an incredulous Brigid that he still thinks he loves her but cannot bring himself to trust her, he declares that he is sending her to jail and may or may not be waiting when she is freed. They are locked in an embrace when the police arrive to take her away.

Considerably more thoughtful and resonant than Hammett's earlier novels, *The Maltese Falcon* is his unquestioned masterpiece. The falcon itself, a contested piece of plunder that, in the novel, has occasioned theft and murder throughout recent history and that in its present form turns out to be a fake, is without doubt one of the strongest and best-developed images in contemporary American fiction. Another equally effective device, absent from the Huston film, is the Flitcraft parable that Spade tells to Brigid early in their relationship as a way of explaining his behavior. Early in his career, he recalls, he was hired to find a Seattle resident named Flitcraft who had disappeared mysteriously one day during the lunch hour, leaving behind a wife and two children. Spade later learned that, during the lunch break, Flitcraft had glimpsed his own mortality after a narrow escape from a falling beam. "He felt like somebody had taken the lid off his life and let him look at the works."

During that same day, he abandoned his family, wandering for two years, after which he fashioned for himself in Spokane a professional and family life very much like the one he had left behind in Seattle. "But that's the part of it I always liked," Spade tells Brigid. "He adjusted himself to beams falling, and then no more of them fell, and he adjusted himself to them not falling." Predictably, Spade's narrative has little effect on Brigid; for the reader, however, it does much to explain Hammett's approach to Spade as character and his own developing sense of the novelist's art. During that stage of his career, Hammett moved from "looking at the works" (*Red Harvest*) to a mature sense of contingency in which one's own deeply held convictions are all that matter.

The Glass Key • Acknowledged to have been Hammett's personal favorite among his five published novels, *The Glass Key* is the only one not to feature a trained detective as protagonist. A rather unlikely hero at first glance, Ned Beaumont is tubercular, an avid gambler without a regular job. His principal occupation is that of friend, conscience, and unofficial assistant to Paul Madvig, an amiable politician of forty-five who, one suspects, without Beaumont's help would have made even more mistakes than he already has. Himself the father of a grown daughter, Madvig is currently unmarried and in love with Janet Henry, daughter of an aristocratic and powerful United States senator. Janet has done little to encourage Madvig's attentions, and Beaumont, for his part, is determined to prevent his friend from making a fool of himself. Complications arise with the brutal murder of Taylor Henry, Janet's brother, who may or may not have been in love with Madvig's daughter Opal. As usual in Hammett's novels, there is an underworld connection; Taylor, it seems, was deeply in debt to a professional gambler at the time of his death.

As Madvig's loyal friend and aide, Beaumont sets out to discover the truth behind Taylor Henry's murder, displaying detective instincts worthy of Sam Spade or the Continental Op. Amid serious encounters with angry gangsters and corrupt police, Ned perseveres in his efforts to clear Madvig's name of suspicion in the murder, fully aware that he may well be a suspect himself. Meanwhile, to both Madvig's and Beaumont's consternation, Janet Henry appears to be falling in love with Beaumont, if only because he seems to be proof against her charms. As the action proceeds, it becomes increasingly clear to Beaumont that Taylor Henry could only have been killed by the senator, who has somehow prevailed upon Madvig to accept the burden of suspicion. When Beaumont finally confronts the senator with his suspicions, Henry admits to killing his son in a fit of anger and tampering with evidence at the scene of the crime; he asks only that Beaumont give him five minutes alone with his loaded revolver. Predictably, Beaumont refuses: "You'll take what's coming to you." Beaumont decides to leave town permanently, and, in a surprise twist at the end, he agrees to take Janet with him; the relationship awaiting them can only be surmised.

Like *The Maltese Falcon*, *The Glass Key* is a thoughtful and resonant novel, rich in memorable scenes and images. The glass key itself occurs in a dream that Janet has shortly after the start of her problematical relationship with Ned: She dreams that they arrive at a locked house piled high with food that they can see through the windows, yet when they open the door with a key found under the mat the house turns out to be filled with snakes as well. At the end of the novel, Janet reveals that she has not told Ned all of her dream: "The key was glass and shattered in our hands just as we got the door open, because the lock was stiff and we had to force it." Just as the Maltese Falcon dominates the book bearing its name, the glass key comes to symbolize the dangerous fragility of Janet's life and especially of her relationships with men—Paul Madvig, her father, and finally Ned Beaumont. Born to wealth and privilege, Janet is potentially dangerous to herself and others for reasons that Hammett suggests are outside her control; she does not share in her father's venality and is quite possibly a decent person beneath the veneer of her upbringing.

Not easily deceived, Ned Beaumont has been skeptical about the Henrys from the beginning; early in the book, he warns Paul against deeper involvement with either Janet or her father:

> Read about it in the *Post*—one of the few aristocrats left in American politics. And his daughter's an aristocrat. That's why I'm warning you to sew your shirt on when you go to see them, or you'll come away without it, because to them you're a form of lower animal life and none of the rules apply.

To Beaumont, the Henrys are thoughtless and dangerous, much like Tom and Daisy Buchanan as seen by Nick Carraway in F. Scott Fitzgerald's *The Great Gatsby* (1925). Janet, however, develops considerably during the course of the novel, and at the end there is just the barest chance that a change of scenery will allow her to work out a decent life in Ned Beaumont's company.

The Thin Man • Fifth and last of Hammett's novels, *The Thin Man* is the only one to have been written during his acquaintance with Lillian Hellman, whose witty presence is reflected throughout the novel. Thanks to the successful film version and various sequels, *The Thin Man* is, next to *The Maltese Falcon*, the most famous of Hammett's novels; it is also the least typical.

The narrator and protagonist of *The Thin Man* is Nick Charles (born Charalambides and proud of his Greek extraction), a former detective in his early forties who has married the rich and beautiful Nora, nearly young enough to be his daughter. Contrary to popular belief, the novel's title refers not to Charles himself but to one Clyde Miller Wynant, suspected of various crimes throughout the novel until the end, when he is revealed to have been the real killer's first victim: Wynant, an inventor, is described as being tall and painfully thin; at the end of the novel, his bones are found buried with clothes cut to fit a much larger man. In the filmed sequel, however, the title presumably refers to the dapper detective himself.

Peopled with a cast of café-society characters in addition to the usual underworld types, *The Thin Man* is considerably lighter in tone and texture than Hammett's earlier novels. Nick Charles, although clearly descended from Beaumont, Spade, and the Op, is nearly a playboy by comparison, trading lighthearted jokes and double entendres with his wife and boon companions. Close parallels may be drawn between Charles and the author himself, who by the time of *The Thin Man* had achieved sufficient material success to obviate his need to work. Lillian Hellman observes, however, that the actual writing of *The Thin Man* took place during a period of abstemious, almost monastic seclusion that differed sharply from Hammett's usual pattern of behavior during those years, as well as from the carefree life ascribed to Nick and Nora in the novel.

Most of the action of *The Thin Man* turns upon the certifiably eccentric personality of the title character, Clyde Wynant, a former client of Nick during his latter years as a detective. Among the featured characters are Wynant's former wife, son, and daughter, as well as his lawyer, Herbert Macaulay. In particular, the Wynants are memorable, deftly drawn characters, nearly as eccentric in their own ways as the missing *paterfamilias*. Wynant's son, Gilbert, about eighteen, is notable for his voracious reading and morbid curiosity concerning such matters as murder, cannibalism, and abnormal psychology. Dorothy Wynant, a year or two older than Gilbert, keeps trying to parlay a former girlhood crush on Nick Charles into something more serious. Their mother, known as Mimi Jorgensen, is a vain, treacherous woman cut from the same cloth as Brigid O'Shaughnessy of *The Maltese Falcon*; she too makes repeated claims upon Nick's reluctant attentions.

Throughout the novel, Mimi and her children coexist uneasily in a state of armed truce that occasionally erupts into open warfare, providing scenes of conflict between parent and child considered rather daring at the time. Among the featured characters, only Macaulay appears sane or even remotely sympathetic, yet it is he who ultimately stands accused of the financial double-dealing and multiple murders originally attributed to Wynant, not to mention the murder of Wynant himself.

Like Hammett's earlier novels, *The Thin Man* is realistic in its portrayal of urban life during Prohibition, when the criminal element was even more visible and overt in its actions than in later times. Despite the witty urbanity of his characters, Hammett harbors few illusions concerning human nature. When Nora asks Nick at the end of the novel what will become of Mimi and her children, he replies, "Nothing new. They'll go on being Mimi and Dorothy and Gilbert just as you and I will go on being us and the Quinns will go on being the Quinns." The novel ends with Nora telling Nick that his explanation is "pretty unsatisfactory." Perhaps it is, Hammett implies, but that is the nature of life.

Partly because of failing health and the pressures of work in Hollywood, Hammett published no fiction after *The Thin Man*. His reputation thus rests on a small and somewhat uneven body of work, redeemed by frequent flashes of brilliance. Notable for their influence upon the work of Raymond Chandler, Ross Macdonald, and a host of lesser writers in the mystery genre, Hammett's novels have also exercised an immeasurable influence on novelists and filmmakers outside the genre.

David B. Parsell

Other major works

SHORT FICTION: *Secret Agent X-9*, 1934 (with Alex Raymond); *The Adventures of Sam Spade, and Other Stories*, 1945; *The Continental Op*, 1945; *The Return of the Continental Op*, 1945; *Hammett Homicides*, 1946; *Nightmare Town*, 1948; *The Creeping Siamese*, 1950; *Woman in the Dark*, 1951; *A Man Named Thin, and Other Stories*, 1962; *The Big Knockover: Selected Stories and Short Novels*, 1966 (Lillian Hellman, editor); *Nightmare Town: Stories*, 1999 (Kirby McCauley, Martin H. Greenberg, and Ed Gorman, editors); *Crime Stories, and Other Writings*, 2001; *Lost Stories*, 2005.

SCREENPLAYS: *City Streets*, 1931 (with Oliver H. P. Garrett and Max Marcin); *Mister Dynamite*, 1935 (with Doris Malloy and Harry Clork); *After the Thin Man*, 1936 (with Frances Goodrich and Albert Hackett); *Another Thin Man*, 1939 (with Goodrich and Hackett); *Watch on the Rhine*, 1943 (with Lillian Hellman).

NONFICTION: *The Battle of the Aleutians*, 1944 (with Robert Colodny); *Selected Letters of Dashiell Hammett, 1921-1960*, 2001 (Richard Layman with Julie M. Rivett, editors).

EDITED TEXTS: *Creeps by Night*, 1931 (also known as *Modern Tales of Horror, The Red Brain*, and *Breakdown*).

Bibliography

Bruccoli, Matthew J., and Richard Layman. *Hardboiled Mystery Writers: Raymond Chandler, Dashiell Hammett, Ross Macdonald.* New York: Carroll and Graf, 2002. A handy supplemental reference that includes interviews, letters, and previously published studies. Illustrated.

Dooley, Dennis. *Dashiell Hammett.* New York: Frederick Ungar, 1984. A particularly useful study for those interested in Hammett's short fiction, which is covered in half of this book. His major novels are also discussed in the context of his life and his works considered in the context of their times. Contains notes, a bibliography, and an index.

Gale, Robert L. *A Dashiell Hammett Companion.* Westport, Conn.: Greenwood Press, 2000. An encyclopedia devoted to Hammett. Includes bibliographical references and an index.

Gregory, Sinda. *Private Investigations: The Novels of Dashiell Hammett.* Carbondale: Southern Illinois University Press, 1985. The first chapter discusses Hammett, his Pinkerton experiences, and the hard-boiled detective genre. Subsequent chapters focus on each of his five major novels. Foreword by Francis M. Nevins, Jr. Includes a preface and a conclusion, notes, a bibliography, and an index.

Johnson, Diane. *Dashiell Hammett: A Life.* New York: Random House, 1983. The most comprehensive biography of Hammett, this book adds considerable information to the public record of Hammett's life but does not provide much critical analysis of the works. More than half the volume deals with the years after Hammett stopped publishing fiction and during which he devoted most of his time to leftist political activism.

Marling, William. *The American Roman Noir: Hammett, Cain, and Chandler.* Athens: University of Georgia Press, 1995. Comparative study of Hammett, James Cain, and Raymond Chandler as noir writers

Metress, Christopher, ed. *The Critical Response to Dashiell Hammett.* Westport, Conn.: Greenwood Press, 1994. A generous compilation of reviews and general studies, with a comprehensive introduction, chronology, and bibliography.

Nolan, William F. *Hammett: A Life at the Edge.* New York: Congdon and Weed, 1983. Author of the first full-length study of Hammett in 1969, Nolan here builds upon his earlier work and that of others to present a convincing portrait of a singularly private man with a code of honor that paralleled those of his detectives. The discussions of the works are straightforward and sound.

Nyman, Jopi. *Hard-Boiled Fiction and Dark Romanticism.* New York: Peter Lang, 1998. Studies the fiction of Hammett, James M. Cain, and Ernest Hemingway. Includes bibliographical references

Panek, LeRoy Lad. *Reading Early Hammett: A Critical Study of the Fiction Prior to the "Maltese Falcon".* Jefferson, N.C.: McFarland, 2004. An absorbing analysis of Hammett's earliest work, including magazine writing and essays on various topics, and particular focus on Hammett's Continental Op character.

Skenazy, Paul. "The 'Heart's Field': Dashiell Hammett's Anonymous Territory." In *San Francisco in Fiction: Essays in a Regional Literature,* edited by David Fine and Paul Skenazy. Albuquerque: University of New Mexico Press, 1995. A consideration of the importance of history and place in Hammett's fiction. Argues that it is wrong to associate Hammett's concern with expedience, environment, habit, training, and chance with a specifically Wild West tradition.

Symons, Julian. *Dashiell Hammett.* San Diego: Harcourt Brace Jovanovich, 1985. A brief but substantive book by a leading English writer of crime fiction and criticism. Symons believes that Hammett created "A specifically American brand of crime story . . . that transcends the form and limits of [its] genre and can be compared with the best fiction produced in America between the two world wars." His considerations of the works support this judgment. Contains a useful select bibliography.

Wolfe, Peter. *Beams Falling: The Art of Dashiell Hammett.* Bowling Green, Ohio: Bowling Green State University Press, 1980. Especially good in his analyses of Hammett's short fiction, Wolfe surpasses other writers in showing the relationship of each work to the total output. The author of books on other crime-fiction writers (Raymond Chandler, John le Carré, and Ross Macdonald), Wolfe has a knowledge and appreciation of the genre that are apparent in this excellent study.

Nathaniel Hawthorne

Born: Salem, Massachusetts; July 4, 1804
Died: Plymouth, New Hampshire; May 19, 1864

Principal long fiction • *Fanshawe: A Tale*, 1828; *The Scarlet Letter*, 1850; *The House of the Seven Gables*, 1851; *The Blithedale Romance*, 1852; *The Marble Faun*, 1860; *Septimius Felton*, 1872 (fragment); *The Dolliver Romance*, 1876 (fragment); *The Ancestral Footstep*, 1883 (fragment); *Doctor Grimshawe's Secret*, 1883 (fragment).

Other literary forms • Many of Nathaniel Hawthorne's short stories were originally published anonymously in such magazines as the *Token* and the *New England Magazine* between 1830 and 1837. Several collections appeared during his lifetime, including *Twice-Told Tales* (1837; expanded 1842), *Mosses from an Old Manse* (1846), and *The Snow-Image and Other Twice-Told Tales* (1851). Houghton Mifflin published the complete works in the Riverside edition (1850-1882) and the Old Manse edition (1900). Hawthorne also wrote stories for children, collected in *Grandfather's Chair* (1841), *Biographical Stories for Children* (1842), *True Stories from History and Biography* (1851), *A Wonder-Book for Boys and Girls* (1852), and *Tanglewood Tales for Boys and Girls* (1853). With the help of his sister Elizabeth, he edited the *American Magazine of Useful and Entertaining Knowledge* (1836) and *Peter Parley's Universal History* (1837) and, as a favor to would-be president Franklin Pierce, wrote a biography for the presidential campaign. His last completed work was *Our Old Home* (1863), a series of essays about his sojourn in England. At the time of his death, he left four unfinished fragments: *Septimius Felton* (1872), *The Dolliver Romance* (1876), *The Ancestral Footstep* (1883), and *Doctor Grimshawe's Secret* (1883).

Achievements • Few other American authors, with the possible exception of Henry James, have engaged in so deliberate a literary apprenticeship as Hawthorne. After an initial period of anonymity during his so-called "solitary years" from 1825 to 1837, he achieved an unfaltering reputation as an author of short stories, romances, essays, and children's books. He is remembered not only for furthering the development of the short-story form but also for distinguishing between the novel and the romance. The prefaces to his long works elucidate his theory of the "neutral ground"—the junction between the actual and the imaginary—where romance takes place. He is noted for his masterful exploration of the psychology of guilt and sin; his study of the Puritan heritage contributed to the emerging sense of historicity that characterized the American Renaissance of the mid-nineteenth century. Hawthorne is unrivaled as an allegorist, especially as one whose character typologies and symbols achieve universality through their psychological validity. Although he has been faulted for sentimentality, lapses into archaic diction, and gothicism, Hawthorne's works continue to evoke the "truth of the human heart" that is the key to their continuing appeal.

Biography • Nathaniel Hawthorne was born in Salem, Massachusetts, on July 4, 1804. On his father's side, Hawthorne was descended from William Hathorne, who settled in Massachusetts in 1630 and whose son John was one of the judges in the 1692

Salem witchcraft trials. Hawthorne's father, a sea captain, married Elizabeth Clarke Manning in 1801. Mrs. Hathorne's English ancestors immigrated to the New World in 1679; her brother Robert, a successful businessman, assumed responsibility for her affairs after Captain Hathorne died of yellow fever in Suriname in 1808.

After his father's death, Hawthorne, his two sisters Elizabeth Manning and Maria Louisa, and his mother moved into the populous Manning household, a move that on one hand estranged him from his Hathorne relatives and on the other provided him with an attentive family life, albeit an adult one, for the eight aunts and uncles living there were unmarried at that time. Perhaps the adult company accounted in part for his literary tastes, as did his less than regular education. Although he attended a school taught by Joseph Emerson Worcester, a renowned philologist of the time, Hawthorne led a sedentary existence for almost three years after being lamed at the age of nine. During his enforced inactivity, he spent long afternoons reading Edmund Spenser, John Bunyan, and William Shakespeare, his favorite authors.

When Hawthorne was twelve, his mother moved the family temporarily to Raymond, Maine, where the Mannings owned a tract of land. The outdoor activity occasioned by nearby Lake Sebago and the surrounding forest land proved beneficial to Hawthorne; quickly recovering his health, he became an able marksman and fisherman. During these years, interrupted by schooling with the Reverend Caleb Bradley, a stern man not to Hawthorne's liking, Hawthorne accumulated Wordsworthian memories of the wilderness and of village life that were to be evoked in his fiction. Recalled to Salem, he began in 1820 to be tutored for college by the lawyer Benjamin Lynde Oliver, working, in the meantime, as a bookkeeper for his Uncle Robert, an occupation that foreshadowed his later business ventures. He continued his reading, including such authors as Henry Fielding, Sir Walter Scott, William Godwin, Matthew "Monk" Lewis, and James Hogg, and produced a family newspaper, *The Spectator*, characterized by humorous notices and essays and parodies of sentimental verse. The first member of his family to attend college, he was sent to Bowdoin, where he graduated eighteenth in a class of thirty-eight. Known for his quietness and gentle humor, he disliked declamations, was negligent in many academic requirements, and, indeed, was fined for playing cards. His fellow students at Bowdoin included Henry Wadsworth Longfellow and Franklin Pierce, who later was elected president of the United States.

Hawthorne had determined early on a career in letters. Returning to Salem upon graduation, he began a self-imposed apprenticeship, the so-called "solitary years." During this time, Hawthorne privately published *Fanshawe*, a work that he so thoroughly repudiated that his wife, Sophia, knew nothing of it; he published many short stories anonymously and unsuccessfully attempted to interest publishers in such collections as *Seven Tales of My Native Land*, *Provincial Tales*, and *The Storyteller*. As a means of support he edited the *American Magazine of Useful and Entertaining Knowledge* and compiled *Peter Parley's Universal History*. Not until the publication of *Twice-Told Tales* under the secret financial sponsorship of his friend Horatio Bridge did Hawthorne's name become publicly known. The label "solitary years" is somewhat of a misnomer, for, as his journals indicate, Hawthorne visited with friends, went for long walks and journeys, and, most important, met Sophia Peabody, the daughter of Dr. Nathaniel Peabody. For Hawthorne, Sophia was the key by which he was released from "a life of shadows" to the "truth of the human heart." Four years passed, however, before they could marry—four years in which Hawthorne became measurer in the Boston Custom House, which he called a "grievous thraldom," and then, although not sympathetic to the burgeoning transcendental movement, joined the utopian community Brook Farm (April, 1841), investing one thousand dollars in an attempt to establish a home for himself and Sophia.

After little more than six months, Hawthorne gave up the communal venture and, settling in the Old Manse at Concord, married Sophia on July 19, 1842. His financial difficulties were exacerbated by the birth of his daughter Una in 1844; finally, in 1846, when his son Julian was born and *Mosses from an Old Manse* was published, he was appointed surveyor of the Salem Custom House, a post he held from 1846 to 1849, when a political upset cost him his job. With more time to write and with the pressure to support a growing family, Hawthorne began a period of intense literary activity; his friendship with Herman Melville dates from that time. *The Scarlet Letter,* whose ending sent Sophia to bed with a grievous headache, was finished in February, 1850.

Library of Congress

The House of the Seven Gables appeared in 1851, the year Hawthorne's daughter Rose was born; by the end of the next year, Hawthorne had completed *The Blithedale Romance,* two volumes of children's tales, *The Life of Franklin Pierce,* and a collection of stories, *The Snow-Image and Other Twice-Told Tales.*

From 1853 to 1857, Hawthorne served as United States consul at Liverpool, England, a political appointment under President Franklin Pierce. After four years of involvement with the personal and financial problems of stranded Americans, Hawthorne resigned and lived in Rome and Florence from 1857 to 1858, where he acquired ideas for his last romance, *The Marble Faun.* After returning with his family to the United States, Hawthorne worked on four unfinished romances, *Doctor Grimshawe's Secret, Septimius Felton, The Dolliver Romance,* and *The Ancestral Footstep,* in which two themes are dominant: the search for immortality and the American attempt to establish title to English ancestry. His carefully considered essays on the paucity of American tradition, the depth of British heritage, and the contrast between democracy and entrenched class systems were first published in *The Atlantic Monthly* and then collected as *Our Old Home.* After a lingering illness, he died at Plymouth, New Hampshire, on May 19, 1864, during a trip with Franklin Pierce. He was buried at Sleepy Hollow Cemetery in Concord, Massachusetts.

Analysis • Central to Nathaniel Hawthorne's romances is his idea of a "neutral territory," described in the Custom House sketch that precedes *The Scarlet Letter* as a place "somewhere between the real world and fairy-land, where the Actual and the Imaginary may meet, and each imbue itself with the nature of the other." A romance, according to Hawthorne, is different from the novel, which maintains a "minute fidelity . . . to the probable and ordinary course of man's experience." In the neutral territory of romance, however, the author may make use of the "marvellous" to heighten atmospheric effects, if he or she also presents "the truth of the human heart." As long as the writer of romance creates characters whose virtues, vices, and sensibilities are distinctly human, he or she may place them in an environment that is out of the ordinary—or, that is, in fact, allegorical. Thus, for example, while certain elements—the stigma of the scarlet letter, or Donatello's faun ears—are fantastical in conception, they represent a moral stance that is true to nature. Dimmesdale's guilt at concealing his adultery with Hester Prynne is, indeed, as destructive as the wound on his breast, and Donatello's pagan nature is expressed in the shape of his ears.

A number of recurring thematic patterns and character types appear in Hawthorne's novels and tales, as Randall Stewart suggests in the introduction to *The American Notebooks by Nathaniel Hawthorne* (1932). These repetitions show Hawthorne's emphasis on the effects of events on the human heart rather than on the events themselves. One common motif is concern for the past, or, as Hawthorne says in the preface to *The House of the Seven Gables*, his "attempt to connect a bygone time with the very present that is flitting away from us." Hawthorne's interest in the Puritan past was perhaps sparked by his "discovery," as a teenager, of his Hathorne connections; it was certainly influenced by his belief that progress was impeded by inheritance, that "the wrong-doing of one generation lives into the successive ones, and . . . becomes a pure and uncontrollable mischief." For Hawthorne, then, the past must be reckoned with, and then put aside; the eventual decay of aristocratic families is not only inevitable, but desirable.

Hawthorne's understanding of tradition is illustrated in many of his works. In *The Scarlet Letter*, for example, he explores the effect of traditional Puritan social and theological expectations on three kinds of sinners: the adultress (Hester), the hypocrite (Dimmesdale), and the avenger (Chillingworth), only to demonstrate that the punishment they inflict on themselves far outweighs the public castigation. Hester, in fact, inverts the rigidified Puritan system, represented by the scarlet letter, whose meaning she changes from "adultress" to "able." Probably the most specific treatment of the theme, however, is found in *The House of the Seven Gables*, in which the Pyncheon family house and fortune have imprisoned both Hepzibah and Clifford, one in apathy and one in insanity; only Phoebe, the country cousin who cares little for wealth, can lighten the burden, not only for her relatives but also for Holgrave, a descendent of the Maules who invoked the original curse. In *The Marble Faun*, Hawthorne goes to Italy for his "sense of the past," although Hilda and Kenyon are both Americans. The past in this novel is represented not only in the setting but also in Donatello's pagan nature; at the end, both Miriam and the faun figure engage in a purgatorial expiation of the past.

Another recurring theme is that of isolation. Certainly Hawthorne himself felt distanced from normal social converse by his authorial calling. The firsthand descriptions of Hawthorne extant today present him more as an observer than as a participant, a stance over which he himself agonized. In writing to Longfellow about his apprenticeship years, he complained that he was "carried apart from the main current of life" and that "there is no fate in this world so horrible as to have no share in either its joys or sorrows. For the last ten years, I have not lived, but only dreamed about living." For Hawthorne, Sophia was his salvation, his link to human companionship. Perhaps that is why he wrote so evocatively of Hester Prynne's isolation; indeed, Hester's difficult task of rearing the elfin child Pearl without help from Dimmesdale is the obverse of Hawthorne's own happy domestic situation. Almost every character that Hawthorne created experiences some sense of isolation, sometimes from a consciousness of sin, sometimes from innocence itself, or sometimes from a deliberate attempt to remain aloof.

According to Hawthorne, this kind of isolation, most intense when it is self-imposed, frequently comes from a consciousness of sin or from what he calls the "violation of the sanctity of the human heart." For Hawthorne, the "unpardonable sin" is just such a violation, in which one individual becomes subjected to another's intellectual or scientific (rather than emotional) interest. Chillingworth is a good example; as Hester's unacknowledged husband, he lives with Dimmesdale, deliberately intensifying the minister's hidden guilt. In *The Blithedale Romance*, Coverdale's voyeurism (and certainly his name) suggests this kind of violation, as does Westervelt's manipulation of Priscilla and Hollingsworth's of Zenobia. Certainly, Clifford's isolation in insanity is the fault of Judge Pyncheon. There is also the implication that the mysterious model who haunts Miriam in *The Marble Faun* has committed the same sin, thereby isolating both of them. One of the few characters to refuse such violation is Holgrave, who, in *The House of the Seven Gables*, forbears to use his mesmeric powers on Phoebe.

Such a set of recurring themes is bolstered by a pervasive character typology. Although literary works such as those by Edmund Spenser, John Milton, William Shakespeare, and John Bunyan form the historical context for many of Hawthorne's characters, many are further developments of his own early character types. *Fanshawe*, for example, introduced the pale, idealistic scholarly hero more fully developed in Dimmesdale. Others, personifications of abstract qualities, seem motivated by purely evil ends. Westervelt is one type; sophisticated and learned in mesmerism, he takes as his victim the innocent Priscilla. Chillingworth, whose literary ancestry can probably be traced to Miltonic devil-figures, is old and bent but possesses a compelling intellect that belies his lack of physical strength. Finally, the worldly Judge Pyncheon manifests a practical, unimaginative streak that connects him to Peter Hovenden of Hawthorne's short story "The Artist of the Beautiful." As for Hawthorne's heroines, Hilda and Phoebe embody the domesticity that Hawthorne admired in Sophia; Priscilla, like Alice Pyncheon before her, is frail and easily subjugated; and Hester, Zenobia, and Miriam exhibit an oriental beauty and intellectual pride.

Fanshawe • Three years after Hawthorne graduated from Bowdoin College, he anonymously published the apprenticeship novel *Fanshawe* at his own expense. Although he almost immediately repudiated the work, it remains not only a revealing biographical statement but also a testing ground for themes and characters that he later developed with great success.

"No man can be a poet and a bookkeeper at the same time," Hawthorne complained in a letter he wrote while engaged in his Uncle Robert's stagecoach business before college. Just such a dichotomy is illustrated in *Fanshawe*, in which the pale scholar fails to rejoin the course of ordinary life and, in effect, consigns himself to death, while the active individual Edward Walcott wins the heroine, Ellen Langton, and so becomes, to use Hawthorne's later words, part of "The magnetic chain of humanity." To be sure, Fanshawe is an overdrawn figure, owing, as Arlin Turner points out, something to Gorham Deane, a Bowdoin schoolmate, and much to Charles Maturin's gothic novel *Melmoth the Wanderer* (1820), from which Ellen's guardian, Dr. Melmoth, takes his name. In repudiating the book, however, Hawthorne is less repudiating the gothic form than he is an early, faulty conception of a writer's life. Certainly, Hawthorne recognized the tension between the intellectual and the practical lives, as his letters and journals suggest, especially when he was at the Boston and Salem Custom Houses and at the consulate in Liverpool. Moreover, as Frederick Crews notes, Fanshawe and Walcott are "complimentary sides," together fulfilling Hawthorne's twin desire for "self-abnegation" and "heroism and amorous success." Nevertheless, as the pattern of his own life makes clear, Hawthorne did not retire (as did Fanshawe) to an early grave after the solitary apprenticeship years; rather, he married Sophia Peabody (fictionally prefigured in Ellen Langton) and, in becoming involved in the ordinary affairs of life, merged the figures of Fanshawe and Walcott.

The plot of the novel—the abduction of Ellen by the villainous Butler—introduces Hawthorne's later exploration of the misuse of power, while the configuration of characters foreshadows not only the scholar figure but also two other types: the dark villain, whose sexual motivation remains ambiguous, and the innocent, domestic young heroine, later developed as Phoebe and Hilda. The fact that Fanshawe should rescue Ellen, appearing like Milton's Raphael over the thickly wooded valley where Butler has secluded her, suggests that he is able to enter the world of action; but that he should refuse her offer of marriage, saying, "I have no way to prove that I deserve your generosity, but by refusing to take advantage of it," is uncharacteristic in comparison with Hawthorne's later heroes such as Holgrave and Kenyon. It may be that after his marriage to Sophia, Hawthorne could not conceive of a triangle existing when two "soul mates" had found each other, for in similar character configurations in *The House of the Seven Gables* and *The Marble Faun*, both Holgrave and Kenyon have no rivals to fear for Phoebe and Hilda.

In setting, however, *Fanshawe* is a precursor to the later novels, as well as an unformulated precedent for Hawthorne's famous definition of romance. Probably begun while Hawthorne was enrolled at Bowdoin, the novel has as its setting Harley College, a picturesque, secluded institution. Formal classroom tutoring is not the novel's central interest, however, just as it was not in Hawthorne's own life; nor is the novel completely a roman à clef in which actual people and places are thinly disguised. Rather, as is the case in the later novels in which Salem itself, Brook Farm, and Rome are the existing actualities on which Hawthorne draws, so in *Fanshawe* the setting is an excuse for the psychological action. To be sure, the later, sophisticated, symbolic effects are missing, and the interpenetration of the actual by the imaginary is not as successful as in, for instance, *The Scarlet Letter*; nevertheless, although what later becomes marvelous is here simply melodramatic, the imagination plays a large, if unformulated, role in the novel's success.

The Scarlet Letter • Begun as a tale and completed shortly after Hawthorne's dismissal from the Salem surveyorship, *The Scarlet Letter* is prefaced by an essay titled "The Custom House" in which Hawthorne not only gives an imaginative account of his business experience but also presents a theory of composition. The essay is thus a distillation of the practical and the imaginative. It includes scant praise for the unimaginative William Lee, the antediluvian permanent inspector whose common-place attitude typified for Hawthorne the Customs operation. In writing, however, Hawthorne exorcised his spleen at his political dismissal that, coupled with charges of malfeasance, was instigated by the Whigs who wanted him replaced; as Arlin Turner comments, "The decapitated surveyor, in becoming a character in a semifictional account, had all but ceased to be Hawthorne." The writer, in short, had made fiction out of his business experiences. He also had speculated about the preconceptions necessary for the creator of romances; such a man, he decided, must be able to perceive the "neutral territory" where the "actual" and the "imaginary" meet. The result of that perception was *The Scarlet Letter.*

In the prefatory essay to the book, Hawthorne establishes the literalism of the scarlet letter, which, he says, he has in his possession as an old, faded, tattered remnant of the past. Just as Hawthorne is said by Terence Martin to contemplate the letter, thus generating the novel, so the reader is forced to direct his attention to the primary symbol, not simply of Hester's adultery or of her ability, but of the way in which the restrictions of the Puritan forebears are transcended by the warmth of the human heart. Through this symbol, then, and through its living counterpart, Pearl, the daughter of Hester and Dimmesdale, Hawthorne examines the isolating effects of a sense of sin, using as his psychological setting the Puritan ethos.

With Hester's first public appearance with the infant Pearl and the heavily embroidered scarlet letter on her breast, the child—Hester's "torment" and her "joy"—and the letter become identified. Hester's guilt is a public one; Dimmesdale's is not. To admit to his share in the adultery is to relinquish his standing as the minister of the community, and so, initially too weak to commit himself, he pleads with Hester to confess her partner in the sin. She does not do so, nor does she admit that Chillingworth, the doctor who pursues Dimmesdale, is her husband. Three solitary people, then, are inexorably bound together by the results of the sin but are unable to communicate with one another.

The Puritan intention of bringing the sinner into submission has the opposite effect upon Hester, who, with a pride akin to humility, tenaciously makes a way for herself in the community. As an angel of mercy to the suffering, the sick, and the heavy of heart, she becomes a living model of charity that the townspeople, rigidly enmeshed in their Puritan theology, are unable to emulate. In addition, she exercises a talent for fine embroidery, so that even the bride has her clothing embellished with the sinner's finery. Hester's ostracization hardens her pride until, as she says to Dimmesdale in the forest, their act has a "consecration of its own." The adultery, in short, achieves a validation quite outside the letter of the Puritan law, and Hester finds no reason not to suggest that Dimmesdale run away with her in a repetition of the temptation and the original sin.

In the meantime, Dimmesdale has not had the relief of Hester's public confession. As veiled confessions, his sermons take on an ever growing intensity and apparent sincerity, gaining many converts to the church. Under Chillingworth's scrutiny, however, Dimmesdale's concealed guilt creates a physical manifestation, a scarlet letter inscribed in his flesh. Although Hester's letter has yet to work its way inward to repentance, Dimmesdale's is slowly working its way outward. Chillingworth himself, initially a scholar, becomes dedicated to the cause of intensifying the minister's sufferings. Although Chillingworth eventually takes partial responsibility for Hester's sin, admitting that as a scholarly recluse he should not have taken a young wife, he inexorably causes his own spiritual death. He joins a line of scientist-experimenters who deprive their victims of intellectual curiosity, violating "the truth of the human heart" and severing themselves from "the magnetic chain of humanity." He becomes, as Harry Levin notes, the lowest in the hierarchy of sinners, for while Hester and Dimmesdale have at least joined in passion, Chillingworth is isolated in pride.

As Terence Martin suggests, the scaffold scenes are central to the work. For Dimmesdale, public abnegation is the key: Standing as a penitent on the scaffold at midnight is insufficient, for his act is illuminated only by the light of a great comet. His decision to elope with Hester is also insufficient to remove his guilt; what he considers to be the beginning of a "new life" is a reenactment of the original deed. In the end, the scaffold proves the only real escape from the torments devised by Chillingworth, for in facing the community with Hester and Pearl, the minister faces himself and removes the concealment that is a great part of his guilt. His "new life" is, in fact, death, and he offers no hope to Hester that they will meet again, for to do so would be to succumb to temptation again. Only Pearl, who marries a lord, leaves the community permanently; as the innocent victim, she in effect returns to her mother's home to expiate her mother's sin.

Like Fanshawe, then, Dimmesdale causes his own demise, but he is provided with motivation. In Pearl, Hawthorne was influenced perhaps by the antics of Una, his first child, but even her name, which is reminiscent of the medieval Pearl-Poet's "pearl of great price"—his soul—indicates that she is emblematic. Likewise, the minister's name is indicative of the valley of the shadow of death, just as Chillingworth's suggests his cold nature. The successful meshing of the literal and allegorical levels in this tale of the effects of concealed sin and the universality of its theme continues to lend interest to the work.

The House of the Seven Gables • As Hawthorne notes in his preface to *The House of the Seven Gables*, he intends to show the mischief that the past causes when it lives into the present, particularly when coupled with the question of an inheritance. Hawthorne's mood is similar to that of Henry David Thoreau when, in *Walden* (1854), Thoreau makes his famous plea to "simplify," evoking the image of Everyman traveling on the road of life, carrying his onerous possessions on his back. The family curse that haunts Hepzibah and Clifford Pyncheon, the hidden property deed, and even Hepzibah's dreams of an unexpected inheritance are so centered on the past that the characters are unable to function in the present. In fact, says Hawthorne, far more worrisome than the missing inheritance is the "moral disease" that is passed from one generation to the next.

This "moral disease" results from the greed of the family progenitor, Colonel Pyncheon, who coveted the small tract of land owned by one Matthew Maule. Maule's curse—"God will give him blood to drink"—comes true on the day the new Pyncheon mansion, built on the site of Maule's hut, is to be consecrated. The Colonel dies, presumably from apoplexy but possibly from foul play, and from that day, Hawthorne says, a throwback to the Colonel appears in each generation—a calculating, practical man, who, as the inheritor, commits again "the great guilt of his ancestor" in not making restoration to the Maule descendants. Clifford, falsely imprisoned for the murder of his uncle Jaffrey Pyncheon, the one Pyncheon willing to make restitution, is persecuted after his release by Judge Pyncheon, another of Jaffrey's nephews and Jaffrey's real murderer, for his presumed knowledge of the hiding place of the Indian deed giving title to their uncle's property.

In contrast to these forces from the past, Hawthorne poses Phoebe, a Pyncheon country cousin with no pretensions to wealth but with a large fund of domesticity and a warm heart. Almost certainly modeled on Sophia, Phoebe, like Hilda in *The Marble Faun*, possesses an unexpected power, a "homely witchcraft." Symbolically, as Crews suggests, she neutralizes the morbidity in the Pyncheon household and eventually stands as an "ideal parent" to Hepzibah and Clifford. Indeed, Phoebe brings her enfeebled relatives into the circle of humanity.

If Phoebe represents the living present, Holgrave, the daguerreotypist and descendant of the Maules, represents the future. Like Clifford, however, who is saved by his imprisonment from an aesthetic version of the unpardonable sin, Holgrave runs the risk of becoming merely a cold-blooded observer. Like Hawthorne, Holgrave is a writer, boarding at the House of the Seven Gables to observe the drama created as the past spills into the present and turning Pyncheon history into fiction. He is, nevertheless, a reformer. In an echo of Hawthorne's preface, he would have buildings made of impermanent materials, ready to be built anew with each generation; likewise, he would merge old family lines into the stream of humanity. Although Holgrave's progressive views become mitigated once he marries Phoebe, he is rescued from becoming a Chillingworth by his integrity, his conscience, and his reverence for the human soul. Although he unintentionally hypnotizes Phoebe by reading her his story of Matthew Maule's mesmerism of Alice Pyncheon, he eschews his power, thereby not only saving himself and her from a Dimmesdale/Chillingworth relationship but also breaking the chain of vengeance that was in his power to perpetuate. The chain of past circumstances is also broken by the death of Judge Pyncheon, who, unlike Holgrave, intended to exercise his psychological power to force Clifford to reveal where the Indian deed is hidden. Stricken by apoplexy (or Maule's curse), however, the Judge is left in solitary possession of the house as Clifford and Hepzibah flee in fear.

Holgrave's integrity and death itself thus prevent a reenactment of the original drama of power and subjection that initiated the curse. As Holgrave learns, the Judge himself murdered his bachelor uncle and destroyed a will that gave the inheritance to Clifford. Although exonerated, Clifford's intellect cannot be recalled to its former state, and so he remains a testimonial to the adverse effects of "violation of the human heart."

During Hepzibah and Clifford's flight from the scene of the Judge's death, Phoebe, representing the present, and Holgrave, the future, pledge their troth, joining the Pyncheon and Maule families. Hawthorne's happy ending, although deliberately prepared, surprised many of his critics, who objected that Holgrave's decision to "plant" a family and to build a stone house were motivated only by the dictates of the plot. F. D. Matthiessen, for example, suggests that Hawthorne's democratic streak blinded him to the implication that Holgrave was simply setting up a new dynasty. On the other hand, for Martin, the decision is foreshadowed; Holgrave's is a compromise position in which he maintains the importance of the structure of society while suggesting that the content be changed, just as a stone house might be redecorated according to its owners' tastes. In marrying Holgrave, Phoebe incorporates Pyncheon blood with the "mass of the people," for the original Maule was a poor man and his son a carpenter.

The Blithedale Romance • The only one of Hawthorne's romances to be told by a first-person narrator, *The Blithedale Romance* is grounded in Hawthorne's abortive attempt to join the utopian Brook Farm. Like Hawthorne, Miles Coverdale notes the disjunction between a life of labor and a life of poetry; like Hawthorne, he never wholeheartedly participates in the community. In fact, to Crews, the work displays "an inner coherence of self-debate." Coverdale is the isolated man viewed from inside; as a self-conscious observer, he is the most Jamesian of all of Hawthorne's characters. As Martin notes, Hawthorne sacrifices certain aesthetic advantages in allowing Coverdale to tell his own story. Although his name is as evocative as, for example, Chillingworth's, Coverdale loses symbolic intensity because many of his explanations—his noting, for example, that his illness upon arriving at Blithedale is a purgatory preparing him for a new life—sound like figments of an untrustworthy narrator's imagination.

As in his other romances, Hawthorne begins with a preface. Although he points out the realistic grounding of the romance, he maintains that the characters are entirely imaginary. He complains that since no convention yet exists for the American romance, the writer must suffer his characters to be compared to real models; hence, says Hawthorne, he has created the Blithedale scenario as a theatrical device to separate the reader from the ordinary course of events (just as the gothic writer did with his medieval trappings). In effect, Coverdale, isolated as he is, serves as the medium who moves between two worlds.

Coverdale's destructive egocentricism is evident throughout the work. His unwillingness to grant a favor to Old Moodie loses him an early acquaintanceship with Priscilla; he cements his position as an outsider by belittling Priscilla and by spying on Zenobia; finally, seeing the intimacy that develops between Priscilla and Hollingsworth after Zenobia's suicide, he retires to enjoy his self-pity. As a minor poet, an urban man who enjoys his cigars and fireplace, he is out of place in the utopian venture; in fact, after his purgatorial illness, he wakes up to death-in-life rather than to reinvigoration. As he moves from Blithedale to the city and back again, his most active participation in the events is his searching for Zenobia's body.

Zenobia herself harks back to Hester, another in the line of Hawthorne's exotic, intellectual women. Like Miriam in *The Marble Faun*, Zenobia has a mysterious past to conceal. She is dogged by Westervelt, her urbane companion whose mesmeric powers become evident in his attempted despoliation of Priscilla. Coverdale imagines her as an orator or an actor; indeed, she is a female reformer whose free and unexpected rhetoric seems to bypass convention. Priscilla, on the other hand, is a frail version of Phoebe and Hilda; she is pliant, domestic, and biddable—hence her susceptibility to Westervelt's powers and her brief tenure as the Veiled Lady. Like Zenobia (whose sister she is revealed to be), she believes in Hollingworth's reformism, but less as a helpmate than as a supporter. In coming to Blithedale, Priscilla really does find the life that is denied to Coverdale, but in falling in love with Hollingsworth, she finds spiritual death.

Hollingsworth is related to Hawthorne's scientist figures. With Holgrave he wants to change society, but his special interest is in criminal reformation. It is Zenobia who, at the end of the novel, realizes that Hollingsworth has identified himself so closely with his plan that he has *become* the plan. Hollingsworth encourages Zenobia's interest in him because of her wealth; he spurns Coverdale's friendship because Coverdale objects to devoting himself entirely to the monomaniacal plan. It is, however, Hollingsworth who rescues Priscilla from Westervelt, exercising the power of affection to break mesmerism, but with him Priscilla simply enters a different kind of subjection.

Indeed, all the main characters suffer real or metaphorical death at the end of the book. Westervelt, like Chillingworth, is frustrated at his victim's escape; Zenobia's suicide has removed her from his power. Priscilla becomes a handmaiden to the ruined ideal of what Hollingsworth might have been, and Hollingsworth becomes a penitent, reforming himself—the criminal responsible for Zenobia's death. Even Coverdale relinquishes a life of feeling; his final secret, that he loves Priscilla, seems only to be fantasizing on the part of the poet who was a master of missed opportunities and who was more comfortable observing his own reactions to a lost love than in pursuing her actively himself.

The Marble Faun • In *The Marble Faun*, the product of a sojourn in Rome, Hawthorne seems to have reversed a progressively narrowing treatment of the effect of the past. In *The Scarlet Letter*, he deals with Puritan theology; in *The House of the Seven Gables*, a family curse; and in *The Blithedale Romance*, the effects of Coverdale's self-created past. In his last completed work, however, he takes the past of all Rome; in short, he copes with a length of time and complexity of events unusual in his writing experience. Hawthorne's reaction to Rome, complicated by his daughter Una's illness, was mixed. He never, as he put it, felt the city "pulling at his heartstrings" as if it were home.

Italy would seem to present to Hawthorne not only the depth of the past he deemed necessary for the flourishing of romance but also a neutral territory, this time completely divorced from his readers' experience. It can be said, however, that while *The Marble Faun* is Hawthorne's attempt to come to terms with the immense variety of the Italian scene, he was not completely successful. In his preface, he once again declares that the story is to be "fanciful" and is to convey a "thoughtful moral" rather than present a novelistic, realistic picture of Italian customs. He inveighs against the "commonplace prosperity" and lack of "antiquity" in the American scene, a lack that satisfies the kind of reforming zeal pictured in Holgrave but mitigates against the writer of romance.

Hawthorne broadens his canvas in another way as well; instead of presenting one or two main characters, he gives the reader four: Donatello, presumably the living twin of the sculptor Praxiteles' marble faun; Miriam Schaeffer, the mysterious half-Italian painter pursued by the ill-fated Brother Antonio; Kenyon, the American sculptor; and Hilda, the New England copyist. Donatello's double is not found elsewhere in the romances; in fact, he seems to be a male version of both Phoebe and Hilda. Unlike the two women, however, he comes in actual contact with evil and thereby loses his innocence, whereas Hilda's and Phoebe's experiences are vicarious. Perhaps the nearest comparison is Dimmesdale, but the minister is portrayed after he chooses to hide his guilt, not before he has sinned. In Donatello's case, Hawthorne examines the idea of the fortunate fall, demonstrating that Donatello grows in moral understanding after he murders the model, a movement that seems to validate Miriam's secular interpretation of the fall as necessary to the development of a soul more than it validates Hilda's instinctive repudiation of the idea. For some critics, such as Hyatt Waggoner and Richard Fogle, the *felix culpa* or fortunate fall is indeed the theme of *The Marble Faun*; Crews, however, emphasizes Hawthorne's unwillingness to confront the problem, noting that Kenyon is made to accept Hilda's repudiation without question. In the final analysis, Hawthorne does indeed seem reluctant to examine the ramifications of the theme.

Like Zenobia and Hester, Miriam is presented as a large-spirited, speculative woman whose talents are dimmed by a secret past, symbolized by the blood-red jewel she wears. Supposedly, Miriam (unlike Hester), has run away from a marriage with a much older man, but, Hawthorne suggests, her family lineage reveals criminal tendencies. She is followed by Brother Antonio, a wandering devil-figure whom she meets in the catacomb of St. Calixtus and whom she employs as a model. The crime that links Miriam to Donatello is not, in this case, adultery, but rather murder. Donatello, who accompanies Miriam everywhere, throws the model from the Tarpeian Rock, the traditional death-place for traitors, saying later that he did what Miriam's eyes asked him to do. Linked in the crime and initially feeling part of the accumulated crimes of centuries, they become alienated from each other and must come separately to an understanding of their own responsibility to other human beings. During this time, Donatello retires to Monte Beni, the family seat, to meditate, and Miriam follows him, disguised.

Just as Miriam and Donatello are linked by their complicity, Kenyon and Hilda are linked by a certain hesitation to share in the other pair's secrets, thereby achieving an isolation that Hawthorne might earlier have seen as a breaking of the magnetic chain of humanity. Unnoticed as she observes the murder, Hilda nevertheless becomes a vicarious participant. She rejects Miriam's friendship, maintaining that she has been given an unspotted garment of virtue and must keep it pristine, but she does agree to deliver a packet of Miriam's letters to the Palazzo Cenci. For his part, Kenyon compensates for his earlier coldness to Miriam by effecting a reconciliation between her and Donatello. Visiting Monte Beni, he is struck by Donatello's air of sadness and maturity and believes that the pagan "faun," whose power to talk to animals was legendary, has come to an understanding of good and evil and has thereby escaped the possibility of a sensual old age to which the throwback Monte Beni eventually succumbs. Kenyon encourages his friend to work out his penitence in the sphere of human action and reunites him with Miriam under the statue of Pope Julius III in Perugia.

In the meantime, Hilda, suffering the pains of guilt for the murder as if she were the perpetrator, paradoxically gains comfort from confession in St. Peter's. After she goes to the Palazzo Cenci to deliver Miriam's letters, however, she is incarcerated as a hostage for Miriam. Her disappearance is the novel's analogue to Donatello's self-imposed isolation; her experience in the convent, where she is detained, convinces her of her need for Kenyon. In searching for Hilda, Kenyon undergoes his own purgation, meeting the changed Donatello and Miriam in the Compagna and learning about Miriam's past. On Miriam's advice, he repairs to the Courso in the height of the carnival; it is there that he is reunited with Hilda. Her freedom means the end of Miriam and Donatello's days together, for Donatello is imprisoned for the murder of Brother Antonio.

As did Sophia for Hawthorne, Hilda becomes Kenyon's guide to "home"; she is Hawthorne's last full-length evocation of the New England girl on whose moral guidance he wished to rely.

Patricia Marks

Other major works

SHORT FICTION: *Twice-Told Tales*, 1837 (expanded 1842); *Mosses from an Old Manse*, 1846; *The Snow-Image, and Other Twice-Told Tales*, 1851.

NONFICTION: *Life of Franklin Pierce*, 1852; *Our Old Home*, 1863; *The American Notebooks*, 1941; *The French and Italian Notebooks*, 1980; *Letters of Nathaniel Hawthorne*, 1984-

1987 (4 volumes); *Selected Letters of Nathaniel Hawthorne*, 2002 (Joel Myerson, editor).

CHILDREN'S LITERATURE: *Grandfather's Chair*, 1841; *Biographical Stories for Children*, 1842; *True Stories from History and Biography*, 1851; *A Wonder-Book for Boys and Girls*, 1852; *Tanglewood Tales for Boys and Girls*, 1853.

EDITED TEXTS: *Peter Parley's Universal History*, 1837.

MISCELLANEOUS: *Complete Works*, 1850-1882 (13 volumes); *The Complete Writings of Nathaniel Hawthorne*, 1900 (22 volumes); *The Centenary Edition of the Works of Nathaniel Hawthorne*, 1962-1997 (23 volumes).

Bibliography

Bell, Millicent, ed. *Hawthorne and the Real: Bicentennial Essays.* Columbus: Ohio State University Press, 2005. Collection of origial essays on the literary heritage of Hawthorne.

Bloom, Harold, ed. *Hester Prynne.* Philadelphia: Chelsea House, 2004. Collection of critical essays about Prynne that have been assembled for student use.

Charvat, William, et al., eds. *The Centenary Edition of the Works of Nathaniel Hawthorne.* Columbus: Ohio State University Press, 1963-. This continuing multivolume edition of Hawthorne's works will, when complete, contain the entire canon. Somewhat unevenly accomplished by a variety of editors, the volumes contain a considerable amount of textual apparatus as well as biographical and critical information. Volumes 9, 10, and 11 give the texts of all known Hawthorne short stories and sketches.

Davis, Clark. *Hawthorne's Shyness: Ethics, Politics, and the Question of Engagement.* Baltimore: Johns Hopkins University Press, 2005. Exploration the often overlooked theme of shyness in Hawthorne's writings.

Doubleday, Neal Frank. *Hawthorne's Early Tales: A Critical Study.* Durham, N.C.: Duke University Press, 1972. Doubleday focuses on what he calls "the development of Hawthorne's literary habit," including Hawthorne's literary theory and the materials from which he fashioned the stories of his twenties and early thirties. The index, while consisting chiefly of proper names and titles, includes some features of Hawthorne's work ("ambiguity," "irony," and the like).

Frye, Steven. *Historiography and Narrative Design in the American Romance: A Study of Four Authors.* Lewiston, N.Y.: Edwin Mellen Press, 2001. Comparative study of four nineteenth century American writers: James Fenimore Cooper, William Gilmore Simms, Lydia Maria Child, and Nathaniel Hawthorne.

Keil, James C. "Hawthorne's 'Young Goodman Brown': Early Nineteenth-Century and Puritan Constructions of Gender." *The New England Quarterly* 69 (March, 1996): 33-55. Argues that Hawthorne places his story in the seventeenth century to explore the nexus of past and present in the attitudes of New Englanders toward theology, morality, and sexuality. Points out that clear boundaries between male and female, public and private, and work and home were thresholds across which nineteenth century Americans often passed.

Kelsey, Angela M. "Mrs. Wakefield's Gaze: Femininity and Dominance in Nathaniel Hawthorne's 'Wakefield.'" *ATQ*, n.s. 8 (March, 1994): 17-31. In this feminist reading of Hawthorne's story, Kelsey argues that Mrs. Wakefield finds ways to escape and exceed the economy of the male gaze, first by appropriating the look for herself, then by refusing to die, and finally by denying her husband her gaze.

Mackenzie, Manfred. "Hawthorne's 'Roger Malvin's Burial': A Postcolonial Reading." *New Literary History* 27 (Summer, 1996): 459-472. Argues that the story is postcolonial fiction in which Hawthorne writes about the emerging American nation and recalls European colonial culture; claims that Hawthorne rehearses the colonialist past in order to concentrate and effectively "expel" its inherent violence.

McKee, Kathryn B. "'A Small Heap of Glittering Fragments': Hawthorne's Discontent with the Short Story Form." *ATQ,* n.s. 8 (June, 1994): 137-147. Claims that Hawthorne's "Artist of the Beautiful" and "Downe's Wooden Image" are examples of his dissatisfaction with the short story as a form; argues that the fragile articles at the center of the tales mirror the limitations Hawthorne saw in the short-story genre.

Mellow, James R. *Nathaniel Hawthorne and His Times.* Boston: Houghton Mifflin, 1980. In this substantial, readable, and illustrated biography, Mellow provides a number of insights into Hawthorne's fiction. Refreshingly, the author presents Sophia Hawthorne not only as the prudish, protective wife of the Hawthorne legend but also as a woman with an artistic sensibility and talent of her own. Mellow's book is a good introduction to a very interesting man. Suitable for the student and the general reader.

Miller, Edward Havilland. *Salem Is My Dwelling Place: A Life of Nathaniel Hawthorne.* Iowa City: University of Iowa Press, 1991. A large biography of more than six hundred pages, illustrated with more than fifty photographs and drawings. Miller has been able to draw on more manuscripts of family members and Hawthorne associates than did his predecessors and also developed his subject's family life in more detail. He offers interpretations of many of the short stories.

Millington, Richard H., ed. *The Cambridge Companion to Nathaniel Hawthorne.* New York: Cambridge University Press, 2004. Collection of new essays on a variety of aspects of Hawthorne's life and writings.

Moore, Margaret B. *The Salem World of Nathaniel Hawthorne.* Columbia: University of Missouri Press, 1998. Margaret Moore explores the relationship between Salem, Massachusetts, and its most famous resident, author Nathaniel Hawthorne.

Muirhead, Kimberly Free. *Nathaniel Hawthorne's "The Scarlet Letter": A Critical Resource Guide and Comprehensive Annotated Bibliography of Literary Criticism, 1950-2000.* Lewiston, N.Y.: Edwin Mellen Press, 2004. Collection of modern critical essays on Hawthorne with a very useful annotated biliography of secondary sources.

Newberry, Frederick. "'The Artist of the Beautiful': Crossing the Transcendent Divide in Hawthorne's Fiction." *Nineteenth-Century Literature* 50 (June, 1995): 78-96. Argues that the butterfly's appearance is Hawthorne's endorsement of the transcendent power of imagination over nineteenth century empiricism.

Pennell, Melissa McFarland. *Student Companion to Nathaniel Hawthorne.* Westport, Conn.: Greenwood Press, 1999. A handy student guide to Hawthorne's writings that includes bibliographical references and an index.

Scharnhorst, Gary. *The Critical Response to Hawthorne's "The Scarlet Letter."* New York: Greenwood Press, 1992. Includes chapters on the novel's background and composition history, on the contemporary American reception, on the early British reception, on the growth of Hawthorne's reputation after his death, on modern criticism, and on *The Scarlet Letter* on stage and screen.

Swope, Richard. "Approaching the Threshold(s) in Postmodern Detective Fiction: Hawthorne's 'Wakefield' and Other Missing Persons." *Critique* 39 (Spring, 1998): 207-227. Discusses "Wakefield" as a literary ancestor of "metaphysical" detective fiction, a postmodern genre that combines fiction with literary theory.

"Wakefield" raises many of the questions about language, subjectivity, and urban spaces that surround postmodernism.

Thompson, G. R. *The Art of Authorial Presence: Hawthorne's Provincial Tales.* Durham, N.C.: Duke University Press, 1993. Argues that for Hawthorne the art of telling a story depends on a carefully created fiction of an authorial presence. Examines Hawthorne's narrative strategies for creating this presence by using contemporary narrative theory. Analyzes a small number of early Hawthorne stories and the criticism that has amassed about Hawthorne's fiction.

Wineapple, Brenda. *Hawthorne: A Life.* New York: Alfred A. Knopf, 2003. An analysis of Hawthorne's often contradictory life that proposes that many of Hawthorne's stories are autobiographical.

Joseph Heller

Born: Brooklyn, New York; May 1, 1923
Died: East Hampton, New York; December 12, 1999

Principal long fiction • *Catch-22*, 1961; *Something Happened*, 1974; *Good as Gold*, 1979; *God Knows*, 1984; *Picture This*, 1988; *Closing Time*, 1994; *Portrait of an Artist, as an Old Man*, 2000.

Other literary forms • Joseph Heller's first published piece was a short story in *Story Magazine* (1945), and during the late 1940's, he placed several other stories with *Esquire* and *The Atlantic Monthly*. His enthusiasm for the theater accounts for the topic of his master's thesis at Columbia University, "The Pulitzer Prize Plays: 1917-1935," and he wrote three plays that deal directly or indirectly with the material he used in *Catch-22*. *We Bombed in New Haven*, a two-act play, was first produced by the Yale School of Drama Repertory Theater in 1967. It later reached Broadway and was published in 1968. *Catch-22: A Dramatization* (1971) was first produced at the John Drew Theater in East Hampton, Long Island, where Heller spent his summers. *Clevinger's Trial*, a dramatization of chapter 8 of *Catch-22*, was produced in London in 1974. Only *We Bombed in New Haven* enjoyed a modicum of critical and commercial success. Heller also contributed to a number of motion-picture and television scripts, the best known of which is *Sex and the Single Girl* (1964), for which he received his only screen credit.

Achievements • Heller's reputation rests largely on his first novel, *Catch-22*, the publication of which vaulted Heller into the front ranks of postwar American novelists. Critics hailed it as "the great representative document of our era" and "probably the finest novel published since World War II." The phrase "catch-22" quickly entered the American lexicon; more than eight million copies of the novel have been printed; and it has been translated into more than a dozen languages. In 1970, director Mike Nichols's film adaptation of Heller's tale sparked renewed interest in the novel itself and launched it onto the best-seller lists.

   Catch-22 was one of the most widely read and discussed novels of the 1960's and early 1970's; its blend of humor and horror struck a responsive chord, particularly with the young, during the upheavals of the Vietnam War era. Critic Josh Greenfield, writing in 1968, claimed that it had "all but become the chapbook of the sixties." Within the context of Vietnam, the novel seemed to be less about World War II than about the Asian war over which America was so furiously divided. *Catch-22*, then, remains the classic fictional statement of the antiwar sentiments of its time.

   Although some have compared *Catch-22* to Norman Mailer's *The Naked and the Dead* (1948), James Jones's *The Thin Red Line* (1962), and other essentially naturalistic war tales written by Heller's contemporaries, its conception of war in basically absurdist terms and its crazy-quilt structure suggest affinities rather with such works as Kurt Vonnegut's *Slaughterhouse-Five* (1969). Heller's fiction is frequently described as "black comedy." In the tradition of Nathanael West, Günter Grass, Ralph Ellison, and Thomas Pynchon, Heller stretches reality to the point of distortion.

   In his novels, as well as in his plays, Heller displays a worldview that shares much with twentieth century existentialist thought: The world is meaningless, it simply exists; humankind by its very nature seeks meaning; the relationship between humanity and its world is thus absurd; when a person recognizes these facts, he or she experiences what Jean-Paul Sartre termed the "nausea" of modern existence. In all of his work, Heller argues for "massive resistance" to routine, regimentation, and authority in whatever form. He affirms, no matter how much that affirmation may be qualified by pain and defeat, the sanctity of the individual. He writes not so much about the life of a soldier (as in *Catch-22*), the life of a businessman (as in *Something Happened*), or the life of a would-be politician (as in *Good as Gold*) as about the threats posed to individual identity by the institutions of modern life.

Biography • Joseph Heller was born in Brooklyn, New York, on May 1, 1923, the son of Russian-Jewish immigrants only recently arrived in America. His mother then barely spoke English; his father drove a delivery truck for a bakery until, when Heller was only five, he died unexpectedly during a routine ulcer operation. The denial of this death in particular and the bare fact of mortality in general were to color Heller's later life and work. The youngest of three children, Heller spent his boyhood in the Coney Island section of Brooklyn, an enclave of lower-and middle-class Jewish families, in the shadow of the famed amusement park. Both his family and his teachers recognized Heller as a bright but bored student; he tinkered with writing short stories while still in high school.

In 1942, at the age of nineteen, Heller joined the U.S. Army Air Corps. He spent one of the war years flying sixty missions over Italy as a wing bombadier in a B-25 squadron stationed on Corsica. This proved to be the crucial year of his life; it provided him with the materials, and the bitterly sardonic attitude, out of which he forged his major work—*Catch-22*—as well as his three plays. Moreover, his sixty missions, many of them brutal and bloody (including the series of raids on Bologna that form the core of *Catch-22*), profoundly affected the attitude toward death that informs all of his work.

Demobilized in 1945, after reaching the rank of first lieutenant, Heller married fellow Brooklynite Shirley Held, with whom he had two children. Heller spent the next seven years within academe. Under the G.I. Bill, he attended college, first at the University of Southern California and then at New York University, where he received his bachelor's degree in 1948. He then moved farther up Manhattan to take a master's degree at Columbia University before receiving one of the first Fulbright fellowships to study at Oxford. He returned to the United States to teach English at Pennsylvania State University between 1950 and 1952.

During the remainder of the 1950's, Heller was employed in the advertising departments of *Time, Look*, and *McCall's* magazines successively. In 1954, he began writing, at night and during odd hours, the manuscript that would be published eight years later as *Catch-22*. Almost forty when *Catch-22* finally appeared, Heller ironically referred to himself as an "aging prodigy."

Heller abandoned his successful advertising career during the 1960's and returned to teaching. His position as Distinguished Professor of English at the City University of New York afforded him both the salary to support his family and the free time to devote to his writing. During those years, he began work on a second novel, wrote several motion-picture and television scripts (usually adaptations of the work of others and often using a pseudonym), and completed his first play, *We Bombed in New Haven*.

Mariana Cook

Something Happened, Heller's second novel, took thirteen years to complete before appearing in 1974. Never fully at ease with academic life, Heller resigned his chair at CUNY in 1975, and in 1979 he published his third novel, *Good as Gold*. Although he has occasionally lectured on the college circuit and has served as writer-in-residence at both Yale University and the University of Pennsylvania, Heller was basically a reclusive writer, uncomfortable at literary gatherings and suspicious of the trappings of literary success. His life and work seem guided by Ralph Waldo Emerson's dictum that "a foolish consistency is the hobgoblin of little minds."

In December, 1981, Heller was diagnosed as a victim of Guillain Barré syndrome, a sometimes fatal condition involving progressive paralysis. He was hospitalized for several months but eventually recovered. That experience led to another book, *No Laughing Matter* (1986), written with his friend Speed Vogel, describing his condition and its resolution. Heller's illness also led to his second marriage, to one of his nurses, Valerie Humphries, in 1987.

God Knows returns to the irreverence and defiance of logic that characterized *Catch-22*. Its narrator, the biblical King David, speaks in modern jargon and in his extended version of his life and career displays knowledge of events long after his own time. *Picture This* is a protracted meditation on the ironies of history and of human life, focusing on the Netherlands of Rembrandt's time and the Athens of Aristotle.

In 1994, more than thirty years after publishing *Catch-22*, Heller published *Closing Time*, a sequel to *Catch-22*. Set during the late 1980's, this novel revisits both the characters from Heller's first novel and the experiences of Heller's generation of New York Jews, for whom World War II was a formative experience. In *Closing Time*, both groups come face to face with their own mortality and the fate of a world governed by flawed human institutions. Heller's final novel, *Portrait of an Artist, as an Old Man*, which was published posthumously, in 2000, is about a successful novelist's struggle to find inspiration for his latest book.

Now and Then: From Coney Island to Here (1998) is an autobiographical account of Heller's life from his boyhood days in Coney Island through the period following the publication of *Catch-22*. Devotees of *Catch-22* may be disappointed to find that Heller spends only part of one chapter on his wartime experience, while much of the early sections of the memoir chart the geography of Coney Island in elaborate detail. Heller made his final home in East Hampton, Long Island, where he died on December 12, 1999.

Analysis • At first glance, Joseph Heller's novels seem quite dissimilar. Heller's manipulation of time and point of view in *Catch-22* is dizzying; it is a hilariously macabre,
almost surreal novel. *Something Happened*, on the other hand, is a far more muted book
composed of the slow-moving, pessimistic broodings of an American business executive. *Good as Gold* is part remembrance of family life in the impoverished sections
of Coney Island and part savage satire of contemporary American political life.
Throughout Heller's work, however, all his characters are obsessed with death and
passionately searching for some means to deny, or at least stay, their mortality.
Heller's characters, like those of Saul Bellow, cry out to assert their individuality, their
sense of self, which seems threatened from all sides. Yossarian, for example, in *Catch-
22*, finds the world in conspiracy to blow him out of the sky. The worlds of *Catch-22*,
Something Happened, and *Good as Gold* are not so much chaotic as absurdly and illogi-
cally routinized. In such an absurd world of callous cruelty, unalloyed ambition, and
blithe disregard for human life, Heller maintains, the individual has the right to seek
his own survival by any means possible.

Catch-22 • Although *Catch-22*'s most obvious features are its antiwar theme and its
wild, often madhouse humor, the novel itself is exceedingly complex in both meaning and form. In brief, the plot concerns a squadron of American airmen stationed
on the fictional Mediterranean island of Pianosa during World War II. More specifically, it concerns the futile attempts of Captain John Yossarian, a Syrian American
bombardier, to be removed from flying status. Every time he approaches the number
of missions necessary to complete a tour of duty, his ambitious commanding officers
increase it. Yossarian tries a number of ploys to avoid combat. He malingers, feigns
illness, and even poisons the squadron's food with laundry soap to abort one mission. Later, after the gunner Snowden dies in his arms during one particularly lethal
mission, Yossarian refuses to fly again, goes naked, and takes to walking backward on
the base, all in an attempt to have himself declared insane.

Yossarian is motivated by only one thing—the determination to stay alive. He sees
his life threatened not only by the Germans who try to shoot him out of the sky but
also by his superior officers, who seem just as intent to kill him off. "The enemy," he
concludes at one point, "is anybody who's going to get you killed, no matter which
side he's on." When Yossarian attempts to convince the camp's medical officer that
his fear of death has driven him over the brink and thus made him unfit to fly, he first
learns of the "catch" that will force him to keep flying: "There was only one catch and
that was Catch-22, which specified that a concern for one's own safety in the face of
dangers that were real and immediate was the process of a rational mind." As Doc
Daneeka tells Yossarian, "Anyone who wants to get out of combat duty isn't really
crazy."

Most of the large cast of characters surrounding Yossarian are, by any "reasonable" standard, quite mad. They include Colonel Cathcart, who keeps raising the
number of missions his troops are required to fly not for the sake of the war effort but
for his own personal glory; Major Major Major, who forges Washington Irving's name
to official documents and who is pathologically terrified of command; and Milo
Minderbinder, the mess officer, a black marketeer who bombs his own base under
contract with the Germans. These supporting characters most often fall into one of
four categories. The ranking officers—Cathcart, Dreedle, Korn, Black, Cargill, and
Scheisskopf—appear more concerned with promotion, neat bombing patterns, and
their own petty jealousies than with the war itself or the welfare of their men. A sec-

ond group, including Doc Daneeka, Minderbinder, and Wintergreen, are also concerned with pursuing the main chance. They are predatory but also extremely comic and very much self-aware. Another group, including Nately, Chief Halfoat, McWatt, Hungry Joe, and Chaplain Tappman, are (like Yossarian himself) outsiders, good men caught within a malevolent system. The dead—Mudd, Snowden, Kraft, and "the soldier in white"—constitute a final group, one that is always present, at least in the background.

It is the military system—which promulgates such absurdly tautological rules as "Catch-22"—that is Yossarian's real enemy. He and the other "good" men of the squadron live in a world that is irrational and inexplicable. As the company's warrant officer explains, "There just doesn't seem to be any logic to their system of rewards and punishments. . . . They have the right to do anything we can't stop them from doing."

As the novel progresses, the victims, increasingly aware of the menace posed by this system, carry their gestures of rebellion to the point of open defiance. Yossarian is the most blatant in this regard: He moans loudly during the briefing for the Avignon mission; he insists that there is a dead man in his tent; he goes naked during the Avignon mission itself and then again during the medal ceremony afterward; he halts the Bologna raid by putting soap in the squadron's food and by moving the bomb-line on the squadron's map; and he requests that he be grounded and eventually refuses to fly. Finally, he deserts, hoping to reach sanctuary in neutral Sweden.

In the world of *Catch-22*, then, the reader is forced to question the very nature of sanity. Sanity is commonly defined as the ability to live within society and to act appropriately according to its rules. If those rules—such as Catch-22—are patently false, however, then adhering to them is in truth an act of insanity, for the end result may be death or the loss of freedom. The world of *Catch-22* is, to Yossarian, a spurious culture, as anthropologists would call it, one that does not meet the basic needs of its members—above all, the need to survive. Authority, duty, and patriotism are all called into question, and Heller demonstrates that when those in authority lack intelligence or respect for life, as is the case with Yossarian's commanding officers, obeying authority can only be self-defeating. Heller thus argues that in an absurd universe, the individual has the right to seek his own survival; he argues that life itself is infinitely more precious than any cause, however just. When Yossarian decides that he has done his part to defeat the Nazis (and after all, he has flown many more missions than most other airmen), his principal duty is to save himself. Yossarian's desertion, then, is a life-affirming act.

As critic Robert Brustein noted, *Catch-22* "speaks solidly to those who are disaffected, discontented, and disaffiliated, and yet who want to react to life positively. With its occasional affirmations couched in terms of pain and cynical laughter, it makes nihilism seem natural, ordinary, even appealing." Thus the surface farce of *Catch-22*, when peeled away, reveals a purpose that is literally deadly serious.

If the basic plot of *Catch-22* is fairly simple, its narrative technique and structure most certainly are not. The novel appears to be a chronological jumble, flashing forward and backward from the central event—the death of Snowden—which marks Yossarian's final realization of the mortal threat posed by Catch-22. Time in the novel exists not as clock time but rather as psychological time, and within Yossarian's stream-of-consciousness narrative, events in the present intermingle with cumulative repetitions and gradual clarifications of past actions. For example, in chapter 4, the bare facts of Snowden's death are revealed, that he was killed over Avignon when

Dobbs, his copilot, went berserk and grabbed the plane's controls at a crucial moment. Yossarian returns to this incident throughout the novel, but it is not until the
penultimate chapter that he reconstructs the story in full. In this fashion, Heller
seeks to capture the real ways in which people apprehend the world, incompletely
and in fragments.

Catch-22 is intricately structured despite its seeming shapelessness. Until chapter
19, almost everything is told in retrospect while Yossarian is in the hospital; chapter
19 itself begins the movement forward in time leading to Yossarian's desertion. The
gradual unfolding of the details of Snowden's death provides another organizing device. Such structural devices as parallelism, doubling, and—most important—repetition, force the reader to share Yossarian's perpetual sense of déjà vu, the illusion of
having previously experienced something actually being encountered for the first
time. The ultimate effect of such devices is to reinforce the novel's main themes:
Yossarian is trapped in a static world, a world in which nothing seems to change and
in which events seem to keep repeating themselves. He does not move *through* his
experiences but rather seems condemned to a treadmill existence. The only way to
resist this world is to escape it, to desert.

Something Happened • Heller himself once revealed that he considered Bob Slocum,
the protagonist-narrator of his second novel, *Something Happened*, to be "the antithesis of Yossarian—twenty years later." Indeed, the scene shifts dramatically from the
dusty, littered airfields of Pianosa to the green, well-kept lawns of suburban Connecticut. In *Something Happened*, Heller details—some say monotonously details—the
inner life of an outwardly successful man and, in doing so, seeks to expose the bankruptcy of contemporary middle-class American culture.

Slocum works as a middle-level marketing research manager in a large company.
He is middle-aged, married, and the father of three children. Although he is by all
appearances successful, Slocum's extended monologue of memories, self-analysis,
and carpings at the world reveal that he is anything but happy: "I keep my own counsel and drift speechlessly with my crowd. I float. I float like algae in a colony of green
scum, while my wife and I grow old." He sees his life as a series of humiliating failures
of nerve, of unfulfilled expectations and missed opportunities. Slocum harks back
repeatedly and with regret to his adolescent yearnings for an office girl—later a
suicide—with whom he had worked shortly after finishing high school. He now
wishes in vain that he could desire someone or something as desperately as he once
desired her.

Slocum despises his present job and mistrusts his associates yet politics shame-
lessly for promotion; he feels bound to his family yet commits numerous adulteries.
He is hopelessly at odds with himself and his life. For example, he loves his family in a
temporizing kind of way, but he also fears that he has made them all unhappy. His
wife, bored and restless, feels isolated in the suburbs and turns to alcohol. His
sixteen-year-old daughter is sullen and promiscuous. One son is hopelessly brain-
damaged and an insufferable burden to Slocum; the other, Slocum seems truly to
want to love, but he cannot help browbeating him. The novel reaches its bleak climax
when this latter son is hit by a car and lies bleeding in the street. Slocum cradles the
boy in his arms and, at the moment when he feels he can express his love, inadvertently smothers him.

There is no real resolution in *Something Happened*. At novel's end, Slocum has not
changed or learned anything of importance. Unlike Yossarian, who is threatened

from without, Slocum is his own worst enemy. His sense of alienation, of loss, of failure, is unrelieved.

Critical opinion of *Something Happened* has been mixed. Those who admire the
novel most often praise its exact and mercilessly honest replication of the banality
and vacuousness of everyday life among the American middle classes, and they argue
that Heller, as in *Catch-22*, nicely fuses form and meaning. Others find the novel irri-
tatingly tedious and pessimistic and consider the character of Slocum seriously
flawed, unlikable, and unheroic by any standard. Many reviewers could not resist
quipping that a more appropriate title for Heller's novel would be *Nothing Happens*.

Good as Gold • Heller's third novel, *Good as Gold*, savagely satirizes the aspirations of
the Jewish intellectual community in America. The comic dimension of *Catch-22*,
so absent from *Something Happened*, returns. Bruce Gold is a forty-eight-year-old
Brooklyn-born English professor who desperately wants to make—or at least have—
money. Like Bob Slocum, Gold has problems with his family, which, he knows, considers him a failure because he is not rich. Much of the novel takes place within the
Gold family itself, which Gold finds oppressive, if at times amusingly so.

Gold is in most ways a fool—albeit a cynical one—a hypocrite, and a congenital social climber. He is a 1970's version of Budd Schulberg's Sammy Glick. One evidence
of this is his engagement to a wealthy WASP socialite with political connections. Gold
himself harbors political ambitions. He hungers to replace his alter-ego and arch-
nemesis Henry Kissinger as secretary of state, and hopes that his fiancé's tycoon-
father will help him in his quest for political power. Heller savages both Gold and
Kissinger, and for precisely the same reason: They represent to him those in the Jewish community who want to escape their heritage while at the same time exploiting
it (to further his financial, academic, and political fortunes, Gold wants to write a
"big" book about the Jewish experience in America, about which he knows next to
nothing).

Gold understands his own hypocrisy but promptly dismisses it. Yet, when Gold is
eventually offered Kissinger's former cabinet position, he experiences a change of
heart. Prompted by the death of his older brother, Gold refuses the post and returns
to New York and his family. Like Yossarian, Gold is able to restore his own integrity by
deserting.

Heller's work has been compared to that of artists as varied as Eugène Ionesco and
the Marx Brothers; *Good as Gold* lies closer to the latter than to the former. Until his
decision to renounce his political ambitions, Gold is very much the comic intellectual, pathetically incapable of coping with the difficulties in which he finds himself.
The humor of *Good as Gold* is painted with the broadest brush of Heller's career, but
its target is his familiar one: the means by which institutions in the modern world co-
erce the individual and the way in which individuals—such as Slocum and, until his
turnabout, Gold—become co-conspirators in their own demise.

God Knows • *God Knows* is Heller's rewriting of a major element of the Old Testament, the story of David. As in all of his fiction, Heller focuses here on the human insistence on repeating earlier mistakes and on the ironies of life. His David is a
prototypical wise guy, looking back over his life from his deathbed; his language veers
from that of the King James version of the Bible to twentieth century slang as he presents his side of various stories, from his encounter with Goliath to his problems with
King Saul to his troubles with his children and his various wives.

David's first wife, Saul's daughter Michal, was a shrew to whom he refers as the first Jewish American Princess. He misses Abigail, his second wife, the only one who loved him completely; she has been dead for many years. Bathsheba, the great passion of his life, has turned into an overweight nag, bored with sex and interested only in trying to persuade David to name their son, Solomon, as his successor. Solomon, in David's eyes, is an idiot, a humorless man with no original thoughts who writes down everything his father says and later pretends that they are his ideas. The old king's only solace is the young virgin Abishag the Shunnamite, who waits on him and worships him.

David complains about his present state, remembers his days of glory, and rationalizes his deeds, avoiding responsibility for any evil that has befallen others but claiming credit for benefits. His knowledge is modern. He maintains, for example, that Michelangelo's famous statue of him is a nice piece of work but it is not "him." His language is laden with quotations from William Shakespeare, Robert Browning, T. S. Eliot, and many others, and he seems to have direct knowledge of most of ancient and modern history.

God Knows is Heller's most engaging fiction since *Catch-22*. Suspense is maintained by David's reluctance to name Solomon as his successor, as he must do, and by the question of whether he will ever hear the voice of God, which he desperately wants. Heller's David is not an admirable man, but he is a fascinating one and an interesting commentator not only on his own life but on human frailty and ambition as well. He is cynical, his faith in God and humanity having left him years before, but even as he complains about the pains of old age, his memory keeps reminding him of the enjoyments of the life he has led.

Picture This • *Picture This* is neither conventional fiction nor history but a kind of extended meditation on human weakness. Its inspiration is the famous painting *Aristotle Contemplating the Bust of Homer,* by the Dutch painter Rembrandt van Rijn. Heller presents many historical facts, chiefly about the Greece of the time of Aristotle, Plato, and Socrates, as well as the Netherlands of the time of Rembrandt, and he draws frequent parallels between events of those periods and those of the modern age. In discussing the Athenian wars, for example, he makes clear his conviction that the motivations, the mistakes, and the stupidities are parallel to those made by the United States in the years since World War II.

Picture This contains much authentic information, most of which is intended to demonstrate human greed and weakness. Heller seems to be fascinated by the financial aspects of Rembrandt's life, in which great success was frittered away and in which a life of luxury ended with enormous debts; he also writes at length about Rembrandt's marriage and his mistresses. In writing about Greece in the Golden Age, he focuses on the failings of government. The great leader Pericles, in his view, led Athens into self-destructive wars. Pericles was personally noble, but he did his city no good. The tyrant Creon was even worse. Much of what Plato wrote about he could not have observed.

Unlike either *Catch-22* or *God Knows, Picture This* fails to provide a leavening of irreverent humor to lighten Heller's dark view of human existence. The only fictional elements in the book are imaginary dialogues between some of the historical figures and the fantasy that Aristotle exists in the painting of him and can observe Rembrandt and his labors; these imaginary flights are only occasionally humorous. Otherwise, the irony in *Picture This* is unrelenting and bitter.

Closing Time • Though *Closing Time* is more humorous, Heller's irony remains bitter, as a World War II generation contemplating the later years of their lives takes the whole world down with them, courtesy of an incompetent U.S. president who, at the novel's conclusion, launches a nuclear strike under the mistaken impression that he is playing a video game. Prior to that apocalyptic finale, readers are reintroduced to Yossarian, who, in the thirty years since the events of *Catch-22*, has been working as an ethics adviser for Milo Minderbinder's multinational corporation. He has been married, had four children, and divorced. As he faces retirement and realizes he is not long for the world, he worries about the future of his children, begins an affair with a younger nurse, and resolves "to live forever, or to die trying."

In terms of genre, *Closing Time* is a difficult book to characterize. As a sequel to *Catch-22*, it takes familiar characters such as Yossarian, Chaplain Tappman, and Milo Minderbinder through an absurdist parody of business, medicine, government, and the military. The addition of two World War II veteran characters (Sammy Singer and Lew Rabinowitz) with only ancillary connections to the main plot brings a nostalgic realism to the novel, more in keeping with Heller's subsequent memoir, *Now and Then*, than with the Yossarian sections of the novel. *Closing Time* also is Heller's most self-consciously postmodern novel, as real-life figures, such as author Kurt Vonnegut, are intertwined with fictional ones; references are made not only to the events of *Catch-22* but also to the novel itself and the entry of the term "catch-22" into the popular lexicon. At its best, this generic combination allows Heller to range widely in his criticism of contemporary society (as in a priceless explanation Yossarian is given of the Freedom of Information Act). However, too often these various formats seem at odds with each other, leading to a novel that moves both slowly and in too many directions.

Richard A. Fine
Updated by Jim O'Loughlin

Other major works

SHORT FICTION: *Catch as Catch Can: The Collected Stories and Other Writings*, 2003 (Matthew J. Bruccoli and Park Bucker, editors).

PLAYS: *We Bombed in New Haven*, pr. 1967; *Catch-22: A Dramatization*, pr. 1971; *Clevinger's Trial*, pb. 1973.

SCREENPLAYS: *Sex and the Single Girl*, 1964 (with David R. Schwartz); *Casino Royale*, 1967 (with others); *Dirty Dingus Magee*, 1970 (with others).

NONFICTION: *No Laughing Matter*, 1986 (with Speed Vogel); *Now and Then: From Coney Island to Here*, 1998; *A Portrait of the Artist, as an Old Man*, 2000.

Bibliography

Aldridge, John W. *The American Novel and the Way We Live Now.* New York: Oxford University Press, 1983. Aldridge's overview of American fiction after World War II gives Heller's work high marks, praising his skeptical view of modern society and the imaginative qualities of his novels.

Bloom, Harold, ed. *Joseph Heller's "Catch-22."* New York: Chelsea House, 2001. A collection of critical assessments.

Bruccoli, Matthew J., and Park Buker. *Joseph Heller.* Pittburgh: Oak Knoll Books, 2002. A bibliography of Heller's works and criticism.

Craig, David M. *Tilting at Mortality: Narrative Strategies in Joseph Heller's Fiction.* Detroit:

Wayne State University Press, 1997. An examination of the ethical dimensions of Heller's work, linking his distinctive stylistic features to his preoccupation with questions of death, meaning, and identity.

Dougherty, D. C. "Nemeses and McGuffins: Paranoia as Focal Metaphor in Stanley Elkin, Joseph Heller, and Thomas Pynchon." *Review of Contemporary Fiction* 15, no. 2 (1995): 70-79. Reflects on the methods and motives of using paranoia as a governing metaphor in modern fiction.

Friedman, John, and Judith Ruderman. "Joseph Heller and the 'Real' King David." *Judaism* 36, no. 3 (1987): 296-302. Explores Heller's relationship to his Jewishness and its representation in *God Knows*.

Hidalgo Downing, Laura. "Negation as a Stylistic Feature in Joseph Heller's *Catch-22*: A Corpus Study." *Style* 37 (Fall, 2003): 318-341, 352. Thoughtful exploration of the negation motif in Heller's most famous novel.

LeClair, Thomas. "Joseph Heller, *Something Happened*, and the Art of Excess." *Studies in American Fiction* 9 (Autumn, 1981): 245-260. This essay focuses on Heller's second novel, defending its repetitive quality as a stylistic device, necessary to the portrayal of the dullness and mediocrity of the life of its protagonist and the other characters.

Potts, Stephen W. *From Here to Absurdity: The Moral Battlefields of Joseph Heller.* 2d ed. San Bernardino, Calif.: Borgo Press, 1995. This insightful and accessible overview of Heller's novels and plays emphasizes the continuities throughout Heller's writings, despite the various genres within which he has worked. As a moralist and political cynic, Heller creates characters whose personal crises drive them either to confront or to conform to governing orthodoxy.

Saurian, Adam J. *Conversations with Joseph Heller.* Jackson: University Press of Mississippi, 1993. Collection of lengthy interviews with Heller.

Scoggins, Michael C. "Joseph Heller's Combat Experiences in *Catch-22*." *War, Literature, and the Arts: An International Journal of the Humanities* 15 (2003): 213-227. Study of the relationship of Heller's actual combat experiences in World War II and the combat passages in his novel *Catch-22*.

Seed, David. *The Fiction of Joseph Heller.* New York: St. Martin's Press, 1989. Broad survey of Heller's novels.

Woodson, Jon. *A Study of Joseph Heller's "Catch-22": Going Around Twice.* New York: P. Lang, 2001. Uses the New Criticism and mythological criticism that Heller was familiar with to argue that *Catch-22* is in essence a retelling of the epic of Gilgamesh in much the same way that James Joyce's *Ulysses* was a retelling of Homer's *Odyssey*.

Ernest Hemingway

Born: Oak Park, Illinois; July 21, 1899
Died: Ketchum, Idaho; July 2, 1961

Principal long fiction • *The Sun Also Rises*, 1926; *The Torrents of Spring*, 1926; *A Farewell to Arms*, 1929; *To Have and Have Not*, 1937; *For Whom the Bell Tolls*, 1940; *Across the River and into the Trees*, 1950; *The Old Man and the Sea*, 1952; *Islands in the Stream*, 1970; *The Garden of Eden*, 1986; *True at First Light*, 1999.

Other literary forms • Ernest Hemingway will be best remembered for his novels and short stories, though critical debate rages over whether his literary reputation rests more firmly on the former or the latter. In his own time, he was known to popular reading audiences for his newspaper dispatches and for his essays in popular magazines. He wrote, in addition, a treatise on bullfighting (*Death in the Afternoon*, 1932), which is still considered the most authoritative treatment of the subject in English; an account of big-game hunting (*Green Hills of Africa*, 1935); two plays (*Today Is Friday*, 1926, and *The Fifth Column*, 1938); and reminiscences of his experiences in Paris during the 1920's (*A Moveable Feast*, 1964).

Achievements • There is little question that Hemingway will be remembered as one of the outstanding prose stylists in American literary history, and it was for his contributions in this area that he was awarded the Nobel Prize in Literature in 1954, two years after the publication of *The Old Man and the Sea*. The general reader has often been more intrigued by Hemingway's exploits—hunting, fishing, and living dangerously—than by his virtues as an artist. Ironically, he is often thought of now primarily as the chronicler of the "lost generation" of the 1920's, a phrase that he heard from Gertrude Stein and incorporated into *The Sun Also Rises* as one of its epigraphs. The Hemingway "code," which originated as a prescription for living in the post-World War I decade, has become a catchphrase for academicians and general readers alike.

Biography • Ernest Miller Hemingway was the first son of an Oak Park, Illinois, physician, Clarence Edmonds Hemingway, and Grace Hemingway, a Christian Scientist. As a student in the Oak Park public schools, Hemingway received his first journalistic experience writing for *The Trapeze*, a student newspaper. After serving as a reporter for the Kansas City *Star* for less than a year, he enlisted as an ambulance driver for the American Red Cross and was sent in 1918 to serve on the Italian front. He received a leg wound that required that he be sent to an American hospital in Milan, and there he met and fell in love with Agnes Von Kurowski, who provided the basis for his characterization of Catherine Barkley in *A Farewell to Arms*. In 1921, Hemingway married Hadley Richardson. They moved to the Left Bank of Paris, lived on her income from a trust fund, and became friends of Gertrude Stein and other Left Bank literary figures.

The Paris years provided Hemingway with material for the autobiographical sketches collected after his death in *A Moveable Feast*. Also in the Paris years, he met the people who would become the major characters in his roman à clef, *The Sun Also Rises*. Hemingway dedicated the novel to Hadley, divorced her (in retrospect, one of the saddest experiences in his life), and married Pauline Pfeiffer in 1927. During the 1930's, Hemingway became attached to the Loyalist cause in Spain, and during the years of the Spanish Civil War, he traveled to that country several times as a war correspondent. His feelings about that war are recorded in *For Whom the Bell Tolls*, which was an enormous popular success.

In 1940, Hemingway divorced Pauline and married the independent, free-spirited Martha Gellhorn, whom he divorced in 1945, marrying in that same year Mary Welsh, his fourth wife. The 1952 publication of *The Old Man and the Sea* is usually regarded as evidence that the writing slump that Hemingway had suffered for nearly a decade was ended. The last years of his life were marked by medical problems, resulting to a great extent from injuries that he had sustained in accidents and from years of heavy drinking. In

©The Nobel Foundation

1961, after being released from the Mayo Clinic, Hemingway returned with his wife Mary to their home in Ketchum, Idaho. He died there on July 2, 1961, of a self-inflicted shotgun wound.

Analysis • "All stories, if continued far enough, end in death, and he is no true story teller who would keep that from you," Ernest Hemingway wrote in *Death in the Afternoon*. He might have added that most of his own stories and novels, if traced back far enough, also begin in death. In *The Sun Also Rises*, death from World War I shadows the actions of most of the main characters; specifically, death has robbed Brett Ashley of the man she loved before she met Jake, and that fact, though only alluded to in the novel, largely accounts for her membership in the lost generation. *A Farewell to Arms* begins and ends with death: Catherine Barkley's fiancé was killed before the main events of the novel begin, and her own death at the end will profoundly influence the rest of Frederic Henry's life. The Caporetta retreat scenes, often referred to as the "death chapters" of *A Farewell to Arms*, prompt Frederic Henry to give up the death of war for what he believes to be the life of love. In *For Whom the Bell Tolls*, death is nearby in every scene, a fact suggested first by the image of the bell in the novel's title and epigraph, the bell whose tolling is a death knell. Perhaps most important in *For Whom the Bell Tolls*, Robert Jordan's choice to die as he does comes from his reflections on the heroic death of his grandfather compared with what he sees as the cowardly suicide of his father. Finally, Santiago's memories of his dead wife in *The Old Man and the Sea* play in and out of his mind as he confronts the possibility of his own death in his struggle against the great marlin and the sea.

Indeed, in Hemingway's work, as Nelson Algren observes, it seems "as though a man must earn his death before he could win his life." However, it would be a mistake to allow what may appear to be Hemingway's preoccupation—or, to some, obsession—with death to obscure the fact that he is, above all, concerned in his fiction with the quality of individual life, even though it must be granted that the quality and intensity of his characters' lives seem to increase in direct proportion to their awareness of the reality of death.

There is a danger, however, in making so general an observation as this. Hemingway's attitudes about life, about living it well and living it courageously in the face of death, changed in the course of his most productive years as a writer, those years between 1926 and 1952, which were marked by the creation of his three best novels and the Nobel Prize-winning novella *The Old Man and the Sea*. During this period, Hemingway shifted away from what many consider the hedonistic value system of Jake, Brett, Frederic, and Catherine, a system often equated with the Hemingway code, to a concern with the collective, almost spiritual value of human life reflected in the actions of Robert Jordan and Santiago. If the constant in Hemingway's works, then, is the fact that "all stories, if continued far enough, end in death," the variable is his subtly changing attitude toward the implications of this fact, no better gauge of which can be found than in the ways his characters choose to live their lives in his major novels.

"Big Two-Hearted River" • The best prologue to Hemingway's novels is a long short story, "Big Two-Hearted River," which has been described as a work in which "nothing happens." By the standards of the traditional, heavily plotted story, very little does happen in "Big Two-Hearted River," but the main reason for this is that so much has happened before the story opens that Nick, Hemingway's autobiographical persona, has been rendered incapable of the kind of action one usually associates with an adventure story. Death has occurred: not literal human death, but the death of the land, and with it the death of Nick's old values. It has been brought about by the burning of once-lush vegetation that covered the soil and surrounded the water of Nick's boyhood hunting and fishing territory. Presented with this scene, Nick must find a way of living in the presence of it, which he does by granting supremacy to his senses, the only guides he can trust. He earns the right to eat his food by carrying the heavy backpack containing it to his campsite; after working with his own hands to provide shelter, he can savor the cooking and eating of the food. He can then catch grasshoppers, which have adapted to the burning of the woods by becoming brown, and use them as natural bait for fishing. Then he can catch fish, clean them, eat them, and return their inedible parts to the earth to help restore its fertility.

It is appropriate that "nothing happens" in this prologue to Hemingway's novels because the dilemma of his main characters is that "nothing" is going to happen unless a modern Perceval removes the plagues of the people and restores fertility to the land. The task for Hemingway's characters, particularly those in his early works, is to establish a code by which they can live in the meantime. Nick, like T. S. Eliot's Fisher King, who sits with his back to an arid plain at the end of *The Waste Land* (1922), is shoring up fragments against his ruins: He is developing a personal system that will enable him to cope with life in the presence of a burned-out, infertile land. Also, like Eliot and many other lost-generation writers, Hemingway suggests that the actual wasteland is a metaphor for the spiritual and psychological impotence of modern humanity, since the state of the land simply mirrors the condition of the postwar human psyche. Like the grasshoppers in "Big Two-Hearted River," who have changed color to adapt outwardly to the changing of the land, Nick must adjust internally to the altered condition of his psyche, whose illusions have been destroyed by the war, just as the land has been destroyed by fire.

The Sun Also Rises • An understanding of the principles set forth in "Big Two-Hearted River" is perhaps essential to an understanding of the life-in-death/death-in-life philosophy that Hemingway presents in his major novels, particularly in *The Sun Also Rises* and *A Farewell to Arms*. Bringing these principles in advance to *The Sun Also Rises* enables a reader to see the mythical substructure that lies beneath the apparent simplicity of the story line. On the face of it, *The Sun Also Rises* tells the story of Jake Barnes, whose war wound has left him physically incapable of sexual activity, though it has done so without robbing him of sexual desire. Jake has the misfortune to fall in love with the beautiful and, for practical purposes, nymphomaniac Lady Brett Ashley, who loves Jake but must nevertheless make love to other men. Among these men is Robert Cohn, a hopeless romantic who, alone in the novel, believes in the concept of chivalric love.

Hemingway explores the frustration of the doomed love affair between Jake and Brett as they wander from Paris and its moral invalids to Pamplona, where Jake and his lost-generation friends participate in the fiesta. Jake is the only one of the group to have become an *aficionado*, one who is passionate about bullfighting. In the end, though, he betrays his *aficion* by introducing Brett to Pedro Romero, one of the few remaining bullfighters who is true to the spirit of the sport—one who fights honestly and faces death with grace—and this Jake does with full knowledge that Brett will seduce Romero, perhaps corrupting his innocence by infecting him with the jaded philosophy that makes her "lost." Predictably, she does seduce Romero, but less predictably she lets him go, refusing to be "one of these bitches that ruins children." Finally, she and Jake are left where they started, she unrealistically musing that "we could have had such a damned good time together"—presumably if he had not been wounded—and he, perhaps a little wiser, responding, "Yes. . . . Isn't it pretty to think so."

Few will miss the sense of aimless wandering from country to country and bottle to bottle in *The Sun Also Rises*. The reader who approaches Jake's condition as a logical extension, symbolically rendered, of Nick's situation in "Big Two-Hearted River," however, will more fully appreciate Hemingway's design and purpose in the novel. As is the case in "Big Two-Hearted River," the death with which *The Sun Also Rises* begins and ends is less a physical death than it is living or walking death, which, granted, is most acute in Jake's case, but that afflicts all the characters in the novel. They must establish rules for playing a kind of spiritual solitaire, and Jake is the character in the novel who most articulately expresses these rules, perhaps because he is the one who most needs them. "Enjoying living," he says, "was learning to get your money's worth and knowing when you had it." In a literal sense, Jake refers here to the practice of getting what one pays for with actual money, but in another sense, he is talking more abstractly about other kinds of economy—the economy of motion in a good bullfight, for example.

To see how thoroughly Hemingway weaves this idea of economy into the fabric of the novel, one needs only to look at his seemingly offhand joke about writing telegrams. On closer examination, the joke yields a valuable clue for understanding the Hemingway code. When Jake and Bill, his best friend, are fishing in Burguete, they receive a telegram from Cohn, addressed simply, "Barnes, Burguete": "Vengo Jueves Cohn" [I come Thursday]. "What a lousy telegram!" Jake responds. "He could send ten words for the same price." Cohn thinks that he is being clever by writing in Spanish and saving a word, an assumption as naïve as the one that leads him to shorten the name and address to "Barnes, Burguete." The address was free, and Cohn could have included full name and address, thus increasing the probability that Jake would get the message. As a response to Cohn's telegram, Jake and Bill send one equally wasteful: "Arriving to-night." The point is that the price of the telegram includes a laugh at Cohn's expense, and they are willing to pay for it.

After the Burguete scene, there is no direct discussion of the price of telegrams, but through this scene, Hemingway gives a key for understanding how each character measures up to the standards of the code. Ironically, Bill, with whom Jake has laughed over Cohn's extravagance and whom Jake admires, is as uneconomical as Cohn. From Budapest, he wires Jake, "Back on Monday"; his card from Budapest says, "Jake, Budapest is wonderful." Bill's wastefulness, however, is calculated, and he is quite conscious of his value system. In his attempt to talk Jake into buying a stuffed dog, Bill indicates that, to him, things are equally valueless: Whatever one buys, in essence, will be dead and stuffed. He is a conscious spendthrift who has no intention of conserving emotions or money. He ignores the fact that letters, cards, and telegrams are designed to accommodate messages of different lengths and that one should choose the most appropriate (conservative) form of communication available. At first, it seems strange that Jake can accept as a true friend one whose value system is so different from his, but just as Frederic Henry in *A Farewell to Arms* will accept the priest, whose code is different, so can Jake accept Bill. Both the priest and Bill are conscious of their value systems. Thus, if Bill's extravagance appears to link him with the wasteful Cohn, the similarity is a superficial one. Like Jake—and unlike Cohn, who still believes in the chivalric code—he has merely chosen extravagance as a way of coping, knowing that whatever he gets will be the equivalent of a stuffed dog. Morally, Bill is less akin to Cohn than he is to Rinaldi in *A Farewell to Arms*, who continues his indiscriminate lovemaking, even though he knows it may result in syphilis. Just as Frederic Henry remains true to Rinaldi, so Jake remains true to Bill.

Standing midway between Bill and Cohn is Brett's fiancé Michael, whose values, in terms of the code, are sloppy. Like Cohn, Mike sends bad telegrams and letters. His one telegram in the novel is four words long: "Stopped night San Sebastian." His letters are in clipped telegraphese, filled with abbreviations such as "We got here Friday, Brett passed out on the train, so brought her here for 3 days rest with old friends of ours." Michael could have gotten more for his money in the telegram by using the ten allotted words, just as he could have sent a letter without abbreviations for the same price. The telegram and the letter suggest that although he is conscious of the *principle* of economy, he simply has no idea how to be economical. Thus, when Brett says of Michael that "He writes a good letter," there is an irony in her comment that Jake acknowledges: "I know. . . . He wrote me from San Sebastian." In juxtaposing the telegram and the letter, Hemingway shows Michael to be a man without a code, a man who, when asked how he became bankrupt, responds, "Gradually and then suddenly," which is precisely how he is becoming emotionally bankrupt. He sees it coming, but he has no code that will help him deal directly with his "lostness."

Unlike Cohn, Bill, and Mike, both Brett and Jake send ten-word telegrams, thus presumably getting their money's worth. When Brett, in the last chapters of the

novel, needs Jake, she wires him: "COULD YOU COME HOTEL MONTANA MA-
DRID AM RATHER IN TROUBLE BRETT"—ten words followed by the signature.
This telegram, which had been forwarded from Paris, is immediately followed by another one identical to it, forwarded from Pamplona. In turn, Jake responds with a
telegram that also consists of ten words and the signature: "LADY ASHLEY HOTEL
MONTANA MADRID ARRIVING SUD EXPRESS TOMORROW LOVE JAKE." Interestingly, he includes the address in the body of the telegram in order to obtain the
ten-word limit. The sending of ten-word telegrams indicates that Jake and Brett are
bonded by their adherence to the code; since they alone send such telegrams, the
reader must see them as members of an exclusive society.

Ironically, to Jake and Brett, the code has become a formalized ritual, something
superimposed over their emptiness. They have not learned to apply the code to every
aspect of their lives, the most striking example of which is Brett's ten-word (exclud-
ing the signature) postcard at the beginning of chapter 8: "Darling. Very quiet and
healthy. Love to all the chaps. Brett." The postcard has no word limit, except that dictated by the size of one's handwriting. Brett, however, in the absence of clearly labeled values, must fall back on the only form she knows: in this case, that of the ten-
word telegram, which is here an empty form, a ritual detached from its meaningful
context.

Jake and Brett, then, come back full circle to their initial frustration and mark
time with rituals to which they cling for not-so-dear life, looking in the meantime for
physical pleasures that will get them through the night. However, if this seems a low
yield for their efforts, one should remember that Hemingway makes no pretense in
The Sun Also Rises of finding a cure for "lostness." In fact, he heightens the sense of it
in his juxtaposition of two epigraphs of the novel: "You are all a lost generation" from
Gertrude Stein, and the long quotation from Ecclesiastes that begins "One generation passeth away, and another generation cometh; but the earth abideth forever. . . .
The sun also ariseth, and the sun goeth down. . . . " As Hemingway maintained, the
hero of *The Sun Also Rises* is the abiding earth; the best one can hope for while living
on that earth, isolated from one's fellows and cut off from the procreative cycle, is a
survival manual. Finally, that is what *The Sun Also Rises* is, and this is the prescription
that it offers: One must accept the presence of death in life and face it stoically, one
must learn to exhibit grace under pressure, and one must learn to get one's money's
worth. In skeleton form, this is the foundation of the Hemingway code—the part of
it, at least, that remains constant through all of his novels.

A Farewell to Arms • Many of the conditions that necessitated the forming of a code
for Jake and Brett in *The Sun Also Rises* are still present in *A Farewell to Arms*, and
there are obvious similarities between the two novels. Like Jake, Frederic Henry is
wounded in the war and falls in love with a woman, Catherine Barkley, whose first
love, like Brett's, has been killed before the main events of the novel begin. However,
there has been a subtle change from *The Sun Also Rises* to *A Farewell to Arms* in Hemingway's perception of the human dilemma. The most revealing hint of this change is
in the nature of the wound that Frederic receives while serving as an ambulance
driver on the Italian front. Unlike Jake's phallic wound, Frederic's is a less debilitat-
ing leg wound, and, ironically, it is the thing that brings him closer to Catherine, an
English nurse who treats him in the field hospital in Milan. Though their relationship begins as a casual one, viewed from the beginning by Frederic as a "chess game"
whose object is sexual gratification, it evolves in the course of Catherine's nursing

him into a love that is both spiritual and physical. Catherine's pregnancy affirms at least a partial healing of the maimed Fisher King and the restoration of fertility to the wasteland that appeared in *The Sun Also Rises.*

With this improved condition, however, come new problems, and with them a need to amend the code practiced by Jake and Brett. Frederic's dilemma at the beginning of the novel, how to find meaning in life when he is surrounded by death, contains clear-cut alternatives: He can seek physical pleasure in the bawdy houses frequented by his fellow soldiers, including his best friend Rinaldi, or he can search for meaning through the religion practiced by the priest from the Abruzzi; he can do either while fulfilling his obligation to the war effort. His choices, simple ones at first, become limited by forces beyond his control. First, he must discard the possibility of religion, because he cannot believe in it; then, he must reject the life of the bawdy houses, both because it is not fulfilling and because it often brings syphilis. These are choices that even a code novice such as Frederic Henry can make, but his next decision is more difficult. Knowing that Catherine is pregnant and knowing that he loves her, how can he continue to fight, even for a cause to which he feels duty-bound? Catherine, who had earlier lost her fiancé to the war and who had refused to give herself to him completely because of her sense of duty to the abstract virtue of premarital sexual purity, has prepared Frederic for his decision, one forecast by the title *A Farewell to Arms.* Frederic's choice is made easier by the disordered and chaotic scenes that he witnesses during the Caporetta retreat, among them the shooting of his fellow officers by carabinieri. Partly because Catherine has initiated him into the life of love, then, and partly because he needs to escape his own death, Frederic deserts the Italian army in one of the most celebrated baptismal rites in American literature: He dives into the Tagliamento River and washes away his anger "with any obligation," making what he terms a separate peace.

If Hemingway were a different kind of storyteller, the reader could anticipate that Frederic and Catherine would regain paradise, have their child, and live happily ever after. In fact, however, no sooner have they escaped the life-in-death of war in Italy to the neutrality of Switzerland, where the reader could logically expect in a fifth and final chapter of the novel a brief, pleasant postscript, than does the double edge hidden in the title become clear. Catherine has foreseen it all along in her visions of the rain, often a symbol of life but in *A Farewell to Arms* a symbol of death: "Sometimes I see me dead in it," she says. The arms to which Frederic must finally say farewell are those of Catherine, who dies in childbirth. "And this," Frederic observes, "is the price you paid for sleeping together. . . . This was what people get for loving each other."

Some will take this ending and Frederic Henry's observations about love at face value and accuse Hemingway of stacking the odds against Frederic and Catherine, maintaining finally that Hemingway provides a legitimate exit from the wasteland with a code that could work and then barricades it capriciously. There is, however, ample warning. From the beginning of the novel, Hemingway establishes Catherine as one who knows well the dangers of loving, and from the time of her meeting with Frederic, she balances them against the emptiness of not loving. In most ways, Catherine is a model of the code hero/heroine established in *The Sun Also Rises*: She stoically accepts life's difficulties, as evidenced by her acceptance of her fiancé's death; and she exhibits grace under pressure, as shown in her calm acceptance of her own death. In giving herself to Frederic, she adds a dimension to the code by breaking through the isolation and separateness felt by Jake and Brett; finally, even though she does not complete the re-creative cycle by giving birth to a child conceived in love, she at least brings the possibility within reach. The reader must decide whether Frederic will internalize the lessons he has learned through Catherine's life and allow his own initiation into the code, which now contains the possibility of loving, to be accomplished.

There are some tenets of Hemingway's philosophy through the publication of *A Farewell to Arms* about which one is safe in generalizing. The most obvious and most important of these is his belief that the only things in life that one can know about with certainty are those things that can be verified through the senses, as Jake can confirm that he has had good food or good wine and as Frederic can verify that being next to Catherine feels good. Hemingway refuses to judge this belief in the primacy of the senses as moral or immoral, and Jake articulates this refusal with mock uncertainty during a late-night Pamplona monologue on values: "That was morality; things that made you disgusted after. No, that must be immorality." The point is that in referring observations about life to the senses, one relieves oneself of the need to think about abstractions such as love and honor, abstractions that the main characters in the first two novels carefully avoid. Frederic, for example, is "always embarrassed by the words sacred, glorious, and sacrifice and the expression in vain." With such a perspective, the value of life can be rather accurately measured and described in empirical terms. Similarly, death in such a system can be described even more easily, since there is nothing in death to perceive or measure, an idea vividly rendered in Frederic's remarks about his farewell to Catherine: "It was like saying good-by to a statue."

In looking back on Catherine's death, Frederic or the reader may conclude that it had sacrificial value, but until the 1930's, Hemingway was reluctant in his novels to identify death with an abstract virtue such as sacrifice or to write about the value of an individual life in a collective sense. By 1937, however, and the publication of what most critics regard as his weakest novel, *To Have and Have Not*, Hemingway's attitudes toward life and death had changed. Harry Morgan, the "have not" spokesman of the novel, finally with much effort is able to mutter at the end, "One man alone ain't got . . . no chance." After saying this he reflects that "it had taken him a long time to get it out and it had taken him all his life to learn it." The major works to come after *To Have and Have Not*, namely, *For Whom the Bell Tolls* and *The Old Man and the Sea*, amplify Morgan's view and show Hemingway's code characters moving toward a belief in the collective values of their own lives.

For Whom the Bell Tolls • The epigraph of *For Whom the Bell Tolls*, which was taken from a John Donne sermon and that gives the novel its title, points clearly to Hemingway's reevaluation of the role of death in life:

> No man is an *Iland*, intire of it selfe; every man is a peece of the *Continent*, a part of the *maine*. . . . And therefore never send to know for whom the bell tolls; It tolls for thee.

Regardless of the route by which Hemingway came to exchange the "separate peace" idea of *The Sun Also Rises* and *A Farewell to Arms* for the "part of the *maine*" philosophy embraced by Robert Jordan in *For Whom the Bell Tolls*, one can be sure that much of the impetus for his changing came from his strong feelings about Spain's internal strife, particularly as this strife became an all-out conflict during the Spanish Civil War (1936-1939). This war provides the backdrop for the events of *For Whom the Bell*

Tolls, and the novel's main character, like Hemingway, is a passionate supporter of the Loyalist cause. The thing that one immediately notices about Jordan is that he is an idealist, which sets him apart from Jake and Frederic. Also, unlike Jake, who wanders randomly throughout Europe, and unlike Frederic, whose reasons for being in Italy to participate in the war are never clearly defined, Jordan has come to the Sierra de Guadaramas with the specific purpose of blowing up a bridge that would be used to transport ammunition in attacks against the Loyalists. Thrown in with the Loyalist guerrillas of Pablo's band at the beginning of the novel, Jordan is confronted with the near-impossible task of accomplishing the demolition in three days, a task whose difficulty is compounded by Pablo's resistance to the idea and, finally, by increased Fascist activity near the bridge.

Potentially even more threatening to Jordan's mission is his meeting and falling in love with the beautiful and simple Maria, who is in the protection of Pablo's band after having been raped by the Falangists who killed her parents. Again, however, Jordan is not Frederic Henry, which is to say that he has no intention of declaring a separate peace and leaving his duty behind in pursuit of love. He sees no conflict between the two, and to the degree that Hemingway presents him as the rare individual who fulfills his obligations without losing his ability to love, Jordan represents a new version of the code hero: the whole man who respects himself, cares for others, and believes in the cause of individual freedom. Circumstances, though, conspire against Jordan. Seeing that his mission stands little hope of success and that the offensive planned by General Golz is doomed to failure by the presence of more and more Fascists, he attempts to get word through to Golz, but the message arrives too late. Although he manages successfully to demolish the bridge and almost escapes with Maria, his wounded horse falls, rolls over, and crushes Jordan's leg. He remains at the end of the novel in extreme pain, urging the others not to stay and be killed with him, and waiting to shoot the first Fascist officer who comes into range, thus giving Maria and Pablo's group more time to escape.

Jordan is perhaps Hemingway's most ambitious creation, just as *For Whom the Bell Tolls* is his most elaborately conceived novel. Its various strands reflect not only what had become the standard Hemingway subjects of personal death, love, and war, but also his growing concern with the broader social implications of individual action. Jordan's consideration of his mission in Spain clearly demonstrates this: "I have fought for what I believe in for a year now," he says. "If we win here we will win everywhere." How well Hemingway has woven together these strands remains a matter of critical debate, but individually the parts are brilliant in conception. One example of the many layers of meaning contained in the novel is the Civil War framework, which leads the reader not only to see the conflict of social forces in Spain but also to understand that its analogue is the "civil war" in Jordan's spirit: The reader is reminded periodically of the noble death of Jordan's grandfather in the American Civil War, compared to the "separate peace" suicide of Jordan's father. Jordan debates these alternatives until the last scene, when he decides to opt for an honorable death that gives others a chance to live. This, Hemingway seems finally to say, gives Jordan's life transcendent value.

The Old Man and the Sea • F. Scott Fitzgerald theorized early in his friendship with Hemingway that Hemingway would need a new wife for each "big book." As Scott Donaldson observes, the "theory worked well for his [Hemingway's] first three wives (Hadley: *The Sun Also Rises*; Pauline: *A Farewell to Arms*; Martha: *For Whom the Bell Tolls*) but breaks down in Mary's case" because *The Old Man and the Sea* does not qualify as a "big book." It does qualify, however, as a major epilogue to the "big books," much as "Big Two-Hearted River" qualifies as their prologue. In the prologue, Hemingway outlines the dilemma of modern humankind and establishes the task with which he is confronted in a literal and figurative wasteland. For Nick in the story, Hemingway posits a swamp, which Nick may fish "tomorrow" and which is a symbolic representation of life with all its complexities, including male-female relationships. In the "big books," Hemingway leads the reader through the wasteland, showing first, in *The Sun Also Rises*, the risk of personal isolation and despair in a life cut off from the regenerative cycles of nature. In *A Farewell to Arms*, he dramatizes the vulnerability of the individual even in a life where there is love, and finally, in *For Whom the Bell Tolls*, he presents a "whole man" who recognizes the value of individual sacrifice for the survival of the human race. In the epilogue, *The Old Man and the Sea*, Hemingway carries this principle to its final step and issues, through Santiago, his definitive statement about the role of life in death.

It is no surprise that *The Old Man and the Sea* takes the form of a parable and that its old man takes the form of the archetypal wise man or savior common to most cultures, mythologies, and religions. Although others who surround Santiago depend on gadgets to catch their fish, Santiago relies only on his own endurance and courage. He goes eighty-four days before hooking the marlin, against whose strength he will pit his own for nearly two full days, until he is finally able to bring him to the boat and secure him there for the journey from the Gulf Stream. Numerous critics have noted the similarities between Santiago and Christ. Santiago goes farther out than most men, symbolically taking on a burden for humankind that most men could not or would not take on for themselves.

When Santiago returns to land from his ordeal, secures his boat, and heads toward his shack, Hemingway describes his journey explicitly in terms of Christ's ascent to Calvary: "He started to climb again and at the top he fell and lay for some time with the mast across his shoulder." Moreover, Santiago talks with the boy Manolin about those who do not believe in him or his ways in terms that are unmistakably religious: Of the boy's father, who does not want his son to be with the old man, Santiago remarks, "He hasn't much faith." In all of this, Hemingway is leading the reader to see that some, in going out "too far," risk their lives in order to transmit to others the idea that "a man can be destroyed but not defeated." Finally, it is of little importance that sharks have reduced Santiago's great fish to a skeleton by the time he has reached land because the human spirit that has been tested in his battle with the fish has in the end prevailed; those who are genuinely interested in that spirit are rarely concerned with ocular proof of its existence. Santiago's legacy, which must stand as Hemingway's last major word on the human condition, will go to Manolin and the reader, since, as the old man tells him, "I know you did not leave me because you doubted"; he did not doubt that man's spirit can prevail.

Hemingway, then, traveled a great distance from the nihilistic philosophy and hedonistic code of *The Sun Also Rises* to the affirmative view of humankind expressed in *The Old Man and the Sea*. His four major works, if read chronologically, lead the reader on an odyssey through the seasonal cycle of the human spirit. "All stories, if continued far enough, end in death," and Hemingway never stops reminding the reader of that fact. He does add to it, though, in his later work, the hope of rebirth that waits at the end of the journey, a hope for which nature has historically provided the model. The reader of Hemingway's work may find the idea of metaphorical rebirth less a solace for the individual facing literal death than Hemingway seems to suggest it can be. Few, however, will leave Hemingway's work without feeling that he, at least, speaks in the end with the authority of one who has earned, in Carlos Baker's words, "the proud, quiet knowledge of having fought the fight, of having lasted it out, of having done a great thing to the bitter end of human strength."

Bryant Mangum

Other major works

SHORT FICTION: *Three Stories and Ten Poems*, 1923; *In Our Time*, 1924, 1925; *Men Without Women*, 1927; *Winner Take Nothing*, 1933; *The Fifth Column and the First Forty-nine Stories*, 1938; *The Snows of Kilimanjaro, and Other Stories*, 1961; *The Nick Adams Stories*, 1972; *The Complete Stories of Ernest Hemingway*, 1987.

PLAYS: *Today Is Friday*, pb. 1926; *The Fifth Column*, pb. 1938.

NONFICTION: *Death in the Afternoon*, 1932; *Green Hills of Africa*, 1935; *A Moveable Feast*, 1964; *By-Line: Ernest Hemingway, Selected Articles and Dispatches of Four Decades*, 1967; *Ernest Hemingway: Selected Letters, 1917-1961*, 1981; *Dateline, Toronto: The Complete "Toronto Star" Dispatches, 1920-1924*, 1985; *The Dangerous Summer*, 1985; *Ernest Hemingway on Writing*, 1999 (Larry W. Phillips, editor); *Hemingway on Fishing*, 2000 (Nick Lyons, editor); *Hemingway on Hunting*, 2001 (Sean Hemingway, editor); *Hemingway on War*, 2003 (Seán Hemingway, editor); *Dear Papa, Dear Hotch: The Correspondence of Ernest Hemingway and A. E. Hotchner*, 2005 (Albert J. DeFazio III, editor); *Hemingway and the Mechanism of Fame: Statements, Public Letters, Introductions, Forewords, Prefaces, Blurbs, Reviews, and Endorsements*, 2006 (Matthew J. Bruccoli, editor).

Bibliography

Berman, Ronald. *Fitzgerald, Hemingway, and the Twenties*. Tuscaloosa: University of Alabama Press, 2001. An explication of the cultural context of the era and how the works of these two American writers are imbued with the attitudes and icons of their day.

Bloom, Harold, ed. *Ernest Hemingway*. Broomall, Pa.: Chelsea House, 2000. Includes articles by a variety of critics who treat topics such as Hemingway's style, unifying devices, and visual techniques.

_____. *Ernest Hemingway*. Philadelphia: Chelsea House, 2005. Collection of critical essays about Hemingway that have been assembled for student use.

Burgess, Anthony. *Ernest Hemingway*. New York: Thames and Hudson, 1999. Originally published in 1978 as *Ernest Hemingway and His World*, this study of Hemingway by a major British novelist includes bibliographical references and an index.

Dubus, Andre. "A Hemingway Story." *The Kenyon Review*, n.s. 19 (Spring, 1997): 141-147. Dubus, a respected short-story writer himself, discusses Hemingway's "In Another Country." States that, whereas he once thought the story was about the futility of cures, since becoming disabled he has come to understand that it is about healing.

Hays, Peter L. *Ernest Hemingway*. New York: Continuum, 1990. A brief but instructive overview of Hemingway's life and his achievement as a writer. Offers brief critical summaries of the novels and many short stories. Contains a useful chronology.

Koch, Stephen. *The Breaking Point: Hemingway, Dos Passos, and the Murder of José Robles*. New York: Counterpoint, 2005. Study of the split that occurred between Heming-

way and novelist John Dos Passos after Dos Passos's poet friend José Robles was executed during the Spanish Civil War.

Lamb, Robert Paul. "The Love Song of Harold Krebs: Form, Argument, and Meaning in Hemingway's 'Soldier's Home.'" *The Hemingway Review* 14 (Spring, 1995):
18-36. Claims that the story concerns both war trauma and a conflict between
mother and son. Discusses the structure of the story; argues that by ignoring the
story's form, one misses the manner of Hemingway's narrative argument and the
considerable art that underlies it.

Leonard, John. "'A Man of the World' and 'A Clean, Well-Lighted Place': Hemingway's Unified View of Old Age." *The Hemingway Review* 13 (Spring, 1994): 62-73.
Compares the two Hemingway stories in terms of the theme of age. Notes also the
themes of aloneness, consolation of light, loss of sexuality and physical prowess,
depression, violence, and the need for dignity.

Reynolds, Michael. *The Young Hemingway.* New York: Blackwell, 1986. First part of
Reynolds's five-volume biography of Hemingway.

_____. *Hemingway: The Paris Years.* New York: Blackwell, 1989.

_____. *Hemingway: The American Homecoming.* New York: W. W. Norton, 1992.

_____. *Hemingway: The 1930's.* New York: W. W. Norton, 1997.

_____. *Hemingway: The Final Years.* New York: W. W. Norton, 1999. Reynolds's
monumental and painstaking multivolume biography is devoted to the evolution
of Hemingway's life and writing.

Vernon, Alex. *Soldiers Once and Still: Ernest Hemingway, James Salter, and Tim O'Brien.*
Iowa City: University of Iowa Press, 2004. Comparative study of the war stories of
representatives of three generations of American novelists.

Wagner-Martin, Linda, ed. *Hemingway: Seven Decades of Criticism.* East Lansing: Michi-
gan State University Press, 1998. A collection of essays ranging from Gertrude
Stein's 1923 review of Hemingway's stories to recent responses to *The Garden of
Eden.* Includes essays on "Indian Camp," "Hills Like White Elephants," and *In Our
Time* as self-begetting fiction.

John Hersey

Born: Tianjin, China; June 17, 1914
Died: Key West, Florida; March 24, 1993

Principal long fiction • *A Bell for Adano*, 1944; *The Wall*, 1950; *The Marmot Drive*, 1953; *A Single Pebble*, 1956; *The War Lover*, 1959; *The Child Buyer*, 1960; *White Lotus*, 1965; *Too Far to Walk*, 1966; *Under the Eye of the Storm*, 1967; *The Conspiracy*, 1972; *My Petition for More Space*, 1974; *The Walnut Door*, 1977; *The Call*, 1985; *Antonietta*, 1991.

Other literary forms • John Hersey is as well known for his nonfiction as he is for his novels. As a young journalist in World War II, Hersey wrote for *Time* and *Life*, interviewing such figures as Japan's Foreign Minister Matsuoka, Ambassador Joseph Grew, and Generalissimo Chiang Kai-shek. His first book, *Men on Bataan* (1942), was written in New York from files and clippings; his second, *Into the Valley: A Skirmish of the Marines* (1943), from his own experiences. *Hiroshima* (1946), generally considered to be his most important book, was based on a series of interviews. After *Hiroshima*, he concentrated on writing novels for twenty years, though he often employed the techniques of interviewing and research to establish a factual basis for his novels. *Here to Stay: Studies in Human Tenacity* (1962) reprinted *Hiroshima* and a number of other interviews with people who had survived similar horrors, such as the Warsaw Ghetto. *The Algiers Motel Incident* (1968) was based on research and interviews concerning the Detroit police killing of three black people during a period of riots. *Letter to the Alumni* (1970) was a portrait of Yale University during May Day demonstrations, and *The President* (1975) followed President Gerald R. Ford on a typical day. *Life Sketches* (1989) is a book of autobiographical pieces. Hersey's collections of short stories include *Fling, and Other Stories* (1990). *Blues* (1987), also classified as short fiction, is an idiosyncratic book about bluefishing, cast in the form of a dialogue between a fisherman and a curious stranger and interspersed with poems by Elizabeth Bishop, James Merrill, and others. Hersey also edited *The Writer's Craft* (1974), an anthology of famous writers' comments on the aesthetics and techniques of literary creation.

Achievements • Hersey's primary achievement was his mastery of the nonfiction novel. Although all the particular techniques of the nonfiction novel have been used for centuries, Hersey can be said to have anticipated the form as it was practiced during the 1960's and 1970's, the era of the New Journalism and of such novels as Gore Vidal's *Burr* (1973) and E. L. Doctorow's *Ragtime* (1975), to cite only two examples. At the beginning of his career as a writer, Hersey was a reporter and based his books on events and people he had observed. Rather than merely recounting his experiences, Hersey molded characters and events to fit a novelistic form, basing, for example, *A Bell for Adano* on what he observed of the American military government at Licata, Sicily. This attention to realistic detail and psychological insight characterizes his best writing and enriches his more imaginative novels, such as *White Lotus*, although these novels were not nearly as well received. Hersey's humanistic perspective is also an important trait of his works and provides a sense of values.

Biography • John Richard Hersey was born in Tianjin, China, on June 17, 1914, to Roscoe and Grace Baird Hersey. His father, a Young Men's Christian Association (YMCA) secretary, and his mother, a missionary, took him on a trip around the world when he was three years old, but most of the first decade of his life was spent in the missionary compound, where, although isolated to an extent from the community, he learned to speak Chinese before he spoke English. From the time he learned to read and write, he amused himself by playing reporter and writing his family news and daily events at the British Grammar School and the American School in Tianjin. Despite his early life abroad, Hersey considered his life there "no more exciting than the average child's."

In 1924, Hersey, who knew of the United States only from secondhand accounts and what could be gleaned from books and magazines, was enrolled in the Briarcliff Manor public schools in New York. Three years later, he entered the Hotchkiss School in Lakeville, Connecticut, and graduated in 1932. After receiving his bachelor's degree from Yale in 1936, he went on to study eighteenth century English literature on a Mellon Scholarship at Clare College, Cambridge. During this time, he became determined to be a reporter for *Time*, because it seemed "the liveliest enterprise of its type." While waiting for an opening, he became the secretary and driver of Sinclair Lewis in the summer of 1937, the same summer that the Japanese invaded Manchuria. Born in China, Hersey was a natural choice for covering the Sino-Japanese War, and he served as a staff member for *Time* from the fall of 1937 until he was assigned to the Chungking bureau under Theodore White in 1939, where he began the itinerant life he would lead throughout World War II.

An enthusiastic, courageous reporter, Hersey often found himself in mortal danger as he covered the war in the South Pacific in 1942, the Sicilian invasion and Mediterranean theater in 1943, and Moscow between 1944 and 1945. Twice, he went down in planes; once he crashed into the Pacific, nearly losing the notes he had taken on Guadalcanal. He was treading water when his notebooks from the sunken plane surfaced only a few feet in front of him. Among other stories that he covered was the first account of PT 109 and its young lieutenant, John F. Kennedy, an account that Kennedy would later use in his campaign for Congress. During one trip to the United States from Asia, he married Frances Ann Cannon on April 27, 1940. They had four children (Martin, John, Ann, and Baird) before being divorced in 1958, when he married Barbara Day Addams Kaufman, with whom he had a daughter, Brook.

In 1942, Hersey published his first book, *Men on Bataan*, basically a morale-builder for an America that had suffered serious setbacks at Pearl Harbor and in the Philippines. Hersey wrote the book only a month after the fall of Corregidor, when most of the men who had actually been on Bataan were imprisoned or assigned to new posts in the Pacific rim. In New York, he combined *Time-Life* files, letters to the servicemen's families, and a few interviews with reporters and other witnesses to write the book, which had a generally favorable if not overenthusiastic reception. In 1943, he published *Into the Valley*, based on his own experiences with the Marines at the Matanikau River on Guadalcanal. With his experience in actual combat, *Into the Valley* had a substantially different tone from that of *Men on Bataan*, which often tended to jingoism. The extent of Hersey's closeness to combat can be measured by his receiving a letter of commendation from the secretary of the Navy for his work removing wounded during the fighting.

A Bell for Adano, the first book Hersey published as fiction, followed in 1944, based on his observations of the American military governance of Licato, Sicily. The novel was later turned into a Broadway play and a motion picture. Hersey missed much of the praise because of his continuing assignments as a journalist. During the last year of the war, he observed the evidence of Nazi atrocities in Warsaw and Tallinn that would later lead to his novel *The Wall.* Just as V-E Day occurred, Hersey was awarded the Pulitzer Prize for *A Bell for Adano* and emerged from World War II an extremely successful writer.

During the rest of 1945 and 1946, Hersey was assigned to China and Japan, where he wrote for *Life* and *The New Yorker* and gathered material for what would be his most famous book, *Hiroshima,* the carefully understated story of six people who were in the city when the first atomic bomb was dropped. The editor of *The New Yorker,* William Shawn, had intended to run *Hiroshima* as a three-part article; he later changed his mind, however, and decided to print the entire text alone. Nothing else would share the issue with *Hiroshima* except advertising. This dramatic step was kept a secret from the regular staff as Shawn and Hersey sequestered themselves in the office from 10:00 A.M. to 2:00 P.M., Hersey rewriting while the text was fed to a harried makeup man.

Hiroshima became a phenomenon. The Book-of-the-Month Club distributed free copies to its members. It was read aloud in four hourlong radio programs. Physicist Albert Einstein ordered one thousand copies, businessman Bernard Baruch was said to have ordered five hundred, and the mayor of Princeton, New Jersey, sought three thousand reprints. The Belgian Chamber of Commerce ordered five hundred copies to distribute to officials in Brussels. Three London newspapers requested serial rights. *Hiroshima,* with its concentration on ordinary people trying to cope with the horror of the first atomic blast, made Hersey known worldwide, except in Japan, where the book was banned by the American military government. Hersey donated many of his proceeds from the book to the American Red Cross. Nearly twenty years later, in 1965, when Hersey was invited to the White House Festival of the Arts by President Lyndon Johnson, *Hiroshima* was still considered Hersey's most profound work; he read sections of it at the White House gathering in a dramatic protest against the escalation of the war in Vietnam.

The year following *Hiroshima,* Hersey became one of the founders, writers, and editors of *'47—The Magazine of the Year.* It only survived one issue. Hersey became increasingly involved in politics, an involvement that would continue throughout his career. He vigorously supported the United Nations and became a member of such organizations as the Authors' League. During the 1950's, he became a speechwriter for politician Adlai Stevenson and actively campaigned for his election by serving as chairman of Connecticut Volunteers for Stevenson. Long before the Watergate affair made it fashionable to question the roles of the FBI and CIA, Hersey was a member of the Committee to End Government Secrecy. He also became interested in education, becoming a member of various educational committees and study groups, including the Westport, Connecticut, Board of Education.

Writing *The Wall* left Hersey little time for journalism during the late 1940's, though he published a few items such as a profile of Harry S. Truman in *The New Yorker.* After extensive research, Hersey published *The Wall* in 1950, repeating the success of *A Bell for Adano* by winning such awards as the Anisfield-Wolf Award, the Daroff Memorial Fiction Award of the Jewish Book Council of America, and the Sidney Hillman Foundation Award. *The Wall,* like *A Bell for Adano,* was later dramatized and then made into a motion picture.

During the early 1950's, Hersey was one of America's most famous writers and was placed in the awkward position of trying to write up to the increasingly higher level expected of him. He began to rely more heavily on his imagination, which tended toward allegorical situations. *The Marmot Drive*, set in Tunxis, a rural New England town, made a political allegory of the town's attempt to rid itself of a threatening colony of woodchucks. A number of Hersey's later books, including *The Child Buyer, White Lotus, Too Far to Walk, Under the Eye of the Storm, The Conspiracy, My Petition for More Space*, and *The Walnut Door*, have been criticized for their reliance on an underlying allegory or parable to support the plot.

From the 1950's on, Hersey was associated with Yale University, with Berkeley College from 1950 to 1965 as a nonteaching fellow, and with Pierson College from 1965 to 1970, as master. In the latter position, Hersey served as a counselor, confidant, resident administrator, social director, and intellectual mentor for the students, among whom was his son John, Jr. His closeness to the students allowed him the perceptions he revealed in *Letter to the Alumni*, which was a factual description of the May Day demonstrations of 1969, when Yalies supported the Black Panthers.

After leaving Yale and Connecticut, Hersey lived in Key West until his death there in 1993, involving himself in political issues of the day, especially those directly affecting writers. Although he was not a recluse, Hersey generally avoided media attention, only occasionally speaking in public or granting interviews.

Analysis • Critics have generally agreed that John Hersey's greatest strengths as a novelist derive from two sources: the observational skills he developed as a journalist and his belief in the importance of individual human beings in difficult situations. Reviewers throughout his career have praised his attention to realistic detail, which rivals that of William Dean Howells. Hersey gets very close to the realistic details of the lives of his characters, so that in his most successful works (both fiction and nonfiction), the reader gets a strong sense of "being there."

When Hersey recaptured his memories of China in the novel *A Single Pebble*, in 1956, he was praised for his acute observations and simple handling of realistic detail, as he would be for nonfictional works such as *Here to Stay, The Algiers Motel Incident, Letter to the Alumni*, and *The President*. Throughout his career, however, Hersey insisted that he mentally separated and saw a clear difference between the way he wrote fiction and the way he wrote nonfiction. He saw the fiction as his chance to make more profound statements of lasting value—tending to push the works into the allegorical realm—although, ironically, most critics have seen his most profound themes in his more journalistic works, whether fiction or nonfiction, such as *Hiroshima, The Wall*, and *A Single Pebble*.

Sometimes, however, Hersey has been criticized for having insufficiently explored his characters in the apparent belief that documentary evidence sufficiently explains them. He has also been charged with cluttering his narratives with excessive detail. Although *A Single Pebble* was generally positively received, one of the criticisms leveled at it was its heavy use of nautical terms that the main character would readily understand but that are confusing to most readers. A similar criticism was leveled at *The War Lover* by a reviewer who asked if Hersey's accounts of twenty-three bombing raids, heavily laden with hour-by-hour details, were really necessary to develop his theme.

Ironically, in his 1949 essay for *The Atlantic Monthly*, "The Novel of Contemporary History," Hersey presented an aesthetic that established the primacy of character over realistic detail. "Palpable facts," he wrote, "are mortal. . . . The things we remember . . . are emotions and impressions and illusions and images and characters: the elements of fiction." He went on to argue that the aim of the novelist of contemporary history was not to illuminate events, but to illuminate the human beings caught up in the events. This concern with the individual gives Hersey great sensitivity to suffering, a sympathy that, combined with his liberal political views, makes his thematic intentions manifest in nearly all of his works, leading to the accusation that Hersey is too allegorical, too moralistic, and too "meaningful" to be taken seriously as a creative artist. Although some critics hoped he would reverse the general trend of antimoralism and experimentalism in the postmodern fiction of the 1950's and 1960's, the more Hersey tried to escape the reportorial style, the less critically successful his novels became, though they continued to sell well.

A Bell for Adano • The genesis of Hersey's first novel, *A Bell for Adano*, was a journalistic assignment in wartime Italy. During the Sicilian campaign, he visited the seaport of Licata, where he observed the workings of the American Military Government and filed a story for *Life* titled "AMGOT at Work," which was printed on August 23, 1943, along with photographs. The article described a typical day in the life of an anonymous Italo-American major from New York as he tried to cope with the problems of governing the newly liberated town. Obviously impressed by the major's common sense, fairness, and accessibility to the local people, Hersey wrote *A Bell for Adano*, based upon the article, within six weeks of the *Life* publication.

A comparison of the article with the book provides an interesting insight into Hersey's work methods in those days. He retained every person in the article and expanded several of the problems. The major became Major Victor Joppolo; Licata became Adano. The central problem of the novel is Joppolo's attempt to find a bell to replace the seven-hundred-year-old bell melted down for bullets by the Nazis. Introducing the unsympathetic character of General Marvin, Hersey was clearly making reference to General George Patton, who was known among reporters for his having slapped two shell-shocked soldiers. Because Joppolo disobeys Marvin's orders, he is reassigned to North Africa after getting Adano its bell. Hersey also invented a romantic interest for Joppolo, an invention that later led to a lawsuit by the original major.

With the exception of *Hiroshima*, *A Bell for Adano* is Hersey's most widely read book. Published by Alfred A. Knopf in early 1944, it was a huge success, mostly because of its representation of the ordinary American as good-hearted, sentimental, and rigorously fair. The book reminded the reader that the war was a struggle to preserve democracy, that government was only as good as the people who govern, and that Americans were better than fascists. Despite all the praise, Hersey understood the effect the political situation of the time was having on the evaluation of his work. In 1944, he was in the Soviet Union and wrote an article on the role of Soviet writers in the war effort, saying "Not a word is written which is not a weapon." One sees, perhaps, in Hersey's ambivalent feelings about his instantaneous success, a motivation for his continual effort to increase the literary merit of his fiction, an effort that, in the estimate of many readers, worked against his best qualities.

Not all reviewers joined the chorus of praise for Hersey's first novel. Malcolm Cowley said that *A Bell for Adano* should be read as a tract and should not be expected to meet the criteria for a novel as well. Diana Trilling ascribed the book's success to its "folk-idealisms and popular assumptions" that surfaced because of the speed of its composition; she saw "very little writing talent" in the novel. These criticisms, though not entirely without justification, did not diminish Hersey's instant reputation as an important novelist.

Shortly after his assignment to Moscow by *Time-Life* in 1945, Hersey and several other reporters were given a tour of the Eastern Front by the Red Army. He saw the ruins of the Warsaw Ghetto, interviewed the survivors of the Lodz Ghetto, and saw signs of the atrocities at Tallinn and Rodogoscz. He knew immediately that he would have to write a novel on what he had seen, though his interviews with survivors of Auschwitz convinced him he could never write about the death camps themselves. Later, he wrote, his time spent in Hiroshima "lent urgency to what had been a vague idea." Another possible source of inspiration for *The Wall* may have come from Hersey's childhood friendship with Israel Epstein, who first interested Hersey in the history of the Jews and later became a staunch supporter of the Chinese revolution, editing the English-language magazine *China Reconstructs.*

Hersey went to the survivors in Eastern Europe and discovered a wealth of diaries, medical records, and other documentary evidence, most of which was untranslated from the original Polish and Yiddish. He hired Mendel Norbermann and L. Danziger to translate directly from the text onto a wire recorder and did further research himself, reading *The Black Book of Polish Jewry* (1943), the works of Sholom Aleichem, the Old Testament, and the Orthodox prayer book, among other sources. Immersed in the moving experience of listening to the tapes, he began writing and soon found the number of characters, themes, and action had grown far too complicated. Four-fifths of his way through the novel, he scrapped what he had written to retell the story through the point of view of Noach Levinson, chronicler of life in the ghetto from November, 1939, to May, 1943, when the last of the buildings was leveled.

The Wall • Hersey has observed that "Fiction is not afraid of complexity as journalism is. Fiction can deal with confusion." In *The Wall*, Hersey confronted a multiplicity of emotions, attitudes, customs, and events beyond a journalist's interest. The novel derives its power from this confrontation with the ragged edges of reality, and a number of critics consider it to be Hersey's greatest work. Although many reviewers expressed reservations about the length of the book and its numerous characters, most praised Hersey's compassion and argued that the strong feelings that emerged from the sustained reading of it more than made up for the technical faults of the book. Leslie Fiedler, however, said that *The Wall* lacked the strength of inner truth, depending too heavily on statistical, objective material, and he particularly criticized Hersey's themes as unconvincing.

Although Hersey argued in *The Atlantic Monthly* that fiction allowed the writer to deal with confusion and complexity, most of his novels after *The Wall* were criticized for their overly simplistic, message-bearing, allegorical intent. Hersey's works continued to sell very well, but he never earned the esteem of literary critics. Most critics consider Hersey's work to be without sufficient technical expertise. Some defenders of his work, however, compare it to that of John Dos Passos and argue that his humanistic themes are too valuable to ignore.

J. Madison Davis

Other major works

SHORT FICTION: *Blues,* 1987; *Fling, and Other Stories,* 1990; *Key West Tales,* 1994.

NONFICTION: *Men on Bataan,* 1942; *Into the Valley: A Skirmish of the Marines,* 1943; *Hiroshima,* 1946; *Here to Stay: Studies in Human Tenacity,* 1962; *The Algiers Motel Incident,* 1968; *Letter to the Alumni,* 1970; *The President,* 1975; *Aspects of the Presidency: Truman and Ford in Office,* 1980; *Life Sketches,* 1989.

EDITED TEXTS: *Ralph Ellison: A Collection of Critical Essays,* 1974; *The Writer's Craft,* 1974.

Bibliography

Fiedler, Leslie. "No! in Thunder." In *The Novel: Modern Essays in Criticism,* edited by Robert Murray Davis. Englewood Cliffs, N.J.: Prentice-Hall, 1969. In discussing authors from his point of view that "art is essentially a moral activity," the controversial Fiedler accuses Hersey of being the author of "The Sentimental Liberal Protest Novel" who fights for "slots on the lists of best sellers" with his "ersatz morality." The essay makes for lively reading at best.

Huse, Nancy L. *The Survival Tales of John Hersey.* Troy, N.Y.: Whitston, 1983. An eminently readable and informed study on Hersey that is useful in understanding the scope and development of Hersey as a writer. Explores the relationship between art and moral or political intentions. Includes extensive notes and a bibliography.

Sanders, David. "John Hersey." In *Contemporary Novelists,* edited by James Vinson. New York: St. Martin's Press, 1982. Covers Hersey's work from wartime journalist to novelist. Cites *The Wall* as his greatest novel and considers him the "least biographical of authors." A rather dense study but helpful in quickly establishing themes in Hersey's writings. A chronology and a bibliography are provided.

_____. *John Hersey Revisited.* Boston: Twayne, 1991. Begins with Hersey's career as reporter and novelist, while subsequent chapters discuss his major fiction and nonfiction, including his later stories. Includes chronology, notes, and bibliography.

Sharp, Patrick B. "From Yellow Peril to Japanese Wasteland: John Hersey's *Hiroshima.*" *Twentieth Century Literature* 46, no. 4 (2000): 434-453. Discusses the role of *Hiroshima* in changing American attitudes toward the Japanese and nuclear weapons.

Oscar Hijuelos

Born: New York, New York; August 24, 1951

Principal long fiction • *Our House in the Last World*, 1983; *The Mambo Kings Play Songs of Love*, 1989; *The Fourteen Sisters of Emilio Montez O'Brien*, 1993; *Mr. Ives' Christmas*, 1995; *Empress of the Splendid Season*, 1999; *A Simple Habana Melody: From When the World Was Good*, 2002.

Other literary forms • Although he produced several short stories, Oscar Hijuelos published only long fiction after his first book, *Our House in the Last World*, which developed from a story line written on scraps of paper as he worked as a clerk for an advertising agency.

Achievements • Hijuelos attained a large audience after winning a 1990 Pulitzer Prize in fiction for his second novel, *The Mambo Kings Play Songs of Love*. He was the first Latino author to receive that honor. His novel was also nominated for the National Book Award and for the National Book Critics Circle's annual fiction prize. In 1990, Hijuelos received a Guggenheim grant, and he was honored at the Kennedy Center in Washington, D.C., with a National Hispanic Heritage Award in 2000.

Although Latino authors are often neglected by mainstream publishers and media, Hijuelos broke through ethnic barriers with his persistence, his style, and his Pulitzer Prize. On the strength of his first novel, Hijuelos received several grants from the National Endowment for the Arts, and the American Academy of Arts and Letters Rome Prize provided him with a stipend for living in Italy for a year of composition and reflection.

Through Hijuelos's observations, dark memories, and radiant storytelling, readers can appreciate Cuban immigrant culture. *The Mambo Kings Play Songs of Love* demonstrates the acceptance of Hispanic literature beyond the previous limited scope of small Latino presses. Critics labeled the book a breakthrough for Latino writers. Hijuelos challenges the reader to interpret the soft voices of an emerging literary culture.

Biography • The Hijuelos family hailed from the Oriente province of Cuba, home of entertainer Desi Arnaz and Cuban dictators Fulgencio Batista y Zaldívar and Fidel Castro—wild roots for the New York-born, iconoclastic author. At the age of four, Oscar and his mother, Magdalena, visited Cuba, and upon their return he developed nephritis, a critical-stage kidney inflammation. Bedridden, Oscar lingered in a children's hospital for two long years. This separation from family and language removed Oscar from Hispanic connections; the theme of separation would later saturate his novels.

Oscar's father Pascual drank heavily, leaving Magdalena to raise her children in a rough, lower-class neighborhood of New York. Hijuelos laments his youth, in which most fathers he knew were drunk, limousines came only for funerals, and "the working class hate[d] everyone else." He recalls the area where he played, caught between the affluence of the Columbia University campus and the habitat of muggers, thieves, and junkies of Morningside Park. Hijuelos hid from this hell by reading, watching television, and observing the traits of his family, as a partially sober father arose to cook at the Biltmore Hotel each day. Affection flooded the household, even with the dysfunction of poverty and neighborhood chaos. Forced to speak English outside his home, Hijuelos easily abandoned his Cuban tongue, although his parents expected Spanish discourse in the home. Thereby alienated, Hijuelos neglected thoughtful conversations with either parent, a theme that would recur in his work.

Frederick Tuten, director of the City University of New York's creative writing program, remarked that this "intense writer" does not "create books from nothing; he's lived." Attending college while working, Hijuelos created his style and honed his skill by writing long responses to assignments, exaggerating the length to fulfill his personal need for expression. After receiving his master's degree in 1976 from the City University of New York, Oscar moved just a few blocks away from his humble childhood home to begin life as an author, supported by work as an inventory controller in an advertising agency.

Hijuelos is a mystery to some Latino writers because he chose to distance himself from their coterie. Hispanic writers must meet two differing sets of standards: acceptance from the American reading public and from Latin American counter-

parts. With his works mostly devoid of political motives, Hijuelos has drawn criticism for not drawing sufficient attention to his Latin roots. Even with this controversy, Hijuelos was adopted by many as the voice of Latinos, the symbol of their culture in America.

Analysis • Oscar Hijuelos represents a new generation of Cuban American writers. His Latino roots enrich his chronicles of the immigrant experience. Latino writers often face quandaries when choosing the language for their literary expression (Spanish or English), when committing to traditions of their descendants, and when chronicling immigrant life in their new world. Hijuelos balances the sensitivities of the American reader and the expectations of the Latino by presenting characters who, removed from the security of their Cuban homeland, are tossed into the diversity and adversity of big-city life; they survive and still bring grace to their daily existence. Hijuelos's two shorter novels, *Our House in the Last World,* his autobiographical debut, and *Mr. Ives' Christmas,* an exploration of spirituality, provide balance to his long works. Proud of his heritage, yet conscious of the limited parameters of his youth, the author places his characters in situations that pronounce their independence but accept their assimilation into a new culture.

Our House in the Last World • *Our House in the Last World* explores the questions of identity and perspective through the travails of the Santinio family, who are seeking fortune by moving from Cuba to New York City. The father, Alejo, expects the younger son, Héctor, to live a macho existence and to be "Cuban," while his mother, Mercedes, smothers him with her anxieties and loses her capability to develop her personality. Hijuelos offers two views of innocence: that of the wonder and confusion of a family facing a new life in an unknown world, and that of their children's bewilderment in a harsh environment.

The novel begins in the ticket office of a film house in Holguín, Cuba. Mercedes, twenty-seven, almost past the age of marriage, meets Alejo, who woos her, marries her, and moves her to New York, where they share an apartment with other Cubans who come and go. Some attain status and wealth, while the Santinios remain impoverished. Alejo becomes a sot, a gluttonous man who allows his sister to wage a harsh campaign against his wife. Mercedes transfers the memory of her father onto Alejo, and it is only after Alejo's death near the end of the novel that she is free to realize her dreams as her own.

The older son, Horatio, epitomizes the image of the man he thinks his mother demands. A womanizer and philanderer, he finally adopts a military lifestyle as an escape from fear of failure. Héctor contracts a near-fatal disease while on holiday in Cuba, and the months of hospitalization that follow embitter him toward the culture of his homeland and all things Cuban. Mercedes becomes unbearably overprotective, and his anxieties prevent him from reacting to the drunken excesses of his father and the hysteria of his mother. Castro has taken over Cuba during this time, and Mercedes and Alejo are disengaged from the lost world of their youth; New York will hold them until death.

Hijuelos embraces these characters with pure affection and gentleness, as he allows the relatives to flow through the Santinios' life. He describes their downslide from hope to resignation, from effort to insanity, and from love to harassment. Love does not conquer all, but it does provide a basis for life. The Santinios are a tribute to perseverance.

The Mambo Kings Play Songs of Love • Oscar Hijuelos's life in the advertising agency had little to do with his passion for writing. When he first began thinking of the story that would become *The Mambo Kings Play Songs of Love,* he knew that an uncle and an elevator operator would be his models. The uncle, a musician with Xavier Cougat during the 1930's, and a building superintendent, patterned after an elevator operator and musician, merge to become Cesar Castillo, the Mambo King. Cesar's brother, Néstor, laconic, retrospective, lamenting the loss of a Latina lover he left behind in Cuba, writes a song in her memory that draws the attention of Desi Arnaz, who will change their life.

As the book opens, Cesar rots with his half-empty whiskey glass tipped at the television beaming old reruns; he seeks the *I Love Lucy* spot featuring him and Néstor as the Mambo Kings. Néstor has tragically died. Cesar pathetically reveals his aging process, the cirrhosis, the loss of flamboyant times. Cesar's old, scratchy records, black, brittle, and warped, resurrect his music stardom. He laments his brother's death by leafing through fading pictures.

In *The Mambo Kings Play Songs of Love,* Hijuelos presents pre-Castro Cubans, who, after World War II, streamed in torrents to New York, their experiences creating a historical perspective for future Third World immigration. All communities may strive for the American Dream, but in Latino quarters, music, the mainstream of a culture, sought to free the oppressed. The Castro brothers become, for a moment, cultural icons with their appearance on *I Love Lucy.* The fame short-lived, Cesar comforts his ego with debauchery, and Néstor dies ungracefully and suddenly. Ironically named, the Hotel Splendour is where Cesar commits suicide—in Cuban culture, a respectable ending to life. Latino culture encourages the machismo of men such as Cesar, and Hijuelos may be asking his countrymen to review that attitude.

The Fourteen Sisters of Emilio Montez O'Brien • *The Fourteen Sisters of Emilio Montez O'Brien* again paints Hijuelos's theme of immigrant life in America, this time on the canvas of a small rural town. Family traditions pass down, hopes spring eternal, and sadness and attempts to assimilate fade as the book's characters meet disappointment and victories to varying degrees. Nelson O'Brien leaves Ireland, sister in tow, for the better life promised in America. Weakened by the journey and her general frailty, the sister dies, leaving Nelson to wander aimlessly, until he retreats to Cuba to take pictures of the Spanish-American War. He meets the sixteen-year-old Mariela Montez and courts her every Sunday for seven weeks. Seducing her with stories of his Pennsylvania farm and with her first sexual experiences, Nelson persuades her to marry and move to the farm, offering a telescope as a token of their future.

The Montez O'Brien household is fertile, and fourteen magnetic sisters charge the home with a feminine aura. Finally, the lone son, Emilio, is born. Mostly told through the older daughter's eyes, the story portrays the ferocity of Nelson's ambition and character through the overbearing feminine mystique that surrounds his life, his decisions, and his focus on the future. Emilio, on the other hand, becomes a gentle soul who adores and is adored by his sisters. The sisters grow, many without mates, into expected positions in the world—entertainers, homekeepers, expectant mothers, recluses, gluttons—carrying the name and bravado of their father with them. Emilio attracts women and suffers the vanity of his charm and good looks, eventually becoming an actor in B-films. His drunken tendencies and a sordid affair with a pregnant teen turn his life sour. Scandalized, he lies in reclusiveness until finding his soulmate in an improbable café in an Alaskan fishing village. She dies before the novel's end, breaking Emilio's heart but allowing the sisters to provide him with solace. Hijuelos finishes the novel succinctly, with both realized tragedies and continuing dreams for the future.

Mr. Ives' Christmas • Hijuelos somberly presents Mr. Ives, a character unlike the romanticized Cesar, the macho Mambo King. Mr. Edward Ives sensitively and sanely goes through his life with no malice toward fellow man or woman. He seeks those rewards he has become accustomed to earning, but one date, Christmas Eve, consistently seems to interfere with his life. A widowed print maker visits Ives on Christmas Eve when he is an orphaned child and, a few Christmases later, adopts him. His adoptive father idyllically rears the dark-skinned child, inspires him to pursue his love for drawing, and eventually guides him to the Arts Student League, where he meets, on Christmas Eve, his future wife.

The picture-postcard family image is grotesquely distorted years later when, on Christmas Eve, the Iveses' seventeen-year-old son is gunned down as he leaves church choir practice. A fourteen-year-old Puerto Rican gunman kills the boy for ten dollars. Mr. Ives devotes his life to obsessive attempts to rehabilitate the murderer.

Symbolically, Mr. Ives's favorite book is a signed copy of Charles Dickens's *A Christmas Carol* (1843). Hijuelos strongly relies on this book to link the two tales. The author emulates Dickens's populous canvases and uses Dickens's love of coincidence and contrivance as a metaphor for God's mysterious workings. The temperance of Mr. Ives engenders his longing for grace, a gift for contemplation, and a world curiosity. Hijuelos also draws heavily on images from his New York neighborhood, his coterie of friends, and the milieu of gangs, muggers, and drug addicts at the end of his street. *Mr. Ives' Christmas* speaks of faith—a faith that mysteriously probes emotions, tested by death and the opportunity of forgiveness.

Empress of the Splendid Season • In *Empress of the Splendid Season*, Lydia Espana is banished from her Cuban home by her father, a small-town alcalde, because she overstayed her allowed time at a dance with a young man. Disheartened, she makes her way to New York and in time marries and gains employment as a cleaning lady. In near poverty, she and her chronically ill husband, a waiter, attempt to maintain respectability and keep food on the table for their two children. Lydia resorts to fantasy as a coping mechanism, envisioning herself as the "Empress of the Splendid Season," a poetic term of endearment used by her husband during the early days of their romance. Hijuelos describes Lydia's passage from privileged girlhood to a widowed old age through her relationships with family, friends, and employers. A wealthy employer sends her son to a prestigious university. He becomes a successful psychologist but is unhappy and feels disconnected from the world. Lydia's daughter grows into a rebellious young woman who later marries an Anglo and moves to the suburbs. She chooses to rear Lydia's grandchildren far from her Cuban roots. Hijuelos again digs beneath the core of tenement life, bringing a magical mystique into his characters' lives through rich text and powerful prose.

A Simple Habana Melody: From When the World Was Good • This 2002 novel begins in 1947, as Israel Levis returns by ship from Spain to his native Cuba. A popular musician best known for "Rosas Puras," a rumba hit that he wrote in 1928, Levis is only fifty-seven, but internment for fourteen months in Buchenwald concentration camp has rendered him a frail old man. Most of the novel consists of Levis's melancholic recollections of happier times in Havana and Paris.

Levis was a creative force within the vibrant Cuban culture of the 1920's. Though he also composed operas, symphonies, and ballets, he became best known for a song he wrote in a few hours for the singer Rita Valladares; in "Rosas Puras," he expresses unfulfilled longing for a beautiful woman whom he could never bring himself to woo, though she was attracted to him. A devout Catholic dominated by his widowed mother, the fleshy Levis channels strong sexual urges into visits to brothels and into his music. He also suppresses erotic interest in other men. After Manny Cortez, his friend and librettist, is assassinated by agents of dictator Gerardo Machado, Levis leaves for Paris, hoping to be closer to Valladares, who is now performing there.

During the 1930's, a vogue for things "tropical" helps make Levis the toast of Europe. He tours widely with his own orchestra, making his home in a luxury hotel in Paris. Valladares stars in the zarzuela that Levis creates out of "Rosas Puras," but, while continuing to pine for her, he cannot allow himself to express with her the vigorous sensuality that he enjoys with hired women. Indifferent to politics, Levis immerses himself in music and the libertine pleasures of Paris. He relishes his renown and friendships with other artists, including Igor Stravinsky, Maurice Ravel, and Gary Cooper.

By the time that Germany conquers France in 1940, most other foreigners have left. Levis remains, however, writing and performing, even when Sarah Rubinstein, a Jew who has become his lover, is forced to flee. Because of Levis's association with Sarah and because his own name sounds Jewish, the Gestapo classifies him as a Jew and forces him to submit to humiliating restrictions. In 1943, he is transported to Buchenwald. Except to note that scraps of food slipped to Levis as reward for occasional command performances probably kept him alive, Hijuelos leaves it to the reader to imagine details of life and death in the camp.

Most of *A Simple Habana Melody* is thus an ailing older man's ruminations over his vanished prime. For Levis, Havana in the 1920's and Paris in the 1930's represented moments "when the world was good"—as the novel's full title suggests. No longer able to compose or to perform sexually, the Levis who repatriates to Cuba has lost two elements essential to his personal identity, religious faith and joie de vivre. What most torments him now, awaiting death, is realizing his naïveté in believing that goodness prevails over evil. The world is more complex than the simple Habana melody that defined the life of Israel Levis.

Craig Gilbert
Updated by Steven G. Kellman

Bibliography

Barbato, Joseph. "Latino Writers in the American Market." *Publishers Weekly* 238, no. 6 (February, 1991): 17-21. An accurate impression of Latino writers in the American market. Multiple interviews with thoughtful questions and answers.

Chávez, Lydia. "Cuban Riffs: Songs of Love." *Los Angeles Times Magazine* 112 (April, 1993): 22-28. A penetrating look at Hijuelos as a man and as a writer. Conversational style with serious revelations by this thought-provoking author.

Héctor, James. "Oscar Hijuelos." In *Latino and Latina Authors*, edited by Alan West-Durán, María Herrera-Sobek, and César Salgado. Vol. 2. New York: Charles Scribner's Sons, 2004. Brief review of Hijuelos's life and work.

Hill, Christine M. *Ten Hispanic American Authors*. Berkeley Heights, N.J.: Enslow, 2002. Chapters on ten major Latino authors, including Hijuelos.

Kevane, Bridget. *Latino Literature in America*. Westport, Conn.: Greenwood Press, 2003. Broad survey of Latino literature that helps to place Hijuelos in perspective.

Patteson, Richard F. "Oscar Hijuelos: 'Eternal Homesickness' and the Music of Memory." *Critique* 44, no. 1 (2002): 38-48. Analyzes the themes of music and memory in *The Mambo Kings*.

Pérez-Firmat, Gustavo. *Life on the Hyphen: The Cuban-American Way*. Austin: University of Texas Press, 1994. A scholarly study of Hijuelos and other Cuban American writers and performers who have become cultural figures.

Shirley, Paula W. "Reading Desi Arnaz in *The Mambo Kings Play Songs of Love*." *MELUS* 20 (September, 1995): 69-78. An intriguing look at a fictional Desi Arnaz, relating his Cuban roots to the Castillo brothers in *The Mambo Kings Play Songs of Love.* The relationship offers some interesting comparisons between the real Arnaz and Hijuelos's fictional Cuban immigrants.

Shorris, Earl. *Latinos: A Biography of the People.* 1992. Reprint. New York: W. W. Norton, 2001. Focuses on the commercial and critical success of Hijuelos and his literary themes.

Silber, Joan. "Fiction in Review." *The Yale Review* 84, no. 4 (October, 1996): 151-157. Scholarly comparison of Hijuelos's *The Mambo Kings Play Songs of Love* to John Updike's *In the Beauty of the Lilies* (1996).

Socolovsky, Maya. "The Homelessness of Immigrant American Ghosts: Hauntings and Photographic Narrative in Oscar Hijuelos's *The Fourteen Sisters of Emilio Montez O'Brien.*" *Proceedings of the Modern Language Association* 117, no. 2 (2002): 252-264. Uses theories of photography to analyze Hijuelos's depiction of photography and immigrant experience in his novel.

Rolando Hinojosa

Born: Mercedes, Texas; January 21, 1929

Principal long fiction • *Estampas del valle, y otras obras/Sketches of the Valley, and Other Works*, 1973 (English revision, *The Valley*, 1983); *Klail City y sus alrededores*, 1976 (*Klail City: A Novel*, 1987); *Mi querido Rafa*, 1981 (*Dear Rafe*, 1985); *Rites and Witnesses*, 1982; *Partners in Crime: A Rafe Buenrostro Mystery*, 1985; *Claros varones de Belken*, 1986 (*Fair Gentlemen of Belken County*, 1986); *Becky and Her Friends*, 1990; *The Useless Servants*, 1993; *Ask a Policeman*, 1998; *We Happy Few*, 2006.

Other literary forms • Rolando Hinojosa is known primarily for his long fiction in both English and Spanish. He has also written "verse novels," such as *Korean Love Songs from Klail City Death Trip* (1978; printed 1980). Hinojosa produced the book *Agricultural Workers of the Rio Grande and Rio Bravo Valleys* in 1984.

Achievements • After the death of Tomás Rivera in 1984, Rolando Hinojosa became considered the dean of Mexican American belles lettres and selflessly advanced Mexican American literature throughout the United States, Latin America, and Europe. His works have been translated into German, French, Italian, English, and Spanish, and they have been anthologized by numerous presses. He has received many accolades, including the Premio Quinto Sol award in 1972, the Casa de las Américas Prize in 1976, and the Lon Tinkle Award for Lifetime Achievement from the Texas Institute of Letters in 1998. He has lectured and read from his work widely and has had several doctoral dissertations and master's theses written about his works. In 1998, the University of Illinois bestowed its Distinguished Achievement Award on him. His distinctively concise literary style, in English and Spanish (or a combination of the two), is marked by irony, satire, stark realism, and a cutting wit. Although his works are often quite experimental, Hinojosa has masterfully incorporated various genres into his novels, including sketches, reportage, poetry, and murder mysteries. Among all Mexican American authors, he is arguably the most accomplished and versatile.

Biography • Rolando Hinojosa was born in the Lower Rio Grande Valley of South Texas to mixed ethnic parents. On his Mexican Texan father's side, he descended from the first Spanish Mexican land-grant settlers, who settled the region in 1749. On his mother's side were Anglo-Texan settlers who arrived in South Texas in 1887. He studied English and Spanish in Texan and Mexican schools. He was therefore raised to be both bilingual and bicultural in a family fostering a rich reading environment with literature from both sides of the U.S.-Mexican border and the Atlantic. This family background influenced his future literary and cultural interests.

At the age of seventeen, he enlisted in the U.S. Army, and after serving his time he entered the University of Texas at Austin under the G.I. Bill. His education would be interrupted by the Korean War, however. After his tour of duty in Korea, he returned to Austin and in 1953 received his bachelor's degree in Spanish literature. He then married, had a son, taught high school, and worked at several other jobs; he later divorced. After completing a master's degree in Spanish literature at New Mexico Highlands University in 1962, he remarried and entered a doctoral program in 1963 at the University of Illinois, Urbana. There he received a doctoral degree in Spanish literature in 1969; he wrote his dissertation on the Spanish writer Benito Pérez Galdós.

Hinojosa then began his college teaching career at Trinity University in San Antonio, Texas. In 1970, he taught Spanish at Texas A&I University in Kingsville, Texas, where he later served as chair of the Spanish Department, dean of the College of Arts and Sciences in 1974, and vice president of academic affairs in 1976. His wife's decision to enter law school caused them to move to the University of Minnesota, where he chaired a Chicano studies program and taught creative writing as an English professor. In 1981 he returned to the University of Texas at Austin as a professor of English, teaching Chicano literature, literature of the

Courtesy, University of Texas at Austin

Southwest, and creative writing. In 1986 he became Ellen Clayton Garwood Chair of the English department. His second wife divorced him in 1988, after raising two daughters with him. Hinojosa continued to write, and by 2006, he had published ten novels, including *We Happy Few* (2006), a tragicomic story set in a Texas university near the state's border with Mexico.

Analysis • Beginning in 1970, Hinojosa published fiction, nonfiction, and poetry, primarily in small Mexican American presses and journals. His major work comprises a series of short novels that he titled The Klail City Death Trip series, after publishing *Korean Love Songs from Klail City Death Trip*, which he referred to as a novel in verse form. The Klail City Death Trip series is distinguished by Hinojosa's having published several novels in both Spanish and English. The series as of 1999 constituted nine serial works.

The different language renditions do not always represent the same narrative. Significant differences between the two versions of the same novel exist in the narrative sequence of chapters, with some chapters deleted, others added, and others rearranged. Thus, both language editions should be read for a comprehensive and more accurate understanding of The Klail City Death Trip series. Some novels, moreover, suffer from egregious publishing errors, due to Arte Público Press failing to copyedit texts before going to press, with large passages repeated and other significant passages completely left out.

The works in the series were not published in strict chronological order. *Fair Gentlemen of Belken County*, for instance, was written prior to *Dear Rafe* but was published one year after.

The Valley • With *The Valley*, Hinojosa begins his serial project by introducing a host of characters, some of whom are extensively developed in succeeding novels. This novel is made up of four loosely connected sections of sketches that give readers a wide sense of the character of the Mexican Texan people inhabiting the fictional Belken County in "The Valley," the area north of the Mexican border in south Texas. Here, the people of various towns are shown at home, in their communities, carrying on with their daily lives. Two cousins, Jehú Malacara and Rafe Buenrostro, are introduced for the first time, characters whose lives are examined in greater detail in later novels. Both characters are orphans, with Jehú being raised by various people unrelated to him, while Rafe and his brothers are raised by their uncle Julian.

Klail City • *Klail City* continues with the same format and purpose as *The Valley*, with three sections of sketches. Hinojosa continues to develop his two main characters' lives, but with this novel, he develops a theme that permeates the entire series: the historical conflict between Anglo-Texans and Mexican Texans over the land and the laws governing their lives. In this novel, readers are informed of the cause of Rafe's father's death, murder by a member of a rival Mexican American clan, the Leguizamóns. Although Jesús Buenrostro's murder is avenged by his brother Julian, the clans' animosity toward each other remains undiminished as The Klail City Death Trip series progresses. Also introduced in this novel is a greater conflict, the Korean War, which will later affect the main characters' lives, especially Rafe's.

The Useless Servants • *The Useless Servants*, in prose, extensively shows Rafe's day-to-day life in the Korean War. The masterfully written realism of the battlefield makes both *Korean Love Songs from Klail City Death Trip* and *The Useless Servants* extraordinary testaments to the horror and senselessness of war. One fact that does not escape Rafe and other Mexican Texan soldiers in Korea, however, is that even while defending their country, they are still subjected to racism by their Anglo-American counterparts.

Dear Rafe • *Dear Rafe* jumps ahead in the serial narrative and portrays Jehú as a principal, though elliptical, character. Incorporating the epistolary and reportage genres, Hinojosa provides multiple perspectives from which readers see the financial, real estate, and political maneuvers enhancing the Anglo-American power structure, as represented by the Klail, Blanchard, Cook (KBC) clan. Employed as a loan officer in a Klail City bank owned by the most powerful Anglo-Texan family in the Valley, Jehú apprentices under bank president Noddy Perkins. Through liaisons Jehú has with three women, he works the system to his clan's advantage by covertly acquiring lands that would otherwise fall into the hands of the rivaling Leguizamón clan or the KBC clan.

In the first half of the novel, readers gain an understanding of the events by reading a series of letters written by Jehú to Rafe, who is interned in a veterans hospital for problems arising from wounds suffered in Korea. In the second half, readers are shown a series of interviews conducted with more than a dozen primary and secondary characters by P. Galindo, who has access to Jehú's letters. The novel's main action involves Noddy backing a Mexican Texan, Ira Escobar, against an Anglo-Texan for county commissioner, something the Anglo-Amerian power structure had never done before. As the action progresses, Jehú comes to understand that Ira has been backed for political office because he is an easily manipulated puppet. More important, Noddy brings Ira's Anglo-Texan opponent, Roger Terry, to his knees to control him, through a political ruse, as the Valley's new U.S. congressman, which was Noddy's intention all along. Jehú , however, leaves the bank, disgusted with how local politics are run, apparently causing P. Galindo to conduct his interviews. Jehú returns to the bank three years later, as is revealed in *Partners in Crime.*

Rites and Witnesses • This novel's action precedes that of *Dear Rafe* and fills in gaps in the lives of both Rafe and Jehú, incorporating reportage, letters, and sketches, with chapters alternating between action in Korea and events foreshadowing *Dear Rafe.* Noddy Perkins approaches Jehú to run for county commissioner, but Jehú is wise enough to refuse the offer, causing Noddy to recruit Ira Escobar later.

Partners in Crime • With *Partners in Crime* Hinojosa changes direction by writing a murder mystery. A lieutenant in Belken County's homicide squad, Rafe, with his squad, investigates and solves gang-land killings related to drug-running in the Valley. No longer a place where adverse race relations dominate, the Valley's economy has become corrupted by Mexican drug dealers' laundered money. The cooperation of law-enforcement agencies on both sides of the border becomes the focus of The Klail City Death Trip series. In this novel the head of the Mexican law-enforcement agency, Lisandro Solís, is responsible for the killings and the drug-running. In the end he escapes persecution but reappears in *Ask a Policeman.*

Fair Gentlemen of Belken County • Written before *Dear Rafe* but not published until 1986, this novel of longer sketches continues filling gaps in Rafe and Jehú's lives after their return from Korea. The texture of the Valley's Mexican Texan culture is brilliantly shown in this novel. Although the life of the prominent Mexican Texan elder, Esteban Echevarría, ends, his legacy and wisdom are preserved and honored by Rafe and Jehú.

Becky and Her Friends • Using reportage, like the second half of *Dear Rafe, Becky and Her Friends* provides more than two dozen interviews with various people associated with Becky Escobar, who, by her marriage to Ira, is kin to the rival Leguizamón clan. At the beginning of the novel, Becky throws out her husband Ira and asks him for a divorce. They divorce, and as the interviews progress, readers learn the circumstances surrounding her astounding transformation from an utterly anglicized and naïve Mexican Texan to a Mexicanized and independent woman. She is then employed as a business manager by Viola Barragán, a wealthy and successful Mexican Texan businesswoman who figures prominently in previous novels. Under Viola's guidance, Becky asserts her independence and marries Jehú, with whom she had an affair during the political campaigns in *Dear Rafe.* Readers also learn that Rafe has married Noddy Perkins's daughter Sammie Jo, thus cementing, through these two marriages, a resolution between formerly rivaling clans. More important, lands formerly split by these rivaling clans are reunited.

Ask a Policeman • In *Ask a Policeman,* another murder mystery, Rafe has been promoted to chief inspector of the Belken County homicide squad. He and his squad again solve drug-related gangland killings, including the murder of Lisandro Solís, who escaped prosecution for his part in the drug-running and killings depicted in *Partners in Crime.* This time, the chief law-enforcement officer on the Mexican side, María Luisa (Lu) Cetina, contributes to the successful apprehension of the guilty parties, which include Lisandro's brother and Lisandro's twin sons, as well as Canadian and Central American assassins.

Jaime Armin Mejía

Other major works
POETRY: *Korean Love Songs from Klail City Death Trip,* 1978 (printed 1980, includes some prose).
EDITED TEXTS: *Tomás Rivera, 1935-1984: The Man and His Work,* 1988 (with Gary D. Keller and Vernon E. Lattin).
MISCELLANEOUS: *Generaciones, Notas, y Brechas/Generations, Notes, and Trails,* 1978; *Agricultural Workers of the Rio Grande and Rio Bravo Valleys,* 1984.

Bibliography
Calderón, Héctor. "Texas Border Literature: Cultural Transformation and Historical Reflection in the Works of Américo Paredes, Rolando Hinojosa, and Gloria Anzaldua." *Disposito* 16, no. 41 (1991): 13-27. An exploration of Hinojosa's work in the broader contex of Mexican-American border culture
Hernandez, Guillermo E. *Chicano Satire: A Study in Literary Culture.* Austin: University of Texas Press, 1991. This work explores how satire figures into the works of three Chicanos: Luis Miguel Valdez, José Montoya, and Rolando Hinojosa. It provides insights into The Klail City Death Trip series, but only some of the books.
Lee, Joyce Glover. *Rolando Hinojosa and the American Dream.* Denton: University of North Texas Press, 1999. A good book-length work in English on Hinojosa's works. Attempts to bring a biographical and psychological analysis to the Klail City Death Trip series.
Saldivar, José David, ed. *The Rolando Hinojosa Reader: Essays Historical and Critical.* Houston: Arte Público Press, 1985. This work contains essays by Hinojosa and by a small number of scholars treating Hinojosa's works. Shows how early scholars analyzed The Klail City Death Trip series.
Saldívar, Ramón. *Chicano Narrative: The Dialectics of Difference.* Madison: University of Wisconsin Press, 1990. One of the most important works of Chicano literary criticism, this book contains a chapter treating *Korean Love Songs from Klail City Death Trip* and The Klail City Death Trip series. Saldivar's analysis covers many of the most significant Chicano literary texts.
Zilles, Klaus. *Rolando Hinojosa: A Reader's Guide.* Albuquerque: University of New Mexico Press, 2001. A guide to the Valley and its inhabitants, focusing on the theme of oral history represented in the series.

William Dean Howells

Born: Martinsville (now Martin's Ferry), Ohio; March 1, 1837
Died: New York, New York; May 11, 1920

Principal long fiction • *Their Wedding Journey*, 1872; *A Chance Acquaintance*, 1873; *A Foregone Conclusion*, 1875; *The Lady of Aroostook*, 1879; *The Undiscovered Country*, 1880; *Doctor Breen's Practice*, 1881; *A Modern Instance*, 1882; *A Woman's Reason*, 1883; *The Rise of Silas Lapham*, 1885; *Indian Summer*, 1886; *April Hopes*, 1887; *The Minister's Charge: Or, The Apprenticeship of Lemuel Barker*, 1887; *Annie Kilburn*, 1888; *A Hazard of New Fortunes*, 1889; *The Shadow of a Dream*, 1890; *An Imperative Duty*, 1891; *The Quality of Mercy*, 1892; *The Coast of Bohemia*, 1893; *The World of Chance*, 1893; *A Traveler from Altruria*, 1894; *A Parting and a Meeting*, 1896; *The Day of Their Wedding*, 1896; *An Open-Eyed Conspiracy: An Idyl of Saratoga*, 1897; *The Landlord at Lion's Head*, 1897; *The Story of a Play*, 1898; *Ragged Lady*, 1899; *Their Silver Wedding Journey*, 1899; *The Kentons*, 1902; *The Son of Royal Langbirth*, 1904; *Miss Bellard's Inspiration*, 1905; *Through the Eye of the Needle*, 1907; *Fennel and Rue*, 1908; *New Leaf Mills*, 1913; *The Leatherwood God*, 1916; *The Vacation of the Kelwyns*, 1920; *Mrs. Farrell*, 1921.

Other literary forms • William Dean Howells was unquestionably one of the most versatile and productive writers of the nineteenth century. In addition to approximately forty novels, Howells produced several volumes of short fiction, among them *A Fearful Responsibility, and Other Stories* (1881) and *Christmas Every Day and Other Stories Told for Children* (1893). He also wrote more than thirty dramas, including *The Parlor Car* (1876), *The Mouse-Trap and Other Farces* (1889), and *Parting Friends* (1911), which generally were designed to be read aloud rather than performed. In addition, one of Howells's earliest and most enduring passions was the writing of poetry. His first published collection was *Poems of Two Friends* (1860, with John J. Piatt); nearly fifty years later, he published *The Mother and the Father* (1909).

The genre that first brought Howells to public attention was travel literature, including *Venetian Life* (1866) and *Italian Journeys* (1867); other volumes continued to appear throughout his career. Howells also continues to be renowned as a perceptive critic and literary historian. Still of literary value are *Criticism and Fiction* (1891), *My Literary Passions* (1895), *Literature and Life* (1902), and *My Mark Twain* (1910). In addition, a substantial number of Howells's critical essays appeared in *Harper's* magazine from 1886 to 1892, and between 1900 until his death in 1920. Finally, Howells wrote biographies such as *Lives and Speeches of Abraham Lincoln and Hannibal Hamlin* (1860), as well as several autobiographical works, including *My Year in a Log Cabin* (1893) and *Years of My Youth* (1916).

Achievements • Howells is remembered today as an important early exponent of realism in fiction. Reacting against the highly "sentimental" novels of his day, Howells—both in his own fiction and in his criticism—advocated less reliance on love-oriented stories with formulaic plots and characters and more interest in emphasizing real people, situations, and behavior. This is not to say that Howells shared the naturalists' interest in sex, low-life, and violence, for in fact he was quite reserved in his dealings

Library of Congress

with these aspects of life. He did, however, acknowledge their existence, and in so doing paved the way for Theodore Dreiser, Stephen Crane, and the modern realistic novel. Inspired by his reading of European literature (notably Leo Tolstoy), Howells also argued that fiction could be a tool for social reform. Finally, in his influential positions at *The Atlantic Monthly* and *Harper's*, Howells was able to offer help and encouragement to rising young American authors, including Crane and Henry James.

Howells's later years were full of recognition: He received an honorary Litt. D. from Yale University (1901), as well as from Oxford (1904) and Columbia (1905); he received the L.H.D. from Princeton in 1912. He was elected first president of the American Academy of Arts and Letters in 1908, and seven years later he received the Academy's gold medal for fiction.

Biography • Although early in his career he was accepted into the charmed literary circles of Boston and New York, William Dean Howells was born and reared in the Midwest, and he never fully lost touch with his midwestern background. He was born on March 1, 1837, in Martinsville (now Martins Ferry), Ohio, the second of eight children. His early life was singularly unstable: Because his father was something of a political radical whose principles jeopardized the prosperity of every newspaper with which he was associated, the family was periodically compelled to move away from one conservative Ohio village after another. Despite such instability, Howells found the variety of experiences enriching and was able to make the most of the spotty formal education he received. His exposure to the written word came at an early age: When Howells was only three, his father moved the little family to Hamilton, Ohio, where he had acquired a local newspaper, the *Intelligencer*; by the age of six, the precocious William was setting type in his father's printing office, and not long after that he began to compose poems and brief sketches. In 1850, the family made one of their more fortunate moves by establishing themselves in a one-room log cabin in the utopian community at Eureka Mills near Xenia, Ohio. It was a welcome interlude in the family's struggle to find a political, economic, and social niche that would satisfy the father, and Howells would remember it fondly much later in *My Year in a Log Cabin*. The next move was to Columbus, where young Howells acquired a position as a compositor on the *Ohio State Journal*. Already beginning to diversify his literary endeavors, the fourteen-year-old Howells was also writing poetry in the manner of Alexander Pope.

In 1852, Howells's father bought a share in the Ashtabula *Sentinel* and moved it to Jefferson, Ohio. For once, his principles did not clash with those of the community:

The little newspaper was a success, and it was to remain in the Howells family for forty years. While living in Jefferson, a community composed largely of well-educated transplanted New Englanders, the teenage Howells embarked on a plan of intensive self-education which included studies of Pope, Oliver Goldsmith, Oliver Wendell Holmes, Edgar Allan Poe, and Heinrich Heine. As much as this program compromised his social life, Howells derived enormous intellectual benefits from it, and several of the townspeople of Jefferson even offered to help finance a Harvard education for this gifted lad; his father declined the offer, however, and Howells remained at Jefferson, publishing his stories pseudonymously beginning in 1853.

As his father gradually rose in Ohio state politics (he was elected clerk of the House of Representatives in 1855), Howells rose with him, and in 1857 he was offered a permanent position as a correspondent on the Cincinnati *Gazette*. Howells, not yet twenty years old, was too emotionally dependent upon his family and too much of a hypochondriac to stay more than a few weeks at the *Gazette*, but when in the following year he received another opportunity in journalism, this time from the *Ohio State Journal*, he was able to accept the offer from his previous employer and to succeed. In addition to his duties as a reporter and editor, Howells found time to write sketches and verse, and some of his writings appeared in *The Atlantic Monthly*, the prestigious Boston-based journal of which he was to become editor in chief many years later.

The year 1860 was the most significant one of his life: He met Elinor Mead of Brattleboro, Vermont, whom he would marry two years later in Paris; he published his first book, *Poems of Two Friends*, coauthored with John J. Piatt; and—at the urging of the volume's Cincinnati publisher, Frank Foster—Howells prepared a campaign biography of Abraham Lincoln. Although assembled out of information Howells had gleaned from printed sources rather than from Lincoln himself, and written in only a few weeks, the book proved to be a moving and inspiring account of his fellow midwesterner. With its royalties, the resourceful and ambitious Howells financed a trip to America's two literary meccas, Boston and New York, where he arranged to meet some of the most important writers and editors of the day, and he returned to Ohio confirmed in his desire to pursue a career in literature.

Following the outbreak of the Civil War, Howells—temperamentally ill-suited to army life—decided to seek a foreign diplomatic post. Cashing in on the success of his popular Lincoln biography, the twenty-four-year-old Howells managed to be appointed as the American consul at Venice, a pleasant and remunerative position he held for four years. Howells was able to draw on his Italian experiences in a series of travel essays that were collected in book form as *Venetian Life* and *Italian Journeys*. When he returned to the United States in the summer of 1865, he was sufficiently established as a writer to be able to embark on a freelance writing career in New York. After a brief stint at the newly founded *The Nation*, Howells was lured to Boston and a subeditorship at *The Atlantic Monthly* under James T. Fields; after five years he became editor in chief (1871-1881). By the age of thirty, Howells was already a prominent member of Boston's literati. He received an honorary master's degree from Harvard in 1867 and was forging friendships with such literary figures as Henry James (whom he met in 1866) and Mark Twain, destined to become a lifelong friend.

At about that time (the late 1860's) Howells came to accept the fact that there was no market for his poetry; so, while he continued to write travel literature, he began to prepare descriptive sketches that would evolve rapidly into the literary form to which he was particularly well suited: the novel. The first product of this transitional period was *Their Wedding Journey*, which was serialized in *The Atlantic Monthly* in 1871 and published in book form in 1872. *Their Wedding Journey*, which manages to straddle both travel literature and fiction, features Basil and Isabel March (based upon William and Elinor Howells), characters who would recur throughout Howells's fiction, most notably in *A Hazard of New Fortunes*. After *Their Wedding Journey*, Howells produced novels with almost machinelike speed and regularity. *A Chance Acquaintance* is a psychological romance that served to demythologize the idea of the "proper Bostonian" that Howells had so admired in his youth; *A Foregone Conclusion*, in which a young American girl clashes with traditional European society, anticipates James's *Daisy Miller* by three years; two "international novels" that contrast American and Italian values and lifestyles are *The Lady of Aroostook* and *A Fearful Responsibility, and Other Stories; The Undiscovered Country* probes spiritualism and the Shakers; *Doctor Breen's Practice* is the social and psychological study of a woman physician.

In 1881, Howells found himself caught in the dissolution of his publisher's partnership, Osgood and Houghton, so he left *The Atlantic Monthly* and began to serialize stories in the *Century* magazine. During this period, Howells began to focus increasingly on ethical problems, and during the 1880's he produced in rapid succession the novels that are generally held to be his greatest achievements in fiction. In 1882, *A Modern Instance* appeared, the so-called "divorce novel" that is now regarded as Howells's first major work in long fiction. During its composition, he suffered a breakdown, in part the result of the worsening health of his daughter Winny, who would die only a few years later at the age of twenty-six. An extended trip to Italy proved disappointing, but it enabled Howells to recover sufficiently to write another major novel, *The Rise of Silas Lapham*, followed immediately by the book he enjoyed writing most, *Indian Summer*. As a comedy of manners set in Italy, *Indian Summer* was both a reversion to Howells's earliest fictional style and subject matter, as well as a welcome change from the intense social realism that characterized his fiction during the 1880's.

By that time, Howells was living permanently in New York and was a member of the editorial staff of *Harper's*. In January, 1886, he began a regular feature in *Harper's* called the Editor's Study, which continued until 1892 and served as the organ through which he campaigned for realism and a greater social consciousness in fiction. Howells had in fact so reoriented himself away from Boston, the cynosure of his youth, that he turned down a professorship at Harvard and wrote his first novel set in New York, *A Hazard of New Fortunes*, regarded as one of his finest works. Howells's novels during the 1890's were even more insistently illustrative of his strong social consciousness than those of the previous decade. *The Quality of Mercy* is the study of a crime (embezzlement) that is to be blamed less on the individual who committed it than on the society that created him; *An Imperative Duty* deals with miscegenation; *A Traveler from Altruria* and its belated sequel, *Through the Eye of the Needle*, were written within the literary tradition of the utopian novel. Late in his career, Howells tended to resurrect and rework earlier material (the March family of *Their Wedding Journey*, Howells's earliest novel, reappeared in *Their Silver Wedding Journey*); one of his finest character studies is that of Jeff Durgin in the late novel *The Landlord at Lion's Head*, the only work by Howells that clearly shows the influence of naturalism.

After a lecture tour through the West, Howells, in 1900, began to write a regular column, the "The Editor's Easy Chair," for *Harper's*, and continued to do so until his death in 1920. His last major works were *My Mark Twain*, an appreciative account of his friend published in 1910 (the year of the deaths of Mark Twain and Elinor

Howells), and the posthumous *The Vacation of the Kelwyns*, published in 1920. Howells died in New York City on May 11, 1920, still productive until his death; although he realized that his creative powers had long since dimmed, he nevertheless had managed to maintain over much of his extraordinary life his well-deserved position as the "Dean of American Letters."

Analysis • Throughout his career as a fiction writer, William Dean Howells worked against the sentimentality and idealization that pervaded popular American literature in the nineteenth century. He pleaded for characters, situations, behavior, values, settings, and even speech patterns that were true to life. While twentieth century readers came to take such elements for granted, the fact remains that in Howells's day he was regarded as something of a literary radical. One indication of his radicalism was his preference for character over plot in his fiction: He was far less interested in telling a good story (albeit his stories are good) than in presenting flesh-and-blood characters who think, feel, make mistakes, and are products of genetic, social, and economic conditions—in other words, who are as imperfect (and as interesting) as real people. Howells did not indulge in meticulous psychological analyses of his characters, as did his friend Henry James, and his plots tend to be far more linear and straightforward than are the convoluted and carefully patterned ones of James. Nevertheless, he was an innovative and influential writer who changed the quality of American fiction.

A Modern Instance • A hallmark of Howells's advocacy of realism was his interest in topics that were taboo in Victorian times. Such a topic was divorce, which in the nineteenth century was still regarded by much of society as scandalous and shameful, and that Howells used as the resolution of his first major novel, *A Modern Instance*. This was not a "divorce novel" per se, as was maintained by several of Howells's shocked contemporaries, but in an era when "they married and lived happily ever after" was a fictional norm, the divorce of Bartley and Marcia Hubbard was quite unpalatable. Given the situation of the characters, however, the breakup was almost inevitable—in a word, "realistic." As William M. Gibson explains in his excellent introduction to the Riverside edition of *A Modern Instance* (1957), the story apparently germinated when Howells saw an impressive performance of Euripides' *Medea* in Boston in the spring of 1875, and in fact the working title of the novel was *The New Medea*. The novel's genesis and working title are significant, for the story's female protagonist harbors a passion which is both overpowering and destructive.

Marcia Gaylord, the only child of Squire Gaylord and his self-effacing wife, Miranda, grows up in Equity, Maine, in an era when the state's once-impressive commercial prominence has all but decayed. Her domineering but indulgent father and her ineffectual mother have failed to mold Marcia's personality in a positive way, and this lack of a strong character, interacting with an environment caught in economic, cultural, political, and spiritual decline, compels Marcia to leave Equity while rendering her utterly unequipped to deal with the outside world. Not surprisingly, she becomes enamored of the first attractive young man to happen her way: Bartley Hubbard, editor of the newspaper of Equity. Superficially, Hubbard has all the earmarks of the hero of a romantic novel: Orphaned young, he is intelligent enough to have succeeded at a country college, and with his education, charm, and diligence, he seems well on his way to a career in law. There, however, the Lincolnesque qualities end. Ambitious, manipulative, shrewd, unscrupulous, and self-centered, Bartley is the worst possible husband for the shallow Marcia, and after a courtship rife with spats, jealousy, and misunderstandings (even the short-lived engagement is the result of misinterpreted behavior), the ill-matched pair elope and settle in Boston.

The remainder of the novel is an analysis of the characters of Marcia and Bartley as they are revealed by the social, professional, and economic pressures of Boston, and a concomitant study of the deterioration of their marriage. Marcia is motivated by her sexual passion for Bartley and her deep emotional attachment to her father— an attachment so intense that she names her daughter after him and attempts to force Bartley into following in his footsteps as a lawyer. Locked into the roles of wife and daughter, Marcia has no separate identity, no concrete values, no sense of purpose. As Marcia struggles with her disordered personality, Bartley's becomes only too clear: His success as a newspaperman is the direct result of his being both shrewd in his estimation of the low level of popular taste, and unscrupulous in finding material and assuming (or disavowing) responsibility for it.

Bartley's foil is a native Bostonian and former classmate, Ben Halleck. A wealthy man without being spoiled, a trained attorney too moralistic to practice law, and a good judge of character who refuses to use that talent for ignoble ends, Halleck is all that Bartley Hubbard could have been under more favorable circumstances. Even so, Ben does not fit into the world of nineteenth century America: As is graphically symbolized by his being crippled, Ben cannot find a satisfying occupation, a meaningful religion, or a warm relationship with a woman. In fact, it is Howells's trenchant indictment of the social, economic, and spiritual problems of nineteenth century America that not a single character in *A Modern Instance* is psychically whole. To further compound his difficulties, Ben loves Marcia, having adored her for years after noticing her from afar as a schoolgirl in Maine. In his efforts to aid her by lending money to Bartley and pressuring her to stand by her husband, Ben unwittingly contributes to Bartley's abandonment of Marcia, to her resultant emotional crisis, and to the devastating divorce in Indiana.

Carefully avoiding the traditional happy ending, Howells completes his story with a scene of human wreckage: Bartley, unscrupulous newspaperman to the end, is shot to death by a disgruntled reader in Arizona; Squire Gaylord, emotionally destroyed by defending his daughter in the divorce suit, dies a broken man; Ben, unsuccessful as a schoolteacher in Uruguay, flees to backwoods Maine to preach; and Marcia returns to the narrow world of Equity, her beauty and spirit long vanished. Interesting, complex, and bitter, *A Modern Instance* so strained Howells's emotional and physical well-being that he suffered a breakdown while writing it. The "falling off" of energy and style in the second part of the novel that so many commentators have noticed may be attributed to the breakdown, as well as to the related stress engendered by the serious psychosomatic illness of his beloved daughter Winny; it should be borne in mind, however, that the novel's singularly unhappy ending cannot be attributed to either crisis. The book's conclusion, planned from the story's inception, was itself meant to be a commentary on a nation buffeted by spiritual, social, and economic change.

The Rise of Silas Lapham • On a level with *A Modern Instance* is Howells's best-known novel, *The Rise of Silas Lapham*. Serialized in the *Century* magazine from November, 1884, to August, 1885, and published in book form in the late summer of 1885, *The Rise of Silas Lapham* takes a realistic look at the upheavals in late nineteenth century America by focusing on the archetypal self-made man. Colonel Silas Lapham of

Lumberville, Vermont, has made a fortune in the paint business by virtue of hard work, honest dealings, and the help and guidance of a good woman, his wife, Persis. The sentimental portrait of the self-made American captain of industry is significantly compromised, however, by the fact that Lapham owes much of his success to simple luck (his father accidentally found a superb paint mine on his farm) and to an early partner's capital (Rogers, a shadowy and rather demonic figure whom Lapham "squeezed out" once his paint business began to thrive). Even more compromising is the fact that Lapham's great wealth and success cannot compensate for his personality and background: Boastful, oafish (his hands are "hairy fists"), and devoid of any aesthetic sensibility, Lapham seeks to buy his way into proper Boston society by building a fabulous mansion on the Back Bay and encouraging a romance between his daughter and Tom Corey, a Harvard graduate with "old" Boston money.

The Coreys are, in fact, foils of the Laphams: Tom's father, Bromfield Corey, is also indirectly associated with paint (he has a talent for portraiture), but having inherited substantial wealth, he has never worked, preferring instead to live off the labors of his ancestors. Ultimately, neither man is acceptable to Howells: Lapham, for all his substantial new wealth, is vulgar and ambitious; Bromfield Corey, for all his old money and polish, is lethargic and ineffectual. The wives do not fare much better. Persis Lapham is burdened with a Puritan reserve that at vital moments renders her incapable of giving her husband emotional support, and Anna Corey, despite her fine manners, is stuffy and judgmental.

The most admirable characters in the novel are two of the five children. Penelope Lapham is a quick-witted, plain girl with a passion for reading George Eliot, while Tom Corey is an educated, enterprising young man who sincerely wants an active business career. Although clearly Pen and Tom are ideally suited to each other, their relationship almost fails to materialize because virtually everyone in the novel—and the reader as well—naturally assumes Tom to be attracted to young Irene Lapham, who is strikingly pretty, beautifully attired, and considerably less intellectually endowed than her sister. In his campaign for realism in literature, Howells intentionally blurs the distinctions between the world of reality (where people like Pen and Tom fall in love) and the world of sentiment (where beautiful, empty-headed Irene is the ideal girl). The blurring is so complete that the Laphams, brainwashed by the romanticized standards of nineteenth century American life, almost deliberately scuttle Pen's relationship with Tom simply because pretty Irene had a crush on him first. The level-headed Reverend Sewell, with his realistic belief in the "economy of pain," is needed to convince the parties involved that they were acting out of "the shallowest sentimentality" rather than common sense in promoting Irene's match with Tom.

As part of his questioning of nineteenth century sentimentality, Howells specifically attacks one of its most graphic manifestations, the self-made man. In the heyday of the Horatio Alger stories, Howells presents a protagonist who to many Americans was the ultimate role model: a Vermont farm lad who became a Boston millionaire. Howells's undermining of Lapham is, however, so meticulous and so complete—he even opens the novel with Lapham being interviewed by sardonic Bartley Hubbard (of *A Modern Instance*) for the "Solid Men of Boston" series in a local pulp newspaper—that the reader is left uncertain whether to admire Lapham for his sound character and business achievements, or to laugh at him for his personality flaws and social blunders. This uncertainty is attributable to the unclear tone of the novel, as George Arms points out in his excellent introduction to *The Rise of Silas Lapham* (1949). The tone is, in fact, a major flaw in the novel, as are some episodes of dubious worth (such as the ostensible affair between Lapham and his typist) and Howells's disinclination to develop some potentially vital characters (such as Tom Corey's uncle and Lapham's financial adviser, James Bellingham). A more fundamental problem is Howells's refusal to face squarely the matter of morality: He never fully resolves the complex relationship between Lapham and his ex-partner Rogers, a relationship that raises such questions as whether good intentions can serve evil ends, and to what extent one has moral obligations toward business associates, friends, and even strangers.

Not surprisingly, the end of the novel is less than satisfying: Tom Corey marries Pen Lapham and moves to Mexico, where presumably the disparity in their backgrounds will be less glaring; the financially ruined Laphams return to the old Vermont farm, where ostensibly they are far happier than they were as wealthy Bostonians; and pretty young Irene endures spinsterhood. Despite these problems and an overreliance on dialogue (at times the novel reads like a play), *The Rise of Silas Lapham* is indeed, as Arms remarks, "a work of competence and illumination" that rightly deserves its status as an outstanding example of late nineteenth century realistic fiction.

A Hazard of New Fortunes • Four years after *The Rise of Silas Lapham*, Howells published the novel that he personally believed to be his best and "most vital" book: *A Hazard of New Fortunes*. A long novel (more than five hundred pages), it features a rather unwieldy number of characters who all know one another professionally or socially (indeed, the "it's a small world" motif is rather strained at times); who possess widely varying degrees of social consciousness; and who come from a number of geographical, economic, and intellectual backgrounds. This cross section of humanity resides in New York City, and the interaction among the remarkably diverse characters occurs as a result of three catalysts: a new magazine titled *Every Other Week*; a boardinghouse run by the Leightons; and a period of labor unrest among the city's streetcar workers.

The magazine subplot nicely illustrates Howells's extraordinary ability to interweave characters, plot, and themes around a controlling element. *Every Other Week* is a new magazine to be published under the general editorship of one Fulkerson. As its literary editor, he hires Basil March, a transplanted middle-class Indianian who has left his position as an insurance agent in Boston to begin a new life at the age of fifty in New York; as its art editor, there is young Angus Beaton, a shallow ladies' man and dilettante who cannot escape his humble background in Syracuse; the translator is Berthold Lindau, an elderly, well-read German who had befriended March as a boy and lost a hand in the Civil War; and the financial "angel" of the magazine is Jacob Dryfoos, an uncultured midwestern farmer who has made a fortune through the natural gas wells on his land, and who forces his Christlike son, Conrad, to handle the financial aspects of the magazine as a way of learning about business. The magazine's cover artist is Alma Leighton, a feminist whom Beaton loves, and a frequent contributor of articles is Colonel Woodburn, a ruined Virginian who boards with the Leightons and whose daughter marries Fulkerson.

Each individual associated with *Every Other Week* perceives the magazine in a different light; each is attracted to it (or repulsed by it) for a different reason. As *Every Other Week* becomes a success, Howells allows it to drift out of the focus of the novel, leaving the reader to observe the interactions (usually clashes) of the various characters' personalities, interests, and motives. Lindau, whose social consciousness calls for unions and socialism, is in essential agreement with Conrad Dryfoos, although the latter disdains the German's advocacy of violence; both men clash with Jacob Dryfoos, who, no longer in touch with the earthy Indiana lifestyle of his early years, believes that prounion workers should be shot. The artist Beaton—who loves the feline quality of Conrad's sister Christine as much as he loves the independence of Alma Leighton and the goodness of socialite worker Margaret Vance—does not care about economic and social matters one way or another, while Colonel Woodburn advocates slavery.

The character whose attitudes most closely parallel those of Howells himself is Basil March, whose social consciousness grows in the course of the novel as he witnesses the poverty of the New York slums, the senseless deaths of Lindau and Conrad, and the pathetic, belated efforts of Jacob Dryfoos to correct his mistakes through the lavish spending of money. In many respects, March is a projection of Howells's attitudes and experiences, and his tendency at the end of the novel to make speeches to his wife about labor, religion, and injustice is a reflection of Howells's reading of Tolstoy. Even so, it would be incorrect to perceive March as the story's main character. That distinction most properly belongs to Jacob Dryfoos, a sort of Pennsylvania Dutch version of Silas Lapham whose values, home, lifestyle, and attitude have been undermined forever by the finding of gas deposits on his farm.

Although much of Howells's fiction deals with social and personal upheaval in late nineteenth century America, nowhere is it more poignantly depicted than in *A Hazard of New Fortunes*. In the light of this poignancy, it is to Howells's credit that the novel does not turn into a cold social tract: The characters are flesh-and-blood rather than caricatures. The novel contains considerable humor, most notably in the early chapters dealing with the Marches house-hunting in New York. There is also a surprising emphasis on feminism and a concomitant questioning of marriage and the false behavioral ideals propagated by sentimental fiction. In addition, Howells provides psychological probing (particularly in the form of fantasizing) such as one would expect of James more readily than Howells, and above all there is the aforementioned interweaving of characters, incidents, and themes.

Of Howells's approximately forty novels written during his long career, at least half a dozen—including *A Modern Instance, The Rise of Silas Lapham*, and *A Hazard of New Fortunes*—have endured, a testament not only to their brilliant, realistic evocation of life in late nineteenth century America but also to the distinctive skills, interests, and sensibility of the "Dean of American Letters."

Alice Hall Petry

Other major works

SHORT FICTION: *A Fearful Responsibility, and Other Stories*, 1881; *Christmas Every Day, and Other Stories Told for Children*, 1893; *Selected Short Stories of William Dean Howells*, 1997.

PLAYS: *The Parlor Car*, pb. 1876; *A Counterfeit Presentment*, pb. 1877; *Out of the Question*, pb. 1877; *The Register*, pb. 1884; *A Sea-Change*, pb. 1887; *The Mouse-Trap, and Other Farces*, pb. 1889; *A Letter of Introduction*, pb. 1892; *The Albany Depot*, pb. 1892; *The Unexpected Guests*, pb. 1893; *A Previous Engagement*, pb. 1897; *An Indian Giver*, pb. 1900; *Room Forty-five*, pb. 1900; *The Smoking Car*, pb. 1900; *Parting Friends*, pb. 1911; *The Complete Plays of W. D. Howells*, pb. 1960 (Walter J. Meserve, editor).

POETRY: *Poems of Two Friends*, 1860 (with John J. Piatt); *Poems*, 1873; *Samson*, 1874;

Priscilla: A Comedy, 1882; *A Sea Change: Or, Love's Stowaway*, 1884; *Poems*, 1886; *Stops of Various Quills*, 1895; *The Mother and the Father*, 1909; *Pebbles, Monochromes, and Other Modern Poems, 1891-1916*, 2000 (Edwin H. Cady, editor).

NONFICTION: *Lives and Speeches of Abraham Lincoln and Hannibal Hamlin*, 1860; *Venetian Life*, 1866; *Italian Journeys*, 1867; *Tuscan Cities*, 1885; *Modern Italian Poets*, 1887; *A Boy's Town*, 1890; *Criticism and Fiction*, 1891; *My Year in a Log Cabin*, 1893; *My Literary Passions*, 1895; *Impressions and Experiences*, 1896; *Stories of Ohio*, 1897; *Literary Friends and Acquaintances*, 1900; *Heroines of Fiction*, 1901; *Literature and Life*, 1902; *Letters Home*, 1903; *London Films*, 1905; *Certain Delightful English Towns*, 1906; *Roman Holidays*, 1908; *Seven English Cities*, 1909; *Imaginary Interviews*, 1910; *My Mark Twain*, 1910; *Familiar Spanish Travels*, 1913; *New Leaf Mills*, 1913; *Years of My Youth*, 1916; *Eighty Years and After*, 1921; *The Life and Letters of William Dean Howells*, 1928 (M. Howells, editor); *A Realist in the American Theatre: Selected Drama Criticism of William Dean Howells*, 1992 (Brenda Murphy, editor); *Selected Literary Criticism*, 1993 (3 volumes); *Letters, Fictions, Lives: Henry James and William Dean Howells*, 1997 (Michael Anesko, editor).

CHILDREN'S LITERATURE: *Christmas Every Day, and Other Stories Told for Children*, 1893.

Bibliography

Abeln, Paul. *William Dean Howells and the Ends of Realism*. New York: Routledge, 2005. Study of the place of Howells in the late nineteenth century American realist movement.

Cady, Edwin H. *The Realist at War: The Mature Years, 1885-1920, of William Dean Howells*. Syracuse, N.Y.: Syracuse University Press, 1958. These two volumes by Cady are standbys for Howells's life and the shaping of his theories of literature.

_____. *The Road to Realism: The Early Years, 1837-1885, of William Dean Howells*. Syracuse, N.Y.: Syracuse University Press, 1956. Study of Howells's life up to the time that he published *The Rise of Silas Lapham*.

Cady, Edwin H., and Louis J. Budd, eds. *On Howells*. Durham, N.C.: Duke University Press, 1993. Essays on materials and form in Howells's fiction, on the equalitarian principle, on individual novels such as *The Rise of Silas Lapham*, *Their Wedding Journey*, and other novels.

Cady, Edwin H., and Norma W. Cady. *Critical Essays on W. D. Howells, 1866-1920*. Boston: G. K. Hall, 1983. Gathers together important criticism on Howells. Includes reviews by contemporaries such as Henry James, George Bernard Shaw, and Mark Twain, as well as commentaries by modern critics, such as Van Wyck Brooks, H. L. Mencken, and Wilson Follett. Contains essays by advocates and detractors of Howells.

Crowley, John W. *The Dean of American Letters: The Late Career of William Dean Howells*. Amherst: University of Massachusetts Press, 1999. A biography by a noted Howells scholar. Includes bibliographical references and an index.

_____. *The Mask of Fiction: Essays on W. D. Howells*. Amherst: University of Massachusetts Press, 1989. Examines Howells's unconscious in his writings, incorporating both the "probing psychologism" of the 1890's and the deeper psychic integration of his later light fiction. An important contribution to critical studies on Howells.

Eble, Kenneth E. *William Dean Howells*. 2d ed. Boston: Twayne, 1982. An excellent introduction to Howells in the Twayne series, that is devoted almost entirely to the major novels.

Goodman, Susan and Carl Dawson. *William Dean Howells: A Writer's Life.* Berkeley: University of California Press, 2005. This broad and compelling biography of the literary giant is an important resource for study of Howells's life and work. Illustrated and includes bibliography.

Nettels, Elsa. *Language and Gender in American Fiction: Howells, James, Wharton, and Cather.* Charlottesville: University Press of Virginia, 1997. Elsa Nettels examines American writers struggling with the problems of patriarchy.

Olsen, Rodney D. *Dancing in Chains: The Youth of William Dean Howells.* New York: New York University Press, 1991. Olsen provides a careful study of the middle-class roots of Howells's fiction, showing how his society shaped him and how his fiction not only appealed to that society but also was an expression of it. Includes very detailed notes.

Stratman, Gregory J. *Speaking for Howells: Charting the Dean's Career Through the Language of His Characters.* Lanham, Md.: University Press of America, 2001. Analyzes the use of dialogue in Howells's work. Includes bibliographical references and an index.

Zora Neale Hurston

Born: Eatonville, Florida; January 7, 1891
Died: Fort Pierce, Florida; January 28, 1960

Principal long fiction • *Jonah's Gourd Vine*, 1934; *Their Eyes Were Watching God*, 1937; *Moses, Man of the Mountain*, 1939; *Seraph on the Suwanee*, 1948.

Other literary forms • In addition to her four novels, Zora Neale Hurston produced two collections of folklore, *Mules and Men* (1935) and *Tell My Horse* (1938), and an autobiography, *Dust Tracks on a Road* (1942). Hurston also published plays, short stories, and essays in anthologies and in magazines as diverse as *Opportunity*, the *Journal of Negro History*, The *Saturday Evening Post*, the *Journal of American Folklore*, and the *American Legion Magazine*. Finally, she wrote several articles and reviews for such newspapers as the *New York Herald Tribune* and the *Pittsburgh Courier*. Hurston's major works have only been reissued in the late twentieth century. Some of her essays and stories have also been collected and reprinted. Although the anthologies *I Love Myself When I Am Laughing...* (1979) and *The Sanctified Church* (1981) helped to bring her writing back into critical focus, some of her works ceased to be readily available, and her numerous unpublished manuscripts can only be seen at university archives and the Library of Congress.

Achievements • Hurston was the best and most prolific black woman writer of the 1930's. Her novels were highly praised. Even so, Hurston never made more than one thousand dollars in royalties on even her most successful works, and when she died in 1960, she was penniless and forgotten. Hurston's career testifies to the difficulties of a black woman writing for a mainstream white audience whose appreciation was usually superficial and for a black audience whose responses to her work were, of necessity, politicized.

Hurston achieved recognition at a time when, as Langston Hughes declared, "the Negro was in vogue." The Harlem Renaissance, the black literary and cultural movement of the 1920's, created an interracial audience for her stories and plays. Enthusiasm for her work extended through the 1930's, although that decade also marked the beginning of critical attacks. Hurston did not portray African Americans as victims stunted by a racist society. Such a view, she believed, implies that black life is only a defensive reaction to white racism. Black and left-wing critics, however, complained that her unwillingness to represent the oppression of African Americans and her focus, instead, on an autonomous, unresentful black folk culture served to perpetuate minstrel stereotypes and thus fueled white racism. The radical, racial protest literature of Richard Wright, one of Hurston's strongest critics, became the model for black literature during the 1940's, and publishers on the lookout for protest works showed less and less interest in Hurston's manuscripts. Yet, when she did speak out against American racism and imperialism, her work was often censored. Her autobiography, published in 1942, as well as a number of her stories and articles were tailored by editors to please white audiences. Caught between the attacks of black critics and the censorship of the white publishing industry, Hurston floundered, struggling through the 1940's and 1950's to find other subjects. She largely dropped out of public view during the 1950's, though she continued to publish magazine and newspaper articles.

The African American and feminist political and cultural movements of the 1960's and 1970's provided the impetus for Hurston's rediscovery. The publication of Robert Hemenway's excellent book, *Zora Neale Hurston: A Literary Biography* (1977), and the reissue of her novels, her autobiography, and her folklore collections seem to promise the sustained critical recognition Hurston deserves.

Library of Congress

Biography • Zora Neale Hurston was born on January 7, 1891. Her family lived in the all-black Florida town of Eatonville in an eight-room house with a five-acre garden. Her father, the Reverend John Hurston, mayor of Eatonville for three terms and moderator of the South Florida Baptist Association, wanted to temper his daughter's high spirits, but her intelligent and forceful mother, Lucy Potts Hurston, encouraged her to "jump at de sun." When Hurston was about nine, her mother died. That event and her father's rapid remarriage to a woman his daughter did not like prematurely ended Hurston's childhood. In the next few years, she lived only intermittently at home, spending some time at a school in Jacksonville and some time with relatives. Her father withdrew all financial support during this period, forcing her to commence what was to be a lifelong struggle to make her own living.

When Hurston was fourteen, she took a job as a wardrobe girl to a repertory company touring the South. Hurston left the troupe in Baltimore eighteen months later and finished high school there at Morgan Academy. She went on to study part-time at Howard University in 1918, taking jobs as a manicurist, a waitress, and a maid in order to support herself. At Howard, her literary talents began to emerge. She was admitted to a campus literary club, formed by Alain Locke, a Howard professor and one of the forces behind the Harlem Renaissance. Locke brought Hurston to the attention of Charles S. Johnson, another key promoter of the Harlem Renaissance. Editor of *Opportunity: A Journal of Negro Life*, he published one of her stories and encouraged her to enter the literary contest sponsored by his magazine.

With several manuscripts but little money, Hurston moved to New York City in 1925, hoping to make a career of her writing. Her success in that year's *Opportunity* contest—she received prizes for a play and a story—won her the patronage of Fanny Hurst and a scholarship to complete her education at Barnard College. She studied anthropology there under Franz Boas, leading a seemingly schizophrenic life in the next two years as an eccentric, iconoclastic artist of the Harlem Renaissance on one hand and a budding, scholarly social scientist on the other.

The common ground linking these seemingly disparate parts of Hurston's life was her interest in black folk culture. Beginning in 1927 and extending through the 1930's, she made several trips to collect black folklore in the South and in the Bahamas, Haiti, and Jamaica. Collecting trips were costly, however, as was the time to write up their results. Charlotte Osgood Mason, a wealthy, domineering white patron to a number of African American artists, supported some of that work, as did the Association for the Study of Negro Life and History and the Guggenheim Foundation. Hurston also worked intermittently during the 1930's as a drama teacher at Bethune Cookman College in Florida and at North Carolina College, as a drama coach for the WPA Federal Theatre Project in New York, and as an editor for the Federal Writers' Project in Florida.

Mules and Men and several scholarly and popular articles on folklore were the products of Hurston's collecting trips during the late 1920's and early 1930's. In 1938, she published *Tell My Horse*, the result of trips to Haiti and Jamaica to study hoodoo. As a creative writer, Hurston devised other outlets for her folk materials. Her plays, short stories, and three of her novels, *Jonah's Gourd Vine*, *Their Eyes Were Watching God*, and *Moses, Man of the Mountain*, make use of folklore. She also presented folk materials in theatrical revues, but even though the productions were enthusiastically received, she could never generate enough backing to finance commercially successful long-term showings.

Hurston's intense interest in black folklore prevented her from sustaining either of her two marriages. She could not reconcile the competing claims of love and work. She married Herbert Sheen, a medical student, in 1927 but separated from him a few months later. They were divorced in 1931. She married Albert Price III in 1939, and they too parted less than one year later. Other romantic relationships ended for the same reason.

During the 1940's, Hurston lost her enthusiasm for writing about black folk culture. She wrote her autobiography and in 1948 published her last novel, *Seraph on the Suwanee*, a work that turns away from black folk culture entirely. The last decade of her life took a downward turn. Falsely accused of committing sodomy with a young boy, Hurston, depressed, dropped out of public view. Through the 1950's, she lived in Florida, struggling for economic survival. She barely managed to support herself by writing newspaper and magazine articles, many of which expressed her increasing political conservatism, and by working as a maid, a substitute teacher, and a librarian. In 1959, she suffered a stroke. Too ill to nurse herself, she was forced to enter a welfare home. She died there on January 28, 1960.

Analysis • For much of her career, Zora Neale Hurston was dedicated to the presentation of black folk culture. She introduced readers to hoodoo, folktales, lying contests, spirituals, the blues, sermons, children's games, riddles, playing the dozens, and, in general, a highly metaphoric folk idiom. Although she represented black folk culture in several genres, Hurston was drawn to the novel form because it could convey folklore as communal behavior. Hurston knew that much of the unconscious artistry of folklore appears in the gestures and tones in which it is expressed and that it gains much of its meaning in performance. Even *Mules and Men*, the folklore collection she completed just before embarking on her first novel (although it was published after *Jonah's Gourd Vine*), "novelizes" what could have been an anthology of disconnected folk materials. By inventing a narrator who witnesses, even participates in, the performance of folk traditions, she combated the inevitable distortion of an oral culture by its textual documentation.

Hurston's motives for presenting black folklore were, in part, political. She wanted to refute contemporary claims that African Americans lacked a distinct culture of their own. Her novels depict the unconscious creativity of the African American proletariat or folk. They represent community members participating in a highly expressive communication system that taught them to survive racial oppression and, moreover, to respect themselves and their community. At the beginning of Hurston's second novel, for example, the community's members are sitting on porches. "Mules and other brutes had occupied their skins" all day, but now it is night, work is over, and they can talk and feel "powerful and human" again: "They became lords of sounds and lesser things. They passed nations through their mouths. They sat in judgment." By showing the richness and the healthy influence of black folk culture, Hurston hoped not only to defeat racist attitudes but also to encourage racial pride among black people. Why should African Americans wish to imitate a white bourgeoisie? The "Negro lowest down" had a richer culture.

Hurston also had a psychological motive for presenting black folk culture. She drew the folk materials for her novels from the rural, southern black life she knew as a child and subsequently recorded in folklore-collecting trips during the late 1920's and 1930's. She had fond memories of her childhood in the all-black town of Eatonville, where she did not experience poverty or racism. In her autobiographical writings, she suggests that she did not even know that she was "black" until she left Eatonville. Finally, in Eatonville, she had a close relationship with and a strong advocate in her mother. In representing the rich culture of black rural southerners, she was also evoking a happier personal past.

Although the novel's witnessing narrator provided Hurston with the means to dramatize folklore, she also needed meaningful fictional contexts for its presentation. Her novels are a series of attempts to develop such contexts. Initially, she maintained the southern rural setting for black folk traditions. In her first novel, *Jonah's Gourd Vine*, she re-created Eatonville and neighboring Florida towns. Hurston also loosely re-created her parents' lives with the central characters, John and Lucy Pearson. Though Hurston claimed that an unhappy love affair she had had with a man she met in New York was the catalyst for her second novel, *Their Eyes Were Watching God*, the feeling rather than the details of that affair appear in the novel. The work takes the reader back to Eatonville again and to the porch-sitting storytellers Hurston knew as a child.

Moses, Man of the Mountain • With her third novel, *Moses, Man of the Mountain*, however, Hurston turned in a new direction, leaving the Eatonville milieu behind. The novel retells the biblical story of Moses via the folk idiom and traditions of black rural southerners. Hurston leaves much of the plot of the biblical story intact—Moses does lead the Hebrews out of Egypt—but, for example, she shows Moses to be a great hoodoo doctor as well as a leader and lawgiver. In effect, Hurston simulated the creative processes of folk culture, transforming the story of Moses for modern African Americans just as slaves had adapted biblical stories in spirituals. Hurston may have reenacted an oral and communal process as a solitary writer, but she gave an imaginative rendering of the cultural process all the same.

Seraph on the Suwanee • *Seraph on the Suwanee*, Hurston's last novel, marks another dramatic shift in her writing. With this novel, however, she did not create a new context for the representation of folk culture. Rather, she turned away from the effort to present black folklore. *Seraph on the Suwanee* is set in the rural South, but its central characters are white. Hurston apparently wanted to prove that she could write about white people as well as black people, a desire that surfaced, no doubt, in response to the criticism and disinterest her work increasingly faced during the 1940's. Yet, even when writing of upwardly mobile southern "crackers," Hurston could not entirely leave her previous mission behind. Her white characters, perhaps unintentionally, often use the black folk idiom.

Although Hurston's novels, with the exception of the last, create contexts or develop other strategies for the presentation of folklore, they are not simply showcases for folk traditions; black folk culture defines the novels' themes. The most interesting of these thematic renderings appear in Hurston's first two novels. Hurston knew that black folk culture was composed of brilliant adaptations of African culture to American life. She admired the ingenuity of these adaptations but worried about their preservation. Would a sterile, materialistic white world ultimately absorb African Americans, destroying the folk culture they had developed? Her first two novels demonstrate the disturbing influence of white America on black folkways.

Jonah's Gourd Vine • *Jonah's Gourd Vine*, Hurston's first novel, portrays the tragic experience of a black preacher caught between black cultural values and the values imposed by his white-influenced church. The novel charts the life of John Pearson, laborer, foreman, and carpenter, who discovers that he has an extraordinary talent for preaching. With his linguistic skills and his wife Lucy's wise counsel, he becomes pastor of the large church Zion Hope and ultimately moderator of a Florida Baptist convention. His sexual promiscuity, however, eventually destroys his marriage and his career.

Though his verbal skills make him a success while his promiscuity ruins him, the novel shows that both his linguistic gifts and his sexual vitality are part of the same cultural heritage. His sexual conduct is pagan, and so is his preaching. In praying, according to the narrator, it was as if he "rolled his African drum up to the altar, and called his Congo Gods by Christian names." Both aspects of his cultural heritage speak through him. Indeed, they speak through all members of the African American community, if most intensely through John. A key moment early in the novel, when John crosses over Big Creek, marks the symbolic beginning of his life and shows the double cultural heritage he brings to it. John heads down to the Creek, "singing a new song and stomping the beats." He makes up "some words to go with the drums of the Creek," with the animal noises in the woods, and with the hound dog's cry. He begins to think about the girls living on the other side of Big Creek: "John almost trumpeted exultantly at the new sun. He breathed lustily. He stripped and carried his clothes across, then recrossed and plunged into the swift water and breasted strongly over."

To understand why two expressions of the same heritage have such different effects on John's life, one has to turn to the community to which he belongs. Members of his congregation subscribe to differing views of the spiritual life. The view most often endorsed by the novel emerges from the folk culture. As Larry Neal, one of Hurston's best critics, explains in his introduction to the 1971 reprint of the novel, that view belongs to "a formerly enslaved communal society, non-Christian in background," which does not strictly dichotomize body and soul. The other view comes out of a white culture. It is "more rigid, being a blend of Puritan concepts and the fire-and-brimstone imagery of the white evangelical tradition." That view insists that John, as a preacher, exercise self-restraint. The cultural conflict over spirituality pervades his congregation. Although the deacons, whom Hurston often portrays satirically, pressure him to stop preaching, he still has some loyal supporters among his parishioners.

White America's cultural styles and perceptions invade Pearson's community in other ways as well. By means of a kind of preaching competition, the deacons attempt to replace Pearson with the pompous Reverend Felton Cozy, whose preaching style is white. Cozy's style, however, fails to captivate most members of the congregation. Pearson is a great preacher in the folk tradition, moving his congregation to a frenzy with "barbaric thunder-poems." By contrast, Cozy, as one of the parishioners complains, does not give a sermon; he lectures. In an essay Hurston wrote on "The Sanctified Church," she explains this reaction: "The real, singing Negro derides the Negro who adopts the white man's religious ways. . . . They say of that type of preacher, 'Why he don't preach at all. He just lectures.'"

If Pearson triumphs over Cozy, he nevertheless ultimately falls. His sexual conduct destroys his marriage and leads to an unhappy remarriage with one of his mistresses, Hattie Tyson. He is finally forced to stop preaching at Zion Hope. Divorced from Hattie, he moves to another town, where he meets and marries Sally Lovelace, a woman much like Lucy. With her support, he returns to preaching. On a visit to a friend, however, he is tempted by a young prostitute and, to his dismay, succumbs. Although he has wanted to be faithful to his new wife, he will always be a pagan preacher, spirit *and* flesh. Fleeing back to Sally, he is killed when a train strikes his car.

In its presentation of folklore and its complex representation of cultural conflict, *Jonah's Gourd Vine* is a brilliant first novel, although Hurston does not always make her argument sufficiently clear. The novel lacks a consistent point of view. Though she endorses Pearson's African heritage and ridicules representatives of white cultural views, she also creates an admirable and very sympathetic character in Lucy Pearson, who is ruined by her husband's pagan behavior. Hurston did not seem to know how to resolve the cultural conflict she portrayed—hence, the deus ex machina ending. It was not until she wrote her next novel, *Their Eyes Were Watching God*, that Hurston learned to control point of view and presented a solution to the problem of white influences on black culture.

Their Eyes Were Watching God • The life of Janie Crawford, the heroine of *Their Eyes Were Watching God*, is shaped by bourgeois values—white in origin. She finds love and self-identity only by rejecting that life and becoming a wholehearted participant in black folk culture. Her grandmother directs Janie's entrance into adulthood. Born into slavery, the older woman hopes to find protection and materialistic comforts for Janie in a marriage to the property-owning Logan Killicks. Janie, who has grown up in a different generation, does not share her grandmother's values. When she finds she cannot love her husband, she runs off with Jody Stark, who is on his way to Eatonville, where he hopes to become a "big voice," an appropriate phrase for life in a community that highly values verbal ability. Jody becomes that "big voice" as mayor of the town, owner of the general store, and head of the post office. He lives both a bourgeois and a folk life in Eatonville. He constructs a big house—the kind white people have—but he wanders out to the porch of the general store whenever he wants to enjoy the perpetual storytelling that takes place there. Even though Janie has demonstrated a talent for oratory, however, he will not let her join these sessions or participate in the mock funeral for a mule that has become a popular character in the townspeople's stories. "He didn't," the narrator suggests, "want her talking after such trashy people." As Janie tells a friend years later, Jody "classed me off." He does so by silencing her.

For several years, Janie has no voice in the community or in her private life. Her life begins to seem unreal: "She sat and watched the shadow of herself going about tending store and prostrating itself before Jody." One day, after Stark insults her in front of customers in the store, however, she speaks out and, playing the dozens, insults his manhood. The insult causes an irreconcilable break between them.

After Jody's death, Janie is courted by Tea Cake Woods, a laborer with little money. Though many of her neighbors disapprove of the match, Janie marries him. "Dis ain't no business proposition," she tells her friend Pheoby, "and no race after property and titles. Dis is uh love game. Ah done lived Grandma's way, now Ah mens tuh live mine." Marriage to Tea Cake lowers her social status but frees her from her submissive female role, from her shadow existence. Refusing to use her money, Tea Cake takes her down to the Everglades, where they become migrant workers. She picks beans with him in the fields, and he helps her prepare their dinners. With Tea Cake, she also enters into the folk culture of the Everglades, and that more than anything else enables her to shed her former submissive identity. Workers show up at their house every night to sing, dance, gamble, and, above all, to talk, like the folks in Eatonville on the front porch of the general store. Janie learns how to tell "big stories" from listening to the others, and she is encouraged to do so.

This happy phase of Janie's life ends tragically as she and Tea Cake attempt to escape a hurricane and the ensuing flood. Tea Cake saves Janie from drowning but, in the process, is bitten by a rabid dog. Sick and crazed, he tries to shoot Janie. She is forced to kill him in self-defense. Not everything she has gained during her relationship with Tea Cake, however, dies with him. The strong self-identity she has achieved while living in the Everglades enables her to withstand the unjust resentment of their black friends as well as her trial for murder in a white court. Most important, she is able to endure her own loss and returns to Eatonville, self-reliant and wise. Tea Cake, she knows, will live on in her thoughts and feelings—and in her words. She tells her story to her friend Pheoby—that storytelling event frames the novel—and allows Pheoby to bring it to the other members of the community. As the story enters the community's oral culture, it will influence it. Indeed, as the novel closes, Janie's story has already affected Pheoby. "Ah done growed ten feet higher from jus' listenin' tuh you," she tells Janie. "Ah ain't satisfied wid mahself no mo'."

In her novels, Hurston did not represent the oppression of black people because she refused to view African American life as impoverished. If she would not focus on white racism, however, her novels do oppose white culture. In *Their Eyes Were Watching God*, Janie does not find happiness until she gives up a life governed by white values and enters into the verbal ceremonies of black folk culture. Loving celebrations of a separate black folk life were Hurston's effective political weapon; racial pride was one of her great gifts to American literature. "Sometimes, I feel discriminated against," she once told her readers, "but it does not make me angry. It merely astonishes me. How *can* any deny themselves the pleasure of my company? It's beyond me."

Deborah Kaplan

Other major works

SHORT FICTION: *Spunk: The Selected Short Stories of Zora Neale Hurston*, 1985; *The Complete Stories*, 1995.

PLAYS: *Color Struck*, pb. 1926; *The First One*, pb. 1927; *Mule Bone*, pb. 1931 (with Langston Hughes); *Polk County*, pb. 1944, pr. 2002.

NONFICTION: *Mules and Men*, 1935; *Tell My Horse*, 1938; *Dust Tracks on a Road*, 1942; *The Sanctified Church*, 1981; *Folklore, Memoirs, and Other Writings*, 1995; *Go Gator and Muddy the Water: Writings*, 1999 (Pamela Bordelon, editor); *Every Tongue Got to Confess: Negro Folk-tales from the Gulf States*, 2001; *Zora Neale Hurston: A Life in Letters*, 2002 (Carla Kaplan, editor).

MISCELLANEOUS: *I Love Myself When I Am Laughing . . . and Then Again When I Am Looking Mean and Impressive: A Zora Neale Hurston Reader*, 1979.

Bibliography
Awkward, Michael, ed. *New Essays on "Their Eyes Were Watching God."* New York: Cambridge University Press, 1990. Essays by Robert Hemenway and Nellie McKay on the biographical roots of the novel and by Hazel Carby on Hurston's use of anthropology. Rachel Blau DuPlessis provides a feminist perspective.

Bloom, Harold, ed. *Zora Neale Hurston*. New York: Chelsea House, 1986. From the series Modern Critical Views. An excellent collection of criticism of Hurston's work and life. Includes early commentary by Franz Boas and Langston Hughes, as well as later studies.

Boyd, Valerie. *Wrapped in Rainbows: The Life of Zora Neale Hurston*. New York: Charles Scribner's Sons, 2003. Good, up-to-date biography of Hurston.

Campbell, Josie P. *Student Companion to Zora Neale Hurston*. Westport, Conn.: Greenwood Press, 2001. A handy student guide to Hurston's writings that includes bibliographical references and an index.

Chinn, Nancy, and Elizabeth E. Dunn. "'The Ring of Singing Metal on Wood': Zora Neale Hurston's Artistry in 'The Gilded Six-Bits.'" *The Mississippi Quarterly* 49 (Fall, 1996): 775-790. Discusses how Hurston uses setting, ritual, dialect, and the nature of human relationships in the story; argues that the story provides a solution to the problem of reconciling her rural Florida childhood with her liberal arts education and training.

Cobb-Moore, Geneva. "Zora Neale Hurston as Local Colorist." *The Southern Literary Journal* 26 (Spring, 1994): 25-34. Discusses how Hurston's creation of folk characters enlarges the meaning of local color; shows how Hurston proves that while physical bodies can be restricted, the imagination is always free.

Cooper, Jan. "Zora Neale Hurston Was Always a Southerner Too." In *The Female Tradition in Southern Literature*, edited by Carol S. Manning. Urbana: University of Illinois Press, 1993. Examines the hitherto neglected role that Hurston played in the Southern Renaissance between 1920 and 1950. Argues that Hurston's fiction is informed by a modern southern agrarian sense of community. Suggests that the Southern Renaissance was a transracial, cross-cultural product of the South.

Croft, Robert W. *A Zora Neale Hurston Companion*. Westport, Conn.: Greenwood Press, 2002. Designed for student use, this handbook contains detailed summaries and analyses of Hurston's major works and other useful reference features.

Cronin, Gloria L., ed. *Critical Essays on Zora Neale Hurston*. New York: G. K. Hall, 1998. A useful collection. Includes bibliographical references and an index.

Gates, Henry Louis, Jr. *The Signifying Monkey: A Theory of Afro-American Literary Criti-*

cism. New York: Oxford University Press, 1988. The chapter on Hurston discusses her best-known novel, *Their Eyes Were Watching God*, as a conscious attempt to rebut the naturalistic view of black people as "animalistic" that Gates claims Hurston saw in Richard Wright's fiction.

Glassman, Steve, and Kathryn Lee Siedel, eds. *Zora in Florida.* Orlando: University of Central Florida Press, 1991. This collection of essays by seventeen Hurston scholars explores the overall presence and influence of Florida in and on the works of Hurston. This collection grew out of a Hurston symposium held in Daytona Beach, Florida, in November, 1989, and includes an excellent introduction to the importance of Florida in the study of Hurston.

Hemenway, Robert E. *Zora Neale Hurston: A Literary Biography.* Urbana: University of Illinois Press, 1977. Perhaps the best extant work on Hurston. Hemenway's painstakingly researched study of Hurston's life and literary career was crucial in rescuing Hurston from neglect and establishing her as a major American writer. Although some of the facts of Hurston's chronology have been corrected by later scholarship, Hemenway's study is the most valuable introduction to Hurston's work available. Includes a bibliography of published and unpublished works by Hurston.

Hill, Lynda Marion. *Social Rituals and the Verbal Art of Zora Neale Hurston.* Washington, D.C.: Howard University Press, 1996. Chapters on Hurston's treatment of everyday life, science and humanism, folklore, and color, race, and class. Hill also considers dramatic reenactments of Hurston's writing. Includes notes, bibliography, and an appendix on "characteristics of Negro expression."

Howard, Lillie P. *Zora Neale Hurston.* Boston: Twayne, 1980. A good general introduction to the life and works of Hurston. Contains valuable plot summaries and commentaries on Hurston's works. Supplemented by a chronology and a bibliography.

Hurston, Lucy Anne. *Speak, So You Can Speak Again: The Life of Zora Neale Hurston.* New York: Doubleday, 2004. A brief biography written by Hurston's niece. Most notable for the inclusion of rare photographs, writings, and other multimedia personal artifacts. Also contains an audio CD of Hurston reading and singing.

Hurston, Zora Neale. *Zora Neale Hurston: A Life in Letters.* New York: Doubleday, 2002. A collection of more than five hundred letters, annotated and arranged in chronological order.

Lyons, Mary E. *Sorrow's Kitchen: The Life and Folklore of Zora Neale Hurston.* New York: Charles Scribner's Sons, 1990. Perhaps the only straightforward biography of Hurston, written with the younger reader in mind. Especially useful for those who need a primer on Hurston's background in all-black Eatonville.

McGlamery, Tom. *Protest and the Body in Melville, Dos Passos, and Hurston.* New York: Routledge, 2004. Comparative study of common motifs in the writings of American novelists Herman Melville, John Dos Passos, and Zora Neale Hurston.

Miles, Diana. *Women, Violence, and Testimony in the Works of Zora Neale Hurston.* New York: P. Lang, 2003. Examination of the complex interaction between protofeminist and violence themes in Hurston's writings.

Newsom, Adele S. *Zora Neale Hurston: A Reference Guide.* Boston: G. K. Hall, 1987. A catalog of Hurston criticism spanning the years 1931-1986, arranged chronologically with annotations. This source is an invaluable aid to serious scholars of Hurston. Also contains an introduction to the criticism on Hurston. An especially useful resource for all inquiries.

Walker, Pierre A. "Zora Neale Hurston and the Post-Modern Self in *Dust Tracks on a Road.*" *African American Review* 32 (Fall, 1998): 387-399. Uses poststructuralist theory to discuss Hurston's autobiography, showing how she avoids certain autobiographical conventions; argues that Hurston focuses on the life of her imagination, on the psychological dynamics of her family, on retelling community stories, on portraying the character of certain friends, and on her ambiguous pronouncements about race.

West, Margaret Genevieve. *Zora Neale Hurston and American Literary Culture.* Gainesville: University Press of Florida, 2005. A chronicle of Hurston's literary career and a look at why her writing did not gain popularity until long after her death.

John Irving

Born: Exeter, New Hampshire; March 2, 1942

Principal long fiction • *Setting Free the Bears*, 1969; *The Water-Method Man*, 1972; *The 158-Pound Marriage*, 1974; *The World According to Garp*, 1978; *The Hotel New Hampshire*, 1981; *The Cider House Rules*, 1985; *A Prayer for Owen Meany*, 1989; *A Son of the Circus*, 1994; *A Widow for One Year*, 1998; *The Fourth Hand*, 2001; *Until I Find You*, 2005.

Other literary forms • John Irving is best known for his long fiction. Some of his few published short stories found their way into his novels, attributed to one or another of the novel's main characters. The rest of the stories, some originally published in magazines, were collected in the volume *Trying to Save Piggy Sneed* (1996), a miscellany that also includes occasional essays and fragments of autobiography.

Achievements • When *The World According to Garp* became a best-seller in 1978, prompting the reissue of his three previous novels, Irving captured the attention of literary critics as well as of the popular audience. His life and works were profiled in *Time*, *Saturday Review*, and *Rolling Stone*, and his novels entered what he calls in *The World According to Garp*, "that uncanny half-light where 'serious' books glow, for a time, as also 'popular' books." Various aspects of Irving's work appeal to different audiences, making him difficult to classify as either "serious" or "popular." The sometimes ribald, occasionally grotesque humor and the explicit sexuality of the novels give them a sensational appeal and made Irving—and his novelist character T. S. Garp—cult heroes. On the other hand, Irving's representation of random violence in the modern world, his emphasis on love and family responsibilities, and his use of writers as major characters have prompted serious examination of his work among academic critics. *The Hotel New Hampshire* delighted Irving fans with its continuation of established motifs and themes—bears, wrestling, Vienna, children—but critics and reviewers took a cautious approach to the novel, not certain whether to place Irving in the first rank of contemporary novelists or to chide him for reiterating his themes and allowing the trivial and the clichéd to coexist with the profound.

Irving's work is of uneven quality: *Setting Free the Bears*, his first novel, is in some sections overwritten and self-indulgent, and his third novel, *The 158-Pound Marriage*, is limited in scope. He is nonetheless a figure to be reckoned with in contemporary American fiction, in part because of his confrontation with issues that occupy public attention. *The Cider House Rules* deals in large part with the issue of abortion, and Irving avoids the polemic of the modern abortion debate by setting the novel in the first half of the twentieth century. *A Prayer for Owen Meany* is set against the backdrop of the Vietnam War and has a strong antiwar bias. The novel makes fresh the literary cliché of the hero as Christ figure by choosing in Owen Meany a character who seems superficially ill-suited for such heroism. The blend of contemporary issues, bizarre yet believable characters, and an old-fashioned devotion to good storytelling distinguishes Irving's novels.

Biography • John Winslow Irving was born on March 2, 1942, in Exeter, New Hampshire, to F. N. and Frances Winslow Irving. His father taught Russian history at Exeter Academy, where Irving attended prep school. At Exeter, he developed two lifelong interests, writing and wrestling, and became convinced that both required the same skills: practice and determination. Though not an outstanding student, he developed an appreciation of hard, steady work and a love of literature. Of his early apprenticeships Irving remarked in a *Rolling Stone* interview, "I was a very dull kid. But I really learned how to wrestle and I really learned how to write. I didn't have an idea in my head." After being graduated from Exeter at the age of nineteen, Irving spent a year at the University of Pittsburgh, where the wrestling competition convinced him that writing was a better career choice.

In 1962, Irving enrolled at the University of New Hampshire, where he began to work with authors Thomas Williams and John Yount, but a desire to see more of the world caused him to drop out. After an intensive summer course in German at Harvard University, he left for Vienna, where he enrolled at the Institute of European Studies. During his two years in Vienna, Irving married Shyla Leary, a painter whom he had met at Harvard, studied German, and became seriously devoted to writing. Living in an unfamiliar place sharpened his powers of observation; as he said in a 1981 *Time* interview, "you are made to notice even the trivial things—especially the trivial things." He returned to the University of New Hampshire, worked again with Thomas Williams, and graduated cum laude in 1965. From there, with his wife and son, Colin, Irving went to the University of Iowa Writers' Workshop, where he earned an M.F.A. degree in creative writing in 1967. During his time at Iowa, Irving continued wrestling with Dan Gable, the Iowa coach who won a medal at the 1976 Munich Olympics. Encouraged by writer-in-residence Kurt Vonnegut, he also completed his first published novel, *Setting Free the Bears*, which is set in Austria.

Setting Free the Bears was well received by critics and sold well (6,228 copies) for a first novel. A projected film of the book did not materialize, and Irving moved his family back to New England. After a brief period of teaching at Windham College, he taught at Mount Holyoke College until 1972, and for 1971 to 1972 was awarded a Rockefeller Foundation grant. *The Water-Method Man*, published in 1972, did not sell as well as *Setting Free the Bears*, but Irving was invited to be a writer-in-residence at the University of Iowa from 1972 to 1975, and for 1974 to 1975 he received a fellowship from the National Endowment for the Arts. During that time, Irving published his third novel, *The 158-Pound Marriage*, which was set in Iowa City. Sales of *The 158-Pound Marriage*, which Irving considers his weakest novel, were poor, and Irving returned to New England to begin a second period of teaching at Mount Holyoke.

The turning point in Irving's career came in 1978, with the publication of *The World According to Garp*. Discouraged by the seeming reluctance of Random House to promote his novels, he moved to E. P. Dutton and the guidance of Henry Robbins, its editor in chief. Although Dutton promoted the novel in ways that normally disenchant the serious reviewer (bumper stickers, T-shirts), the critical reaction was good and the public reception overwhelming; combined hardback and paperback sales reached three million in the first two years. In 1982, *The World According to Garp* was made into a film, with Irving playing a bit part as a wrestling referee. The success of the novel allowed Irving to devote more of his time to writing, and in 1981 Dutton published his fifth novel, *The Hotel New Hampshire*. Although some critics expressed disappointment in the novel, it was a best-seller and a Book-of-the-Month Club selection. The author of *The World According to Garp* had become a household word.

©Marion Ettlinger

Irving's four subsequent novels—*The Cider House Rules, A Prayer for Owen Meany, A Son of the Circus,* and *A Widow for One Year*—were also bestsellers and book-club selections. As predicted by his earlier performance, he managed both to sustain a popular following and to provoke frequent scholarly interest; articles about and reviews of his work have appeared in journals as diverse as *Novel, The Sewanee Review,* and the *Journal of the American Medical Association.* In *Trying to Save Piggy Sneed,* a collection of essays and short fictional pieces originally published elsewhere, Irving updates his biography with mention of divorce, remarriage, and the birth of a third son. Like Johnny Wheelwright, the narrator of *A Prayer for Owen Meany,* Irving lived for a time in Toronto but then transferred his main residence to his native state of New Hampshire. In 1998, shortly after publication of *A Widow for One Year,* the Modern Library issued a commemorative edition of *The World According to Garp* with a new introduction by the author. In 2005, Irving published his most autobiographical work, *Until I Find You,* a story centering on a son's search for his father.

Analysis • John Irving's fiction is distinguished by a highly personal fusion of seemingly incongruous elements. Irving's settings, actions, and characters are often bizarre and violent. The world he presents is frequently chaotic and unpredictable, full of sudden death and apparently meaningless collisions of people, values, ideologies, and objects. Among his characters are the Ellen Jamesians (*The World According to Garp*), who cut out their tongues to protest the rape and mutilation of a little girl; a blind bear-trainer named Freud (*The Hotel New Hampshire*); and a motorcyclist who locks a zoo attendant in a cage with an anteater (*Setting Free the Bears*). Characters die in excruciating ways: stung to death by thousands of bees, killed in airplane crashes, assassinated in parking lots. Irving himself has referred to *The World According to Garp* as "an X-rated soap opera." Balancing the sensational and pessimistic elements of the novels, however, is a core of humane values. Irving does not posit a violent and arbitrary world but rather one in which violence and havoc are present in sufficient quantities to demand constant vigilance. His characters may behave strangely, but their motives are usually pure. Infidelity exists, but so does real love; children deserve protection; human kindness is paramount. Despite his characterization of *The World According to Garp* as "X-rated," Irving denies that it presents an unbelievable world: "People who think *Garp* is wildly eccentric and very bizarre are misled about the real world. I can't imagine where they've been living or what they read for news."

Irving is essentially a storyteller and often uses an omniscient narrator who feels free to interrupt the narrative. In *Setting Free the Bears*, he uses elements of the tall tale and the fairy tale, and all of his novels are characterized by broad situational comedy rather than wit. At the same time, especially in *Setting Free the Bears* and *The World According to Garp*, he writes self-conscious fiction which reflects on its own making. As Michael Priestly has commented, "Irving resembles both the Victorian novelist ('dear reader') and the 'new novelist' who writes fiction about fiction." Many issues with which his novels deal are quite contemporary: feminism, sex-change operations, political assassination. Of equal importance, however, are romantic impulses such as freeing the animals in a zoo, rescuing the afflicted, and guarding one's loved ones against harm. The tension between tradition and novelty, reverence and blasphemy, contributes to the singularity of Irving's work.

A group of common motifs and images give Irving's novels coherence as a body of work. Wrestling is the dominant sport and is the avocation of a number of characters. Bears are set free, as indicated by the title of his first novel, to reappear in a number of guises in later books. At least one character in each novel is a writer—most notably T. S. Garp in *The World According to Garp*. There are always children to be guarded from serious injury, though efforts to protect them are not always successful. Vienna is a frequent locale for Irving's fiction, as are Iowa and New Hampshire. These characters and motifs suggest a strong autobiographical current in Irving's fiction, and although the ingredients of his own life are transmuted by his imagination, his novels provide a rough outline of his progress from student in Vienna to graduate student in Iowa to successful novelist. Wary of readers believing that his novels are generally autobiographical, Irving has said that "people with limited imaginations find it hard to imagine that anyone else has an imagination. Therefore, they must think that everything they read in some way *happened*."

The enormous reality of Irving's characters, more than their possible identification with the author, is the central interest for his novels. Even his most bizarre characters are not caricatures; rather, they are believable people with extraordinary characteristics. Jenny Fields, Garp's mother, sets out to be impregnated by a terminally ill patient so that she will have to endure no further sexual contact, yet her action is presented as practical rather than perverse. Lilly, the youngest Berry child in *The Hotel New Hampshire*, never reaches four feet in height, but her family—and the reader—regards her not as a freak but merely as small. Irving illustrates the diversity in the human family by presenting some of its most extreme members in his fiction, but instead of creating a circus, he urges tolerance. Violence is given the same matter-of-fact approach as are other extremes in Irving's fiction. It is present, if unwelcome, merely because it exists as a part of life. Irving is never sentimental or dramatic about motorcycle accidents, terrorists' bombs, bees that kill, or gearshifts that blind children; these are the risks of living.

The humor in Irving's novels serves both to make the bizarre and violent elements more acceptable and to reinforce the duality of his vision. No contemporary novelist better exemplifies Dorothy Parker's requisites for humor: "a disciplined eye and a wild mind." Early in his career, Irving relied heavily on slapstick comedy, such as the adventures of Siggy Javotnik in the Heitzinger Zoo in *Setting Free the Bears* and Bogus Trumper's duck hunt in *The Water-Method Man*. Increasingly, he turned to irony and wit as major devices of humor, but all the novels have a strong element of fantasy; dreams or nightmares become reality. Comedy and tragedy are woven closely together. Irving, always sensitive to public opinion, built into *The World According to*

Garp a defense against those who would accuse him of treating serious subjects too lightly. Mrs. Poole, of Findlay, Ohio, writes to T. S. Garp to accuse him of finding other people's problems funny; Garp replies that he has "nothing but sympathy for how people behave—and nothing but laughter to console them with." By insisting that life is both comically absurd and inevitably tragic, Irving espouses an acceptance of extremes. He has been described by Hugh Ruppersburg as a "stoic pessimist," a label that at this point seems appropriate, but his major contribution to the American novel is the product of imagination rather than philosophy: the creation of truly memorable people and situations that extend the reader's understanding of human existence. In the words of T. S. Garp, "a writer's job is to imagine everything so personally that the fiction is as vivid as our personal memories." At this job, Irving has succeeded admirably.

Setting Free the Bears • Unlike many first novels, *Setting Free the Bears* is not an autobiographical account of the author's early years. Although it is set in Austria and draws on Irving's experience there as a student, the novel is an exuberant and imaginative account of the adventures of Hannes Graff, the narrator, and his friend Siggy Javotnik as they ride a motorcycle through Austria. The middle section of the novel consists of alternating chapters of two documents written by Siggy: "The Zoo-Watch," an account of Siggy's vigil at the Heitzinger Zoo, and "The Highly Selective Autobiography of Siegfried Javotnik," which documents his family's history from the mid-1930's to the early 1960's. Siggy, who lives in the past—"I rely on pre-history for any sense and influence"—has only one dream for the future: to free the animals from the Heitzinger Zoo. After Siggy's death from multiple bee stings, Graff accomplishes Siggy's dream and, after the ensuing chaos, rides off on his motorcycle. The novel is a youthful fantasy, full of grand adventures and characters of mythic stature: The characters have no futures and only a tenuous relationship with the present.

The basic topic of the novel is freedom. Part of Siggy's "pre-history" deals with the liberation of Austria from the Germans during World War II. In 1967, the year the frame narrative takes place, Graff frees the fairy-tale princess Gallen from her aunt's house and takes her to Vienna. Finally, Graff frees the animals from the zoo and what Siggy has assumed is their torture by the night guard, O. Schrutt. At the end of the novel, the Rare Spectacled Bears are loping across an open field to take up life in the woods, but if they survive, they will be the only ones who are free. Siggy, like the rest of his family, is dead. Gallen has sold her lovely reddish hair for money to live on while she waits for Graff to return to Vienna, and Graff is rootless and aimless on his motorcycle. In his attempt to create the perfect world denied by his ancestors by war, Siggy has become impossibly idealistic, and Graff has succumbed to his idealism, a fact he realizes at the end of the novel: "What worse awareness is there than to know there would have been a better outcome if you'd never done anything at all?" The suggestion is that freedom is best achieved by letting life run its natural course without human interference.

The nature of the novelist, however, is to interfere—that is, to impose an order on life by structuring it into novelistic form. *Setting Free the Bears* is a novel about writing. Late in his autobiography, Siggy reveals that it is more fiction than fact. Graff becomes, in a sense, Siggy's literary executor; as Graff reveals in the "P.S." at the beginning of part three, it has been his editorial decision to interleave sections of the autobiography with sections of the zoo-watch notebook. As the naïve editor-narrator, Graff does not comprehend the relationship between the two documents, though the parallels between the two types of imprisonment—war and the zoo—are apparent to the reader. Graff's attempts to impose order on Siggy's life are far more successful than Siggy's own attempts, but ultimately all that Siggy has written may be fiction—it is fiction in one sense—so Graff is left trying to order a phantom existence.

In keeping with Irving's insistence on the elusive nature of reality, the novel has a dreamlike quality. Many of the characters live fantasy lives. Graff dreams of the lovely Gallen; Siggy dreams of freeing the animals from O. Schrutt. Within Siggy's autobiography, a chicken-farmer dressed in feather-covered pie plates imagines he looks like an eagle, representing Austria's independence. Elements of fantasy, which here dominate the novel, are characteristic of Irving's later novels as well, though the line between fantasy and reality is more sharply drawn in his later work. *Setting Free the Bears* is further removed from traditional realistic fiction than any of Irving's other novels. Like "The Pension Grillparzer," T. S. Garp's first piece of fiction in *The World According to Garp*, it is a story told for the sake of telling a story. In an interview with Greil Marcus of *Rolling Stone*, Irving said, "I had no idea who the people in *Setting Free the Bears* were, or how they were going to get from A to Z." The careful plot structure of the novel suggests that at some point Irving envisioned the whole quite clearly, but the imaginative power evidenced here continued to be an important element in his fiction.

The Water-Method Man • Deserving of more attention than has yet been given it, *The Water-Method Man* is Irving's most consistently comic novel. "I wanted," Irving has said, "to write a book that was absolutely comic: I wanted it to be intricate and funny and clever and I wanted it to go on and on and on." Fred "Bogus" Trumper, also known to various friends as "Bogge" and "Thump-Thump," is the narrator and main character of the novel, which is an account of his misadventures in Iowa, Austria, New York, and Maine. Bogus Trumper is a charming failure searching for meaning and order in his life. He has tried marriage to a skiing champion appropriately nicknamed "Biggie," fatherhood, a doctoral program in comparative literature, and filmmaking. In desperation one night, he begins to write a diary, which becomes the first-person portions of the novel. As he had in *Setting Free the Bears*, Irving alternates sections of two different pieces of writing, but in *The Water-Method Man* this device is simpler; the first-person autobiographical chapters tell of Trumper's past; the third-person narrative sections tell of his present.

The somewhat improbable metaphor for Bogus's wayward life is his penis. For years he has had problems with painful urination and orgasm; a urologist discovers that his urinary tract is "a narrow, winding road." Rejecting the alternative of surgery, Trumper chooses the "water method," which consists of flushing his system with large amounts of water. This treatment alleviates his problem rather than curing it and represents all the other unfinished business in his life. Also serving as an analogue to Trumper's life is the subject of his doctoral thesis, an Old Low Norse saga, *Akthelt and Gunnel*, which he is translating—or rather pretending to translate. His actual translation has stopped at the point where he realized the impending doom of the characters; after that, he began to invent a lusty saga with parallels to his own life. When Trumper finally achieves order and peace in his life, Irving signals the change with Trumper's corrective surgery and his completion of a faithful translation of *Akthelt and Gunnel*. He is able to come to terms with the people and events around him.

Any serious message in *The Water-Method Man*, however, is incidental to the comic dimensions of the novel. Much of the humor is ribald, though Irving's skill enables him to avoid obscenity. Several of the most memorable sequences involve equally memorable minor characters, such as Merrill Overturf, Trumper's diabetic friend who drowns while trying to find a Nazi tank he insists was sunk in the Danube, and Dante Calicchio, the New York limousine driver who takes Trumper to Maine. Though briefly sketched, these characters demonstrate Irving's ability to make the incidental character or situation come alive. The almost complete absence of violent or grotesque incidents makes *The Water-Method Man* unique in Irving's canon. Scenes such as the one in which Bogus Trumper skis into an Alpine parking lot, which in Irving's other novels would have some shocking, tragic outcome, are here handled as they are in comic strips: Everyone walks away unscathed. The closest approach to serious emotional involvement comes in the scenes between Trumper and his young son, Colm. The pressured responsibilities of parenthood become a major topic in Irving's later novels, as does the relationship between life and art, here represented by Bogus Trumper's attempt to find order in writing translations (both real and fake), autobiographies, letters, and making films. The fact that Trumper is ultimately at peace with himself makes *The Water-Method Man* one of Irving's most optimistic novels.

The 158-Pound Marriage • In contrast to the boisterous comedy of *The Water-Method Man*, Irving's third novel is painfully serious. *The 158-Pound Marriage* is Irving's shortest novel to date and also the most conventional in both form and subject matter. It is the story of two couples who swap partners regularly for a period of time, an experiment that sours all the relationships involved. Irving has said that the book is about "lust and rationalization and restlessness," and it mirrors the moral floundering of the early 1970's in which it is set. Severin and Edith Winter mistakenly conceive the exchange as a means of saving their own marriage by introducing sexual variety to erase the memory of Severin's previous affair with a ballet dancer. Almost inevitably, the individuals become emotionally involved with their "temporary" partners, and this places both marriages in jeopardy. The first-person narrator, a novelist, considers himself a cuckold by the end of the novel (T. S. Garp's second novel in *The World According to Garp* is titled *The Second Wind of the Cuckold*) and is going to Vienna to attempt a reconciliation with his wife, Utch. Whatever the outcome of this effort, their marriage will never be the same.

Despite the significance of Irving's message about contemporary life, *The 158-Pound Marriage* is his weakest novel because he fails to take advantage of his strengths as a novelist. Instead of merging the comic and the tragic, as he does in his best work, Irving steers a course between them; as a result, the novel has a flatness rather than the peaks and valleys of emotion which Irving is capable of evoking. Only in the histories of the characters that the narrator provides at the beginning does Irving's usual inventiveness emerge. Severin and Utch have exotic yet similar backgrounds. Both were children in wartime Vienna; Severin is the son of an obscure Austrian painter and a model, and Utch is the daughter of a clever farm woman who hid Utch in the belly of a dead cow to protect her from rape at the hands of the invading Russians. Instead of being raped, the seven-year-old was christened Utchka ("calf") and virtually adopted by a Russian officer occupying Vienna. When the narrator meets Utch, she is working as a tour guide in Vienna. Edith meets Severin when she is sent by an American museum to purchase some of his father's paintings. The coincidence of the two couples' meeting and becoming intimately involved with one another years afterward lends interest to the early sections of the novel, but Irving does not manage to sustain this interest.

As the title suggests, wrestling is a major motif in *The 158-Pound Marriage.* Severin Winter is a wrestling coach as well as a professor of German, and the jargon of the sport dominates the novel, as it does his speech. "Wrestling," the narrator says, "was a constant metaphor to him," and the tedious struggle of a wrestling match becomes an apt metaphor for the struggle to maintain human relationships. Were this Irving's only novel, one would have little sense of the mastery of tone and style of which he is capable; however, his next two novels amply display that mastery.

The World According to Garp • By far Irving's most successful novel, *The World According to Garp* is the best example of his ability to wed the bizarre and the commonplace, the tragic and the comic. The novel deals with the extremes of human experience, embodying that dualism of vision which is Irving's greatest strength as a writer. Titled in the working draft *Lunacy and Sorrow,* it has been called "a manic, melancholic carnival of a book," and Irving manages to keep the reader poised between laughter and tears. The seriousness of *The World According to Garp* lies in its thematic concerns: the elusive nature of reality and the human need to find or impose order on existence. The "lunacy" in the novel derives from the extremes to which people will go to achieve order and meaning; the "sorrow" arises from the ultimate human inability to control destiny. The last line—"in the world according to Garp we are all terminal cases"—conveys the stoic acceptance of misfortune and disaster that Irving posits as necessary for survival, yet the lightly ironic tone of this concluding sentence also reflects the novel's utter lack of sentimentality or melodrama.

T. S. Garp, the main character, is an unlikely hero. On one hand he is a fairly typical twentieth century man, a husband and father who worries about his children, pursues his career, jogs regularly, and has a penchant for young female baby-sitters. He loves his wife, is good to his mother, and has a few close friends. These bare facts, however, do not explain Garp, nor, Irving suggests, would such a sketch be adequate to represent most people. Garp is the son of Jenny Fields, nurse, daughter of a wealthy family, author of an autobiography, and finally sponsor of a haven for women with special needs. Garp's father, a fatally injured ball turret gunner during World War II, enters the picture only long enough to impregnate Jenny Fields. Jenny then rears the boy at the Steering School, where she is the school nurse.

After Garp graduates from Steering, mother and son go to Vienna, where Jenny writes her autobiography, *A Sexual Suspect,* and Garp writes "The Pension Grillparzer." *A Sexual Suspect,* the beginning and end of Jenny Fields's writing career, catapults her to fame as a feminist writer and finally leads to her assassination by a reactionary gunman during a political rally. "The Pension Grillparzer" launches Garp on a career as a writer and also makes possible his marriage to Helen Holm, daughter of the wrestling coach at Steering, with whom he has two sons, Duncan and Walt. Because of his mother's fame, Garp becomes a close friend of Roberta Muldoon, a transsexual who was formerly Robert Muldoon, tight end for the Philadelphia Eagles. He also encounters the Ellen Jamesians, a radical feminist group who protest rape with self-mutilation. After an automobile accident that kills Walt and blinds Duncan in one eye, Garp and Helen adopt the real Ellen James, who eventually becomes a writer. Garp himself is killed at the age of thirty-three by an Ellen Jamesian who is angered by Garp's rejection of the group's extremist practices.

Despite this grim outline, *The World According to Garp* is often humorous and occasionally wildly comic. The humor usually grows out of human foibles: Dean Bodger catching a dead pigeon as it falls from the Steering infirmary roof and mistaking it for the body of young Garp; Jenny Fields failing to recognize a well-dressed woman as a prostitute on the streets of Vienna; Garp sprinting down the streets of his neighborhood to overtake astonished speeders who endanger the lives of his children, or dressing as a woman to attend the "feminist funeral" of his mother. When the comic and tragic merge, the result is black humor in the tradition of Nathanael West. At the climax of the novel, for example, when Garp's car crashes into that of Michael Milton, Helen, in the act of performing oral sex on Milton, bites off his penis, effectively ending the affair that she has been trying to conclude, and providing an ironic counterpoint to the tonguelessness of the Ellen Jamesians.

Humor and tragedy may coexist because the nature of reality is always in question. The title of the novel suggests that the world presented in the novel may be only Garp's idiosyncratic version of reality. The short stories and the fragment of Garp's novel *The World According to Bensenhaver* are different versions of reality—those created by T. S. Garp the novelist. Ultimately, the novel presents a version of the world according to John Irving. The fact that things are not always what they seem is further evidenced in many of the novel's details. Garp's name is not really a name at all. The initials T. S., though echoing those of T. S. Eliot, do not stand for anything, and "Garp" is merely a sound made by Garp's brain-damaged father. Roberta Muldoon is occasionally uncertain whether to behave as a female or male. Jenny Fields does not set out to be a feminist but is regarded as one by so many people that she takes up the cause. Given this confusion between reality and illusion, order is difficult to achieve. As a novelist, Garp can control only the worlds of his fiction; he cannot protect his family and friends from disaster. Garp is in many ways an old-fashioned knight attempting to deal with rapists in parks and speeding automobiles on suburban streets. Like his character Bensenhaver, who appoints himself special guardian of a family after he retires from the police force, Garp imagines himself the particular guardian of children and the enemy of rape.

Of particular interest to modern readers is the prominence of feminism in *The World According to Garp*. Irving's depiction of the movement is broad and essentially sympathetic, including not only its extremes, such as the Ellen Jamesians, but also the changes in social and family relationships brought about by revisions in sex roles. Jenny Fields wants to be a single parent, but artificial insemination and single-parent adoptions are not available to her in the mid-1940's. Her choice of a fatally wounded patient as the father for her child is born of pragmatism rather than feminist philosophy; only later, as she writes her autobiography, is she able to articulate the need for tolerance of those with nontraditional ways. Garp himself is a house-husband. While Helen teaches at the university, he writes at home, takes care of his sons, and cooks. He therefore must deal with public suspicion that he is an unemployed failure, and his own situation enables him to understand the plight of many women and to see the damage done to the feminist cause by extremists such as the Ellen Jamesians.

The major flaw in *The World According to Garp* is its lack of a coherent structure. The examples of Garp's own writing, though interesting and thematically related to the rest of the novel, remain undigested lumps in the chronological narrative. In part, Irving has attempted too much by hoping to fuse the story of a writer's development with all the other issues in the novel. In addition, he is reluctant to let go of his characters, so that the novel continues past the point of its dramatic conclusion.

Chapter 19, "Life After Garp," traces all the main characters to their inevitable ends rather than leaving the reader's imagination to envision them. Art, as the novel insists, is a way of ordering reality, but here the two become confused. There is some suggestion that Garp is a Christlike figure—his almost-virgin birth, his death at the age of thirty-three—but the evidence is too thin to sustain a reading of the final chapter as the "lives of the disciples."

The Hotel New Hampshire • Shortly before T. S. Garp is killed in *The World According to Garp*, he has begun a new novel called *My Father's Illusions*, an apt title for *The Hotel New Hampshire*. Depending less on dreams and violence and more on the imaginative creation of real human types, the novel has a calmer, less urgent tone than *The World According to Garp*. Although themes and motifs present in Irving's earlier novels reappear in *The Hotel New Hampshire*, this novel is far less dependent on autobiography and has a more cohesive focus. Critics and reviewers expressed disappointment with the novel, one calling it "a perverse *Life with Father*, a savage situation comedy." It seems likely, however, that the very absence of much of the perversity and savagery that characterized *The World According to Garp* has made it seem less vital. The tone of *The Hotel New Hampshire* is more assured, its humor more sophisticated, its presentation of life more realistic than in much of Irving's other work.

Like *The World According to Garp*, *The Hotel New Hampshire* deals with illusion and reality—specifically with one man's dreams for his family. Win Berry is a man with improbable hopes. As his son John, the narrator, says of him, "the first of my father's illusions was that bears could survive the life lived by human beings, and the second was that human beings could survive a life led in hotels." The Berry family lives in three hotels during the course of the novel, which spans the period from 1920, when Win Berry meets Mary Bates, to 1980, when the surviving Berry children are grown and have become successful at various pursuits. (Egg, the youngest, is killed in a plane crash along with his mother; Lilly, the smallest, commits suicide.) All the Berry children are marked by a childhood spent in the hotels created by their father's dreams: first a converted school in Dairy, New Hampshire, then a dubious pension in Vienna. Finally, Win Berry, by this time blind—as he in some ways has been all his life—returns to the Maine resort where he first met Mary Bates, shielded by his children from the knowledge that it has become a rape crisis center. The familiar Irving motifs and images are prominent in *The Hotel New Hampshire*. Win Berry's father, Iowa Bob, is a wrestling coach whose strenuous view of life contrasts sharply with his son's dreaminess; bears appear in both actual and simulated form. Near the beginning of the novel, Win Berry buys a bear named State O'Maine from a wanderer named Freud, who eventually lures Win and his family to the second Hotel New Hampshire in Vienna; there they meet Susie-the-bear, a young American who wears a bear suit as a protection against reality.

Several critics have referred to the fairy-tale quality of *The Hotel New Hampshire*, and various elements contribute to that quality: a trained bear, a dog named Sorrow who reappears in different forms, and several heroic rescues, including the Berry family's rescue of the Vienna State Opera House from terrorists who intend to bomb it. The novel partakes of the atmosphere of fantasy present in *Setting Free the Bears* and "The Pension Grillparzer"; the latter, in fact, contains the germ of this novel. Despite the premature deaths of three members of the Berry family, there is little of the bleakness or desperation of *The World According to Garp*. In part, this is the result of the narrator's point of view. John Berry, the middle child, is the keeper of the family records, and thus the one who orders their experience in writing. Though he is patient with other people's fantasies, John has few of his own, and he casts a mellow light over the experience of the family. Irving has compared him to Nick Carraway in F. Scott Fitzgerald's *The Great Gatsby* (1925), but he resembles more nearly the narrative voice in some of J. D. Salinger's work, taking the strange behavior of his family for granted and delighting in their unusual talents and proclivities. John is closest to his sister Franny (another Salinger echo); in fact, they have a brief incestuous relationship, in part intended to ease Franny back into heterosexual relationships following her rape as a teenager.

Although the tone of *The Hotel New Hampshire* is gentler than that of *The World According to Garp*, Irving presents many of the same social problems and situations: rape (which Irving has called "the most violent assault on the body and the head that can happen simultaneously"), murder, race relations, sex roles, and the modern family. The difference between this fifth novel and those that preceded it is that Irving seems to have become reconciled to the need for illusion as a means of survival. No longer are dreams only irresponsible fantasies or terrible nightmares; they are what enable most people, in the refrain of the novel, to "keep passing the open windows" rather than taking a suicidal plunge. By treating contemporary anxieties with the traditional devices of the storyteller, Irving conveys an age-old message about the purpose of art: It can provide an illusion of order that may be more important—and is certainly more readily attained—than order itself.

The Cider House Rules • John Irving's two novels following *The Hotel New Hampshire* deal more insistently with moral and ethical issues, although they also contain the bizarre characters and situations that have become hallmarks of his fiction. *The Cider House Rules* concerns, as the title suggests, the rules by which people are to conduct their lives, but just as the list of rules posted in the cider house ("Please don't smoke in bed or use candles") is consistently ignored, so Dr. Wilbur Larch, one of the novel's central characters, breaks the rules by performing abortions in rural Maine during the 1920's. As he dealt with the issue of rape in *The World According to Garp*, Irving here approaches the issue of abortion inventively: Wilbur Larch is no back-alley abortionist but a skilled obstetrician who also runs an orphanage for the children whose mothers prefer to give birth, and he seeks to have the children adopted.

Homer Wells, the other central character, is an orphan who is never adopted, and who grows up in the orphanage absorbing the most basic lesson taught there: that one must "be of use." His final usefulness is to replace Dr. Larch when the elderly man dies, but even here he breaks the rules, for although he is a skilled obstetrician and abortionist, he has no medical degree, and so takes over the position with an assumed identity. Partly because of the precarious nature of his own existence, Homer has opposed abortion all his life, until he feels that he must perform one for a black teenager who has been raped by her father. Just as the illiterate apple pickers cannot read the rules of the orchard where Homer spends his young adulthood, Irving suggests that the rules that people should follow are those that are derived from human encounter rather than those that are arbitrarily imposed.

The apple orchard setting is part of a muted Garden of Eden theme in the novel. Homer falls in love with Candy, the daughter of the orchard's owner, and she gives birth to his child shortly before she marries another man. No one, however, is cast out of the garden; Irving instead creates another of his oddly mixed families when Homer moves in with Candy, her husband Wally, and the child, a boy named Angel.

Here, too, Homer proves to have been "of use," because a serious illness during World War II prevents Wally from fathering children, and he and Candy rear Angel as their own. Despite its strong proabortion-rights stance, *The Cider House Rules*, like Irving's previous fiction, evokes a special reverence for children. The children in Wilbur Larch's orphanage are cared for lovingly, Homer dotes on his son, Angel, and it is the plight of the pregnant girl, Rose Rose, that converts Homer to the prochoice position of Wilbur Larch.

A Prayer for Owen Meany • As *The Cider House Rules* is set against the political and social realities of the first half of the twentieth century, *A Prayer for Owen Meany* chronicles even more directly those of the next two decades—from the escalation of the Vietnam War to the advent of heavy-metal rock music, and from the early spread of television culture to the presidency of Ronald Reagan. In its overtly religious imagery, the novel posits the need for some kind of salvation during these turbulent years. *A Prayer for Owen Meany* is more complex structurally than the straightforward storytelling of *The Cider House Rules*, features the quick juxtapositions of violence and comedy of Irving's earlier work, and is ambitious in its creation of an unlikely Christ figure.

A Prayer for Owen Meany details the friendship—from childhood during the 1950's to Owen Meany's death during the 1960's—of two boys who grow up in Gravesend, New Hampshire, at opposite ends of the social scale: Owen's reclusive family owns the local granite quarry, whereas John Wheelwright's family boasts of Mayflower origins and functions as the local gentry. Their roles are reversed and confused, however, in the course of the narrative: Owen, a diminutive boy who even as an adult is never more than five feet tall, and whose voice—rendered by Irving in capital letters—is a prepubescent squeak, becomes a Christ figure with powers over life and death, whereas John leads a rather uneventful adult life as a schoolteacher in Toronto, even remaining a virgin, as Owen does not.

Imagery and actions identifying Owen Meany with Christ begin early in the novel and accumulate rapidly to the climactic scene of his death. When he is a small child, his size and lightness seem to the other children a "miracle"; for the same reason, he is cast as the Christ child in a church Christmas pageant. Owen's father tells John that Owen's was a virgin birth—that his parents' marriage was never consummated—and Owen "plays God" to save John from being drafted during the Vietnam War by cutting off one of his fingers with a diamond wheel used to engrave granite monuments. Owen foresees the date of his own death and has a recurrent dream that he will die saving small children; the fact that both predictions are accurate lends to Owen a God-like foreknowledge.

A Prayer for Owen Meany is far from being a solemn theological tract. Irving's characteristically ebullient humor erupts throughout the novel in slapstick scenes, in boyish pranks, and even in the ironic contrast between Owen's small voice and the large print in which it leaps authoritatively from the page. The blending of the serious and the comic reaches its apotheosis early in the novel, when the one ball that Owen Meany ever hits in Little League baseball kills John Wheelwright's mother, Tabitha. The fact that Owen Meany is the agent of John's mother's death does not mar the boys' friendship; indeed, it brings them closer together, partly because John knows that Owen worshiped his mother (and for the rest of his life keeps her dressmaker's dummy in his bedroom as a kind of ministering angel), and partly because the event has an inevitability that foretells Owen's later powers over life and death.

A Prayer for Owen Meany is a mixture of realism and fabulism, of commentary on contemporary American culture and evocation of the magic of childhood and friendship. Religious imagery permeates but does not overwhelm the novel, which takes its tone from the narrator's somewhat self-mocking stance and his obvious delight in recalling the "miracle" of Owen Meany. The novel is indeed a "prayer" for, and to, Owen, who, in refusing to flinch from his own destiny, has given John Wheelwright the courage to face his own life with equanimity.

After turning fifty, Irving published two major novels that confirmed his standing reputation, both satisfying his supporters and irritating his detractors. In *A Son of the Circus*, Irving took advantage of a recent stay in India to revisit his familiar concerns with illness, crime, violent death, and bizarre sexual practices from a somewhat different perspective; in *A Widow for One Year*, he returned to the basic premises and purview of *The World According to Garp*, this time with a female novelist as the central character. In both novels, Irving continues his investigation into the relationship of process to product in fiction.

A Son of the Circus • In *A Son of the Circus*, Irving takes as his main character an orthopedic surgeon who, born in India and trained in postwar Vienna, has long since become a Canadian citizen, with his main practice in Toronto. As the omniscient narrator repeatedly points out, Farrokh Daruwalla, M.D., is in fact a stateless person, never "at home," regardless of where he might be. A member of the Parsi ethnic minority in India, Farrokh happened to be in Vienna studying medicine at the moment of Indian independence in 1947, when Vienna itself was partitioned among the Allied occupying forces in the aftermath of World War II. Although reasonably successful as a surgeon and medical researcher, Farrokh remains curiously adrift in life well into his late fifties in part because of the tangled legacy of his father, Lowji, who was killed by car bomb in 1969.

When the action of *A Son of the Circus* begins, Farrokh is back in India on one of his occasional extended visits, overseeing his second career as a "closet" writer of continuity for detective films starring his brother's adopted son, an actor best known by the name of his character, Inspector Dhar. One of twin sons born to a forgettable (and long forgotten) American actor who was filming on location in India in 1949, Inspector Dhar—also known as John Daruwalla or John D.—grew to maturity under the care of the entire Daruwalla family, although he was technically adopted only by Farrokh's elder brother, also a physician. Dhar's twin, it seems, was taken to California by their mother soon after birth.

A series of murders, combined with threats against Dhar, keep deterring Farrokh from telling John D., a.k.a. Dhar, what he has come to Bombay to tell him, to wit, that John D. has a twin brother who, as a Jesuit priest in training, has been posted to Bombay, and that the brothers are likely to meet. In the meantime, the hapless Jesuit, mistaken for Dhar, is the subject of numerous assaults.

Farrokh, like his father before him, retains membership in the exclusive Duckworth Club, an anomaly left over from the days of the British Empire, and it is there that various threads of his life, including his sponsorship of Inspector Dhar, become entangled. It is there that Rahul, a *hijra* (transsexual) prostitute permanently disguised as Mrs. Dogar, threatens and commits murder; it is also at the club that Farrokh and John D., with the help of a police inspector and his American wife (who witnessed one of Rahul's murders twenty years earlier), set a trap for Rahul and bring the murders to an end. Throughout the narrative, Farrokh's active imagination keeps playing tricks on him, proposing fictional alternatives to what is actually taking place. Unlike the Inspector Dhar series, however, Farrokh's later scenarios will remain unfilmed, upstaged by equally unpredictable reality.

A Widow for One Year • In *A Widow for One Year,* Irving centers his narration around Ruth Cole, a successful American novelist whose career in some respects reflects his own, as well as that of the fictional T. S. Garp. The tale begins in 1958 when Ruth is four years old, having been conceived as the "replacement" for two adolescent brothers recently killed in a freak auto accident. Her father, Ted Cole, a successsful writer and illustrator of children's books, is also a womanizer and a borderline alcoholic; Ruth's mother, Marion, has put her own literary ambitions aside in favor of her husband's career. By 1958, however, a trial separation is under way; Ted has moved out of their house and hired sixteen-year-old Eddie O'Hare to serve as his driver and secretary. True to form, however, Ted has an ulterior motive: Eddie, it seems, bears a strong resemblance to the Coles' lost sons, and Ted believes Eddie might fall unwittingly into the role of Marion's lover, which he does.

Marion, meanwhile, plans simply to leave Long Island for good, destination unknown. Rearing Ruth with the help of a Latin couple formerly employed by one of his ex-mistresses, Ted has stopped writing, having depended first upon the boys and later upon Ruth for questions that would generate new stories. To stay in shape, he plays endless games of squash in a court above his detached garage. In *A Widow for One Year,* squash, for obvious reasons, replaces wrestling as the sport of choice and contest.

Eddie O'Hare, forever marked by his idyll with Marion, reaches a modest level of success with novels about the love of a young man for a woman old enough to be his mother. Throughout the novel, the implication of incest, or incest-by-proxy, is never far from the characters' minds.

By 1990, the next year of her life to be portrayed in depth, Ruth, a novelist, has long since become even better known as a writer than her father: a mainstream novelist with strong popular appeal, not unlike a female John Irving. Ted, at the age of seventy-seven, is still playing squash and chasing younger women. Marion, true to her word, has been out of sight since 1958 and, as far as Ruth and Ted are concerned, might well have died in the meantime. Eddie O'Hare, however, suspects that Marion is living in Canada, publishing mystery novels under her mother's maiden name. It is in 1990 that Ruth and Eddie meet again, for the first time as adults. Eddie helps to fill many of the gaps in Ruth's memory of Marion. Now in her mid-thirties, Ruth is contemplating marriage for the first time, in part to experience motherhood, and remains puzzled by her mother's disappearance from her life. Ruth emerges from the conversation inclined to accept the marriage proposal of her editor, Allan Albright, eighteen years her senior and divorced.

Ruth learns that her father has taken his own life by literally running himself to death on the squash court while his Volvo idled in the garage below. His suicide, presumably provoked by a quarrel with Ruth over his sleeping with her best friend, apparently frees Ruth to marry Allan, with whom she will soon have a son, named Graham after the British novelist Graham Greene. Allan dies in his sleep when the boy is three years old, thus bringing Ruth a widowhood predicted by one of her angry detractors on the lecture circuit. Within a year, however, Ruth meets her second husband, an Amsterdam policeman. As it happens, the recently retired Harry Hoekstra is a voracious reader, favoring mysteries but also fond of such authors as Ruth Cole and even Eddie O'Hare. He is also familiar with the Canadian mysteries of Alice Somerset, now known by Eddie and Ruth to be the pseudonymous Marion Cole. Ruth and Eddie, meanwhile, remain concerned that nothing has managed to lure Marion out of hiding; what finally does coax her out is Ruth's decision to sell Ted's house so that she can move to Vermont with Graham and Harry. Marion does in fact come back to Eddie, with whom she will share the cost of the house, thus keeping it "in the family" for the foreseeable future.

As in *The World According to Garp*, the narrative of *A Widow for One Year* is frequently interrupted by excerpts of prose attributed to one or another of the main characters—short stories or fragments of novels by Ruth, children's books by Ted, even detective fiction ascribed to "Alice Somerset." Like other Irving protagonists, including the frustrated novelist-scenarist Farrokh Daruwalla, M.D., Ruth Cole exemplifies the creative tension between invention and experience in the writing process, a subject Irving treats at some length in the title essay of *Trying to Save Piggy Sneed*. Arguably, Ruth's childhood "reconstructions" of the lives of her dead brothers, together with her efforts to fill the void left by Marion's long absence, have turned her into a "natural" writer, a person for whom creative writing is less an option than a need.

Nancy Walker
Updated by David B. Parsell

Other major works

SCREENPLAY: *The Cider House Rules*, 1999.

NONFICTION: *The Imaginary Girlfriend*, 1996; *My Movie Business: A Memoir*, 1999.

CHILDREN'S LITERATURE: *A Sound Like Someone Trying Not to Make a Sound*, 2004 (illustrated by Tatjana Hauptmann).

MISCELLANEOUS: *Trying to Save Piggy Sneed*, 1996.

Bibliography

Campbell, Josie R. *John Irving: A Critical Companion*. Westport, Conn.: Greenwood Press, 1998. Part of the Critical Companions to Popular Contemporary Writers series, Campbell's book covers Irving's career through *A Widow for One Year*, showing both the popular and the literary sources and appeal of his novels.

Harter, Carol C., and James R. Thompson. *John Irving*. Boston: Twayne, 1986. Part of the Twayne United States Authors series, this clearly written study of Irving's fiction through *The Cider House Rules* emphasizes the mixture of popular and artistic appeal in the novels. The volume includes an annotated bibliography.

Johnson, Brian D. "Iron John: Stepping into the Lion's Den with John Irving, Our Almost-Canadian Writer, Wrestler, and Macho-Feminist Guy." *Maclean's* 114, no. 30 (July, 2001): 40. Brief but interesting Canadian perspective on Irving.

Miller, Gabriel. *John Irving*. New York: Frederick Ungar, 1982. Part of the Ungar Modern Literature series, this is a useful biographical and critical study of Irving's career through *The Hotel New Hampshire*. It includes a chronology through 1982, a 1981 interview with Irving, and a bibliography of both primary and secondary sources.

Priestley, Michael. "Structure in the Worlds of John Irving." *Critique* 23, no. 1 (1981): 82-96. Priestley analyzes the ways the novelist—and his characters—seek to impose order on their fictional worlds in Irving's first four novels.

Reilly, Edward C. *Understanding John Irving.* Columbia: University of South Carolina Press, 1991. A concise exposition of Irving's work through *A Prayer for Owen Meany*, Reilly's volume is part of a continuing series devoted to world literature and situates Irving's work with regard to both British and continental traditions.

Van Gelder, Lindsy. Review of *A Widow for One Year*, by John Irving. *The Nation* 127 (May 11, 1998): 52-55. A thoughtful feminist reading of Irving's sole novel with a female protagonist, Van Gelder's review ends on an unexpectedly positive, if still ironic, note.

Henry James

Born: New York, New York; April 15, 1843
Died: London, England; February 28, 1916

Principal long fiction • *Roderick Hudson*, 1876; *The American*, 1876-1877; *An International Episode*, 1878-1879 (novella); *Daisy Miller*, 1878; *The Europeans*, 1878; *Confidence*, 1879-1880; *The Portrait of a Lady*, 1880-1881; *Washington Square*, 1880; *The Bostonians*, 1885-1886; *The Princess Casamassima*, 1885-1886; *The Reverberator*, 1888; *The Tragic Muse*, 1889-1890; *The Awkward Age*, 1897-1899; *The Spoils of Poynton*, 1897; *What Maisie Knew*, 1897; *In the Cage*, 1898; *The Turn of the Screw*, 1898; *The Sacred Fount*, 1901; *The Wings of the Dove*, 1902; *The Ambassadors*, 1903; *The Golden Bowl*, 1904; *The Outcry*, 1911; *The Ivory Tower*, 1917; *The Sense of the Past*, 1917.

Other literary forms • Fiction was assuredly where Henry James's essential talent and interest lay, and it was the form to which he devoted almost all of his literary efforts. His more than twenty novels (the count is inexact because some of his middle-length pieces, such as *The Turn of the Screw* and *Daisy Miller*, can be categorized as novellas) and roughly 112 tales attest his lifetime of dedication to this genre. Despite this clear emphasis on fiction, however, James was seduced by his desire to regain his lost popularity with the general public and his wish to attempt a kind of writing that he had studied for many years, writing drama. For a five-year period, from 1890 to 1895, he concentrated on playwriting; during this time he wrote no novels but continued to publish short stories. Although his failure to gain a public with his plays somewhat embittered James (an emotion that has been exaggerated by some biographers; he always had loyal and appreciative readers and friends), he never lost confidence in the legitimacy of his art, and he returned to fiction with what many scholars believe to be a stronger, more ambitious inspiration, resulting in what has been called the "major phase" of his writing. It is perhaps indicative of the primacy of fiction in James's career that his most successful play was *The American* (1891), an adaptation of his earlier novel.

Unlike many creative writers, James produced an enormous volume of critical writings, chiefly literary, in which he not only studied the works of other authors (the most noteworthy are Nathaniel Hawthorne, Walt Whitman, Ralph Waldo Emerson, Ivan Turgenev, Gustave Flaubert, George Eliot, Anthony Trollope, Robert Louis Stevenson, Honoré de Balzac, and Guy de Maupassant) but also performed a detailed analysis of his own work. This latter effort appears primarily in the form of the prefaces to the New York edition (1907-1909) of his novels and tales. Inasmuch as the New York edition occupies twenty-six volumes, these prefaces provide a considerable body of critical material that has proved to be of great value to James scholars. His often reprinted essay "The Art of Fiction" (1884) presents his general theories on the art. Aside from his literary criticism, James wrote numerous studies and critiques on other subjects, such as painting (which greatly interested him) and travel.

In the late twentieth century, James's books and travel sketches attained critical admiration for their graceful style and penetrating insight into times that have gone and places that will never be the same. As might be expected, his studies of Italy,

France, and England (the foreign countries that most intrigued him) are detailed and entertaining. More surprising is his finest work in this genre, *The American Scene* (1907), the fruit of a long visit to the United States; he toured the country extensively (partly to visit friends and places that he had not seen and others that he had not been to for a long time, and partly to deliver lectures on literary topics). His account of America at the turn of the century fuses the poignance of a native's return with the distance and objectivity of a European perspective.

Achievements • James was the first American novelist to bring to the form a sense of artistic vocation comparable to Flaubert's. Except for the wide popularity of *Daisy Miller*, which appealed to audiences both in Europe and in the United States, no work of James achieved a

Library of Congress

wide readership in his lifetime. This fact, though it caused him pain, did not impel this most discriminating of writers to lower his standards in order to appeal to a mass audience. Those who did appreciate his work tended to be the better educated, more sophisticated readers, though even some of these occasionally had blind spots concerning James's novels—his brother William, for example, once wrote to James that his fiction was "bloodless." Except for the disastrous essay into drama, James adhered to his principles, always convinced that what he was doing would improve the quality of the novel and even raise the standards of conscientious readers. Events after his death have proved him right.

With the growth of courses of study in modern American literature, James earned the wide readership that was denied him during his lifetime, and after World War II, critical studies and biographical works devoted to him proliferated in staggering numbers. This is not to say that James is without his critics. He has frequently been criticized for a lack of scope and feeling, for concentrating his formidable talents on the psychological maneuverings of the privileged few. His later style has often been judged impenetrable, grotesquely mannered—though some critics regard his late novels as the highest achievements of the novelist's art, unsurpassed before or since.

There can be no question of James's influence on the subsequent course of the novel. He refined the novelistic art, purified it, and gave it directions never thought of before his time. Four areas of emphasis have especially attracted scholars in their attempts to isolate the essential contributions to the art of fiction with which James can be credited: point of view, psychological realism, style, and the connection of moral and aesthetic values. Throughout his career, James experimented with the varieties of consciousness (the word can be found everywhere in his fiction and criticism) through which stories can be told. The completely objective point of view, in which the reader is presented solely with what anyone present would see and hear, and the first-person point of view, in which a character tells the story as he perceives it, were both traditional, and James used them frequently.

As James's writing became more complex and dense, though, he endeavored to relate the action more in terms of what goes on in people's minds, the most impressive example of such a "center of consciousness" being Lambert Strether in *The Ambassadors*. As Percy Lubbock noted as early as 1921 in *The Craft of Fiction*, James achieves in *The Ambassadors* a point of view remarkable for its appropriateness to the story told and astounding in its focus on Lambert Strether's consciousness, which is made possible by James's using the third-person limited point of view but relating the hero's thoughts and feelings in a way that he himself could never manage—in short, the reader sees Strether's perceptions both from the inside and from the outside, with James gently guiding attention to the more important features of Strether's cognition. This sort of advanced work in viewpoint did two important things: It helped to prepare the way for the stream-of-consciousness novel, and it deepened the psychological realism that was to be James's chief intellectual contribution to the novel form.

Realism was in the literary air when James was starting out as a writer, but he focused his attention on fidelity to the movements of consciousness in a way that no previous writer had done. In a James novel, what is most significant is not what transpires in the plot, per se, but rather the attitudes and emotions and discoveries that unfold in the consciousnesses of the characters. Even in a work in the objective mode, such as *The Awkward Age*, which consists almost entirely of dialogue, what interests the attentive reader is the tides of feeling and realization that are implied by the speech. James appreciated the realistic aspects of the novels of Stendhal, Balzac, and Flaubert, but he resisted the naturalistic emphasis on the scientific and empirical—he believed Émile Zola to be misguided and unliterary. Indeed, James became a necessary counterfoil to this powerful literary movement in the later years of the nineteenth century.

As a stylist, James introduced the scrupulous craftsmanship of Flaubert to English-language readers. Like Flaubert, he weighed every phrase, every nuance of diction and rhythm, every comma. Indeed, for James, style was a moral imperative. Joseph Conrad, a great admirer of James (the feeling was reciprocated, but with less enthusiasm), once asserted that the American writer was "the historian of fine consciences." Certainly, no one who reads James closely could fail to note the delicate but constant attention paid to right and wrong in the novels. What might escape detection, however, is that James evidently believed that ethics are, in somewhat intricate ways, related to aesthetics. This does not mean that all the "good" characters are beautiful and the evil ones ugly. On the contrary, in many instances, physically attractive characters such as Christina Light (*Roderick Hudson*) and Kate Croy (*The Wings of the Dove*) are sources of much wickedness (such characters are also usually very charming); while less prepossessing ones, such as Madame Grandoni (*The Princess Casamassima*) and Henrietta Stackpole (*The Portrait of a Lady*), appear to represent the forces of virtue.

The true relationship between beauty and morality in James rests on his evident conviction that those elements of life that are positive and benevolent, such as freedom and personal development, have within them great beauty—and James takes considerable pains to express these qualities fully and with impressive aesthetic form. The appreciation of Fleda Vetch, in *The Spoils of Poynton*, for the beautiful appurtenances and objets d'art of the country house in the title constitutes, to some degree, a basis for the acts of renunciation and self-effacement that provide evidence of her virtue. Ever determined not to oversimplify, James offers such concatenations cautiously. This most subtle of moralists was equally understated in his presentation of beauty, revealing the ways in which it can conceal evil as well as the ways in which it can enrich life and give it greater meaning. After reading James, one cannot doubt the sincerity of his avowal, in his 1915 letter to H. G. Wells, that "It is art that *makes* life, makes interest, makes importance, for our consideration and application of these things, and I know of no substitute whatever for the force and beauty of its process."

Biography • If one wished to create for oneself a background and early life that was appropriate for preparing to be an important and dedicated American novelist during the later years of the nineteenth century and the early years of the twentieth, one might very well choose just the sort of family and early experience that fate created for Henry James. The family circumstances were comfortable (his grandfather, William James, had amassed one of the three largest fortunes in New York), and his father, Henry James, Sr., his mother, Mary Robertson Walsh James, his older brother, William, and his younger siblings, Garth Wilkinson, Robertson, and Alice, were all lively, articulate, and stimulating. It has been speculated that the very effervescence of his siblings helped to develop in Henry a tendency toward observation rather than participation, a trait that may have contributed to his decision never to marry and certainly helped to lead him to the vocation to which he devoted his life.

Another important feature of James's youth was his father's belief in the merit of unsystematic but broadly based education. The future novelist thus enjoyed the benefits of instruction by tutors as well as in excellent European institutions (made possible by a four-year stay, 1855-1858, on the Continent, in Switzerland, England, and France). Early on, the elder Henry James, an unorthodox philosopher and writer, observed of his son that "Harry is not so fond of study, properly so-called, as of reading. He is a devourer of libraries." The fact that this parent was not insistent on a more traditional attitude toward education is to his credit; though James was largely self-educated (his only true conventional schooling was a brief period at Harvard Law School, in 1862-1863)—resulting in some ignorances of extended areas of knowledge, such as the sciences, and in specialized concentrations, represented by his phenomenally wide reading in nineteenth century fiction but in little literature written before that era—it is generally agreed that he was one of the best informed of the major literary men of his time.

Apart from several later trips to Europe, which finally led him to the decision to move there in 1875 and to remain there for the rest of his life (except for a number of trips to America, where he never established a home), James led, for his first thirty years, a largely domestic life in the family circle. In his early twenties he had decided to become a writer; his initial publication is thought to be an unsigned story that appeared in 1864. This was the first of an endless stream of tales, reviews, essays, and novels (James became so proficient at French that he also translated a few works, which achieved publication); even during the period of his attempts to write plays he was turning out short pieces regularly. He was closely attached to his older brother William, a relationship that endured until William's death, in 1910, and to Alice and his cousin Mary ("Minny") Temple, whom James thought to be "the very heroine of our common scene." This charming young lady may have been the only real romantic love of James's life—it has been suggested that her death at the age of twenty-four, in 1870, had much to do with James's resolution never to marry—and he immortalized her in Milly Theale, the ailing heroine of *The Wings of the Dove*, and perhaps in all the bright, appealing American girls who come to grief in his novels.

James was never very close to his younger brothers, a fact that has been attributed partly to his inability to serve in the army during the Civil War (because of "an obscure hurt," which was probably nothing more dramatic than a back injury—James had a painful back for all of his early manhood), in which "Wilky" and "Bob" fought, but also to the fact that he was simply temperamentally unsuited to association with these essentially unhappy men, both of whom died before him. Alice James became an invalid. The element of sadness in these three lives underlines the note of tragedy that can be found in much of James's fiction. There is no reason to doubt that, when James wrote to a friend, in 1896, "I have the imagination of disaster—and see life indeed as ferocious and sinister," he had had this grim attitude for many years, perhaps from as far back as his youth. Certainly, touches of the sinister abound in his novels.

After James's removal to Europe, the rest of his life became chiefly a matter of hard work, important friendships with literary figures (he seems to have known nearly everyone of importance in French and English belles lettres of his time, from Stevenson to George Sand, from George Eliot to Zola—and he wrote many essays about their work), and extraordinary ranges of travel. After a year in Paris, in 1875, James decided that his art would flourish more fully in England, where he took up residence, first in London, later in Rye, Sussex. He chose this relatively remote location because, he claimed, the vigorous social life of London was draining his energy and time from writing—typically, though, it is known that he greatly enjoyed that social contact, once boasting that during a single winter he dined out 107 times. Despite the claims of some critics and biographers—most notably Van Wyck Brooks, in *The Pilgrimage of Henry James* (1925)—that James abandoned his native land to become an uncritical lover of Europe and especially of England, a careful reading of his novels reveals that he was very clear-sighted about the weaknesses and flaws in English "high" society.

Whatever one's judgment about the validity of the reasons for James's resolve to live and work in Europe, it is plain that his art was largely determined by the European experience. Abroad, James found what he believed to be lacking in America, at least for a novelist of manners interested in cultural phenomena. In his biography of Hawthorne, James listed, perhaps with tongue at least partly in cheek, those items that could be studied only in Europe, since they did not exist in America: "No sovereign, no court . . . no aristocracy, no church, no clergy, no army, no diplomatic service, no country gentlemen, no palaces, no castles, nor manors, nor old country-houses . . . no literature, no novels, no museums, no pictures, no political society, no sporting class." Though this list offers some hint of James's sense of humor, the works themselves are sure evidence that he was convinced that Europe provided him with indispensable materials for his novels.

James never made a great deal of money from his writing, but he always lived comfortably (he was so confident of his financial security that he turned over his share of the estate of his father, who died in 1882, to Alice). He was a generous friend, both with money and advice, to his many acquaintances and to young writers hoping to succeed. He had what some biographers call a genius for friendship, which his enormous correspondence attests. His fondness for congenial associates, particularly literary ones, did not, however, blind him to their weaknesses nor subdue his pride in his accomplishments. He once wrote home that, as to his friend Flaubert, "I think I easily—more than easily—see all round him intellectually." Such a boast may help to explain James's remarkable adherence to his absolute belief in his powers and in the rightness of his efforts.

While public taste was going in one direction (downward, in his view), James's technique was headed precisely the opposite way. This firmness has since been justified, and even in his lifetime the admiration of such respected writers as Conrad and William Dean Howells did much to console him for his lack of popularity. On James's seventieth birthday, April 15, 1913, some 270 friends presented him with a "golden bowl" and asked him to sit for a portrait by John Singer Sargent (which is now in the National Portrait Gallery, in London). More formal honors were an honorary degree from Harvard University (1911) and one from Oxford (1912); perhaps the most lofty distinction was the Order of Merit, presented to James by King George V, in 1916, the year of the author's death (from heart trouble and pneumonia). This decoration was given in recognition of James's valued service to England during the opening years of World War I; James believed that the United States was dishonorable for not becoming involved.

As death approached—James wrote of it, "So here it is at last, the distinguished thing!"—he was still engaged in writing; he left two unfinished novels, *The Ivory Tower* and *The Sense of the Past*, and a number of unpublished essays and stories, all of which have since been printed. This continuation of his labors right to the end was fitting, for never before, or since, was there a man of whom it is so appropriate to say that his work *was* his life.

Analysis • Henry James's distinctive contributions to the art of the novel were developed over a long career of some fifty years. Leon Edel, possibly the most renowned and respected James scholar, has indicated that James's mature writing can be divided into three periods (with three subdivisions in the middle phase). Through the publication of *The Portrait of a Lady*, in 1880-1881, James was chiefly interested in the now famous "international theme," the learning experiences and conflicts of Americans in Europe and Europeans in America (the former situation being by far the more frequent). This first period is represented by *Roderick Hudson, The American, Daisy Miller*, and *The Portrait of a Lady*; of these *Daisy Miller* and *The Portrait of a Lady* are probably the best examples of James's early work.

The more complex second period falls into three parts. The first, roughly from 1881 through 1890, displays James's concern with social issues (not the sort of topic for which he is known), as in *The Bostonians* and *The Princess Casamassima*, the former about women's rights in the United States and the latter concerning the class struggle in England. The second of these subperiods is that during which he created plays (many of which have never been performed) and produced a variety of short stories.

The final subdivision is that marked by the appearance of short and midlength fictions dealing with the problems of artists in their relationships with society (he had already touched on this subject in *Roderick Hudson*) and of occasionally bizarre stories, such as *The Turn of the Screw* and "The Altar of the Dead," about men, women, and children who are obsessed, haunted, and perhaps insane. Some of these pieces were written during James's calamitous endeavor with drama. The final period, called "the major phase," from about 1896 till the close of his career, shows James returning to the international theme. The themes of this period are most obviously exhibited in the three large novels of his later years: *The Ambassadors* (which was written before the next novel but published after it), *The Wings of the Dove*, and *The Golden Bowl*.

During this extended development and shifting of interests and enthusiasms, James was continuously trying to refine his presentation of character, theme, and event. In his critical writing he stated that he finally recognized the value of "the *indirect* presentation of his main image" (he is here speaking of Milly Theale, in *The Wings of the Dove*, who is seen largely through the eyes of other characters and about whom the reader learns, even of her death, chiefly by report). Several critics, perhaps the most famous being F. R. Leavis, in *The Great Tradition* (1948), believe this "recognition" to be a grave error; they claim that James refined his presentation beyond clear comprehension (thus the common accusation of excessive ambiguity) and eventually beyond interest. Others—perhaps the most salient is F. W. Dupee, in *Henry James* (1951)—aver that these three late novels are James's masterpieces, works in which his study of the complexities of moral decisions reaches an elevation never attained by another author.

Two aspects of James's fiction have received little attention: Not much has been written about his humor, which is usually ironic but often gentle. A fine example is his presentation of Mrs. Lavinia Penniman, the foolish aunt of Catherine Sloper in *Washington Square* and a widow "without fortune—with nothing but the memory of Mr. Penniman's flowers of speech, a certain vague aroma of which hovered about her own conversation." This romantic, meddling woman is depicted by James humorously, but with a clear indication of the harm that her interference causes. The image of her "flowers of speech" suggests another neglected style: the repetition of certain key words and images throughout his canon. Readers can easily become distracted by frequently encountered "flower" images such as the foregoing one and key words such as "figured" (as in "it figured for him"), "lucid" or "lucidly" (as in "he said it lucidly"), "idea" (as in "he had his idea of"), and a phrase such as "She took it in" to signify an understanding of a remark. Also, "theory"—in a phrase such as "She had a theory that"—appears many times. It is not surprising that certain terms might emerge frequently in a canon as large as James's, but his evident affection for particular expressions such as the foregoing ones does seem odd in a writer whose repertoire of verbal expression appears to be boundless. It would, for example, be hard to think of another writer, who, in characterizing the grim conversation of Mrs. Bowerbank, in *The Princess Casamassima*, would be able to suggest it by noting, "her outlook seemed to abound in cheerless contingencies."

All in all, though, there is little of James's subject matter and technique that has escaped the close inspection of scholarship. Possibly the greatest shift of critical emphasis in James scholarship has been the increasing awareness of the moral thrust of his work. Early critics frequently charged that no consistent moral attitude was clearly expressed in his work. In later times, this concern evaporated, with a realization that James was an insightful moralist who understood that general rules are of little use in dealing with complex social and personal situations. He tended to treat each novel as a sort of special problem, to be worked out by the characters. From his total production, though, two "principles" have issued: The author was a firm believer in freedom and in personal development. To become a true hero or heroine in a James novel, a character must achieve a state of self-realization (again, an acute act of consciousness is needed), must recognize the truth and face it bravely, must act freely (without emotional dependence on others), and must renounce any personal gain in order to promote the welfare of others. In this way, the person attains true personal development and achieves as much freedom as James believed the world could offer—he did not subscribe to the doctrine that human liberty is unlimited. The basic moral conflict in his novels is essentially between powerful, often heartless or thoughtless, oppressors, such as Gilbert Osmond in *The Portrait of a Lady* and Olive Chancellor in *The Bostonians*, and their "victims," such as Isabel Archer, in the former work, and Verena Tarrant, in the latter.

James's reputation, already high, is continuing to rise and is likely to continue to do so. The dramatizations of several of his works in the cinema (*Daisy Miller, The Europeans, Washington Square, The Portrait of a Lady*, and *The Wings of the Dove*) and on television (*The Ambassadors, The Turn of the Screw*, "The Author of Beltraffio," *The Spoils of Poynton*, and *The Golden Bowl*) are perhaps superficial indices of increasing acclaim, but the burgeoning of critical attention is not. There is no question that James belongs, in F. R. Leavis's phrase, squarely in the "great tradition" of the novel.

Daisy Miller • *Daisy Miller*, which established James's reputation as a leading novelist both in England and the United States, announces several of his recurring themes and motifs. The story is an uncomplicated one, from the standpoint of plot. Frederick Winterbourne, a sophisticated young American who lives in Europe, meets Daisy Miller, who is visiting Europe with her mother and younger brother; Mr. Miller is back in Schenectady, New York, presumably making enough money to allow his family to travel comfortably. The essence of the novella is the relationship that develops between the young, cosmopolitan expatriate (a not uncommon type in James's fiction) and the pretty, naïve, and willful girl.

In *Daisy Miller* a central issue is whether Winterbourne could have prevented the tragedy that ends Daisy's life. As he gets to know her better and comes to like her, he becomes increasingly distressed at Daisy's refusal to heed the warnings of Mrs. Costello, his aunt, and Mrs. Walker, another Europeanized American society matron (it is significant that the people who most condemn Daisy are not native Europeans but expatriates). Daisy stubbornly continues to consort with the gigolo Giovanelli, who is seen with her all about Rome, much to the dismay of the society people, who are scandalized by such "loose" behavior—even the Romans joke about it in a subdued fashion, which only irritates Winterbourne the more. He tries to warn Daisy that she is seen too much with Giovanelli—"Everyone thinks so"—but she refuses to take his cautions seriously: "I don't believe a word of it. They're only pretending to be shocked. They don't really care a straw what I do." This perverse attitude finally leads to Daisy's death, when she goes, against Winterbourne's urging, to the Colosseum at night (a place that, after dark, was reputed to have a miasma often fatal to foreigners) and contracts a mortal fever. When Winterbourne angrily asks Giovanelli why he took Daisy to such a dangerous place, the Italian answers, "*she*—she did what she liked."

The complexity of the moral nuances of the story is revealed when one remembers that Winterbourne, who is regarded as quite the perfect young gentleman and is welcomed in the best society, has a mistress back in Geneva. Clearly, in that "best" society what matters is not virtue (Daisy is quite guiltless of any actual wrongdoing) but the appearance of it—Winterbourne may not be virtuous, but he is discreet. The old theme of appearance versus reality thus emerges in this story, but with social implications not found in the work of other authors. To James, one of the most difficult problems for Americans trying to come to terms with Europe is that the appearance of virtue often counts for more than the reality. This problem is seen quite plainly in *The Reverberator*, written ten years later, in which an American businessman is puzzled that a French family is upset over some scandalous things said about them in a newspaper; so far as he is concerned, such things do not matter so long as they are not true.

James's realism is most evident in the close of the story. Winterbourne is remorseful over Daisy's death. He regrets that he did not try harder to understand her and correct her misconceptions. He tells his aunt, "She would have appreciated one's esteem." Then, he applies the lesson to himself: "I've lived too long in foreign parts." So far, the story has seemed to advance a moral thesis about the corruption of innocence and the valuable truths that can be learned. James closes the novella, however, on a note that proves how realistic his vision of human nature was: "Nevertheless he soon went back to live at Geneva, whence there continue to come the most contradictory accounts of his motives of sojourn: a report that he's 'studying' hard—an intimation that he's much interested in a very clever foreign lady." James had no illusions about people.

The Portrait of a Lady • Although *Daisy Miller* is told in the first person, from Winterbourne's consciousness, *The Portrait of a Lady*, a much longer and more complicated fiction, is related through the minds of a number of characters. This book is probably the most generally admired of all James's full-length novels. It carries the "international theme" to what some consider its highest level of expression, and it offers the reader one of the most impressive characters in James's work, the delightful Isabel Archer, the "lady" of the title. Again, James is psychologically realistic: Although Isabel is honest, intelligent, and sensitive, she is not without fault; she does have "an unquenchable desire to think well of herself." She is an "innocent abroad" who is "affronting her destiny." This fate is to be given, first, the chance to visit Europe (offered by Mrs. Lydia Touchett, her wealthy aunt who lives in Europe) and, then, a great deal of money (provided by the will of Mr. Daniel Touchett, at the suggestion of his son Ralph, who becomes very fond of Isabel). This combination of high connections—Mr. Touchett associates with a number of prominent English families, most significantly that of Lord Warburton—opportunities for travel, and comfortable circumstances is common in James's novels.

In *The Portrait of a Lady*, James studies the relationships of the characters in great detail. When Lord Warburton proposes to Isabel, the situation is examined closely, and her rejection of him prepares for later plot developments and revelations of character. As is often the case with James, the money that Isabel inherits is both a blessing and a curse. It permits her to travel and to live almost lavishly, but it also attracts to her one of the few outright villains in James's fiction. Gilbert Osmond appears to be charming, modest, intelligent, and sensitive. He proves to be proud, arrogant, idle, and cruel. In a powerful enunciation of the international theme, Osmond courts Isabel cleverly, appealing to her sense of the artistic wonders of Europe, of which he seems to be a fine judge. He wins her hand, partly through the efforts of Madame Serena Merle, an American expatriate (as is Osmond) who, Isabel later discovers, was once Osmond's mistress (they could not marry, since neither was wealthy—the topic of marrying for money is one that James explored as thoroughly as any writer ever had and with greater insight). Mme Merle is eager for Osmond to marry well, since they have a daughter, Pansy, whom she wishes to see well placed in the world. With James's usual subtlety and with his use of a device that again proves effective in *The Golden Bowl,* Isabel first suspects the unacknowledged intimacy between Mme Merle and Osmond when she sees them through a window, in a room in which she is standing and he is seated—such social touches mark James's fiction repeatedly; to him, the social graces were a great deal more than simply pleasant decorations on the fringes of human intercourse.

The marriage is a failure. Osmond comes to resent Isabel, and eventually she despises him. In the famous chapter 42, Isabel examines the grim condition of her life. In an extended passage of what is clearly a precursor of the stream-of-consciousness technique, James causes Isabel to review the terrible errors she has made—"It was her deep distrust of her husband—this was what darkened her world"—and to consider how foolish her pride has made her: Ralph Touchett, among others, warned her against Osmond. Isabel's stubbornness and refusal to heed wise advice reminds one of Daisy Miller's similar folly. The plot becomes more complex when Lord Warburton directs his affections to Pansy. Naturally, Osmond is highly in favor of such a marriage, since Warburton is very rich. Isabel incurs her husband's even more intense hatred by discouraging the English peer with the simple argument that he and Pansy do not really love each other. Here, European corruption (expressed in an American expatriate, as is often the case in James's fiction) is opposed to American innocence and emotional integrity.

The conclusion of this novel is among James's most subtle and ambiguous. Isabel returns to England to visit the deathbed of Ralph Touchett. His death has been prepared for by the announcement in the first chapter that he is in poor health. In fact, Ralph is one of James's truly virtuous characters, as is shown by his renunciation of any thought of marrying Isabel, whom he loves, because of his failing physical condition. Isabel admits to Ralph that he was right and that she committed a monumental error in marrying Osmond. Ralph, typically, blames himself for having provided her with the money that tempted Osmond; Isabel refuses this excuse, recognizing that the mistake was her own.

The puzzling aspect of the last pages of the novel is that Isabel determines to go back to Osmond as his wife. Several explanations have been offered, all of them proving the profound depth of James's penetration of human motives. The most dramatic is that Isabel's confrontation with her old lover from America, Casper Goodwood, is so violent—he seizes her and kisses her passionately—that it frightens her (perhaps arousing an unsettling sexuality in her nature) into returning to a life that may be despicable but is safe. Another, more likely reason for the decision is that Isabel has become fond of Pansy and has promised to come back and help her to advance in life along sound and honorable lines. The most subtle reason may be that Isabel is simply too proud to admit her blunder openly to the world, which a separation would do, and prefers to live in misery rather than escape to what she would regard as shame. Whatever the true cause of her resolution (and they might all be operative), she starts back to Rome immediately. In the last passage of the book, however, Isabel's old friend and confidante, Henrietta Stackpole, suggests to Caspar that he must have patience—evidently a hint that this loyal friend of Isabel believes that she will not stay with Osmond forever.

Scholars who believe that James attained the peak of his treatment of the international theme in this novel point to the delicate illumination of Isabel's growing awareness of the sinister undertones of life and to the gallery of superb portraits of ineffectual innocence (as in Ralph, who is all good will and yet helps to ruin Isabel's life), black evil (in Mme Merle and Osmond), and admixtures of positive and negative traits, as in Mrs. Touchett, who is essentially well intentioned but is supremely intransigent (she does not live with the mild-mannered Mr. Touchett, and "the edges of her conduct were so very clear-cut" that they "had a knife-like effect"). Even if the reader is not quite ready to agree with the judgment of F. R. Leavis that this novel, along with *The Bostonians*, is one of "the two most brilliant novels in the language," it seems difficult to deny that *The Portrait of a Lady* is the articulate treatment of the "international theme" in American literature.

The Bostonians • James omitted *The Bostonians* from the New York edition because it deals with purely American subjects, Americans in the United States; it has no trace of the international theme. *The Bostonians* was undervalued by critics as well as by its author, and it has taken many years for readers to recognize the novel as, in Leavis's words, "a wonderfully rich, intelligent and brilliant book." Aside from focusing on a social topic, a rare instance of this emphasis in James, *The Bostonians* also treats skillfully another subject much on his mind during this era: the problems and aberrations of obsessed, disturbed people. The conflict between the old-fashioned conservative southerner, Basil Ransom, and his New England cousin, Olive Chancellor, makes for a novel full of tension and animation. Some of the modern interest in the book results from what has been judged a nearly lesbian relationship between Olive and Verena Tarrant, the attractive girl who is the source of the antagonism. As Irving Howe suggests in his introduction to the Modern Library edition of *The Bostonians* (1956), the fact that people of James's era did not have modern terms of reference such as "lesbian" does not mean that they knew less about these kinds of relationships.

The social problem underlined by the novel is that of women's rights, the difficulty being that women had few of them. Today, the victories that have been won for the right of women to vote, hold office, and the like are taken for granted, but a reading of *The Bostonians* makes clear how much painful and dreary effort went into creating these advances. As usual, however, James treats the issue specifically, in terms of individual people. In discussing the book later, James said that he took too long to get the story going and provided too much background for the characters. Many current readers, however, judge the background both necessary and interesting. It is, for example, important that Ransom be presented in both a positive and negative light, in order to prepare adequately for the somewhat ambiguous resolution of the plot. As a southerner who has come North to practice the law in a location that will provide him with opportunities not available in the war-ravaged South (it is a clever touch that James causes him to be a Civil War veteran, now living in the region populated by his recent enemies; in this way James emphasizes Basil's sense of alienation and loneliness), Ransom is both appealing—he has "a fine head and such magnificent eyes"— and repelling: "He was very long . . . and he looked a little hard and discouraging, like a column of figures."

Ransom proves very hard and discouraging. After he meets Verena Tarrant, the daughter of a "mesmeric healer" of dubious integrity (James's depiction of this character is further evidence of his rich fund of humor), who has become, by some natural inspiration, an eloquent platform speaker on behalf of the movement to extend the rights of women, the stage is set for the great contention. Olive Chancellor reluctantly allows Basil to become acquainted with Verena—by this time, the well-to-do Boston spinster has already been overwhelmed by the innocent charm of the naïve girl. Thus the battle lines are drawn early. Ransom soon realizes that Verena should be married, preferably to him, instead of wasting her life on a fruitless and, in his opinion, misguided cause. Ransom believes that the highest destiny to which a woman can aspire is "to make some honest man happy." He finds a formidable opponent in Olive, whose zeal for reform inspires her widowed sister, Mrs. Luna, who believes the whole movement to be ridiculous (since she is very interested in romantic relationships with men, particularly Ransom, for a time), to remark that "she would reform the solar system if she could get hold of it." The wit that James displays at the expense of the movement may seem to indicate that he too thinks it ridiculous, but, as usual, the author is fair, offering a warm and sensitive picture of Miss Birdseye (a character who caused James to be much criticized in his own time, since many readers believed her to be based closely on a highly respected member of the Peabody family of Boston—James always denied the charge), an old reformer who has been pursuing the cause for decades.

Verena and Basil meet but a handful of times before the climax of the novel, but their dialogues are artfully designed by the author to reveal that Verena, who has been welcomed into Olive's home as a permanent guest (the Boston spinster, while having no gift for oratory herself, is fully committed to Verena's promulgation of the cause—she is also deeply and possessively committed to Verena personally, having once cried passionately, "Promise me not to marry!"), is slowly becoming interested in Ransom. Finally, when he believes that he can afford to marry, a conviction that seems somewhat optimistic, since his career has advanced very slowly, and because his belief is based on the publication of only one essay on political and social philosophy, he proposes to Verena. James has not been widely accused of depending on coincidences in his plots, as Charles Dickens and Thomas Hardy, for example, have been, but a number of them do appear. In this case, Verena turns to Olive and away from Basil chiefly because Miss Birdseye, of whom she is very fond, dies shortly after the proposal.

These circumstances lead to the highly dramatic scene at the Boston Music Hall, where Verena is scheduled to address a large crowd. Ransom, learning of the planned address, arrives, manages to get backstage (to the door of the dressing room, which is guarded by a large Boston policeman, provided by the fearful and distraught Olive), and forcefully urges Verena to go away with him. She ultimately accedes to his coercion (he seizes her and almost pushes her out the door), leaving Olive weeping and desolate. James, in his customary evenhanded dealing with themes and characters, makes it clear that the marriage of Basil and Verena will certainly be anything but "happy ever after." Verena is in tears when she is ushered from the theater by her lover, and in the last sentence of the book, James provides a typically ominous forecast of their future: "It is to be feared that with the union, so far from brilliant, into which she is about to enter, these were not the last she was destined to shed." Many readers find it astonishing that James could have so underrated this penetrating study of social movements and human beings torn between personal loyalties and abstract ideals. The climactic final scene is the most dramatic and lively that James ever wrote. This is, though, clearly not the end of the story. As Conrad has said, "One is never set at rest by Mr. Henry James's novels. His books end as an episode in life ends. You remain with the sense of the life still going on."

The Ambassadors • *The Ambassadors*, which James considered "frankly, quite the best, 'all round,' of my productions," is now generally rated as one of his masterpieces (some critics believe it to be far and away the most accomplished work of the major phase). Like many of his novels, it was based on an incident in real life. In his notebooks, James recalls being told of a visit that his old friend William Dean Howells made to Paris in his later years. According to the anecdote, told to James by Jonathan Sturges, Howells, overcome by the beauty of Paris, remarked to his youthful friend, "Oh, you are young, you are young—be glad of it: be glad of it and *live*. Live all you can: it's a mistake not to." This passage, and the rest of the speech, is almost word-for-word that made by the middle-aged Lambert Strether, the hero of *The Ambassadors*, to Little Bilham (a character thought to have been based on Sturges) in the beautiful Parisian garden of the artist Gloriani (a character carried over from *Roderick Hudson*; James sometimes became so interested in a character that he revived him for a later novel).

Strether is indeed an "ambassador." He has been given the unenviable assignment (by his formidable patroness, Mrs. Abel Newsome) of persuading her son, Chadwick Newsome, to return to his family and commercial responsibilities in Woollett, Massachusetts (probably representing Worcester, Massachusetts). The primary subject of this novel is joie de vivre; this quality is just what Strether finds when he arrives in Paris, where he has not been since he was a young man. It has been observed that one of the salient aspects of James's fiction is irony. Nowhere is this quality more in evidence than in *The Ambassadors*. Chad Newsome, Strether discovers, has been made a gracious gentleman by his life in Paris; Strether, charmed by the beauty and enchantment of the city, cannot in good conscience urge Chad to leave delightful Paris for dull Woollett. The irony lies in the fact that Chad is quite willing and, finally, eager to return home to make a great deal of money (the family business is very successful; it manufactures some useful article that is, typically, unidentified by James), while Strether longs to remain in Paris. Indeed, his delay in dispatching Chad home impels Mrs. Newsome to send her intimidating daughter, Mrs. Sarah Pocock, and her husband to take up the commission, since Strether has evidently failed. Thus the forces of philistinism are present, enlivening the conflict.

This conflict is chiefly in the mind of Strether, since, in this novel, James undertook to employ the third-person limited point of view to its fullest effect. As usual, the situation is not as simple as it appears. It is not merely residence in Paris that has "civilized" Chad; it has also been his mistress, Mme Marie de Vionnet. Strether, before he knows of the intimacy between his young friend and this sophisticated and charming lady, develops an intense admiration and affection for her. Even after he learns of the liaison, accidentally seeing the two rowing on a river near an inn where they are staying, Strether is still entranced by Marie de Vionnet. When Chad decides to return home and abandon his mistress (who has been reviled, to Strether's dismay, by Mrs. Pocock, who refers to Chad's relationship with her as "hideous"), Strether recognizes her tragedy ("You are fighting for your life!") and is extremely sympathetic. He has, however, his own problems. Thanks to Mrs. Newsome's already aroused suspicions and Sarah Pocock's expected damning report, Strether sees that his comfortable position in Woollett (and possibly eventual marriage to his widowed employer) is very likely gone: "It probably *was* all at an end."

The renunciation theme, so prominent in James's novels, is perhaps more powerfully formulated at the close of this novel than in any other of his books. Despite the appeal of Paris, and the hinted offer of an agreeable marriage to Maria Gostrey, an

American expatriate who had befriended Strether when he first landed in Europe, this highly moral and responsible man resolves to return to Woollett, where he believes his duty to lie. He cannot help Mme de Vionnet. He cannot help himself. This sort of ethical resolution may seem foolish to modern readers, but it is believable in the novel, and the circumstances suggest James's belief that, in current terms, there is a price tag on everything, even happiness. The novel, then, is not only a tribute to Paris and the life of cultural elevation that it can provide but also the necessity of responsible and considerate action. James admitted that he learned a great deal from George Eliot; he shared her conviction that duty is absolute in the ethical universe. The temptation of Strether is almost overwhelming, but his New England sense of duty compels him to conquer it. It is difficult to think of another novelist, or, indeed, another novel, that illuminates so brightly the significance of conscientious moral choices.

Henry James's contributions to the evolution of the modern novel are of staggering magnitude and diversity. Perhaps his greatest contribution was best summed up by Ezra Pound shortly after James's death: "Peace comes of communication. No man of our time has so labored to create means of communication as did the late Henry James. The whole of great art is a struggle for communication."

Fred B. McEwen

Other major works

SHORT FICTION: *A Passionate Pilgrim*, 1875; *The Madonna of the Future*, 1879; *The Siege of London*, 1883; *Tales of Three Cities*, 1884; *The Author of Beltraffio*, 1885; *The Aspern Papers*, 1888; *The Lesson of the Master*, 1892; *The Private Life, Lord Beaupre, The Visits*, 1893; *The Real Thing*, 1893; *Terminations*, 1895; *Embarrassments*, 1896; *The Two Magics: The Turn of the Screw and Covering End*, 1898; *The Soft Side*, 1900; *The Better Sort*, 1903; *The Novels and Tales of Henry James*, 1907-1909 (24 volumes); *The Finer Grain*, 1910; *A Landscape Painter*, 1919; *Travelling Companions*, 1919; *Master Eustace*, 1920; *Stories of Writers and Other Artists*, 1944; *Henry James: Selected Short Stories*, 1950; *Henry James: Eight Tales from the Major Phase*, 1958; *The Complete Tales of Henry James*, 1962-1965 (12 volumes; Leon Edel, editor); *The Figure in the Carpet, and Other Stories*, 1986; *The Jolly Corner, and Other Tales*, 1990; *The Uncollected Henry James: Newly Discovered Stories*, 2004.

PLAYS: *Daisy Miller*, pb. 1883 (adaptation of his novel); *The American*, pr. 1891, pb. 1949 (adaptation of his novel); *Guy Domville*, pb. 1894, privately; pr. 1895, pb. 1949; *The Reprobate*, pb. 1894, pr. 1919; *Theatricals: Tenants and Disengaged*, pb. 1894; *Theatricals, Second Series: The Album and The Reprobate*, pb. 1895; *The High Bid*, pr. 1908, pb. 1949; *The Other House*, wr. 1909, pb. 1949; *The Outcry*, wr. 1909, pr. 1917, pb. 1949; *The Saloon*, pr. 1911, pb. 1949 (one act); *The Complete Plays of Henry James*, pb. 1949 (Leon Edel, editor).

NONFICTION: *Transatlantic Sketches*, 1875; *French Poets and Novelists*, 1878; *Hawthorne*, 1879; *Portraits of Places*, 1883; *A Little Tour in France*, 1884; *The Art of Fiction*, 1884; *Partial Portraits*, 1888; *Essays in London*, 1893; *William Wetmore Story and His Friends*, 1903; *English Hours*, 1905; *The American Scene*, 1907; *Views and Reviews*, 1908; *Italian Hours*, 1909; *A Small Boy and Others*, 1913 (memoirs); *Notes of a Son and Brother*, 1914 (memoirs); *Notes on Novelists*, 1914; *The Middle Years*, 1917; *The Art of the Novel: Critical Prefaces*, 1934 (R. P. Blackmur, editor); *The Notebooks of Henry James*, 1947 (F. O.

Matthiessen and Kenneth B. Murdock, editors); *The Scenic Art,* 1948 (Allan Wade, editor); *Henry James Letters,* 1974-1984 (5 volumes; Leon Edel, editor); *Henry James: Literary Criticism,* 1984; *The Art of Criticism: Henry James on the Theory and Practice of Fiction,* 1986; *The Complete Notebooks of Henry James,* 1987; *Dear Munificent Friends: Henry James's Letters to Four Women,* 1999 (Susan E. Gunter, editor); *Henry James on Culture: Collected Essays on Politics and the American Social Scene,* 1999 (Pierre A. Walker, editor); *Dearly Beloved Friends: Henry James's Letters to Younger Men,* 2001 (Susan E. Gunter and Steven H. Jobe, editors).

Bibliography

Anesko, Michael. *"Friction with the Market": Henry James and the Profession of Authorship.* New York: Oxford University Press, 1986. A thoughtful and well-researched specialized study. Covers with great skill the social and economic aspects of James's career as a novelist, essayist, dramatist, and critic. Erudite but still quite useful for the general reader.

Bailie, Ronnie. *The Fantastic Anatomist: A Psychoanalytic Study of Henry James.* Atlanta: Rodopi, 2000. A look at James and his works from the psychological perspective. Bibliography and index.

Bloom, Harold, ed. *Henry James.* New York: Chelsea House, 1987. Bloom has compiled what he considers the best in criticism available on James, presented in order of original publication. Contains much insight from knowledgeable sources on this important American novelist.

Flannery, Denis. *Henry James: A Certain Illusion.* Brookfield, Vt.: Ashgate, 2000. An analysis of illusion in the works of James. Bibliography and index.

Freedman, Jonathan, ed. *The Cambridge Companion to Henry James.* New York: Cambridge University Press, 1998. A reference work that provides extensive information on James's life and literary influences and also details his works and the characters contained in them. Bibliography and index.

Greenwood, Christopher. *Adapting to the Stage: Theatre and the Work of Henry James.* Burlington, Vt.: Ashgate, 2000. An analysis of James's dramatic works and of his works that have been adapted for the stage. Bibliography and index.

Harden, Edgard F. *A Henry James Chronology.* New York: Palgrave Macmillan, 2005. Detailed chronology of James's life and work.

Moore, Harry Thornton. *Henry James.* New York: Thames and Hudson, 1999. A biography that covers the life and works of James.

Nettels, Elsa. *Language and Gender in American Fiction: Howells, James, Wharton, and Cather.* Charlottesville: University Press of Virginia, 1997. Elsa Nettels examines American writers struggling with the problems of patriarchy.

Novick, Sheldon M. *Henry James: The Young Master.* New York: Random House, 1996. A controversial biography that provoked considerable debate. Novick explores James's career up to *The Portrait of a Lady,* delving more daringly into James's sexual life than other biographers. Includes notes and bibliography.

Pollak, Vivian R., ed. *New Essays on "Daisy Miller" and "The Turn of the Screw."* Cambridge, England: Cambridge University Press, 1993. Includes feminist and psychological approaches as well as a study of the stories in the context of the Victorian period. Contains an introduction and bibliography.

Rawlings, Peter. *Henry James and the Abuse of the Past.* New York: Palgrave Macmillan, 2005. Exploration of James's distortions of Civil War stories in his autobiographical and fictional writings by one of the leading British Henry James scholars.

Rowe, John Carlos. *The Other Henry James.* Durham, N.C.: Duke University Press, 1998. A biography of James that examines his political and social views and looks at his portrayal of gender and sex roles.

Stevens, Hugh. *Henry James and Sexuality.* New York: Cambridge University Press, 1998. A study of sexuality as it presents itself in James's work, including homosexuality and sex roles. Bibliography and index.

Tambling, Jeremy. *Henry James.* New York: St. Martin's Press, 2000. From the series Critical Issues. Includes bibliographical references and an index.

Sarah Orne Jewett

Born: South Berwick, Maine; September 3, 1849
Died: South Berwick, Maine; June 24, 1909

Principal long fiction • *Deephaven*, 1877 (linked sketches); *A Country Doctor*, 1884; *A Marsh Island*, 1885; *The Country of the Pointed Firs*, 1896; *The Tory Lover*, 1901.

Other literary forms • In addition to her novels, Sarah Orne Jewett wrote several collections of short stories and sketches, most of which were published initially in periodicals such as *The Atlantic Monthly*. The best-known of these collections are *Old Friends and New* (1879), *Country By-Ways* (1881), *A White Heron, and Other Stories* (1886), and *The King of Folly Island and Other People* (1888). Jewett also wrote a series of children's books, including *Play Days: A Book of Stories for Children* (1878), *The Story of the Normans* (1887), and *Betty Leicester: A Story for Girls* (1890). The posthumous *Verses: Printed for Her Friends* was published in 1916. Finally, Jewett was a voluminous writer of letters. Among the collections of her private correspondence are the *Letters of Sarah Orne Jewett* (1911), edited by Annie Fields, and the *Sarah Orne Jewett Letters* (1956), edited by Richard Cary.

Achievements • Jewett is remembered today as perhaps the most successful of the dozens of so-called "local-color" or "regional" writers who flourished in the United States from approximately 1870 to 1900. She is especially noted for her remarkable depictions of the farmers and fishermen of Maine coastal villages at the end of the nineteenth century. Although Jewett was writing from firsthand observation (she was born and reared in Maine), she was not one of the common folk of whom she wrote. Wealthy, articulate, and well-read, Jewett was an avid traveler who moved within prominent literary circles. Her sophistication imbued her best work with a polish and a degree of cosmopolitanism that renders it both readable and timeless; as a result, Jewett's reputation has been preserved long after the names of most other regional writers have been forgotten. Jewett is also regarded as something of a technical innovator. As modern critics of fiction attempt to establish specific criteria for novels and short stories, Jewett's best work—notably her classic *The Country of the Pointed Firs*—is seen as straddling both fictional categories. As such, her work is of great interest to contemporary literary theorists.

Biography • Sarah Orne Jewett was born in South Berwick, Maine, on September 3, 1849, the second of three daughters of a country doctor. The colonial mansion in which she was born and reared had been purchased and lavishly furnished by her paternal grandfather, Theodore Furber Jewett, a sea captain turned shipowner and merchant whose fortune enabled Sarah to live in comfort and to travel and write at leisure throughout her life. Her father and maternal grandfather were both practicing physicians who early imbued Sarah with a love of science and an interest in studying human behavior, as well as a passion for literature. Her formal education was surprisingly sporadic: Because she had little patience with classroom procedures and tended to be sickly, her father generally permitted Sarah to be absent from her elementary school and to accompany him on his medical rounds in the Berwick area. This proved to be an education in itself, for her father spoke to her of literature and history, the two fields that became the great interests of her life, as well as of botany and zoology. Beginning in 1861, she attended the Berwick Academy, a private school; although for a while she considered pursuing a career in medicine, her formal education was in fact completed with her graduation from the academy in 1865.

Under no pressure either to earn a living or to marry, Jewett went on trips to Boston, New York, and Ohio and began to write stories and sketches under various pseudonyms, including "Alice Eliot" and "Sarah O. Sweet." Her first published story, "Jenny Garrow's Lovers," was a melodrama that appeared in Boston's *The Flag of Our Union* in 1868, and the eighteen-year-old author was sufficiently encouraged by this to begin submitting children's stories and poems to such juvenile magazines as *St. Nicholas* and the *Riverside Magazine for Young People*, as well as adult stories and sketches to *The Atlantic Monthly*. Her tale "Mr. Bruce" was published in *The Atlantic Monthly* in December, 1869. The first of her Maine sketches, "The Shore House," appeared in that magazine in 1873, and a successful series of them rapidly followed. At the urging of *The Atlantic Monthly* editor William Dean Howells, she collected and revised them for publication in book form as *Deephaven*. By that time, Jewett was beginning to establish a circle of literary friends that eventually would include James Russell Lowell, John Greenleaf Whittier, Oliver Wendell Holmes, and Harriet Beecher Stowe, whose *The Pearl of Orr's Island* (1862) that Jewett had read when she was thirteen or fourteen is believed to have inspired Jewett's attempts to record Maine life.

Unquestionably the most significant of her literary relationships was that with James T. Fields of Ticknor and Fields, the Boston publishing house. When Fields died in 1881, his widow Annie established a close lifelong friendship with Jewett. The relationship inspired long visits to Annie's Boston residence at 148 Charles Street, as well as summer vacations at the Fieldses' cottage in Manchester-by-the-Sea. In addition, Jewett and Fields traveled extensively: In 1882, they visited England, Ireland, France, Italy, Switzerland, Belgium, and Norway, and they met Alfred, Lord Tennyson, and Christina Rossetti. On other trips to Europe in 1892 and 1898, Jewett met Samuel L. Clemens, Rudyard Kipling, and Henry James, and in 1900 the pair traveled to Greece and Turkey.

Meanwhile, Jewett continued to write. *A Country Doctor* was published in 1884, and a visit to Florida with Fields in 1888 led to several stories with southern settings. Jewett was strongest, however, in her fictional re-creation of Maine coastal life, as is evident from the popular and critical success of *The Country of the Pointed Firs*, published in 1896. She received an honorary Litt.D. degree from Bowdoin College in 1901, the same year she published her first (and only) historical novel, *The Tory Lover*. In 1902, an accident virtually ended her career: On her birthday, Jewett was thrown from a carriage when the horse stumbled, and she sustained serious head and spinal injuries. She never fully recovered either her physical health or her literary powers; only two brief pieces were published during the remaining few years of her life, although she was able to write letters and to encourage the literary endeavors of the young Willa Cather. In March, 1909, she had a stroke while staying at Fields's Boston home; transported to South Berwick, Jewett died on June 24 in the house where she was born.

Analysis • The proper classification of Sarah Orne Jewett's first effort at long fiction, *Deephaven*, remains problematic even after a century. In some circles it is regarded as a

novel, while many literary historians regard it as a collection of short
stories, a contention immediately
attributable to the book's genesis.
It originated as a popular series of
sketches that appeared in *The Atlantic Monthly* beginning in 1873.
William Dean Howells encouraged
Jewett to combine the sketches and
flesh them out with a suitable
dramatic framework and continuity, and the result—which was titled
Deephaven after the composite
Maine seaport in which the
sketches are set—was an immediate
popular success. Even if a reader
were unaware of the book's origins,
however, he or she still might be inclined to perceive it as a collection
of stories, for the individual chapters—and, at times, even portions
of chapters—tend to function as
discrete fictional units rather than
as elements subsumed within a satisfying whole. *Deephaven*'s confusing fictional status is caused in part
by its young author's inexperience
with revision, and as such it may be
perceived as a flawed book; the fictional hybrid quality of *Deephaven*, however, ultimately became Jewett's stylistic trademark, and for many readers this blurring of the
traditional distinctions between the novel and the short story is precisely the source of
much of the charm and uniqueness of Jewett's work.

James Notman

Deephaven • Regardless of whether one reacts to *Deephaven* as seriously flawed or
charmingly eclectic, the fact remains that structurally speaking it is a sort of fictional
quilt: The individual chapters retain much of their original discreteness, while the
fictional framework that was constructed around them is patently an afterthought; in
other words, the seams show. Jewett introduces two young ladies of Boston, Kate Lancaster and Helen Denis, who spend an extended summer vacation in Deephaven,
Maine, at the home of Kate's late grandaunt, Katharine Brandon. The two women
are wealthy, educated, and affectionate twenty-four-year-olds: All of this background
is revealed in a flurry of exposition within the first chapter or two, and in fact one
learns nothing more of the women in the course of the next 250 pages. Their sole
function in the story is to react to Deephaven and to record those reactions, and although Kate and Helen fulfill this function dutifully, their characterizations suffer
accordingly. One has no sense of them as flesh-and-blood humans; indeed, they disappear from the text while some salty sea captain or rugged farmer, encouraged by
an occasional "Please go only on!" from Kate, recounts a bit of folklore or personal
history.

This narrative frame, however annoying and contrived a technique it may be, suited Jewett's interests and purposes: Never skillful at portraying upper-class urbanites, she was strongest at presenting the colorful, dignified, and occasionally grim lives of common people clinging to a dying way of life in coastal Maine in the late nineteenth century. These farmers, villagers, and seafarers were a source of perennial interest to Jewett, and the rich variety of their lifestyles, skills, and experiences were elements that she lovingly recorded, even as they were dying before her eyes. Ultimately, it is this impulse to record various aspects of a cross section of American life, rather than poor judgment or technical incompetence, which must be cited as the source of Jewett's distinctive fragmentary style.

That style was rapidly being crystallized in the creation of *Deephaven*. As noted, the two outsiders who react to the coastal village almost disappear from the text despite the fact that this is a first-person narration, but frankly they are not missed. The book dissolves rapidly into a series of character studies, anecdotes, events, and descriptions of the landscape or homes. Individual characters are far more memorable than the volume in toto: The reader is inclined to recall Mrs. Kew, the lighthouse keeper; the widower Jim Patton, who repairs carpets; Danny the red-shirted fisherman, whose only friend was a stray cat; the "Kentucky Giantess," a local girl turned sideshow attraction; Captain Sands, a firm believer in thought-transference and the power of dreams; and Miss Sally Chauncey, the insane survivor of a once prosperous family. Each character is painfully aware of the passing of the economic and cultural prominence of Deephaven and, concomitantly, the passing of each one's way of life; accordingly, each (rather incredibly) recounts his or her life's high points, along with bits of folklore and anecdotes, to the two vacationing Boston ladies.

In addition to offering poignant and often penetrating studies of common folk, Jewett provides accounts of events that are symptomatic of the passing of Deephaven. These accounts include a circus full of tired performers and exhausted (or dead) animals and a lecture on the "Elements of True Manhood" written for young men but addressed to a town whose young men have all died or departed to find new lives in urban factories or in the West. Finally, Jewett provides extended descriptions, often of home interiors. As a symbol of the luxurious life of the past, she offers a chapter-long discussion of the house of the deceased Aunt Kate (an analysis so meticulous that it mentions the tiny spiders on the wallpaper), along with a companion study of the home of the mad Miss Sally, whose crumbling, furnitureless mansion is decorated with frames without paintings. Clearly this is not the sunny, sentimental world that is generally—and erroneously—attributed to local-color writing of the late nineteenth century. Although Jewett is often accused of avoiding the less positive aspects of life, this is certainly not the case with *Deephaven*: one finds a world of despair, poverty, unemployment, disease, alcoholism, insanity, and death. This is not gratuitous misery, but life as Jewett perceived it in coastal Maine.

Despite the book's rather unexpected acknowledgement of the unpleasant in life, however, it was warmly received, not only because of the limitations Jewett set for herself (she was surely no literary naturalist when compared to Émile Zola, Stephen Crane, or Jack London), but because of the two protagonists through whose eyes the reader experiences Deephaven. Early in the book, as they giggle and kiss their way through the alien environment of Deephaven, Kate and Helen generate a sentimentalized and frankly vacuous aura that is in keeping with the book's initial focus on the superficially picturesque aspects of the town; later in the story, as Jewett progressively focuses more on the grim side of life, the two girls begin to lapse frequently into improbable dialogues. For example, it is after a poor, unemployed widower dies of alco-holism that Kate reveals the lesson she's learned: "Helen, I find that I understand better and better how unsatisfactory, how purposeless and disastrous, any life must be that is not a Christian life. It is like being always in the dark, and wandering one knows not where, if one is not learning more and more what it is to have a friendship with God." Kate and Helen are ingenuous and often preachy; they offer a romanti-cized counterbalance to the realistic world of Deephaven. As such, the book was ren-dered palatable to a Victorian audience, but as a result, it appears disjointed, dated, and sentimental to modern readers. With the notable exception of *The Country of the Pointed Firs*, these unfortunate qualities tend to pervade all of Jewett's attempts to write fiction of substantial length.

A Country Doctor • Jewett's second effort at long fiction, and her one book that is most amenable to classification as a novel, is *A Country Doctor*. However, the book is marred by technical problems. Poorly proportioned, it concentrates so much on the childhood of its heroine, Nan Prince, that her adult activities as a determined medi-cal student and successful physician are simply matters of unconvincing hearsay. Structurally unimaginative, it offers a dry chronological account and a glaring pau-city of psychological depth: The strength of character that Nan ostensibly possesses is scarcely glimpsed as she facilely combats with laughter or thin logic the feeble at-tempts of acquaintances and townspeople to dissuade her from embarking on a "man's" career instead of assuming the more "natural" role of wife and homemaker. Even so, *A Country Doctor* was Jewett's favorite work, and it is easy to understand why. Despite its flaws, the book is in several respects representative of her finest work; its focal character, Dr. John Leslie, is a loving portrait of Jewett's own father, Dr. Theo-dore Herman Jewett.

The technical problems in *A Country Doctor* are apparent from even the most cur-sory reading. As Jewett herself acknowledged, she was far more adept at the delinea-tion of character than at the development of plot, but even so, the characters in *A Country Doctor* are not generally handled effectively. Four of the characters to whom the reader is initially introduced—the twins Jacob and Martin Dyer and their wives (who coincidentally are sisters)—are interesting rural types and fascinating exam-ples of the power of early sibling relationships, heredity, and environment in the determination of adult character and behavior. Also interesting is Grandmother Thacher, the death of whose troubled prodigal daughter Adeline leaves her with the infant Nan, and whose son John, a country lawyer, is old long before his time. How-ever, Jewett does not utilize the potential of these characters: The four Dyers are for-gotten not long after they are introduced, Grandmother Thacher dies while Nan is still young, and the child's Uncle John is dispatched a few pages after he makes his belated appearance in the story.

Jewett clearly wished to devote her time and energy not to secondary characters, but to Dr. Leslie himself, and in fact she succeeded so well in this endeavor that she inadvertently blurred the focus of the novel. The very title *A Country Doctor* appar-ently was designed to do double duty, referring to both Dr. Leslie and Dr. Nan Prince, his ward after the deaths of her grandmother and uncle; in fact, however, Jewett's primary concern was the presentation of Dr. Leslie. His portrait is vivid and touch-ing: A widower well into middle age, Leslie is a trusted, competent physician much loved in the community of Oldfields, Maine. If he possesses any character flaws or troubles, aside from occasional grief for his wife or qualms over the stress his ward will encounter as a doctor, he conceals them nicely. Even the transparently contrived visit from his former classmate and foil, the well-traveled surgeon Dr. Ferris, fails to convince Leslie that his life might have been more productive, happy, or exciting away from Oldfields.

Living with the obligatory salty housekeeper in an old house full of books and flowers, Dr. Leslie readily adopts the orphaned Nan and interprets her "wildness" as simply "natural" behavior—and in this respect he not only is in keeping with the autobiographical elements of the book but also serves to express several of Jewett's own theories. For much as Dr. Leslie is Jewett's father, young Nan is Sarah herself, and their unusual fictional relationship mimics the real one. Like Dr. Leslie, Dr. Jewett permitted his daughter to be absent from school and took her with him on his rounds, educating her with his discussions of science, literature, history, and psychology. Like Nan, Sarah was far more comfortable out of doors than in a classroom, and at an early age she decided to pursue a career as a physician rather than marry; although Sarah later abandoned her plans for medicine, the similarities between her own situation and the fictional one are quite pronounced.

Perhaps for this reason, the elements of the book that are least satisfying are those that are not derived from Jewett's personal experiences. The opening chapter, in which the wretched Adeline Thacher Prince decides against drowning herself and young Nan, and with her last breath returns home to die on her elderly mother's doorstep, is blatant melodrama. Nan's eventual reconciliation with her wealthy, long-lost aunt (also named Nan Prince) is a fairy-tale motif that does not even offer psychological tension to make it worthwhile. Finally, Nan's ostensible love affair with the milquetoast George Gerry utterly lacks credibility, let alone passion. In theory, the relationship has much literary potential: George is the son of Aunt Nancy Prince's former lover, much as Nan is the daughter of Aunt Nancy's once-beloved brother, and both young people desire to better themselves; but George is a dull, admittedly mercenary lawyer in equally dull Dunport, and he is so threatened by Nan's blithely setting a farmer's dislocated shoulder—George "felt weak and womanish, and somehow wished it had been he who could play the doctor"—that it is clear that the tension Jewett seeks to create between Nan's personal desire to become a physician and society's desire to make her a wife simply cannot materialize. George is a cipher; marriage is never a serious issue; and the single-mindedness with which Nan pursues her career, although obviously meant to demonstrate the strength of her character, compromises the chances for any development of her personality or the generation of interest in the plot. Indeed, the two elements that would have had extraordinary potential for the development of both character and plot—Nan's admission into medical school, and the difficulties she must overcome as a student—are simply ignored.

Part of the problem with *A Country Doctor* is that Jewett downplays plot in her desire to utilize the book as a sort of lecture platform. Much as the two girls in *Deephaven* (transparently speaking for Jewett herself) occasionally lapse into brief lectures on Christianity, the advantages of rural life, and the like, so too the characters in *A Country Doctor* embark on improbable discussions on behalf of the author. For example, in the chapter titled "At Dr. Leslie's," one learns of Jewett's ideas about child-rearing and heredity. As Dr. Leslie talks about young Nan at incredible length with his old classmate Dr. Ferris, one finds that Nan's guardian seeks to rear her in a deliberately "natural" way. Leslie's interest in her "natural" growth is grounded in his scientific predisposition: He feels that "up to seven or eight years of age children are simply bundles of inheritances," and Nan presents a unique case for study: Grandmother Thacher was "an old fashioned country woman of the best stock," but there had been "a very bad streak on the other side" that led to Nan's mother being marginally insane, tubercular, and alcoholic. Whereas Dr. Leslie's desire to let Nan grow naturally stems from scientific curiosity, Nan's desire is eventually traced to a religious impulse: She feels it is her God-given (and hence "natural") duty to become a doctor, and indeed her final words in the story are "O God . . . I thank thee for my future."

In addition to injecting some of her ideas about child-rearing, heredity, and theology into the story, Jewett also presents her ideas about feminism ("It certainly cannot be the proper vocation of all women to bring up children, so many of them are dead failures at it; and I don't see why all girls should be thought failures who do not marry"), about the shortcomings of urban life (Nan's mother degenerates as a result of moving to Lowell to work), and about the economic deterioration of New England (the once-thriving Dunport is dying, albeit in a picturesque fashion). In short, *A Country Doctor* is typical of Jewett's work in that it shows her incapacity to sustain plot; her occasional inability to present and develop characters who are both believable and interesting; and her unfortunate tendency to preach or theorize. These difficulties were happily under control when Jewett came to write *The Country of the Pointed Firs*.

The Country of the Pointed Firs • *The Country of the Pointed Firs* is unquestionably Jewett's masterpiece: An immediate popular and critical success, it is the only one of Jewett's five volumes of long fiction that is widely known today, and it is at the center of the perennial theoretical controversy as to how one should differentiate between a true novel and a collection of related short stories. As noted above, this situation exists with regard to *Deephaven*, but with an important difference: *Deephaven* was Jewett's first book, and so its hybrid quality is generally attributed at least in part to its author's inexperience. On the other hand, *The Country of the Pointed Firs* is clearly a more mature effort: Tight in structure, consistent in tone, complex in characterization, and profound in thought, it demonstrates how two decades of writing experience had honed Jewett's judgment and technical skill. Thus, the impression that *The Country of the Pointed Firs* somehow manages to straddle the two traditionally separate fictional classifications must be regarded as intentional. *The Country of the Pointed Firs* is considerably more than a text for fictional theorists—it is a delightful book that shows Jewett at the height of her literary powers.

A comparison of *The Country of the Pointed Firs* with *Deephaven* gives some indication of the extent of those powers, for essentially *The Country of the Pointed Firs* is a masterful reworking of the earlier book. The premise is the same in both stories: A female urbanite visits a Maine coastal community for a summer and records her impressions. In *Deephaven*, the reader follows the experiences of two rather silly young women from Boston; in *The Country of the Pointed Firs*, there is only one visitor from an unspecified city, and even alone she is more than a match for Kate and Helen. A professional writer, she is by nature and training far more perceptive than the *Deephaven* girls. Well into middle age, she also has the maturity and experience to comprehend the residents of Dunnet Landing, who themselves are people who have led quite full, if not always pleasant, lives. The narrator of *The Country of the Pointed Firs* has credibility; one can believe that she enters into the world of Dunnet Landing and that people are willing to impart to her their most private and painful thoughts, whereas it is almost impossible to believe that any thinking person could be so intimate with giggly

Kate and Helen. By the same token, although one knows little of the background and personal life of the narrator of *The Country of the Pointed Firs* (the reader is never told her name), one does know what goes on in her mind—her reactions, concerns, interests, misgivings—and as such she seems more like a real person than a fictional creation.

Closely aligned with this is the fact that the narrator of *The Country of the Pointed Firs* stays in focus throughout the story. Even though the book often breaks into little vignettes, character studies, or anecdotes, one never loses sight of the narrator, not only because she is the controlling consciousness who records the events at Dunnet Landing, but also because one knows how she reacts to what she sees and hears. Those reactions are not always positive: She is initially annoyed by Captain Littlepage's account of the mythical Arctic place where souls reside; she is startled (and a bit disappointed) by the modernity of Elijah Tilley's cottage; and she feels the pang of young Johnny Bowden's glance of "contemptuous surprise" as she fails to recognize a local symbol pertaining to fishing.

The narrator's revelation of her inner life is perhaps most apparent in her dealings with Mrs. Almira Todd, the owner of the house where she stays for the summer. Whereas in *Deephaven* Kate and Helen stay in a relative's mansion and bring their Boston servants to run the household for them, the narrator of *The Country of the Pointed Firs* has a close link with the community in the form of her landlady: They live, eat, visit, and occasionally work together (Mrs. Todd grows and sells medicinal herbs), a situation that enables the narrator to acquire extensive firsthand knowledge of the people and lore of Dunnet Landing. Even so, she is aware that, as a nonnative, she can never truly be admitted into the community; she feels rather out of place at Mrs. Begg's funeral and at the Bowden family reunion, and her acute awareness of her being privy to many of the more intimate or concealed aspects of the community (such as Mrs. Todd's admission that she did not love her husband), while simultaneously being denied knowledge of many others, shows her to be a more complex, perceptive, and thoughtful character than either Kate or Helen could ever be. It also shows that Jewett was able to comprehend and convey the fundamental fact that life is far less cut and dried, far more rich and contradictory, than was indicated in her earlier fiction. This is perhaps most evident in her treatment of Dunnet Landing itself.

Jewett goes to great lengths to emphasize the local aspects of Dunnet Landing that make it unique in time and place. She carefully records local dialect by spelling phonetically; she presents characters whose values, interests, and activities mark them as a dying breed living in an isolated area; she reveals the ways in which the region's unusual environment and situation result in so-called "peculiar people," including the woman who designed her life around the fantasy that she was the twin of Queen Victoria. Although emphasizing the uniqueness of this late nineteenth century coastal Maine village, however, Jewett also emphasizes its universality: "There's all sorts o' folks in the country, same's there is in the city," declares Mrs. Todd, and it is clear that the reader is supposed to derive from *The Country of the Pointed Firs* a deeper comprehension of the universality of human nature and experience. It is significant in this regard that the reader is never told the year in which the events take place, and Jewett habitually draws analogies between the people of Dunnet Landing and those of biblical, classical, and medieval times.

Jewett's ability to strike a consistently happy balance between the universal and particular is quite remarkable, and equally remarkable is her talent for maintaining a tone that is profound without being obscure, touching without being sentimental. For once, Jewett also avoids preachiness: Captain Littlepage's discussion of the Arctic "waiting-place" inhabited by human souls does not lead into a lecture on Christian views of the afterlife nor a debate between matters of scientific fact and religious faith. Littlepage and his recital, like all the characters, anecdotes, and events of the novel, are allowed to speak for themselves, and the effect is a powerful one. Whether or not Willa Cather was justified in maintaining that *The Country of the Pointed Firs*, Nathaniel Hawthorne's *The Scarlet Letter* (1850), and Mark Twain's *Adventures of Huckleberry Finn* (1884) were the only American books destined to have "a long, long life," it is true that *The Country of the Pointed Firs* does show Jewett in perfect control of her material and sure in her use of technique. Unquestionably, she had found the fictional milieu in which she functioned best. Given this achievement, it is all the more lamentable that in her next book Jewett deliberately abandoned the milieu.

The Tory Lover • Jewett's final attempt at long fiction proved to be her worst book. Usually classified as a historical romance or costume novel, *The Tory Lover* was transparently intended to cash in on the unprecedented and highly remunerative vogue for historical romances that characterized the American fiction market throughout the 1890's and the early years of the twentieth century; in fact, the long out-of-print book was reissued in 1975 (under the title *Yankee Ranger*) for precisely the same reasons on the eve of the American Bicentennial. *The Tory Lover* is virtually a casebook for students of the mishandling of fictional material and technique, and as such it is a perennial embarrassment to even the most devoted advocates of Jewett's work.

As usual, Jewett demonstrates her inability to handle plot, or, as she accurately lamented to Horace Scudder in 1873, "I have no dramatic talent . . . It seems to me I can furnish the theater, and show you the actors, and the scenery, and the audience, but there never is any play!" Whereas *The Country of the Pointed Firs* is strong precisely because it lacks—and in fact does not need—a plot in the usual sense of the word, *The Tory Lover* is virtually all plot, and it suffers accordingly. Although the book is set in the opening months of the American Revolution (1777), Jewett is unable to convey the excitement and tension of that most stirring era in American history. Surprisingly, little happens in this overly long story: At the urging of his girlfriend Mary Hamilton, Roger Wallingford of Berwick, Maine, declares himself to be in support of the American cause; he ships out to England on the *Ranger* under Captain John Paul Jones, is captured during Jones's attempt to burn Whitehaven, and is imprisoned at Plymouth, eventually winning a full pardon thanks to the efforts of assorted English noblemen.

Although this story line is potentially rich with exciting scenes, none materializes. The transatlantic crossing is quite dull, despite Jewett's desperate efforts to render credible the novel's obligatory villain, Dickson. The disgruntled crew's unsuccessful attempt to overthrow Captain Jones, instead of being excitingly dramatized, is reduced to a comment: "There had been an attempt at mutiny on board, but the captain had quelled that, and mastered the deep-laid plot behind it." Similarly, Roger Wallingford's imprisonment, which lasts for much of the novel, is barely mentioned, and his daring and bloody escape is a matter of hearsay. Jewett's attempts to generate intrigue, mystery, or tension are no more successful. Wallingford's pardon is the result of the written request of a resident of Berwick, one Master Sullivan, but his relationship to the powerful noblemen who actually secure the pardon is never explained, and the effect generated is more annoyance than mystery. Likewise, the tension between Captain Jones and Wallingford that results from Jones's wearing Mary's ring is resolved a few pages later when Wallingford bluntly reveals the source of his ill temper. Finally, the book's climax—the evil Dickson's admission of his role in the thwarting of Jones and the arrest of Wallingford—is not in the least surprising or convincing: Quite simply, the drunken Dickson boasts of his deeds in a public house, and his fellow sailors toss him into the street. A few paragraphs later, the book abruptly ends.

Plot had never been Jewett's strong suit, but even the characterization in *The Tory Lover* is lamentable. The story's heroine, Mary Hamilton, is constantly described as "beautiful," "bright," and "charming"; but the repeated use of vague adjectives does not constitute characterization. The very little that she thinks, says, and does reveals virtually nothing about her. In this regard, she is perhaps ideally suited to her equally wooden lover, Roger Wallingford, who repeatedly is said to be "gentlemanly" and "handsome," but who in fact is not in the least missed as he languishes for much of the novel in a British prison. Even the historical figures who would be expected to have intrinsic interest, such as Benjamin Franklin and John Paul Jones, are nothing more than flaccid bundles of adjectives who are irritating in their very lifelessness. Jewett also introduces a series of dull, obligatory stock characters (Dickson as the villain, Madam Wallingford as the grande dame, Old Caesar as the loyal black servant), as well as a plethora of characters who are simply dropped a few pages after they first appear: Dr. Ezra Green, the *Ranger*'s literary surgeon; wealthy Colonel Jonathan Hamilton, Mary's allegedly dashing brother; Gideon Warren, the Berwick sailor who is reunited with Wallingford in the Plymouth prison.

Ultimately, *The Tory Lover* is a cluttered, confusing pastiche of unexciting events and lifeless characters; it is to Jewett's credit that she was able to acknowledge her inability to write historical romance. There is every indication that she agreed with Henry James's negative reaction to *The Tory Lover*: "Go back to the dear Country of the Pointed Firs, *come* back to the palpable present *intimate* that throbs responsive, and that wants, misses, needs you, God knows, and suffers woefully in your absence." Jewett's devastating buggy accident occurred before she could act on James's admonition, however, and *The Tory Lover* stands as her last, but far from best, work.

Alice Hall Petry

Other major works

SHORT FICTION: *Old Friends and New*, 1879; *Country By-Ways*, 1881; *The Mate of the Daylight, and Friends Ashore*, 1884; *A White Heron, and Other Stories*, 1886; *The King of Folly Island and Other People*, 1888; *Strangers and Wayfarers*, 1890; *Tales of New England*, 1890; *A Native of Wimby*, 1893; *The Life of Nancy*, 1895; *The Queen's Twin*, 1899; *Stories and Tales*, 1910; *The Uncollected Short Stories of Sarah Orne Jewett*, 1971.

POETRY: *Verses: Printed for Her Friends*, 1916.

NONFICTION: *Letters of Sarah Orne Jewett*, 1911 (Annie Fields, editor); *Sarah Orne Jewett Letters*, 1956 (Richard Cary, editor).

CHILDREN'S LITERATURE: *Play Days: A Book of Stories for Children*, 1878; *The Story of the Normans*, 1887; *Betty Leicester: A Story for Girls*, 1890.

Bibliography

Blanchard, Paula. *Sarah Orne Jewett: Her World and Her Work*. Reading, Mass.: Addison-Wesley, 1994. Offers biographical information and critical interpretation of Jewett's works.

Cary, Richard, ed. *Appreciation of Sarah Orne Jewett: Twenty-nine Interpretive Essays*. Waterville, Maine: Colby College Press, 1973. This book collects a good cross section of the major writing on Jewett from 1885 until 1972. Contains biographical sketches, extended reviews, examinations of her technique, interpretations of some individual works, and evaluations of her career.

Church, Joseph. *Transcendent Daughters in Jewett's "Country of the Pointed Firs."* Madison, N.J.: Fairleigh Dickinson University Press, 1994. An excellent examination of Jewett's novel. Includes bibliographical references and an index.

Howard, June, ed. *New Essays on "The Country of the Pointed Firs."* Cambridge, England: Cambridge University Press, 1994. Essays interpreting the novel. Provides bibliographical references.

Joseph, Philip. "Landed and Literary: Hamlin Garland, Sarah Orne Jewett, and the Production of Regional Literatures." *Studies in American Fiction* 26 (Autumn, 1998): 147-170. Compares some of Garland's early stories with the stories in Jewett's *The Country of the Pointed Firs* to examine ideological conflict within literary regionalism. Argues that while Garland's support for social reform leads him to challenge some of the conventions of late nineteenth century realism, Jewett does not see class differences as a hindrance to U.S. destiny.

Matthiessen, F. O. *Sarah Orne Jewett*. Boston: Houghton Mifflin, 1929. This short biographical study may be the most readily available in libraries. Matthiessen surveys Jewett's life without going into great detail.

Mobley, Marilyn Sanders. *Folk Roots and Mythic Wings in Sarah Orne Jewett and Toni Morrison*. Baton Rouge: Louisiana State University Press, 1991. A critical study that asserts the importance of myth and folklore in the work of two women of different races and generations who draw on the cultural roots of their people.

Morgan, Jeff. *Sarah Orne Jewett's Feminine Pastoral Vision: "The Country of the Pointed Firs."* Lewiston, N.Y.: Edwin Mellen Press, 2002. Incisive study of Jewett's most important and most studied novel.

Nagel, Gwen L., ed. *Critical Essays on Sarah Orne Jewett*. Boston: G. K. Hall, 1984. This collection includes sixteen contemporary reviews of Jewett's books, reprints of eight critical essays from 1955 to 1983, and eight original essays. These deal with biography as well as interpretation. The introduction surveys the history of critical writing on Jewett.

Nagel, Gwen L., and James Nagel. *Sarah Orne Jewett: A Reference Guide*. Boston: G. K. Hall, 1978. Introduced with a survey of criticism on Jewett, this reference guide lists and annotates writing about Jewett from 1873 to 1976. It is invaluable as a source for secondary writing and for forming impressions of how Jewett's reputation has developed. For discussions of criticism since 1976, see *American Literary Scholarship: An Annual*.

Roman, Margaret. *Sarah Orne Jewett: Reconstructing Gender*. Tuscaloosa: University of Alabama Press, 1992. A survey of Jewett's life and art, focusing on her rejection of the limited role of women in the nineteenth century. Argues that "The White Heron" presents doubts that men and women can join together and suggests hope for a symbolic androgyny instead. Argues that Jewett rejects male/female sexual categories in her fiction.

Sherman, Sarah Way. *Sarah Orne Jewett: An American Persephone.* Hanover, N.H.: University Press of New England, 1989. A full-length, penetrating study of Jewett that discusses the source of the mythic quality in her work. Sherman tells how Jewett came to terms with the culture that defined her womanhood, and sees the myth of Demeter and Persephone as a central symbol.

Silverthorne, Elizabeth. *Sarah Orne Jewett: A Writer's Life.* Woodstock, N.Y.: Overlook Press, 1993. Silverthorne describes the increasing interest in Jewett's treatment of women, ecology, and regional life. Silverthorne had access to letters and manuscripts unavailable to previous biographers, and she takes full advantage of Jewett scholarship.

James Jones

Born: Robinson, Illinois; November 6, 1921
Died: Southampton, New York; May 9, 1977

Principal long fiction • *From Here to Eternity*, 1951; *Some Came Running*, 1957; *The Pistol*, 1959; *The Thin Red Line*, 1962; *Go to the Widow-Maker*, 1967; *The Merry Month of May*, 1971; *A Touch of Danger*, 1973; *Whistle*, 1978.

Other literary forms • James Jones published one much underrated collection of short fiction, *The Ice-Cream Headache, and Other Stories*, in 1968. Despite the excellence of several of these stories, he did not return to short fiction, primarily because of the difficulty of writing openly about sex in mass circulation magazines. He wrote two book-length works of nonfiction, *Viet Journal* (1974) and *WWII* (1975). The first is an account of Jones's experiences and observations while a war correspondent in Vietnam. *WWII*, a much more important work, is an analysis of the graphic art produced during World War II. The book contains some of Jones's finest writing, as well as an extended analysis of the central concept underlying his best fiction, "the evolution of a soldier." Jones also contributed essays to *Esquire, Harper's*, and the *Saturday Evening Post*, among other journals; the subject matter of these pieces ranges widely, from theories of fiction to skin diving.

Achievements • Jones's first novel, *From Here to Eternity*, was a spectacular success, both with critics and with the popular reading audience. As several reviewers pointed out, its frank treatment of sexuality and military brutality broke important new ground for American literary naturalism. Although the novel had its detractors, it won the National Book Award for fiction. *From Here to Eternity* appeared just in time to ride the crest of the new wave in paperback publishing, and in November, 1953, *Newsweek* reported that the paperback reprint of Jones's novel had gone through five printings of "1,700,000 copies . . . in the past six weeks." The popularity of the novel was augmented by its adaptation into one of the most highly regarded American films of the 1950's. Directed by Fred Zinnemann and with unforgettable performances by Montgomery Clift, Burt Lancaster, and Deborah Kerr, among others, the film version won the Best Picture award from the Motion Picture Academy of Arts and Sciences and the New York Film Critics in 1953. Jones himself became an international celebrity.

During the next twenty-five years, Jones remained an enormously popular writer. He and Norman Mailer were sometimes praised for having inspired a revitalized American literary realism. Nevertheless, Jones never regained the critical acceptance he enjoyed with his first novel. His much anticipated second novel, *Some Came Running*, was denounced as a failure. Occasionally thereafter, his work received positive and intelligent reviews. His tightly constructed 1959 novella *The Pistol* was seen by some perceptive critics as refuting the recurring charge that Jones could not control his material. Such reviewers as Maxwell Geismar and Lewis Gannett emphasized the structural brilliance and emotional power of his 1962 combat novel *The Thin Red Line*. Even *Time* magazine, a perennially hostile critic of Jones's work, praised his

1975 nonfictional analysis of wartime art, *WWII.* Nevertheless, when he died in 1977, Jones had been largely ignored by the critical establishment for some time. Academic critics especially dismissed him as an outdated naturalist no longer relevant in an age of literary innovation and experimentation. To the reading public, however, he remained quite relevant. Indeed, it seems quite likely that Jones's public acceptance was a factor in the academy's dismissal of him as a serious writer.

Jones was, in fact, a most serious and significant writer. Nevertheless, the critical neglect of Jones at the time of his death cannot be attributed solely to academic hostility toward popular success. The last three novels published in his lifetime, *Go to the Widow-Maker,* *The Merry Month of May,* and *A Touch of Danger,* added little to his total achievement. *A Touch of Danger* is a detective novel in the Dashiell Hammett-Raymond Chandler "hard-boiled" tradition. A competent work, it was never intended as anything more than popular entertainment. In contrast, *Go to the Widow-Maker,* inspired by Jones's devotion to skin diving, and *The Merry Month of May,* focusing on the 1968 Paris student rebellion, are quite ambitious civilian novels. Like *Some Came Running,* each is intended as a serious investigation of the novelist's belief that the American male is devoted to an adolescent cult of masculinity. Jones's vision of American sexual maladjustment, while honest and insightful, was simply not original enough to serve as the primary focus of a long novel, although the concept works well as a major subtheme in his army fiction.

In part because of the time he devoted to civilian novels, the major achievement of Jones's career was unrecognized at the time of his death. *From Here to Eternity* and *The Thin Red Line* were always intended as the first two volumes in a trilogy. *Whistle,* the concluding volume of the trilogy, was published posthumously in 1978 and inspired a reappraisal of Jones's lasting contribution to American literature. His army trilogy began to receive, in the late twentieth century, its proper recognition as the most important fictional treatment of American involvement in World War II. Moreover, *From Here to Eternity* has attained the status of a modern classic, and *The Thin Red Line* is frequently praised as the best American "combat novel." *The Thin Red Line* was adapted into a well-received 1998 film directed by Terrence Malick.

Biography • Born in Robinson, Illinois, on November 6, 1921, James Jones grew up in a proud and socially prominent family. When he was a junior at Robinson High School, however, the family's position abruptly deteriorated, largely because of the Samuel Insull stock scandal. Even though his father, Ramon, was never professionally successful and became an alcoholic before ultimately committing suicide, Jones was fond of him. In sharp contrast, he felt contemptuous of, and rejected by, his mother, Ada Blessing Jones.

After he graduated from high school in 1939, Jones, on the advice of his father, joined the United States Air Force and was stationed in Hawaii, where he transferred to the infantry. His army career was not distinguished; he once summarized his record of two promotions and subsequent reductions back to the lowest enlisted grade: "Apted Cpl 13 May 42 Red to Pvt 3 Dec 43, Apt Sgt 1 Mar 44 Red to Pvt 20 May 44." Nevertheless, in more than one way, Jones's military experience was crucial in his development as an artist. Primarily, he developed a complex love-hate relationship with the United States Army that later gave his military fiction a unique tension. Moreover, he was present at Schofield Barracks, Hawaii, on December 7, 1941, and witnessed the birth of a new and terrifying world. Later, Jones saw combat on Guadalcanal, the brutality of which inspired his concept of "the animal nature of man."

Wounded on Guadalcanal in 1943, he was sent back to the States and, on July 6, 1944, received his military discharge. Greatly shaken both by the combat horror he had experienced and by the continuing dissolution of his family, Jones met Mrs. Lowney Handy of Marshall, Illinois, in late 1943 or early 1944, and began one of the strangest, and ultimately most publicized, apprenticeships in the history of American letters. A 1953 *Newsweek* essay described Lowney Handy as "a more dynamic version of Sinclair Lewis's Carol Kennicott in 'Main Street,'" and she does appear to have waged a one-woman crusade against small-town midwestern provincialism. Certainly, she and her husband, Harry Handy, supported Jones during a seven-year period in which he worked at his ambition of becoming a writer.

The young soldier had discovered Thomas Wolfe at the Schofield Barracks Post Library and realized he "had been a writer all his . . . life without knowing it or having written." With Lowney Handy's encouragement, Jones wrote a first novel, which he submitted to Maxwell Perkins, the legendary editor at Charles Scribner's Sons. Perkins rejected this first novel but encouraged Jones to concentrate on a work about the old peacetime army. After Perkins's death, Jones profited from the help and encouragement of editor Burroughs Mitchell, and when Scribner's published *From Here to Eternity* in 1951, its author became an instant celebrity. Initially, he used his new wealth to establish a writers' colony at Marshall. Lowney Handy assumed the directorship of the colony and imposed an iron discipline upon her new protégés.

Jones, however, grew bored and skeptical in Marshall, seeing the cynicism of some of the writers and the failure of Mrs. Handy's methods to create universally good writing or even cooperation among the writers. His introduction to the beautiful actor Gloria Mosolino made almost inevitable a bitter and painful break with the Handys. In 1957, Jones and Gloria Mosolino were married at the Olofson Hotel in Haiti. The couple lived for a few months in New York City before moving to Paris in 1958. For the next sixteen years, the Joneses were the center of the American expatriate community in Paris. Whether his books were critically praised or attacked made no difference to Jones's new status as international celebrity.

Jones's break with Lowney Handy and his love affair with Gloria are fictionalized in his autobiographical novel *Go to the Widow-Maker*, and Paris is the setting of his ambitious 1971 work *The Merry Month of May*. Nevertheless, he always wrote best about the army. In 1973, he went to Vietnam as a war correspondent and, the following year, published *Viet Journal*, a nonfictional account of what he had seen in that tragic country. Also in 1974, he and his wife and two children returned home to the United States. Jones was increasingly determined to complete what he had long envisioned as the central work of his career, a trilogy about the United States Army, of which *From Here to Eternity* and *The Thin Red Line* constituted the first two volumes.

On May 9, 1977, Jones died of congestive heart failure in Southampton, New York. He had not quite completed *Whistle*, the third volume of his trilogy. It was possible, however, for Willie Morris, a writer, editor, and longtime friend, to finish the manuscript from Jones's notes and tapes. When *Whistle* was published in February, 1978, James Jones's army trilogy took its place as the most important American fictional treatment of World War II.

Analysis • Critics, especially academics, have increasingly dismissed James Jones as a "war novelist" committed to outdated naturalistic techniques. Though Ihab Hassan provides an extensive and largely favorable discussion of *From Here to Eternity* in *Radi-*

cal Innocence, his 1961 examination of post-World War II American fiction, two important subsequent studies of the contemporary American novel, Tony Tanner's *City of Words* (1971) and Josephine Hendin's *Vulnerable People* (1978), ignore Jones completely. This neglect arises, in part, from oversimplified and incorrect perceptions of his work. For example, as the term is most commonly used, Jones is not strictly a "war novelist." Of his eight novels, only one, *The Thin Red Line*, is primarily devoted to a description of military combat, while four have peacetime civilian settings. Although it is true that army life provides the background of his best fiction and World War II its controlling event, his reactions to the army and the war exhibit the complexity and ambiguity essential to meaningful art.

Especially during the 1950's, Jones often permitted himself to be depicted as an advocate of masculine toughness in life and literature. A 1957 *Life* magazine article emphasized the novelist's devotion to knives and boxing and declared his prominence in the literary cult of violence. However, a careful reader of Jones's fiction will discover an artist deeply concerned about the capacity of human beings for self-destruction. In a 1974 interview, Jones discussed his belief that humanity was doomed by two interrelated forces: its own animal nature and the anonymous power of modern technological society. He stressed "the ridiculous misuse of human strength that can include many subjects, not only physical strength, but technology, and all of the things that we live by." After defining morality as the refusal to give another pain "even though one suffers himself," he forecast the inevitable failure of such an idealistic ethical code:

> In all of us, there is this animal portion . . . which is not at all adverse to inflicting cruelty on others. This can be quite enjoyable at times. . . . It's in myself . . . it's in all of us.

Modern man, Jones believed, is caught in both an external and an internal trap. Human strength, which has its source in the "animal nature of man," has been translated into an awesome technology that ironically threatens the extinction of human individuality, if not the actual obliteration of humankind. In his civilian novels, Jones's characters habitually seek the few remaining "frontiers" of individualism (for example, skin diving), only to discover the impossibility of escaping their own "animal" heritage. An element of brutal and destructive competition is thereby introduced into the "frontier," which is perverted and ultimately doomed. It is in his army fiction, however, that Jones most memorably dramatizes the tragic vulnerability of contemporary man.

In a 1967 *Paris Review* interview, Jones said: "I've come to consider bravery as just about the most pernicious of virtues. Bravery is a horrible thing. The human race has it left over from the animal world and we can't get rid of it." His army fiction underscores the destructiveness of this "most pernicious of virtues." Strength and bravery are essential qualities of the traditional hero. In more romantic ages, these two virtues were often perceived as the very foundation of manhood. Today's all-pervasive technology makes such romantic concepts of heroism archaic and dangerous. The dominant social mechanism of the modern world is bureaucracy, which can hardly permit heroism, since bureaucracy denies individuality. Jones saw modern warfare as the inevitable product of a bureaucratic, highly technological society. In it, death falls from the sky in a totally "random" and "anonymous" manner. For Jones, a fundamental and dismaying truth was implicit in this impersonal rain of death: In such a technological hell, the traditional Western concepts of the individual and the self no longer hold their old importance. The question he examines throughout his most important fiction is whether they still have any validity at all.

The army trilogy • The major achievement of Jones's career is his army trilogy: *From Here to Eternity, The Thin Red Line*, and the posthumously published *Whistle*. His novella *The Pistol* and several of the short stories in his collection *The Ice-Cream Headache, and Other Stories* also have military settings. The thematic focus in all Jones's army fiction is upon the evolution of the soldier, a concept that is given a full and convincing nonfictional elaboration in *WWII*. In Jones's view, warfare constitutes man's total capitulation to his animal nature. The traditional concepts of the individual and the self must be discarded in combat: The army trains the soldier to function on a primitive, subhuman level of consciousness. This training is a reversal of evolution; it is a process by which the army systematically dehumanizes the enlisted man. Such dehumanization is necessary for the soldier's acceptance of his own anonymity and probable death in combat. In World War II's anonymous, technological warfare, the enlisted man became more clearly expendable and anonymous than he had ever been. Throughout his military fiction, Jones is intent upon describing the manner in which the army, by using technology and its awareness of the enlisted man's inherent animalism, carried out the dehumanization process.

The three novels that constitute the army trilogy depict three major stages in the evolution of a soldier. It is important to note here that Jones intended the three novels to be seen as constituting a special kind of trilogy. He wished that each "should stand by itself as a work alone," "in a way that . . . John Dos Passos's three novels in his fine USA trilogy do not." At least in *From Here to Eternity* and *The Thin Red Line*, the first two novels in his own trilogy, Jones clearly achieved this ambition.

The army trilogy's most innovative feature is the presence of three character types in all three volumes. Of these three character types, two are of overriding importance. First Sergeant Milt Warden of *From Here to Eternity* is transformed into Sergeant "Mad" Welsh in *The Thin Red Line* and into Sergeant Mart Winch in *Whistle*. Private Robert E. Lee Prewitt of *From Here to Eternity* becomes Private Witt in *The Thin Red Line* and Private Bobby Prell in *Whistle*. John W. Aldridge, sometimes a perceptive critic of Jones's fiction, understands a more important reason than Prewitt's death in *From Here to Eternity* for the characters' different names in each of the novels: Increasingly brutal experiences, he writes, have "transformed [them] into altogether different people." In other words, as they reach new and more dehumanizing stages in the evolution of a soldier, their inner selves undergo transformation.

There is a fundamental level on which Jones's character types remain constant. Warden/Welsh/Winch is Jones's realist, who comprehends the inevitability of his own destruction as well as that of his fellow enlisted men. He is burdened by a deep concern for others, but he attempts to hide that concern behind a surface cynicism. Just as he anticipates, his inability to deny his compassion ultimately drives him mad. Private Prewitt/Witt/Prell is the determined and increasingly anachronistic individualist who regularly defies army bureaucracy in the name of his personal ethical code. In *From Here to Eternity*, which focuses on the old peacetime army, he is a romantic figure refusing to compromise with a corrupt bureaucracy. In *The Thin Red Line*, a grim account of combat on Guadalcanal, he is reduced to an animalistic level; his defiance seems insane and pointless rather than romantic. Primarily through his analysis of these two character types, Jones analyzes the contemporary validity of the interrelated concepts of the self and the individual.

From Here to Eternity • The central factor in the critical and popular success of *From Here to Eternity* was its vivid characterization. As Maxwell Perkins had anticipated, Sergeant Milt Warden and Private Robert E. Lee Prewitt are unforgettable figures. They are not, however, the novel's only memorable characters. Private Angelo Maggio and "the women," Alma Schmidt and Karen Holmes, are also strong individuals determined to preserve their integrity in an anonymous, bureaucratic world. *From Here to Eternity* is easily Jones's most romantic novel. In it, he depicts a world that ceased to exist on December 7, 1941; the novel's setting is Hawaii, and its climax is the Japanese attack on Pearl Harbor. For most of the novel, modern technological destruction has not made its appearance, and individualism seems a vital concept that is to be preserved in spite of "old Army" corruption. On the surface, the novel's roster of unforgettable characters seems to guarantee the survival of this traditional Western value.

Warden always knows, however, what is coming. He sees the inevitable destruction of the self and struggles to suppress his instinctive sympathy for Private Prewitt's defiance of the army. Prewitt's integrity is so strong that ultimately even Warden has to respect it. Nevertheless, the sergeant's admiration for his "bolshevik" private is a largely nostalgic response; he identifies with this defiant individualism while remaining aware that it is doomed.

Because his individualism is related to much that is crucial to Western values, Prewitt does, in fact, emerge as the dominant character in the novel. In the beginning, his quarrel with the army is almost absurdly simple. His commanding officer, Dynamite Holmes, is determined that Prewitt will become a member of the regimental boxing team; the private is equally determined not to box, even if his refusal means that he must give up playing the bugle, his "calling." Prewitt undergoes prolonged and systematic mental and physical abuse without acquiescing to Holmes's insistence that he box. Ultimately, this vicious "Treatment" does force him past his breaking point and into a mistake that enables Holmes to have him sentenced to the stockade, where he experiences further brutality at the hands of Sergeant Fatso Judson. Judson is one of the most unforgettable sadists in American literature, and Prewitt decides that he must be destroyed. The reader can hardly disagree with this decision; still, it assures Prewitt's own doom.

Much of *From Here to Eternity*'s unique power derives from the levels of symbolic meaning contained within the deceptively simple Prewitt-Holmes conflict. Boxing is a metaphor for the animal nature of man, while Prewitt's "calling" to play the bugle comes to represent that uniquely individualistic integrity that makes possible artistic creation. Throughout the novel, Prewitt is something of a romantic folk hero; he is the personification of "the good soldier," the proud enlisted man. When he plays taps on the bugle or helps in the collective composition of "The Re-Enlistment Blues," he is also giving artistic expression to the enlisted man's pain and loneliness. His desire to play the bugle symbolizes the urge to create a distinctive proletarian art. Warden sees the army's destruction of Prewitt as an illustration of animalism negating man's potential for lasting creativity. Yet, because Prewitt's death occurs just after the Japanese attack on Pearl Harbor, the sergeant has no real opportunity to mourn him. Because Warden understands that December 7, 1941, represented the end of traditional individualism and self-expression, Prewitt's death seems to him almost an anticlimax.

The Thin Red Line • The mood of doomed romanticism so vital to *From Here to Eternity* is completely missing from the second volume of Jones's army trilogy, *The Thin Red Line*, a grimly detailed account of brutal combat. The bolshevik private in this novel is Witt, whose defiance has no relevance to art or to any idealistic values. In a real sense, the novel's main character is "C-for-Charlie Company," all the members of which are forced to submerge themselves into an anonymous mass. *The Thin Red Line* has been called the best American combat novel, and such high praise is deserved. The novel offers an unforgettable account of the sheer animalism of war. The sexuality of all the men of Charlie Company is systematically translated into brutal aggression toward the enemy. In fact, the only meaningful difference among the characters is the degree to which they are aware that such a transformation is taking place.

The one most aware is the superficially cynical first sergeant, Edward "Mad" Welsh. Like Milt Warden in *From Here to Eternity*, "the First" continually wonders how much of his basic self can be denied without a resultant loss of sanity. He has come very close to finding an answer to this question; one source of Jones's title is an old midwestern saying: "There's only a thin red line between the sane and the mad." Welsh's sanity is still intact, but it is being severely strained by his unrelenting awareness of the dehumanization process that he and his men are undergoing. They are threatened not only by the fanatical determination of the Japanese enemy and by the deadly accidents of warfare, but also by the gross incompetence of their own officers. Writing out of a proletarian consciousness, Jones depicted the officer class as incompetent, if not actually corrupt, in all of his army fiction.

The Thin Red Line is Jones's most structurally sound novel, focusing upon the American struggle to capture an area of Guadalcanal known as "The Dancing Elephant." The brutality of combat is documented in complete naturalistic detail. Nevertheless, a majority of the central characters are alive when the novel ends with Charlie Company preparing to invade New Georgia. It is only here that the reader comes to share with Mad Welsh an awful knowledge—for those men who did not die on Guadalcanal, another Japanese-occupied island awaits, and then another and another. Thus, ultimate survival seems out of the question, and madness becomes a form of escape from too much awareness.

Although no one individual American soldier could confidently expect to survive the war, the majority of the soldiers did survive to return home. Such men returned to a country that, Jones believed, was being irrevocably changed by an unprecedented wave of material prosperity. Thus, men who had accepted the inevitability of their own deaths and whose sexuality had been converted into unrestrained animalism returned to a vital, challenging economy that could not afford the time for their reorientation. They faced what Jones, in *WWII*, called "The De-Evolution of a Soldier," the final and most difficult stage of the soldier's evolution: the acceptance of life and healthy sexuality by men who, after a long and excruciating process, had been converted to death-dealing and death-accepting savagery. *Whistle* focuses on this last, and nearly impossible, transformation.

Whistle • In large part because Jones was unable to finish it before his death in May, 1977, *Whistle* lacks the power of *From Here to Eternity* and *The Thin Red Line*. Nevertheless, as completed from Jones's notes, by Willie Morris, it stands as a memorable conclusion to the army trilogy. The novel focuses upon the return home of four characters, all members of Charlie Company and all veterans of the kind of brutal combat depicted in *The Thin Red Line*. The war is not over, but the stateside economic boom is well under way. Although Marion Landers is not one of Jones's three major recurring character types, he is nevertheless reminiscent of Geoffrey Fife in *The Thin Red Line* and Richard Mast in *The Pistol*. All three men are stunned by their forced realization that modern technological combat negates the heroism assigned in romantic myth to warfare. John Strange completes the least successful of the three character types introduced in *From Here to Eternity*. Like his predecessors, Maylon Stark and Mess Sergeant Storm, Strange (nicknamed Johnny Stranger) is unable to care for anyone but himself, even though he has perfected a mask of compassion. Stark/Storm/Strange is the exact opposite of First Sergeant Warden/Welsh/Winch.

Jones's bolshevik private in *Whistle* is Bobby Prell, who has recaptured much of the Prewitt quixotic idealism that had hardened into animal stubbornness in the characterization of Witt. Very seriously wounded, Prell is battling the army that wishes to give him the Congressional Medal of Honor—the army that also insists on amputating his leg. Although not convinced that he deserves the medal, Prell is certain that he should keep his leg, even if refusing amputation means certain death. Certainly, his conflict is elemental and significant; still, Prell never attains a stature comparable to that of Prewitt. Given Jones's vision, Prell must, in fact, seem largely anachronistic. Pearl Harbor marked the death of the romantic rebel as hero.

The truly memorable figure in *Whistle* is Sergeant Mart Winch, the culmination of Jones's depiction of "the First." Throughout most of *Whistle*, Winch functions as Warden and Welsh did, secretly protecting his men by elaborate manipulation of army bureaucracy. He is forced to see, however, the severe limitations of his ability to protect anyone in a new and nightmarish world. After Landers and Prell are shattered by their inability to adjust to civilian society, Winch surrenders to insanity. Thus, he crosses "the thin red line" and is destroyed by the madness that had threatened to engulf Warden and Welsh. The cumulative characterization of "the First" is the most brilliant achievement in Jones's fiction; it is the heart of the army trilogy. Jones called the vision underlying his trilogy "quite tragic" and talked of the impossibility of an affirmative contemporary literature. He described a world so thoroughly converted to dehumanizing bureaucracy and technology that it drives to insanity those men who still believe in such traditional Western values as the self and individualism.

James R. Giles

Other major works
    SHORT FICTION: *The Ice-Cream Headache, and Other Stories*, 1968.
    NONFICTION: *Viet Journal*, 1974; *WWII*, 1975.

Bibliography
Aldrich, Nelson W., ed. *Writers at Work: The Paris Review Interviews*. 3d ser. New York: Viking Press, 1967. Jones talks about his methods of composition and defends his novels and his own brand of realistic writing against critical attacks. He also believes that an academic education can hurt a writer. Although he was living in Europe at the time of the interview, he considers himself an American.
Carter, Steven R. *James Jones: An American Literary Orientalist Master*. Urbana: University of Illinois Press, 1998. A deeply probing study of Jones's spiritual evolution and philosophy and his concern with individual salvation and growth. Includes bibliography.

Giles, James R. *James Jones*. Boston: Twayne, 1981. Examines each of Jones's novels in detail and gives a brief biography of the novelist. Sees a central division between the he-man and the sophisticate in Jones's life and art. Contains an excellent bibliography.

Hassan, Ihab. *Radical Innocence*. Princeton, N.J.: Princeton University Press, 1961. Describes the hero of *From Here to Eternity*, Prewitt, as a passive sufferer and compares his alienation to that of black Americans. Hassan likes the novel but not the subliterary psychology in which Jones indulges.

Jones, Peter G. *War and the Novelist*. Columbia: University of Missouri Press, 1976. Praises James Jones's *From Here to Eternity* and *The Thin Red Line* highly, describing them as accurate portrayals of Army life and combat and as possessing psychological insights.

McShane, Frank. *Into Eternity: The Life of James Jones*. Boston: Houghton Mifflin, 1985. McShane provides the most thorough and detailed of the biographical works devoted to Jones.

Morris, Willie. *James Jones: A Friendship*. 1978. Reprint. Urbana: University of Illinois Press, 1999. The friendship between these two writers occurred late in Jones's life. They both lived on Long Island and were drawn into conversations about life and art. Jones reveals much about his early military career.

William Kennedy

Born: Albany, New York; January 16, 1928

Principal long fiction • *The Ink Truck*, 1969; *Legs*, 1975; *Billy Phelan's Greatest Game*, 1978; *Ironweed*, 1983; *The Albany Cycle*, 1985 (includes *Legs*, *Billy Phelan's Greatest Game*, and *Ironweed*); *Quinn's Book*, 1988 (continues the Albany cycle); *Very Old Bones*, 1992 (continues the Albany cycle); *The Flaming Corsage*, 1996 (continues the Albany cycle); *Roscoe*, 2002 (continues the Albany cycle).

Other literary forms • In addition to the novels cited above, William Kennedy's non-fiction *O Albany! An Urban Tapestry* (1983), pamphlets for the New York State Library, Empire State College, and the *Albany Tricentennial Guidebook* (1985) largely center on his native Albany, New York. He wrote the screenplays for *The Cotton Club* (1984), with Francis Coppola and Mario Puzo, and *Ironweed* (1987), adapted from his novel of the same title. Kennedy collaborated with his son, Brendan, on the children's books *Charlie Malarkey and the Belly Button Machine* (1986) and *Charlie Malarkey and the Singing Moose* (1994).

Achievements • Before becoming known as a novelist, Kennedy worked as a newspaperman in Albany, New York, a city in which politics plays an important role. He struggled at writing for years while teaching as an adjunct at the State University of New York (SUNY) at Albany. He brought all these traditions to his writing: the bite of the newsman, the literary allusions of the professor, and the mysticism of the American Irishman. His first books—*The Ink Truck*, *Legs*, and *Billy Phelan's Greatest Game*—drew some notice but sold sluggishly, so *Ironweed* was rejected by thirteen publishers until writer Saul Bellow, Kennedy's teacher and mentor, persuaded Viking to reconsider. Viking reissued the previous two novels along with *Ironweed* as *The Albany Cycle*, and *Ironweed* won the National Book Critics Circle Award in 1983 and the Pulitzer Prize in fiction in 1984. Kennedy's 2002 novel *Roscoe* earned him a PEN/Faulkner Award nomination.

In 1983, Kennedy received a MacArthur Foundation Fellowship. This unsolicited "genius" award freed him for creative work; he used part of the proceeds to start a writers' institute in Albany, later funded by New York State with him as director. His novels' characters are drawn from the world of bums and gangsters and have been compared in brilliance to those of James Joyce and William Faulkner. *The Albany Cycle*, with its interlocking characters and spirit of place, has been compared to Faulkner's Yoknapatawpha stories and Joyce's *Dubliners* (1914) and *Ulysses* (1922). Kennedy's style won praise as a combination of naturalism and surrealism, yet critics faulted what they call his overwriting and pandering to the public's demand for violence, explicit sex, and scatological detail. Critics generally agree that *Ironweed* is among Kennedy's best novels, fusing the style, characterization, attention to detail, and mysticism of the first two novels and focusing them with mastery. Kennedy would continue to add to his Albany cycle, publishing *Quinn's Book* in 1988, *Very Old Bones* in 1992, and *The Flaming Corsage* in 1996.

Courtesy, Penguin Books

Biography • William Kennedy was born of Irish Catholic heritage in Albany, New York, on January 16, 1928. He graduated from Siena College in 1949 and went to work for the Glens Falls, New York, *Post Star* as sports editor and columnist, followed by a stint as reporter on the Albany *Times Union* until 1956. He went to Puerto Rico to work for the *Puerto Rico World Journal*, then for the *Miami Herald* (1957), returning to Puerto Rico as founding managing editor of the San Juan *Star* from 1959 to 1961. Deciding to make fiction writing his career and Albany his literary source and center, he returned to the Albany *Times Union* as special writer and film critic from 1963 to 1970, while he gathered material and wrote columns on Albany's rich history and its often scabrous past. Upon the success of *Ironweed*, he was promoted to professor of English at State University of New York at Albany, in 1983. The university and the city sponsored a "William Kennedy's Albany" celebration in September, 1984.

In 1993, Kennedy was elected to the American Academy of Arts and Letters. He added sixth and seventh novels to the Albany cycle with the publication of *The Flaming Corsage* in 1996 and *Roscoe* in 2002. Meanwhile, he continued to work in other genres, writing, with his son Brendan, his second book for children, *Charlie Malarkey and the Singing Moose*.

Analysis • William Kennedy's fiction is preoccupied with spirit of place, language, and style, and a mystic fusing of characters and dialogue. The place is Albany, New York, the capital city—nest of corrupt politics; heritor of Dutch, English, and Irish immigrants; home to canallers, crooks, bums and bag ladies, aristocrats, and numbers-writers. Albany, like Boston, attracted a large Irish Catholic population, which brought its churches, schools, family ties, political machine, and underworld connections.

Kennedy's style has been compared to that of sixteenth century French novelist François Rabelais for its opulent catalogs and its ribald scatology. Kennedy is not, however, a derivative writer. As his books unfold, one from another, he makes novel connections, adeptly developing the hallucinations of Bailey, the protagonist of *The Ink Truck*, the extrasensory perception of Martin Daugherty, one of the central consciousnesses of *Billy Phelan's Greatest Game*, and the ghosts of his victims visiting Francis Phelan on his quest for redemption in *Ironweed*.

The Ink Truck • Kennedy's first published novel, *The Ink Truck,* connects less strongly to these themes and styles than do later works. The novel focuses on the headquarters of a Newspaper Guild strike committee on the one-year anniversary of its strike against the daily newspaper of a town resembling Albany. Only four Guild members remain: Bailey, Rosenthal, Irma, and Jarvis, their leader. Bailey, the proverbial blundering Irish reporter, mixes his libido and marital problems with his earnest belief in the strike, now bogged down in trivialities.

Bailey's relationship with his wife is strained and crazed: She is madly jealous, as she has reason to be. Bailey mixes idealism about the strike with several sexual romps and psychic encounters, punctuated by savage beatings from the scabs and company agents determined to break the strike.

Bailey's fantasy is to open the valve on the ink truck coming to the newspaper plant, bleeding the newspaper's black blood into the snow of the mean streets. In the Guild room near the paper plant, Bailey attempts to revive his affair with Irma, another of the few remaining strikers. Joined by Deek, a collegiate type and an executive's son who wants to join the strike, the four members try to harass the paper's owners, whose representative, Stanley, refuses to grant their demands, which, by this time, have become niggling. As they attempt to block the ink truck in the snow and release the ink, everything goes wrong. When Bailey sets fire to the vacant store where the gypsies congregate, Putzina, the queen, is fatally burned, and she dies in the hospital amid a wild gypsy rite. Antic writing celebrates Bailey's subsequent kidnapping by the gypsies so that they seem comic despite the violence. Bailey escapes after cooperating with the company secretary in her sexual fantasy but is disillusioned when he finds that he must sign an apology to the newspaper company for the action of some members.

More setbacks emerge: Bailey takes back the apology, then finds that the motor has been taken out of his car. Rosenthal's house has been trashed viciously. Bailey, expelled from the Newspaper Guild, goes home to find that his wife, Grace, has put all of his belongings on the curb to be pilfered. His uncle Melvin refuses to help but invites him to an elaborate pet funeral for his cat. Just after this event, the cat's body disappears, a ludicrous culmination of all Bailey has lost: Guild, Guild benefits, apartment, and wife. Going literally underground, Bailey takes a job shelving books in the State Library, where Irma visits him to tell him that despite all setbacks, he, Rosenthal, and Deek are being hailed as the Ink Truck Heroes. In this aspect, Bailey prefigures the gangster hero, Legs Diamond, and the hero as transfigured bum, Francis Phelan, of the later books.

Becoming a media hero, Bailey makes one more futile try at the ink truck. In a grand finale, the orgiastic end-of-strike party hosted by Stanley becomes another humiliation for Bailey. Kennedy's low-key and inconclusive ending leaves the characters where they began: looking at the place on the wall of the Guild Room where a sign hung over the mimeograph machine saying DON'T SIT HERE. Bailey tries to make sense of his experiences, but even the reader cannot understand. Some of the richest of these experiences—a religious pilgrimage by trolley car and a trip backward in time to a cholera epidemic in 1832—seem almost gratuitous, loose ends without much relationship to the rest of the story. Bailey realizes that "all the absurd things they'd all gone through, separately or together . . . were fixed in time and space and stood only for whatever meaning he, or anyone else, cared to give them."

Legs • Kennedy's next novel, *Legs*, develops clearer patterns and meanings, though with the same mixture of realism and surrealism as in *The Ink Truck*. Kennedy demonstrates the truth of his 1975 novel's epigraph, "People like killers," a quote from Eugène Ionesco, through his portrayal of John "Jack" Diamond, also known as "Legs," an idolized, flamboyant underworld figure, a liquor smuggler during Prohibition, a careless killer, and a tough womanizer. Finally brought to justice by New York governor Franklin D. Roosevelt, Jack was mysteriously executed gangland style in Albany in December, 1931.

The story begins in a seedy Albany bar, where four of the book's characters meet in 1974 to reminisce about the assassination of their gangster-hero, Jack "Legs" Diamond. The novel is a fictionalization of Jack's life, superimposing fictional characters, fictional names for real people, and Kennedy's imagination on real events. Three of the four in the frame story are minor, therefore surviving, members of Jack's entourage. The fourth member of the group is Marcus Gorman, Jack's attorney, mouthpiece, and friend, who gave up a political career to lend respectability and a capacity for legal chicanery to Jack. Marcus is the narrator of the novel, providing a less-than-intimate portrait, yet one filtered through a legal mind accustomed to the trickery of the profession as it was practiced then in Albany.

The book is tightly crafted, with parallel scenes, apt literary allusions, well-constructed flashbacks, foreshadowing throughout, and, always, the map of Albany and its neighboring Catskills in mind. The sordid historical account is elevated with signs and coincidences: Marcus, employed by Jack after he successfully represented another gangster, visits Jack in the Catskills after speaking at a police communion breakfast in Albany; a copy of Rabelais is in the Knights of Columbus Library frequented by Marcus in Albany; one is in Jack's bookcase at his Catskills hideaway. Literary allusions combined with Bonnie-and-Clyde violence produce Kennedy's most transcendental effects. Marcus seems a divided consciousness: He regrets the straight-and-narrow life of Irish Catholic Albany and a secure role in politics, yet he has a way of suborning witnesses, getting them to pretend insanity, and ignoring obvious hints about Jack's grislier killings (such as the garage murder of an erstwhile ally).

Jack Diamond became a mythical imaginative popular hero, a "luminous" personality who appealed to the crowds and remained their darling even in his final trials. He survived assassination attempts, though his murder is foretold from the beginning. The story is interwoven with parallels and coincidences. Kiki, Jack's gorgeous mistress, engages in a monologue reminiscent of Molly Bloom's in Joyce's *Ulysses* when she learns (from a newspaper she has hidden in her closet) that Jack really kills people. Then, when Jack is shot in a hotel (he recovers), Kiki leaves for a friend's apartment and hides in her closet from both the police and the rival gangsters.

Finally, Jack comes to trial over his torture of a farmer in the matter of a still. The farmer complains, and a grand jury is called by Roosevelt. Though he is acquitted of the assault on the farmer, a federal case against him nearly succeeds because of the testimony of an aide Jack betrayed. Following this, Jack is shot and killed in a rooming house in Albany.

Part of the novel's theme relates to the legal profession. Marcus insists that he defends those who pay his fee. In Jack's second trial, he uses an old nun, a courthouse regular, telling the court in a rambling summation that this old nun came to tell him how compassionate Jack Diamond was. Though a complete fabrication, these emotional touches win juries.

Kennedy's manic touch is evident in his portrayal of scenes on an ocean liner as Jack and Marcus try to conclude a drug deal, in the Kenmore bar in Albany in its art deco heyday, and of the singing of "My Mother's Rosary" at the Elk's Club bar in Albany. The final coda is a lyrically written, but puzzling, apotheosis: Jack, dead, gradually emerges from his body, in a transfiguration worthy of a Seigfried or a Njall of Nordic sagas.

Billy Phelan's Greatest Game • Kennedy's next novel, *Billy Phelan's Greatest Game*, tells the story of another of Albany's historical crimes—the real kidnapping of the political boss Dan O'Connell's nephew—through the framework of a series of games of chance played by a young hanger-on of the city's underside. He is Billy Phelan, son of an absent father, Francis, who will be the protagonist of *Ironweed*. The other consciousness of the book is Martin Daugherty, old neighbor of the Phelans and a newspaperman. The time frame covers several days in late October, 1938, the time of the greatest game—the kidnapping.

Family interrelationships loom importantly in this novel. Billy Phelan has lost his father, Francis, by desertion twenty-two years before; Martin's father, a writer with an insane wife and a lovely mistress, now lies senile in a nursing home. The politically powerful McCall family almost loses their only heir, the pudgy, ineffectual Charlie. Martin lusts after his father's mistress, who plays sexual games with him. Similarly, Billy's lady friend, Angie, cleverly outwits him by pretending to be pregnant, to see what Billy will do. They have never, she says, really talked about anything seriously. Billy reminisces about rowing down Broadway in a boat, during a flood in 1913, with his father and uncle. Soon, he finds his father in a seedy bar, along with his companion Helen, and gives Helen his last money for his father.

This novel frames and mirrors an unsavory crime in the lives of ordinary, yet complicated, human beings. Kennedy's wealth of language, his handiness with an anecdote, sometimes leads him to leave loose ends in his otherwise tightly constructed narratives. For example, Martin Daugherty has extrasensory perception; moreover, he lusts after his father's former mistress Melissa, who also has a taste for women. These details are interesting, yet, unlike the appearance of the vagrant Francis Phelan, these anecdotes do not further the plot or embellish the theme. Kennedy's novels unfold in a profusion of ideas, one from the other, both in language and in plot. The same time frame and some of the same characters appear in *Ironweed*, the final book of the cycle and the Pulitzer Prize winner.

Ironweed • *Ironweed* takes place immediately after the events in *Billy Phelan's Greatest Game*, on Halloween and All Saint's Day, 1938, just after the radio broadcast of Orson Welles's adaptation of H. G. Wells's *The War of the Worlds* (1898). The dates are not randomly chosen: The story, though on the surface the saga of a failed, homeless man, is actually a religious pilgrimage toward redemption from sin. Ironweed is described in an epigraph as a tough-stemmed member of the sunflower family, and Francis, like the weed, is a survivor. These analogies, like the Welles broadcast, hinge on a question of belief important to this novel.

Unlike Kennedy's previous books, *Ironweed* has no narrator or central consciousness. The main character, Francis Phelan, first left home after he killed a man during a transit strike by throwing a stone during a demonstration against the hiring of scab trolley drivers. Subsequently he returned, but left for long periods when he played professional baseball. Later, he disappeared for twenty-two years after he dropped his infant son while diapering him; the child died, yet Francis's wife, Annie, never told anyone who dropped Gerald. Francis and another bum, Rudy, dying of cancer, get jobs digging in St. Agnes's Cemetery, where Gerald and other relatives are buried.

Reason and fact are supremely important in the book, yet within one page Francis's mother, a disagreeable hypocrite, twitches in her grave and eats crosses made from weeds, and the infant Gerald converses with his father and wills him to perform acts of expiation, as yet unknown, that will cease his self-destructiveness and bring forgiveness. Francis has killed several people besides the scab driver, yet it is not for these crimes that he needs forgiveness but for deserting his family. The rest of the book chronicles his redemption. Throughout, shifts to fantasy occur, triggered by passages of straight memory and detailed history. Ghosts of the men Francis killed ride the bus back to Albany, yet they do not seem as horrible to Francis as a woman he finds near the mission, freezing in the cold. He drapes a blanket around her, yet later he finds her dead, mangled and eaten by dogs.

During the night, Francis meets with his hobo "wife," Helen, a gently educated musician (she once went to Vassar) with enough energy, though dying of a tumor, to sing proudly in a pub on their rounds. In the mission, Francis gets a pair of warm socks; on the street, Helen is robbed of the money given to her by Francis's son Billy. Then follows a nightmare search through the cold streets for shelter for the delicate Helen. In desperation, Francis goes to a friend's apartment, where he washes his genital region in the toilet and begs a clean pair of shorts. The friend refuses them shelter, so Francis leaves Helen in an abandoned car with several men, though he knows she will be molested sexually.

The next day, Francis gets a job with a junkman. While making his rounds, he reads in a paper about his son Billy getting mixed up in the McCall kidnapping. Making the rounds of old neighborhoods, buying junk from housewives, releases a flood of memories for Francis: He sees his parents, his neighbors the Daughertys in their house, now burned, where one day the mad Katrina Daugherty walked out of her house naked to be rescued by the seventeen-year-old Francis. Because of this memory, he buys a shirt from the ragman to replace his filthy one. While he is buying the shirt, Helen goes to Mass, then listens to records in a record store (stealing one). Retrieving money she has hidden in her bra, Helen redeems the suitcase at the hotel. In her room, she recalls her life, her beloved father's suicide, her mother's cheating her of her inheritance, and her exploiting lover/employer in the music store. Washing herself and putting on her Japanese kimono, she prepares to die.

Francis, meanwhile, revisits his family, bringing a turkey bought with his earnings from the day's job. He bathes, dresses in his old clothing his wife has saved, looks over souvenirs, meets his grandson, gets his daughter's forgiveness as well as his wife's, and is even invited to return. He leaves, however, and finds Rudy; together they look for Helen. Finding Helen registered at Palumbo's Hotel, Francis leaves money with the clerk for her. The final violent scene occurs in a hobo jungle, as it is being raided by Legionnaires. Francis kills Rudy's attacker with his own baseball bat and carries the fatally injured Rudy to the hospital. Returning to the hotel, Francis discovers Helen dead and leaves swiftly in a freight car.

The ending, typical of Kennedy's novels, is inconclusive. The reader can assume either that Francis leaves on a southbound freight or that he returns to his wife Annie's house and lives hidden in the attic. The use of the conditional in narration of this final section lends the necessary vagueness. Nevertheless, in *Ironweed*, the intricacy of poetry combines with factual detail and hallucinatory fugues to create a tight structure, the most nearly perfect of *The Albany Cycle* and its appropriate conclusion. The parallelism, for example, of a discussion of the temptations of Saint Anthony with the name of the Italian Church of St. Anthony, where Helen hears Mass on her last day of life, shows the craftsmanship of the author. The interconnections of theme, plot, and character in the three Albany novels, their hallucinatory fantasies, their ghostly visitations, ennoble the lowest of the low into modern epic heroes.

Quinn's Book • Kennedy's next novel, *Quinn's Book*, also centers on Albany. Spanning a period from the late 1840's to the mid-1860's, *Quinn's Book* is a historical novel infused with Magical Realism, deliberately extravagant in style. The narrator and protagonist, Daniel Quinn, an orphan, relates his adventures and his gradual progress toward maturity. Ultimately he becomes a writer, encouraged by his editor on the *Albany Chronicle*, Will Canady (whose name suggests that he is the author's alter ego). Coming-of-age tale, picaresque, novel of education, *Künstlerroman*: *Quinn's Book* partakes of all these genres and more, generally stopping just short of parody. It is Kennedy's most explicit celebration of the transformative power of art.

Very Old Bones • In *Very Old Bones*, Kennedy focuses on the Phelan family history, his narrator a third-generation, albeit unacknowledged, Phelan. Orson Purcell, child of Peter Phelan and his landlady, Claire Purcell, has come to the family home in Albany to care for the ailing Peter. Orson brings a troubled soul to the house that was home to his father, but not to him. Uncertain of his identity, he has suffered two breakdowns and alternately mythologizes and demonizes his wife Giselle, a talented photographer.

In the house on Colonie Street, Orson composes a family history, a "memoir," while his father struggles to complete the Malachi Suite, a series of paintings that document a tragic but pivotal event in the family's past. The two artists find solutions to the mysteries of their own lives by unearthing "very old bones," not unlike the construction crews who have discovered the skeleton of a mastodon beneath Albany's old water filtration plant.

The event that provides the key to so many Phelan mysteries is the 1887 "exorcism" murder of Lizzie McIlhenny at the hands of her demented husband Malachi, brother of Kathryn Phelan. The story helps to explain the unremitting joylessness of the Phelan matriarch, an unwilling spectator of the horror. In addition, the four paintings in the suite depict the patterns of belief that have informed the behavior of successive generations of Phelans: a distrust of happiness, a keen awareness of the dark forces afoot in the world, and a conviction that the past is always buried in a very shallow grave.

The Flaming Corsage • *The Flaming Corsage*, the sixth novel in the Albany Cycle, begins with a cryptic account of the so-called Love Nest killings in 1908, a scandalous event in which the playwright Edward Daugherty is injured by his friend Giles Fitzroy, who then kills his own wife and himself.

The complex of causes resulting in the killings had been set in motion a generation earlier when Emmett Daugherty saved the life of his employer who, in gratitude, promised to educate Emmett's children. Thus, Edward Daugherty, a well-educated child of Albany's Irish North, is positioned not only to court the granddaughter of his patron but also to incur the envy of his colleague, Maginn, a Claggert-like figure whose machinations lead to the killings.

The union of Edward and Katrina is doomed because it defies the ethnic, religious, and class divisions of Albany, but the turning point in their marriage is the fire in the Delavan Hotel that indirectly claims the lives of Katrina's sister and father. Katrina herself is scarred when a flaming stick pierces her breast and sets her corsage afire. Finding in the accidental tragedy an indictment of her own and Edward's behavior, Katrina withdraws from her husband and unwittingly sets in motion a new train of causation that will contribute to other deaths fourteen years later.

In *The Flaming Corsage*, Kennedy's characters continue to seek "God's own symmetry" in random tragedies while failing to anticipate the consequences of their own behavior. Love, like the flaming arrow that wounds Katrina, is more often a cause of than a cure for the sadness of life.

Roscoe • Kennedy's seventh novel of the Albany cycle, *Roscoe* is the story of Roscoe Conway, the boisterous, engaging, and rogue politician who has made the Democratic Party what it is in 1930's and 1940's Albany. The book begins in 1945, as Roscoe has decided, finally, to retire from politics. A series of barriers, however, stand in the way, and the retirement has to be delayed.

Things fall apart when Roscoe's best friend, steel magnate Elisha Fitzgibbon, commits suicide, and his former wife, the sister of Elisha's widow, returns to add mayhem to an already volatile situation. Meanwhile, Roscoe is working to get Alex Fitzgibbon, Elisha's son, back into the office of mayor. He is also attempting to patch up a feud between Democratic leader Patsy McCall and his brothers, characters who previously appeared in *Billy Phelan's Greatest Game*. On top of this, Roscoe is also trying to heal the divide between McCall stooge Mac McEvoy and Roscoe's brother O.B., Albany's chief of police, over credit for the killing of Jack "Legs" Diamond.

Another element that adds confusion and chaos to Roscoe's life is his longtime love for Elisha's widow, Veronica. Now that Elisha is dead, Roscoe finally works up the courage to make a move on Veronica, and he is very close to winning her heart. As if that were not enough, Roscoe also receives visitations from his dead father, Felix, and the reader is reminded how commonplace it is for the living to communicate with the dead in Kennedy's Albany.

In some ways, *Roscoe* is the book that Kennedy has always needed and wanted to write. It is an investigation into the nature of a certain kind of politician, the kind that seemingly no longer exists. Hot-blooded Roscoe bears much in common with legendary politicians of old such as Jimmy Walker and Fiorello La Guardia, and he injects vibrancy and comic energy into Kennedy's otherwise dark vision of the post-World War II Albany political machine. More than that, though, the novel is about Roscoe's Irishness and about the archetypal Irish American Democrat of the first half of the twentieth century. Whether one reads *Roscoe* as historical fiction, as a tale about power in the vein of William Shakespeare's *Henry IV* (c. 1597-1598), or as a simple legal thriller, *Roscoe* is a successful contribution to the Albany cycle, one that cements Kennedy's place among America's greatest literary regionalists and also helps shed light on a time when politicians were as flawed and crooked as ever, yet full of a vivacity and originality that has all but disappeared from the American political landscape.

In interviews, Kennedy has stressed the importance to him of writing about past events instead of current events in the interest of avoiding the trap of writing mere journalism. With *Roscoe,* the reader sees why this formula works for Kennedy. He allows himself enough distance, enough freedom, to mold and shape these characters into unique and spirited creations. An exposé on a recent or current political figure would surely backfire for precisely all the reasons that *Roscoe* works so well.

Anne Mills King
Updated by Kathleen N. Monahan and William Boyle

Other major works

SHORT FICTION: "The Secrets of Creative Love," 1983; "An Exchange of Gifts," 1985; "A Cataclysm of Love," 1986.

SCREENPLAYS: *The Cotton Club,* 1984 (with Francis Coppola and Mario Puzo); *Ironweed,* 1987 (adaptation of his novel).

NONFICTION: *Getting It All, Saving It All: Some Notes by an Extremist,* 1978; *O Albany! An Urban Tapestry,* 1983 (also known as *O Albany! Improbable City of Political Wizards, Fearless Ethnics, Spectacular Aristocrats, Splendid Nobodies, and Underrated Scoundrels,* 1983); *The Capitol in Albany,* 1986; *Riding the Yellow Trolley Car: Selected Nonfiction,* 1993; *Conversations with William Kennedy,* 1997 (Neila C. Seshachari, editor).

CHILDREN'S LITERATURE: *Charlie Malarkey and the Belly Button Machine,* 1986 (with Brendan Kennedy); *Charlie Malarkey and the Singing Moose,* 1994 (with Brendan Kennedy); *Roscoe and Me: The Specific and the Impossible,* 2003.

Bibliography
Giamo, Benedict. *The Homeless of "Ironweed": Blossoms on the Crag.* Iowa City: University of Iowa Press, 1996. Giamo explores the theme of homelessness and social problems in literature, focusing on *Ironweed.* Includes a bibliography.
Kennedy, Liam. "Memory and Hearsay: Ethnic History and Identity in *Billy Phelan's Greatest Game* and *Ironweed.*" *MELUS* 18 (Spring, 1993): 71-83. The author focuses on *Billy Phelan's Greatest Game* and *Ironweed* to explore Kennedy's presentation of ethnic identity. In a tightly knit community such as Albany's Irish North End, family, civic, and ethnic history blend into an inchoate, yet powerful, force. The author points to Kennedy's insistence on the role of the past in the motives and impulses of his characters.
Kennedy, William. "The Art of Fiction CXI: William Kennedy." Interview by Douglas R. Allen and Mona Simpson. *Paris Review* 31 (Winter, 1989): 34-59. Conducted in two sessions, in 1984 and 1988, this wide-ranging interview provides an excellent introduction to Kennedy's work. He discusses his experience as a newspaper writer, the vicissitudes of his literary career, and his development as a novelist. Includes Kennedy's observation that he does not regard *Legs, Billy Phelan's Greatest Game,* and *Ironweed* as a trilogy but rather as works in an ongoing cycle.
_____. *Conversations with William Kennedy.* Edited by Neila C. Seshachari. Jackson: University Press of Mississippi, 1997. Part of the Literary Conversations series, this book of interviews with Kennedy is insightful. Includes an index.
Lynch, Vivian Valvano. *Portraits of Artists: Warriors in the Novels of William Kennedy.* San Francisco: International Scholars, 1999. Engaging survey of Kennedy's writing career that emphasizes his use of Irish and American themes.
Michener, Christian. *From Then into Now: William Kennedy's Albany Novels.* Scranton, Pa.: University of Scranton Press, 1998. Discusses the theme of city life in Kennedy's works. Contains a bibliography and an index.

Nichols, Loxley F. "William Kennedy Comes of Age." *National Review* 27 (August 9, 1985): 78-79. An excellent short piece on Kennedy with much useful information. Discusses *The Ink Truck*, which Nichols considers Kennedy's most atypical work. Also analyzes Jack Diamond's death in *Legs*. Explores *Ironweed* in the light of its mythical allusions and describes *O Albany!* in terms of the "pervasive vitality of the past."

Reilly, Edward C. *William Kennedy*. Boston: Twayne, 1991. A useful source of biographical, critical, and bibliographical information.

Turner, Tramble T. "*Quinn's Book:* Reconstructing Irish-American History." *MELUS* 18 (Spring, 1993): 31-46. Discusses the presentation of the Irish and the African American in *Quinn's Book*. Similarities between the two outcast communities in the nineteenth century do not prevent racist outbreaks such as the Draft Riot of 1863. The author compares *Quinn's Book* to Toni Morrison's 1987 *Beloved* as commentary on America's past.

Van Dover, J. K. *Understanding William Kennedy*. Columbia: University of South Carolina Press, 1991. Van Dover provides a genealogy for the complex Phelan and Quinn family relationships and a chronology combining events that occur within the novels.

Jack Kerouac

Born: Lowell, Massachusetts; March 12, 1922
Died: St. Petersburg, Florida; October 21, 1969

Principal long fiction • *The Town and the City*, 1950; *On the Road*, 1957; *The Dharma Bums*, 1958; *The Subterraneans*, 1958; *Doctor Sax*, 1959; *Maggie Cassidy*, 1959; *Tristessa*, 1960; *Visions of Cody*, 1960, 1972; *Big Sur*, 1962; *Visions of Gerard*, 1963; *Desolation Angels*, 1965; *Vanity of Duluoz*, 1968; *Pic*, 1971.

Other literary forms • In addition to his novels, Jack Kerouac published *Mexico City Blues* (1959), a poetry collection intended to imitate the techniques of jazz soloists. *Scattered Poems* (1971) and *Old Angel Midnight* (1976) were published posthumously. His nonfiction prose includes *The Scripture of the Golden Eternity* (1960), a homemade sutra written to Gary Snyder; *Book of Dreams* (1961), sketches that recorded his dreams; *Lonesome Traveler* (1960), travel sketches; and *Satori in Paris* (1966).

Achievements • Although some critics have condemned Kerouac as an incoherent, unstructured, and unsound writer, the prophet of a nihilistic movement, his books have continued to be read. The very qualities for which he has been criticized—wildness, sensationalism, and irresponsibility—have been sources of charm to other commentators. He has been described on one hand as pessimistic and bizarre, and on the other as optimistic and fresh. His most prestigious and enthusiastic reviewer has been Malcolm Cowley, who introduced *On the Road* to Viking after it had been turned down by Ace, Harcourt Brace, and Little, Brown. *On the Road*'s respectability is evidenced by its appearance in excerpt form in *The Norton Anthology of American Literature* and its publication as a casebook in The Viking Critical Library series.

Kerouac's unofficial and unwanted title as "King of the Beats" brought him a great deal of the publicity he shunned. As with other aspects of Kerouac's life and works, there was little agreement about what a "Beat" was. Kerouac's friend, Gary Snyder, has described the Beats as a movement that gathered together the myths of freedom espoused by Henry David Thoreau and Walt Whitman, adding some of the notions of Buddhism. John Holmes defined "Beat" as a "nakedness of soul," as "feeling reduced to the bedrock of consciousness." The Beat writers, he added, recognized the need for home, for values, and for faith, and they advocated companionship, courage, and mutual confidence.

To Kerouac, who is generally credited with the invention of the term, "Beat" meant "beatific"—holy and compassionate. Interviewed by Mike Wallace on television, Kerouac declared that the Beats did not fear death and that they wanted to lose themselves as Christ had advised. In *Pageant* magazine, he wrote that the Beats believed that honesty and freedom would lead to a vision of a God of Ecstasy. In a public forum, Kerouac declared that America was changing for the better and warned those who wanted to spit on the Beat generation that the wind would blow the spit back on them. Mass-media writers developed the image of a bearded "beatnik" who wore sweatshirts and jeans, played bongo drums, never bathed, and used the word "like" as a ubiquitous conjunction. Even though the beatniks were a far cry from the intellec-

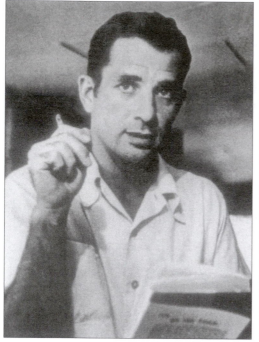

National Archives

tual Beats, they became associated with them in the public eye.

Although Kerouac's public image endangered his critical reception, critics of the late twentieth century recognized him as a powerful and talented writer. His work, as he intended it to be, is one long opus.

Biography • Jean Louis Lebris de Kerouac was born in Lowell, Massachusetts, on March 12, 1922. His mother, Gabrielle Ange Levesque Kerouac, and his father, Leo Alcide Kerouac, were both French Canadians whose families had emigrated from Quebec. Gabrielle's father, a mill worker and an owner of a small tavern, had died when she was fourteen, and she then went to work as a machine operator in a Nashua, New Hampshire, shoe shop. From this moment, and for the rest of her life, "Memere" fought for a higher social status. Leo was an insurance salesman who became a job printer. At the time of Kerouac's birth, his sister Caroline ("Nin") was three, and Gerard, the brother who had been weakened by rheumatic fever, was five.

The year after Kerouac's birth, Leo began publication of *The Lowell Spotlight*, which featured local political and theatrical news. The family was very close; the mother was a teller of tales, and the father was an entertainer who specialized in animal noises. At the age of nine, Gerard became so ill that he was forced to remain in bed. To his younger brother, Gerard was a saint who had once saved a mouse from a trap. As Gerard grew weaker, he grew more angelic in the eyes of everyone in the family, and the lively young Jack suffered by comparison. As Gerard's pain grew worse, Jack began to feel that he was somehow responsible. After Gerard's death, Jack tried futilely to replace him by being especially pious and sensitive.

As he grew older, Kerouac went frequently to films with passes given to Leo. The public library also became another favorite haunt, but the biggest outside influence on Kerouac's childhood was the Roman Catholic Church of his forefathers. He attended parochial school, had visions of Christ and the Virgin Mary, memorized the catechism, and worried about his sins and purgatory. When he became an altar boy, his Jesuit teachers thought that he might become a priest, but when he entered a public junior high school, Jean Kerouac became "Jacky," who could write, and whose favorite radio program was *The Shadow*—the forerunner of Dr. Sax.

As he walked to Lowell High School, where he participated in track and football, Kerouac saw the factories and the failures of his French Canadian neighbors; his father had lost his business and had even been forced to accept a job carrying water buckets for the Works Progress Administration (WPA). Memere, frustrated in her ever present ambitions, placed all of her hopes in her remaining son and urged him to study and to succeed in a way that his father had not. By his senior year, Kerouac was a football star, scoring the winning touchdown for Lowell in the final game against Lawrence High.

Kerouac fell in love with Mary Carney, but he left her behind to accept Columbia University football coach Lou Little's offer to attend Horace Mann Prep School, where he was to add the pounds and knowledge requisite for a Columbia football player. At Horace Mann, Jack wrote papers for his classmates for pay, some of which he spent on his first prostitute. He published short stories in the *Horace Mann Quarterly*, discovered the jazz world in Harlem, and adopted Whitman as his personal bard.

At Columbia, Kerouac studied William Shakespeare under Mark Van Doren, registered for the draft, found another mentor in the works of Thomas Wolfe, and broke his leg in a freshman football game. One day, to the great distress of his parents, who constantly pleaded with him to "get ahead" in the world, Kerouac left Columbia for Washington, D.C., New Haven, and Hartford, Connecticut, and a series of short-lived jobs. While he was a sportswriter for the *Lowell Sun*, he read Fyodor Dostoevski, who became his prophet. He shipped out of Boston as a merchant seaman on the *Dorchester*, where he started a novel called *The Sea Is My Brother*. In 1943, he entered the navy, which discharged him honorably three months later for "indifferent character." In 1944, Kerouac met poet Allen Ginsberg, a Columbia student until he was banned from campus, and William S. Burroughs, with whom he wrote a detective story. He also met Edie Parker, whom he married but from whom he separated shortly thereafter.

After his father died of cancer in 1946, Kerouac started taking Benzedrine and writing *The Town and the City*. He also met Neal Cassady, the "brother" he had been seeking since Gerard's death. After Cassady returned to Denver, Kerouac set out to see America, stopping in Denver before going to San Francisco, where he worked as a security guard, sending his savings to Memere. On a bus bound for Los Angeles, he met Bea Franco, with whom he took a job in Bakersfield picking cotton. From there, he took a bus to Pittsburgh and hitched a ride back to Memere's house, where she took care of him while he wrote. Cassady came east again, and he, Kerouac, and Cassady's first wife, Lu Anne, made their famous "on the road" trip.

At this time, Harcourt Brace announced that they would publish *The Town and the City*. Kerouac used the profits from *The Town and the City* to buy a house for Memere in Colorado, but she left it for New York after seven weeks of misery. Several journeys back and forth from Brooklyn to Colorado followed for Cassady and Kerouac. In 1950, Kerouac married Joan Haverty and began writing *On the Road*, typing it on rolls of teletype paper. In 1952, Janet Michele Kerouac was born to Joan, but it would be ten years before Kerouac admitted paternity.

Kerouac held jobs during the next few years as a brakeman, as a yard clerk, and as a fire watcher, but he depended mostly on his mother for support, despite the gnawing recollection that he had promised his father to take care of her. After several rejections, *On the Road* was published in 1957 and was hailed by *The New York Times* critic Gilbert Millstein as a major novel. During the next six years, Kerouac published twelve more books.

While Kerouac was in New York, he fell in love with Mardou Fox, whose American Indian and black ancestry Memere could never accept. After losing Mardou to the poet Gregory Corso, Kerouac wrote about the affair in *The Subterraneans*. In response to William Burroughs's request, Kerouac typed out "The Essentials of Spontaneous Prose," explaining the writing method he had used.

Kerouac found solace in *Walden: Or, Life in the Woods* (1854) and Thoreau, with whom he shared a rejection of civilization, and he also began to study Buddhism as part of his search for peace from the carping of Memere and the disappointments engendered by unsympathetic editors. He tried to convert the Cassadys, with whom he lived for a time in California, to Buddhism, but he also expressed to Ginsberg, once more in New York, his fear that charlatans might misuse Buddhism for aesthetic purposes. He meditated daily in an effort to reach Nirvana. When he met poet Gary Snyder, a Zen Buddhist whose approach was prayerful, Kerouac felt a harmony he had not known, even with Cassady.

By the time Kerouac married Stella Sampas, the sister of an old friend who was killed in the war, and settled down again in Lowell, he was suffering from three problems: recurring phlebitis, alcoholism, and the adulation of youngsters who invaded his privacy and made him feel old. They expected him to be Dean Moriarty of *On the Road*, but his aging, alcoholic body rebelled.

Meanwhile, Cassady had been arrested for possession of marijuana and sentenced to prison time at San Quentin, whence he complained about Kerouac's lack of attention. After his release, Cassady drank tequila and swallowed Seconals at a Mexican wedding party; the combination caused his death. Kerouac never allowed himself to believe that Cassady was actually dead. In October, 1969, Kerouac's years of heavy drinking caused him to begin to bleed internally, and he died hours later. He had been, in spite of his bizarre habits, a gentle, loving man.

Analysis • Jack Kerouac described himself as "a great rememberer redeeming life from darkness." In one sense, the Beat movement itself issued from his memory. In his June, 1959, *Playboy* essay on "The Origins of the Beat Generation," Kerouac claimed that the guts of the Beats had come from his ancestors—the independent Breton nobles who fought against the Latin French; his grandfather, Jean-Baptiste Kerouac, who used to defy God to put out his kerosene lamp during a thunderstorm; his father, who used to give such loud parties that the Lowell police came for drinks—and from his own childhood, peopled with the Shadow, the Moon Man, and the Marx Brothers.

Kerouac claimed on more than one occasion that his books were actually one book about his entire life. He had intentions to consolidate them, but these plans were not carried out before his death. The areas of life that he remembered and celebrated include the dichotomy between his family and friends in Lowell, Massachusetts, and the Beat friends with whom he carried on such a frenzied, peripatetic relationship. As a rememberer, he never separated the two entirely; the Roman Catholic Bretons and the gentle Leo and Gerard were never far from his consciousness. Kerouac declared that his father had never lifted a hand to punish his children, or even their little pets, and that Gerard had extracted from his younger brother a promise never to hurt or allow anyone else to hurt a living thing. These two strains— the fierceness of the Bretons and the gentleness of his brother and father—culminated in the vitality and the kindness of Jack Kerouac, the former football player who cared so much for his pets as a grown man that his mother feared to tell him that his cat had died.

The Town and the City • When he was ready to write his first published book, *The Town and the City*, Kerouac found it necessary—or more aesthetically pleasing—to

use five boys to present the many facets of his own character. The Kerouac family became the Martins, and Lowell became Galloway, which had a rural setting. The Martins are wealthier than the author's own family; they are also less devout as Roman
Catholics. The mother is French, and the rest of the family is Irish. Most of the vignettes serve to illustrate the love that the Martins feel for one another and Galloway
as a town of "wild, self-believing individuals," the kind about which Walt Whitman
sang.

The style of the novel is romantic and sprawling, in the vein of Thomas Wolfe. Although Kerouac possessed an almost uncanny aptitude for recollecting details, he
enhanced his memory by reviewing his old notebooks. The book was to be more than
a chronicle of the Martin/Kerouac family; it was to be a microcosm of America.
There are three sisters and five brothers in the Martin family, as opposed to the
daughter and two sons of the Kerouacs; the loving, compassionate Mrs. Martin
recalls Kerouac's own mother. Mickey, the youngest child of the Martins, goes to
dinner and the races with his father, just as the young Jack had gone to Rockingham
racetrack with Leo. He also writes novels and publishes newspapers about his imaginary racehorses and baseball teams.

Two of the sisters, Rose and Ruth, have the characteristics of Kerouac's sister Nin,
while the third, Liz, is more like Kerouac's high school sweetheart, Mary Carney.
One story of sibling love involves Charley, who had broken a window with his sling-
shot and is collecting junk to pay for it. Liz and Joe pitch in to help him when they
learn of his plight. Liz eventually elopes with a jazz musician, has a stillborn baby,
divorces her husband, and becomes a blond barmaid.

The central character, Peter, is thirteen when the novel begins, and the story of
his most spectacular high school game is that of his creator. As a result of his prowess,
Peter wins a football scholarship to the University of Pennsylvania, but he leaves to
join the merchant marines. As a student, however, he meets a new circle of friends,
whose habits dismay George Martin just as Kerouac's marijuana-smoking cronies had
bewildered Leo. Peter tries to introduce his mistress Judie to his parents, but their
meeting is interrupted by a policeman who wants Peter to identify the body of Waldo
Meister, a suicide victim. The gulf between the Martin family and Peter's friends is
never closed, but Peter continues to be a loving part of both groups. He nurses his
father during his illness and reacts to his death with grief and disbelief.

Peter's brother Francis is a shy, studious Harvard student who fails the Officers'
Candidate School aptitude test and rebels at being a soldier. When he is confined for
tests, he spots a navy psychiatrist with *The New Republic* under his arm and decides that
he has met a kindred spirit. Convinced that Francis is indeed incapable of taking orders, the doctor helps him obtain his discharge.

In one scene, Levinsky (the Allen Ginsberg character) lectures to Peter in a Times
Square cafeteria about a "post-atomic" disease of the soul, using words taken from an
actual essay by Ginsberg (with permission from Ginsberg).

The novel ends with an unhappy Peter heading West to a new life, on a lonely,
rainy night. The family has figuratively died with the father, and Peter will go wherever the roads lead. According to John Clellon Holmes, the book had originally
ended with the family together, and the "on the road" ending was a last-minute
Kerouac addition, which would lead obviously and naturally into his next book, already in the planning stage.

The Town and the City is frequently compared with Thomas Wolfe's *Look Homeward,
Angel* (1929), and, like Wolfe's book, it required considerable editing, which was ac-

complished by Robert Giroux, who cut one third of the manuscript. In spite of its lukewarm success, Kerouac continued to believe in his own genius. Years later, he learned that the Kerouac family crest included the motto (translated from the French), "Love, Work, and Suffer." He happily noted that these words accurately describe the Martin family.

On the Road • Both the title and the novel were incubating in Kerouac's mind for four years before he sat down to write *On the Road* on a 100-foot roll of paper, in one 120,000 word, single-spaced paragraph. Six more years passed before its publication, and in the decade between conception and birth, America had changed, and so had the writer.

Sal Paradise, the narrator and the Kerouac figure, received his name when Ginsberg wrote a poem containing the line, "Sad paradise it is I imitate." The carelessly written "d" caused "Sad" to look like "Sal." Sal, whose ideals are both romantic and personal, sets out near the beginning of the tale to search for an eden. He is at the same time leaving behind all intimacy and responsibility associated with home and family.

Like Geoffrey Chaucer's pilgrims, everyone Sal meets is described with superlatives: He hears "the greatest laugh in the world"; he observes the most smiling, cheerful face in the world; and he watches a tall Mexican roll the biggest bomber anybody ever saw. While observing these fellow pilgrims, he thinks of himself and his friends as seeking salvation and the promised land. Sal expects to find a direction and purpose on the road that his life has not previously had.

Sal has studied maps of the West, and when he begins his trip, he wants to repeat as closely as possible the path of the old wagon trains. He glories in the names of such cities as Platte and Cimarron and imagines that the unbroken red line that represents Route 6 on his map duplicates the trail of the early American settlers. After a false start on a rainy day, Sal returns to New York, where he had started, and buys a bus ticket to Chicago; the bus is a mode of travel he uses more than once. In Des Moines, Sal awakens nameless and reborn in what seems to be a turning point in his life. This moment that divides his youth from his future occurs, fittingly enough, in mid-America. He goes from Denver to California, where he meets Dean Moriarty, the central figure of the book and the figure that made Neal Cassady a legend.

Dean becomes a part of Sal's life, an extension of his personality, his alter ego; he even insists on sharing his wife with Sal. Three become a crowd, however, and Sal, after several digressions, goes back to the East and his aunt. On the last lap of the journey, he meets a shriveled old man with a paper suitcase who is called "Ghost of the Susquehanna." Sal sees him as an aging reflection of what he himself will become—a bum.

The energy of the book derives from Dean Moriarty, who is never far out of Sal's mind. Dean's accomplishments include skillful driving—often of cars he has stolen for a joyride—talking his way out of any tight situation, seducing women—frequently two at a time—and appreciating jazz. The friends Dean has met in pool halls become the minor heroes of this epic.

In Kerouac's mind, Cassady and America were one entity—vibrant, carefree, and admirable. Through Dean Moriarty, Kerouac chronicles a new kind of existence in postwar America—suggesting a life less dependent upon place and family and more tolerant of impropriety. The hedonist Dean loves and leaves his women in the manner of the stereotyped cowboy who rides off into the sunset. Dean, never complacent, ever free, can be characterized by the fact that he goes to answer his door completely naked. Even when he is employed and has a home address, he seems to be on the move; he is always planning a break from entanglements, often represented by whomever his current wife might be.

Sal sees himself as a disciple to the saint, Dean, and he exults in Dean's uniqueness and eccentricity. Dean's mysticism consists of belief in his father, in God, and IT, which can be communicated by jazz musicians and that has somehow been communicated to Dean through his missing father, who had been a drunk. The search for Dean's father is one of the book's themes, along with the search for God. The roaders are seeking someone to shelter them from life and responsibility, and they approve of those pilgrims (Montana Slim and Remi Boncoeur) who are respectful toward their own fathers.

Perhaps the story would not have been told if Dean had not been such an extraordinary driver, absolutely at home on the road. Sal has no driver's license and when allowed at the wheel guides the car off the road and onto a muddy shoulder. Even though Dean's chief contribution to the conversation seems to be "Wow," he expresses himself eloquently while in control of a car. Never mind if he wears it out; he delivers the car exhausted to its owner, while he travels on jauntily in another vehicle willing to respond to his touch.

Women respond to Dean in the same way, and he sees sex as essential and holy. His problem is that he wants to love several women simultaneously. He sees them as part of his self-improvement schedule, which is not induced by remorse for crimes committed or prison terms spent, but by the demands imposed by his search for a better life. Sal forgives Dean his thefts and other transgressions, reasoning that all Americans are like that.

On the Road is a love story: Sal loves Dean Moriarty, and their movements back and forth across the continent represent in some ways their relationship. Sal sees Dean at first as a source of hope, and he moves toward him, fascinated. He finally assumes some of the responsibility for his friend, and he becomes his defender. After Dean's thumb becomes infected as a result of hitting one of his women, Sal sees him as a mad Ahab. When Dean, Sal, and a friend go to Mexico City, on what is significantly their first North-South journey, Sal becomes ill and is abandoned by Dean, who has to go home to straighten out one of his recurring domestic crises. Sal never denies Dean, but he is less enamored of his sometimes childish friend by the book's end.

Most of the characters Sal meets on the road are attractive in some way; as Huck Finn found people on the river to be sympathetic, Sal feels a communion with the hobos, who eschew competition and jobs for a sense of brotherhood and a simple life. He is disappointed, however, when he sees his first cowboy, whose apparel is his only claim to authenticity. Like Stephen Crane before him, Sal sees that the West is merely trying to perpetuate dead traditions, and that Central City is simply a tourist attraction. Nothing can be as fine as his dreams of the West, and he eventually begins to conclude that the East, after all, may be the place to find contentment and salvation. He returns home in his favorite month, October, realizing that he has acted out an adventure, but that he has experienced no rebirth.

The point of view of *On the Road* is consistently that of Sal, but as he tells the reader about his experiences as they occurred at the time, he also comments on the same events as he sees them now, with a more mature, more disillusioned, more objective eye. Saddened by the realization that the road itself is all important to Dean, he repudiates the idea of movement with no purpose.

Recognizing the vastness and shapelessness of the experience he was about to put on paper, Kerouac sought a suitable form and style. He began to write the book in a conscious imitation of Thomas Wolfe, but he finally decided to emulate Cassady's amorphous, joyous style. He added to that a new, free-association method that he called "sketching," suggested to him by Ed White, who thought it possible to paint with words. Sketching, comparable in Kerouac's view to the improvisation of the jazz musicians he greatly admired, was new, but the story he told was a repetition of the ageless initiation theme. *On the Road* is, however, not simply another *Tom Jones* (Henry Fielding, 1749) or *Adventures of Huckleberry Finn* (Mark Twain, 1884); it reflects the confusion, the sense of search, and the troubled spirit of the Kerouac generation.

The Subterraneans • The title of *The Subterraneans* comes from Ginsberg's name for Greenwich Villagers; its setting is New York, disguised with San Francisco place names. Kerouac claimed that the book is a full confession of the incidents surrounding his love affair with Mardou Fox, a part black, part American Indian subterranean who had been hanging out with drug addicts and musicians. Kerouac fell in love with her, he said, even before they were introduced.

The book, consciously modeled after Fyodor Dostoevski's *Notes from the Underground* (1864), contains Mardou's private thoughts as she has whispered them to Leo Percipied (the Kerouac figure). She imagines herself walking naked in the Village, crouching like a feline on a fence, experiencing a private epiphany, and then borrowing clothes and money to buy herself a symbolic brooch.

Leo (as Kerouac himself always did) sympathizes with minority races and listens to Mardou's thoughts about African Americans, American Indians, and America with a keen perception. The story carries Leo and Mardou on their frenzied movements through the Village in scenes that include meetings with bop musicians, poets, and novelists. A central scene describes Yuri Gligoric's (Gregory Corso) theft of a vendor's pushcart, in which he transports his friends to the home of Adam Moorad (Allen Ginsberg), who is angry at Yuri because of the prank.

Both Mardou and Leo become dissatisfied with their life together, and when Yuri and Leo bicker over her, Leo chooses the incident as an excuse to separate from Mardou. Afterward, he wanders alone to a freight yard, where he has a vision of his mother. Leo finally admits that he felt inadequate sexually in the presence of Mardou, and he concludes, "I go home, having lost her love, and write this book."

Fortified by Benzedrine, Kerouac sat at his typewriter with yet another teletype roll and wrote his confession in "three full moon nights of October." The style of the novel is remarkable for its faithful reproduction of Mardou's syntax and her drawn-out syllables. Kerouac heard in her speech a similarity to bop music, and he found in it what he called the "prose of the future." Impressed by this remarkable language, Burroughs and Ginsberg asked Kerouac to write a description of his spontaneous method of composition, and the result was the essay "The Essentials of Spontaneous Prose."

Reviews of *The Subterraneans* were not favorable. The only affirmation came from Henry Miller, who admired Kerouac's forthrightness. When an editor tried to cut some of the book, Kerouac refused to let him print it, and it was finally published in its original form in March of 1958.

The Dharma Bums • *The Dharma Bums*, a book that Kerouac himself once described as a potboiler, is perhaps the most representative expression of the Beat sensibility in a work of fiction. Its focus is the close intellectual and religious relationship of Ray Smith (Kerouac) and Japhy Ryder (Gary Snyder). Snyder called *The Dharma Bums* a real statement of synthesis, through Kerouac, of the available models and myths of freedom in America: Whitman, Thoreau, and the bums—with Buddhism added as a catalyst. Unlike *The Subterraneans, The Dharma Bums* is not purely confessional, and the literary hand is much more evident in the later work. For example, the author includes an encounter on a freight train with a bum who reads daily the prayers of Saint Teresa, who had been much beloved by Kerouac himself since childhood. He includes this character because the ascetic hobo adds to the book's religious ambience, but he pointedly omits mention of a meeting with an earthy, blond female that occurred the same day and is recounted in his notebook.

Ray Smith remembers an evening of peaceful happiness when he and Japhy sat together on a big glacial rock, elated, hallucinating, yet serious, and surrounded by yellow aspens. It was a cold evening in late autumn, and snow was on the ridges. It was on such an evening that Smith earned the sobriquet of the "Buddha Known as the Quitter," because he failed to climb a mountain. Ryder is another kind of coward. Because he has been a "poor guy" all of his life, he is afraid to enter a restaurant that might have an expensive menu.

The picture of Japhy is painted through faithful reproduction of Gary Snyder's speech and recollections of his poetry. The haiku Japhy composes on the mountainside are repeated verbatim, and one poem addressed to Sean Monahan (actually written by Snyder to Kerouac) is stuck on a nail of his cabin. Monahan is a twenty-two-year-old carpenter whose wife is adept at keeping him and their two children alive and happy on vegetable soup. The Monahans' life is described as "joyous," and they live in their woodland cottage furnished with Japanese straw mats, while they amuse themselves by studying sutras.

The way of life to which Ryder introduces Smith is a religious way, punctuated with prayer, laughter, and poetry, and it is espoused by the social minority who belong to the rucksack revolution. Both Smith and Ryder long to explain the dharma, or the truth of religion and life, to others. The dharma is associated with a nobility of body, mind, spirit, and speech that is surely worthy of their missionary zeal, if it can be attained.

Through Ryder, Smith learns of ecology and earth consciousness. The two discuss their own private religious beliefs. After he learns about the lifestyle of the "rucksack saints" through observation and listening, Smith delineates the mode of living for any would-be followers, listing the spiritual and physical equipment necessary: submission, acceptance, expectancy, rucksacks, tents, and sleeping bags.

Three books, then, shaped Kerouac's public image: *On the Road, The Subterraneans,* and *The Dharma Bums.* Each of them centers on a close relationship between a Kerouac figure and another person, and in each case, an intense dependency is involved. All are testaments of love, all concern America and Americans, all suggest an opportunity to develop emotional maturity, and all describe the existence of a subculture that anticipated the counterculture of the 1960's. However, despite these similarities, there is a progression. Certainly Ray Smith of *The Dharma Bums* is a wiser figure than Sal Paradise of *On the Road.* Ray admires Japhy Ryder, who teaches him about faith, hope, and charity, whereas Sal had worshiped Dean Moriarty, whose human relationships—especially with women—had been characterized by thoughtlessness and selfishness, for all of his charm. Japhy studies Japanese and reads Ezra Pound, whereas Dean had parroted Arthur Schopenhauer, often without understanding. The Buddhist sympathy for all beings and the notion that man is but a speck in the universe are a contrast to Moriarty's selfishness and vanity. In Gary Snyder, the gentle Jack Kerouac found the brother he had lost, and *The Dharma Bums* offers a calmer, more benevolent, albeit less sweeping picture of the country Kerouac wanted his works to celebrate than does the more famous *On the Road.*

Sue L. Kimball

Other major works
POETRY: *Mexico City Blues,* 1959; *Scattered Poems,* 1971; *Old Angel Midnight,* 1976.

NONFICTION: *Lonesome Traveler,* 1960; *The Scripture of the Golden Eternity,* 1960; *Book of Dreams,* 1961, revised 2001; *Satori in Paris,* 1966; *Good Blondes and Others,* 1993, revised and enlarged 1994; *Selected Letters, 1940-1956,* 1995 (Ann Charters, editor); *Selected Letters, 1957-1969,* 1999 (Charters, editor); *Door Wide Open: A Beat Love Affair in Letters, 1957-1958,* 2000; *Book of Haikus,* 2003 (Regina Weinreich, editor).

MISCELLANEOUS: *The Portable Jack Kerouac,* 1995 (Ann Charters, editor); *Some of the Dharma,* 1997; *Book of Sketches,* 2006.

Bibliography
Amburn, Ellis. *Subterranean Kerouac: The Hidden Life of Jack Kerouac.* New York: St. Martin's Press, 1998. A fascinating biography by one of Kerouac's editors, showing how his ambivalent feelings about his sexuality influenced his work. Includes detailed notes and bibliography.

Amram, David. *OffBeat: Collaborating with Kerouac.* New York: Thunder's Mouth Press, 2002. This memoir by a member of the Beat circle sheds a friendly light on Kerouac. An engaging account of a fascinating generation.

Cassady, Carolyn. *Heart Beat: My Life with Jack and Neal.* Berkeley, Calif.: Creative Arts, 1976. Chronicles Cassady's relationship with Kerouac from 1952 through 1953 and the *ménage à trois* between the Cassadys and Kerouac. Reprinted here are letters of Allen Ginsberg, Kerouac, Neal Cassady, and Carolyn Cassady.

_____. *Off the Road: My Years with Cassady, Kerouac, and Ginsberg.* New York: William Morrow, 1990. A personal account, with many anecdotes and recollections written from Carolyn Cassady's perspective. Important for its inside view of the Beat movement.

Charters, Ann. *Kerouac.* 1974. Reprint. New York: St. Martin's Press, 1987. A sympathetic biographical interpretation of his life and work.

Clark, Tom. *Kerouac's Last Word: Jack Kerouac in Escapade.* Sudbury, Mass.: Water Row Press, 1986. A somewhat expressionistic interpretation, but good analytical material. With a supplement of three articles by Kerouac.

Dittman, Michael J. *Jack Kerouac: A Biography.* Westport, Conn.: Greenwood Press, 2004. Highly regarded, concise biography of Kerouac that attempts to pull together all the themes in Kerouac's writings.

French, Warren G. *Jack Kerouac.* Boston: Twayne, 1986. A standard biography from Twayne's United States Authors series.

Giamo, Ben. *Kerouac, the Word and the Way: Prose Artist as Spiritual Quester.* Carbondale: Southern Illinois University Press, 2000. A study of the Beat poet's Roman Catholicism-infused Buddhism and his search for enlightenment.

Lardas, John. *The Bop Apocalypse: The Religious Visions of Kerouac, Ginsberg, and Burroughs.* Urbana: University of Illinois Press, 2001. A study of the spiritualism of three leading figures of the Beat movement.

McNally, Dennis. *Desolate Angel: Jack Kerouac, the Beat Generation, and America.* New York: Random House, 1979. A well-researched and generally sensitive biography that uses the materials of Kerouac's own books as well as comments by his friends to present Kerouac's life.

Nicosia, Gerald. *Memory Babe: A Critical Biography of Jack Kerouac.* New York: Grove Press, 1983. A comprehensive, biographical account of Kerouac's life. Highly regarded for background information on Kerouac and the process of his writing.

Turner, Steve. *Angelheaded Hipster: A Life of Jack Kerouac.* New York: Viking, 1996. Not as authoritative as Amburn, but copiously illustrated and with anecdotes that help illuminate the novels.

Ken Kesey

Born: La Junta, Colorado; September 17, 1935
Died: Eugene, Oregon; November 10, 2001

Principal long fiction • *One Flew over the Cuckoo's Nest*, 1962; *Sometimes a Great Notion*, 1964; *Caverns*, 1990 (with others; as O. U. Levon); *Sailor Song*, 1992; *Last Go Round*, 1994 (with Ken Babbs).

Other literary forms • When Stewart Brand was the editor of *The Last Whole Earth Catalog* in 1971, he asked Ken Kesey to edit *The Last Supplement to the Whole Earth Catalog*. Somewhat reluctant, Kesey agreed if Paul Krassner would be the coeditor. Krassner accepted, and it took almost two months to write, edit, and lay out the five-hundred-page final issue, which contained the best selections from previous issues as well as some new writings by Kesey. The final issue had a total press run of 100,000 copies and is now out of print.

Viking Press and Intrepid Trips jointly published *Kesey's Garage Sale* (1973), a volume based on an American phenomenon: the rummage, yard, or garage sale. The book is a miscellany of essays, poetry, letters, drawings, interviews, prose fiction, and a film script. Although much of the writing was Kesey's, "Hot Item Number 4: Miscellaneous Section with Guest Leftovers" contained a letter by Neal Cassady and poems by Allen Ginsberg and Hugh Romney. Kesey's "Who Flew over What," "Over the Border," and "Tools from My Chest" supply interesting insights into Kesey's beliefs and personality, and more important, they supplement the biographical details in Tom Wolfe's *The Electric Kool-Aid Acid Test* (1968), an informative biographical account of Kesey's Merry Pranksters exploits.

In "Who Flew over What," Kesey answers some of the most common questions about *One Flew over the Cuckoo's Nest*. He admitted that he wrote the novel while a night attendant at the Menlo Park Veterans Hospital, that he wrote part of it while under the influence of drugs, and that Randle Patrick McMurphy, the protagonist, was a fictional character "inspired by the tragic longing of the real men" on the ward. Kesey not only included his only sketches of McMurphy but also provided interesting facts and insights into his job and the actual life on the ward.

"Over the Border" is an innovative film script based on Kesey's second arrest, his flight to Mexico, the arrival of his family and some of the Merry Pranksters, their sojourn in Mexico, and the decision to return to the United States. The characters are easily recognizable: Devlin and Betsy Deboree are Kesey and his wife Faye; Sir Speed Houlihan is Neal Cassady; Claude and Blanch Muddle are Ken Babbs and his wife Anita; the Animal Friends are the Merry Pranksters; and Behema is Carolyn Adams. The script contains examples of Kesey's writing techniques, especially as he switches from scene to scene, as he describes the annual land-crab migration, and as he narrates Deboree's encounter with the Lizard, a Federales prison guard. Augmenting Wolfe's biographical account, the script also reveals Kesey's altered attitudes toward drugs as a means of changing society.

Another interesting section is "Tools from My Chest," parts of which were published originally in either *The Last Whole Earth Catalog* or *The Last Supplement to the Whole Earth Catalog.* These "tools" were figuratively those persons and things that had an impact on Kesey's own life and beliefs and, ultimately, on his writings. Kesey commented on such things as the Bible, the *I Ching*, mantras, the North Star, alcohol, and flowers; about such writers as Ernest Hemingway, William Faulkner (Kesey's declared favorite), Larry McMurtry, and William S. Burroughs; about radicals such as Malcolm X and Eldridge Cleaver; and about entertainers such as Woody Guthrie, Joan Baez, the Jefferson Airplane, and the Beatles. Finally, there are two powerfully written parables about Devlin Deboree.

Another miscellany, *Demon Box*, was published in 1986, and in 1990 Kesey and thirteen of his students published a collaborative novel, *Caverns*, under the pseudonym O. U. Levon. *The Further Inquiry*, also published in 1990, recounts the Merry Pranksters' 1964 cross-country bus trip and memorializes Neal Cassady.

Achievements • Writer Tom Wolfe remarked that Kesey was one of the most charismatic men he had ever met, and others have likewise commented upon Kesey's charisma. In fact, social critics affirmed that there were two important leaders of the 1960's counterculture revolution: Timothy Leary, who had his devotees on the East Coast, and Kesey, with his Merry Pranksters on the West Coast. Leary and his Learyites took themselves seriously, advocated passively dropping out of society, and rejected much that was American, especially American gadgetry. In contrast, Kesey and his Merry Pranksters were pro-America, were more interested in the spontaneous fun of the twentieth century neorenaissance, and took LSD not to become societal dropouts but rather to lead society to new frontiers of social communality.

As a novelist, Kesey achieved both notoriety and distinction as a major voice of his generation. However, some critics argue that his achievement goes further. They point to Kesey's complex characters, rollicking humor, and creative manipulation of point of view as his enduring contribution to American literature.

Biography • Ken Elton Kesey was born in La Junta, Colorado, on September 17, 1935, to Fred A. and Geneva Smith Kesey. Kesey's father shrewdly foresaw that the West Coast would be ideal for business ventures, and he moved his family to Springfield, Oregon, where he founded the Eugene Farmers Cooperative, the largest and most successful dairy cooperative in the Willamette Valley. The father taught his sons, Ken and Joe—the latter being called Chuck—how to wrestle, box, hunt, fish, and swim, and how to float the Willamette and McKenzie rivers on inner-tube rafts.

After attending the Springfield public schools and being voted most likely to succeed, Kesey enrolled in the University of Oregon at Eugene. In 1956, he married his high school sweetheart, Faye Haxby. During his undergraduate years, Kesey was an adept actor and seriously considered pursuing that career. He was also a champion wrestler in the 174-pound division and almost qualified for the Olympics. He received a bachelor's degree in 1957 and wrote *End of Autumn*, an unpublished novel about college athletics. In 1958, he enrolled in the graduate school at Stanford University on a creative writing scholarship and studied under Malcolm Cowley, Wallace Stegner, Frank O'Connor, and James B. Hall.

During his graduate student years, two important things occurred that would influence Kesey's life and writing. The first occurred when he moved his family into one of the cottages on Perry Lane, then the bohemian quarters of Stanford. He met other writers, including Larry McMurtry, Kenneth Babbs, Robert Stone, and Neal Cassady. The second event was that Kesey met Vic Lovell, to whom he would dedicate

© Christopher Felver

One Flew over the Cuckoo's Nest. Lovell not only introduced Kesey to Freudian psychology but also told Kesey about the drug experiments at the veterans' hospital in Menlo Park, California. In 1960, Kesey volunteered, earned twenty dollars per session, and discovered mind-expanding drugs that included Ditran, IT-290, and LSD. Kesey thus experienced LSD two years before Timothy Leary and Richard Alpert began their experiments at Harvard. Lovell also suggested that Kesey become a night attendant on the Menlo Park Veterans Hospital psychiatric ward so that he could concentrate on his writing. While there, he completed "Zoo," an unpublished novel about San Francisco's North Beach. Meanwhile, Kesey became intensely interested in the patients he saw and their lives on the ward. He began writing *One Flew over the Cuckoo's Nest* during the summer of 1960 and completed it in the spring of 1961. More important, as a volunteer and an aide, Kesey stole all types of drugs—especially LSD—which he distributed to his Perry Lane friends.

In June, 1961, Kesey moved his family to Springfield, Oregon, to help his brother start the Springfield Creamery and to save enough money for researching his next novel. Having saved enough money, the Keseys moved to Florence, Oregon, fifty miles west of Springfield, and Kesey began gathering material for *Sometimes a Great Notion.* His research included riding in the pickup trucks, called "crummies," that bussed the loggers to and from the logging sites. At night Kesey frequented the bars where the loggers drank, talked, and relaxed.

One Flew over the Cuckoo's Nest was published in 1962 and was critically acclaimed. In the late spring of 1962 Kesey returned to Perry Lane, where he began writing his second novel and renewed his drug experiments. When a developer bought the Perry Lane area for a housing development, Kesey purchased a home and land in La Honda, California, and invited about a dozen of his closest Perry Lane friends to join him so that they could continue their drug experiments. This group would eventually become Kesey's famous Merry Pranksters or the Day-Glo Crazies.

Sometimes a Great Notion was scheduled for publication in July, 1964, and Kesey and Ken Babbs, who had just returned from Vietnam, had planned a trip to the New York World's Fair to arrive there for the publication of Kesey's second novel. Kesey bought a converted 1939 International Harvester school bus for the trip; it had all the conveniences for on-the-road living. The trip mushroomed and was the final impetus for forming the Merry Pranksters. Besides painting the bus various psychedelic colors, the Pranksters wired it with microphones, amplifiers, speakers, recorders, and motion-picture equipment: The sign on the front proclaimed "Furthur" (sic), and the sign on the back warned: "Caution: Weird Load." Prior to departing for New York, Kesey established the only rules for the trip—everyone would "do his own thing," "go with the flow," and not condemn anyone else for being himself. As an adjunct to the trip, the Pranksters recorded their entire odyssey on tape and film, which would eventually become a film titled *The Movie,* the first acid film recorded live and spontaneously. When the journey ended, there were more than forty-five hours of color film, large portions of which were out of focus, an obvious effect of the drugs. Kesey devoted much of the 1964 spring and the 1965 fall to editing the film.

On April 23, 1965, federal narcotics agents and deputies raided Kesey's La Honda commune. Of the seventeen persons arrested, only Kesey and Page Browning were officially charged with possession of marijuana. When the San Francisco newspapers proclaimed Kesey a great writer, a new leader, and a visionary, Kesey became a celebrity, and people flocked to his La Honda commune. Jerry Rubin and the Vietnam Day Committee even invited him to speak at an antiwar rally at Berkeley in October, 1965. After listening to fiery speeches, the protesters were to march en masse to the Oakland Army Terminal and close it down. While awaiting his turn to speak, Kesey realized that the speaker before him sounded like the Italian dictator Benito Mussolini and was appalled. When he finally spoke, he told the audience simply to turn their backs on the Vietnam War and then played "Home on the Range" on his harmonica. Instead of inciting the crowd, Kesey's speech had the opposite effect, and the march ended quietly in the Berkeley Civic Center Park.

Kesey later met August Owsley Stanley III, who was known as the "Ford of LSD" because he was the first mass manufacturer of quality LSD; this was before LSD was officially declared illegal. With unlimited supplies of LSD, Kesey and his Merry Pranksters could conduct their famous "Can You Pass the Acid Test" experiments. Amid rock music, Day-Glo decorations, strobe lights, and reels from *The Movie,* the Pranksters invited everyone—the straight people and the hippies—to come and try LSD.

While Kesey's lawyers were fighting his original marijuana possession charge, Kesey was arrested in San Francisco on January 10, 1966, again for possession of marijuana. His second arrest carried an automatic five-year sentence without parole. After a clumsily planned suicide hoax (Kesey was high on drugs), he fled to Mexico and was later joined by his family and some of his Prankster friends.

Tired of being a fugitive and of life in Mexico, Kesey disguised himself and entered the United States at Brownsville, Texas. After he was arrested by the FBI in San Francisco on October 20, 1966, he was tried two more times in San Francisco, on November 30, 1966, and in April, 1967; both trials ended in hung juries. His lawyers appealed a *nolo contendere* sentence of ninety days, but Kesey dropped the appeal and served his sentence, first at the San Mateo Jail and then at the San Mateo County Sheriff's Honor Camp. He completed his sentence in November, 1967.

In 1968, Kesey moved his family to Pleasant Hill, Oregon, where he began a book based on his jail experiences. Then titled "Cut the Mother-F——ers Loose," the book was not published until 2003. In August, 1968, Tom Wolfe's *The Electric Kool-Aid Acid Test* was published, and also during this year some of Kesey's letters and other writings appeared in underground publications. Between March and June, 1969, Kesey lived in London, England, and wrote for *Apple.* He also revised the play version of *One Flew over the Cuckoo's Nest,* which had opened in New York but had closed after only eighty-five performances. Early in 1970, however, Lee D. Sandowich, a prominent figure in San Francisco theater circles, saw an amateur production of the play, decided it had potential, and professionally produced the play again at the Little Fox Theatre in San Francisco, where it was a success; the play reopened successfully in a New York Off-Broadway theater. During 1971, Kesey, Babbs, and Paul Foster edited selections for *Kesey's Garage Sale*, and in the spring of 1971, Kesey and Krassner coedited *The Last Supplement to the Whole Earth Catalog*. Late in 1971, a film version of *Sometimes a Great Notion* was released.

In 1974, Kesey was instrumental in organizing the Bend in the River Council, a unique people-politics experiment based on the concept of a town meeting. The council featured about two hundred delegates and various experts who discussed a variety of environmental issues in a forum carried on both radio and television, and listeners telephoned their comments and votes on certain issues. The year 1975 saw the release of the film version of *One Flew over the Cuckoo's Nest*, which won Academy Awards for best picture, best director (Milos Forman), best lead actor (Jack Nicholson), best lead actress (Louise Fletcher), and best adapted screenplay.

During 1978, Kesey edited a magazine called *Spit in the Ocean*, in which he serialized portions of a work-in-progress, a novel titled "Seven Prayers by Grandma Whittier." Devlin Deboree is a secondary character in the work. He remained content to work on his Pleasant Hill, Oregon, farm and produce his yogurt, which was marketed in Oregon, Washington, and northern California. During the 1980's, a three-term teaching assignment with graduate students in the creative writing program at the University of Oregon resulted in the collaborative novel *Caverns* (1990).

After undergoing surgery for cancer of the liver, Kesey died in Eugene, Oregon, on November 10, 2001, at the age of sixty-six. Approximately one thousand people attended his funeral. He was buried in a psychedelically decorated coffin, and former Merry Prankster Ken Babbs gave one of the eulogies. Kesey's manuscripts and papers have been deposited at the University of Oregon.

Analysis • To understand some of the ideas behind the counterculture revolution is to understand Ken Kesey's fictional heroes and some of his themes. Originating with the 1950's Beat generation, the 1960's counterculture youth were disillusioned with the vast social injustices, the industrialization, and the mass society image in their parents' world; they questioned many values and practices—the Vietnam War, the goals of higher education, the value of owning property, and the traditional forms of work. They protested by experimenting with Eastern meditation, primitive communal living, unabashed nudity, and nonpossessive physical and spiritual love. At the core of the protest was the value of individual freedom. One of the main avenues to this new type of life and freedom was mind-expanding drugs, which allowed them to *grok*, a word from Robert A. Heinlein's *Stranger in a Strange Land* (1961) that means to achieve a calm ecstasy, to contemplate the present moment. In that it emphasized some major problems in the United States, the counterculture had its merits, but it was, at best, a child's romantic dreamworld, inevitably doomed, because it did not consider answers to the ultimate question: "After the drugs, what is next?"

From Kesey's counterculture experiences, however, he learned at least two important lessons. First, he learned that drugs were not the answer to changing society and that one cannot passively drop out of life. In "Over the Border," for example, Deboree realizes, as he bobs up and down in the ocean's waves, that man does not become a superman by isolating himself from reality and life. Instead, he must immerse himself in the waves so that he can "ride the waves of existence" and become one with the waves.

Second, Kesey detested the mass society image that seemed to dominate life in twentieth century America. Although Kesey was pro-America and admired American democracy per se, he abhorred those things in society that seemed to deprive people of individuality and freedom. For Kesey, mass society represents big business, government, labor, communication, and religion and thus subordinates the individual, who is stripped of dignity, significance, and freedom. One of the counterculture's protest slogans underscored this plight: "I am a human being. Do not fold, spindle, or mutilate." The system, preachments, and methodologies of the twentieth century had indeed betrayed humankind and left only two choices: People could either passively conform and thus lose their individuality or find some way to exist in the modern wasteland without losing their dignity and freedom.

Kesey came to believe that people must not and cannot isolate themselves from life; they must meet life on its own terms and discover their own saving grace. Kesey's solution is similar to the solutions found in J. D. Salinger's *Catcher in the Rye* (1951), Joseph Heller's *Catch-22* (1961), Saul Bellow's *Mr. Sammler's Planet* (1970), and even John Irving's *The Hotel New Hampshire* (1981). Having their archetypes in the comic book and Western heroes, Kesey's McMurphy in *One Flew over the Cuckoo's Nest* and Hank Stamper in *Sometimes a Great Notion* are vibrant personalities who defy the overwhelming forces of life by constantly asserting their dignity, significance, and freedom as human beings. Each one learns also that no victories are ever won by passively isolating oneself from life or by being self-centered. They, therefore, immerse themselves in life, ask no quarter, and remain self-reliant. McMurphy and Stamper may not be able to save the entire world, but, Kesey believes, they can save themselves and perhaps even part of the world. Their victories may be slight, but they are, nevertheless, victories.

One Flew over the Cuckoo's Nest • In *One Flew over the Cuckoo's Nest*, the oppressive power of the mass society is evident in its setting—a mental ward dominated by the tyrannical Miss Ratched, the big nurse, whom Chief Bromden, the schizophrenic narrator, describes in mechanical metaphors. Her purse is shaped like a toolbox; her lipstick and fingernail polish are "funny orange" like a glowing soldering iron; her skin and face are like an expensively manufactured baby doll's; and her ward is run like a computer. If a patient dares disrupt her smoothly running ward, Nurse Ratched has the ultimate threats—electroshock treatments—and if these fail, she has prefrontal lobotomy operations that turn people into vegetables. Bromden says that the ward is only a "factory for the Combine," a nebulous and ubiquitous force that had ruthlessly destroyed Bromden's father and that is responsible for the stereotyped housing developments along the coast.

Kesey's metaphors are clear. The Combine, the macrocosm, and the hospital ward, the microcosm, are the twentieth century world gone berserk with power; it uses the miracles of modern science not to free people and make their lives better but rather to compel them to conform. It is the mass society that will not tolerate individuality and that will fold, spindle, or mutilate any person who fails to conform.

Into the ward boils McMurphy, the former Marine, logger, gambler, and free spirit who is intimidated by neither the nurse nor her black ward attendants, and who immediately becomes a threat to Nurse Ratched and her ward policies. McMurphy has had himself committed for purely selfish reasons—he disliked the manual labor on the prison work farm, and he wants the easy gambling winnings from the patients, two facts that he candidly admits. Outraged at Ratched's power, McMurphy bets the other patients that he can get the best of her. Certain that he can win his wager, he sings and laughs on the ward, conducts poker games in the tub room, and disrupts the group therapy sessions. He finally succeeds in destroying her composure when he leads the men watching the blank television screen after Nurse Ratched cuts the power source during the first game of the World Series.

These scenes are crucial because they reveal the typical Kesey conflict. A physically powerful, free, and crucible-tested hero comes into conflict with an equally powerful force. It is simply, as most critics have noted, the classic struggle between good and evil, or the epic confrontation reminiscent of Western films. However, the dichotomy is not so simple, because the Kesey hero must learn a further lesson. McMurphy has won his wager, but he has not yet won significant victory, because his actions are selfish ones.

Several important incidents transform McMurphy into a champion of the patients. McMurphy is *committed*, which means that Ratched can keep him on the ward as long as she wishes. Instead of jeopardizing his relatively short sentence, McMurphy conforms and does not disrupt the therapy sessions or life on the ward. When Charles Cheswick argues with the nurse about the cigarette rationing, he gets no support from McMurphy, despairs, and drowns himself in the hospital swimming pool. Cheswick's death plagues McMurphy, even though he is not actually responsible. McMurphy cannot understand why the other patients, who are there voluntarily, do not leave the hospital. Billy Bibbit finally tells McMurphy that they are not big and strong like McMurphy, that they have no "g-guts," and that it is "n-no use." McMurphy begins to realize that he must do something to convert the patients into responsible men again. At the next group therapy session, when Ratched is supposed to win her final victory over him, McMurphy rams his hand through the glass partition in the nurses' station and thereby renews the struggle.

A key passage occurs earlier that not only summarizes Kesey's view of humanity in the modern world but also provides a clue to McMurphy's actions. Scanlon, who is also committed, says that it is a "hell of a life," and that people are damned if they do and damned if they do not. Scanlon adds that this fact puts people in a "confounded bind." At this point, McMurphy is damned either way. If he does nothing, then Ratched has the final victory and McMurphy will become another victim of the Combine, a nonentity like the other patients. If he renews the struggle, he must remain on the ward until the nurse discharges him or kills him. McMurphy chooses, however, the higher damnation, selflessly to give of himself, and in so doing, he also reaffirms his own dignity and significance.

Dedicated to the patients' cause, McMurphy continues to disrupt the ward and ward policy by using what can only be termed McMurphy's therapy. He continues the poker games and organizes basketball games and even a deep-sea fishing trip, during which the men finally learn to laugh at themselves, Nurse Ratched, and the world in general. He fights with an attendant who was bullying one of the patients, and as a result he is given a series of electroshock treatments. Finally, McMurphy physically attacks the nurse when she ironically accuses him of "playing" and "gambling" with the men's lives. When a prefrontal lobotomy turns McMurphy into a vegetable, Bromden sacrificially murders him and then escapes from the hospital.

In Kesey's world, an individual may indeed be damned either way when he or she encounters the overwhelming forces of the mass society, but through accepting responsibility and acting one can still win an important victory. McMurphy's death is not futile, because he has saved his soul by losing it to a higher cause. He did not save

or even change the entire world, but he did save and change part of it: The other patients are no longer cowed and intimidated by Nurse Ratched, and several of them
voluntarily check out of the hospital. Bromden, as McMurphy had promised, has
been "blown back up" to his full size. There is, then, a slight but significant victory.

Sometimes a Great Notion • Kesey remarked that he wanted his style to be a "style of
change," since he wished neither to write like anyone else nor to be part of any movement. Even though *One Flew over the Cuckoo's Nest* was innovative in style and technique, Kesey's second novel is even more innovative. Even though some critics
faulted it for being too rambling and disjointed, *Sometimes a Great Notion* is not only
much longer than but also superior to his first novel. It is Kesey at his best. Ultimately,
what makes the novel superior is its technical complexity.

More than six hundred pages in length, *Sometimes a Great Notion* is reminiscent of
Light in August (1932) and *Absalom, Absalom!* (1936) by William Faulkner, Kesey's favorite author. As did Faulkner, Kesey begins his novel at its climax, with a scene in a
bus depot where Jonathan Bailey Draeger, a labor union official, asks Vivian Stamper,
Hank's wife, about the nature of the Stamper family. This interview between Viv and
Draeger frames the entire narrative. The narrative then shifts to the past, at times as
far back as 1898, when the first Stamper left Kansas to move west. Through these past
scenes, Kesey establishes the family background and relationships, which in turn provide the psychological makeup of the characters. Having rejected traditional narrative forms, Kesey thus moves freely from past to present time. Complementing the
time shifts are the complex points of view. Bromden is the single narrator in *One Flew
over the Cuckoo's Nest*, but in *Sometimes a Great Notion* Kesey uses several points of view.
There is the traditional omniscient viewpoint, then there are the first-person points
of view in the stories of Henry Stamper, Sr., Hank, and Leland Stanford Stamper,
Hank's half brother. Kesey freely shifts abruptly from one viewpoint to another, and
several shifts may occur in one paragraph. In addition, Kesey presents several incidents that are separated in space but are actually simultaneous actions.

Even the conflict in *Sometimes a Great Notion* is more complicated than that of *One
Flew over the Cuckoo's Nest*. The forces aligned against McMurphy are clearly delineated; it is McMurphy versus Nurse Ratched and the Combine, and it is clear who is
good and who is evil. On the other hand, in *Sometimes a Great Notion*, Hank confronts
more subtle and complex forces. He pits himself against the logging union and the
Wakonda, Oregon, community, both of which represent mass society. Hank must also
contend with two natural forces—the weather and the Wakonda River, the latter being one of the major symbols in the novel. The most important conflict, however, is
between Hank and Lee (Leland, his half brother).

Like McMurphy, Hank is a physically powerful man who is self-reliant, answers to
no one but himself, and cherishes his freedom. Like McMurphy, Hank defies those
forces of life that would strip him of his dignity, significance, and freedom. For Hank,
then, the dictatorial pressures of the union and the Wakonda community are the dictates of the mass society. Having signed a contract with Wakonda Pacific, Hank becomes a strikebreaker who is harassed and threatened by union leaders and the
townspeople. Literally, Hank breaks the strike to save the Stamper logging business;
symbolically, he breaks the strike because to do so will assert his independence and
freedom. The results of *any* action Hank chooses to take are undesirable, and he, like
McMurphy, chooses the course of a higher morality.

Kesey uses three major symbols to underscore Hank's bullheaded defiance. The first is the Stamper house itself, which "protrudes" into the Wakonda River on "a peninsula of its own making." The second is the "Never Give an Inch" plaque, painted in yellow machine paint over the plaque's original message: "Blessed Are the Meek for They Shall Inherit the Earth." The plaque with its new dictum is nailed to Hank's bedroom wall by old Henry Stamper. The third symbol is old Henry's severed arm, which is a hanging pole, with all of its fingers tied down except the middle one. As part of Kesey's complex technique, these symbols fuse with the characters' historical and psychological background, with the various narrative viewpoints, and with the major conflicts.

Of the conflicts, the one between Hank and Leland is potentially the most destructive, and it is also important in terms of Hank's and Lee's character development. Through a crack in the bedroom wall, Lee watched his mother and Hank commit adultery, an act that eventually results in the mother's suicide after she and Lee move back East. Lee returns to Wakonda, not to help the Stampers' failing lumber business but actually to take revenge against Hank. Lee decides that he can best hurt Hank by having an affair with Viv, who, even though she loves Hank, cannot tolerate his "teeth-gritting stoicism in the face of pain." She wants to be both loved and needed, and Lee seems to love and need her. Ironically, after the drowning of Joe Ben, Hank swims across the Wakonda instead of using the motorboat, quietly enters the house, and through the same crack in the bedroom wall sees Lee and Viv in bed together. Temporarily overwhelmed by the death of Joe Ben, his father's horrible maiming, the bad weather, and Viv's adultery, Hank decides that he is "tired of being a villain" and that he will fight the union no longer. His surrender is implied, moreover, in the song lyrics from which the title of the novel is taken: "Sometimes I take a great notion/ To jump into the river an' drown." Immediately after the fistfight with Lee, however, Hank decides to take the logs down river, and Lee joins him.

The fight between Hank and Lee embodies the novel's central theme. Hank understands that Lee has arranged events so cleverly that Hank is damned either way, or as Hank says, "whipped if I fight and whipped if I don't." Hank chooses the greater notion and fights. During the fight, his inner strength is rekindled, and he later tells Viv that "a man is always surprised just how much he can do by himself." Concomitantly, during the fight, Lee realizes that he too has regained the strength and pride that he thought had been lost. Each has a new respect for the other, a respect that is based on love—love for the Stamper name, love for individual freedom. Lee and Hank may be defeated by the river, the weather, or the strike itself, but the significant fact is that they, like McMurphy, are acting. They have not saved the entire world, but they have saved themselves, have regained their own dignity and significance; that, in itself, is a victory.

Sailor Song • *Sailor Song* takes place in the remote little fishing village of Kuinak, Alaska, in the early twenty-first century. Largely untouched by ecological catastrophes, Kuinak attracts a big-budget Hollywood company filming a pseudomyth of aboriginal Native American life. *Sailor Song*'s protagonist, Isaak Sallas—a former naval aviator, ex-environmental activist, ex-convict, and ex-husband—has dropped out of mainstream society and lives as a commercial fisherman. Independent, competent, and well intentioned but resolutely uninvolved, Salas is nonetheless caught up in a conflict with Nicholas Levertov, a native of Kuinak controlling the Hollywood company, which proposes not only to make a film but also to transform Kuinak into a spin-off theme park and resort. In Melvillian symbolism, Levertov is an albino, inherently bent not on creation but on desecration, destruction, and revenge. The novel's conflict evolves against a backdrop of Kuinak's uninhibited lifestyle. Kuinak's citizens include Sallas's friend Greer, transplanted from Bimini; members of the Loyal Order of Underdogs, a rowdy but sometimes purposeful organization; Michael Carmody, a displaced English fisherman; and Carmody's wife, Alice the Angry Aleut. Into this community come the filmmakers, including Levertov, his sycophantic assistant, a figurehead director, and the Innupiat star of the film, Shoola.

The novel's loosely connected episodes come together satisfyingly in the denouement. In the opening episode, Sallas rescues a neighbor from Levertov, her vengeful former husband. Later Sallas rescues the marijuana-dealing president of the Underdogs from a charismatic cultist. Later still he rescues Carmody and Greer from their malfunctioning fishing boat. Most important, he saves himself, both literally and metaphorically. However, although Sallas is sometimes characterized in explicitly messianic terms, he is more modern-day Ulysses than Christ figure, while Alice Carmody is an ironically inverted Penelope.

The anticipated final confrontation between Sallas and Levertov never occurs. In the open-ended, understated denouement, a commotion of bears and wild boars may signal Levertov's end. Whether it does or not, Levertov's consuming malice not only defeats itself but also sets loose a worldwide electronic apocalypse ironically transforming civilization to a state much like Kuinak's, a transformation symbolically marked by butterfly-shaped electrical phenomena.

Technically interesting for its symbolism, fluent manipulation of point of view, and command of narrative rhythm, *Sailor Song* clearly expresses Kesey's philosophy of independence, integrity, and perseverance and counters critics' accusations against Kesey of racism or sexism. *Sailor Song* is above all an engaging and thoroughly enjoyable story.

Last Go Round • Kesey wrote *Last Go Round* with Ken Babbs. Much shorter than Kesey's other novels, it is no less artfully written. *Last Go Round*, like *One Flew over the Cuckoo's Nest*, presents only a version of the truth—in this case a version told to a comatose listener by Jonathan E. Lee Spain, the story's protagonist, almost a century after the events being described. Spain's account is supplemented, if not corroborated, by a set of historical photographs of participants in the first Pendleton Round Up, held on three days in September, 1911. Spain, unlike Kesey's other heroes, is young—only seventeen—and the novel recounts his initiation into adulthood. He meets two older rodeo riders, the black cowboy George Fletcher and the Nez Perce Jackson Sundown, who make him their protégé. He rejects the corruption of the cynical showman Buffalo Bill and the malignant strongman Frank Gotch. He is attracted to a young horsewoman, Sarah Meyerhoff, whom he loses. Above all, Jonathan Spain learns. He learns the tricks of the rodeo, the trust that rodeo riders share, and the untrustworthiness of others. He learns the inconsequence of championships, the importance of excellence, and the meaningfulness of peers' approbation. He learns the unpredictability and inexorability of events. Finally, he learns to accept what comes, even while he defines himself by what he has chosen to do, however briefly.

Edward C. Reilly
Updated by David W. Cole

Other major works

PLAY: *Twister*, pr. 1994.

NONFICTION: *The Further Inquiry*, 1990; *Kesey's Jail Journal*, 2003.

CHILDREN'S LITERATURE: *Little Tricker the Squirrel Meets Big Double the Bear*, 1990; *The Sea Lion: A Story of the Sea Cliff People*, 1991.

EDITED TEXTS: *The Last Supplement to the Whole Earth Catalog*, 1971 (with Paul Krassner).

MISCELLANEOUS: *Kesey's Garage Sale*, 1973; *Demon Box*, 1986.

Bibliography

Gilmore, Mikal. "Ken Kesey's Great American Trip." *Rolling Stone*, nos. 885/886 (December 27, 2001-January 3, 2002): 58-62, 144. Brief account of Kesey's famous 1964 cross-country bus trip with other counterculture figures.

Kesey, Ken. *Kesey's Jail Journal: Cut the M************ Loose*. Introduction by Ed McClanahan. New York: Viking, 2003. Memoir of Kesey's incarceration in California on a drug possession charge that he wrote during the mid-1960's but did not finish until shortly before he died. Includes many of his own hand-drawn illustrations.

_____. *"One Flew over the Cuckoo's Nest": Text and Criticism*. Edited by John C. Pratt. New York: Viking, 1973. Contains the text of the novel, related materials, and a selection of early critical responses to the novel, together with a brief bibliography.

Perry, Paul. *On the Bus: The Complete Guide to the Legendary Trip of Ken Kesey and the Merry Pranksters and the Birth of the Counter Culture*. New York: Thunder's Mouth Press, 1990. Lively account of the famous cross-country bus trip that Kesey made with other famous counterculture figures in 1964.

Porter, M. Gilbert. *The Art of Grit: Ken Kesey's Fiction*. Columbia: University of Missouri Press, 1982. In this first full-length study of Kesey, Porter penetrates Kesey's drug-culture image to reveal his accomplishments as an author in the traditional "American mold of optimism and heroism." A highly regarded critical study that offers an astute commentary on Kesey's fiction.

Searles, George J., ed. *A Casebook on Ken Kesey's "One Flew over the Cuckoo's Nest."* Albuquerque: University of New Mexico Press, 1992. A collection of critical articles, most originally published during the 1970's. Also includes a *MAD* magazine satire of the film and a bibliography.

Sherwood, Terry G. "*One Flew over the Cuckoo's Nest* and the Comic Strip." *Critique: Studies in Modern Fiction* 13, no. 1 (1971): 97-109. Sherwood explores Kesey's references to popular culture, particularly comic strip materials, which are not just "casual grace notes but clear indications of his artistic stance." Contains some appreciative criticism but faults Kesey for his belief in the escapist world of the comic strip and his oversimplification of moral dilemmas.

Tanner, Stephen L. *Ken Kesey*. Boston: Twayne, 1983. This study affirms Kesey as a significant writer and a leader of a cultural movement despite his scant output. Presents some biographical details of Kesey's early years and accomplishments, followed by a critical study of major works. Gives particular attention to *One Flew over the Cuckoo's Nest* and *Sometimes a Great Notion*. Selected bibliography is provided.

Vogler, Thomas A. "Ken Kesey." In *Contemporary Novelists*, edited by James Vinson. London: St. James Press, 1976. Describes Kesey's work as "Richly north-western and regional in quality." Presents some critical appraisal of *One Flew over the Cuckoo's Nest* and *Sometimes a Great Notion*. Also refers to *The Last Supplement to the Whole Earth Catalog*, for which Kesey wrote numerous reviews and articles.

Wolfe, Tom. *The Electric Kool-Aid Acid Test*. New York: Farrar, Straus and Giroux, 1968. A notable work in its own right. Wolfe confers on Kesey the charismatic leadership of a cultural movement. Provides important background information on Kesey, the Merry Pranksters, and the milieu of psychedelic experimentation.

Zubizarreta, John. "The Disparity of Point of View in *One Flew over the Cuckoo's Nest*." *Literature Film Quarterly* 22 (Spring, 1994): 62-69. Contrasts the kinds of comedy produced by the film's realistic third-person point of view and the novel's surrealistic, highly unreliable, and ironic first-person point of view. Bibliography.

Jamaica Kincaid

Born: Saint Johns, Antigua; May 25, 1949

Principal long fiction • *Annie John*, 1985; *Lucy*, 1990; *The Autobiography of My Mother*, 1996; *Mr. Potter*, 2002.

Other literary forms • Jamaica Kincaid first gained respect and admiration as the writer of *At the Bottom of the River* (1983), a collection of unconventional but thematically unified short stories. She also wrote two important memoirs, *A Small Place* (1988), about growing up in a Caribbean vacation resort, and *My Brother* (1997), the story of her brother's struggle with acquired immunodeficiency syndrome (AIDS). Additionally, as a staff writer for *The New Yorker* for twenty years, she wrote numerous "Talk of the Town" pieces and frequent articles on gardening.

Achievements • Jamaica Kincaid made writing about her life her life's work. She developed a finely honed style that highlights personal impressions and feelings over plot development. Though she allows a political dimension to emerge from her use of Caribbean settings, her fiction does not strain to be political. Rather, the political issues relating to her colonial background are used to intensify the most important issue of her fiction: the intense bond between mother and daughter. Her spare, personal style simultaneously invites readers to enter her world and, by its toughness, challenges them to do so. Although she made no specific effort to align herself with any ideology, her first book, *At the Bottom of the River* (which in 1983 won the Morton Dauwen Zabel Award from the American Academy and Institute of Arts and Letters), quickly established her as a favorite among feminist and postcolonial critics, who lauded her personal but unsentimental presentation of the world of women and of the Caribbean.

Biography • Jamaica Kincaid was born Elaine Potter Richardson in Saint John's, Antigua, the daughter of Annie Richardson and Roderick Potter, a taxi driver. Her father was not a significant presence in her life. The man she considered her father was David Drew, a cabinetmaker and carpenter whom her mother married shortly after Elaine's birth. Neverthless, she would later write *Mr. Potter*, a fictional biography of her father.

Elaine learned to read at the age of three, and when she turned seven, her mother gave her a copy of the *Concise Oxford Dictionary* as a birthday gift. The birth of her three brothers, Joseph in 1958, Dalma in 1959, and Devon in 1961 (whose death from AIDS in 1996 would provide the focus for *My Brother*), changed her life, not only because it meant that she was no longer an only child but also because she began to realize that her education would never be taken as seriously as that of her brothers. While Elaine's parents made plans for their sons' university training, Elaine was sent to study with a seamstress twice a week.

When she was seventeen, Elaine left for America to become an au pair in Scarsdale, New York. She took classes at Westchester Community College but soon left Scarsdale to take another au pair position looking after the daughters of an upper

East Side, New York, couple (this experience would provide the basic material for *Lucy*). Over the course of the
next few years, she would study photography at the New School for Social
Research and at Franconia College in
New Hampshire before returning to
New York to work briefly for the magazine *Art Direction.*

In 1973 she sold her first professional publication, an interview with
Gloria Steinem published in *Ingenue*
on what life was like for the well-
known feminist at the age of seventeen. Also in 1973, she changed her
name to Jamaica Kincaid, a move
probably inspired by her need to create an anonymous, authorial identity;
significantly, her adopted pen name
marks her as Caribbean to the American reading audience, something her
birth name does not. Also in 1973,
George Trow, a writer for the "Talk of

Sigrid Estrada

the Town" column in *The New Yorker*, started incorporating quotations by her in his
writing (she was his "sassy black friend"), and her writing career was started. She
worked as a freelance writer until she became a staff writer for *The New Yorker* in 1976
(a position she held until a 1995 disagreement with then-editor Tina Brown over the
direction of the magazine led to her resignation). In 1979, she married Allen Shawn,
son of William Shawn, the editor of *The New Yorker* at the time, and the couple moved
to North Bennington, Vermont, where Shawn was on the faculty of Bennington College. The couple had two children, Annie (born in 1985) and Harold (born in 1989).
Aside from being a novelist, Kincaid became a passionate gardener; she wrote on
gardening for *The New Yorker* and edited a book of garden writing, *My Favorite Plant*,
published in 1998.

Analysis • Jamaica Kincaid is known for her impressionistic prose, which is rich with
detail presented in a poetic style, her continual treatment of mother-daughter issues,
and her relentless pursuit of honesty. More so than many fiction writers, she is an autobiographical writer whose life and art are inextricably woven together. She began
her career by mastering the short story, the form from which her longer fiction grew.
Most of the pieces that constitute *At the Bottom of the River* and *Annie John* were first published in *The New Yorker*, as were the chapters of *Lucy*. Though the individual pieces in
each work have a self-contained unity, *Annie John* and *Lucy* also have a clear continuity
from story to story, something less true of the impressionistic writing of *At the Bottom of
the River*; thus, it is often considered a collection of short stories, while *Annie John* and
Lucy are clearly novels. Nonetheless, it was *At the Bottom of the River* that won for
Kincaid the Morton Dauwen Zabel Award for short fiction and that contained "Girl,"
a story written as a stream of instructions from a mother to a daughter, which is her
best-known piece.

Kincaid's native Antigua is central in her writing. This colonial setting strongly relates to her mother-daughter subject matter, because the narrators Annie and Lucy of her first two novels both seem to make a connection between their Anglophile mothers and the colonial English, and also because the childhood experiences of both narrators have been shaped by a colonial background that limits their options and makes their relationships with their mothers that much more intense.

Beginning with *Lucy*, Kincaid cultivates a detachment with which she explores issues of anger and loss, carefully disallowing any easy resolution. Kincaid seems less interested in solving fictional problems than in exploring contrary states of mind that perceive problems. Admittedly, this style is not to everyone's taste, and even quite a few readers who were seduced by Kincaid's earlier works were less pleased with *Lucy* and *The Autobiography of My Mother*. However, even if her incantatory rhythms and her tight focus on bleak, emotional situations in her post-*Annie John* works are not universally appreciated, few readers deny her eye for poetic detail and her ability to achieve a shimmering honesty in her prose.

Annie John • Kincaid's first novel, *Annie John*, is about a talented young girl in Antigua who, while growing into early womanhood, must separate herself from her mother. Fittingly, the book begins with a story of her recognition of mortality at the age of ten. Fascinated by the knowledge that she or anyone could die at any time, she begins to attend the funerals of people she does not know. At one point, she imagines herself dead and her father, who makes coffins, so overcome with grief that he cannot build one for her, a complex image suggesting her growing separation from her family. When, after attending a funeral for a child she did know, Annie neglects to bring home fish, as her mother demanded, Annie's mother punishes her before kissing her good-night. Though this ending kiss suggests a continued bond between mother and daughter, the next chapter places it in a different context. The title "The Circling Hand" refers to her mother's hand on her father's back when Annie accidentally spies her parents making love. Almost as if in contradiction to the reassuring maternal kiss of the earlier story, this chapter offers the rising specter of sexuality as a threat that will separate mother and daughter. Annie learns not only that she must stop dressing exactly like her mother but also that she must someday be married and have a house of her own. This is beyond Annie's comprehension.

Though Annie never fully understands this growing distance from her mother, she contributes to it. For instance, when she becomes friends with a girl at school named Gwen, she does not tell her mother. In part, she is transferring her affections to friends as a natural process of growing up, but as the chapters "Gwen" and "The Red Girl" make clear, she is also seeking comfort to ease the disapproval of her mother. Gwen becomes her best friend, and Annie imagines living with her, but Gwen is replaced briefly in Annie's affections by the Red Girl, who is a friend and cohort with whom Annie plays marbles, against the wishes of her mother.

The growing separation from her mother comes to a crisis in the chapter "The Long Rain," when Annie lapses into an extended depression and takes to her bed. When medicine and the cures of a local conjure woman do nothing to help, Annie's grandmother, Ma Chess, also a conjure woman, moves in with her. The weather remains damp the entire time Annie remains bedridden, and she feels herself physically cut off from other people. When she is finally well enough to return to school, she discovers she has grown so much that she needs a new uniform; symbolically, she has become a new person. Thus it is that the last chapter, "The Long Jetty," begins with Annie thinking, "My name is Annie John," an act of self-naming that is also an act of self-possession. The chapter tells of Annie's last day in Antigua as she prepares to meet the ship that will take her to England, where she plans to study to become a nurse. A sensitive, detailed portrayal of a leave-taking, this chapter serves as a poignant farewell to childhood and to the intimacy with her mother that only a child can know. This last chapter captures perfectly Kincaid's ability to tell a story sensitively without sentimentality.

Lucy • Kincaid's next novel, *Lucy*, is a thematic sequel to her first. Lucy is seventeen when the novel begins, newly arrived in the United States from Antigua to work as an au pair, watching the four girls of Lewis and Mariah, an upper-middle-class New York couple. Although the novel is set entirely outside Antigua and Lucy's mother never appears in it, Lucy's attempt to separate herself from her mother constitutes the main theme of the novel.

Mariah is presented as a loving but thoroughly ethnocentric white woman. A recurring example of this is her attempt to make Lucy appreciate the Wordsworthian beauty of daffodils, unaware that it is precisely because Lucy had to study William Wordsworth's poetry about a flower that does not grow in Antigua that this flower represents the world of the colonizer to her. In fact, Mariah's unselfconscious, patronizing goodwill is exactly what Lucy loves most and yet cannot tolerate about her employer, because it reminds her of her mother.

When Lucy learns that Lewis is having an affair with Mariah's best friend, Dinah, she understands that this idyllic marriage is falling apart. When a letter from home informs her that her father has died, she is unable to explain to Mariah that her anger toward her mother is based on mourning the perfect love she had once felt between them. At the same time, her own sexuality begins to emerge, and she develops interests in young men. Wanting more space, she moves in with her friend Peggy, a young woman who represents a more exciting world to Lucy, cutting short her one-year au pair agreement. The novel ends with Lucy writing her name, Lucy Josephine Potter, in a book and wishing that she could love someone enough to die for that love. This ending clearly signals an act of self-possession (much like the self-naming at the end of *Annie John*), but it also signifies the loneliness of breaking away from others, even to assert oneself. Though *Lucy* is a much angrier novel than *Annie John*, Lucy's anger is best understood in terms of the writer's earlier autobiographical surrogate in *Annie John*; the melancholy that debilitates Annie at the end of her novel is turned into anger by Lucy.

The Autobiography of My Mother • *The Autobiography of My Mother* is a tough, bleakly ironic novel written by a writer at the full height of her powers. It follows Xuela Claudette Richardson, a Caribbean woman who aborted her only pregnancy. If this fact seems to imply that Kincaid has taken a step away from the style of autobiographical fiction, the self-contradictory title and the main character's last name, Richardson, a name she shares with Jamaica Kincaid, both suggest that this story is not very far removed from the facts of Kincaid's own family.

The novel begins with the narrator proclaiming that her mother died the moment she was born, "and so for my whole life there was nothing standing between myself and eternity." This interesting statement reveals as much about the importance of mothers in Kincaid's writing as about the character Xuela. She lives with her father and a stepmother, who hates her and may have tried to kill her with a poisoned necklace, until she is sent at the age of fifteen to live with a wealthy couple. Ostensibly, she is to be a student, but in fact she is to be the man's mistress.

Though the relationship between the colonizer and the colonized is important in all of Kincaid's writing, *The Autobiography of My Mother* brings it to the foreground in different ways. The first words Xuela learns to read are the words "the British Empire," written across a map. Meanwhile, her stepmother refuses to speak to Xuela in anything other than a patois, or provincial dialect, as if to reduce Xuela to the status of an illegitimate subject of the empire. When Xuela eventually marries (after many affairs with men), it is to a man she identifies as "of the victors"—the British. She takes a cruel satisfaction in refusing to love him, even though, according to her, he lived for the sound of her footsteps. Though it is never a relationship based on love, she lives with him for many years, and he becomes for her "all the children I did not allow to be born." Although this is hardly an ideal relationship, it is not a completely empty one.

Toward the end, Xuela declares that her mother's death at the moment of her birth was the central facet of her life. Her ironic detachment from life seems to have been based on this, as if, devoid of the only buffer between herself and the hardship of life that she can imagine—a mother—she further rejects all other comforts and answers that people wish to propose. If Xuela is the least likable of Kincaid's main characters, her tough-as-nails approach to the world nonetheless makes her among the most compelling.

As in Jamaica Kincaid's other fiction, the themes of *The Autobiography of My Mother* explore what happens to a young woman who grows up in a loveless household, in this case the child of a mother who died at her birth. Intermingled with Xuela's immediate story is the story of the Caribbean island of Dominica, a land that once lived under the cold stepparent of colonial rule.

Since Xuela never knew her mother, and since her father is a distant figure in her life, her efforts to tell her mother's story require her to tell her own story, beginning with her father depositing her to be cared for by his laundress, as if she were another bundle of dirty clothes. The laundress has no more warmth for Xuela than she has for her own children. Like others who live in poverty in Dominica, she faces a constant battle for survival, with no time for loving relationships.

As Xuela begins school, some themes emerge that color her life. One is an image of her mother descending a ladder to her; in the vision, Xuela can see only her mother's heels, although gradually she creates a picture of the whole woman in her imagination and at last imagines an entire history for her. At the same time, Xuela begins to think about her father, a remote man who visits her only occasionally, a policeman whose life seems to suggest the possibilities of power. Already the child is beginning to understand the value in being able to make others do what she wants. Finally, as she attends school, Xuela begins to understand the disparity between what she is taught and what is truly relevant to life in Dominica. Her school is a product of English colonial rule, and its subjects are more suitable for England than for a Caribbean island. Throughout her life, Xuela has a painful consciousness of the legacy of colonialism.

Xuela spends her youth first in the laundress's home, then in the household of her father and his second wife and her children, and then in the home of a friend of her father. Her ability to control others is coupled with a growing sexual sense as well as a generalized sensuality. As a result, her adolescence and adulthood are marked by a series of sexual encounters and several pregnancies (which she aborts). No one could call these liaisons love affairs, however, for love is impossible for a young woman who feels as abandoned as Xuela does.

In the last sections of the novel, in old age, Xuela imagines her parents' courtship. Her father was the son of a Scottish sailor and a woman of African parentage; her mother was from the indigenous Carib people. Xuela imagines their clothing (always a subject of interest to her) and how they might have met, at last able to put a face, even though an imaginary one, to her mother's figure. When finally Xuela marries, it is for power and sex rather than for love. She knows that she will never love children of her own but will remain, perhaps like the island of Dominica, an orphan in the world.

Thomas Cassidy
Updated by Ann D. Garbett

Other major works

SHORT FICTION: *At the Bottom of the River,* 1983.

NONFICTION: *A Small Place,* 1988; *My Brother,* 1997; *My Garden (Book),* 1999; *Talk Stories,* 2001; *Among Flowers: A Walk in the Himalaya,* 2005.

CHILDREN'S LITERATURE: *Annie, Gwen, Lilly, Pam, and Tulip,* 1986 (with illustrations by Eric Fischl).

EDITED TEXTS: *The Best American Essays 1995,* 1995; *My Favorite Plant: Writers and Gardeners on the Plants They Love,* 1998; *The Best American Travel Writing 2005,* 2005.

Bibliography

Als, Hilton. "Don't Worry, Be Happy." Review of *Lucy. The Nation* 252 (February 18, 1991): 207-209. Als compares *Lucy* with *A Small Place,* since both are concerned with oppression. Als emphasizes Kincaid's importance as a Caribbean writer who is not afraid to tackle the issues of racism and colonialism at the risk of alienating readers.

Bloom, Harold, ed. *Jamaica Kincaid.* Philadelphia: Chelsea House, 1998. A collection of individually authored chapters on Kincaid, this critical study includes bibliographical references and an index.

Bouson, J. Brooks. *Jamaica Kincaid: Writing Memory, Writing Back to the Mother.* Albany: State University of New York Press, 2005. An examination of Kincaid's life, including her relationship with her mother, her homeland of Antigua, and her conflicting relations with her father and brother.

De Abruna, Laura Nielsen. "Jamaica Kincaid's Writing and the Maternal-Colonial Matrix." In *Caribbean Women Writers,* edited by Mary Condé and Thorunn Lonsdale. New York: St. Martin's Press, 1999. Discusses Kincaid's presentation of women's experience, her use of postmodern narrative strategies, and her focus on the absence of the once-affirming mother or mother country that causes dislocation and alienation.

Ferguson, Moira. *Jamaica Kincaid: Where the Land Meets the Body.* Charlottesville: University Press of Virginia, 1994. Includes bibliographical references and an index.

_____. "A Lot of Memory: An Interview with Jamaica Kincaid." *The Kenyon Review,* n.s. 16 (Winter, 1994): 163-188. Kincaid discusses the inspiration for her writing and the reasons she wrote her first book in an experimental style; describes the influence of the English tradition on fiction in the Caribbean; comments on the nature of colonial conquest as a theme she explores through the metaphor of gardening.

Garis, Leslie. "Through West Indian Eyes." *The New York Times Magazine* 140 (October, 7, 1990): 42. Based on an interview with Kincaid, this six-page article is an excellent source of information about Kincaid's life. Contains details about her childhood in Antigua, her relationship with her mother, her early interest in books, her early years in New York, and her marriage to Allen Shawn. Includes illustrations.

Mistron, Deborah. *Understanding Jamaica Kincaid's "Annie John."* Westport, Conn.: Greenwood Press, 1999. A student casebook, providing literary, cultural, and biographic context for Kincaid's novel.

Paravisini-Gerbert, Lizabeth. *Jamaica Kincaid: A Critical Companion*. Westport, Conn.: Greenwood Press, 1999. Two biographical chapters are followed by penetrating analyses of *At the Bottom of the River, Annie John, Lucy,* and *The Autobiography of My Mother.*

Simmons, Diane. *Jamaica Kincaid*. New York: Twayne, 1994. A clear, lucid critical overview of Kincaid's life and work. A good introduction to her work for nonspecialist readers.

Valens, Keja. "Obvious and Ordinary: Desire Between Girls in Jamaica Kincaid's *Annie John.*" *Frontiers: A Journal of Women's Studies* 25 (June, 2004): 123-150. Study of relationships among young women in Kincaid's first novel.

Stephen King

Born: Portland, Maine; September 21, 1947

Principal long fiction • *Carrie*, 1974; *'Salem's Lot*, 1975; *Rage*, 1977 (as Richard Bachman); *The Shining*, 1977; *The Stand*, 1978, unabridged version 1990; *The Dead Zone*, 1979; *The Long Walk*, 1979 (as Bachman); *Firestarter*, 1980; *Cujo*, 1981; *Roadwork*, 1981 (as Bachman); *The Gunslinger*, 1982, revised 2003 (illustrated by Michael Whelan; first volume of the Dark Tower series); *The Running Man*, 1982 (as Bachman); *Christine*, 1983; *Cycle of the Werewolf*, 1983 (novella; illustrated by Berni Wrightson); *Pet Sematary*, 1983; *The Eyes of the Dragon*, 1984, 1987; *The Talisman*, 1984 (with Peter Straub); *Thinner*, 1984 (as Bachman); *The Bachman Books: Four Early Novels by Stephen King*, 1985 (includes *Rage*, *The Long Walk*, *Roadwork*, and *The Running Man*); *It*, 1986; *Misery*, 1987; *The Drawing of the Three*, 1987 (illustrated by Phil Hale; second volume of the Dark Tower series); *The Tommyknockers*, 1987; *The Dark Half*, 1989; *Needful Things*, 1991; *The Waste Lands*, 1991 (illustrated by Ned Dameron; third volume in the Dark Tower series); *Gerald's Game*, 1992; *Dolores Claiborne*, 1993; *Insomnia*, 1994; *Rose Madder*, 1995; *Desperation*, 1996; *The Green Mile*, 1996 (six-part serialized novel); *The Regulators*, 1996 (as Bachman); *Wizard and Glass*, 1997 (illustrated by Dave McKean; fourth volume in the Dark Tower series); *Bag of Bones*, 1998; *Storm of the Century*, 1999 (adaptation of his teleplay); *The Girl Who Loved Tom Gordon*, 1999; *Black House*, 2001 (with Straub); *Dreamcatcher*, 2001; *From a Buick Eight*, 2002; *Wolves of the Calla*, 2003 (fifth volume of the Dark Tower series); *Song of Susannah*, 2004 (sixth volume of the Dark Tower series); *The Journals of Eleanor Druse: My Investigation of the Kingdom Hospital Incident*, 2004 (written under the pseudonym Eleanor Druse); *The Colorado Kid*, 2005; *Cell*, 2006; *Lisey's Story*, 2006.

Other literary forms • Stephen King published more than one hundred short stories (including the collections *Night Shift*, 1978, *Skeleton Crew*, 1985, and *Nightmares and Dreamscapes*, 1993) and the eight novellas contained in *Different Seasons* (1982) and *Four Past Midnight* (1990). Two of these novellas are central to his work. In *The Body*, a boy's confrontation with mortality shapes his developing identity as a writer. In *The Mist*, King in his satirical and apocalyptic mode brings Armageddon to the Federal Foods Supermarket as an assortment of grade-B film monsters that inhabit a dense fog.

The relations of King's fiction with the electronic media are many and complex. Much of his fiction has been adapted to both the large and small screens, although it usually plays best in the mind's eye. Several of King's screenplays have been produced, including *Maximum Overdrive* (1986), which he directed. A relatively successful mixed-media venture was his collaboration with George Romero on *Creepshow* (1982), a film anthology inspired by the DC Comics' blend of camp and gore and based on King's own book version. *Creepshow II*, written by Romero and based on King's stories, appeared in 1987. King's teleplays include *The Stand* (1994), which was based on his novel, and *Storm of the Century* (1999), which was written expressly for television broadcast. King has published numerous articles and a critical book, *Danse Macabre* (1981).

Achievements • King is perhaps the most widely known American writer of his generation, yet his distinctions include publishing as two authors at once: Beginning in 1966, he wrote novels that were published under the pseudonym Richard Bachman. He won many British Fantasy and World Fantasy Awards, including the latter for overall contributions to the genre in 1980. At first ignored and then scorned by mainstream critics, by the late 1980's his novels were reviewed regularly in *The New York Times Book Review*, with increasing favor. Beginning in 1987, most of his novels were main selections of the Book-of-the-Month Club, which in 1989 created the Stephen King Library, committed to keeping King's novels "in print in hardcover." King was *People* magazine's Writer of the Year in 1980. One of his most appropriate distinctions was the October 9, 1986, cover of *Time* magazine, which depicted a reader, hair on end, transfixed by "A Novel by Stephen King." The cover story on the "King of Horror" correctly suggested that his achievement and the "horror boom" of the 1970's and 1980's are inseparable. Yet, like Edgar Allan Poe, King turned a degenerated genre— a matter of comic-book monsters and drive-in films—into a medium embodying the primary anxieties of his age.

King's detractors attribute his success to the sensational appeal of his genre, whose main purpose, as King readily confesses, is to scare people. He is graphic, sentimental, and predictable. His humor is usually crude and campy. His novels are often long and loosely structured: *It*, for example, contains 1,138 pages. In an environment of "exhaustion" and minimalism, King's page-turners are the summit of the garbage heap of a mass, throwaway culture. Worst of all, he is "Master of Postliterate Prose," as Paul Gray stated in 1982—writing that takes readers mentally to the films rather than making them imagine or think.

On the other hand, King's work provides the most genuine example of the storyteller's art since Charles Dickens. He has returned to the novel some of the popular appeal it had in the nineteenth century and turned out a generation of readers who vastly prefer some books to their film adaptations. As Dickens drew on the popular culture of his time, King reflects the mass-mediated culture of his own. His dark fantasies, like all good popular fiction, allow readers to express within conventional frames of reference feelings and concepts they might not otherwise consider. In imagination, King is not merely prolific; his vision articulates universal fears and desires in terms peculiar to contemporary culture.

Biography • The second son of Donald and Nellie Ruth Pillsbury King, Stephen Edwin King has lived most of his life in Maine, the setting for most of his fiction. Two childhood traumas, neither of which he remembers, may have been formative. In 1949, when he was two years old, his parents separated and his father disappeared. In 1951, he apparently saw a train dismember a neighborhood friend.

King's conservative Methodist upbringing was supplemented early with a diet of comic books and pulp magazines such as *Weird Tales*. When twelve, he began submitting stories for sale. In 1970, he graduated from the University of Maine, Orono, with a bachelor's degree in English and a minor in dramatics. He encountered two lasting influences, the naturalist writers and contemporary American mythology. He also met Tabitha Jane Spruce, whom he married in 1971.

After graduation, he worked in an industrial laundry until 1971, when he became an English instructor at a preparatory school in Hampden, Maine. He wrote at night in the trailer he shared with his wife and two children. During the early 1970's, he sold stories to men's magazines. Then, in 1974, he published *Carrie*, which was followed by several best-sellers and sales of motion-picture rights.

King settled in Maine with his wife, Tabitha King, a novelist and the writer of *Small World* (1981), *Caretakers* (1983), and others. They had three children, Naomi, Joe, and Owen. In addition to writing daily (except Christmas and his birthday), King became active in opposing censorship, composing essays and lecturing on the topic and supporting controversial publications. He also indulged his love of rock and roll, having purchased a local radio station (renamed WZON) and occasionally performing, with writers Dave Barry, Amy Tan, and others, in the Rock-Bottom Remainders.

In 1999, King was struck by a vehicle while walking along a rural road near his home and sustained severe and life-threatening injuries that would require many years of painful surgery and therapy to recover. Nevertheless, he remained upbeat and philosoph-

Tabitha King

ical during his lengthy recovery and eventually returned to productive writing. At the time of his accident, he was writing his memoir *On Writing* (2000). When he finally completed that book, he included in it an account of his life-altering experience.

Analysis • Stephen King may be known as a horror writer, but he calls himself a "brand name," describing his style as "the literary equivalent of a Big Mac and a large fries from McDonald's." His fast-food version of the "plain style" may smell of commercialism, but that may make him the contemporary American storyteller without peer. From the beginning, his dark parables spoke to the anxieties of the late twentieth century. As a surrogate author in *The Mist* explains King's mission, "when the technologies fail, when . . . religious systems fail, people have got to have something. Even a zombie lurching through the night" is a "cheerful" thought in the context of a "dissolving ozone layer."

King's fictions begin with premises accepted by middle Americans of the television generation, opening in suburban or small-town America—Derry, Maine, or Libertyville, Pennsylvania—and have the familiarity of the house next door and the 7-Eleven store. The characters have the trusted two-dimensional reality of kitsch: They originate in clichés such as the high school "nerd" or the wise child. From such premises, they move cinematically through an atmosphere resonant with a popular mythology. King applies naturalistic methods to an environment created by popular culture. This reality, already mediated, is translated easily into preternatural terms, taking on a nightmarish quality.

King's imagination is above all archetypal: His "pop" familiarity and his campy humor draw on the collective unconscious. In *Danse Macabre*, a study of the contemporary horror genre that emphasizes the cross-pollination of fiction and film, he divides his subject according to four "monster archetypes": the ghost, the "thing" (or human-made monster), the vampire, and the werewolf. As with his fiction, his sources are the classic horror films of the 1930's, inherited by the 1950's pulp and film industries. He hints at their derivations from the gothic novel, classical myth, Brothers Grimm folktales, and the oral tradition in general. In an anxious era both skeptical of and hungry for myth, horror is fundamentally reassuring and cathartic; the tale-teller combines roles of physician and priest into the witch doctor as "sin eater," who assumes the guilt and fear of his culture. In the neoprimitivism of the late twentieth century, this ancient role and the old monsters have taken on a new mystique. In *The Uses of Enchantment* (1976), psychologist Bruno Bettelheim argues that the magic and terrors of fairy tales present existential problems in forms children can understand. King's paranormal horrors have similar cathartic and educative functions for adults; they externalize the traumas of life, especially those of adolescence.

Carrie • Stephen King's first published novel, *Carrie*, is a parable of adolescence. Sixteen-year-old Carrie White is a lonely ugly duckling, an outcast at home and at school. Her mother, a religious fanatic, associates Carrie with her own "sin"; Carrie's peers hate her in a mindless way and make her the butt of every joke. *Carrie* concerns the horrors of high school, a place of "bottomless conservatism and bigotry," as King explains, where students "are no more allowed to rise 'above their station' than a Hindu" above caste. The novel is also about the terrors of passage to womanhood. In the opening scene, in the school shower room, Carrie experiences her first menstrual period; her peers react with abhorrence and ridicule, "stoning" her with sanitary napkins, shouting "Plug it up!" Carrie becomes the scapegoat for a fear of female sexuality as epitomized in the smell and sight of blood. (The blood bath and symbolism of sacrifice will recur at the climax of the novel.) As atonement for her participation in Carrie's persecution in the shower, Susan Snell persuades her popular boyfriend Tommy Ross to invite Carrie to the Spring Ball. Carrie's conflict with her mother, who regards her emerging womanhood with loathing, is paralleled by a new plot by the girls against her, led by the rich and spoiled Chris Hargenson. They arrange to have Tommy and Carrie voted king and queen of the ball, only to crown them with a bucket of pig's blood. Carrie avenges her mock baptism telekinetically, destroying the school and the town, leaving Susan Snell as the only survivor.

As in most folk cultures, initiation is signified by the acquisition of special wisdom or powers. King equates Carrie's sexual flowering with the maturing of her telekinetic ability. Both cursed and empowered with righteous fury, she becomes at once victim and monster, witch and White Angel of Destruction. As King has explained, Carrie is "Woman, feeling her powers for the first time and, like Samson, pulling down the temple on everyone in sight at the end of the book."

Carrie catapulted King into the mass market; in 1976 it was adapted into a critically acclaimed film directed by Brian De Palma. The novel touched the right nerves, including feminism. William Blatty's *The Exorcist* (1971), which was adapted into a powerful and controversial film, had touched on similar social fears during the 1960's and 1970's with its subtext of the "generation gap" and the "death of God." Although Carrie's destructive power, like that of Regan in *The Exorcist*, is linked with monstrous adolescent sexuality, the similarity between the two novels ends there. Carrie's "possession" is the complex effect of her mother's fanaticism, her peers' bigotry, and her newly realized, unchecked female power. Like Anne Sexton's *Transformations* (1971), a collection of fractured fairy tales in sardonic verse, King's novel explores the social and cultural roots of evil.

King's *Carrie* is a dark modernization of "Cinderella," with a bad mother, cruel siblings (peers), a prince (Tommy Ross), a godmother (Sue Snell), and a ball. King's reversal of the happy ending is actually in keeping with the Brothers Grimm; it recalls the tale's folk originals, which enact revenge in bloody images: The stepsisters' heels, hands, and noses are sliced off, and a white dove pecks out their eyes. As King knows, blood flows freely in the oral tradition. King represents that oral tradition in a pseudodocumentary form that depicts the points of view of various witnessess and commentaries: newspaper accounts, case studies, court reports, and journals. Pretending to textual authenticity, he alludes to the gothic classics, especially Bram Stoker's *Dracula* (1897). *'Salem's Lot*, King's next novel, is a bloody fairy tale in which Dracula comes to Our Town.

'Salem's Lot • By the agnostic and sexually liberated 1970's, the vampire had been demythologized into what King called a "comic book menace." In a significant departure from tradition, he diminishes the sexual aspects of the vampire. He reinvests the archetype with meaning by basing its attraction on the human desire to surrender identity in the mass. His major innovation, however, was envisioning the mythic small town in American gothic terms and then making it the monster; the vampire's traditional victim, the populace, becomes the menace as mindless mass, plague, or primal horde. Drawing on Richard Matheson's grimly naturalistic novel *I Am Legend* (1954) and Jack Finney's novel *The Body Snatchers* (1955), King focused on the issues of fragmentation, reinvesting the vampire with contemporary meaning.

The sociopolitical subtext of *'Salem's Lot* was the ubiquitous disillusionment of the Watergate era, King has explained. Like rumor and disease, vampirism spreads secretly at night, from neighbor to neighbor, infecting men and women, the mad and the senile, the responsible citizen and the infant alike, absorbing into its zombielike horde the human population. King is especially skillful at suggesting how small-town conservatism can become inverted on itself, the harbored suspicions and open secrets gradually dividing and isolating. This picture is reinforced by the town's name, 'salem's Lot, a degenerated form of Jerusalem's Lot, which suggests the city of the chosen reverted to a culture of dark rites in images of spreading menace.

King's other innovation was, paradoxically, a reiteration. He made his "king vampire," Barlow, an obvious reincarnation of Stoker's Dracula that functions somewhere between cliché and archetype. King uses the mythology of vampires to ask how civilization is to exist without faith in traditional authority symbols. His answer is pessimistic, turning on the abdication of Father Callahan, whose strength is undermined by secret alcoholism and a superficial adherence to form. The two survivors, Ben Mears and Mark Petrie, must partly seek, partly create their talismans and rituals, drawing on the compendium of vampire lore—the alternative, in a culture-wide crisis of faith, to conventional systems. (At one point, Mears holds off a vampire with a crucifix made with two tongue depressors.) The paraphernalia, they find, will work only if the handler has faith.

It is significant that the two survivors are, respectively, a "wise child" (Petrie) and a novelist (Mears); only they have the necessary resources. Even Susan Norton, Mears's lover and the gothic heroine, succumbs. As in *The Shining, The Dead Zone*, and *Firestarter*, the child (or childlike adult) has powers that may be used for good or for evil. Mears is the imaginative, nostalgic adult, haunted by the past. The child and the man share a naïveté, a gothic iconography, and a belief in evil. Twelve-year-old Mark worships at a shrinelike tableau of Aurora monsters that glow "green in the dark, just like the plastic Jesus" he was given in Sunday School for learning Psalm 119. Mears has returned to the town of his childhood to revive an image of the Marsten House lurking in his mythical mind's eye. Spiritual father and son, they create a community of two out of the "pop" remnants of American culture.

As in fairy tales and Dickens's novels, King's protagonists are orphans searching for their true parents, for community. His fiction may reenact his search for the father who disappeared and left behind a box of *Weird Tales*. The yearned-for bond of parent and child, a relationship signifying a unity of being, appears throughout his fiction. The weakness or treachery of a trusted parent is correspondingly the ultimate fear. Hence, the vampire Barlow is the devouring father who consumes an entire town.

The Shining • In *The Shining*, King domesticated his approach to the theme of parent-child relationships, focusing on the threat to the family that comes from a trusted figure within it. Jack Torrance, a writer, arranges to oversee a mountain resort during the winter months, when it is closed due to snow. He moves his family with him to the Overlook Hotel, where he expects to break a streak of bad luck and personal problems (he is an alcoholic) by writing a play. He is also an abused child who, assuming his father's aggression, in turn becomes the abusing father. The much beloved "bad" father is the novel's monster: The environment of the Overlook Hotel traps him, as he in turn calls its power forth. As Jack metamorphoses from abusive father and husband into violent monster, King brilliantly expands the haunted-house archetype into a symbol of the accumulated sin of all fathers.

Christine • In *Christine*, the setting is Libertyville, Pennsylvania, during the late 1970's. The monster is the American Dream as embodied in the automobile. King gives *Christine* all the attributes of a fairy tale for "postliterate" adolescents. *Christine* is another fractured "Cinderella" story, *Carrie* for boys. Arnie Cunningham, a near-sighted, acne-scarred loser, falls "in love with" a car, a passionate (red and white) Plymouth Fury, "one of the long ones with the big fins," that he names Christine. An automotive godmother, she brings Arnie, in fairy-tale succession, freedom, success, power, and love: a home away from overprotective parents, a cure for acne, hit-and-run revenge on bullies, and a beautiful girl, Leigh Cabot. Soon, however, the familiar triangle emerges, of boy, girl, and car, and Christine is revealed as a femme fatale—driven by the spirit of her former owner, a malcontent named Roland LeBay. Christine is the medium for his death wish on the world, for his all-devouring, "everlasting Fury." LeBay's aggression possesses Arnie, who reverts into an older, tougher self, then into the "mythic teenaged hood" that King has called the prototype of 1950's werewolf films, and finally into "some ancient carrion eater," or primal self.

As automotive monster, Christine comes from a variety of sources, including the folk tradition of the "death car" and a venerable techno-horror premise, as seen in King's "Trucks" and *Maximum Overdrive*. King's main focus, however, is the mobile youth culture that has come down from the 1950's by way of advertising, popular songs, film, and national pastimes. Christine is the car as a projection of the cultural self, Anima for the modern American Adam. To Arnie's late 1970's-style imagination, the Plymouth Fury, in 1958 a mid-priced family car, is an American Dream. Her sweeping, befinned chassis and engine re-create a fantasy of the golden age of the automobile: the horizonless future imagined as an expanding network of superhighways and unlimited fuel. Christine recovers for Arnie a prelapsarian vitality and manifest destiny.

Christine's odometer runs backward and she regenerates parts. The immortality she offers, however—and by implication, the American Dream—is really arrested development in the form of a *Happy Days* rerun and by way of her radio, which sticks on the golden oldies station. Indeed, *Christine* is a recapitulatory rock musical framed fatalistically in sections titled "Teenage Car-Songs," "Teenage Love-Songs," and "Teenage Death-Songs." Fragments of rock-and-roll songs introduce each chapter. Christine's burden, an undead 1950's youth culture, means that most of Arnie's travels are in and out of time, a deadly nostalgia trip. As Douglas Winter explains, *Christine* reenacts "the death," during the 1970's, "of the American romance with the automobile."

The epilogue from four years later presents the fairy-tale consolation in a burned-out monotone. Arnie and his parents are buried, Christine is scrap metal, and the true Americans, Leigh and Dennis, are survivors, but Dennis, the "knight of Darnell's Garage," does not woo "the lady fair"; he is a limping, lackluster junior high teacher, and they have drifted apart, grown old in their prime. Dennis narrates the story in order to file it away, all the while perceiving himself and his peers in terms of icons from the late 1950's. In his nightmares, Christine appears wearing a black vanity plate inscribed with a skull and the words, "ROCK AND ROLL WILL NEVER DIE." From Dennis's haunted perspective, *Christine* simultaneously examines and is a symptom of a cultural phenomenon: a new American gothic species of anachronism or déjà vu, which continued after *Christine*'s publication in films such as *Back to the Future* (1985), *Peggy Sue Got Married* (1986), and *Blue Velvet* (1986). The 1980's and the 1950's blur into a seamless illusion, the nightmare side of which is the prospect of living an infinite replay.

The subtext of King's adolescent fairy tale is another coming of age, from the opposite end and the broader perspective of American culture. Written by a fortyish King in the final years of the twentieth century, *Christine* diagnoses a cultural midlife crisis and marks a turning point in King's career, a critical examination of mass culture. The dual time frame reflects his awareness of a dual audience, of writing for adolescents who look back to a mythical 1950's and also for his own generation as it relives its undead youth culture in its children. The baby boomers, King explains, "were obsessive" about childhood. "We went on playing for a long time, almost feverishly. I write for that buried child in us, but I'm writing for the grown-up too. I want grown-ups to look at the child long enough to be able to give him up. The child should be buried."

Pet Sematary • In *Pet Sematary*, King unearthed the buried child, which is the novel's monster. *Pet Sematary* is about the "*real* cemetery," he told Winter. The focus is on the "one great fear" all fears "add up to," "the body under the sheet. It's our body." The fairy-tale subtext is the magic kingdom of our protracted American childhood, the Disney empire as mass culture—and, by implication, the comparable multimedia phenomenon represented by King himself. The grimmer, truer text-within-the-text is Mary Wollstonecraft Shelley's *Frankenstein* (1818).

The novel, which King once considered "too horrible to be published," is also his own dark night of the soul. Louis Creed, a university doctor, moves with his wife, Rachel, and their two children (five-year-old Ellie and two-year-old Gage) to Maine to work at King's alma mater; a neighbor takes the family on an outing to a pet cemetery created by the neighborhood children, their confrontation with mortality. Additionally the "sematary," whose "Druidic" rings allude to Stonehenge, is the outer circle of a Native American burial ground that sends back the dead in a state of soulless half life. Louis succumbs to temptation when the family cat, Church, is killed on the highway; he buries him on the sacred old Native American burial grounds. "Frankencat" comes back with his "purr-box broken." A succession of accidents, heart attacks, strokes, and deaths—of neighbor Norma Crandall, Creed's son Gage, Norma's husband Jud, and Creed's wife Rachel—and resurrections follows.

The turning point is the death of Gage, which Creed cannot accept and that leads to the novel's analysis of modern medical miracles performed in the name of human decency and love. Louis is the father as baby boomer who cannot relinquish his childhood. The larger philosophical issue is Louis's rational, bioethical *creed*; he believes in saving the only life he knows, the material. Transferred into an immoderate love for his son, it is exposed as the narcissistic embodiment of a patriarchal lust for immortality through descendants, expressed first in an agony of sorrow and rage, then ghoulishly, as he disinters his son's corpse and makes the estranging discovery that it is like "looking at a badly made doll." Later, reanimated, Gage appears to have been "terribly hurt and then put back together again by crude, uncaring hands." Performing his task, Louis feels dehumanized, like "a subhuman character in some cheap comic-book."

The failure of Louis's creed is shown in his habit, when under stress, of taking mental trips to Orlando, Florida, where he, Church, and Gage drive a white van as Disney World's "resurrection crew." In these waking dreams, which echo the male bond of "wise child" and haunted father from as far back as *'Salem's Lot*, Louis's real creed is revealed: Its focus is on Oz the Gweat and Tewwible (a personification of death to Rachel) and Walt Disney, that "gentle faker from Nebraska"—like Louis, two wizards of science fantasy. Louis's wizardry is reflected in the narrative perspective and structure, which flashes back in part 2 from the funeral to Louis's fantasy of a heroically "long, flying tackle" that snatches Gage from death's wheels.

In this modernization of *Frankenstein*, King demythologizes death and attacks the aspirations toward immortality that typify contemporary American attitudes. King's soulless Lazaruses are graphic projections of anxieties about life-support systems, artificial hearts, organ transplants—what King has called "mechanistic miracles" that can postpone the physical signs of life almost indefinitely. The novel also indicts the "waste land" of mass culture, alluding in the same trope to George Romero's "stupid, lurching movie-zombies," T. S. Eliot's poem about the hollow men, and *The Wizard of Oz*: "headpiece full of straw." Louis worries that Ellie knows more about Ronald McDonald and "the Burger King" than the "*spiritus mundi*." If the novel suggests one source of community and culture, it is the form and ritual of the children's pet "sematary." Its concentric circles form a pattern from their "own collective unconsciousness," one that mimes "the most ancient religious symbol of all," the spiral.

It • In *It*, a group of children create a community and a mythology as a way of confronting their fears, as represented by It, the monster as a serial-murdering, shape-shifting boogey that haunts the sewers of Derry, Maine. In 1958, the seven protagonists, a cross-section of losers, experience the monster differently, for as in George Orwell's *Nineteen Eighty-Four* (1949), It derives its power through its victim's isolation and guilt and thus assumes the shape of his or her worst fear. (To Beverly Rogan It appears, in a sequence reminiscent of "Red Riding Hood," as her abusive father in the guise of the child-eating witch from "Hansel and Gretel.")

In a scary passage in *Pet Sematary*, Louis dreams of Walt Disney World, where "by the 1890s train station, Mickey Mouse was shaking hands with the children clustered around him, his big white cartoon gloves swallowing their small, trusting hands." To all of *It*'s protagonists, the monster appears in a similar archetypal or communal form, one that suggests a composite of devouring parent and mass-culture demigod, of television commercial and fairy tale, of 1958 and 1985: as Pennywise, the Clown, a cross between Bozo and Ronald McDonald. As in *Christine, Pet Sematary*, and *Thinner*, the monster is mass culture itself, the collective devouring parent nurturing its children on "imitations of immortality." Like Christine, or Louis's patched-up son, Pennywise is the dead past feeding on the future. Twenty-seven years after its original reign of terror, It resumes its seige, whereupon the protagonists, now professionally successful and, significantly, childless yuppies, must return to Derry to confront as adults their childhood fears. Led by horror writer Bill Denborough (partly based on King's friend and collaborator Peter Straub), they defeat It once more, individually as a sort of allegory of psychoanalysis and collectively as a rite of passage into adulthood and community.

It was attacked in reviews as pop psychology and by King himself as a "badly constructed novel," but the puerility was partly intended. The book summarizes King's previous themes and characters, who themselves look backward and inward, regress and take stock. The last chapter begins with an epigraph from Dickens's *David Copperfield* (1849-1850) and ends with an allusion to William Wordsworth's "Intimations of Immortality," from which King takes his primary theme and narrative device, the look back that enables one to go forward. During the 1970's, King's fiction was devoted to building a mythos out of shabby celluloid monsters to fill a cultural void; in the postmodern awareness of the late 1980's, he began a demystification process. *It* is a calling forth and ritual unmasking of motley Reagan-era monsters, the exorcism of a generation and a culture.

Other 1980's Novels • As for King the writer, *It* was one important rite in what would be a lengthy passage. After *It*'s extensive exploration of childhood, however, he took up conspicuously more mature characters, themes, and roles. In *The Eyes of the Dragon* (written for his daughter), he returned to the springs of his fantasy, the fairy tale. He told much the same story as before but assumed the mantle of adulthood. This "pellucid" and "elegant" fairy tale, says Barbara Tritel in *The New York Times Book Review* (February 22, 1987), has the "intimate goofiness of an extemporaneous story" narrated by "a parent to a child." In *The Tommyknockers*, King again seemed to leave familiar territory for science fiction, but the novel more accurately applies technohorror themes to the 1980's infatuation with technology and televangelism. In *The Dark Tower* cycles, he combined the gothic with Western and apocalyptic fiction in a manner reminiscent of *The Stand*. Then with much fanfare in 1990, King returned to that novel to update and enlarge it by some 350 pages.

King and Bachman • The process of recapitulation and summing up was complicated by the disclosure, in 1984, of Richard Bachman, the pseudonym under whose cover King had published five novels over a period of eight years. Invented for business reasons, Bachman soon grew into an identity complete with a biography and photographs (he was a chicken farmer with a cancer-ravaged face), dedications, a narrative voice (of unrelenting pessimism), and if not a genre, a naturalistic mode in which sociopolitical speculation combined or alternated with psychological suspense. In 1985, when the novels (with one exception) were collected in a single volume attributed to King *as* Bachman, the mortified alter ego seemed buried. Actually Bachman's publicized demise only raised a haunting question of what "Stephen King" really was.

Misery • *Misery*, which was conceived as Bachman's book, was King's first novel to explore the subject of fiction's dangerous powers. After crashing his car on an isolated road in Colorado, romance writer Paul Sheldon is "rescued," drugged, and held prisoner by a psychotic nurse named Annie Wilkes, who is also the "Number One Fan" of his heroine Misery Chastain (of whom he has tired and killed off). This "Constant Reader" becomes Sheldon's terrible "Muse," forcing him to write (in an edition especially for her) *Misery's* return to life. Sheldon is the popular writer imprisoned by genre and cut to fit fan expectations (signified by Annie's amputations of his foot and thumb). Like Scheherazade, the reader is reminded, Sheldon must publish or literally perish. Annie's obsession merges with the expectations of the page-turning real reader, who demands and devours each chapter, and as Sheldon struggles (against pain, painkillers, and a manual typewriter that throws keys) for his life, page by page.

Billed ironically on the dust jacket as a love letter to his fans, the novel is a witty satire on what King has called America's "cannibalistic cult of celebrity": "[Y]ou set the guy up, and then you eat him." The monstrous Reader, however, is also the writer's muse, creation, and alter ego, as Sheldon discovers when he concludes that *Misery Returns*—not his "serious" novel *Fast Cars*—was his masterpiece. Just as ironically, *Misery* was King's first novel to please most of the critics.

The Dark Half • *The Dark Half* is an allegory of the writer's relation to his genius. The young writer-protagonist Thaddeus Beaumont has a series of headaches and seizures, and a surgeon removes from his eleven-year-old brain the incompletely absorbed fragments of a twin—including an eye, two teeth, and some fingernails. Nearly thirty years later, Beaumont is a creative writing professor and moderately successful literary novelist devoted to his family. For twelve years, however, he has been living a secret life through George Stark, the pseudonym under which he emerged from writer's block as the author of best-selling crime novels. Stark's purely instinctual genius finds its most vital expression in his protagonist, the ruthless killer Alexis Machine. Beaumont is forced to disclose and destroy his now self-destructive pseudonym, complete with gravesite service and papier mâché headstone. A series of murders (narrated in Stark's graphic prose style) soon follows. The pseudonym has materialized, risen from its fictional grave literally to take Thad's wife and children (twins, of course) hostage. What Stark wants is to live in writing, outside of which writers do not exist. However, the writer is also a demon, vampire, and killer in this dark allegory, possessing and devouring the man, his family, friends, community.

Drawing on the motif of the double and the form of the detective story—on Robert Louis Stevenson's *The Strange Case of Dr. Jekyll and Mr. Hyde* (1886) and Sophocles' *Oedipus Rex* (c. fifth century B.C.E.), as well as *Misery* and *Pet Sematary*—King gluts the first half of the book with Stark/Machine's gruesome rampages. The last half is psychological suspense and metafiction in biological metaphor: the struggle of the decently introspective Beaumont against the rawly instinctual Stark for control of both word and flesh, with the novel taking shape on the page as the true author reclaims the "third eye," King's term for both child's and artist's inward vision. Once again, the man buries the terrible child in order to possess himself and his art. The book ends in a "scene from some malign fairy tale" as that child and alter ego is borne away by flocks of sparrows to make a last appearance as a black hole in the fabric of the sky.

In dramatizing the tyrannies, perils, powers, and pleasures of reading and writing, *Misery* and *The Dark Half* might have been written by metafictionists John Fowles (to whose work King is fond of alluding) or John Barth (on whom he draws directly in *It* and *Misery*). Anything but abstract, however, *The Dark Half* is successful both as the thriller that King's fans desired and as an allegory of the writer's situation. Critic George Stade, in his review of the novel for *The New York Times Book Review* (October 29, 1989), praised King for his tact "in teasing out the implications of his parable." *The Dark Half* contains epigraphs instead to the novels of George Stark, Thad Beaumont, and "the late Richard Bachman," without whom "this novel could not have been written." Thus reworking the gothic cliché of the double, King allows the mythology of his own life story to speak wittily for itself, lending a subtle level of self-parody to this roman à clef. In this instance, his blunt literalness ("word become flesh, so to speak," as George Stark puts it), gives vitality to what in other hands might have been a sterile exercise.

Gerald's Game* and *Dolores Claiborne • Some have criticized King's negative depiction of women, which King himself admitted in 1983 was a weakness. A decade later, King would address, and redress, this in his paired novels *Gerald's Game* and *Dolores Claiborne*. Both present a strong but besieged female protagonist, and both feature the total solar eclipse seen in Maine in 1963, during which a moment of telepathy, the books' only supernaturalism, links the two women.

Gerald's Game is the story of Jessie Burlingame, a young wife who submits to her husband's desire for bondage in a deserted cabin, only to have him die when she unexpectedly struggles. Alone and helpless, Jessie confronts memories (including the secret reason she struck out at Gerald), her own fears and limitations, and a ghastly visitor to the cabin who may or may not be real. In a bloody scene—even by King's standards—Jessie frees herself and escapes, a victory psychological as well as physical. The aptly named Dolores Claiborne is trapped more metaphorically, by poverty and an abusive husband, and her victory too is both violent and a sign of her developing independence and strength.

Initial reaction from critics was sometimes skeptical, especially given the prurient aspect of Jessie's plight and the trendy theme of incestuous abuse in both novels. However, King examined family dysfunction in works from *Carrie* and *The Shining* to *It*, and he continued his commitment to women's issues and realistic strong women in *Insomnia*, *Rose Madder*, and other novels. Archetypal themes also strengthen the two books: Female power must overcome male dominance, as the moon eclipses the sun; and each woman must find her own identity and strength out of travail, as the darkness gives way to light again. (King uses mythology and gender issues more explicitly in *Rose Madder*, which evenly incorporates mimetic and supernatural scenes.)

The books are daring departures for King in other ways. In contrast to King's sprawling *It* or encyclopedic *The Stand*, these books, like *Misery*, tightly focus on one setting, a shorter period of time, and a small cast—here *Misery*'s duet is replaced by intense monologues. In fact, all of *Dolores Claiborne* is her first-person narrative, without even chapter breaks, a tour de force few would attempt. Moreover, King challenges our ideas of the genre horror novel, since there is little violence, none of it supernatural and all expected, so that suspense is a function of character, not plot (done previously by King only in short fiction such as "The Body" and "The Last Rung of the Ladder").

Character and voice have always been essential to King's books, as Debbie Notkin, Harlan Ellison, and others have pointed out. Dolores Claiborne is especially successful, her speech authentic Mainer, and her character realistic both as the old woman telling her story and as the desperate yet indomitable wife, the past self whose story she tells. In these novels, King reaches beyond childhood and adolescence as themes; child abuse is examined, but only from an adult point of view. Dolores and Jessie—and the elderly protagonists of *Insomnia*—reveal King, perhaps having reconciled to his own history, exploring new social and psychological areas.

Bag of Bones • *Bag of Bones*, which King calls a "haunted love story," opens with narrator Mike Noonan recounting the death of his wife, Jo, who collapses outside the Rite Aid pharmacy from a brain aneurysm. Both are relatively young, and Jo, Mike learns, was pregnant. Because Mike is unable to father children, he begins to question whether Jo was having an affair. As Mike slowly adjusts to life without Jo, he is forced to make another adjustment. Formerly a successful writer of gothic romance fiction, he now finds that he is unable to write even a simple sentence. In an attempt to regain his muse and put Jo's death behind him, Mike returns to Sarah Laughs (also referred to as "TR-90" or the "TR"), the vacation cabin he and Jo purchased soon after he became successful. As Mike quickly learns, Sarah Laughs is haunted by ghosts, among them the ghost of blues singer Sarah Tidwell.

While at Sarah Laughs, Mike meets Mattie Devore, her daughter Kyra, and Mattie's father-in-law, Max Devore, a withered old man of incalculable wealth who is accustomed to getting anything he wants. Having rescued Kyra from walking down the middle of Route 68, Mike quickly becomes friends with both Kyra and Mattie. Mattie is the widow of Lance Devore, Max's stuttering son. Lance had nothing to do with his father after learning that his father had tried to bribe Mattie into not marrying him. After Lance's death from a freak accident, Max returned to Mattie's life in an attempt to get acquainted with his granddaughter, Kyra. The truth is, however, that Max wants to gain custody of Kyra and take her away to California; he will do whatever it takes to accomplish that.

To help Mattie fight off Max's army of high-priced lawyers, Mike uses his own considerable resources to retain a lawyer for Mattie named John Storrow, a young New Yorker unafraid to take on someone of Max Devore's social stature. As Mike is drawn into Mattie's custody battle, he is also exposed to the ghosts that haunt the community. As Mike sleeps at night, he comes to realize that there are at least three separate spirits haunting his cabin. One, he is sure, is Jo, and one, he determines, is Sarah Tidwell. The third manifests itself only as a crying child, and Mike cannot tell whether it is Kyra or some other child. Mike and Kyra share a special psychic connection that allows them to share dreams and even to have the same ghosts haunting their homes—ghosts who communicate by rearranging magnetic letters on each of their refrigerator doors.

As Mike becomes further embroiled in the custody battle with Max Devore, his search to determine the truth about Jo's affair finally leads him to a set of journals Jo was keeping, notes from a research project that was her real reason for sneaking away to Sarah Laughs. Jo's notes explain how everyone related to the people who murdered Sarah Tidwell and her son have paid for this sin by losing a child of their own. Sarah Tidwell's ghost is exacting her revenge by murdering the children of those who murdered her own child. Mike, related to one of the people who murdered Sarah's child, has been drawn into this circle of retribution from the beginning, and the death of his unborn daughter, Kia, was not the accident it seemed to be. Mike also realizes that Kyra, the last descendant of this tragedy, is to be the final sacrifice used to put Sarah Tidwell to rest. Mike's return to the ironically named Sarah Laughs, it seems, has been a carefully orchestrated tragedy. Everything is tied to the ghost Sarah Tidwell's purposes, even Mike's writer's block. Mike's writing abilities return while he is at Sarah Laughs, but by the end of the novel he realizes it was simply to lead him to the information he needed to put Sarah's spirit to rest. Sarah's ghost may have destroyed his wife and child, but Jo's ghost gives him the means to save Kyra.

The usual King trademarks that fans have come to expect are present in *Bag of Bones*. The novel, moreover, shares much with the southern novel and its themes. Guilt is a predominant theme of many southern works, especially those of William Faulkner, Edgar Allan Poe, and Tennessee Williams. Racism, not a theme usually associated with northern writers, has been successfully transplanted by King via the traveling Sarah Tidwell. By the end of the novel the evils of the community have become so entrenched in the soil (another similarity to Faulkner's fiction) that they begin to affect Mike himself, and he has to fight the urge to kill Kyra. Only by reburying the past—in this case, by literally reburying Sarah Tidwell's body—can matters finally be put to rest. Mike dissolves Sarah's body with lye and her spirit finally leaves Sarah Laughs. Jo's spirit also leaves, and all is quiet once more at the cabin.

By the 1980's, King had become a mass-media guru who could open an American Express commercial with the rhetorical question "Do you know me?" At first prompted to examine the "wide perceptions that light [children's] interior lives" (*Four Past Midnight*) and then the cultural roots of the empire he had created, he proceeded to explore the phenomenon of fiction, the situations of reader and writer. During the 1990's, King continued to develop as a writer of both supernatural horror and mimetic character-based fiction. His novels after *Dolores Claiborne*—from *Insomnia* through *Lisey's Story*—all provide supernatural chills while experimenting with character, mythology, and metafiction.

Financially invulnerable, King became almost playful with publishing gambits: *The Green Mile* was a serial, six slim paperbacks, in emulation of Charles Dickens and as a self-set challenge; Richard Bachman was revived when *The Regulators* was published in 1996. Although he is still thought of as having no style, actually King maintained his compelling storyteller's voice (and ability to manipulate his reader emotionally) while maturing in the depth and range of his themes and characters.

King, perhaps more than any other author since Faulkner and his fictional Yoknapatawpha County, also creates a sense of literary history within the later novels that ties them all together. In *Bag of Bones*, King references several of his other novels, most notably *The Dark Half, Needful Things*, and *Insomnia*. For longtime fans, this serves both to update King's readers concerning their favorite characters and to unify King's body of work. King's ironic sense of humor is also evident. When Mike's literary agent tells him of all the other best-selling novelists who have novels coming out in the fall of 1998, the most notable name missing from the list is that of Stephen King himself.

Linda C. Badley
Updated by Bernadette Lynn Bosky

Other major works

SHORT FICTION: *Night Shift*, 1978; *Different Seasons*, 1982; *Skeleton Crew*, 1985; *Dark Visions*, 1988 (with Dan Simmons and George R. R. Martin); *Four Past Midnight*, 1990; *Nightmares and Dreamscapes*, 1993; *Hearts in Atlantis*, 1999; *Everything's Eventual: Fourteen Dark Tales*, 2002.

SCREENPLAYS: *Creepshow*, 1982 (with George Romero; adaptation of his book); *Cat's Eye*, 1984; *Silver Bullet*, 1985 (adaptation of *Cycle of the Werewolf*); *Maximum Overdrive*, 1986 (adaptation of his short story "Trucks"); *Pet Sematary*, 1989; *Sleep Walkers*, 1992.

TELEPLAYS: *The Stand*, 1994 (based on his novel); *Storm of the Century*, 1999; *Rose Red*, 2002.

NONFICTION: *Danse Macabre*, 1981; *Black Magic and Music: A Novelist's Perspective on Bangor*, 1983; *Bare Bones: Conversations on Terror with Stephen King*, 1988 (Tim Underwood and Chuck Miller, editors); *On Writing: A Memoir of the Craft*, 2000; *Faithful: Two Diehard Red Sox Fans Chronicle the 2004 Season*, 2004 (with Stewart O'Nan).

CHILDREN'S LITERATURE: *The Girl Who Loved Tom Gordon: A Pop-up Book*, 2004 (text adaptation by Peter Abrahams, illustrated by Alan Dingman).

MISCELLANEOUS: *Creepshow*, 1982 (adaptation of the DC Comics); *Nightmares in the Sky*, 1988.

Bibliography

Beahm, George W. *Stephen King from A to Z: An Encyclopedia of His Life and Work*. Kansas City, Mo.: Andrews McMeel, 1998. Comprehensive reference source on King's life and writings.

Bloom, Harold, ed. *Stephen King: Modern Critical Views*. Philadelphia: Chelsea House, 1998. This is the best single collection of essays about King, many collected from other sources listed here, but including previously unreprinted pieces from journals or non-King-specific books. High-quality pieces cover a range of themes and King's works through *Needful Things*. Good chronology, bibliography, and index.

Collings, Michael R. *Scaring Us to Death: The Impact of Stephen King on Popular Culture*. 2d rev. ed. San Bernardino, Calif.: Borgo Press, 1997. Examines King's influence on the rise of horror fiction in the United States.

_____. *The Work of Stephen King: An Annotated Bibliography and Guide*. San Bernardino, Calif.: Borgo Press, 1996. Provides both a good chronology and useful descriptions of some of King's hard-to-find works, as well as a copious, annotated list of secondary sources.

Docherty, Brian, ed. *American Horror Fiction: From Brockden Brown to Stephen King*. New

York: St. Martin's Press, 1990. This collection of essays places King's works into context with other American horror writers.

Hohne, Karen A. "The Power of the Spoken Word in the Works of Stephen King." *Journal of Popular Culture* 28 (Fall, 1994): 93-103. Discusses the tension in King's work between slang speech, which codifies a knowledge rejected by those in power, and monologic orality, which embodies that power; claims his works illustrate the tension between official and unofficial languages and ideologies that exists not only in literature but also throughout society.

Hoppenstand, Gary, and Ray B. Browne, eds. *The Gothic World of Stephen King: Landscape of Nightmare.* Bowling Green, Ohio: Bowling Green State University Press, 1987. The collection of academic criticism of King includes an introduction by Hoppenstand and essays on themes ("Adolescent Revolt," "Love and Death in the American Car"), characters ("Mad Dogs and Firestarters," "The Vampire"), genres (King's "Gothic Western," techno-horror), technique ("Allegory"), and individual works.

King, Stephen. *Bare Bones: Conversations on Terror with Stephen King.* Edited by Tim Underwood and Chuck Miller. New York: McGraw-Hill, 1988. Though many of the interviews collected in this volume become somewhat repetitive, they provide a good sense, in King's own words, of what he is trying to do in his fiction and why he does it. The interviews were held between 1979 and 1987; the opening transcript of a talk King gave at the Billerica Public Library is most useful.

Magistrale, Tony. *Hollywood's Stephen King.* New York: Palgrave Macmillan, 2003. Study of the adaptations of King's stories to the screen that is organized by themes and pays close attention to how King's texts are altered. Includes an interview with King.

_____. *Landscape of Fear: Stephen King's American Gothic.* Bowling Green, Ohio: Bowling Green State University Press, 1988. Placing King in an American gothic tradition with Edgar Allan Poe, Nathaniel Hawthorne, Herman Melville, and William Faulkner, this study treats sociopolitical themes such as "The Betrayal of Technology," individual accountability, innocence betrayed, and survival in the novels through *It.* The text is supplemented by a bibliography of scholarship from 1980 to 1987.

_____. *Stephen King: The Second Decade, "Danse Macabre" to "The Dark Half."* New York: Twayne, 1992. Discusses King's work during the 1980's, including his nonfictional analysis of the horror genre in *Danse Macabre,* his Richard Bachman books, *Misery,* and the novellas of the *Dark Tower* saga. Also includes a 1989 interview in which King discusses fairy-tale references in his work, as well as his treatment of sexuality, masculinity, and race; discusses critical and popular reaction to his fiction.

_____, ed. *The Dark Descent: Essays Defining Stephen King's Horrorscape.* Westport, Conn.: Greenwood Press, 1992. This academic collection of interpretive essays covers subjects such as homophobia, treatment of female characters, and dialogic narratives in King's work; the sixteen pieces examine most of King's novels and some short fiction. Individual essay bibliographies, book bibliography, and book index.

Miller Power, Brenda, Jeffrey D. Wilhelm, and Kelly Chandler, eds. *Reading Stephen King: Issues of Censorship, Student Choice, and Popular Literature.* Urbana, Ill.: National Council of Teachers of English, 1997. Examines issues at the heart of horror fiction. Includes bibliographical references and an index.

Russell, Sharon. *Revisiting Stephen King.* Westport, Conn.: Greenwood Press, 2002. Analyses of King's later works, from *The Green Mile* through *Dreamcatcher.*

Spignesi, Stephen J. *The Complete Stephen King Encyclopedia: The Definitive Guide to the Works of America's Master of Horror.* Chicago: Contemporary Books, 1991. First published with the title *The Shape Under the Sheet,* this is an important guide for all students of King. Includes bibliographical references and indexes.

Vincent, Ben. *The Road to "Dark Tower": Exploring Stephen King's Magnum Opus.* New York: NAL Trade, 2004. Full analysis of King's six-volume Dark Tower cycle.

Wiater, Stanley, Christopher Golden, and Hank Wagner. *The Stephen King Universe: A Tale-by-Tale Examination of the Interconnected Elements in His Work.* St. Martin's Press, 2001. A critical feast of all things King. The authors explore the common themes, places, and characters that run through King's novels. Resources include a biographical chronology, a bibliography, and an index.

Barbara Kingsolver

Born: Annapolis, Maryland; April 8, 1955

Principal long fiction • *The Bean Trees*, 1988; *Animal Dreams*, 1990; *Pigs in Heaven*, 1993; *The Poisonwood Bible*, 1998; *Prodigal Summer*, 2000.

Other literary forms • Barbara Kingsolver, known primarily for her long fiction, has also written travel articles, book reviews, essays, and poetry. Her nonfiction book *Holding the Line: Women in the Great Arizona Mine Strike of 1983* (1989) presents a compelling picture of the plight of miners in southern Arizona's copper-mining "company towns." The form of her poetry collection *Another America/Otra America* (1992)— with Kingsolver's poetry and its Spanish translations printed on facing pages—invites awareness of diverse perspectives. *Homeland and Other Stories* (1989), a short-story collection, contains previously published and new work, most of which depicts the vagaries and pressures of different mother/daughter relationships. Some of the stories encompass fathers, brothers, and husbands as well, but all explore how family, past and present, affects the identity and perspective of the main character or the narrator in each story. Essays included in *High Tide in Tucson: Essays from Now or Never* (1995) offer thoughts on parenting, home ownership, cultural habits, travel, and writing.

Achievements • Kingsolver has won many writing awards. In 1986 the Arizona Press Club gave her its feature-writing award. She received American Library Association awards in 1989 for *The Bean Trees* and in 1990 for *Homeland and other Stories*. The Edward Abbey Ecofiction Award (1990) for *Animal Dreams* and the prestigious PEN Western Fiction Award (1991) added to her reputation. In 1993 and 1994 she received the Los Angeles Book Award and Mountain and Plains Booksellers Association Award for *Pigs in Heaven*. She also received an Enoch Pratt Library Youth Book Award for *The Bean Trees*. Her other awards include the Enoch Pratt Library Lifetime Achievement Medal in 2005; the 2002 International IMPAC Dublin Literary Award for *Prodigal Summer*; an award for the Best American Science and Nature Writing in 2001; a National Humanities Medal in 2000; the 1999 Patterson Fiction Prize; a *New York Times* Ten Best Books selection for *The Poisonwood Bible* in 1998; a citation of accomplishment from the United Nations National Council of Women in 1989. In 1995, De Pauw University conferred an honorary doctorate on her. She spent two semesters as a visiting writer at Emory and Henry College. True to her activist principles, she is the founder of the Bellwether Prize, given in support of literature of social change.

Biography • Barbara Kingsolver was born in Annapolis, Maryland, in 1955. Her childhood was spent mostly in eastern Kentucky's rural Nicholas County. She began writing before she entered high school. In 1977 she earned an undergraduate degree in biology magna cum laude from De Pauw University in Indiana. Work toward her master of science degree at the University of Arizona in Tucson (1981) included a creative writing class. Between her stints as a student she lived for a time in Greece and France. After completing her master's degree she worked as a science writer for the University of Arizona and began to write feature articles, which appeared in publica-

tions such as *Smithsonian, Harpers,* and *The New York Times.* In 1985 she married Joseph Hoffman. She wrote *The Bean Trees* in insomniac interludes when she was pregnant with their daughter, Camille. Kingsolver subsequently was divorced; she then married Steven Hopp, and they settled in Tucson, Arizona. Kingsolver has been a political activist all her adult life.

Analysis • Kingsolver's long fiction is best characterized as contemporary versions of the *Bildungsroman* with a feminist twist. The main character ventures forth to develop herself and find her place in her community. Many books by women that incorporate such a quest portray punishment for women who explore issues of sexuality or who discover meaningful work in the world. Often these *Bildungsromane* reiterate a main female character's struggle with the patriarchal response to her journey, as in *The Awakening* (1899) by Kate Chopin, or emphasize the price in intimacy and passionate relationships a woman pays for fully developing her skills, as in Willa Cather's *O Pioneers!* (1913). In both instances, female writers highlight the tension between an individual and society to suggest women's dilemmas finding legitimate voices and strengths in their lives and times.

Kingsolver's work departs from the punitive mold. Tension emerges as her female characters seek synthesis, a coming together that will meld place, memory, and the present moment to create personal identity. Her narratives also orchestrate the play between inner and outer landscapes. In *The Bean Trees,* Taylor Greer moves across Kentucky and through Oklahoma, landing in Tucson with a baby who will change her emotional geography. On the third page of *Animal Dreams,* the still mysterious Cosima announces her destination as Grace, Arizona—the site of her early life, stage for the novel's action, and catalyst of self-knowledge. *Pigs in Heaven* includes another flight by Taylor and Turtle. Ultimately, it depicts their trek to the deep Cherokee past, which threatens Taylor's role as a mother and unlocks Taylor's and Turtle's ties to their own histories and identities. *The Poisonwood Bible* evokes the Belgian Congo of the 1960's in rich detail, juxtaposing it with the southern U.S. landscape of memory and the recent past of Nathan Price's wife and four daughters. Patriarchy, instead of creating the frame of reference as in earlier fictions, emerges referentially in Kingsolver's books as part of a female consciousness.

Kingsolver's women negotiate new places for themselves within their personal, domestic, and social contexts. They acquire self-understanding through social interaction and introspection; these things bring harmony within and without. Her main female characters weather negotiation with themselves and their environments. They display character flaws, lapses in judgment, anger, and personal fears as well as idealism, generous hearts, moral consciences, and affection. Her women reach equilibrium rather than glorious redemption. Their personal insights are fragile in the way that most real-life understandings are, remaining constant only until new discoveries or crises initiate adjustment or expansion. Such shifts do not destroy each woman's cumulative advancement toward wholeness. Kingsolver's journeying women increase their poise and certainty at a rate commensurate with their courage and individual learning curves.

Taylor, Cosima (Codi), and the Price women all passionately pursue relationships spawned by family identity. Coming into their own carries an intrinsic connection to family, community, and state. In all Kingsolver's books, the personal is acutely political. Codi, of *Animal Dreams*, discovers her true origins as she works with older Hispanic women in Grace to end toxic environmental contamination. Leah, in *The Poisonwood Bible*, redefines her cultural and religious allegiances as she takes up residence in the "liberated" Congo. Kingsolver's long fiction is overtly political, her short stories obliquely so. (Her short fiction often focuses on the domestic sphere of women's lives—situations replete with social and matrimonial expectations dictated by patriarchal values before the revolutions of the 1960's began to change sensibilities.) Her women live in the real world, and her narratives include male activity in women's ruminations or the narration of events. Male perspectives surface primarily because they affect the female characters and move the plot forward. *The Poisonwood Bible*, in which the Price entourage is dragged off to Africa, seems an exception. However, the women tell the entire story of their father's and husband's misguided mission, controlling perspective and interpretation.

Kingsolver's fiction places relationships—between parents and children, spouses and families—in the foreground and sets them against the larger social milieu. Kingsolver gives no credence to the opinion that art is apolitical. The inherent inequities and racism faced by Hispanic, Native American, and African persons surface, not as the chief lament of her main characters or as the narrative frame for their lives, but as elements in their situations.

The Bean Trees • Marrietta Greer, the traveling woman of *The Bean Trees*, sees herself as part of life in Pittman County, Kentucky, but she has flair. She leaves town five years after high school graduation in a "'55 Volkswagen bug with no windows to speak of, and no back seat and no starter." She heads west in search of a new name and new location, believing that mysterious signs will appear to help her along. She takes her new name from Taylorville, Illinois, where she runs out of gas. Deciding to go west until the car stops running, she reaches the "Great Plain," as she calls it, and finds herself in a broken-down car in Oklahoma. She appreciates the irony of landing in Cherokee territory: Her maternal grandfather had provided the one-eighth Cherokee blood required for her to qualify for tribal membership, and the idea of moving to the Cherokee Nation had become a family joke—their last hope if they face destitution. Before Taylor leaves a Cherokee bar in Oklahoma, a pleading American Indian woman deposits a child in her front seat and drives off. Taylor calls the silent child Turtle because she attaches herself to Taylor anywhere she can get a grip and holds on as fiercely as a mud turtle when it bites. Turtle has been fiercely abused. Chapter 2 introduces Lou Ann Ruiz, pregnant, living in Arizona, and struggling in a failing marriage with Angel. Taylor arrives in Arizona in chapter 3 and, through the auspices of Mattie (a woman who runs Jesus Is Lord Used Tires), Taylor and Lou Ann form a supportive and zany household. The two friends become involved in Mattie's clandestine work with illegal Central American refugees.

The Bean Trees reorients readers toward daily experience, juxtaposing ordinary picnics, car repairs, and kitchen scenes with such events as the chilling account of Estevan and Esperanza's daughter being snatched by the Guatemalan government. Kingsolver's relatively uneducated but compassionate people live mundane lives, but many of their activities focus on the human terms of political injustice. The novel braids the stories of ordinary women following their consciences, and it gives the lie to the idea that massive amounts of money and large organizations are needed to eradicate inhumanity. The novel's end offers a typical array of Kingsolver anomalies. Turtle is illegally but justly adopted; family has been redefined, and readers accept the safe place that Taylor and Lou Ann inhabit; the politics of safe houses and churches aiding immigrants and refugees escaping crushing cruelty seems noble despite its clandestine nature; and money has nothing to do with feeling cared about and connected.

Animal Dreams • Cosima (Codi) and Homer Noline share this book in alternating sections that detail Codi's return to Grace, Arizona, to care for Homer, her physician father, who is succumbing to Alzheimer's disease. Alternation between an omniscient narrator for the Doc Homer sections and first-person narration for Codi emphasizes postmodern disjunction of perspective, but Kingsolver uses memory to create links between the sections and characters that override the break in form. The personal, communal, and global politics of *Animal Dreams* are syncopated as well. Personally, Codi discovers her tie to the nine Gracela sisters who founded Grace. She also comes to terms with a baby she had buried alone when she was fifteen. Communally, she connects with the older women of the Stitch and Bitch Club, who alert her to the Black Mountain Mining Company's toxic presence in Grace. Together they challenge and defeat the corporate polluter. Hallie's letters from Nicaragua weave the theme of human rights throughout *Animal Dreams*. As usual in Kingsolver's fiction, the scenes take place in domestic and familiar public places—kitchens, attics, front yards, schools, and trains—where personal circumstances allow a focus on larger social and political issues. There are no pat answers. An ordinary woman seeking justice dies, but the Stitch and Bitch ladies triumph. Codi moves toward a full life. All Souls Day and the Corn Dance rituals unite the past and present and provide time for Codi to seek and find answers. *Animal Dreams* articulates the complicated intersection of private and public identities and offers hope.

Pigs in Heaven • *Pigs in Heaven* revisits Taylor and Turtle's lives. They are on a road trip visiting Hoover Dam when Turtle's glimpse of a near-fatal fall that involves a spectacular rescue makes celebrities of Taylor and Turtle. Notoriety brings the Cherokee Nation into the story, and soon Taylor is traveling to keep Turtle from being "repossessed" by Cherokee lawyer Annawake Fourkiller. Taylor maintains telephone contact with her mother, Alice, and lives hand-to-mouth while avoiding Ms. Fourkiller. To expedite matters, Alice travels to Oklahoma to reestablish her tie with a Cherokee cousin. She falls in love with an American Indian man named Cash Stillwater. Telephone calls and negotiations result in Taylor and Turtle meeting with Annawake, Cash, Alice, and the Child Welfare Services. In a bizarre twist, Cash turns out to be Turtle's grandfather and proposes to Alice. The solution of joint custody and Alice and Cash's determination to be married unite everyone with their pasts, both deep and recent.

Chapters in *Pigs in Heaven* establish irregular intervals between Taylor and Turtle's adventures and accounts of Taylor's mother, who is beginning her own road trip away from her second husband as the novel starts. Taylor runs until she must return to Oklahoma, and Alice travels to Cherokee ground to reunite with her cousin. Throughout, Kingsolver relies on the threads of Cherokee blood, Alice and Taylor's telephone calls, and the history of the Cherokee Nation to bind the plot lines. She employs a style that combines an omniscient narrator in equal parts with dialogue and with sequences that seem to be half narrated and half in the voice of the character under consideration. The ritual Cherokee stomp dance and the U.S. government's mistreatment of the Cherokees make readers consider how the past carries forward as both repetition and renewal.

The Poisonwood Bible • In *The Poisonwood Bible* the ill-fated Price women follow two men, a husband and their father, to the Belgian Congo just as fighting for liberation breaks out in earnest. The *Bildungsroman* in this case involves the simultaneous creation of five separate journeys to the self within the framework of the family's African journey. The book is an ambitious undertaking, as Kingsolver creates the voices of six-year-old Ruth May, twelve-year-old twins Leah and Ada, and fifteen-year-old Rachel Price. She then follows them to adulthood (all but Ruth May, who dies of malaria), through the tumult of Congolese revolution and U.S. manipulation.

The surviving sisters fare better than their parents do. Leah marries the university-educated Congolese rebel who was her teacher and remains in the country. Her thoughts outline the Congo's grinding poverty and the sheer energy it takes to survive in a society preyed upon by a colonial power and then by capitalist interests. Ada becomes a doctor, and Rachel runs a hotel for the Europeans who remain in Africa fomenting unrest. Ironically, she, the most self-centered and resentful daughter, comes closest to emulating her father despite her financial success. Orleanna Price returns to America a drifting and unsteady shadow of herself.

After his family escapes, Nathan Price sinks into madness and wanders wildly for years. Kingsolver provides an intimate portrait of the stupidity of Nathan Price; his attempted exploitation of the Congolese stands as a metaphor for the plundering of the Congo. Rich details of landscape and tribal culture, including the traditional philosophy that shapes Congolese life, surface through the disparate voices of the Price girls. The tragedy of the Price family's lives, the ruin of Congolese tribal structure, and the breakdown of national order are concentric circles. The failure of private communication within the Price family and between the Prices and their African neighbors both prefigures and contributes to the failure and destruction of an ancient society in a ruthlessly short period of time.

Prodigal Summer • In this 2000 novel, Eddie Bondo and Deanna Wolfe share a love of nature, and they begin their interlude as lovers before he even knows her name. Deanna is a Forest Service employee serving as a resident biologist-ranger overseeing a section of the Zebulon National Forest. She has a deep knowledge of the people and ecology of Zebulon Valley and a stake in the wildlife balance, which she suspects that Eddie will threaten.

Then readers meet Lusa, Cole Widener's "over-educated" wife whom he brought back to his family's farm from Lexington, Kentucky. Lusa and Cole fight about her

unwillingness to mix with local people, and Cole feels the sting of her idea that the
world they inhabit is stultifying. Her Arabic background and her love of moths and
insects set Lusa apart from the family. Cole defends his people and the ways of farmers, as well as his closed-minded family, when Lusa tries to tell him her problems.
Cole's accident while driving a grain truck for Southern States changes Lusa's life
forever and adds another point of conflict with the family, since she inherits the
farm.

The third pair of antagonists, Garnett Walker and Nannie Land Rawley, tussles
over whether to spray weeds along Highway 6. She is afraid that the toxins will drift
onto her organic apples, and he wants the spraying done to protect his chestnut seed-
lings.

Kingsolver considers this her most difficult novel, as the issues being considered
are more important in the book than the characters themselves. She has said that it
has no main character and encourages readers to look beyond the tensions of the human interaction. Over the course of the novel, the five chief characters remaining after Cole's death explore their sexuality in relationships, through memory, and by
reputation. Their relationships prompt talk based on ideas like those found in T. R.
Paine's work on keystone predators. The effect of removing even one such predator
from an environment is profound, upsetting the fragile ecological balance beyond
repair. All the human tensions in the novel relate in some way to balance and the
sensible use of the land, as well as respect for all living things. The novel reminds
readers that their interdependence with nature is inescapable.

Karen L. Arnold
Updated by Marilyn Kongslie

Other major works

SHORT FICTION: *Homeland, and Other Stories*, 1989.
POETRY: *Another America/Otra America*, 1992.
NONFICTION: *Holding the Line: Women in the Great Arizona Mine Strike of 1983*, 1989;
High Tide in Tucson: Essays from Now or Never, 1995; *Last Stand: America's Virgin Lands*,
2002 (photographs by Annie Griffiths Belt); *Small Wonder*, 2002.
EDITED TEXTS: *The Best American Short Stories, 2001*, 2001.

Bibliography

Aay, Henry. "Environmental Themes in Ecofiction: *In the Center of the Nation* and *Animal Dreams.*" *Journal of Cultural Geography* 14 (Spring, 1994). Aay's comparative
study of Kingsolver's novel and *In the Center of the Nation* (1991) by Dan O'Brien is
one of the few scholarly discussions of Kingsolver's work.
Cockrell, Amanda. "Luna Moths, Coyotes, Sugar Skulls: The Fiction of Barbara
Kingsolver." *The Hollins Critic* 38, no. 2 (2001): 1-15. Analysis of symbols in
Kingsolver's fiction.
DeMarr, Mary Jean. *Barbara Kingsolver: A Critical Companion*. Westport, Conn.: Greenwood Press, 1999. A good overview of Kingsolver's work, emphasizing her eco-
feminism.
Draper, James P. "Barbara Kingsolver." In *Contemporary Literary Criticism: Yearbook
1993*. Vol. 81. Detroit: Gale Research, 1994. A collection of critical views of
Kingsolver's work.

Eisele, Kimi. "The Where and Why of Literature: A Conversation with Barbara Kingsolver." *You Are Here* 2, no. 2 (1999): 10-15. Interview with Kingsolver after she had published her first four novels.

Fleischner, Jennifer, ed. *A Reader's Guide to the Fiction of Barbara Kingsolver: "The Bean Trees," "Homeland and Other Stories," "Animal Dreams," "Pigs in Heaven."* New York: Harper Perennial, 1994. A good resource for the student new to Kingsolver's work.

Kingsolver, Barbara. Interview by Lisa See. *Publishers Weekly* 237 (August 31, 1990): 46. Kingsolver discusses her early literary influences and her research and writing methods.

_____. "Barbara Kingsolver." Interview by Robin Epstein. *Progressive* 60 (February, 1996): 33-38. An informative interview with Kingsolver; Kingsolver believes that most readers do not think that her writing is overly political; she feels that she has a responsibility to discuss her beliefs with the public.

Marshall, John. "Fast Ride on 'Pigs.'" Review of *Pigs in Heaven*, by Barbara Kingsolver. *Seattle Post-Gazette*, July 26, 1993, p. 1. This review gives an overview of Kingsolver's writing.

Ryan, Maureen. "Barbara Kingsolver's Lowfat Fiction." *Journal of American Culture* 18, no. 4 (Winter, 1995): 77-123. Ryan compares Kingsolver's first three novels and first short-story collection.

Wagner-Martin, Linda. *Barbara Kingsolver's "The Poisonwood Bible": A Reader's Guide.* New York: Continuum, 2001. A penetrating guide to Kingsolver's most popular novel.

Jerzy Kosinski

Born: Lodz, Poland; June 14, 1933
Died: New York, New York; May 3, 1991

Principal long fiction • *The Painted Bird*, 1965; *Steps*, 1968; *Being There*, 1971; *The Devil Tree*, 1973, revised 1981; *Cockpit*, 1975; *Blind Date*, 1977; *Passion Play*, 1979; *Pinball*, 1982; *The Hermit of 69th Street: The Working Papers of Norbert Kosky*, 1988.

Other literary forms • Jerzy Kosinski was a professional sociologist, educated in Poland and the Soviet Union. His first two books in English were studies of collectivized life in Soviet Russia, *The Future Is Ours, Comrade* (1960) and *No Third Path* (1962), both published under the pen name "Joseph Novak." Kosinski discussed some of his critical views in two short booklets, *Notes of the Author on "The Painted Bird"* (1965) and *The Art of the Self: Essays à Propos "Steps"* (1968).

Achievements • Kosinski is among that small group of serious, difficult, absolutely uncompromising writers who attained critical acclaim and, at the same time, great popular success; his novels regularly appeared on best-seller lists and have won such prizes as the National Book Award (1969) and the French Prix du Meilleur Livre Étranger (best foreign book, 1966). His first, most popular, and probably best, novel, *The Painted Bird*, about a child growing up through sheer determination in a very hostile world, is one of those works, such as Daniel Defoe's *Robinson Crusoe* (1719) or Mark Twain's *Adventures of Huckleberry Finn* (1884), that immediately touch some basic part of every reader. His later novels expressed contemporary experiences so directly that they seem to have been written out of the day's headlines. Charges of excessive violence and sensationalism are sometimes directed against Kosinski's work, but he argued cogently that life, no matter how much people have numbed themselves to it, is violent and sensational, and it is better to face the implications of those realities than to run and hide from them. In fact, it is only in experiencing life fully that one can extract value from it. His existential theme is that only when one lives conscious of the knowledge of one's coming death is one fully alive. Kosinski's achievements have been clouded by charges that he falsified his biography and failed to credit his translators. Nevertheless, Kosinski's reputation will continue to grow as critics and thoughtful readers better understand his intentions.

Biography • Jerzy Nikodem Kosinski was born in Lodz, Poland, on June 14, 1933. His life was as incredible as any of his novels, which he claimed were, to some degree, autobiographical. In 1939, when he was six, World War II began. He was Jewish, and his parents, believing he would be safer in the remote eastern provinces of Poland, paid a large sum of money to have him taken there. He reached eastern Poland, where—by his own, disputed account—he was immediately abandoned; his parents thought he was dead. Instead, at this very young age, he learned to live by his wits in an area where the peasants were hostile and the Nazis were in power. The extreme experiences of that time were given artistic expression in his first novel, *The Painted Bird*. Kosinski survived the ordeal, and his parents found him in an orphanage at the end of the war.

The stress of his experience had rendered him mute, and his irregular, wandering life had left him unfit to live normally with other people. Finally, in the care of his family, Kosinski regained his speech, and, studying with his philologist father, he completed his entire basic formal education in a year and entered the University of Lodz, where he eventually earned advanced degrees in history and political science.

By that time, Poland was an Iron Curtain country with a collectivized society. Kosinski had developed a fierce independence and could not endure communal life in which the individual was under scrutiny at every step. He knew he could not remain without getting into serious trouble with the government, so he put together an elaborate scheme to escape. Making the cumbersome

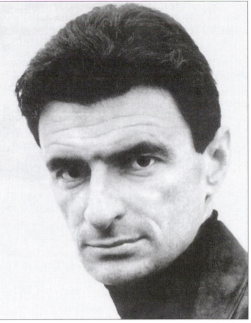

National Archives

bureaucracy work in his favor, Kosinski invented a series of sponsors, all highly regarded scientists according to the documents he forged for them, to write him letters of recommendation, which eventually enabled him to get a passport to study in the United States. He arrived in New York on December 20, 1957, twenty-four years old, with $2.80 in his pocket and a good textbook knowledge of English, though little experience in speaking the language. He lived any way he could, stealing food when necessary and constantly studying English. By March, he was fluent in the language, and within three years he had published *The Future Is Ours, Comrade,* a study of Soviet life that sold extremely well. Suddenly he was moderately wealthy, but that was only the beginning. Mary Hayward Weir, the young widow of steel magnate Ernest Weir and one of the wealthiest women in the United States, read his book and wrote him a letter of praise. They met and were soon married. All at once he was wealthy beyond his own dreams, owning villas in several countries, a vast yacht, a private jet. "I had lived the American nightmare," he said, "now I was living the American dream."

Five years later, in 1968, Mary Weir died of a brain tumor. The wealth, held by her in trust, went back to the estate. Kosinski had, during his marriage, written his first two novels, *The Painted Bird* and *Steps,* and he was a well-known, celebrated author. Needing to earn a living, he taught at Yale, Princeton, and Wesleyan Universities. He continued to write novels; they continued to sell well, so that he was able to leave teaching to write fulltime. He was remarried, to Katherina von Frauenhofer, in 1987.

Kosinski's life then fell into an active but regular and disciplined pattern. In season, he traveled to Switzerland to ski or to the Caribbean to play polo, and he made extensive American tours, granting innumerable interviews and publicizing his books. He was also internationally active in civil rights cases and served for two terms (the maximum allowed) as president of the International Association of Poets, Playwrights, Editors, Essayists, and Novelists (PEN). The rest of the time he spent working in his small apartment in Manhattan.

On May 3, 1991, Jerzy Kosinski, suffering from a serious heart disorder and discouraged by changes of dishonesty and plagiarism and by a growing inability to work, apparently chose to end his own life.

Kosinski often wrote that the world is an arena of violence and pure chance, which was certainly true of his own life. In addition to the numerous violent fluctuations of his early life, on a 1969 trip his baggage was misplaced, by chance, delaying his plane flight. His eventual destination was the home of his friends Roman Polanski and Sharon Tate; had it not been for the delay, he would have been there the fateful night the Charles Manson gang murdered everyone in that house.

Always a highly visible figure, Kosinski became during the early 1980's the subject of unwelcome publicity. In an article in *The Village Voice* (June 29, 1982), Geoffrey Stokes and Eliot Fremont-Smith charged that a number of Kosinski's novels had been written in part by various editorial assistants whose contributions he failed to acknowledge and indeed systematically concealed. Stokes and Fremont-Smith further charged that Kosinski's accounts to interviewers of his traumatic childhood experiences, his escape from Poland, and his first years in America have been contradictory and in some cases verifiably untrue. Finally, they suggested that Kosinski's acclaimed first novel, *The Painted Bird*, was actually written in Polish and then rendered into English by an unacknowledged translator. Kosinski denied all the charges. In *The Hermit of 69th Street*, which its protagonist calls a *"roman à tease,"* he responds indirectly to the controversy by reflecting on the writer's craft, which, he concludes, is largely a process of borrowing and recasting narrative material.

Analysis • The themes and techniques of Jerzy Kosinski's fiction are adumbrated in the sociological studies he published within five years of his arrival in the United States. As a highly regarded Polish sociology student in the mid-1950's, Kosinski was granted permission to travel widely in the Soviet Union to interview people about their experiences in collectivized living. It was assumed by the authorities that he would write a thesis praising communism, but, in fact, he found it abhorrent; his notes provided material for *No Third Path* and *The Future Is Ours, Comrade*, indictments of the system that he could never have published had he remained behind the Iron Curtain. The studies are diaries of his travels and consist mainly of his interviews with the people he met, people from every walk of life, some of whom were thriving in conformity within the system while others were in trouble because of their opposition to it. The interviews are not arranged chronologically; rather, each is located at the point where it can best support the theme under discussion.

This arrangement is typical of the structure of Kosinski's novels. The protagonist, who often has a great deal in common with Kosinski himself, is a loner, able to travel freely through all walks of life. Because he is secretly at war with his society, he is unable to stop and settle or to have more than a fleeting relationship with each person he encounters. The brief scenes in the novels are not arranged chronologically, but each vignette is one more stone in a mosaic; taken together, these vignettes constitute a powerful statement of Kosinski's recurring theme.

That theme is exactly the same as that of the sociological studies on collective life: the struggle of the individual to retain his or her individuality in a mass society. Central to Kosinski's novels are the ideas of the German philosopher Martin Heidegger, who profoundly influenced the existentialists. Heidegger said that one has no control over what is given one in life—where and when one is born, whether one is healthy or the reverse, intelligent or the reverse—that it is all a matter of chance. It is one's responsibility, however, to make the most of the particular life one is given. Daily life, petty responsibilities, the routine of work and family life, all have the effect of dulling one to the passage of time, and with it, the passage of one's opportunity to make the most of one's brief life. It is soothing, in a way, to be lulled and numbed into inattentiveness to coming pain and dissolution, yet to live in such a state is really not to live at all. According to Heidegger, one only lives fully when confronted by the terror of approaching death. The Kosinski hero purposely and unflaggingly thrusts himself into the terror-ridden present moment of his life, heroically refusing the deceptive and deadening temptations of his society to give up his lonely individuality and crawl under the umbrella of its collective "safety."

The Painted Bird • While Kosinski was living in immense wealth with his wife Mary Hayward Weir, he began writing *The Painted Bird*, a novel about an orphaned outcast. "It was an attempt to somehow balance the reality of my past with the reality of my present. She [Mary], in turn, learned of my past through my writing." This statement suggests an autobiographical impulse for writing *The Painted Bird*; in other statements, however, Kosinski has made it clear that it was a novel, a work of art he was writing, not a memoir.

The child protagonist of the novel, never named, is dark haired and dark eyed, and he speaks the educated dialect. The peasants among whom he is abandoned are blond and blue eyed and speak a barely comprehensible peasant dialect. He stands out from them at a glance, and they suspect he is a gypsy or a Jew; the penalty for hiding such a person from the Nazis is severe, so they are not pleased to have him around. Further, the peasants are suspicious of strangers, and superstitious, and they believe his dark coloring indicates an evil eye. He has no choice, however, but to live among them, suffer their unmotivated violence, and take the blame for any natural catastrophes, surviving in any way he can.

At one point he lives with Lekh, the birdcatcher. When Lekh is angry, he takes out his anger by capturing a bird, the strongest and handsomest of the flock, painting it in brilliant rainbow colors, and then releasing it among its drab brown congeners. They fall on it at once and peck it to death. The examples of the perils of being a "painted bird" are constantly brought home to the boy, who is aware that his visible difference from the others marks him as a painted bird. In one of Kosinski's nonfiction works, *No Third Path*, he describes a man he met in the Soviet Union who survives because he is able to remain as one of the masses, always staying in the exact center of the crowd, never calling attention to himself. In that way, life could be "waited through," as he phrased it, without too much inconvenience. There is safety, then, in not being a painted bird, yet it is safety gained through a denial of life.

In the winter there is no work for the boy to do in the villages. He is simply another mouth to feed, and his presence is unwelcome. Instead, he wanders freely over the countryside, wrapped in his collection of rags and bits of fur. He is warmed and protected by his "comet," a tin can with a wire handle. The can is punched full of holes so that by swinging it he can force air through it, thus keeping alight the sticks and bits of dry moss he uses to fuel it. No one else ventures out in the deep snow; he can easily break into barns and steal potatoes and other vegetables, then find shelter for the night under the roots of a tree and cook his food with his comet. At these times, even though he is only seven or eight years old, he feels a marvelous happiness at his freedom and independence, his ability to face life directly and survive. In the summer, he is forced to move back into the village, and his torments begin again. His only hope is to try to blend into the society—valuable months of his life need to be "waited through."

Toward the end of the war, when the Germans have retreated, he is found and briefly adopted by a Soviet army battalion. The stresses of his experience have left him mute; he has psychically cut himself off from communication with others. Two soldiers in the army have particularly taken him under their care: Gavrila, the political officer, and Mitka the Cuckoo, the sharpshooting instructor. They are the first human beings in memory to treat him kindly, and he worships them and wants to model his life after theirs. He cannot, however, because they are diametrically opposite to each other. Gavrila lectures him daily on the advantages of the collective: No one stands alone, but the entire society is a unit. Individuals can make mistakes, but not when they give themselves up to the wise decisions of the community. As long as they are careful to remain within the center of the collective, they will march ahead to a marvelous new future. The boy wants to believe what his hero Gavrila tells him, but he is uneasy. His experiences in the villages, putting himself in the power of the mass, have all been unfortunate, whereas his life seemed fullest and most satisfying when he was by himself, making his own decisions. Mitka the Cuckoo—his name suggesting that he, like the boy, is a painted bird—was a sniper behind enemy lines; because of this, he had to develop to the fullest his instincts to be solitary and to depend on no one but himself. Like the boy, he has always been a loner in a hostile world but able to take care of himself. In the end it is this philosophy that wins the boy.

The boy survives, when so many other children did not, because of his miraculously tough emotional health. He does not despair or curse his fate. Instead, he accepts his world as it is and desperately tries to learn how to survive in it. In this respect, *The Painted Bird* is a *Bildungsroman* in which the boy, always an empiricist, struggles to find the underlying principle of life. He believes at one time that it might be love, at another time religion, and finally that it might be evil, but each time he is disillusioned. At the end, his speech gone, he believes that hatred and revenge against one's enemies are the keys to survival. The war is over, and his parents have found him in an orphanage; it seems he has survived. Yet, hatred and cynicism possess him completely. They give him a certain power: the power to have survived. Yet, one wonders whether he really is a survivor if he has been so deeply scarred that he can no longer relate to other human beings.

How can this story about experiences apparently so remote from those of most of its readers have moved those readers so deeply? Perhaps a clue to this can be found in a statement Kosinski made: "I think it is childhood that is often traumatic, not this or that war." Perhaps the novel is best read as an allegory of childhood, and the war—as so often occurs in works of fiction—as symbolic of the struggle and engagement with life. Children—who are small, weak, powerless, and ignorant of adult ways—are often deeply alienated from the ruling adult society (adults, after all, may be the prototypes for the terrifying giants found in the most powerful children's tales). Learning to live in a society, in enemy territory, can be a deeply scarring struggle. Reconciliation and the reopening of communications come, if at all, with the slow painful dawning of maturity.

Steps • *Steps* was the first novel Kosinski began writing, but feeling too close in time to some of the experiences he was recording in it, he set it aside and instead wrote

The Painted Bird. Steps, which won a National Book Award, is engrossing but puzzling for the reader. The book consists of nearly fifty brief vignettes. Many of the scenes report perverse or violent sexual encounters or ruthless acts of revenge. Each scene is brief, and each has little or no connection with the successive scenes. There is no certain indication that the main character in one scene will reappear in the next one. Kosinski never comments on the action, forcing readers to decide for themselves how they are to judge the characters.

These puzzling features are explained by Kosinski's aesthetic and philosophical principles. The short vignettes force readers to concentrate their attention on the individual scenes themselves, rather than, as in a conventionally plotted book, taking the scene as a whole. Society tries to "plot" one's life, Kosinski suggests, in such a way as to make one look to the future, but while one waits for the future to come, one has missed one's real life, which takes place in the present moment. The protean narrator of the scenes presents another philosophical point. He is different each time he appears; indeed, some critics have claimed that there are several different protagonists, but Kosinski has specifically stated that one protagonist links all the scenes: Identity, the nature of the self, is fluid. Finally, there is no authorial judgment of the actions of the protagonist. Kosinski makes it a point in all his novels to give the absolute minimum of advice to readers, thus implicating readers continuously in the action, forcing them to examine their own values.

Perhaps an exception to this system is in the scenes of revenge. In many of his novels, Kosinski seems to advocate an ethic of revenge. If a person has hurt one, physically or spiritually, that individual must strike back or lose his or her sense of self. Selfhood seems to be very much an absolute value to Kosinski. It must be defended against the collective and in personal encounters as well, particularly in sexual encounters. Kosinski believes that human beings reveal themselves most completely in their sexual relations, and therefore these relations play a large role in his novels. The longest series of repeated, connected scenes in *Steps* is a series of thirteen italicized passages, sprinkled throughout the novel, which consist of elaborate pre- and postcoital dialogues between a man and a woman who are trying desperately to sort out their relationship.

The difficulty in a relationship is to find the means by which one may give him- or herself to another while still retaining one's selfhood. Kosinski presents this problem in terms reminiscent of Jean-Paul Sartre's existential psychology: In any relationship between two people, one must be the subject, and the other the object. To be the object is to give up one's selfhood and be nothing. To be the subject is to manipulate and diminish the other. There is a desperate struggle then for people to retain their selfhood—in other words, to become the subject and make the other the object. If one is successful in the struggle, he or she survives as an individual, but only at the cost of destroying the other. Relationships in this novel, and in all of Kosinski's novels, tend to be manipulative and destructive. Though the characters do not seem to find a way out of their dilemma, and though the novel offers no solutions, it seems that Kosinski is critical of his characters for their failure, for he has elsewhere defined love as "the attempt to be simultaneously subject and object . . . the willing relinquishment of the single subject to a new subject created from two single ones, each subject enhanced into one heightened self."

Steps is thus Kosinski's purest novel. It has no "plot," but instead it draws the reader's attention to the present moment of each incident as it unfolds; it has a protean narrator who is a new person in relation to each new set of experiences with which he is confronted; it presents human life as a struggle to maintain selfhood, to avoid being diluted into some larger mass, or, on the individual level, to avoid being dominated and made into an object in personal relationships; and finally, it offers no authorial judgments, throwing the reader entirely to his or her own resources.

Being There • *Being There*, at twenty-three thousand words, is a novella rather than a novel. Short in length, stripped and pure in language, and simple in outline, the story is told as a parable or moral allegory, which indeed it is. Chance, the protagonist, is consistent as a character because he has no character. Because he is mentally disabled, he is incapable of change or growth. No situation makes an impression on him, and therefore no situation alters him. He has never in his life been outside a rich man's estate, where he has remained to tend the garden. He works in the garden by day and watches television by night. When the rich man dies, however, the executors of the estate release Chance. He is tall, handsome, soft-spoken, and wears his former employer's cast-off suits. The wife of a billionaire financier invites Chance into her house thinking he must be a rich businessman. That night, the president of the United States visits the financier and is introduced to Chance. In every situation, Chance acts the way he has seen someone on television act in a similar situation. Every question he is asked, he answers in terms of gardening, since that is what he knows. His simple statements about flowers growing are taken as profound metaphorical statements about the economy. The president quotes him in his national speech that night, and he is immediately pursued by all the media, invited to talk shows, and courted by foreign ambassadors; by novel's end, there are plans to run him for high office, since he looks good on television and does not seem to have a past that might prove an embarrassment.

This amusingly absurd tale is in fact Kosinski's indictment of the mass media, especially television, which, as a sociologist, he frequently attacked in lectures and essays. The first evil of television, according to Kosinski, is that it presents viewers with an immediately accessible image and therefore does not induce them to do any thinking for themselves (an infant child, Kosinski reminds his readers, can watch the same programs they do). This mindless image is ultimately deadly, because it suggests that experience is *outside*, something that happens only to other people. Through lulling viewers into believing that wrecks and bombings and deaths can happen only to others, television robs them of the angst needed to live life fully. Further, television can make mere images so attractive that it can persuade viewers to vote for any well-made-up puppet it puts before them. Into the empty, simplified, television image, viewers pour all their hopes and wishes, as the characters around Chance fill in his blank personality, making him into the person they want him to be. The comedy loses its humor when Kosinski suggests how easily this completely empty puppet could find itself sitting in the Oval Office, world destruction within the push of a single button.

Unlike television or films, which present the audience directly with an external image, novels, when they are read properly, force readers to re-create the scenes inside their heads, to generate their own images. This act of re-creation allows the reader to experience directly the action of the novel; when a character dies, the reader must, to an extent, experience that death. Kosinski was so opposed to the way the image falsifies and separates people from experience that he long refused to have any of his novels made into films. Under extraordinary and repeated persuasion from actor Peter Sellers, he at last agreed to allow *Being There* to be made into a film, starring Sellers, in 1979. There is a kind of ironic appropriateness in a story dealing entirely with the effect of visual images being portrayed in visual images.

Blind Date • *Blind Date* is typical, and indeed is probably the best, of a later group of Kosinski novels (the others in this group are *Cockpit, Passion Play,* and *Pinball*). The novel is presented in what can be called a standard Kosinski format: a series of incidents that finds the mobile lone-wolf protagonist in various countries, frequently flashing back to the past, moving from adventure to adventure, from woman to woman. In this group of novels, Kosinski begins to move toward more conventional plotting, and his protagonists are softened and made more human, more vulnerable. They are growing older and are no longer capable of some of the feats of their youth. Human relationships become less of a battleground, and at least the possibility of love is present. The theme of revenge, so prominent in earlier novels, begins to diminish. Where it is still present, it has been sublimated. The protagonist, giving up acts of personal revenge, raises himself to be a sort of "scourge of God," taking impersonal revenge against enemies of humanity. The earlier novels made frequent use of autobiographical materials, which these later novels continue to do, but there is a new element. The later novels come more programmatically to represent Kosinski's spiritual biography, and the protagonist, for all the indirection of art, comes more and more to stand for Kosinski himself.

The novel *Blind Date* and its protagonist Levanter are transitional in this scheme. Levanter as a young man is just as egotistic and manipulative as earlier Kosinski heroes have been. In summer camp, for example, he binds and brutally rapes a girl with whom he is infatuated, but he refuses to talk to her because he is too shy. That event, however, is seen in flashback. When the novel opens, Levanter is middle aged, and though he is still capable of violence, the violence has a social dimension. When he learns that the minister of internal affairs of a small dictatorship, a man famous for tortures and murders, is staying incognito at the same ski resort he is, Levanter manages, through an elaborate scheme, to have him killed. When a champion fencer from an Iron Curtain country is imprisoned because of information given against him by an informant, Levanter kills the informer by skewering him on just such a sword as the fencer has used.

Levanter, particularly as he grows older, is not so ruthlessly manipulative in his personal relationships as previous protagonists. If Tarden, the protagonist of the previous novel, *Cockpit,* had raped a girl, he would never have looked back. Instead, Levanter again meets the girl he had raped a year later (she had never seen his face), and their relationship continues to the point of true love; when he kisses her in the way the rapist had, however, she recognizes him and leaves in a rage. He feels then that he has missed a real opportunity and regrets his earlier action.

Levanter had met the girl the second time through sheer chance, another in a series of chance events in the novel. For example, in the novel's opening, Levanter meets a woman whose piano playing reminds him of the way his mother once played. By chance, that woman had been instructed under the same teacher as his mother, and Levanter and the woman feel this establishes a link between them. They go their separate ways, but toward the end of the novel, by sheer chance, Levanter meets her again; this time they complete the relationship begun earlier, one of total fulfillment for both.

These chance meetings, which have the ironic effect of giving the novel a conventional plot, seem like the most banal and improbable coincidences until the reader realizes that chance is actually the governing principle of the novel. The novel's epigraph is a quotation from Jacques Monod's *Chance and Necessity* (1972) in which he argues that every moment in life is the chance convergence of completely unrelated chains of random events, and therefore there is no "plot" to life, no inevitability, no prediction. *Blind Date* reiterates more directly than any of Kosinski's other novels the Heideggerian notion that human beings are on earth only through sheer chance, that their time here, whether long or short, must end with death, and therefore they must get the most possible out of each moment as it is lived. What is new in the novel is the social dimension: One way human beings make their life meaningful is by trying to make the lives of those around them meaningful as well. The earlier Kosinski protagonists fought desperately and ruthlessly to preserve the self, even if it meant destroying their closest personal relationships. The later protagonists, among whom Levanter again is a transitional figure, take more risks with the self, even hesitantly offering it in love. As a sign of this mellowing, Levanter actually seeks to rectify the cruelty he had practiced as a youth. As a first step he dedicates himself to punishing totalitarians; later, he seeks to undo his own totalitarian act of raping the girl at summer camp. In the novel's greatest coincidence, he realizes that the pianist is that very girl from the summer camp, who, as a result of the rape, has never been able to achieve sexual fulfillment. He binds her now, gently, and, this time with her permission, reenacts the rape, at last freeing her to be fully herself.

At this point a romantic novel might have ended, but such an end would be a falsification. Life can only end with death, which is the only predictable and almost inevitable conclusion to life's "plot." An aging Levanter is skiing when an unexpected late-season surge of bad weather catches him inadequately dressed. He is lost in the fog and slowly gives in to the cold, feeling he has played life's game very well and is now perhaps titled to a rest.

Norman Lavers

Other major works
SCREENPLAY: *Being There*, 1979 (adaptation of his novel; with Robert C. Jones).
NONFICTION: *The Future Is Ours, Comrade*, 1960 (as Joseph Novak); *No Third Path*, 1962 (as Novak); *Notes of the Author on "The Painted Bird,"* 1965; *The Art of the Self: Essays à Propos "Steps,"* 1968; *Passing By: Selected Essays, 1962-1991*, 1992; *Conversations with Jerzy Kosinski*, 1993 (Tom Teicholz, editor).
EDITED TEXTS: *Sociologia Amerykánska: Wybór Prae, 1950-1960*, 1962.

Bibliography
Bruss, Paul. *Victims: Textual Strategies in Recent American Fiction.* Lewisburg, Pa.: Bucknell University Press, 1981. Explores the strategies of three writers, including Kosinski, and their alliance with the idealist tradition. Examines Kosinski's early fiction with regard to his use of language, as well as his novels *Steps, Cockpit*, and *Blind Date*. A selected bibliography of primary and secondary sources is provided.
Fein, Richard J. "Jerzy Kosinski." In *Contemporary Novelists*, edited by James Vinson. London: St. James Press, 1976. Includes comments by Kosinski and critical appraisal of his most distinguished novels. Fein honors the vision of Kosinski and sees his works as "strange hymns to suffering."
Lavers, Norman. *Jerzy Kosinski.* Boston: Twayne, 1982. An appreciative critical study that considers Kosinski a major writer. Discusses his fiction and nonfiction novels

with some biographical information and provides considerable critical commentary on *The Painted Bird*. Contains a selected bibliography. A useful introduction to the beginning reader of Kosinski.

Lilly, Paul R., Jr. *Words in Search of Victims: The Achievement of Jerzy Kosinski*. Kent, Ohio: Kent State University Press, 1988. A full-length appreciative critical study of Kosinski's novels with much of interest and value for the Kosinski scholar. Includes a discussion of the controversy with *The Village Voice*, which attacked Kosinski's authenticity and compositional methods.

Lupack, Barbara Tepa. *Plays of Passion, Games of Chance: Jerzy Kosinski and His Fiction*. Bristol, Ind.: Wyndham Hall Press, 1988. Innovative analysis of Kosinski's fiction

Sloan, James Park. *Jerzy Kosinski: A Biography*. New York: Dutton, 1996. An essential work on Kosinski, this iconoclastic study challenges many of Kosinski's claims about his own life but maintains an essential admiration for Kosinski's writing.

Tepa Lupack, Barbara, ed. *Critical Essays on Jerzy Kosinski*. New York: G. K. Hall, 1998. Thoughtful essays on Kosinski's writing. Includes bibliographical references and an index.

Margaret Laurence

Born: Neepawa, Manitoba, Canada; July 18, 1926
Died: Lakefield, Ontario, Canada; January 5, 1987

Principal long fiction • *This Side Jordan*, 1960; *The Stone Angel*, 1964; *A Jest of God*, 1966; *The Fire-Dwellers*, 1969; *The Diviners*, 1974.

Other literary forms • Margaret Laurence published two short-story collections, *The Tomorrow-Tamer* (1963) and *A Bird in the House* (1970), and two children's books, *Jason's Quest* (1970) and *The Christmas Birthday Story* (1980). She also produced a translation of Somali folktales and poems, *A Tree for Poverty: Somali Poetry and Prose* (1954); a travelogue, *The Prophet's Camel Bell* (1963); and a study of Nigerian novelists and playwrights, *Long Drums and Cannons: Nigerian Dramatists and Novelists, 1952-1966* (1968). A collection of her essays, *Heart of a Stranger*, appeared in 1976. Because of her work on Nigerian fiction and drama, she is well known to students of African literature.

Achievements • From the beginning of her writing career, Laurence received much popular and critical recognition. *This Side Jordan* won the Beta Sigma Phi prize for a first novel by a Canadian; *The Stone Angel* received both critical and popular acclaim; *A Jest of God* was awarded the Governor-General's Award in 1966 and was adapted for motion pictures as *Rachel, Rachel; The Diviners*, despite less than universal critical acclaim, was at the top of the best-seller list for more than sixty consecutive weeks. Along with her popularity, Laurence enjoyed an international reputation as a consistently accomplished fiction writer. Her special contribution to the novel was recognized by Jack McClelland of the Canadian publishing house of McClelland and Stewart when he first read *This Side Jordan*. The stories that were gathered in *The Tomorrow-Tamer* and *A Bird in the House* originally appeared separately in such Canadian, American, and British journals as *Prism, The Atlantic Monthly*, and *Queen's Quarterly*. Laurence also won respect as a lecturer and critic. United College, University of Winnipeg, made her an Honorary Fellow, the first woman and the youngest to be so honored. She received honorary degrees from McMaster, Dalhousie, Trent, University of Toronto, and Carleton University and served as writer-in-residence at several Canadian universities. Her works have been translated into French, German, Italian, Spanish, Dutch, Norwegian, Danish, and Swedish.

Biography • Margaret Laurence was born Jean Margaret Wemyss on July 18, 1926, in Neepawa, Manitoba. Laurence's mother's family was of Irish descent and her father's Scottish. Although she was separated from the "old country" on both sides by at least two generations, her early memories, like those of Vanessa MacLeod in the short stories in *A Bird in the House* and of Morag Gunn in *The Diviners*, are of a proud and lively Scottish ancestry.

When Laurence was four, her mother died, and her aunt, Margaret Simpson, left a respected teaching career in Calgary and went home to care for her niece. A year later, she and Robert Wemyss were married. They had one son, Robert, born only two years before his father died of pneumonia. In 1938, Margaret Simpson Wemyss took the two children and moved in with her father, the owner of a furniture store. This domestic situation in slightly altered form provides the setting for the Vanessa MacLeod stories in *A Bird in the House.* Laurence lived in Grandfather Simpson's house until she went to United College, University of Winnipeg, in 1944.

John Simpson was a fierce and autocratic man of eighty-two when his widowed daughter and her two children moved in with him. Laurence resented his authority over her and her stepmother; this relationship fostered Laurence's empathy with women struggling toward freedom. All of her heroines—Hagar Shipley, Rachel Cameron, Vanessa MacLeod, Stacey MacAindra, and Morag Gunn—struggle against oppressive forces, and Laurence's recurring theme of the lack of communication between men and women, as well as between women and women, is rooted in the domestic situation in Grandfather Simpson's house. It appears in her first novel, *This Side Jordan,* as the problem between the colonialists and the Africans, between husbands and wives, and between relatives. At the beginning of her last novel, *The Diviners,* the problem of communication—searching for the right words—is a major frustration that Morag, the protagonist, faces as a writer.

The encouragement and honest criticism given to Laurence by her stepmother were a great help to the girl, who started writing at an early age. At United College, she took honors in English, while her involvement with "The Winnipeg Old Left" during and after her college years reflected her dedication to social reform. Social awareness—the realization that men and women are constrained by social structures and exploit and are exploited by others through these systems—developed from her awareness that the hopes of her parents' generation had been crushed by the Great Depression and that her own generation's prospects were altered radically by World War II. After she graduated, she worked for one year as a reporter for the *Winnipeg Citizen.* Her experience covering the local labor news consolidated her social and political convictions and advanced theoretical problems to personal ones.

In 1948, Laurence married Jack Laurence, a civil engineer from the University of Manitoba. They left Canada for England in 1949 and went to the British Protectorate of Somaliland in 1950, where he was in charge of a dam-building project. In 1952, they moved to the Gold Coast (now Ghana), where they lived until 1957. A daughter, Jocelyn, was born when they were on leave in England in 1952, and a son, David, was born in Ghana in 1955. Out of these African years came several early works, including *The Tomorrow-Tamer, This Side Jordan,* the translations of folktales, and the travel journal *The Prophet's Camel Bell.* Of the last, Laurence said that it was the most difficult work she ever wrote because it was not fiction. The importance of this work lies in its theme—the growth in self-knowledge and humility in an alien environment. During the years in Africa, Laurence read the Pentateuch for the first time, and these books of the Bible became a touchstone for her, especially pertinent to the African works and to a lesser extent to her Manawaka fiction. Here she developed the patience and discipline of a professional writer.

In 1962, Laurence and her children left Jack Laurence in Vancouver and moved to London. They remained in England until 1968, when Laurence returned to Canada to be writer-in-residence at Massey College, University of Toronto. She was affiliated with several other Canadian universities in the years that followed. In 1987, Laurence died in Lakefield, Ontario.

**Analysis • ** The major emphasis of Margaret Laurence's fiction changed considerably between her early and later works. In a 1969 article in *Canadian Literature,* "Ten

Years' Sentences," she notes that after she had grown out of her obsession with the nature of freedom, the theme of the African writings and *The Stone Angel*, her concern "had changed to that of survival, the attempt of the personality to survive with some dignity, toting the load of excess mental baggage that everyone carries. . . . " In the same article, she remarks that she became increasingly involved with novels of character, that her viewpoint altered from modified optimism to modified pessimism, and that she had become more concerned with form in writing.

The more profound psychological realism of her later novels developed after a general awareness of the intractable problems of emerging African nations had matured both the Africans and their observers. The characters in the African works were products of a now dated optimism that forced them into preconceived molds. The later novels reveal modified pessimism, but their vitality comes from Laurence's developing concern with psychological realism, which authenticates the characters and their voices. After *This Side Jordan*, the point of view is consistently in the first person, the protagonist's, and is strictly limited to the protagonist's consciousness. Although Hagar in *The Stone Angel* and Stacey in *The Fire-Dwellers* are stereotypes, a stubborn old lady and a frantic middle-aged housewife, Laurence makes them both compelling protagonists through accurate psychological portrayals.

A theme of major importance that Laurence did not fully develop until *The Diviners* is the nature of language. Rachel's concern with name calling in *A Jest of God* anticipates the larger exploration in *The Fire-Dwellers*, in which Laurence experiments with a variety of voices, using language in a variety of ways. Exterior voices, many of them bizarre, interrupt and are interrupted by Stacey's inner voices—her monologues, her memories of voices from the past, her challenges, threats, and prayers to God. The exterior voices include radio and television news, snatches of her children's conversations, the characteristic dialects of various socioeconomic groups, the half-truthful promotions of her husband's company, and the meaningfully unfinished conversations between her and her husband. In order to allow language to be discussed explicitly, Laurence makes the protagonist of *The Diviners* a novelist.

In her first three novels Laurence uses biblical allusions to provide a mythic framework for a psychological study of character and situation. All these allusions are from the Old Testament, which made a lasting impression on her when she read it for the first time in Africa. The names she chooses for the characters in the early fiction—Adamo, Jacob, Abraham, Nathaniel, Joshua, Hagar, Ishmael, and Rachel—provide ready-made dilemmas whose traditional solutions appear contrived and psychologically unrealistic. In *This Side Jordan*, Joshua's Ghanian father proclaims that his son will cross the Jordan into the Promised Land, confidently assumed to be both an independent, prosperous Ghana and a Christian heaven. These allusions contribute to the sacramental overtones in the early works, particularly at the end of *The Stone Angel*.

Biblical myth is replaced in *A Bird in the House* and *The Diviners* by the myths of Scottish immigrants and Canadian pioneers and Indians. Vanessa in *A Bird in the House* lives with the sentimentally mythologized memories of her grandparents. The dispossessed Scots and the dispossessed Métis Indians provide a personal mythology for young Morag Gunn in *The Diviners*, which her foster father, Christie Logan, embellishes to give the orphan girl an identity. Christie himself becomes mythologized in the mind of Morag's daughter Pique. The theme of the search for one's true origins plays a prominent part throughout Laurence's fiction, but the issues become increasingly complex. Whereas a clear dichotomy between his Christian and African backgrounds divides Nathaniel Amegbe in *This Side Jordan*, Morag in *The Diviners*, a recognized novelist who was an orphan brought up by a garbage collector, is seriously perplexed by the bases of her identity. Nathaniel hopes for, and apparently receives, both worldly and spiritual rewards in a successful if simplistic reconciliation of his dual heritage. In contrast, Morag painfully learns to reject the heroic Scottish ancestress Christie had invented for her without rejecting him; she realizes that she has invented a hopelessly confused web of self-fabricated personal myth that she has to reconcile with her Canadian roots in her search for self-identity.

Throughout all her works, Laurence explores themes concerning the role of women, the injustices of sex-role stereotyping, and the inequality of opportunity. The changing roles of women in the late twentieth century are a problem for Morag, who is jealous of her daughter's sexual freedom. Although the protagonists of Laurence's later novels are women—women who have not always been treated well by the men in their lives—men are never treated harshly in her work, even though the point of view is limited to the female protagonist's consciousness. Stacey generously concludes that perhaps her uncommunicative husband is tormented by fears and doubts much like her own. Morag never speculates about Jules Tonnerre's motives—a strange lack of curiosity for a novelist. Although Laurence's protagonists are oppressed, they never simply blame the men in their lives or the male-dominated society for their oppression. Men, almost to a man, are given the benefit of the doubt.

This Side Jordan • Laurence's first novel, *This Side Jordan*, was begun in Ghana in 1955, finished in Vancouver, and published in 1960. The setting of the novel is Ghana just before independence. The protagonist, Nathaniel Amegbe, had boarded at a Roman Catholic mission school since he was seven and is now caught between two cultures, between loyalty to the fading memory of tribal customs and loyalty to the Christian mission that educated him and gave him the opportunity to better himself, in a European sense, by teaching in the city. His predicament is balanced by that of Johnnie Kestoe, a newly arrived employee of an English-based export-import firm who is trying to forget his slum-Irish background and to rise in the firm despite his antipathy for Africans. Both men have wives expecting their first child. Many of Nathaniel's dilemmas are resolved in the end, even his fears that his father's soul might be assigned to hell. In part, his resolution results from the salvation metaphor of "crossing the Jordan," a feat he hopes his newborn son will accomplish.

Nathaniel's interior monologues reveal the conflicts his dual loyalties have produced. Laurence uses this device more and more in the ensuing novels, and it culminates in *The Diviners* with its complex narrative techniques. Both Johnnie and Nathaniel move through the novel to a greater realization of self by means of humbling experiences, and both achieve worldly success, a naïvely optimistic conclusion made at the expense of psychological realism.

The Stone Angel • *The Stone Angel* was published in 1964, two years after Laurence and her children moved to London. Laurence, in "A Place to Stand On" from *Heart of a Stranger*, states that the dominant theme of this novel is survival, "not just physical survival, but the preservation of some human dignity and in the end some human warmth and ability to reach out and touch others." The monument Hagar Shipley's father had built for her mother's tomb in the Manawaka cemetery is a stone angel, gouged out by stonemasons who were accustomed to filling the needs of "fledgling pharaohs in an uncouth land." Laurence's horror at the extravagance of the pharaohs' monuments at Luxor, recorded in "Good Morning to the Grandson of Rameses the Second" in *Heart of a Stranger*, is similar to her reaction to the material ambitions of the stern Scotch-Irish prairie pioneers.

The story of Hagar Shipley is told in the first person and covers the three weeks before her death, but in these weeks, long flashbacks depict scenes of Hagar's life in chronological order. Laurence gives sacramental overtones to the events of Hagar's last days: She confesses to a most unlikely priest in a deserted cannery over a jug of wine; in the hospital where she dies, she is able to overcome her pride and to enjoy and empathize with her fellow patients; after she accepts a previously despised minister sent by her son, she has an epiphany—"Pride was my wilderness, and the demon that led me there was fear"; and just before her death, she wrests from her daughter-in-law her last drink. Such sacramental overtones are not unusual in Laurence's works, but in her later works they become more subtle and complex than they are here.

Hagar Shipley is an old woman, an enormously fat, physically feeble old woman, grotesque and distorted in both body and spirit. She is mean spirited as well as mean about her money and her possessions—almost a stereotype, an unlikely heroine, certainly not one who would seem to attract the sympathy of the reader. Hagar does, however, attract the reader; the genuineness of her portrayal makes her believable because of her total honesty, and the reader empathizes with her plight, which she finally recognizes as self-made. The reader feels compassion for her in spite of and because of her pettiness. Her voice, even in her old age, is still strong, willful, and vital, and the development of her self-awareness and self-knowledge is gripping.

The Stone Angel is the first work in which Manawaka, Laurence's fictionalized hometown of Neepawa, Manitoba, serves as the childhood setting of the protagonist. She makes Manawaka a microcosmic world, the childhood home of all her later protagonists, whose memories and friends carry over from one work to another. The mythic heritage of Hagar in *The Stone Angel*—the Scotch-Irish pioneers and Méti Indians in Manitoba—is shared by Vanessa in *A Bird in the House*, Rachel in *A Jest of God*, Stacey in *The Fire-Dwellers*, and Morag in *The Diviners*, although Hagar is old enough to be the grandmother of the other four. Every one of these women leaves Manawaka in a search for identity and spiritual freedom, but none is able to escape her heredity and childhood environment entirely. The effects of environment and heredity were increasingly explored as Laurence became more and more concerned with the nature of identity. The Manawaka setting gave Laurence the opportunity to develop characters whose parents or grandparents engaged in a strenuous battle to open the frontier, founded what they hoped would be dynasties, and lived to see them fall because of the Great Depression. These stubborn and proud people begot children who had to find their own identities without the visible mansions their parents had built to proclaim theirs. Pride in personal success became in the next generation pride in family and origin, and Hagar's inheritance from her father showed that the strength of the pioneer generation could destroy as well as build. The recognition of the double-edged nature of this strength enables Hagar, a stone angel in her former blindness, to feel at the end some human warmth for those around her.

A Jest of God • *A Jest of God* was written in Buckinghamshire, England, in 1964 and 1965, and was published the next year. The action takes place during a summer and fall during the 1960's in Manawaka. Laurence creates a woman protagonist learning to break through the entrapments oppressing her.

Only through the first-person point of view could Laurence manage to reenact Rachel Cameron's fearful responses to everything around her and her self-mocking evaluations of her responses; she is afraid even of herself. When she reflects upon the way she thinks, upon her paranoia and her imagination, she warns herself that through her own distortions of reality she will become strange, weird, an outcast. She continues to tell herself that she must stop thinking that way. Her fear about her own responses to ordinary life keeps her in a state near hysteria. Except for the recognizable quality of her perceptions and the color and richness of her imagination, she could indeed be dismissed as a stereotyped old-maid schoolteacher, the butt of the town's jokes. She lives with her widowed mother, renting the upper story of her dead father's former funeral parlor.

The mythic framework for the psychological study of Rachel is the Old Testament story in which Rachel is "mourning for her children"—in the novel, the children she has never had. When she is confident enough to love Nick Kazlik, whom she needs more as a father for her children than as a lover, he tells her that he is not God; he cannot solve her problems. Neither he nor the possibility of the child he might give her can overcome her sense of isolation, of which the lack of children is only the symbol; her sense of isolation seems to be based on her lack of spiritual fulfillment, isolation from God. God's word is evaded in the church she and her mother attend, and she is totally horrified by fundamentalist irrationality. In the end, Rachel recognizes her own self-pity to be a horrendous sort of pride, and she starts to learn instead to feel compassion for others because they are as isolated as she.

Rachel's situation could set the stage for a tragedy, but Laurence's heroines do not become tragic. They live through their crises, endure, and in enduring gain strength. Rachel gains strength from the loss of Nick, which she never understands, and from the loss of what she hoped and feared would be Nick's baby. After Rachel has decided not to commit suicide when she thinks she is pregnant, she discovers that what she had thought was a baby was a meaningless tumor, not even malignant— a jest of God. Despite, or perhaps because of, this grotesque anticlimax, Rachel is able to make the decision to leave Manawaka; she applies for and earns a teaching position in Vancouver. At the end, she is traveling with her mother, her "elderly child," to a new life in Vancouver.

The Fire-Dwellers • *The Fire-Dwellers* was written in England between 1966 and 1968; the protagonist of the novel, Stacey MacAindra, is Rachel Cameron's sister. She is an ordinary woman—a middle-class contemporary housewife in Manawaka, anxious over all the possible and impossible perils waiting for her and her family. She overcomes stereotyping through the recognizable, likable, and spontaneous qualities of her narrative voice. Laurence's narrative technique is more complex in *The Fire-Dwellers* than in any of her earlier works. The first-person narration is fragmented by a variety of interruptions—Stacey's inner voices, snatches of Stacey's memories set to the side of the page, italicized dreams and fantasies, incomplete conversations with Mac, her husband, and radio and television news. At times, she is concentrating so completely on her inner voice that she feels a physical jolt when external reality breaks into her inner fantasies.

The title refers, as Stacey's lover Luke implies, to Stacey: She is the ladybird of the nursery rhyme who must fly away home because her house is on fire and her children will burn. Although Sir James Frazer's *The Golden Bough* (1890-1915) lies unopened beside Stacey's bed at the end of the book, as it did in the beginning, Stacey seems to understand intuitively the explanation of the primitive sexuality of fire. Stacey burns from sexual frustration and fears the burning of an atomic bomb, a threat ever present on the news. Newspaper pictures from Vietnam of a horrified mother trying to remove burning napalm from her baby's face appear again and again in Stacey's mind. Counterpointing the fire metaphor is that of water, here regenerative as well as destructive, which foreshadows its more important position in *The Diviners*.

Unlike the other Manawaka protagonists, Stacey could never be considered grotesque; she considers herself quite ordinary, and, at first glance, most people would agree, despite her apocalyptic fears. The world around her, however, is grotesque. The frightening events in the lives of Stacey's neighbors and friends are counterpointed by the daily news from the Vietnam War. Almost a symbol of Stacey's inability to communicate her fears, her two-year-old, Jen, cannot or will not speak. No wonder Stacey hides her drinks in the Mix-Master. Her interior dialogue convincingly portrays a compassionate woman with a stabilizing sense of humor that makes the limited affirmation of the conclusion believable; Mac and his equally uncommunicative son Duncan are brought together by Duncan's near-death, and Jen speaks her first words: "Hi, Mum. Want tea?"

The Diviners • Laurence worked on *The Diviners* from 1969 to 1973, at the old house she bought on the Otonabee River near Peterborough, Ontario. Unlike the earlier Laurence protagonists, apparently ordinary women, almost stereotypes who turn out to be extraordinary in their own way, Morag Gunn is an extraordinarily gifted writer who has quite ordinary and common concerns. She is also unlike her Manawaka "sisters" in that she is an orphan reared by the town's garbage collector; thus she is an outsider who bears the scorn and taunts of the town's wealthier children such as Stacey Cameron and Vanessa MacLeod. She shares her humble status with the disreputable half-breed Indians, the Tonnerres, and learns the injustice of the inequality of opportunity at first hand.

The title, *The Diviners*, refers explicitly to gifted individuals, artists such as Morag who contribute to a greater understanding of life, as well as to her friend, Royland, a true water diviner. Indeed, Morag discovers that many of her acquaintances are, in some way, themselves diviners. At the end of the book, when Royland tells Morag he has lost the gift of divining, Morag muses, "At least Royland knew he had been a true diviner. . . . The necessity of doing the thing—that mattered."

The Diviners is the longest and the most tightly structured of Laurence's novels; it has three long parts framed by a prologue and epilogue. The plot is commonplace; Morag spends a summer worrying about her eighteen-year-old daughter Pique, who has gone west to "find" herself. In this action, Morag is only an observer, as all mothers must be in this situation. Her own story is enclosed within the action in the present, with chronological flashbacks such as those in *The Stone Angel*. The novel is presented in the first person, but with two new techniques: "Snapshots," meditations on the few snapshots Morag has from her youth; and "Memorybank Movies," Morag's memories from her past. The snapshots cover the lives of her parents, before Morag was born through her early childhood and their deaths. Aware that she embroidered stories about the snapshots as a child, Morag looks at a snapshot, remembers her make-believe story, and then muses, "I don't recall when I invented that one." This comment, early in the novel, establishes the mythologizing of one's past as an important motif.

Morag's future as a writer is foreshadowed by her retelling of Christie Logan's tales when just a girl, adapting them to her own needs. In the prologue, Morag the novelist worries about diction, the choice of the proper words: "How could that colour be caught in words? A sort of rosy peach colour, but that sounded corny and was also inaccurate." Morag uses her hometown for setting and characters, just as Laurence herself does; the theme of where one belongs is as important to Morag as a writer as it is to Laurence.

The title of Morag's second novel, *Prospero's Child*, foreshadows the motif of the end-frame. Royland loses his gift of witching for water and hopes to pass it on to A-Okay Smith. Morag realizes that she will pass on to Pique her gift, just as Christie Logan's manic prophecies influenced her creativity. Among all Laurence's heroines, Morag Gunn is the closest in experience and interests to Laurence herself. Each successive protagonist, from Hagar and Rachel and Vanessa to Stacy, came closer and closer to Laurence's own identity. She said that she realized how difficult it would be to portray a protagonist so much like herself, but *The Diviners* is a risky novel, an ambitious book that only an established writer could afford to produce.

Because Laurence depicts human problems in terms of sex roles, the gender of the characters in the Manawaka novels is particularly important. The women protagonists of all of these novels clearly demonstrate Laurence's persistent investigation of the role of women in society. The sex lives of Laurence's women are fully integrated parts of their identities without becoming obsessive or neurotic. All of her protagonists enjoy their sexuality but, at the same time, suffer guiltily for it. Laurence did not admit a connection with the women's liberation movement. Morag Gunn, however, a single head of a household with an illegitimate dependent child, could not have been as readily accepted by readers and admired before the feminist movement as she was after.

Similarly, although Laurence employs Christian motifs and themes throughout her fiction, she did not embrace institutional Christianity. Like psychologist Carl Jung, Laurence seems to find God in the human soul, defining religion in terms of a Jungian "numinous experience" that can lead to a psychological change. Salvation is redefined as discovery of self, and grace is given to find a new sense of life direction.

Presenting her characters as beings caught between the determinism of history and their free will, as individuals who are torn between body and spirit, fact and illusion, Laurence portrays life as a series of internal crises. Through the development of her protagonists, Laurence celebrates even the crises as she celebrates her protagonists' progress. The search for self involves both the liberation from and the embracing of the past. Survival with dignity and the ability to love, she remarks in *Heart of a Stranger*, are themes almost inevitable for a writer of her stern Scotch-Irish background. Because these themes are of immense contemporary importance, her works explore problems that have universal appeal, a fact that goes far to explain her tremendous popularity.

Judith Weise

Other major works

SHORT FICTION: *The Tomorrow-Tamer*, 1963; *A Bird in the House*, 1970.

NONFICTION: *The Prophet's Camel Bell*, 1963 (pb. in U.S. as *New Wind in a Dry Land*, 1964); *Long Drums and Cannons: Nigerian Dramatists and Novelists, 1952-1966*, 1968; *Heart of a Stranger*, 1976; *Intimate Strangers: The Letters of Margaret Laurence and Gabrielle Roy*, 2004 (Paul G. Socken, editor).

CHILDREN'S LITERATURE: *Jason's Quest,* 1970; *Six Darn Cows,* 1979; *The Olden Days Coat,* 1979; *The Christmas Birthday Story,* 1980.
EDITED TEXTS: *A Tree for Poverty: Somali Poetry and Prose,* 1954.

Bibliography

Buss, Helen M. *Mother and Daughter Relationships in the Manawaka Works of Margaret Laurence.* Victoria, B.C.: University of Victoria, 1985. A Jungian reading of the four Manawaka novels and *A Bird in the House,* this book raises interesting issues about the mother-daughter relationships that Laurence depicts, although at times the archetypal readings can be somewhat dense. Includes a select bibliography of criticism on Laurence and some later feminist criticism that informs the critic's work.

Coger, Greta M. K., ed. *New Perspectives on Margaret Laurence: Poetic Narrative, Multiculturalism, and Feminism.* Westport, Conn.: Greenwood Press, 1996. Collection of critical essays on a wide variety of aspects of Laurence's life and work.

Gunnars, Kristjana, ed. *Crossing the River: Essays in Honour of Margaret Laurence.* Winnipeg, Manitoba: Turnstone Press, 1988. Twelve previously unpublished essays by Canadian and international writers and critics pay tribute to Laurence's life and work. Includes some interesting new insights.

Irvine, Lorna M. *Critical Spaces: Margaret Laurence and Janet Frame.* Columbia, S.C.: Camden House, 1995. Irvine provides chapters on early review and critiques, maturing opinions, biographical and critical studies, and the role of politics, gender, and literary study. Includes a detailed bibliography.

Kertzer, J. M. "Margaret Laurence and Her Works." In *Canadian Writers and Their Works: Fiction Series,* edited by Robert Lecker, Jack David, and Ellen Quigley. Toronto: ECW Press, 1987. This study is divided into the four parts, "Laurence's Works" being the longest and most thorough section. Despite its scholarliness, this study's clear style and extensive bibliography make it invaluable.

King, James. *The Life of Margaret Laurence.* Reprint. Toronto: Random House Canada, 2002. A good, updated biography of the author. Includes bibliographical references and an index.

Morley, Patricia. *Margaret Laurence.* Boston: Twayne, 1981. An extremely helpful and complete study of Laurence's work, which the author approaches by first arguing that Laurence, despite the fact that her work tends to focus on two very disparate places, Africa and Canada, has shown a consistent development of ideas and themes. She then looks at the African works, followed by the Manawaka cycle. Includes a complete chronology up to 1980, biographical information, an index, and an annotated select bibliography. A useful reference tool.

Nicholson, Colin, ed. *Critical Approaches to the Fiction of Margaret Laurence.* Vancouver: University of British Columbia Press, 1990. An excellent collection of critical essays on Laurence, most written specifically for this book. They cover such topics as Laurence's place in the Canadian tradition in fiction, her work on Africa, close readings of specific works, comparison with Tillie Olsen and Jack Hodgins, and the use of autobiography in her writing. Includes a helpful preface and an index.

Riegel, Christian, ed. *The Writing of Margaret Laurence: Challenging Territory.* Edmonton: University of Alberta Press, 1997. Essays on Laurence's African stories, the novels, and Laurence's Scots Presbyterian heritage and other early influences. Includes a bibliography.

Sorfleet, John R., ed. "The Work of Margaret Laurence." *Journal of Canadian Fiction* 27 (1980). This issue, devoted to Laurence, comprises four stories, a letter and an essay by Laurence, and nine essays by Canadian critics on various aspects of her fiction.

Thomas, Clara. *The Manawaka World of Margaret Laurence.* Toronto: McClelland and Stewart, 1976. A close reading of the works in the Manawaka cycle combined with an argument that although Laurence's characters talk Canadian, Laurence cannot be restricted to the category of Canadian or prairie writer, as her concerns, experiences, and philosophy are far from limited to one nation, or even one continent. Supplemented by a complete bibliographic checklist.

Verduyn, Christl, ed. *Margaret Laurence: An Appreciation.* Peterborough, Ont.: Broadview Press, 1988. The eighteen essays in this invaluable book chronicle the evolution of Laurence's vision in both her fiction and the chief social concerns of her life. The essay topics range from studies of her early African-experience stories to Laurence's own address/essay "My Final Hour."

Woodcock, George. *Introducing Margaret Laurence's "The Stone Angel": A Reader's Guide.* Toronto: ECW Press, 1989. A close reading of the novel *The Stone Angel,* the first of the Manawaka series. Examines the novel's plots, characters, themes, origins, comparisons, and critical reception, as well as Laurence's work as a whole. Includes a useful chronology of Laurence's life, a brief biography, and an index.

_____, ed. *A Place to Stand On: Essays by and About Margaret Laurence.* Edmonton: NeWest Press, 1983. A thorough, rich exploration of Laurence's craft and works, containing essays by Laurence and various critics published over more than twenty years. The book is highlighted by interviews with Laurence. Also includes a useful bibliography.

Harper Lee

Born: Monroeville, Alabama; April 28, 1926

Principal long fiction • *To Kill a Mockingbird*, 1960.

Other literary forms • In addition to the novel that made her famous, Lee wrote for magazines, including *Vogue* and *McCall's*.

Achievements • Although based entirely on one novel, the only one she has ever published, Harper Lee's success has been phenomenal. According to a survey of reading habits conducted in 1991 by the Book-of-the-Month Club and the Library of Congress's Center for the Book, researchers found that Lee's *To Kill a Mockingbird* was "most often cited as making a difference in people's lives, second only to the Bible." In 1961, *To Kill a Mockingbird* won a Pulitzer Prize in fiction, the Brotherhood Award of the National Conference of Christians and Jews, the Alabama Library Association Award, and the British Book Society Award. By 1962 it had become a Literary Guild selection and a Book-of-the-Month-Club choice, it had won the Bestsellers' Magazine Paperback of the Year award, and it was featured in the *Reader's Digest* series of condensed books. In the same year Lee was given an honorary doctorate by Mount Holyoke College. She would receive another honorary doctorate in 1990 from the University of Alabama and would continue to receive honors for *To Kill a Mockingbird* into the twenty-first century.

Initially enjoying seventy-three weeks on the national best-seller lists, *To Kill a Mockingbird* has been translated into at least ten languages. In 1962 it was made into a motion picture starring Gregory Peck, which won several Academy Awards. President Lyndon Johnson appointed Lee to the National Council on the Arts in 1966, on which she served for five years. In 1970 playwright Christopher Sergel published a stage version of Lee's novel, *Harper Lee's To Kill a Mockingbird: A Full-Length Play*, with Dramatic Publications. The play was professionally performed on both sides of the Atlantic Ocean during the 1980's and 1990's.

Biography • The third daughter and youngest child of Amasa Coleman Lee, an attorney and newspaper publisher, and Frances Finch Lee, reportedly a somewhat eccentric pianist, Nelle Harper Lee grew up in Monroeville, Alabama, attended public school there, then went to Huntington College for Women in Montgomery for a year before transferring to the University of Alabama in 1945. Lee edited the college newspaper, the *Rammer Jammer*, and spent a year as an exchange student at Oxford University.

In 1950 she entered law school, no doubt with the intention of following in her father's footsteps. However, after one year she decided to abandon the study of law and go to New York City to pursue a career in writing. Throughout the early 1950's Lee worked by day as a reservation clerk for Eastern Airlines and British Overseas Airways, living in a cramped flat with no hot water, and writing in her free time. During this period she also made many trips to Monroeville to be with her ailing father, who died in 1962. Happily, Amasa Lee did live long enough to see *To Kill a Mockingbird* become a hugely successful book.

In a short article published in *Mc-Call's* in December, 1961, called "Christmas to Me," Lee recounts how she missed her home and family, contrasting New York City with memories of Monroeville during the Christmas season. However, she made some very close friends in her adopted home, and she spent Christmas with one of these families, who surprised her with a monetary gift. On the accompanying card were the words, "You have one year off from your job to write whatever you please. Merry Christmas." She was overwhelmed, but her benefactors believed that their faith in Lee's ability was well founded.

Lee used this time carefully: A methodical writer, she composed a few pages each day and revised them carefully, completing three short fictional sketches by 1957. After being advised that she must do more to transform this work into a novel, she continued to write for two and a half years, until

To Kill a Mockingbird went to press in 1960, dedicated to her father and to her older sister, Alice, a partner in the family law firm.

Writer Truman Capote spent a great part of his childhood in Monroeville, staying each summer with relatives whose house was in close proximity to the Lees'. The character of Charles Baker Harris, nicknamed Dill, in *To Kill a Mockingbird* is an accurate portrait of the young Capote, who remained close to Lee throughout his life. During the early 1960's Lee went with Capote to Kansas to help him research *In Cold Blood* (1966), which chronicles the murders of the Clutter family in Holcomb, Kansas; Capote dedicated the book to Lee and another lifelong friend, Jack Dunphy. Much of what is known about Lee is revealed in Capote's works and in those written about him by others.

Lee was invited to write the screenplay for the film version of *To Kill a Mockingbird*, but she declined. She was, however, very pleased with screenwriter Horton Foote's script, about which she said, "If the integrity of a film adaptation is measured by the degree to which the novelist's intent is preserved, Mr. Foote's screenplay should be studied as a classic." She was so delighted by Gregory Peck's portrayal of Atticus Finch that she honored his performance and resemblance to her father by giving him Amasa Lee's gold pocket watch, which was inscribed, "To Gregory from Harper, 1962."

Although *To Kill a Mockingbird* has sold more than fifteen million copies, Lee never produced another book. As she told her cousin Richard Williams, when he questioned her about this, "When you have a hit like that, you can't go anywhere but down." Although known in her hometown as a friendly and jovial woman, Lee consistently refused all attempts to interview her. In 1995, when HarperCollins released the thirty-fifth-anniversary edition of *To Kill a Mockingbird*, Lee declined to write an introduction, stating, "The book still says what it has to say: it has managed to survive the years without preamble."

Into the twenty-first century, Lee continued stay out of the public eye. She divided her time between a New York apartment and a modest house in Monroeville, which she shared with her sister, Miss Alice.

Analysis • Lee's only novel, *To Kill a Mockingbird*, has gained stature over the years, becoming thought of as more than merely a skillful depiction of small-town southern life during the 1930's with a coming-of-age theme. Claudia Durst Johnson, who has published two books of analysis on *To Kill a Mockingbird*, suggests that the novel is universally compelling because Lee's overall theme of "threatening boundaries" covers a wide spectrum, from law to social standing, from childhood innocence to racism.

The narrator of the book is Scout (Jean Louise) Finch, who is discussing childhood events with her adult brother, Jem, as the story begins. She then slips effortlessly into the role of the six-year-old tomboy who matures over the three years of the book's action. In the first half of the novel, Scout and Jem, along with their childhood companion, Dill, are fascinated by their mysterious neighbor, Boo (Arthur) Radley. Because no one has seen Boo in many years, the youngsters construct a gothic stereotype of him, imagining him as huge and ugly, a monster who dines on raw squirrels, sports a jagged scar, and has rotten yellowing teeth and bulging eyes. They make plans to lure Boo from his "castle" (in reality the dark, shuttered Radley house), but in the course of their attempts to breach the boundaries of his life, they begin to discover the real Boo, an extremely shy man who has attempted to reach out to the children in a number of ways, and who, in the final chapters of the book, saves their lives.

The second half of the book is principally concerned with the trial of Tom Robinson, a young African American unfairly accused of raping a white woman. Racial tensions in the neighborhood explode; Scout and Jem are shocked to find that not only their peers but also adults they have known their whole lives are harshly critical of their father, Atticus, who provides the legal defense for the innocent man.

Throughout both sections of *To Kill a Mockingbird* Lee skillfully shows other divisions among people and how these barriers are threatened. Obviously, it is not a matter of race alone that sets societal patterns in their provincial Alabama town. For example, when Atticus's sister, Alexandria, visits the family, she makes it clear that she is displeased by Scout's tomboyish appearance, since she feels a future "southern belle" should be interested in more ladylike clothing and more feminine behavior. Furthermore, as Jem tells Scout later, there is a strict caste system in Maycomb, with each group threatened by any possible abridgements of the social order. As Jem suggests, there are the "old" families—the gentry, who are usually educated, frequently professional, but, given the era, often cash-poor. On the next level down are the "poor but proud" people, such as the Cunninghams. They are country folk who pay their bills with crops and adamantly refuse all charity. Beneath them is the group commonly called "poor white trash," amply represented by Bob Ewell, "the only man ever fired by the WPA for laziness," and his pitiful daughter Mayella, the supposed victim of the rape. At the lowest rung of the social ladder are African Americans, although many are clearly superior to some of the poor white trash, who have only their skin color as their badge of superiority. They are represented by Tom Robinson, the accused rapist, and Calpurnia, the housekeeper for the motherless Finch family.

In addition to the clearly defined social castes, there are deviants, such as Dolphus Raymond, a white man involved in a long relationship with a black woman. He pretends to be an alcoholic to "give himself an excuse with the community" for his lifestyle. There is Mrs. Henry Lafayette Dubose, a member of the upper class who became a morphine addict, whose one desire is to overcome her habit before her death. Also featured is Miss Maudie, the friendly neighbor who seems to represent, along with Atticus, the best hope for change in the community.

Lee uses many symbols in the book, none more pervasive than the mockingbird of the title. The bird is characterized as an innocent singer who lives only to give pleasure to others. Early in the novel, when Atticus gives Jem and Scout air rifles, he makes it clear that it would be a sin to harm a mockingbird, a theme reiterated by Miss Maudie. Two of the main characters are subtly equated with the birds: Boo Radley and Tom Robinson, both innocents "caged for crimes they never committed." Atticus himself is a symbol of conscience. Unlike his sister, he is a nonconformist, an atypical southerner, a thoughtful, bookish man at odds with his environment. He constantly tells his children that they can understand other people only by walking in their shoes. He is mindful of majority opinion but asserts, "The one thing that doesn't abide by majority rule is a person's conscience."

Sometimes, violent action is necessary to alter boundaries. This is foreshadowed early in the novel when Atticus finds it necessary to shoot a rabid dog. However, later, when he faces the mob from Old Sarum, who are intent on lynching Tom Robinson, he simply sits in front of the jail, ostensibly reading a newspaper. Atticus seems very calm, upset only by the appearance of the children and Jem's refusal to take Dill and Scout home, not by the men who threaten violence. After Scout recognizes Mr. Cunningham and mentions Walter, his son, as her school friend, the group leaves. Braxton Underwood, owner of the *Maycomb Tribune*, leans out of his window above the office holding a double-barreled shotgun, saying, "I had you covered all the time, Atticus," suggesting that there may well be occasions in which force is appropriate.

Tried before a jury of white men, in an echo of the 1931 Scottsboro Nine case, which convicted nine innocent black men of raping two white women, Tom Robinson is found guilty in spite of proof that he could not have committed the crime. However, even here there is a bit of hope for change to come, because the jury does not reach a quick decision, deliberating for three hours in a case involving the strongest taboo in the South, a black man sexually molesting a white woman. Tom, however, does not believe that Atticus's legal appeals will save him, and again violence erupts when he is shot and killed while trying to escape from the prison exercise yard.

Although Lee set her novel in a very isolated locale, which she calls Maycomb, in an era when her notion of crossing racial and social boundaries does not always seem imminently attainable, the world of 1960, when *To Kill a Mockingbird* appeared, was radically different. The Civil Rights movement had begun: The United States Supreme Court had ruled against school segregation in the 1954 *Brown v. Board of Education* decision, and there had been a successful bus boycott in Montgomery, Alabama, in 1955-1956, which brought activist Martin Luther King, Jr., to public attention. Finally, people who believed in the importance of applying law fairly and breaking racial boundaries (as Atticus Finch did) were being heard.

There was some criticism of the melodramatic ending of the novel, in which Bob

Ewell attacks the Finch children, who are in costume returning from a school Halloween pageant. Jem's arm is broken in the scuffle, and Scout is saved from the attacker by Boo Radley, who kills Ewell with his own knife. However, in addition to providing closure for the plot, Lee uses this ending to confirm her view of Atticus and his moral character. At first, when Sheriff Heck Tate comes to the Finch home to learn the details of the evening's happenings, Atticus mistakenly assumes that Jem has killed Bob while defending Scout. Heck tries to reassure Atticus, saying, "Bob Ewell fell on his knife. He killed himself." Atticus believes that the sheriff is suggesting a cover-up for Jem, which he refuses, saying, "I can't live one way in town and another way in my home." Finally he realizes that it was Boo Radley who had stabbed Bob with a kitchen knife, not Jem. Atticus then agrees out of kindness to the reclusive Boo to go along with the sheriff's version of the death. When he tells Scout that Mr. Tate was right, she says, "Well, [telling the truth would] be sort of like shootin' a mockingbird, wouldn't it?"

Most literary critics have written of *To Kill a Mockingbird* in glowing terms. One critic has suggested that Atticus is the symbol of the future, of the "new" South that will arise when it takes into account all human experience, discarding the old romantic notions of an isolated regionalism in favor of a wider Emersonian view of the world.

Edythe M. McGovern

Bibliography

Bloom, Harold, ed. *To Kill a Mockingbird*. Philadelphia: Chelsea House, 1999. Part of the Modern Critical Interpretations series, this volume includes a number of critical essays concerning the novel.

Johnson, Claudia Durst. *To Kill a Mockingbird: Threatening Boundaries*. New York: Twayne, 1994. A thesis regarding Lee's feelings about the South.

_____. "The Secret Courts of Men's Hearts: Code and Law in Harper Lee's *To Kill a Mockingbird*." *Studies in American Fiction* 19, no. 2 (Autumn, 1991): 129-139.

_____. *Understanding "To Kill a Mockingbird": A Casebook to Issues, Sources, and Historical Documents*. Westport, Conn.: Greenwood Press, 1994. Useful for those doing penetrating studies of the novel.

Moates, Marianne M. *A Bridge of Childhood: Truman Capote's Southern Years*. New York: Holt, 1989. Clearly shows Capote as character Dill Harris, reiterating childhood episodes that Lee used in the book.

O'Neill, Terry. *Readings on "To Kill a Mockingbird."* San Diego, Calif.: Greenhaven Press, 2000. A collection of essays useful for students.

Shields, Carol. *Mockingbird: A Portrait of Harper Lee*. New York: Henry Holt, 2006. This biography tells of the events that led to Harper's writing of *To Kill a Mockingbird*, as well as her decision to shun the spotlight that shone on her after its publication.

Ursula K. Le Guin

Born: Berkeley, California; October 21, 1929

Principal long fiction • *Planet of Exile,* 1966; *Rocannon's World,* 1966; *City of Illusions,* 1967; *A Wizard of Earthsea,* 1968; *The Left Hand of Darkness,* 1969; *The Lathe of Heaven,* 1971; *The Tombs of Atuan,* 1971; *The Farthest Shore,* 1972; *The Dispossessed: An Ambiguous Utopia,* 1974; *Very Far Away from Anywhere Else,* 1976; *The Eye of the Heron,* 1978; *Leese Webster,* 1979; *Malafrena,* 1979; *The Beginning Place,* 1980; *Always Coming Home,* 1985; *Tehanu: The Last Book of Earthsea,* 1990; *Searoad: Chronicles of Klatsand,* 1991; *Four Ways to Forgiveness,* 1995 (four linked novellas); *The Telling,* 2000; *The Other Wind,* 2001.

Other literary forms • In Ursula K. Le Guin's body of work are many books written for children and young adults, among them *A Wizard of Earthsea, The Tombs of Atuan,* and *The Farthest Shore* (the first three books of the Earthsea series); *Very Far Away from Anywhere Else, Leese Webster,* and *The Beginning Place.* Her other publications include novellas, such as *The Word for World Is Forest* (1972); several volumes of poetry, *Wild Angels* (1975), *Hard Words, and Other Poems* (1981), *In the Red Zone* (1983), and *Wild Oats and Fireweed: New Poems* (1988); and a number of volumes of short stories, including *The Wind's Twelve Quarters* (1975), *Orsinian Tales* (1976), *The Compass Rose* (1982), *Buffalo Gals and Other Animal Presences* (1987), *A Fisherman of the Inland Sea* (1994), and *Unlocking the Air, and Other Stories* (1996). Le Guin's essays on the nature and meaning of fantasy, her own creative process, science fiction, and gender politics are collected in *From Elfland to Poughkeepsie* (1973), *The Language of the Night: Essays on Fantasy and Science Fiction* (1979; edited by Susan Wood), *Dancing at the Edge of the World: Thoughts on Words, Women, and Places* (1988), and *Napa: The Roots and Springs of the Valley* (1989). Her numerous book reviews have appeared in *The New York Times Book Review, The Washington Post Book World, The New Republic,* and other respected publications. Her collaboration with the photographer Roger Dorband, *Blue Moon over Thurman Street* (1993), documents in words and pictures the human ecology of the city street on which she lived for more than a quarter of a century.

Achievements • The high quality of Le Guin's work was apparent from the beginning of her writing career. Brian Attebery, a fellow writer, has stated that even her first published novels are superior to most works of science fiction written at that time. Public recognition of Le Guin's work began with the *Boston Globe* Horn Book Award for *A Wizard of Earthsea* in 1969. Le Guin soon amassed numerous prestigious awards. They include Nebula and Hugo Awards for *The Left Hand of Darkness* (1969, 1970); the Newbery Silver Medal Award for *The Tombs of Atuan* (1972); a Hugo Award for *The Word for World Is Forest* (1973); a National Book Award for Children's Books for *The Farthest Shore* (1973); a Hugo Award for "The Ones Who Walk Away from Omelas" (1974); a Nebula Award for "The Day Before the Revolution" (1974); Nebula, Jupiter, and Hugo Awards for *The Dispossessed* (1974, 1975); a Jupiter Award for "The Diary of the Rose" (1976); a Gandalf Award for achievement in fantasy (1979); and the Kafka Award in 1986. Le Guin also won a Hugo Award for "Buffalo Gals, Won't You Come Out Tonight?" (1988); a Pilgrim Award for body of work, awarded by the Science

Courtesy, Allen and Unwin

Fiction Research Association (1989); a Pushcart Prize for "Bill Weisler" (1991-1992); a Nebula Award for *Tehanu* (1990); and a Nebula Award for "Solitude" (1995). In addition to receiving these honors, Le Guin was a writer-in-residence at the Clarion West workshop at the University of Washington and a teaching participant in a science-fiction workshop at Portland State University. A number of science-fiction conventions, literary conferences, and universities recognized her literary stature by inviting her to teach and speak.

Biography • Ursula Kroeber Le Guin was born into a close, intellectual family in Berkeley, California, on October 21, 1929. Her father, Alfred, was an anthropologist distinguished for his studies of native California tribes and was curator of the Museum of Anthropology and Ethnology of the University of California. Her mother, Theodora Krackaw Kroeber, was a respected writer with an advanced degree in psychology and a special affinity for Native American subjects and sensibilities. It was Le Guin's father who befriended Ishi, the last survivor of the native Californian Yahi people, and it was her mother who wrote *Ishi in Two Worlds* (1961), an anthropological study of Ishi's life and times, as well as the simpler popular narrative *Ishi, Last of His Tribe* (1964). The interest that Le Guin's fiction shows in communication across great barriers of culture, language, gender, and ideology is a natural branching-off from her parents' lifelong passion for understanding worldviews other than the dominant Euro-American competitive materialism. Her use of songs, stories, folktales, maps, and depictions of material culture to flesh out fictional worlds is also congruent with her parents' professional focus.

The Kroeber family seems to have enjoyed an enviable degree of closeness, reasonable financial security, and an abundance of intellectual stimulation. During the academic year, they lived in a large, airy house in Berkeley. Their summers were spent in their Napa Valley home, Kishamish. To these forty acres flocked writers, scholars, graduate students, relatives, and American Indians.

Living among so many people rich in knowledge and curiosity, and having access to an almost unlimited supply of books, Le Guin began writing and reading quite young. She did not discover science fiction, however, until she was twelve. When she found, while reading Lord Dunsany one day, that people were still creating myths, Le Guin felt liberated, for this discovery validated her own creative efforts.

In 1947, Le Guin entered Radcliffe College in Cambridge, Massachusetts. After she graduated magna cum laude in 1951, she entered Columbia University, where she majored in French and Italian Renaissance literature. After completing her master's degree in 1952, she began work on a doctoral program. En route to France as a

Fulbright fellow, she met Charles Le Guin, a historian from Georgia also on a Fulbright. They were married in Paris on December 22, 1953.

When they returned from France, the Le Guins lived in Georgia. Ursula taught French at Mercer University in Macon, and Charles completed his doctoral degree in French history at Emory University. Afterward, they moved to Idaho, where their first child, Elisabeth, was born in 1957. Caroline, their second daughter, arrived in 1959, the year Charles accepted a position at Portland State University and the family moved to a permanent home in Oregon. A third child, Theodore, would be born in 1964.

Ursula, who had never stopped writing but had yet to find a proper market for her efforts, became reacquainted with science fiction when a friend encouraged her to borrow from his library. Cordwainer Smith's story "Alpha Ralpha Boulevard" proved to be a catalyst, a type of fiction approaching Le Guin's own attempts. Le Guin began thinking, not only about writing, but also about publishing her work in something other than obscure magazines.

Since she had begun to write, she had been trying to get her work published, but except for one story, "An die Musick," and a few poems, her work was returned, some of it characterized as "remote." Her breakthrough came when *Fantastic* published "April in Paris" in September, 1962. The following year, *Fantastic* published her first genuine science-fiction story, "The Masters." After that time, Le Guin's literary output steadily increased, and her recognition as one of America's outstanding writers was assured.

Throughout her career, Le Guin has been reserved about the details of her personal life, maintaining that they are expressed best through her fiction. Although she has been involved in political activities, most of Le Guin's efforts are devoted to writing. As her recognition has increased, she has become a strong advocate for improving the quality of fantasy and science fiction. She seems determined that readers of this genre will not be cheated on their voyages of discovery. She has also become a firmer, more definite advocate for feminism as she has matured as a writer and a woman. Early works (such as *The Left Hand of Darkness*) may have grappled delicately with gender issues through "gender-bending" imagination; later works (such as *Tehanu* and *Four Ways to Forgiveness*) have dealt quite explicitly with the impossibility of real love in the absence of equality, the oppression of unshared housework, and the importance of language itself in creating freedom or bondage.

During her writing career, however, Le Guin's work expanded significantly outside the genre of science fiction. From "pro-choice" parables reprinted in *Ms.* magazine to advice to fellow authors, both from her book of essays *Dancing at the Edge of the World*, Le Guin was prolifically diverse in her output.

Analysis • When Ursula K. Le Guin has Genly Ai state in *The Left Hand of Darkness* that "truth is a matter of the imagination," she is indirectly summarizing the essential focus of her fiction: explorations of the ambiguous nature of truth through imaginative means. Few other contemporary authors have described this process with the force and clarity of Le Guin. Her subject is always humankind and, by extension, the human environment, since humanity cannot survive in a vacuum; her technique is descriptive, and her mode is metaphoric. The worlds Le Guin creates are authentic in a profoundly moral sense as her characters come to experience truth in falsehood, return in separation, unity in variety. Frequently using a journey motif, Le Guin sends her characters in search of shadows, rings, theories, or new worlds—all of which are metaphors for undiscovered elements of the self. Along the way, Le Guin demands that they learn the paradoxes inherent in life, the ambiguous nature of creation, and the interrelatedness of all that seems to be opposed. Once made, these discoveries allow her characters to be integrated into themselves and their worlds.

In the end, her characters stand for no one, no concrete meaning; they simply are. Le Guin offers her readers characters motivated by intellectual curiosity, humanism, and self-determination, a nonviolent, nonexploitative philosophy capable of encompassing the unknown and complex cultures in relation to one another.

Unity is what Le Guin's characters seek: not a simple sense of belonging but a complex sense of wholeness. Much of her outlook is derived from the Daoist philosopher Lao-tzu, who maintained that scientific, ethical, and aesthetic laws, instead of being imposed by any authority, "exist in things and are to be discovered." Thus, Le Guin's characters must learn to recognize the true natures (or true names) of people or objects—none of which yields easily to the protagonist—before apprehending their essence and role in the world. Dao (Tao) is the ultimate unity of the universe, encompassing all and nothing. Built upon paradox, Daoist philosophy proposes that apparently opposing forces actually complete each other. Discovering this in a world enamored of dualist thought, however, requires attaining an attitude of actionless activity, an emptying of the self and at the same time the fullest self-awareness. This compassionate attitude establishes a state of attraction, not compulsion: a state of being, not doing. Indeed, because the cycle of cause and effect is so strong, the Daoist sage never tries to do good at all, for a good action implies an evil action. Discovering the correlation of life/death, good/evil, light/dark, male/female, and self/other requires a relativist judgment. The Native American lore Le Guin absorbed as a child also contributed to her sense of unity. In her writing, she has drawn upon her rich knowledge of myths and the work of Carl Jung as well as her own fertile imagination to create intricate metaphors for psychic realities. In her own words, "Outer Space, and the Inner Lands, are still, and will always be, my country."

Rocannon's World • Le Guin has described *Rocannon's World,* her first published novel, as "definitely purple," an odd mixture of space age and bronze age, the product of an author unsure of her direction and materials. Drawing heavily on Norse mythology, the novel originated from a short story, "Dowry of the Angyar," published in 1964. The story begins when a woman named Semley leaves her husband and child to claim her dowry, a gold and sapphire necklace. During her search, Semley time-travels to another planet, where Rocannon, an ethnologist, struck by her beauty and bearing, gives her the necklace, a museum piece on his planet. Semley returns home, believing that she has been gone only overnight. To her dismay, though, she discovers that she has been gone for sixteen years. Her husband is dead; her daughter a grown stranger.

The remainder of the novel concerns Rocannon's exploration of Semley's planet, known to him as Formalhaut II, with the aid of Semley's grandson Mogien. After his ship is destroyed by rebels from the planet Farady, Rocannon must warn the League of All Nations of their rebellion. To do so, he must locate the rebel ship in order to use their ansible, an instantaneous transmitter, since his has been destroyed.

This episodic tale moves from adventure to adventure, as Rocannon learns that appearance often belies reality, that knowledge is not gained without sacrifice. The price he pays for increased understanding (the gift of mind-speech through which he can hear the voices of his enemy) is costly: Mogien's life. Through his efforts, however, the planet is saved. Rocannon, a man changed forever by his knowlege, never returns to his own planet, and he dies without knowing that the planet he rescues is given his name.

Often her own best critic, Le Guin has cited this novel to illustrate the flaws of mixing science fiction with fantasy, of ignoring the limitations imposed by plausibility, of excessive caution in creating a new myth, and of reliance on stereotyped characters and situations. Although this novel lacks the rich complexity of her later works, it does contain elements Le Guin develops in subsequent novels. A readily apparent trait is that her focus is not on theoretical or applied science but rather on social science: how different individuals, races, and cultures perpetuate diffusion through lack of communication and how her main character surmounts these genuine yet arbitrary barriers. For example, as an ethnologist, Rocannon is interested in learning about all kinds of human behavior; nevertheless, he assumes superiority over his "primitive" guides. Experience, however, leads him to admire the individual qualities of Mogien, Kyo, and the Fiians. During their journey, his admiration of and loyalty to them increase to such an extent that loyalty becomes a prominent theme, one developed more thoroughly in *The Left Hand of Darkness*, with the relationship of Mogien and Rocannon prefiguring that of Genly Ai and Estraven (as well as other pairs of characters).

The most important goal in the novel, though, is to locate the other, often presented as the enemy, unify it with the self, and thus receive personal gain. The mindspeech Rocannon learns to hear expresses his fear. Though once he listens to the voices of his enemies he will never regain the self-sufficient confidence he had before embarking on his journey, he earns a vital awareness of his human limitations. Rocannon's sense of adventure is tempered by responsibility; his gain requires loss. In the end, Rocannon feels that he is a temporary resident on an alien planet. His sense of displacement denotes his lack of completion as a character. The novel ends without any resolution. In her next two novels, Le Guin shows greater control over her materials: less dependence upon others' stories and more considered ideas and direction. Where *Rocannon's World* indicates a major theme of self-exploration, *City of Illusions* develops this theme, bringing it closer to its fullest realization in *The Dispossessed*.

City of Illusions • *City of Illusions* begins dramatically in the blank terror of mental darkness experienced by Ramarren and ends in an even larger exterior darkness when Falk-Ramarren, returning to his home planet, departs for his unknown future. In the intervening time, Le Guin presents vivid scenes of an America largely undeveloped and peopled by disparate tribes, all of whom distrust one another and are united only in their universal fear of the Shing, an alien group that maintains division through that terror. Themes of communication, truth, self-discovery, and self-unification are central to this novel.

Using the quest motif, Le Guin has Falk nurtured by the pacific Forest Dwellers, who instill in him their set of values. When he leaves to discover his former identity, Falk confronts differing values, conflicting truths. Along the way, he receives the same warning from those who befriend him: trust no one; go alone. Although he neglects to heed this advice always, these warnings prepare him in part to withstand the considerable powers of the Shing, whose authority depends on self-doubt. Falk is able to recover his past self and retain his present self when he discovers that "there is in the long run no disharmony, only misunderstanding, no chance of mischance but only the ignorant eye." After he achieves this state of understanding, his two identities merge; he becomes Falk-Ramarren to return to his world with the truth—or rather truths—he apprehends.

Le Guin's Daoist beliefs are given full exposure in this novel, where Falk-Ramarren not only reads the *Tao Te Ching* (late third century B.C.E), called the Old Canon, and looks for The Way, but also demonstrates the strength of passivity and enters a state of actionless activity to find himself. Stoical and silent, he prefigures Shevek of *The Dispossessed*. Le Guin's use of setting is also significant as it is employed to reflect psychological states. Her description of the Shing buildings in Es Toch suggests the illusory quality of this alien race and Falk's ambiguous state of mind. This novel fails, however, to measure up to later works. The Shing, for example, meant to personify evil, are all but unbelievable. Their ambiguity lapses into confusion; their "power" is unsubstantiated. Falk's sudden compassion for them is thus rather surprising. Another mark of this novel's early place in Le Guin's career is her heavy-handedness regarding her source. Not only does she thinly disguise the *Tao Te Ching* but she also employs puns and even paraphrases passages to stress her meaning. In her later novels, she achieves better results through greater restraint and insight.

The Left Hand of Darkness • Le Guin arrived at a denser, more original expression of Daoist thought in *The Left Hand of Darkness*. In this novel, she brings together previously expressed themes in a striking metaphor. Time levels, separate in former books, coexist in this novel, as do polarized political systems, philosophies, and genders. Genly Ai, the man sent to bring the planet of Genthen into the Ekumen (formerly the League of All Worlds), must, like Falk, come to see the relativity of truth. To do so, he must cross barriers of thought, barriers he is at first incapable of recognizing. Even when he does, Ai is reluctant to cross, for he must abandon his masculine-scientific-dualist training to become a relativist. He must believe that "truth is a matter of the imagination."

Ai's difficulty in arriving at this conclusion is complicated by his alien existence on Genthen, where he is not merely an outsider; he is a sexual anomaly, a pervert as far as the local beings are concerned. Being a heterosexual male in an androgynous culture adds immeasurably to Ai's sense of distrust, for he cannot bring himself to trust "a man who is a woman, a woman who is a man." The theme of androgyny enriches this novel, not simply because it develops the complex results of an androgynous culture but also because it demonstrates how gender affects—indeed prejudices—thought and explores the cultural effects of this bias. Initially, Ai can see only one gender, one side at a time. This limited vision leaves him vulnerable to betrayal, both by himself and by others. Through his friendship with Estraven, Ai begins to respect, even require, those qualities he at first denigrates until he and Estraven become one, joined in mindspeech. Ai's varied experiences on Genthen teach him that apparently polarized qualities of light/dark, male/female, rational/irrational, patriot/traitor, life/death are necessary complements. The order of the universe requires both.

The Left Hand of Darkness consolidates Daoist ideas expressed in Le Guin's previous books, places them in a dramatically unique culture, and develops them with a finesse lacking in her earlier novels. Ai discovers what Falk does: a fuller recognition of self through merger with the other. He does so, however, in a much more complete way because Le Guin complicates *The Left Hand of Darkness* with questions of opposing political systems, the nature and consequences of sexism, the issue of personal and political loyalty, and the interrelatedness of different periods of time. While retaining her basic quest structure, Le Guin has Genly Ai construct his "report" by using multiple sources: Estraven's diary, folktales, ancient myths, reports from previous investigatory teams. This adds texture and depth by dramatizing the multiplicity of truth and the unity of time. In a sense, this mixture of sources, added to the seasonlessness of Genthen, where it is always winter, and the relentless journey over the Gobrin Ice, constructs a center of time for the reader, an objective correlative to Ai's state of mind. Within a circular framework, a sense of wholeness is achieved. Ai will set the keystone in the arch, the image that opens *The Left Hand of Darkness*, by adding Genthen to the Ekumen. Later, he cements his personal bond to Estraven by visiting his home, ostensibly to return Estraven's diary but actually to assuage a sense of betrayal for not having Estraven publicly absolved of his "crime" of supporting the Ekumen instead of his king. At the novel's end, however, when Ai meets in Estraven's son the father's limitless curiosity, Ai's journey begins anew.

Robert Scholes stated that one of the great strengths of *The Left Hand of Darkness* is that it "asks us to broaden our perspectives toward something truly ecumenical, beyond racism and sexism, and even speciesism." Clearly, Le Guin opened up new territory for science-fiction writers to explore.

The Dispossessed • In *The Dispossessed*, her next novel in what is called her Hainish cycle, she presses even further, bringing to full realization her heroic figure of the Daoist sage in the protagonist Shevek. Stoic, persistent, curious, and humane, he shares qualities with Falk, Estraven, and Genly Ai. Shevek's character and journey, however, differ from his predecessors' in several important respects. Shevek's sense of alienation is tempered by his mature love for his partner Takver. No matter how alone he is on his journey, Shevek can and does turn to their mutually supportive relationship for solace. Shevek's sense of individual integrity is also more conscious than that of previous characters. Already aware of himself and his value, he is able to expand beyond both. Most important, Shevek has a clearly defined sense of purpose—a need to unbuild walls through communication—and a certainty of return. Early in the novel, Le Guin assures her readers that "he would most likely not have embarked on that years-long enterprise had he not had profound assurance that return was possible . . . that the very nature of the voyage . . . implied return." Buttressed by this conviction, Shevek goes forth, his empty hands signifying his spiritual values, and effects a revolution in both senses of the word: a completed cycle and a dynamic change. When he discovers his theory of temporal simultaneity, Shevek gives it away, for he knows that its value is not in its scarcity but in its general use.

The Dispossessed is not simply a vehicle for Daoist philosophy; it is just as significantly a political novel. Le Guin subtitles the novel *An Ambiguous Utopia*, indicating her focus, and she directs her reader's attention by alternating chapters on Anarres, Shevek's home planet, and Urras, where he resides throughout much of the novel. Scenes from Anarres are recalled through flashback as Shevek, surrounded by an alien political and social system repugnant to much in his nature, reflects upon himself in relation to his culture. Anarres, founded by libertarian followers of Odo, a radical Urrasti thinker, is at once dedicated to individual freedom and to the good of the whole. There is no formal government, only a system of individually initiated syndicates, a Division of Labor to keep track of job needs, and the Production Distribution Committee to oversee production loosely. On Anarres nothing is owned; everything is shared. Because everyone is equal, there is no discrimination, no exploitation, but there are stringent societal responsibilities that all Anarresti share. Because Anarres is virtually a desert, with plant life so scarce that no animals are indigenous, careful conservation, voluntary labor, and a sense of duty to the whole are required of everyone.

By contrast, Urras is wealthy, lush with water, teeming with life. Its capitalistic system, however, encourages exploitation because profit is the motivating force. As a result, Urras has an entrenched class system, with women and workers considered inferior to the intellectual and governing classes, and a power structure intent on maintaining control. Although much of this authority is exerted by custom, some is imposed by force. Shevek, unaccustomed to any type of exploitation, violence, discrimination, or conspicuous waste, needs to experience fully the benefits and detriments of Urras before he can make necessary connections. After he recognizes that the seeds of his freedom germinated in the rich soil of Urras, he can declare his brotherhood with the Urrasti and offer them what he can: a way to the only future he knows, that of Anarres. Speaking from deep within himself, Shevek tells Urrasti rebels "You must come to it alone, and naked, as the child comes into his future, without any past, without any property, wholly dependent on other people for his life. . . . You cannot make the Revolution. You can only be the Revolution."

The Earthsea series • The Earthsea series has been categorized by many as "young adult fiction." Le Guin does write often and well for young audiences, and the fact that the three original books of the series (*A Wizard of Earthsea*, *The Tombs of Atuan*, and *The Farthest Shore*) were quite short, were populated by sorcerers and dragons, and used the vocabulary and syntax of high fantasy, tended to identify them as children's literature, at least on the surface. However, their subtle spiritual, mythic, psychological, and philosophical underpinnings and the elegant simplicity of the writing make the books challenging and satisfying to adult readers as well.

In *A Wizard of Earthsea*, Le Guin introduces Ged, a natural-born wizard whose insensitive family does not realize his innate gift. Ged becomes a sorcerer's apprentice to the mage Ogion but ultimately is forced to leave before completing his studies because he keeps casting spells before learning their complications. His inner conflicts are revealed through his struggle to find and to name what he believes to be a mysterious shadow pursuing him. Le Guin's essay "The Child and the Shadow" (in *The Language of the Night*) discusses her depiction of this archetypal Jungian "dark brother of the conscious mind."

In *The Tombs of Atuan*, Ged meets Tenar (known as Arha), the child-priestess of the dark Nameless Ones. Ged has gone to the Labyrinth of the Nameless Ones to recover a Ring that is necessary to the well-being of Earthsea, but he becomes a prisoner in the Labyrinth. Ged and Tenar help each other out of their different sorts of darkness and bondage, return the Ring to its rightful place, and become firm friends. Tenar finds a refuge with Ged's old master, Ogion. Tenar is as powerful as Ged in her own way. Yet, she too leaves her apprenticeship with Ogion before completing her training, though for a different reason. Ged is forced to leave; Tenar chooses to leave for the fulfillment of married life.

Le Guin's understanding of identity and its relationship to naming is revealed in the theme that runs throughout the Earthsea series: To know the true name of someone gives one power over him. Hence, characters have "use" names as well as real names. Real names are usually only told at the moment of death or to someone who is completely trusted.

Tehanu • In 1990, *Tehanu: The Last Book of Earthsea* was published, formally (or so Le Guin has said) bringing the adventures of Tenar and Ged to an end. *Tehanu* is markedly different from the earlier books in the series, however, in that it is written unequivocally for adults. Perhaps Le Guin wanted to aim it at the audience who had grown up reading her books and was now older and mature—like Tenar and Ged, no longer rash in their actions and fearless with the immortality of youth.

In *Tehanu*, the fourth book of Le Guin's Earthsea series, Tenar has been widowed. She is called to assist in the treatment of a badly burned and sexually abused young girl, whom Tenar adopts and names Therru. A visit to the now-dying mage Ogion elicits the information that there is a powerful and dangerous presence in Therru. The dramatic return of Ged aboard the back of the dragon Kalessin, however, occupies Tenar's mind, as she must nurse him. He has lost the powers of archmagery and is now an ordinary man, vulnerable to violence, grief, depression, aging, and sexual love.

Tehanu is, like much of Le Guin's work, a careful compendium of names, spells, and physical transformations. (As a venture in world-making, *Tehanu* resembles *Always Coming Home,* a work intended primarily for adults. Purporting to write the history of several peoples in the distant future, *Always Coming Home* is accompanied by tape-recordings of poems and stories, and the text is supplemented by illustrations and glossaries of terms.) *Tehanu*, however, deals more directly with the dark themes of child molestation and abuse and death than do the earlier volumes in the series.

Four Ways to Forgiveness • Just as *Tehanu* deepens Earthsea to include the difficult realities of violence, oppression, sex, and aging, *Four Ways to Forgiveness* deepens Le Guin's exploration of the ways that power creates deep gulfs between the powerful and the powerless. As in *The Dispossessed,* Le Guin uses the device of two planets, Werel and Yeowe, connected by kinship and history, to illustrate the separate "worlds" created by privilege and exploitation. *Four Ways to Forgiveness* is a novel in the form of four interconnected novellas. Each of the four sections is, in its own way, a love story and could stand alone as a tale of alienation healed. Taken together, the four tales present the larger story of an entire society mending, a new whole being conceived through the union of opposites, and the whole being born through blood and pain.

The first story, "Betrayals," tells of two aging survivors of Yeowe's long, bitter struggle for emancipation. They each have retreated to live in seclusion and "turn to silence, as their religion recommended them to do" in old age. When the man becomes ill, the woman nurses him. When her house burns down, he takes her in. In helping each other, they learn to see each other. Seeing each other, they learn to love each other. Like *Tehanu*, "Betrayals" explores the issues of what loves and graces are left for old age, after the many inevitable losses of life.

The second section, "Forgiveness Day," is the love story of a brash young Ekumenical diplomat on Werel and a stolid, traditional soldier of the ruling class. Their path to partnership gives the author a chance to examine sexism and racism from the point of view of a woman who has been raised in an egalitarian society and from the point of view of a male military defender of the privileged group. To the woman, the rules of behavior that enforce power and powerlessness seem bizarre; to the man, they seem completely natural. Through sharing a difficult ordeal, the two learn to appreciate each other and build a lasting loving partnership. As they work through the difficulties in their relationship, the author demonstrates for the reader how mental practices of power and privilege make true friendship and love impossible.

The third section, "A Man of the People," follows the career of a Hainish historian as he leaves the comfortable provincial village in which he was born. He studies the history of the diverse cultures of the universe, travels widely, and finally goes to Yeowe as an Ekumenical observer. On Yeowe, he commits himself to the struggle for the long-delayed liberation of women, and in this commitment to a community, he finally experiences the sense of belonging he left behind him when he first left his pueblo. The meditations of the historian on his discipline allow the author to present her ideas on the difference between local cultural knowledge and universal cross-cultural knowledge (both of which she honors), education as revolution, and the interplay between historical observation and activism.

The final piece, "A Woman's Liberation," tells the life story of the Werelian woman who becomes the Hainish historian's wife. This simple first-person telling, reminiscent of the slave narratives collected to support the abolition of slavery in the United States, details the life of an owned woman from childhood in the slave compound to service in the big "House" to the day when she is technically "freed" through the difficulties of staying free and gaining equality. Le Guin uses the final two sections of the book to depict, explicitly and realistically, many of the ugly inhumanities that accompany slavery, such as sexual abuse and other violence. To this author, power and exploitation are not merely theoretical subjects; she seeks to portray the real human suffering that is an essential component of institutionalized privilege.

Karen Carmean
Updated by Donna Glee Williams

Other major works

SHORT FICTION: *The Word for World Is Forest*, 1972; *The Wind's Twelve Quarters*, 1975; *Orsinian Tales*, 1976; *The Water is Wide*, 1976; *Gwilan's Harp*, 1981; *The Compass Rose*, 1982; *The Visionary: The Life Story of Flicker of the Serpentine, with Wonders Hidden*, 1984; *Buffalo Gals and Other Animal Presences*, 1987; *Fish Soup*, 1992; *A Fisherman of the Inland Sea: Science Fiction Stories*, 1994; *Solitude*, 1994 (novella); *Unlocking the Air, and Other Stories*, 1996; *Tales from Earthsea*, 2001; *The Birthday of the World, and Other Stories*, 2002; *Changing Planes*, 2003.

POETRY: *Wild Angels*, 1975; *Hard Words, and Other Poems*, 1981; *In the Red Zone*, 1983; *Wild Oats and Fireweed: New Poems*, 1988; *Blue Moon over Thurman Street*, 1993; *Going Out with Peacocks, and Other Poems*, 1994; *Sixty Odd: New Poems*, 1999; *Incredible Good Fortune: New Poems*, 2006.

NONFICTION: *From Elfland to Poughkeepsie*, 1973; *The Language of the Night: Essays on Fantasy and Science Fiction*, 1979 (Susan Wood, editor); *Dancing at the Edge of the World: Thoughts on Words, Women, and Places*, 1988; *Napa: The Roots and Springs of the Valley*, 1989; *Steering the Craft: Exercises and Discussions on Story Writing for the Lone Navigator or the Mutinous Crew*, 1998; *The Wave in the Mind: Talks and Essays on the Writer, the Reader, and the Imagination*, 2004.

CHILDREN'S LITERATURE: *The Adventure of Cobbler's Rune*, 1982; *The Visionary*, 1984; *A Visit from Dr. Katz*, 1988; *Catwings*, 1988; *Solomon Leviathan's 931st Trip Around the World*, 1988; *Catwings Return*, 1989; *Fire and Stone*, 1989; *A Ride on the Red Mare's Back*, 1992; *More Tales of the Catwings*, 1994; *Wonderful Alexander and the Catwings*, 1994; *Tales of the Catwings*, 1996; *Tom Mouse and Ms. Howe*, 1998; *Tom Mouse*, 1998; *Jane on Her Own: A Catwings Tale*, 1999; *Gifts*, 2004; *Voices*, 2006.

TRANSLATIONS: *Tao Te Ching: A Book About the Way and the Power of the Way*, 1997 (of Laozi); *Selected Poems of Gabriela Mistral*, 2003.

EDITED TEXTS: *Norton Book of Science Fiction: North American Science Fiction, 1960-1990*, 1993; *Selected Stories of H. G. Wells*, 2005.

Bibliography

Cadden, Michael. *Ursula K. Le Guin Beyond Genre: Fiction for Children and Adults*. New York: Routledge, 2005. Broad survey of Le Guin's writings.

Cummins, Elizabeth. *Understanding Ursula K. Le Guin*. Columbia: University of South Carolina Press, 1990. An analysis of Le Guin's work emphasizing the different worlds she has created (Earthsea, the Hannish World, Orsinia, and the West Coast) and how they provide the structure for all of her fiction.

Davis, Laurence, and Peter G. Stillman. *The New Utopian Politics of Ursula K. Le Guin's "The Dispossessed."* Lanham, Md.: Lexington Books, 2005. Examination of political themes in Le Guin's award-winning novel, whose subtitle is *"An Ambiguous Utopia."*

De Bolt, Joe, ed. *Ursula K. Le Guin: Voyager to Inner Lands and to Outer Space*. Port Washington, N.Y.: Kennikat Press, 1979. This volume is a collection of critical essays that discusses Le Guin's work from a variety of perspectives, including anthropology, sociology, science, and Daoist philosophy.

Freedman, Carl. *Critical Theory and Science Fiction*. Hanover, N.H.: Wesleyan University Press, 2000. Le Guin is one of five science-fiction writers whose works are analyzed using contemporary literary theory.

Kaler, Anne K. "'Carving in Water': Journey/Journals and the Images of Women's Writings in Ursula Le Guin's 'Sur.'" *Literature, Interpretation, Theory* 7 (1997): 51-62. Claims that Le Guin's story "Sur" provides a cleverly coded map for women striving to be professional writers; to illustrate the paths that women writers must take into the tundras ruled by male writers, she uses the devices of disorder, dislocation, and reversal in the journey/journal.

Keulen, Margarete. *Radical Imagination: Feminist Conceptions of the Future in Ursula Le Guin, Marge Piercy, and Sally Miller Gearhart*. New York: Peter Lang, 1991. Explores science fiction from a feminist viewpoint in the three authors. Includes bibliographical references and an index.

Le Guin, Ursula. "I Am a Woman Writer; I Am a Western Writer: An Interview with Ursula Le Guin." Interview by William Walsh. *The Kenyon Review*, n.s. 17 (Summer/Fall, 1995): 192-205. Le Guin discusses such topics as the genre of science fiction, her readership, the feminist movement, women writers, and the Nobel Prize.

Reid, Suzanne Elizabeth. *Presenting Ursula K. Le Guin*. New York: Twayne, 1997. This critical biography helps young readers to understand how her childhood, family, and life have helped to shape Le Guin's work.

Rochelle, Warren. *Communities of the Heart: The Rhetoric of Myth in the Fiction of Ursula K. Le Guin*. Liverpool, England: University of Liverpool Press, 2001. Analyzes Le Guin's construction of myth and use of mythological themes in her work.

Wayne, Katherine Ross. *Redefining Moral Education: Life, Le Guin, and Language*. San Francisco: Austin and Winfield, 1996. Focuses on ecological concerns and the depiction of the environment and environmentalism in Le Guin's work.

White, Donna R. *Dancing with Dragons: Ursula K. Le Guin and the Critics*. Columbia, S.C.: Camden House, 1999. Part of the Studies in English and American Literature, Linguistics, and Culture series, this volume examines Le Guin's works and critical reaction to them.

Elmore Leonard

Born: New Orleans, Louisiana; October 11, 1925

Principal long fiction • *The Bounty Hunters,* 1953; *The Law at Randado,* 1954; *Escape from Five Shadows,* 1956; *Last Stand at Saber River,* 1959 (also known as *Lawless River* and *Stand on the Saber*); *Hombre,* 1961; *The Big Bounce,* 1969; *The Moonshine War,* 1969; *Valdez Is Coming,* 1970; *Forty Lashes Less One,* 1972; *Fifty-two Pickup,* 1974; *Mr. Majestyk,* 1974; *Swag,* 1976 (also known as *Ryan's Rules*); *The Hunted,* 1977; *Unknown Man No. 89,* 1977; *The Switch,* 1978; *Gunsights,* 1979; *City Primeval: High Noon in Detroit,* 1980; *Gold Coast,* 1980; *Split Images,* 1981; *Cat Chaser,* 1982; *LaBrava,* 1983; *Stick,* 1983; *Glitz,* 1985; *Elmore Leonard's Double Dutch Treat: Three Novels,* 1986; *Bandits,* 1987; *Touch,* 1987; *Freaky Deaky,* 1988; *Killshot,* 1989; *Get Shorty,* 1990; *Maximum Bob,* 1991; *Rum Punch,* 1992 (also known as *Jackie Brown*); *Pronto,* 1993; *Riding the Rap,* 1995; *Naked Came the Manatee,* 1996 (with 12 other Florida writers); *Out of Sight,* 1996; *Cuba Libre,* 1998; *Be Cool,* 1999; *Pagan Babies,* 2000; *Tishomingo Blues,* 2002; *Mr. Paradise,* 2004; *The Hot Kid,* 2005.

Other literary forms • Elmore Leonard published numerous Western short stories as well as several magazine articles on crime writing and police procedure. More significantly, he developed considerable expertise as a writer of screenplays, both originals and adaptations.

Achievements • Leonard has come to be widely regarded as one of the best crime-fiction writers in the world and is ranked with Dashiell Hammett and Raymond Chandler as a writer who transcends the limitations of category fiction. He is one of those who made hard-boiled crime fiction "respectable," and his storytelling technique has influenced countless others. In 1984, *LaBrava* won the Mystery Writers of America (MWA) Edgar Allan Poe Award as the best novel of the year, and in 1992 the MWA named him a Grand Master, its highest accolade.

Biography • Elmore John Leonard, Jr., was born in New Orleans, Louisiana, but grew up in Detroit, Michigan, a city that forms the background for many of his crime novels. He attended Blessed Sacrament Elementary School and the University of Detroit High School and was drafted into the U.S. Navy in 1943, serving in the Admiralty Islands of New Guinea with the Seabees. After the war, he attended the University of Detroit on the G.I. Bill, majoring in English and philosophy, and, following his graduation in 1950, went to work as a copywriter for a Detroit advertising agency. His growing family made it difficult for him to pursue his ambition to become a freelance writer, but he began writing Western short stories between 5:00 and 7:00 A.M. each day before going to work, and he published his first in 1951: "Trail of the Apache," in *Argosy* magazine. During the ensuing decade, he sold twenty-seven more such stories to pulp magazines and published four Western novels. Though he quit the advertising agency in 1959 to become a full-time writer, for several years he supplemented his fiction income by writing scripts for Encyclopædia Britannica educational films.

Hombre, his last Western novel, was published in 1961, and four years later Twentieth Century-Fox purchased the film rights for ten thousand dollars (it was made into a film starring Paul Newman in 1967). He also sold Columbia the film rights to "3:10 to Yuma," an early story, and *The Tall T* (1957), a novelette, during this period. At the same time, the market for Western fiction was drying up, perhaps because the genre had been overly exploited by television. Leonard, in characteristically pragmatic fashion, switched to writing crime fiction. This was the turning point in his career, for he had never felt entirely at ease with Westerns, and he made the transition effortlessly. His first non-Western novels, *The Big Bounce* and *The Moonshine War*, were published in 1969; Warner Bros. bought the film rights to the former, and Leonard wrote a screenplay (his first) of the latter and sold it. A few years later, in 1972, *Joe Kidd*, a film of his first original screenplay, was released. Thus began Leonard's long relationship with the film industry.

©Linda Solomon

In 1974, after twenty years of heavy drinking, he joined Alcoholics Anonymous; in 1977 he and his wife divorced, and he remarried in 1979. He married his third wife during the early 1990's; they would make their home in Bloomfield Hills, Michigan.

Since the 1980's, Leonard's novels have received widespread critical praise, and he has been described as "the best American writer of crime fiction alive." When *LaBrava* won the Mystery Writers of America Edgar Allan Poe Award in 1984, his reputation as a major crime writer was secured, though he says he writes "novels, not mysteries." He has also been a popular success. In 1985, *Glitz* made *The New York Times* best-seller list, and Warner Books two years later published a first printing of 250,000 copies of *Bandits* in a one-million-dollar deal. A year later, he received three million dollars for *Freaky Deaky*. Film rights purchases continued to be a regular occurrence with Leonard novels, as 1995's *Get Shorty* was a success, and the 1998 film of *Out of Sight* was hailed as one of the year's best.

Analysis • Elmore Leonard's early short stories and novels were conventional in terms of plot and characterization; however, writing Westerns was good training. Knowing nothing about the West, he learned to depend on research that he could embellish with his vivid imagination. This is essentially the method he has employed throughout his writing career. Furthermore, when he switched to crime fiction, he brought some of his hair-trigger, saloon-wrecking cowboy villains into urban settings with startling effects. Examples of these "redneck monsters" are Raymond Gidre in *Unknown Man No. 89*, Clement Mansell in *City Primeval*, Roland Crowe in *Gold Coast*, and Richard Nobles in *LaBrava*. Another type of displaced Western character is Armand Degas in *Killshot*, a half-breed American Indian turned Mafia hit man.

Placing cowboys and American Indians in modern cities such as Miami and Detroit is only one of the many types of contrast Leonard employs to produce effects. In his crime novels the most violent incidents occur in the most peaceful settings, such as family restaurants, supermarkets, and real estate offices, and the worst villainy is often directed against people whose lives had previously been conventional and uneventful. In *Killshot*, a working-class couple suddenly find themselves having their front windows blown out with shotgun blasts; the story ends with a double murder in the cozy breakfast nook of their model kitchen.

In 1959, there were thirty prime-time Western series on television. The public was bound to become surfeited with saloon brawls and shoot-outs on Main Street. It was not until this six-gun overkill forced Leonard to turn to crime fiction that he began to develop the distinctive approach to storytelling that brought him fame and fortune. That approach was influenced by his own involvement in filmmaking, which has one cardinal rule for writers: "Don't tell us: *Show* us."

Hollywood has long exerted a push-pull effect on fiction writers. The cinematic manner of telling stories through action and dialogue has had an incalculable influence on their conscious and unconscious minds, and the big money to be made from sales of motion-picture rights has provided an often irresistible temptation to structure novels so that adaptation from print to film would present no problems. The traits that distinguish Leonard's crime novels are those found in all good films: strong characterization, believable dialogue, and interesting visual effects.

The publication of his crime novel *Fifty-two Pickup* in 1974 was the turning point in his career. He says, "I started to realize that the way to describe anywhere, *anywhere*, was to do it from someone's point of view . . . and *leave me out of it.*" Perhaps not entirely coincidentally, 1974 was also the year he separated from his first wife and began attending Alcoholics Anonymous meetings. In describing his recovery from alcoholism, he also said: "The key is getting out of yourself." Prior to *Fifty-two Pickup*, Leonard had written his fiction in a conventional manner—that is, mostly in the "voice" of an anonymous narrator who sets the scenes, describes his characters' appearance and behavior, and quotes their verbal interchanges. This objective technique was perfected by Ernest Hemingway, whose Spanish Civil War novel *For Whom the Bell Tolls* (1940) had a permanent effect on Leonard's approach to fiction writing. However, Leonard went beyond Hemingway, trying as much as possible to vanish as a narrator and to let his stories be told by the characters themselves. He describes what characters see and hear as well as what they think and feel in language appropriate to each character, so that most of his narration and description reads like dialogue without the quotes.

It would be inaccurate to call this technique "stream of consciousness" or "interior monologue": It is a modification that Leonard describes as his unique "sound." There are no long passages in italics, no stream-of-consciousness ramblings. There are no "pebbles in the pond" or other old-fashioned flashback conventions. Because Leonard generally has the reader inside a character's mind, it is easy to move back and forth in time, as he frequently does. The character simply remembers an earlier event, and the reader is instantly transported back to the past.

Changing from past to present is simply another of Leonard's ways of deliberately keeping the reader off balance. The one consistent feature of a Leonard novel is that nothing ever stays the same. He imitates modern American films, which create the effect of being in continuous motion with changing camera angles, jump cuts, intercuts, tracking shots, aerial shots, flashbacks, and all the other tricks of the trade. His practice of constantly shifting viewpoints is analogous to modern filmmaking, in which scenes are shot simultaneously by several cameras, and strips of film are spliced together to provide visual variety as well as to highlight whatever the director considers most important. Typically, Leonard changes points of view from chapter to chapter; however, he does it within chapters as well, and with an effortlessness that makes lesser writers envious.

The average category fiction writer will describe his or her characters only once, when they first appear, and then rely largely on peculiarities of dialogue to differentiate them from one another for the rest of the book. A standard practice of commercial fiction writers is to give each character some "shtick"—a cane, a monocle, a pipe, a stammer, a foreign accent—to help the reader remember him or her; still, in many category novels the characters become a hopeless jumble in the reader's mind. The reader's interest in a novel depends on the credibility of its characters. Shootings, bombings, and other forms of violence are not effective unless the reader can believe they are happening to real people. In describing each character's appearance and actions through the eyes of another character, Leonard not only eliminates the need for the "intrusive author" but also characterizes both individuals at once. From beginning to end, he never stops characterizing. He also achieves a strong sense that his characters are actually interrelating, because each is seen in turn through the eyes of someone else. That is why Leonard's writing is so much more effective than most category fiction and why he has transcended his genre.

Fifty-two Pickup • In *Fifty-two Pickup*, Leonard was only partially successful in telling his story through the viewpoints of his characters. The "good guys," a middle-class husband and wife who are being victimized by blackmailers, come alive; however, the "bad guys" are two-dimensional characters exuding the all-too-familiar blend of sadism, cynical humor, and innuendo. Leonard knew that he needed to humanize his villains in order to give his novels balance. In his next novel, *Swag*, he tells the story from the points of view of the "bad guys," two likable young men who take up armed robbery for fun and profit.

Swag • *Swag* may be the best novel Leonard has written, although it is far from being his best known. Held in the robbers' viewpoints like a fly in amber, the reader is helplessly but deliciously dragged into one holdup after another and lives out his own secret fantasies about walking into a store with a big Colt .45 automatic and walking out with a bag of cash. The reader experiences all the dangers of the profession and ponders all the intangibles: "What if the clerk dives for a gun?" "What if a customer starts screaming?" "What if an alarm goes off?" "What if a cop drives up?" Here, to quote horror writer Stephen King, is "the kind of book that if you get up to see if there are any chocolate chip cookies left, you take it with you so you won't miss anything."

This kind of story has drawbacks. For one thing, the reader is willing to identify with the "bad guys" only as long as they refrain from killing innocent people. Also, stories such as this one usually end with the protagonists being shot or sent to prison—as in the films *Bonnie and Clyde* (1967) and *Butch Cassidy and the Sundance Kid* (1969). In *Swag*, the antiheroes almost inevitably become overconfident and walk into disaster. Finally, the viewpoint characters in *Swag* seem less like real criminals than like middle-class young men who are playing at being criminals. Such a "Robin

Hood" plot might serve for a single novel but could not be extended to a career technique. Leonard realized that he needed to learn more about the criminal mentality.

In 1978, Leonard spent two and a half months haunting police headquarters in downtown Detroit, soaking up the atmosphere and listening to the way detectives, criminals, lawyers, and witnesses really talked. He also established contacts with working detectives, contacts that have continued to prove useful to him. His later novels show a much better balance between protagonists and antagonists.

Freaky Deaky • Leonard's highly successful *Freaky Deaky* is an example of his mature technique. A detective who specializes in bomb disposal is pitted against a beautiful but treacherous former convict plotting to extort a fortune from a pair of multimillionaire brothers, whom she suspects of informing on her back during the 1960's when they were antiwar activists together. The chapters alternate between the mind of the detective and that of the female extortionist, until all the principals are brought together at the end. The reader sees the world through the bomber's jaundiced eyes and sympathizes with her; however, the reader also sees the world through the detective's eyes and sympathizes with him a bit more. Leonard has become expert at manipulating the sympathies of his reader, which enables him to create more realistic characters. Like people in the real world, the characters in his best novels are not all good or all bad, but mixtures of both.

Killshot • Leonard follows the same blueprint in *Killshot*. The main villain, a half-breed Native American, is a cold-blooded professional killer; however, the reader achieves a strong identification with and even affection for this lonely, unhappy individual, because the reader spends so much time in the killer's mind. Leonard seems to understand the criminal mentality so well that many people have labored under the erroneous impression that he must have an unsavory past. Whereas he once had trouble making his villains seem credible, his problem later in his career has been making his law-abiding characters seem equally credible. In his next novel, *Get Shorty*, he did away with "good guys" altogether.

Get Shorty • In *Get Shorty*, for the first time in his career, Leonard sets a novel in Hollywood, California. Here he reaps a rich harvest from his many years of experience as an author of original scripts, adaptations of other authors' novels, and adaptations of his own novels, and as an author of works that have been adapted by others. Among all of his novels, *Get Shorty* most clearly reveals his intention of making his fiction read like motion pictures. He even incorporates some pages of a screenplay that his sleazy characters are trying to peddle. Some of his Hollywood characters are so hopelessly immersed in the fantasy world of filmmaking that they see everyone as an actor and every event as a sequence of medium shots, closeups, and other types of camera shots with varied lighting effects—even when that other character might be coming to shoot them or throw them off a cliff. Leonard is suggesting that Americans are so brainwashed by films and television images that it is becoming impossible to distinguish between fantasy and reality.

Maximum Bob • With *Maximum Bob*, his next novel, Leonard returns to familiar turf, southern Florida. The title character is a criminal court judge; though corrupt to the core professionally and personally, he metes out sentences that offenders deserve, and he easily wins reelection. In contrast to him, Leonard presents capable, dedicated, and honest policemen, assistant district attorneys, and probation officers; however, they fight a losing battle, buffeted not only by corrupt superiors like Judge Bob Isom Gibbs but also by offenders who cannot be rehabilitated. The forces of good frequently confront this dilemma in Leonard novels, sometimes in a contrast between social haves and have-nots. Also as in other Leonard books, *Maximum Bob* is peopled by assorted grotesques, notable among them the judge's wife, a onetime underwater dancing mermaid who has become a spiritualist with two personalities, one of which is a twelve-year-old 1850's slave with a voice like Butterfly McQueen of the 1939 film *Gone with the Wind*. The major character, though, is completely normal: Kathy Diaz Baker, a young probation officer with carefully honed people skills and analytical crime-solving ability who narrates most of the novel and is its moral conscience. Baker is not the only narrator, however; other characters also so serve, with the effect that a host of figures are developed more fully than they otherwise would have been. Also, in a curious turn, Leonard relates a portion of an episode from an alligator's point of view.

Pronto • Leonard again criticizes aspects of law enforcement in *Pronto*, another novel with a Florida setting, though here he focuses primarily upon organized crime. The main theme of the book is interdependence. Be it Raylan Givens of the U.S. Marshals Service, Buck Torres of the Miami Beach Police Department, or Federal Bureau of Investigation agent McCormick (whose lack of a first name depersonalizes him), success depends upon the cooperation of others, and all grit their teeth when they must enlist the aid of people they consider undesirables. Givens is the focus of a secondary theme, that of fundamental decency. Unimpressed by wealth earned through criminality and corruption, he has a refreshing naïveté tempered only by his determination to redeem a career-damaging error. He is the untainted person of the novel, and that he ultimately prevails—and gets the woman, too—presents an unmistakable thematic message. *Pronto* is of special interest in the Leonard canon for two reasons: It introduces Raylan Givens, who returns in the next novel, *Riding the Rap*, and it marks a singular Leonard reversion to a Western trademark. From start to finish, *Pronto* is a chase. The effect of this elementary plot technique is an immediate creation of tension, with momentum and suspense increasing without letup as the narrative moves to climactic shots two pages before the conclusion.

Cuba Libre • Leonard also returns to his fictional roots in *Cuba Libre*, a Western complete with a shoot-out and prison escape, albeit set in Cuba in 1898 at the time of the Spanish-American War. The protagonist is an Arizona Territory cowboy and erstwhile bank robber who heads to Cuba in order to sell horses and, not incidentally, to smuggle guns to Cuban rebels. This also is a novel with suspense, fast-paced action, and a collection of grotesque characters who somehow seem credible, no small tribute to Leonard's skills at characterization.

Out of Sight • In Leonard's 1996 novel, *Out of Sight*, the trademark gritty realism of Leonard's oeuvre is blended with a romance between criminal Jack Foley and U.S. Marshal Karen Sisco. The novel's opening is widely acknowledged to rank among Leonard's best, as he takes the reader through a daring prison break, modeled on a real escape from that same prison in 1995. As is his practice, the point of view shifts among three different characters in the first three chapters, as the same scene is viewed from three different angles.

The opening sentence of the novel, "Foley had never seen a prison where you could walk right up to the fence without getting shot," immediately locates the reader both psychologically—within Foley's consciousness, attitudes, and experience—and physically—just inside the fence of a medium-security Florida prison. The second chapter begins as Sisco pulls up to the parking area just outside that same fence, looking at the same point from the other side, both literally—outside the prison versus inside—and figuratively—cop versus criminal. As she sits in her car, the headlights from a car pulling into the row behind her hit her rearview mirror. The opening of chapter 3, "Buddy saw the mirror flash and blond hair in his headlights, a woman in the blue Chevy Caprice parked right in front of him," takes the reader inside that second car as it introduces a third major character, Orren "Buddy" Bragg, a former partner of Foley who has arrived to help him escape. The escape itself is thus rendered in great visual depth, as the reader sees Buddy see Sisco see Foley as he emerges from a tunnel by the fence. Such detailed multiple visualizations are especially common in Leonard's later novels, which can resemble screenplays in their rapid cuts from character to character and their close specification of the precise angles and fields of vision from which characters view scenes.

After the successful prison break, the plot takes all these characters to Detroit, where the suspense intensifies as the relatively gentle and sympathetic Foley and Buddy are thrown into an uneasy alliance with a set of violent sociopaths seeking to rob a wealthy financier. Critic James Devlin notes the symbolism of the settings in the novel, as the sunny Florida setting of the opening scenes gives way to the dark and cold of the Detroit scenes. Brutal scenes of rape and murder alternate uneasily with scenes sketching the developing love story between the criminal and the cop pursuing him. For some critics, the conventional story of love at first sight, complete with a film-friendly "meet cute" when Foley and Sisco are locked in the trunk of a getaway car, is a rare misstep by Leonard that ultimately breaks the book into two incompatible halves, one a screwball romantic comedy and the other an usually violent portrait of depravity and urban violence. Although not a hit at the box office, the motion picture adaptation starring George Clooney and Jennifer Lopez earned high praise from film critics such as Roger Ebert for its success in translating "the texture of the pacing and dialogue" and the large cast of colorful characters to the screen.

Bill Delaney
Updated by Gerald H. Strauss and William Nelles

Other major works
SHORT FICTION: *The Tonto Woman, and Other Western Stories*, 1998; *When the Women Come Out to Dance*, 2002; *The Complete Western Stories of Elmore Leonard*, 2004.
SCREENPLAYS: *The Moonshine War*, 1970; *Joe Kidd*, 1972; *Mr. Majestyk*, 1974; *Stick*, 1985 (with Joseph C. Stinson); *Fifty-two Pickup*, 1986 (with John Steppling); *The Rosary Murders*, 1987 (with Fred Walton).
TELEPLAYS: *High Noon Part 2: The Return of Will Kane*, 1980; *Desperado*, 1987.
CHILDREN'S LITERATURE: *A Coyote's in the House*, 2004.

Bibliography
Challen, Paul. *Get Dutch! A Biography of Elmore Leonard*. Toronto: ECW Press, 2000. A biography with some literary evaluation as well.

Devlin, James E. *Elmore Leonard*. New York: Twayne, 1999. A literary biography covering Leonard's Westerns, his use of Florida as a locale for his novels, his worldview, his use of genre formulas and pop-culture references, and his film work.

Geherin, David. *Elmore Leonard*. New York: Continuum, 1989. The first book-length study of Leonard, this volume provides a brief biography and then a critical evaluation of Leonard's works, beginning with his early Western short stories and concluding with more detailed discussions of his novels of the 1980's. It also includes a chronology, notes, a selected bibliography, and an index.

Gorman, Edward. "Elmore Leonard." In *Mystery and Suspense Writers: The Literature of Crime, Detection, and Suspense*, edited by Robin W. Winks and Maureen Corrigan. New York: Charles Scribner's Sons, 1998. An appreciation of Leonard as a mystery writer.

Grella, George. "Film in Fiction: The Real and the Reel in Elmore Leonard." In *The Detective in American Fiction, Film, and Television*, edited by Jerome H. Delamater and Ruth Prigozy. Westport, Conn.: Greenwood Press, 1998. Brief study of the adaptation of Leonard's stories to the screen.

Leonard, Elmore. "Elmore Leonard." Interview by Dennis Wholey. In *The Courage to Change: Personal Conversations About Alcohol with Dennis Wholey*, edited by Wholey. New York: Warner Books, 1986. This interview provides the best available information about Elmore Leonard as a human being. He describes his growing problem with alcohol over two decades and the psychological insights that enabled him to stop drinking. Leonard's hard-won victory over alcoholism has had an important influence on his writing technique and choice of subjects.

_____. "To Write Realistically: An Interview with Elmore Leonard." Interview by Robert E. Skinner. *Xavier Review* 7 (1987): 37-46. Less diffuse than most that have appeared in newspapers and magazines, this article deals primarily with Leonard's realism. The sources of this often praised quality are his extensive preliminary research into potential milieus (including visits and interviews by him or surrogates) and his keen ear for nuances of speech patterns.

Millner, C. "Elmore Leonard: The Best Ear in the Business." *Writer's Digest*, June, 1997, 30-32. Many commentators call attention to Leonard's skill at creating realistic dialogue. Though this article does not offer much in the way of new insights, it is of interest because it is addressed primarily to writers, both professionals and those aspiring to become such.

Most, Glenn. "Elmore Leonard: Splitting Images." *Western Humanities Review* 41 (Spring, 1987): 78-86. This penetrating scholarly analysis of *Split Images* suggests some of the hidden psychological and sociological implications of Leonard's apparently simple writing. It also exemplifies the serious critical attention that Leonard's work has begun to receive.

Pelecanos, George. "The Best of Elmore Leonard." *Sight and Sound* 15, no. 4 (April, 2005): 28-30. Appreciation of Leonard's works at the time of his publication of *The Hot Kid*.

Wilkinson, A. "Elmore's Legs: Where Does Elmore Leonard Get His Atmosphere?" *The New Yorker*, September 30, 1996, 43-47. Writers for many years focused upon a few notable aspects of Leonard's novels; his creation of atmosphere is one of them. This piece is one of many, but it offers some different perspectives and insights into a career that spans decades and has produced more than two dozen novels.

Sinclair Lewis

Born: Sauk Centre, Minnesota; February 7, 1885
Died: Rome, Italy; January 10, 1951

Principal long fiction • *Our Mr. Wrenn: The Romantic Adventures of a Gentle Man*, 1914; *The Trail of the Hawk: A Comedy of the Seriousness of Life*, 1915; *The Innocents: A Story for Lovers*, 1917; *The Job: An American Novel*, 1917; *Free Air*, 1919; *Main Street: The Story of Carol Kennicott*, 1920; *Babbitt*, 1922; *Arrowsmith*, 1925; *Mantrap*, 1926; *Elmer Gantry*, 1927; *The Man Who Knew Coolidge: Being the Soul of Lowell Schmaltz, Constructive and Nordic Citizen*, 1928; *Dodsworth*, 1929; *Ann Vickers*, 1933; *Work of Art*, 1934; *It Can't Happen Here*, 1935; *The Prodigal Parents*, 1938; *Bethel Merriday*, 1940; *Gideon Planish*, 1943; *Cass Timberlane: A Novel of Husbands and Wives*, 1945; *Kingsblood Royal*, 1947; *The God-Seeker*, 1949; *World So Wide*, 1951.

Other literary forms • Sinclair Lewis started writing regularly during his freshman year at Yale University. His stories and poems imitating the manner of Alfred, Lord Tennyson and Algernon Charles Swinburne appeared in the *Yale Literary Magazine*. His short stories began to appear in 1915 in *The Saturday Evening Post*. In 1934, *Jayhawker: A Play in Three Acts* was produced, and in 1935, Harcourt, Brace published the *Selected Short Stories of Sinclair Lewis*. During his lifetime, there were numerous stage and screen adaptations of many of his novels. The year after Lewis's death, Harcourt, Brace published *From Main Street to Stockholm: Letters of Sinclair Lewis, 1919-1930*, containing the novelist's correspondence with that publisher. In 1953, his miscellaneous writings appeared under the title *The Man from Main Street: Selected Essays and Other Writings, 1904-1950*.

Achievements • In 1930, Lewis received the Nobel Prize in Literature, the first United States citizen so honored. He acknowledged in his acceptance address that the Swedish Academy honored American literature with this prize. By awarding it to the novelist who not only added the term "Babbitt" to the American language but also enriched the European vocabulary with his "Main Street," Europe acknowledged America's coming-of-age. There may have been a touch of condescension in the Academy's choice; the image of America that Lewis projected seemed to reinforce the European perception of the United States as a dollar-hunting, materialistic country, alien to cultural refinement.

Lewis's road to fame was stormy. He wrote five novels before he achieved his first big success with *Main Street* in 1920. Critics were divided: *The Dial* neglected his books, and academic critics Fred L. Pattee and Irving Babbitt rejected him, but, at the peak of Lewis's career, V. F. Parrington, T. K. Whipple, Constance Rourke, Walter Lippman, and Lewis Mumford acknowledged his strengths as a writer despite some reservations; H. L. Mencken enthusiastically supported him. English writers paid him tribute; among them were E. M. Forster, Rebecca West, Hugh Walpole, and John Galsworthy. They were joined by such fellow U.S. writers as F. Scott Fitzgerald and Vachel Lindsay. Lewis himself was generous with others; he helped young writers such as Thomas Wolfe and was quick to praise novelists of his own generation. In his

Nobel Prize acceptance speech, which came to be called "The American Fear of Literature," he repudiated the genteel tradition, in which he included William Dean Howells, and praised Theodore Dreiser, Sherwood Anderson, and a score of younger writers. Like all his writings, this speech was regarded as controversial.

Each novel renewed the controversy; some considered him unworthy of the attention and overrated; others denounced his aggressive criticism of United States life, but after *Arrowsmith* he received favorable recognition even in *The Atlantic Monthly, The Nation, The New Republic, The New York Times,* the New York *Herald Tribune,* and *The Literary Review.* Indeed, his popularity in the United States reached unprecedented levels. In one decade, with the help of Harcourt, Brace he became the most widely known novelist in the country. An authentic interpreter of American life, he created self-awareness among people in the United States, yet this role was short-lived. In 1927, Walter Lippman called him a national figure, but by 1942, as Alfred Kazin pointed out, his importance was over. The short period of fame, preceded by long years of preparation, was followed by a painful period of decline marked by ten weak novels.

Biography • Harry Sinclair Lewis was born in Sauk Centre, Minnesota, on February 7, 1885. His father, Edwin J. Lewis, and his mother, Emma F. Kermorr, were both schoolteachers, but Edwin Lewis took a two-year medical course in Chicago and practiced as a country doctor, first in Wisconsin and later in Sauk Centre, a small Minnesota town with a population of 2,500. Harry Sinclair, nicknamed "Red" because of the color of his hair, was the third of three sons. His mother died of tuberculosis when he was three. Edwin Lewis remarried shortly after her death. The future novelist was an awkward, rather ugly, lonely child with little aptitude for sports or any type of physical exercise. He soon became an ardent reader; at an early age, he also started a diary and tried his hand at creative writing.

After a short preparation in the Oberlin Academy, Lewis became a freshman at Yale at the age of seventeen. There, too, he was a loner, even after he became a regular contributor of poems and short stories to the *Yale Literary Magazine.* In the summers of 1904 and 1906, he participated in cattle-boat trips to London, and in his senior year he left Yale. For a month, he worked as a janitor in Upton Sinclair's New Jersey commune, Helicon Hall. Because he had no financial support from his father at that time, he tried to make money, first in New York with his writing and then in Panama with work on the canal construction. Unsuccessful in both attempts, he returned to Yale and graduated in 1908.

Between 1908 and 1915, Lewis traveled from New York to California in search of employment; he also sold story plots to other writers. From 1910 to 1915, he worked in New York for commercial publishers. In 1914, his first novel, *Our Mr. Wrenn,* was published, and on April 15, he married Grace Livingston Hegger. The couple settled in Long Island. In 1915, *The Saturday Evening Post* accepted one of Lewis's short stories for publication, the first of many to be published there. With some money at his disposal, he traveled around the country with Grace, publishing short stories and writing more novels.

The five novels following *Our Mr. Wrenn,* all published under pseudonyms, were unsuccessful, but *Main Street,* Lewis's first novel to be published by Harcourt, Brace suddenly made him famous. Never again did Lewis worry about money. With *Babbitt* his fame was firmly established. He went on a Caribbean tour in preparation for *Arrowsmith,* and from 1923 to 1925 he traveled with Grace in Europe. It is interesting

Library of Congress

to note that Lewis loved publicity. In 1925, while working on *Elmer Gantry*, he defied God from a pulpit in Kansas City, giving God fifteen minutes to strike him down. His refusal of the Pulitzer Prize in 1926—an obvious act of anger over a previous disappointment—became an internationally broadcast event.

In 1927, Lewis separated from Grace and spent much of the next year in Europe. After Grace had obtained a Reno divorce, Lewis married Dorothy Thompson, whom he had met in Berlin, on May 14, 1928. At that time, Thompson was the best-known U.S. newspaperwoman in Europe; she also became the first U.S. journalist to be expelled from Nazi Germany. *It Can't Happen Here*, Lewis's novel about the possibility of fascism in America, was written under Thompson's influence. In 1929, Lewis published *Dodsworth*, a product of his long stay in Europe, which dealt with the American-in-Europe theme. In 1930, Lewis received the Nobel Prize and reached the peak of his fame.

After this period of renown, Lewis's life and career declined. A longtime drinking problem grew worse, and his health rapidly deteriorated. One sign of his restlessness was his break with Harcourt, Brace; he switched to Doubleday. The world around him was changing rapidly; he became increasingly confused, unhappy, and lonely. In 1937, he separated from his second wife, and they were divorced in 1942. Lewis attempted to find a new career in acting and simultaneously had an affair with a young actor. His obsession with the theater is documented in *Bethel Merriday*. With *Kingsblood Royal*, a novel about racism, he once more tried his hand at an urgent contemporary issue, but his energy was decreasing. After World War II, he spent most of his time in Europe. He died in Rome, Italy, on January 10, 1951. His last novel, *World So Wide*, dedicated to "memories in Italy," was published posthumously in 1951.

Analysis • Early reviews praised or condemned Sinclair Lewis for a blend of realism and optimism; indeed, a curious mixture of almost naturalistic realism and a kind of romance characterized Lewis's fiction throughout his career. He failed to solve the dichotomy in his novels, nor did he ever solve it for himself. If his characters sometimes behave as romantic rebels, so did Lewis, rebelling against a philistine lifestyle in which he was deeply rooted and to which he remained attached all his life. The five novels that made him famous, *Main Street, Babbitt, Arrowsmith, Elmer Gantry*, and *Dodsworth*, can be read as a series of variations on the same theme. Lewis exposed a United States dominated by business and petty bourgeois mentality. His characters, still full of nostalgia for the excitement of the frontier, persuade themselves that what they have at the present represents the zenith, the summit of human potential. Descendants of pious pioneer Puritans, Lewis's wealthy Americans of the 1920's are in desperate need of a civilization they can call their own. This transitory stage of the U.S. experience becomes the theme of Lewis's writings.

As Van Wyck Brooks described it, America's coming-of-age in the decade before World War I paved the way for a cultural and moral revolution, heralded by works such as Edgar Lee Masters's *Spoon River Anthology* (1915), Sherwood Anderson's *Winesburg, Ohio* (1919), and Lewis's *Main Street* and *Babbitt*, with its bitter attacks on "boobus Americanus." *Civilization in the U.S.* (1921), edited by Harold Stearns, gave a rather bleak picture of the average U.S. citizen during the 1920's—materialistic, hypocritical, and suffering from emotional and aesthetic starvation. At his best, Lewis portrayed this same world and became himself part of "the revolt from the village."

There were three distinct stages in Lewis's career. As a young novelist, he published five novels between 1914 and 1918, probing the problem of escape or the contradiction between easterners and midwesterners, favoring midwestern sincerity to eastern refinement. The 1920's were highlighted by five novels, extremely successful and ultimately winning Lewis the Nobel Prize in Literature. This glorious decade, however, was followed by a twenty-year period of decline during which he published ten inferior novels. With the passage of time, Lewis became increasingly out of touch with a rapidly changing world. While Lewis was still writing about the period of transition from exciting frontier life to small-town boredom, the United States rapidly proceeded to new phases, to radically different and exciting experiences.

The influences on him were many; he acknowledged a debt to Henry David Thoreau, and among his contemporaries he had much in common with George Bernard Shaw and H. G. Wells. His ability for mimicry and for detailed observation made him a true "photographer" of life. Indeed, his novels are almost historical documents. He documented a fixed period in American history, the frustrations and disillusionments of one generation. However, Lewis never went beyond documentation; he re-created the symptoms but never analyzed them, never provided any formula for a meaningful life. The pattern in his books is always similar: There is a central character who—at any given moment—realizes the emptiness of his or her life and tries to break out of the mechanical boredom of the suffocating environment. The revolt is short-lived and leads nowhere. The escape ends in an impasse because Lewis himself could never solve the strange paradox of his own dislike of and attachment to Sauk Centre. If he was a loner in his native village, he remained lonely at Yale and in Europe as well. Unlike Mencken, who praised and encouraged him, Lewis was not a true iconoclast; deep down he remained attached to the values he exposed.

Lewis was an extremely hard worker; he did extensive research for each novel, carrying notebooks and drawing plans of streets, houses, furniture. All this made it possible for him to evoke a concrete world. This attention to realistic detail extended to the speech of his characters. More than any novelist of his time, Lewis made a systematic effort to record American speech from all levels of society, collecting examples of usage as if he were a student of linguistics. It is no surprise that Virginia Woolf claimed to have discovered the American language in Lewis's works. Lewis's creativity was that of a photographer with an admirable instinct for selecting his subjects but an inability to give a comprehensive evaluation of what he so diligently observed.

In his best novels, Lewis selected the most important issues of American life— villages/small towns in *Main Street*, business in *Babbitt*, science in *Arrowsmith*, religion in *Elmer Gantry*, politics in *It Can't Happen Here*, and finally, after World War II, racism in *Kingsblood Royal*—yet despite these successes, Lewis was not a great writer. As Lewis

Mumford has pointed out, he was well aware of the limitations of his environment, of the lifestyle he depicted, but he lacked the strength and the imagination to overcome those very limitations in himself. The revolt in his fiction is always unsuccessful because it never presents any workable alternatives to the life Lewis opposed; he stopped at faithfully and photographically reproducing spiritual poverty.

Main Street • In the year when Warren Harding was successfully campaigning for the presidency with the pledge of a "return to normalcy," Lewis captured the reading public with his *Main Street*. Stuart Sherman compared the book to Gustave Flaubert's *Madame Bovary* (1857), and Mencken praised the central characters, Carol Milford-Kennicott and her husband Dr. Will Kennicott as "triumphs of normalcy." Although there are surface similarities between the plight of Emma Bovary and that of Carol Kennicott, the two characters are very different and the novels even more so. In Flaubert's novel, the emphasis is on the personal tragedy of the heroine; Lewis, on the other hand, as always, deals with a theme: the "village virus." In fact, Lewis had originally intended to give this title to the book. The village-virus syndrome was a characteristic of a certain period of U.S. life. Describing it with photographic accuracy, Lewis preserved the atmosphere of a short historical stage in U.S. development. Village novels were no rarity in literature before Lewis, but Lewis's sharp satirical approach marked a radical departure from that tradition.

Main Street, the most popular book of 1920, is deeply rooted in the author's life. Gopher Prairie, population three thousand, is modeled on Sauk Centre, Lewis's birthplace. Dr. William Kennicott is based in part on Lewis's father and on his brother Claude, who also became a doctor. Carol is partly Lewis himself, the romantic side of him. Born in Minnesota, she is not exactly a village girl when she first appears in the novel. It is 1906 and she is a student at Blodgett College near Minneapolis. Her studies in professional library work take her to Chicago, the center of a poetic revival in the twentieth century. There she is exposed to the benefits of America's coming-of-age: the Art Institute, classical music, intellectual discussions on Sigmund Freud, Romain Rolland, syndicates, feminism, radically new thinking in philosophy, politics, and art. She has a job at St. Paul's public library when she meets Dr. Kennicott. The bulk of the novel is about their married life in Gopher Prairie, where Will works as a country doctor; it covers the years 1912 to 1920, from World War I and the United States' participation in the war to 1920, the cynical decade of the Jazz Age. The United States was passing into a new period in which the political and economic fiber of the country came to be shaped and determined in cities rather than rural communities. *Main Street* is not so much a chronicle of Carol Kennicott's life between 1912 and 1920 as it is a documentation of the national phenomenon of the village virus.

The village virus is best described by Gopher Prairie's frustrated liberal, Guy Pollock. He defines it as a vicious disease menacing ambitious people who stay too long in places such as Gopher Prairie. The small-town atmosphere breeds boredom, dullness, stupidity, complacency, and vulgarity, causing the inhabitants to wither away spiritually and become the living dead. Only a few of the inhabitants see Gopher Prairie as a menace. All the "important" people of the community—Ole Jensen, the grocer; Ezra Stowbody, the banker; Sam Clark, owner of a hardware store—take pride in Main Street. When she first sees Main Street, Carol is terrified by its repulsive ugliness, but to the others it constitutes the "climax of civilization."

All the people to whom Carol is drawn are outsiders in the community. Except for the resigned Guy Pollock, they all leave, disappointed and frustrated, or else die. Village atheist and political radical Miles Bjornstrom leaves after his wife and child die of typhoid. Before her death, his wife, Bea, formerly Carol's maid, is Carol's only confidante in Gopher Prairie. The young, idealistic teacher Fern Mullins is cruelly driven out of town by Mrs. Bogart, the hypocritical watchdog of Puritan morality, and her son Cy Bogart, the village bully. Erik Valborg, an artistically minded eccentric with whom Carol almost engages in a love affair, leaves because of gossip. Those who always triumph are the Bogarts and Stowbodys; they succeed in slowly killing all of Carol's romantic ambitions.

When Carol arrives in Gopher Prairie, she is determined to bring about changes for the better. Much of the novel is about her frustrated reform efforts. Again and again she tries to initiate new and fresh ideas and plans, but all of them fail because of the all-pervasive spiritual emptiness of Gopher Prairie. People there are not interested in poetry, theater, or intellectual discussions. Will Kennicott proves to be the gentle husband through all of his wife's efforts and failures. Though he does not understand Carol's frustration, he not only stands by her but also tries to help in every way he can.

Carol leaves Gopher Prairie with their son just as the war is ending. Will is there to wave good-bye as the train taking her to Washington, D.C., pulls out of the station. In the nation's capital, Carol is on her own; she tries to find her identity, tries to become a whole person, not simply a wife. She succeeds and enjoys the opportunity of a new life in which she can be active and in which she can use her brain once again, as she did in her girlhood, but she learns something else too: The radical changes in the behavior and attitudes of the young girls around her shock her as much as her behavior once had shocked a sleepy Gopher Prairie. In the end, she returns with Will to their home and settles down in Gopher Prairie, this time permanently. She still has dreams for her baby girl and likes to picture her as a future feminist or scientist; to the end, Carol remains a dreamer rather than a doer.

The last word in the novel belongs to the pragmatic Will Kennicott. He is Lewis's real favorite—the simple country doctor who performs acts of quiet heroism and worries about matters such as putting up storm windows. Lewis is unquestionably drawn to this stable, dependable, and reliable man, representing in his view the best of middle-class America. Lewis only halfheartedly endorses Carol's romantic attempts at beautifying Gopher Prairie because he himself was of divided mind whom to prefer: the artistically minded Carol or the always commonsensical though unsophisticated Will. If the cigarette-smoking modern young girls of the 1920's shocked Carol, Lewis, too, was unable to catch up with new trends. In this sense, *Main Street*, a novel about the village virus, is also an autobiography of Sinclair Lewis's spiritual development or, rather, spiritual stagnation.

The year 1921 was highlighted by an outburst of favorable and unfavorable reactions to this novel. First, there emerged a series of Main Street literature, attacking, burlesquing, and imitating the original, among them Carolyn Wells's *Ptomaine Street*, Meredith Nicholson's *Let Main Street Alone*, and Donald Ogden Stewart's *A Parody Outline of History*. At the same time, dramatized by Harving O'Higgins and Harrier Ford, *Main Street* was performed at New York's National Theater.

Babbitt • Even before he finished *Main Street*, Lewis had started work on *Babbitt*, a novel about a land speculator. From Main Street, U.S.A., "the climax of civilization," the novelist moved to an imaginary city in the Middle West, satirically named Zenith, symbolizing the average U.S. city and its status-symbol-oriented population. Set in the boom decade of the 1920's, the novel concentrates on the new national disease, which came to be called "Babbittry," after the book's protagonist. Webster's dictionary would define a Babbitt as "a seemingly self-satisfied businessman who readily conforms to the norms and ideas of middle-class society." The term "seemingly" is important; it indicates that even in this realistic, satirical presentation of middle-class America and its business culture, Lewis's romantic side is present; it finds outlet in Babbitt's dissatisfaction with his life. Predominantly, though, the almost photographic portrayal of Zenith prevails. While President Warren G. Harding was hoping to plant a Rotary Club in every city and village in the country to ensure the propagation of American ideals, Lewis was provoking the anger of those very Rotary Clubs by holding up a mirror to their Tartuffe-like hypocrisy and their materialistic culture.

Just as *Main Street* killed the friendly village novel by concentrating on the village virus, so *Babbitt* undercut the traditional business novel. With *Babbitt*, Lewis demonstrated that the era of the independent, creative tycoon was over. The tycoon gave way to the joiner, the conformist relying on status symbols and good public relations rather than daring and creative initiative. Babbitt, positively no giant, is almost a pathetic figure in his desperate need for approval. Far from being a tycoon, he lacks any individual ideas. He is a Booster, an Elk, a Presbyterian, a member of the chamber of commerce, a family man—nothing more. Senators of the Republican Party prescribe his political beliefs; national advertisers dictate his preferences in consumer goods. Without all these accessories, he is nobody; Babbitt is spiritually empty. Although he relies on the sham values that make him a "solid citizen," he becomes a pitiful victim of mechanical gadgets; his identity depends on having a car, the most technologically advanced alarm clock, and a royal bathroom.

Lewis worked very hard on this novel, which some critics consider his best. He prepared detailed maps of Zenith, plans of the decoration and furniture of Babbitt's house. The mimicry of language is superb, culminating in Babbitt's famous address at the meeting of the Zenith Real Estate Board. In his speech, Babbitt pours scorn on moth-eaten, old-fashioned Europe and glorifies the city of Success, known "wherever condensed milk and paste-board cartons are known." The pitiful, empty world of Zenith is presented in loosely connected episodes, the sequence of which could almost be changed, and that are held together only by the presence of Babbitt. These episodes take the reader through the most important aspects of middle-class life: politics, leisure, clubs, class, labor, religion, and family.

This apparent contentment, however, is one side of the novel; Babbitt is only "seemingly" satisfied. In reality, this prosperous real estate agent passionately desires something more and different from mere material success. This desire leads to his unsuccessful, vague, romantic rebellion against the Zenith world. Closely linked to his desire for escape is his longstanding friendship with Paul Riesling. Paul is one of those lonely, out-of-the-ordinary characters who emerge in all Lewis novels—creative, individualistic, nonconformist. With Paul, Babbitt escapes to Maine, but the escape does not help; his frustration remains.

Amid this frustration, crisis enters Babbitt's life. Paul is condemned to three years in prison for shooting his wife in what is described as temporary insanity. Without Paul, life seems impossible for Babbitt to bear; he tries to leave Zenith again but very soon returns. Zenith is the only thing in the world he knows; without it he is empty, a nobody. Like Lewis, who could never get rid of Sauk Centre, Babbitt takes Zenith with him wherever he goes. For a while, he tries to outrage Zenith society by drinking heavily and by associating with the wrong people—with the adventuress Tanis Judique and her bohemian friends, called the Bunch. At the same time, Vergil Gunch, one of the exemplary solid citizens, is organizing the Good Citizens' League. Babbitt shocks all his former friends and associates by defying Vergil's request to join their antilabor vigilante organization.

In *Main Street*, Lewis made Carol Kennicott return to Gopher Prairie. In a similar spirit of compromise, he finds a convenient way for Babbitt to give up his empty rebellion. His wife, Myra, has to undergo emergency surgery; her hospitalization pulls Babbitt back to his duties as a solid citizen. To seal his return to normalcy, he joins the Good Citizens' League. At the end of the novel, he is taken by surprise by his younger son; Ted drops out of school and elopes. In a private, man-to-man talk with his son, Babbitt acknowledges that he admires him for doing what he wants. He, Babbitt, never did that in all his life. In *Main Street*, Carol Kennicott's rebellion dwindles to romantic dreams for her daughter; all that remains of Babbitt's rebellion is his pleasure in his son's defiance and an encouragement not to let himself be bullied by Zenith. At the moment, however, Ted does not hold out much promise; rather than going to college he wants to be a mechanic at a factory.

Although *Babbitt* outraged certain sectors of the business community, the novel became an international success. Europeans loved it even more than *Main Street*. They enjoyed seeing the United States portrayed as they believed it was: materialistic, vulgar, standardized, and hopelessly without culture. They enjoyed the language; the British edition even added a glossary of 125 "American" terms. It is interesting to note that even while the novel was being angrily attacked, a number of midwestern cities claimed to have been the model for Zenith. Without offering any cure, simply by diagnosing and photographically reproducing symptoms of a national phenomenon, Lewis promoted self-awareness among his many readers.

Critics who wondered whether Lewis himself was Babbitt, lacking all spiritual ideals, were surprised by *Arrowsmith*, which featured an idealistic hero with spiritual values. In 1922, while gathering material in Chicago for a labor novel, Lewis met Paul de Kruif, a University of Michigan teacher of bacteriology experienced in immunology research. They became friends, and Lewis changed his plans; assisted by Paul de Kruif's expertise, he decided to write a novel on the medical profession. Lewis had some personal experience on which to draw; his father, his brother Claude, an uncle, and a grandfather were doctors. He needed help, however, in the field of scientific research; that is what de Kruif provided. Because a plague in the West Indies was to be an important part of the novel, they took a tour in the Caribbean together. De Kruif stayed with Lewis in England while he was working on *Arrowsmith*, a well-researched novel and his best-plotted one.

Arrowsmith • *Arrowsmith* was an instant success, being the first American novel about a medical researcher. The central character, Martin Arrowsmith, is a real hero with a purpose: He is wholly dedicated to pure science. The plot develops around the dramatic conflict between Martin, a few others of the same mind, and a society based on profit. Arrowsmith, Gottlieb, Sondelius, and Terry Wickett are akin to earlier idealists in Lewis's fiction, to Eric Valborg in *Main Street* and Paul Riesling in *Babbitt*, but there is a significant difference. Eric and Paul are lonely figures; Martin and his associates are not alone and they do not give up; they put up a fight against the commercial standards of a society that does not understand their ideals.

Martin Arrowsmith is introduced on the first page of the novel as a fourteen-year-old boy sitting in a country doctor's office. From his hometown of Elk Mills, the hero moves on to college to pursue his dreams; he regards himself as a "seeker of truth." At the University of Winnemac, young Martin associates with two kinds of people who symbolize the opposing forces of material versus purely scientific values. On one hand, there are the people involved in fraternity life; on the other, there is the German-born biologist, Max Gottlieb, modeled on Jacques Loeb, who allows Martin to work in his lab. Two events disrupt the smooth course of young Martin's drive to achieve his goal. First, he meets a nurse, Leora Tozer, and they fall in love; then, an irritable Gottlieb dismisses him from the laboratory. Martin and Leora marry, and, after an internship in Zenith General Hospital, they settle down in Wheatsylvania, North Dakota, responding to pressure from Leora's family.

As a country practitioner, Martin finds himself in a situation well known to Lewis. The young idealist who hopes to become another Robert Koch is increasingly in the position of a businessman in rivalry with other country doctors. At the same time, Martin's idol Gottlieb is undergoing a similar experience. After his defeat at Winnemac, he is faced with a new crisis in Pittsburgh when he refuses the request of a large pharmaceutical firm to have his antitoxin patented. Finally, a frustrated Martin escapes to Nautilus, Iowa, another Zenith, and then to the Rouncefield Clinic in Chicago. One of his articles catches the attention of Gottlieb, now associated with the McGurk Institute of Biology in New York, and the two are reunited. Martin even finds a new kindred spirit in Terry Wickett. Life at the Rouncefield Clinic and then at the McGurk Institute provides ample occasion for Lewis to describe the internal rivalry in such institutions, the pressures from outside and the search for power and fame.

When a severe plague erupts in the West Indies, Martin's recent discovery catches the attention of the outside world; this is the most dramatic part of the novel. Gottlieb's approach is not philanthropic but scientific. He wants Martin to use the antitoxin only with half of the patients so that its true value can be tested, but on the islands Martin is faced with real people. His faithful assistant Sondelius dies, and so does Leora. He initially intends to be a scientist and not a sentimentalist, but in the end he gives in, hoping to save more lives. On his return to New York, he finds changes at the institute; Gottlieb is pensioned, and the new director is all for "practicalness." The frustrated Martin marries a wealthy socialite, Joyce Lanyon, and they have a baby; however, Martin and his friend Terry find themselves out of place in the institute under the new direction, and Martin does not find in Joyce the companion he had in Leora. The two friends escape to Vermont to fish and to pursue their drive for pure science. While commercial society in Washington and elsewhere continues in its Babbitt-Zenith ways, Martin and Terry discuss quinine research in their boat.

The conclusion is rather romantic, sentimental, and unsatisfactory, but despite this flaw and some misgivings on the part of the medical community, *Arrowsmith* was universally acclaimed. Even the Pulitzer Prize, so far denied Lewis, was his, but he refused to accept it at that time. The retreat to Vermont in *Arrowsmith* was no real solution to the dilemma, but once again Lewis had presented, and called attention to, a genuine problem in American society. *Arrowsmith* celebrates an unwillingness to compromise and a dedication to ideals, which give this novel a heroic dimension missing in all other Lewis novels.

Elmer Gantry • Lewis dedicated *Elmer Gantry* "with profound admiration" to Mencken, and rightly so, because in this novel the romantic side of the novelist is overshadowed by a brutal, iconoclastic, almost fanatical satire. From his idealistic excursion in *Arrowsmith*, Lewis returned to his former mood, except that this time he created in the central character a complete villain. Elmer Gantry is the American Tartuffe. The reader can feel compassion for Carol Kennicott and pity toward Babbitt, but there is absolutely no saving grace for Elmer Gantry, the fundamentalist preacher in Lewis's novel.

Elmer Gantry was probably Lewis's most thoroughly researched novel. In 1922, a preacher named William Stidger suggested to Lewis that he write a novel on the subject of religion. In the anti-Puritan 1920's, religious life was in disarray in America. When Lewis finally decided to write a novel on the topic, he went to Kansas City in search of Stidger, living there for a considerable time in order to prepare material for *Elmer Gantry*. In Kansas City, he visited churches, preached himself, and investigated and worked with a group of fifteen clergymen of various denominations in what he called "Sinclair Lewis's Sunday Work Class." There were tragic events in his own life while he was working on the novel: His father died, his marriage with Grace broke up, and he was literally drunk when writing the final pages in New York.

The most obvious characteristic of the novel is its brutality; there is no trace of that sympathy that mitigated the dark picture in *Main Street* or *Babbitt*; there is no trace of a love/hate relationship with Elmer Gantry. Neither he nor the novel's other major characters have many redeeming qualities. The novel, indeed, is an uncompromising indictment of American religious practices in the early century. This most devastating of Lewis's satires is similar to *Babbitt* in that it is loosely structured and episodic. Its three main parts concern Elmer Gantry's involvement with three different women. In no other Lewis novel is the sexual element as important as in this one; it is Gantry's sexual desire that threatens his rise in religious circles.

The young Elmer Gantry attends a Baptist college and is ordained a minister. As soon as he receives his first pulpit, he becomes sexually involved with a young girl. He gets rid of Lulu by casting doubt on her character, revealing the depths of falsehood and villainy of which he is capable. In the second phase of his religious career, he becomes an evangelist, the partner (religious and sexual) of the female evangelist Sharon Falcon. They are two of a kind who never consider "their converts as human beings"; they regard them as a surgeon regards his patients or as a fisherman regards trout. Sharon dies in a fire, and Elmer Gantry's adventures take him to the Methodist denomination. There, he rises quickly and is promoted to pastorates in larger and larger communities. He is made a doctor of divinity, marries, becomes the first preacher whose sermons are broadcast, and tours Europe. Suddenly his fame and position are almost destroyed by a new love affair. Hettie and her convict husband try to outwit Gantry; they set a trap for him. For a short time he is frightened, but influential and clever friends come to his rescue, and he bounces back. At the end of the novel, he is leading his congregation in prayer, determined "to make these United States a moral nation." Like all true hypocrites, Gantry convinces himself of his sincerity.

Understandably, the novel outraged members of churches all over the United States. Some clergy even called Lewis "Satan's cohort," but the book sold 175,000 copies in fewer than six weeks, and an Academy Award-winning motion picture was made of the novel in 1960.

Dodsworth • With *Dodsworth*, Lewis returned to Zenith. At the beginning of the novel, Sam Dodsworth, a successful businessman in his forties, undergoes a crisis similar to Babbitt's, but there the similarities end. Sam, a Yale graduate, is much better educated than Babbitt and is receptive to the arts. A self-made man, he builds his own company, but, following the prevailing trend in America, his small business is bought by a conglomerate. This causes the active, enterprising Sam to believe himself to be a useless part of a big bureaucratic machine and provides an opportunity for his snobbish wife, Fran, to persuade him to go with her on a long European tour. This trip takes up the major part of the novel, which is a rather shallow treatment of Henry James's "international theme."

Sam Dodsworth does not know how to spend his wealth or his leisure time meaningfully; also, he is painfully gauche. In spite of these flaws, the author's sympathies are with him. Sam is trying hard to please his empty-headed wife. In her utter stupidity, Fran tries to imitate the worst symptoms of the decaying European aristocracy. At the end, she takes a lover and proposes divorce to Sam in hope of an exciting marriage. These plans fail, and Sam is there to rescue her, but their marriage cannot be saved. Lewis condemns the superficiality of European high society, but he is far from criticizing European culture; his satire is concentrated on Fran. Finally, Sam finds an understanding companion in a widow, Edith Cortright, who appreciates his honesty and integrity, likes him for what he is, and does not want to change him into something else. At the end of the novel, they are in Paris discussing marriage, but they are planning to return to the United States, where they know they belong.

Significantly, Lewis always turned back to the middle class for his subject matter. In *It Can't Happen Here,* inspired by Dorothy Thompson's antifascist stand, Lewis exposed the danger inherent in right-wing extremism in the United States; however, at the end of the 1930's, when the new left-wing writers hoped to see him write a proletarian novel, the essentially middle-class Lewis could not accommodate them.

During the long and painful years of his decline, Lewis tried to continue to focus on issues of importance—the career woman (*Ann Vickers*); organized philanthropy (*Gideon Planish*); American marriage (*Cass Timberlane*). American life was changing too rapidly for Lewis, however; he was never able to catch up with the changes. He did hit upon an important theme in *Kingsblood Royal,* but by that time his greatest ability—to re-create the world around him in photographic detail—seemed to have abandoned him.

Lewis's aesthetic shortcomings are obvious, but so are his merits. A writer of international reputation, he made American literature acceptable in Europe, becoming the first American winner of the Nobel Prize in Literature. His *Main Street* was one of the most sensational successes in U.S. publishing history. His biographer, Mark Schorer, describes him as a major force in the liberating of twentieth century American literature. Yet, by the turn of the twenty-first century, he was virtually ignored by critics. A well-balanced, objective evaluation of this controversial novelist is long overdue; the necessary distance in time should soon make it possible.

Anna B. Katona

Other major works

SHORT FICTION: *Selected Short Stories of Sinclair Lewis,* 1935.

PLAY: *Jayhawker: A Play in Three Acts,* pr. 1934 (with Lloyd Lewis).

NONFICTION: *From Main Street to Stockholm: Letters of Sinclair Lewis, 1919-1930,* 1952 (Harrison Smith, editor); *The Man from Main Street: Selected Essays and Other Writings, 1904-1950,* 1953 (Harry E. Maule and Melville H. Crane, editors); *Minnesota Diary, 1942-1946,* 2000 (George Killough, editor).

Bibliography

Bucco, Martin, ed. *Critical Essays on Sinclair Lewis.* Boston: G. K. Hall, 1986. Divided into two large sections of contemporary reviews of Lewis's novels and essay-length studies. The essays deal with the quality of the novels, Lewis's use of humor, his treatment of art and artists and of American businesses and philistinism. Bucco provides an introduction but no bibliography.

_____. *"Main Street": The Revolt of Carol Kennicott.* New York: Twayne, 1993. One of Twayne's masterwork studies, this collection of essays explores closely the characterization in *Main Street* and its effects on literature.

_____. *Sinclair Lewis as Reader and Critic.* Lewiston, N.Y.: Edwin Mellen Press, 2004. Another broad collection of critical essays on Lewis.

DiRenzo, Anthony. *If I Were Boss: The Early Business Stories of Sinclair Lewis.* Carbondale: Southern Illinois University Press, 1997. The introduction provides an excellent overview of Lewis's work in journalism, advertising, and public relations and shows how he developed in his early short fiction the themes that would distinguish his mature novels. The rest of the book makes available stories that have been out of print since their first publication.

Hutchisson, James M. *The Rise of Sinclair Lewis, 1920-1930.* University Park: Pennsylvania State University Press, 1996. A study of the literary career of Sinclair Lewis during the period of his greatest achievement, the 1920's.

Koblas, John J. *Sinclair Lewis: Home at Last.* Bloomington, Minn.: Voyageur Press, 1981. A look at Lewis's life and his midwestern roots, from which he tried to remove himself but to which he continually returned in his fiction. A valuable study, with much insight into the author and the places that were meaningful to him.

Light, Martin. *The Quixotic Vision of Sinclair Lewis.* West Lafayette, Ind.: Purdue University Press, 1975. A respected critic of Lewis, Light examines the conflict of realism and romance, which he terms the quixotic element, in Lewis's work. An invaluable and perceptive critical study of Lewis.

Lingeman, Richard R. *Sinclair Lewis: Rebel from Main Street.* New York: Random House, 2002. A critical biography that analyzes the novels that made Lewis one of the most important American writers in the twentieth century. Lingeman describes in detail the life that made the novelist so unhappy.

Love, Glen A. *Babbitt: An American Life.* New York: Twayne, 1993. Another in Twayne's Masterwork Studies, this volume examines *Babbitt* and its importance in U.S. society.

Parrington, Vernon Louis. *Sinclair Lewis: Our Own Diogenes.* Seattle: University of Washington Press, 1927. Reprint. New York: Haskell House, 1973. An essay on Lewis that discusses his role as the "bad boy of letters." Looks at Lewis's disillusionment through his novels *Babbitt* and *Arrowsmith.* A good example of critical thinking of the 1920's.

Schorer, Mark. *Sinclair Lewis: An American Life.* New York: McGraw-Hill, 1961. The definitive biography.

_____, ed. *Sinclair Lewis: A Collection of Critical Essays.* Englewood Cliffs, N.J.: Prentice-Hall, 1962. A compilation of criticism from H. L. Mencken's "Consolation" (1922) to Geoffrey Moore's "Sinclair Lewis: A Lost Romantic" (1959). A useful complement to the more recent criticism available in Bloom's volume.

Jack London

Born: San Francisco, California; January 12, 1876
Died: Glen Ellen, California; November 22, 1916

Principal long fiction • *A Daughter of the Snows*, 1902; *The Call of the Wild*, 1903; *The Sea-Wolf*, 1904; *The Game*, 1905; *Before Adam*, 1906; *White Fang*, 1906; *The Iron Heel*, 1907; *Martin Eden*, 1908; *Burning Daylight*, 1910; *Adventure*, 1911; *The Abysmal Brute*, 1913; *The Valley of the Moon*, 1913; *The Mutiny of the Elsinore*, 1914; *The Scarlet Plague*, 1915; *The Star Rover*, 1915; *The Little Lady of the Big House*, 1916; *Jerry of the Islands*, 1917; *Michael, Brother of Jerry*, 1917; *Hearts of Three*, 1920; *The Assassination Bureau, Ltd.*, 1963 (completed by Robert L. Fish).

Other literary forms • Jack London's fifty-nine published works include plays, children's fiction, sociological studies, essays, short stories, and novels. Although generally known as a writer of short fiction, London is also remembered for his pioneering work in tramp nonfiction (*The Road*, 1907) and the science-fiction novel (*The Star Rover*). London was also a journalist, serving as a newspaper correspondent for the San Francisco *Examiner* during the Russo-Japanese War in 1904 and, later, during the Mexican conflict in Veracruz in 1915. His accounts of these wars were published in 1970 under the title *Jack London Reports*. London's correspondence was first published in one volume in 1965.

Achievements • Called at one time the "Kipling of the Klondike," London was in the forefront of the move toward naturalistic fiction and realism. His social fiction, which included the first sympathetic and realistic treatment of the convict and the tramp, gave him credence as a spokesman for the working class. As a folk hero, London has achieved a popularity that may make him, along with Mark Twain, a permanent figure in American mythology. London is also extremely popular in Europe and the Soviet Union. His work has been translated into more than fifty languages, and his stories appear in countless anthologies of short fiction. Complete editions of London's work have been published in French, German, and Russian. London's novels, especially *The Sea-Wolf* and *The Call of the Wild*, are taught each year in high school and college English courses; a number of his books remain in print year after year. London's reputation as a solid craftsman—especially of short stories—has now been established firmly, even among literary critics. His novels, still regarded by many as weak and unpolished, gained in stature in the late twentieth century as more and more critics found London's work a subject worthy of discussion.

Biography • Born John Griffith London, Jack London was a sometime tramp, oyster pirate, seaman, socialist, laundryman, and miner. He is as famous for the life he lived and the myths he wove around it as he is for the short stories and novels he wrote. Largely self-educated, London was the product of California ranches and the working-class neighborhoods of Oakland. His rise to literary fame came as a result of the Klondike gold rush. Unsuccessful in his attempt to break into the magazine market, London joined the flood of men rushing toward instant riches in the Yukon. He found little gold but returned after the winter of 1897 with a wealth of memories and notes of the northland, the gold rush, and the hardships of the trail. By 1900, London had firmly established himself as a major American writer.

Also in 1897, London married Elizabeth May Maddern. The couple settled in Oakland, soon adding two daughters to their family. In 1904, seeking new material for his stories and escape from his marriage, which by this time had gone sour, London signed with publisher William Randolph Hearst to cover the impending Russo-Japanese War for Hearst's newspaper the San Francisco *Examiner.* His photographs and accounts of that war were among the first to be published, and he returned to California in triumph, only to face a divorce action.

London's next years were marked by further adventures and travels. In 1905, he journeyed across the United States, lecturing on the need for a socialist revolution. He married Clara Charmian Kittredge that same year, and together they planned a seven-year voyage around the world on a yacht they named *Snark* after Lewis Carroll's mock epic. Ill health forced abandonment of the adventure after only two years, however, and London returned once more to California, this time to create a large ranch complex in Sonoma County.

To support his travels and building program, as well as an extravagant lifestyle, London wrote at a furious pace, publishing fifty books by his fortieth year. His body could not withstand the brutal treatment it received, however, and shortly before his forty-first birthday, London died. His death, officially labeled uremic poisoning and renal colic, was widely rumored to have been suicide. The mysterious circumstances surrounding it have never been explained satisfactorily.

Analysis • Jack London's fame as a writer came about largely through his ability to realistically interpret humanity's struggle in a hostile environment. Early in his career, London realized that he had no talent for invention, that in his writing he would have to be an interpreter of the things that are, rather than a creator of the things that might be. Accordingly, he drew his plots, characters, themes, and settings from real-life experiences and published accounts.

London's career as a novelist began shortly after the turn of the twentieth century with the publication of *A Daughter of the Snows.* It ended nineteen novels later with the posthumous publication of *The Assassination Bureau, Ltd.* in 1963. The novels vary widely in length, subject matter, and (especially) artistic quality, for while London could write bold, violent,

Library of Congress

and sometimes primitive short stories of immense power, depicting the frontier environment and the human struggle within it in memorable fashion, his novels often suffered from weakness of structure and excessive didacticism. London's failure of invention, never a significant problem in his short stories, all too often surfaced in his longer works. Some critics have complained that a few of his novels (such as *Burning Daylight*, for example) are not novels at all, but merely strings of short stories hung together by the merest contrivance.

London's novels characteristically contain at least one of three different settings: the Canadian northland, where he began his literary apprenticeship; the primitive South Seas and Hawaii, where his career began anew following a short decline; and the California wilderness—particularly the Sonoma Valley—where London retreated during the last years of his life.

Each novel also generally contains a philosophical focus. Popular at the time were Charles Darwin's theory of evolution, as interpreted by Herbert Spencer; Friedrich Nietzsche's version of the superman, and, much later, the new psychology of Sigmund Freud and Carl Jung, as well as Karl Marx's theories of a new social order. All fired London's imagination and provided fuel for his characters and plots, and their presence—particularly London's version of the Darwinian "survival of the fittest" motif—lends credence to London's claim for membership in the naturalistic school of fiction.

The Call of the Wild • London was at the height of his powers when he wrote *The Call of the Wild*. He was dealing with the kind of subject matter, theme, and setting with which he was most comfortable. Written with vigor and intensity, the novel was intended originally only as a companion story to "Batard," an earlier short story. The story literally "got away from him," as he explained in a letter to a friend, and he was forced to expand it to its present length. The book was written shortly after his return from the slums of London. Wanting to escape the degradation and poverty he had witnessed there, London returned to the clean, frozen, beautiful world of the North, where the struggle for survival was elemental, uncomplicated, and fierce. The story is that of a dog, Buck, who is kidnapped from his home on a California ranch and taken to the Yukon, where he is forced to pull heavily laden sleds for inhumane masters. In order to survive, Buck must adapt, falling back on primitive instincts. With domesticity stripped from him, Buck learns the ways of his ancestors; he learns the law of the club—that he will be beaten but will survive. Gradually, as he completes his initiation into the primitive, Buck learns to respond. He learns the law of the fang: that he must be quick to use his own fangs, before others use theirs on him. By adapting to his new environment, Buck survives, learns the instincts of his forebears, and finally, hears the true call of the wild.

Incredibly, London's most successful novel was the one least understood by its author. He did not foresee its popularity, and he sold it outright to his publisher for two thousand dollars. He did not like its title, which now has become a recognizable phrase in the English language, nor did he understand the most powerful element in the book—the human allegory.

In *The Call of the Wild*, London was able to incorporate to good advantage the popular notion of the fierce Darwinian struggle for survival of the fittest. Curiously, he modified the Darwinian theme slightly. Buck must struggle to survive, but his survival is not predicated upon ultimate triumph. He must learn how to use his instincts, he must learn to be a good sled dog, but he need not become the team leader in order to survive. Struggle for its own sake also appears in *The Call of the Wild* and in other London novels. The team does not have to kill the snowshoe rabbit; at the time they are sleek and well fed. Yet, they chase after the animal anyway for the sheer sport of the kill. Struggle for its own sake reappears in *The Iron Heel, Martin Eden*, and *The Valley of the Moon.*

The Sea-Wolf • *The Sea-Wolf* drew on London's youthful adventures in the sealing grounds off Japan. The novel concerns the survival of upper-class Humphrey Van Weyden, a man who finds himself, through means beyond his control, aboard *The Ghost*, a sealing schooner on its way to Japan. Van Weyden soon finds that the captain of the schooner, Wolf Larsen, has created a hell-ship, filled with brutality and sordidness, where even the ship's practical purpose—to hunt seals—is lost in the misery of mere survival. Van Weyden survives this environment because, like Buck, he is able to adapt to it, learning new codes of survival, drawing upon unknown instincts, and using to best advantage all the benefits of his upbringing and status: intelligence, optimism, and a capacity to love. Van Weyden's growth is the focus of the novel.

If Van Weyden survives because he, too, has learned the law of the club and the fang, the ship's captain, Wolf Larsen, dies precisely because he cannot adapt. At least, that was London's intention, but it was lost upon many early critics. "I attacked Nietzsche and his super-man idea," London wrote to Mary Austin. "Lots of people read *The Sea-Wolf*, [but] no one discovered that it was an attack upon the super-man philosophy."

The Sea-Wolf is a fine example of literary naturalism. Larsen, a sensitive, intelligent, domineering man, treats his crew with arrogance. He has no inhibitions and also no friends. He is alone, and his life lacks purpose and direction. His aloneness and alienation from nature and from humankind, and, in fact, from himself, lead to his almost inevitable destruction. Without Van Weyden's ability to adapt, Larsen dies.

If London fails to convince his reader that Larsen died because he was a superman, perhaps it is because London did not fully subscribe to the idea himself. The world is full of supermen—London fancied himself one in many ways—and the socialist alternative that London supported intellectually was one he could not accept emotionally. This conflict between the superman idea and socialism erupts full-scale in *Martin Eden*, when London again takes Nietzsche to task.

Although *The Sea-Wolf* may have failed to convey its point to the critics, it did not fail to capture the fancy of the reading public. Next to *The Call of the Wild*, it was (and is) London's most popular book, and it gave the author the financial security he so desperately needed.

The last third of the book is concerned not only with the powerful element of Larsen's degeneration (which Ambrose Bierce called "unforgettable") but also with the introduction of Maud Brewster. London generally had trouble with female characters in his fiction—his editors demanded strict Victorian morals, and London was happy to oblige—and following Maud's introduction, the book is reduced to a sentimental shambles. Although the love story, in great part, ensured the critical failure of the book, it also ensured the book's popular success. As soon as Maud steps aboard, Van Weyden reverts to his earlier stature, as if wholly unaffected by the events that have thus transpired: His growth and adaptation are cast aside. The contradictions of The Sea-Wolf mirror the contradictions of London's own times. The novel is successful in depicting the turn-of-the-century society in which London lived, which was shaking off the morals and ways of the nineteeth century yet still was holding on to vestiges and customs of the earlier time.

White Fang • If *The Call of the Wild* is a novel about a dog who reacquaints himself with his ancestral instincts and learns survival by adaptation, *White Fang* is both its sequel and reverse. *White Fang* is the story of a wolfdog brought from the Alaskan wilderness to California civilization. Just as Buck used his civilized intelligence to survive, so White Fang uses his primitive strength and endurance to survive in a new environment—the world of civilized humanity. Environment is London's primary focus in this novel, as he traces the changes in the animal's behavior as it moves first from the wolf pack to an American Indian village, then to the white settler, and, finally, to the Santa Clara Valley in California. White Fang is tamed by love, and he successfully makes the transition from savage wolf to loving house pet. Although the book does not have the power of *The Call of the Wild*, it does show White Fang's struggle with nature as represented by Native Americans, dogs, white men, and finally, after critical injuries suffered while defending his new benevolent master, death itself.

London was intensely interested in sociology and sociological studies. He wrote one himself, *The People of the Abyss* (1903), and planned another one about the slums of New York City. Much of his interest in the subject can be explained by his belief in socialism, an answer to the problems many sociologists revealed. Thus it is not surprising that he would write *The Iron Heel*, a novel espousing a Marxist solution.

The Iron Heel • Like *The Valley of the Moon*, *The Iron Heel* is a novel set in the California wilderness. The similarities end there, however, for while London would later see his agrarian vision as a solution to the economic troubles of his time, in 1905, he still believed that a socialist revolution was necessary and inevitable. He documented it in this futuristic novel of social science fiction—a twentieth century vision of blood, fire, and destruction.

Basing his story on a small book by W. J. Ghent titled *Our Benevolent Feudalism* (1902), London poured out his private dreams of revolution and glory. If Martin Eden would later die because he was Jack London without socialist fervor, Ernest Everhard, the hero of *The Iron Heel*, cannot live because he lacks the depth and conviction of his own cause. London preaches in *The Iron Heel* without dramatizing his beliefs in convincing action. Indeed, he tried to convince his audience of the righteousness of a cause in which he did not fully believe. Everhard is too superhuman to be credible; Avis Everhard, the widow of the leader of the revolt, is disembodied. Not until the struggle in the book reaches a climax and the battle in the street begins does the novel start to take life.

London used a number of complicated plot structures to convey his point in *The Iron Heel*, and, as usual when dealing with fiction of greater length, he was not entirely successful in sustaining the plot or action. *The Iron Heel* is supposed to be a copy of the Everhard manuscript, a fragment of a paper hidden away by Avis Everhard. This paper was supposed to have been found, some seven centuries later, edited by Anthony Meredith, and then brought to publication as *The Iron Heel*. Covering the period 1912-1913 when the oligarchy rises to power and destroys all forms of free speech and opposition, the paper tells of Everhard's struggle against the oppression and his final flight underground, where he continues the fight, sometimes, as in *The Call of the Wild*, for the sheer sport of it. The novel reaches a bloody climax in Chicago when the mob is slaughtered by the Iron Heel mercenaries.

As might be expected, London's novel was not particularly popular with the reading public. His vision was not accepted by the socialists, either, perhaps because they sensed that the book was written as a halfhearted attempt at reaffirmation. The struggle between man and nature, so convincingly portrayed in *The Call of the Wild*, becomes a struggle between man and man, oppressed and oppressor, and even London was unsure who would really win the battle.

Martin Eden • While sailing around the world on his yacht *Snark*, London attempted a novel to bolster his career, which was sagging badly in 1907. The result, *Martin Eden*, was a profoundly moving novel, but also, as literary critic Franklin Walker would later note, a most puzzling work. Called alternately London's finest and his worst novel, *Martin Eden* was meant as another attack on individualism and the Nietzschean superhero. As in *The Sea-Wolf*, London was only partially able to convey this intention. The rags-to-riches motif runs so strongly through the book that the reader is compelled to identify and sympathize with Martin, a lowly seaman, who without education or culture is thrown into the world of the educated and cultured. His introduction to their world fires his mind, and he yearns for their sophisticated ways, their knowledge, and the woman who brings this world to him. Like London himself, Martin decides that the path to social betterment lies through his writing talent, and the novel masterfully describes Martin's (and London's) literary apprenticeship, early failure, and final success.

Martin Eden is a *Bildungsroman*—a novel of education. It employs the potent cultural myth of rags to riches and masterfully depicts Martin's painful transition from the innocence of unknowing to the power of knowledge. As Martin grows and learns, he finds himself embroiled in the battle of the Iron Heel, pitting man against man, oppressed against oppressor. London offers Martin the key to salvation through the poet Brissenden—socialism—but Martin rejects it, and in so doing seals his fate. By the time Martin's road to success ends, it is too late. Without a reason for living, Martin rejects all that he has sought and, finally, takes his own life.

Martin Eden was written aboard ship and is about a sailor. It is therefore not surprising that the paramount symbol in the novel is water. Beginning life as a sailor, coming from the ocean, Martin must return to his beginnings, and he does so by booking passage on an ocean liner and then committing suicide by drowning in the sea.

London returns to the theme of *The Call of the Wild* in *Martin Eden*, with one peculiar twist. Like Buck, Martin begins life unconscious of himself. He does not know that his grammar is imperfect, that his dress is slovenly, or that his manners are uncouth until Ruth Morse educates him. As he learns about himself, he becomes self-conscious. No longer do the instincts that Buck uses to adapt and survive work for Martin. Unable to adapt to his new environment, Martin returns to the only thing he knows—the sea—and, fulfilling the paradox of knowing and unknowing, dies.

Martin Eden is a profoundly moving work of imaginative realism, but, like much of London's longer work, it suffers from an uneven structure and sometimes clumsy expression. The major flaw of the book, however, is London's failure to convey his point. Readers are so caught by the potent myth, so sympathetic toward Martin and his fight to the top, that they cannot understand Martin's almost inevitable death and feel cheated by it. There is too much of Jack London in Martin Eden, too much of London's own confusion over individualism versus Marxism, to carry the novel, and so it fails, as London did, in the attempt.

The Valley of the Moon • In a May, 1911, letter to editor Roland Phillips, London outlined his plan for *The Valley of the Moon*: The theme of the book would be back to the land, a likely motif, for it paralleled London's own life story. The agrarian vision, London wrote, would be accomplished by a man and a woman, both wage earners, who meet and grow to love each other in the confines of a big city. Hard times befall them, and the woman, in an attempt to regain the good times they had had together, leads them both on a pilgrimage through California that ends, finally, in Jack London's own valley, the Valley of the Moon.

As London matured, he saw a return to the soil as the solution to the great economic problems of the age. He used this agrarian vision to advantage in his writings and also on the acres of his own expanding ranch. The theme runs through much of his work, including not only *The Valley of the Moon* but also *Burning Daylight* and *The Little Lady of the Big House.*

To solve the problems of the city, Saxon and Billy, the two characters in *The Valley of the Moon*, flee, as they must. London saw the strikes, the fierce struggles for economic and human survival, as symptomatic of the greater problem of humankind out of touch with itself. To return to the soil, to gain salvation, men and women must restore rural America. Billy and Saxon set out to do this, but first they must be reborn; London did not advocate an escape to the wilderness but a return to the goodness of nature. To return to Eden, Billy and Saxon must first gain salvation so that they do not spoil Eden as their ancestors once did.

Eden, in this case, is London's own ranch, and once Billy and Saxon arrive they begin applying the principles of agrarian success London fancied himself to be applying. They bring with them the good intentions, motivation, good character, and knowledge necessary to treat the land gently. They do not make the same mistakes the old-style American farmer made; they do not use the land up or wear it out; they apply new methods they have learned from foreigners, Portuguese farmers, to restore the land to its former richness. London realized there was no longer a vast American West. The land beyond the horizon had long been conquered and ruined. It was up to enlightened men and women to restore the land for the reruralization of America that was to come.

Although much more successful as a short-story writer than as a novelist, London's best novels remain alive and vibrant even to this day. His longer fiction was often episodic, disjointed, and loosely structured; his plots were often weak, and many times he let his characters preach rather than act out their philosophy. Nevertheless, London offered a compelling vision of the human condition. The Darwinian struggle for survival was at the forefront of American thought at the turn of the twentieth century; London's fiction mirrored his society, including its contradictions, and led his readers to the primitive arenas where the struggle for survival is best laid bare. London's contribution to the naturalistic tradition and his raw power as a storyteller ensure his continued place in the American literary heritage.

David Mike Hamilton

Other major works

SHORT FICTION: *The Son of the Wolf*, 1900; *The God of His Fathers, and Other Stories*, 1901; *Children of the Frost*, 1902; *The Faith of Men, and Other Stories*, 1904; *Love of Life, and Other Stories*, 1906; *Moon-Face, and Other Stories*, 1906; *Lost Face*, 1910; *South Sea Tales*, 1911; *When God Laughs, and Other Stories*, 1911; *A Son of the Sun*, 1912; *Smoke*

Bellew Tales, 1912; *The House of Pride, and Other Tales of Hawaii*, 1912; *The Night-Born*, 1913; *The Strength of the Strong*, 1914; *The Turtles of Tasman*, 1916; *The Human Drift*, 1917; *The Red One*, 1918; *On the Makaloa Mat*, 1919; *Dutch Courage, and Other Stories*, 1922.

PLAYS: *Scorn of Women*, pb. 1906; *Theft*, pb. 1910; *The Acorn-Planter*, pb. 1916; *The Plays of Jack London*, pb. 2001.

NONFICTION: *The Kempton-Wace Letters*, 1903 (with Anna Strunsky); *The People of the Abyss*, 1903; *The War of the Classes*, 1905; *The Road*, 1907; *Revolution, and Other Essays*, 1910; *The Cruise of the Snark*, 1911; *John Barleycorn*, 1913; *Letters from Jack London*, 1965 (King Hendricks and Irving Shepard, editors); *No Mentor but Myself: Jack London on Writers and Writing*, 1979, revised and expanded 1999 (Dale L. Walker and Jeanne Campbell Reesman, editors).

CHILDREN'S LITERATURE: *The Cruise of the Dazzler*, 1902; *Tales of the Fish Patrol*, 1905.

Bibliography

Auerbach, Jonathan. *Male Call: Becoming Jack London*. Durham, N.C.: Duke University Press, 1996. Auerbach reverses the trend of earlier London studies, emphasizing how London used his writing to reinvent himself. Above all, Auerbach argues, London wanted to become a successful author, and in that respect he shaped his life to suit his art. Includes detailed notes but no bibliography.

Cassuto, Leonard, and Jeanne Campbell Reesman, eds. *Rereading Jack London*. Stanford, Calif.: Stanford University Press, 1996. Essays on London as "representative man," his commitment to authorship, his portrayal of American imperialism, his handling of power, gender, and ideological discourse, his relationship to social Darwinism, and his status as writer/hero. Includes end notes but no bibliography.

Doctorow, E. L. *Jack London, Hemingway, and the Constitution: Selected Essays*. New York: Random House, 1993. A long, thoughtful reflection on London's politics and fiction from the point of view of a major novelist who is sympathetic but also critical of London's example.

Freund, Charles Paul. "Call of the Whites." *Reason* 28 (April, 1997): 52-53. Discusses London as a racist and a propagandist for the overthrow of capitalism; notes how London influenced some of the Weimar Germany's pulp racists.

Hedrick, Joan D. *Solitary Comrade: Jack London and His Work*. Chapel Hill: University of North Carolina Press, 1982. Hedrick interweaves a discussion of London's stories and novels with details of his life in an attempt to see behind London's self-created myth. She does some close reading of the stories and includes a useful bibliography and an index.

Kershaw, Alex. *Jack London: A Life*. New York: St. Martin's Press, 1997. Concentrates on the "powerful drama" of London's life. Includes notes, illustrations, bibliography, and several helpful maps.

Labor, Earle, and Jeanne Campbell Reesman. *Jack London*. Rev. ed. New York: Twayne, 1994. This clear introduction, first published in 1974, takes into account the twenty years of scholarship after the volume first appeared. This volume also takes issue with the widespread belief that the quality of London's work declined in the last decade of his life. Includes chronology, notes, and an annotated bibliography.

London, Jack. *The Letters of Jack London*. Edited by Earle Labor, Robert C. Leitz III, and I. Milo Shepard. 3 vols. Stanford, Calif.: Stanford University Press, 1988. Includes the most significant letters of the thousands London wrote during his lifetime. The editors have thoroughly annotated each letter, explaining references and identifying people. The letters include love letters, letters to editors and publishers, and to fellow writers on London's ideas and methods, as well as to friends and family.

Perry, John. *Jack London: An American Myth.* Chicago: Nelson-Hall, 1981. A detailed biography that is especially good on London's early life and his later adventures as sailor and journalist. Lacks illustrations but includes notes, bibliography, and index.

Stefoff, Rebecca. *Jack London: An American Original.* New York: Oxford University Press, 2002. Examines the life, beliefs, adventures, and works of London. Three-page bibliography and index.

Watson, Charles N. *The Novels of Jack London: A Reappraisal.* Madison: University of Wisconsin Press, 1982. A very good critical overview of London's fiction. Highly readable and accessible to students of all levels.

Alison Lurie

Born: Chicago, Illinois; September 3, 1926

Principal long fiction • *Love and Friendship*, 1962; *The Nowhere City*, 1965; *Imaginary Friends*, 1967; *Real People*, 1969; *The War Between the Tates*, 1974; *Only Children*, 1979; *Foreign Affairs*, 1984; *The Truth About Lorin Jones*, 1988; *The Last Resort*, 1998; *Truth and Consequences*, 2005.

Other literary forms • Besides writing fiction, Alison Lurie distinguished herself in two other areas, children's literature and the semiotics of dress, and her novels reflect both concerns as well. Her interest in children's literature is reflected in *Only Children*, in which two little girls pose their fantasies against the shocking reality exposed to them by their parents, and in *Foreign Affairs*, in which one of the two central characters, Vinnie Miner, spends her sabbatical in England collecting playground rhymes. Real children's rhymes, Lurie observes, are surprisingly subversive, not like the "safe" literature written for children by adults. She developed this insight in a nonfiction work, *Don't Tell the Grown-Ups: Subversive Children's Literature* (1990). Lurie's fascination with the semiotics of clothing (*The Language of Clothes*, 1981) is reflected frequently in the novels, where she pursues the relationship between clothing and personal identity. An especially provocative example can be found in *Imaginary Friends*, where Roger Zimmern, forced by a strange religious group to abandon his normal academic dress in favor of cheap suits, loses his sense of identity.

Achievements • Lurie's fiction has received much praise from critics, and her work has been very popular with the broader reading public. Her first novel, *Love and Friendship*, appeared in 1962 and was followed by several prestigious grants and fellowships: Yaddo Foundation Fellowships in 1963, 1964, and 1966; a Guggenheim grant in 1965-1966; a Rockefeller Foundation grant in 1967-1968; a New York State Cultural Council Foundation grant in 1972-1973. *The War Between the Tates* in 1974 brought Lurie a popular audience and more critical acclaim. An American Academy of Arts and Letters award followed in 1978, and for *Foreign Affairs* she was awarded a Pulitzer Prize in 1985.

All of Lurie's fiction displays a remarkable control of language, a style that surprises and amuses. Both for her wit and for her sharp-edged, satiric depiction of human follies, she has often been compared to Jane Austen.

Biography • Alison Lurie was born September 3, 1926, in Chicago, Illinois, but grew up in White Plains, New York. Her Latvian-born father was a scholar, a teacher, and a socialist who later became the founder and executive director of the Council of Jewish Federations. Lurie's mother, also a socialist, was a former journalist for the Chicago Free Press. Lurie suffered a minor birth injury that affected the hearing in her left ear and also caused some damage to her facial muscles. An avid reader as a child, she began at about the age of thirteen to read the works of such authors as Charles Dickens, George Bernard Shaw, and Jane Austen. In 1947, she graduated from Radcliffe College, where she met many people who later became important literary figures, in-

Jimm Roberts/Orlando

cluding Jonathan Peale Bishop, a teacher, critic, and essayist. She married Bishop in 1948, and they had three children. In 1975, Lurie separated from Bishop, divorcing him ten years later.

Struggling with many discouraging rejections of her writing in her twenties, the turning point in her life came in 1966, when she wrote a memoir of an eccentric friend, V. R. (Bunny) Lang. Thereafter came a succession of novels that garnered high praise, including a Pulitzer Prize for *Foreign Affairs*. A professor of children's literature at Cornell University in Ithaca, New York, where she began teaching in 1969, Lurie divided her time between Ithaca, Key West, and London.

Analysis • Alison Lurie's novels are known for their comedy and satire, and her acute observation is most often trained on the complications of love, marriage, and friendship as they affect the lives of the upper classes, the educated, the academic. Many of her novels take place at the fictional Convers College in New England or at Corinth University in upstate New York (based on Cornell University, where Lurie taught for many years) or concern characters who teach at or have been associated with Corinth. These novels are not, however, all academic satire; the academics often travel to other places or become involved in issues beyond the campus.

Lurie's style is most often detached and ironic, a treatment that has won for her both blame and praise. Her novels, except for *Only Children*, explore the time in which they are written and reflect the events and culture of Lurie's own adult years. The novels typically cover a short space of time, a crisis point in the lives of the characters, but several of the characters are seen at different points in their lives because of Lurie's use of the same characters in different novels—sometimes as major, sometimes as minor characters. Lurie works successfully with a variety of narrative points of view: omniscient narration in *The War Between the Tates*, first-person narration in *Real People*, third-person focus narration in *Imaginary Friends* (expanded to include two focus characters in *Foreign Affairs*). She shows no penchant for either the happy or the unhappy ending, realistically leaving her characters to continue to work out their lives as best they can. In 2006, she returned to some of the themes for which she is best known in *Truth and Consequences*, a novel about academia and adultery set at her fictional Corinth University.

Love and Friendship • At the heart of Lurie's first two novels are couples trying to work out their relationships. Her first novel, *Love and Friendship* (a title taken from Jane Austen), draws out the main lines of the issue. What is love and what is friendship? Are they different in what is best and most enduring? In this novel, the main character, Emmy Turner, "loves" her lover more than she does her husband. In the end, however, she chooses her husband over her lover because he needs her and to him she can be a friend. Indeed, what first led her to enter into a love affair was a frustration with her husband's failure to make a friend of her, to discuss with her his work and his concerns. Ultimately, Lurie suggests, friendship is more satisfying and lasting than love; indeed, love at its best is friendship at its best.

The Nowhere City • In her second novel, *The Nowhere City*, the ending is the opposite, but the implication seems the same. Paul Cattleman rediscovers his wife at the end after much neglect and many adulteries. It is too late, however: Friendship is lost, and with it love; she tells him that she is not angry with him, but she just does not know him anymore.

Real People • Although the love and friendship theme becomes a secondary issue in *Imaginary Friends*, the novel Lurie published after *The Nowhere City*, she made it once again the central focus of *Real People*. In this novel, Janet Belle Spencer, a writer, has taken up residence at Illyria, a haven for writers and artists. She has gone there primarily to work, since she cannot seem to write at home. She is also drawn there by her love for an artist, Ken, with whom she believes she has much more in common than with her insurance-executive husband. The artists' colony of Illyria is an unreal world, however, and Janet discovers that she and Ken are not really friends; she learns much about her writing that she resolves to change. It is at home with her husband, Clark, not at Illyria, she finally realizes, that she will be able to put to work her new understandings.

The War Between the Tates • Love and friendship in marriage are explored most intensively in Lurie's next and most celebrated novel, *The War Between the Tates*. Erica and Brian Tate, a young academic couple, are in their own eyes and in the eyes of their friends the perfect couple, but as middle age looms, Brian becomes increasingly frustrated at not being famous, while the children become rebellious teenagers. True love and friendship appear to be lacking. Finally, Brian has an affair with a student whom he makes pregnant, Erica befriends the student, and both Brian and Erica, but especially Erica, wander through a bewildering maze of events that leave their earlier sense of themselves and their marriage damaged. As the novel ends, they drift back together, confused, "out of love," but basically seeking a peace they can find only with each other.

Only Children • Love and friendship in marriage is the topic once again of *Only Children*, but this time the actions of the adults are seen through the eyes of two little girls, Lolly and Mary Ann, who respond to what they see in the behavior of their elders, especially their parents. In each set of parents there is one serious, deeply dedicated person (Lolly's mother, Mary Ann's father) and one shallow, egotistic, flamboyant hunter of the other sex. The two sets of parents ultimately stay together, but, lacking a love based on friendship, they are merely maintaining a facade, and their example will cripple their children's ability to love.

Foreign Affairs • The love and friendship theme appears again in *Foreign Affairs*, which juxtaposes two main characters, one married and one not. Vinnie Miner, a middle-aged professor, finds love where she had least expected it, in a friendship with a man totally unlike her, a retired sanitary engineer. The other main character, a handsome young man in Vinnie's academic department, begins the novel estranged from his wife, is temporarily dazzled and infatuated by a far more glamorous English-woman, but returns to his wife at the end, finding her superior in trust, honesty, and common decency.

The Truth About Lorin Jones • Love and friendship are very complicated and contra-dictory in *The Truth About Lorin Jones*, a novel that is a departure from her earlier nov-els for a number of reasons. Instead of an academic setting, the setting is the contem-porary art world, and the primary relationship in the novel is one that essentially exists within the mind of Polly Alter, a failed painter who is researching the life of the late Lorin Jones, an artist whose life and loves seem to speak to Polly's own situation. Lorin, who was once Lauren "Lolly" Zimmern, one of the little girls in *Only Children*, has lived a life of professional and personal frustration and is possibly still haunted by the demons of her childhood. The contemporary issues of feminism and lesbianism complicate the lives of both Polly and Lorin, but Lurie adds a new twist to the femi-nist argument by suggesting that it was Lorin who exploited the men in her life, using them as a means to serve her own ambitions. Polly's discovery of the truth about Lorin permits her a new lease on life, as does her romance with Hugh Cameron, a onetime hippie poet who had been Lorin's first husband.

The Last Resort • In Lurie's tenth novel, *The Last Resort*, Jenny Walker, formerly a subservient wife to her distinguished academic husband, faces a crisis in her mar-riage when she increasingly comes under the sway of the charismatic lesbian Lee Weiss. Jenny's attraction to Lee is heightened by the respect and attention Lee ac-cords her, whereas her husband, Wilkie, is content to see her merely as a passive sup-porter of his plans. Wilkie himself, under the impression that he is terminally ill, be-gins to detach himself emotionally from his wife but has a brief flirtation with a young female admirer even as he prepares to commit suicide. Although the couple is re-united at the end of the novel, their relationship has changed. Jenny acquires greater self-confidence and feels she is now in charge of her own life. Wilkie's "greatness" is no longer allowed to dominate their relationship as it once did.

The Academic Microcosm • Lurie's novels concern themselves with relationships be-tween people, and these relationships are at the center of all of her work. However, the lives of Lurie's characters are affected by more than personal forces alone. Con-text, temporal and physical alike, is also central to these novels, and the direction of the lives of Lurie's characters is profoundly affected by the times and the places in which they live. The most persistent context, moreover, is academic, since many of these characters, like Lurie herself, are university professors or members of their families. In this case again, *Love and Friendship* sets a pattern that other novels will follow.

The academic world is also a factor in *The Nowhere City*, although the story takes place in a Los Angeles setting that dominates the novel. Paul, in the end, will retreat to the eastern academic world that he knows (remaking his relationships with his old Harvard friends and taking a teaching post at Convers College), while Katherine, who had initially seemed the more eastern academic of the two, refuses to return there with him and seems to find a new self in Los Angeles.

The War Between the Tates again makes the academy not only a strong backdrop but also an actor in the events. Brian Tate is a highly successful sociology professor at Corinth University in upstate New York; his wife, Erica, is a faculty wife. Their two closest friends, who divorce in the novel, are Leonard Zimmern, an English professor, and Danielle Zimmern, Erica's closest female friend, a part-time faculty member in the French department. The convulsions of American academe during the late 1960's interfere directly in Brian's and Erica's lives. Brian, though very successful academically, has always dreamed of fame as an adviser to governments and presidents, and his middle-aged frustration makes him susceptible to trying to recover his lost youth by mixing socially with his graduate students, increasingly adapting his clothing and other styles to theirs, finally indulging in his affair with Wendy. Erica, like Katherine Cattleman in *The Nowhere City*, attempts to preserve her traditional moral values in the face of all this upheaval and tries not only to adapt herself to these values but also to give direction to Brian and Wendy, even to the point of insisting that Brian divorce her and marry Wendy. She becomes peripherally involved, through her friend Danielle, in the Hens, a local feminist group, and finding the local Hare Krishna guru of the students to be an old school friend, under his guidance has her own adventure with LSD. Brian and Erica, then, experience their marital troubles amid the student rebellions of the 1960's. Though the novel does not probe as deeply as *Imaginary Friends* into the political and intellectual doubts and troubles of academe, these influences are present, shaping their reaction.

In *Foreign Affairs*, the two main characters are again college professors, both from the English department at Corinth University: the middle-aged, internationally famous expert in children's literature, Vinnie Miner, and the young specialist in the eighteenth century, Fred Turner, both on leave to do scholarly work in London. The novel for the most part tells their stories separately, their paths crossing significantly only twice. Although their common background does make their lives cross in significant ways, and while both their lives are shaped by their academic backgrounds, the primary focus of the novel is on other aspects of their lives, which will be discussed below.

The American Macrocosm • The university campus, then, demonstrates the importance of time and place in Lurie's novels. This is also true in a larger sense, since American culture itself, with its regional and sociological tensions, plays just as important a role as the characters do. If *Love and Friendship*, the first novel, works off a Jane Austen theme, it also echoes a peculiarly American, Fitzgeraldian theme in which the different regions and classes of America become important players in the conflicts of the novel. Emmy is New Jersey rich, her lover Will Thomas southern shabby genteel, and her husband Holman Chicago shabby but respectable poor. As the marital couple work out their conflicts with traditions of Convers College playing an important role, these different regional and class conflicts do much to shape their actions and reactions. In *The Nowhere City*, 1960's America, with its new and strange customs and dress, almost overpowers its characters' ability to work out their human problems. Here, Los Angeles is the city in which "nowhere" comes to mean "present but lacking history and future." Strange and mixed new forms of architecture in both house and public building design, styles of hair and dress, sexual lifestyles, artistic forms, even subjects being studied in the universities are all strange, macabre, and new, dividing Katherine and Paul Cattleman as they respond to them so differently. Setting plays just as important a role in *Imaginary Friends*, which brings two very traditional strongholds, the enclosed small town and the principles of academic inquiry, together with the strains of the world without.

Real People, again, though it removes its main characters to an isolated, protected, ideal world of the artists' colony, nevertheless shows that the best work cannot be done in an artificial atmosphere but only when the artists are living and writing truthfully about the world in which they are "real people." Again, too, despite all the 1960's campus shenanigans of *The War Between the Tates* (drugs, strange new lifestyles, clothes, and hairstyles) the novel presents a strong sense that the campus is only reflecting all the major movements, confusions, and displacements of the society at large. In *Only Children*, which is set during the Great Depression, the characters reflect the concerns of that time, including its powerful economic and political conflicts. Bill Hubbard, for example, is an example of the President Franklin D. Roosevelt-type liberal democrat, dedicated to social reforms that will lift the poor, while Dan Zimmern represents the nascent Madison Avenue type, flamboyant and driven to succeed. *Foreign Affairs*, in the experiences of both Vinnie Miner and Fred Turner, discloses the tensions of many cultural mores, especially different class and sexual expectations, complicated further by differences between Great Britain and the United States.

In her ninth and tenth novels, Lurie abandons both the international theme and an academic setting, returning to the world of art and the artist that was her subject in *Real People*.

The Truth About Lorin Jones and *The Last Resort* introduce another setting into Lurie's work, namely Key West, the southernmost point in the continental United States and the site of Lurie's second home. Lurie uses the remoteness and luxury of Key West to place her characters in a distinct setting where they can work out their problems before returning, altered and refreshed, to the "real" world. In this way, Key West operates much like the island in William Shakespeare's *The Tempest* (1611). Lurie also sketches cultural and political differences on the island, delineating the way Key West's sizable homosexual community comes under attack from wealthy, right-wing Republicans who also reside in the area. Issues such as aging and AIDS also are given extended, if sometimes lighthearted, examination.

Literary Influences • The lives of the individual characters are additionally set against the backdrop of the world of literature itself. In *Real People*, Janet Belle Spencer images Ken as the ideal reader of her fiction, largely because he recognizes every literary reference—which in turn is reminiscent of Lurie's own rich texture of literary reference. In this regard, as already observed, she uses the "love and friendship" theme from Jane Austen. Another novelist to whom Lurie is greatly indebted is Henry James, especially in *Imaginary Friends* and *Foreign Affairs*. Indeed, *Imaginary Friends* in many ways duplicates the plot of James's *The Bostonians* (1885-1886), in which a young woman named Verena leads a band of truth-seekers by an extraordinary gift of public speaking, which seems to proceed from a trancelike ability to contact higher powers.

Foreign Affairs enlarges on the Jamesian theme not only by explicitly introducing James's work by name but also by exploring one of his most insistent themes: what happens when basically good, decent Americans encounter a far more culturally sophisticated European society. In James's novels of this type, the balance is struck in favor finally of the basic, honest decency of Americans against the more sophisticated but possibly corrupt world of the Europeans, and Lurie's novel arrives at the same resolution. This exploration is complicated by the fact that, of the two Americans, Vinnie Miner is very sophisticated in the ways of the English, knowing their ways and customs so well that she really feels more culturally at home there than in the United States. Fred Turner, on the other hand, despite his great physical charms and handsomeness and his knowledge of eighteenth century literature, is basically a raw recruit to European culture. Both, however, have "foreign affairs": Vinnie, with an almost illiterate Oklahoman whom she meets on the plane on the way over, so embarrasingly crude that she dreads presenting him to her friends; Fred, with an English aristocrat and actor so elegant and sophisticated that his American life appears crude by comparison. Despite this structural converse, in which Vinnie loves an American far less presentable than her European friends, and in which Fred loves an Englishwoman far more sophisticated than his American wife and friends, both find, despite all of their differences, their American loves superior after all, and their European friends, for all of their sophistication, less satisfying morally as friends and lovers than their American friends. Thus, the pattern of James's international novels, in which superior American decency confronts and ultimately wins out over superior European elegance and sophistication, is repeated here in Lurie's fiction.

The influence of James can also be discerned in *The Truth About Lorin Jones*, which, like *Imaginary Friends*, recalls James's *The Bostonians*. In this case, the competition between male and female for the loyalty of a talented woman is enlarged into an exploration of the politics of lesbian feminist separatism, something only hinted at in the James novel.

Characters • If Lurie's readers often spot resonances from other fiction, they also have the pleasure of recognizing characters they have met in other Lurie novels, for Lurie frequently works with recurring characters. Emmy Turner's four-year-old boy Freddy from *Love and Friendship* is one of the grown-up main characters in *Foreign Affairs*, while Fred's wife Roo in that same novel appeared as a child in the earlier *The War Between the Tates*. Sometimes Lurie will, in a later novel, go back to an earlier period in a character's life: Miranda, the grown-up, married mother of three children in *Love and Friendship*, is seen as a child in the later novel *Only Children*.

Of all the characters that recur, the most persistent one is Leonard Zimmern, first seen in *Real People* as a middle-aged, distinguished critic of American literature living in New York; later, in *The War Between the Tates*, as a friend of Brian and Erica. He is also the father of Roo, a child here but an adult in *Foreign Affairs*. In *Only Children*, the Great Depression-era story, Zimmern is a teenager, and in *Foreign Affairs* he is the father of a grown-up Roo, the famous critic whose harsh article on Vinnie Miner's work in children's literature haunts Vinnie as she goes to England. Roger Zimmern of *Imaginary Friends* is mentioned briefly in *The War Between the Tates* as Leonard Zimmern's cousin. L. D. Zimmern also surfaces in *The Truth About Lorin Jones* as the legal owner of his half sister Lorin's unsold paintings. In addition, *The Truth About Lorin Jones* features the return of Lorin's father, Dan Zimmern of *Only Children*, and Danielle Zimmern, divorced wife of Leonard and Erica's best friend in *The War Between the Tates*. In her next novel, *The Last Resort*, L. D. Zimmern returns as the cousin of Lee Weiss, the lesbian who befriends Jenny Walker. Another continuity in *The Last Resort* is the return of the character of Barbara Mumpson, who first appeared in *Foreign Affairs*. This remarkable amount of recurrence suggests Lurie's strong interest in understanding how her characters came to be who they are, despite her novels' time frames. Her novels, as noted before, cover only short periods of time—one, *Only Children*, takes place in a single weekend. In order to continue her characters' development, then, Lurie often spreads out their lives over several novels, the recurrence of her characters in different novels doing much to tie their lives together.

Imaginary Friends • As in the other novels, all the themes discussed so far are treated as well in *Imaginary Friends*. Their treatment in this novel, however, represents perhaps Lurie's broadest and deepest effort, for the academic backdrop she uses so often elsewhere is broadened here to embrace the most fundamental of human questions, questions of knowledge, of identity, of sanity, and finally of madness. The main character in this novel, sociologist Roger Zimmern—a young, brand-new Ph.D. at a large, upstate New York university—goes to Sophis, a nearby small town, as the research assistant of Thomas McMann, a famous senior professor in his department whom Roger admires despite rumors he has heard about him from other young faculty members and despite the realization that McMann's form of empirical sociology (the case-study method) is passé. To investigate McMann's hypothesis that small groups can build a belief system so powerful that it can withstand, rationalize, and incorporate doubting attacks from within and without, Roger infiltrates, under the cover of a public opinion seeker, a group of religious fundamentalists called the Truth-seekers, whose young leader, Verena, leads and directs through automatic writing from superior beings on another planet, named Varna. McMann is introduced as a businessman friend, also interested in their theories.

Roger's secure identity is overset by his mentor's unscientific attempt to control the experiment in the direction of his hypothesis rather than merely to observe and record. Also tormented by his sexual attraction for Verena, he reaches a point where he no longer knows what he believes in, no longer knows who he is, no longer knows whether there is in his discipline any objective basis for scientific inquiry. He believes that he is going mad but decides that it is, rather, his mentor who is insane, and he unwillingly becomes the primary witness whose testimony results in McMann's being committed to an asylum. The novel ends with Roger maintaining a tenuous but commonsensical hold on his own sanity. Here, Lurie has touched upon questions central not only to academic life but to the lives of everyone else as well: How can one truly observe and know? How real is our own sense of self?

Taken as a whole, Lurie's novels reveal a remarkable uniformity. Her own background in academe provides the most common setting for her novels, and frequently this setting is broadened to reflect the central questions with which Lurie is concerned. Her interest in clothing and identity, in the lives of children, indeed in the lives of all of her characters, is unusual. Her work is best considered not as a series of separate novels but as a continuity in which her characters' lives continue, not ceasing with the end of a particular novel but continuing as do most human lives—growing and changing through time.

June M. Frazer
Updated by Margaret Boe Birns

Other major works
SHORT FICTION: *Women and Ghosts*, 1994.
NONFICTION: *The Language of Clothes*, 1981; *Don't Tell the Grown-Ups: Subversive*

Children's Literature, 1990; *Familiar Spirits: A Memoir of James Merrill and David Jackson,* 2001; *Boys and Girls Forever: Children's Classics from Cinderella to Harry Potter,* 2003.

CHILDREN'S LITERATURE: *The Heavenly Zoo: Legends and Tales of the Stars,* 1979; *Clever Gretchen, and Other Foreign Folktales,* 1980; *Fabulous Beasts,* 1981; *The Black Geese: A Baba Yaga Story from Russia,* 1999 (with Jessica Souhami).

EDITED TEXTS: *The Oxford Book of Modern Fairy Tales,* 1993.

Bibliography

Costa, Richard Hauer. *Alison Lurie.* New York: Twayne, 1992. The first book-length study of Lurie, this overview is an essential resource. Written with Lurie's cooperation, the book includes a biographical sketch and discussion of all her writing, including a thorough examination of her major novels. Also features an extensive bibliography.

Hite, Molly. *The Other Side of the Story: Structures and Strategies of Contemporary Feminist Literature.* Ithaca, N.Y.: Cornell University Press, 1989. A brief entry on Lurie with reference to her novel *Foreign Affairs.* Places Lurie in the genre of women writing in the margins, the metaphor in their novels being minor characters playing major roles.

Newman, Judie. *Alison Lurie: A Critical Study.* Atlanta: Rodopi, 2000. After a chapter of biography, Newman devotes a chapter to each of Lurie's novels through *The Last Resort.*

_____. "Paleface into Redskin: Cultural Transformations in Alison Lurie's *Foreign Affairs.*" In *Forked Tongues: Comparing Twentieth Century British and American Literature,* edited by Ann Massa and Alistair Stead. London: Longman, 1994. Particularly valuable for its discussion of Lurie's theme of transatlantic cultural differences. Offers insights into why Lurie is so popular in England.

Rogers, Katherine M. "Alison Lurie: The Uses of Adultery." In *American Women Writing Fiction: Memory, Identity, Family, Space,* edited by Mickey Pearlman. Lexington: University Press of Kentucky, 1989. An important study of Lurie's novels through *Foreign Affairs.* A feminist analysis, it especially concentrates on the theme of self-examination on the part of Lurie's heroines.

Watkins, Susan. "'Women and Wives Mustn't Go Near It': Academia, Language, and Gender in the Novels of Alison Lurie." *Revista Canaria de Estudios Ingleses* 48 (2004): 129-146. This study of feminist themes in Lurie's novels appears in a journal published by the University of La Laguna in Spain's Canary Islands.

Cormac McCarthy

Born: Providence, Rhode Island; July 20, 1933

Principal long fiction • *The Orchard Keeper*, 1965; *Outer Dark*, 1968; *Child of God*, 1973; *Suttree*, 1979; *Blood Meridian: Or, The Evening Redness in the West*, 1985; *All the Pretty Horses*, 1992; *The Crossing*, 1994; *Cities of the Plain*, 1998; *The Border Trilogy*, 1999 (includes *All the Pretty Horses, The Crossing,* and *Cities of the Plain*); *No Country for Old Men*, 2005; *The Road*, 2006.

Other literary forms • Cormac McCarthy is known almost exclusively as a writer of novels. Short excerpts from his novels in progress sometimes appeared in such literary magazines as *Yale Review, Sewanee Review,* and *TriQuarterly.* He also wrote the script for *The Gardener's Son,* a teleplay in the *Visions* series shown on public television. First broadcast in January, 1977, the drama is based on an actual murder in 1876 in Graniteville, South Carolina. In a story full of dark implications, the disabled Rob McEvoy, son of a poor working family, kills the son of the local textile mill owner. The story was adapted for the big screen in 1996.

Achievements • Few writers have received such critical acclaim as McCarthy without also gaining wide popularity. He has consistently been praised for his carefully crafted work; his unflinching, dark vision; his immense range of vocabulary; and his powers of observation and description. These qualities also won for him rich recognition in the form of prizes and grants. *The Orchard Keeper* won the 1965 William Faulkner Foundation Award as the best first novel by an American writer and helped win for McCarthy an American Academy of Arts and Letters traveling fellowship to Europe in 1965-1966. The following years brought him grants from the Rockefeller, Guggenheim, Lyndhurst, and MacArthur Foundations. McCarthy has been compared to William Faulkner, Edgar Allan Poe, and Mark Twain.

The same qualities in McCarthy that have been praised have also been the cause of criticism and help to explain why he has not been more popular. A slow writer, he took at least twenty years to produce his first five books; thus, McCarthy faded from the public eye between books. His subjects—killings, incest, necrophilia, Knoxville lowlife, and scalp-hunting Western marauders—may repel some readers, and others may find his dark vision too unrelenting and morbid. Finally, his tendencies to ransack the dictionary for unusual words and to describe his dripping horrors in overwritten prose make him sound occasionally like gothic writer H. P. Lovecraft.

In 1992, *All the Pretty Horses* won the National Book Award and the National Book Critics Circle Award for fiction. In 2000, it was adapted to the screen. Although many readers do not enjoy McCarthy's lurid subject matter, his work has been much praised by critics. He is respected for his unflinching moral vision and his sense of humanity.

Biography • Cormac McCarthy was born into a middle-class Roman Catholic family—about as far as one can get from the background of most of his characters (with the notable exception of Suttree). He was born in Providence, Rhode Island, in 1933.

When McCarthy was four, his family moved to the Knoxville, Tennessee, area, where his father was chief legal counsel to the Tennessee Valley Authority (TVA). There, McCarthy grew up, attending parochial school, Catholic High School, and the University of Tennessee. He dropped out of the university after one year, traveled for a year, and then joined the United States Air Force, in which he served for four years. Afterward, he attended the University of Tennessee for three more years but finally left in 1959 without getting a degree.

McCarthy did discover his writing vocation at the University of Tennessee, where he began work on a novel. After the publication of *The Orchard Keeper*, he traveled in Europe for three years, living in London, in Paris, and on the Spanish island of Ibiza. While in Europe, he married Anne de Lisle of Hamble, England. Later, they lived

David Styles

on a small farm in Rockford, Tennessee, just outside Knoxville. McCarthy moved to El Paso, Texas, during the time he was writing *Blood Meridian*.

As *Blood Meridian* and his East Tennessee novels show, McCarthy's work is influenced by the landscape around him, and McCarthy absorbed local talk, color, and tradition. Whether he was more directly influenced by his father's work with the TVA is an interesting question. For many families who had been living in the mountain valleys for generations, the TVA was their first contact with big government—a traumatic one that has still not been forgiven. The permanent flooding of their land by TVA projects, despite "compensation," resulted in massive dislocations within the traditional mountain culture. One of the more gruesome aspects was transferring the contents of cemeteries to higher ground—a scene of the restless dead that seems to be echoed repeatedly in McCarthy's work, as is the theme of the government's bringing of change. Tennessee would continue to be a special place to McCarthy, though in his later years he traveled frequently, living and writing in motels.

Analysis • Like British Catholic writer Graham Greene, Cormac McCarthy is reluctant to develop any optimistic themes. He is also reluctant about stating his themes, although some of his titles offer strong hints. For the most part, he merely tells his stories and leaves it up to the reader to interpret their meanings. As a result, one critic has judged McCarthy to be nihilistic, but surely this judgment is incorrect. McCarthy's reluctance to preach about the good news masks a profoundly moral sensibility that is forced to face the worst in human nature and to recognize the power of evil. In this way, his novels are comparable to the medieval morality play or to such films by Ingmar Bergman as *The Seventh Seal* (1957).

There is also a softer, more modern side to McCarthy's morality. Few writers identify so thoroughly with people beyond the pale—the poor, the homeless and dispossessed, the criminal and degenerate, the outcasts. He manages to find some humanity even in the worst of these and to ascribe their conditions partly to contingency, bad luck, or the operations of respectable society. Their nemesis (besides themselves) is often the law and its officers, who, for them, become additional embodiments of the death and destruction that pursue everyone. McCarthy's refusal to avert his sympathies from the outcasts thus raises some complex social and theological issues.

The Orchard Keeper • McCarthy's first novel, *The Orchard Keeper*, introduces the outcasts as members of the disappearing mountain culture of East Tennessee. Young Marion Sylder lives by bootlegging, and in self-defense he kills a man and disposes of the body in an abandoned peach orchard that symbolizes the dying culture. Old Arthur Ownby, who fondly watches over the orchard, finds the body, but he does not report it. He lets it rest in peace for seven years. The old man also believes in his own peace and privacy, and when these are disturbed by a government holding tank erected on a nearby hill, he shoots his *X* on the tank's side. Both the men live by old mountain codes that, by definition, are outside the law of the intruding modern world. However, the enforcers of the law, who finally arrest and beat Sylder and send the old man to a mental institution, seem degenerate in comparison to them. The novel's theme is also represented in John Wesley Rattner (ironically, the son of the dead man), a boy who hunts and traps, is befriended by the two men, and comes of age in the novel. He decides to cast his loyalties with the old ways even if they have become anachronistic.

Outer Dark • The episodic converging stories and italicized flashbacks of *The Orchard Keeper* recall Faulkner's narrative techniques, and McCarthy's second novel, *Outer Dark*, also owes a debt to Faulkner. The novel takes place in some vaguely Deep South setting early in the twentieth century and deals with the horrible consequences of incest between Culla and Rinthy Holme, brother and sister. Rinthy delivers a baby boy, and Culla abandons it in the woods, where a passing tinker finds and takes it. Culla tells Rinthy that the baby died, but Rinthy digs up the shallow grave, discovers his lie, and intuitively goes in search of the tinker. Culla goes after Rinthy to bring her back. Their wanderings on the roads recall those of Lena Grove and Joe Christmas in Faulkner's *Light in August* (1932). Everyone she encounters befriends Rinthy, who moves along dripping mother's milk for over six months, but Culla meets nothing except suspicion and trouble. These episodes also recall the journey down the river in Mark Twain's *Adventures of Huckleberry Finn* (1884), particularly a wild incident in which a loose ferry is swept down a raging river.

McCarthy's most original and unforgettable creation in *Outer Dark* is a set of three avenging angels, or devils, who rove about the landscape murdering people. On a realistic level, they are lawless, asocial drifters who have gone totally beyond the pale into the "outer dark." They have lost all caring. Appropriately, Culla meets this unholy trio of blood brothers near the novel's end. The three hang the tinker and dispose of the baby (now symbolically scarred as in a Nathaniel Hawthorne story) before Culla's eyes: One slits the baby's throat and another sucks its blood.

Child of God • If *Outer Dark* does not contain horror enough, McCarthy followed it with *Child of God*, which returns to a rural East Tennessee setting. Here, mountain man Lester Ballard loses his farm for failure to pay taxes; embittered and alone, he sinks gradually into necrophilia and then murder. His degeneration is marked by movement from the farm to an abandoned shack that burns, to a cave where he stores his supply of dead women. He is finally captured, dies in a state mental hospital, and is dissected in a medical laboratory. His neighbors, whose choruslike, folksy comments are interspersed throughout the story, always thought him a bit strange, with bad blood. McCarthy suggests that all Lester ever needed, however, was a home and love. Lester was only "a child of God much like yourself perhaps."

Suttree • A short, tightly unified work, *Child of God* contrasts with McCarthy's next novel, *Suttree*, usually considered his masterpiece. *Suttree* displays the variety and range of McCarthy's talent. Set in Knoxville during the 1950's, the novel is a long, rambling work rich in incident, character, language, and mood, including some surprisingly amusing, bawdy humor. However, *Suttree* has certain features in common with *Child of God*. Misery and unhappiness also predominate here, and instead of one child of God, *Suttree* has hundreds—drunks, prostitutes, perverts, petty criminals, and the poor generally, black and white—all dumped together in a slum known as McAnally Flats. The characters have such names as Hoghead, Gatemouth, Worm, and Trippin Through The Dew, and their dialogue is spiced with slang and expletives.

The central character is Cornelius "Buddy" Suttree, scion of a prominent local family. He has deliberately chosen to live in this slum on a houseboat moored in the Tennessee River, from whose filthy waters he catches a few carp and catfish to sell. Why he has made this strange choice gradually becomes clear. On one hand, he has made a mess of his life. He and his parents are no longer on speaking terms, and his wife left him long ago, taking their child (who dies in the novel). Suttree sank to drink and served a term in the prison workhouse. Now he lives in McAnally Flats because, on the other hand, he feels at home there. There, he can find the company of like-minded, fun-loving pals who can help him pass the time and avoid involvement in the pain of life. There he sits, the fisher king in his wasteland, and with dread and longing he awaits the oblivion of death.

A happy flaw in Suttree's character, however, prevents his nihilistic scheme from taking effect: compassion. He cannot avoid feeling compassion for the people around him, such as the ignorant but irrepressible Gene Harrogate, a country boy who serves a term in the workhouse for having sex with a farmer's watermelons and who dynamites the city's sewer system down on himself trying to rob a bank (the "country mouse," as he is first called, soon becomes the "city rat"). Further involvement with people leads to further pain for Suttree—a girl he falls in love with is killed, his long affair with a rich prostitute breaks up, and most of his pals are killed or imprisoned. Deeper emotional commitment on Suttree's part, however, might have saved both the girl and the affair with the prostitute. After a solitary retreat to the Great Smoky Mountains and a near-fatal illness, Suttree decides to embrace life—pain and all—and to leave Knoxville. He leaves just as the McAnally Flats are being torn down to make room for an expressway. His parting words of advice concern the hounds of death: "Fly them."

Blood Meridian • McCarthy's fifth book, *Blood Meridian*, is a historical novel set in the American Southwest and northern Mexico around the middle of the nineteenth century. The novel's protagonist is a nameless character known only as "the kid" (with suggested parallels perhaps to Billy the Kid), who runs away from his Tennessee home when he is fourteen and heads west. His story might be that of Huck Finn after Huck "lit out for the territory" and left civilization behind. After repeated scrapes, always moving west, the kid joins a band of scalping bounty hunters who hunt the Apaches when the Apaches are not hunting them. The massacres go on endlessly, all duly noted in the running summaries that head each chapter.

In some ways, *Blood Meridian* provides a useful retrospective view of McCarthy's work. It returns to the horrors of his earlier novels but seems to relate these to the social themes of *Suttree*. The scalp hunters are, after all, the advance guard of Western civilization. They suggest a terrible moral ambiguity at the heart of civilization, as in the hearts of individuals, that enables it to stamp out Apaches and backward mountaineers and to create such slums as McAnally Flats. Judge Holden, the repulsive and evil philosopher of *Blood Meridian*, argues that God made humanity thus, that morality is irrelevant, and that superior violence shall triumph. The naked judge finally embraces the kid with an apparent death hug inside a privy behind a whorehouse in Fort Griffin, Texas. Readers can probably find a warning in this to flee such philosophers.

The Border trilogy • The American Southwest and northern Mexico also serve as the setting for McCarthy's most ambitious work, the Border trilogy, the sweeping saga of two boys' initiation into manhood immediately before, during, and after World War II. With this work the author sheds the label of southern regional writer by combining universal themes and postmodernist thought with the bold experimental style he exhibited in *Blood Meridian*.

In the opening book, *All the Pretty Horses*, McCarthy paints a splendid yet harsh landscape populated by an equally noble yet coarse cast of characters. Among them are John Grady Cole and Billy Parham, who spend much of their time in search of a cultural identity and Western way of life that is on the verge of extinction. A sense of restlessness permeates the tale as Cole and Parham, despite their determination, seem incapable of attaching themselves to a particular time or place, other than the disappearing open range.

In *The Crossing*, a prequel to *All the Pretty Horses*, the sense of homelessness is similarly pervasive, starting with the opening sequence when Parham becomes obsessed with trapping a renegade she-wolf. After he captures the animal, he decides to release her back into the wild, a symbolic act indicating the wild-at-heart temperaments McCarthy instills in his characters. It is the first of a series of losses experienced by Parham, a list that later would include his parents, brother, and dog.

The thematic "quest" continues in *Cities of the Plain*, as Cole and Parham are united while working as a pair of hired hands on a New Mexico cattle ranch where they quickly become inseparable friends, bound by a love of horses and life on the range. Soon, Cole finds another love in the figure of Magdalena, a Mexican prostitute. In an attempt to rescue her from an abusive pimp, both Cole and Magdalena wind up dead, leaving Parham alone to wander the land, performing odd jobs, before finding himself back in New Mexico an elderly man.

The Border trilogy is unconventional in word and deed and filled with an imaginative succession of contrasts and conflicts that drive the author's narrative to its conclusion. Throughout his story he is able to juxtapose competing cultures, languages, and moral codes to create a milieu that spawns extraordinary actions and stretches of dialogue, such as the series of tales by the priest, the blind man, and the gypsy in *The*

Crossing. The mystic element of these exchanges underscores the thread of the natural versus the supernatural running through the story. Yet, whenever otherworldly elements edge closer to becoming the balm for his protagonists' troubles, there is always the landscape to return them to reality. As critics have noted, the surrounding land becomes another of McCarthy's characters with contrasting features of its own, from august mountains to desolate plains. It is not an oversimplification to conclude that much of the trilogy becomes a matter of when humankind and nature meet and that the author's characters do not change or grow over the course of his story. Rather, they are blended into the ever-present landscape that, in the end, is destined to unite them.

Cities of the Plain • Set in the early 1950's around El Paso, Texas, and across the border in Juarez, Mexico, *Cities of the Plain* brings together the protagonists of the first two novels of the Border trilogy. Billy Parham, now in his thirties, and John Grady Cole, now nineteen, both find themselves working on a ranch in the Tularosa Basin, an area threatened by U.S. government appropriation for military purposes. "Anyway this country aint the same," Billy tells John Grady. "The war changed everthing. I don't think people even know it yet."

The central action revolves around John Grady's single-minded obsession with a young Mexican epileptic prostitute, Magdalena, an obsession that readers understand better in the light of his experiences in *All the Pretty Horses*. The extent to which John Grady is devoted to this woman and willing to sacrifice for her shows how difficult it can be to distinguish between foolishness and heroism. Grady's powerful emotions propel him along the path of romance, despite cautions and counsel offered by older men such as Billy, Mac the ranch owner, and the maestro, a blind Mexican musician who subscribes to a kind of fatalist philosophy: "Men imagine that the choices before them are theirs to make. But we are free to act only upon what is given. Choice is lost in the maze of generations and each act in that maze is itself an enslavement for it voids every alternative and binds one ever more tightly into the constraints that make a life."

There are plenty of signs that the relationship will not work; the narrative bears the usual markings of tragedy. The most stubborn, insurmountable obstacle turns out to be Eduardo, the girl's pimp who is also in love with her. Despite her mortal fear of Eduardo, Magdalena finally arranges to escape with John Grady. The price of her defiance is death: She is caught and killed in her attempt to flee. When John Grady finds out what happened, he seeks revenge, going after Eduardo. An extremely graphic knife fight between the two men ends with a critically wounded Grady killing his rival. Despite Billy's attempt to save him, Grady dies from his wounds. Neither energies nor the beings housing them stay within prescribed boundaries. Grady's obsession, the woman's epilepsy, Eduardo's capacity for jealousy and desire for triumph over his rival—all are displays of excess, and, while this excess leads to tragedy, it at least is vivid proof of life's intensity, perhaps preferable to a dull, lifeless, modern existence, void of tragic potential.

As do the first two novels in the trilogy, *Cities of the Plains* discloses the complex dynamics between the United States and Mexico, fraught with tensions, mutual suspicions and fascinations. Both Billy and John Grady, fully aware of cultural differences, register a real appreciation of their neighbors south of the border. Billy recounts the extraordinary generosity and hospitality of ordinary Mexicans:

I was just a kid. I rode all over northern Mexico. . . . I liked it. I liked the country and I liked the people in it. I rode all over Chihuahua and a good part of Coahuila and some of Sonora. I'd be gone weeks at a time and not have hardly so much as a peso in my pocket but it didn't make no difference. Those people would take you in and put you up and feed you and feed your horse and cry when you left. You could of stayed forever. They didn't have nothin. Never had and never would. But you could stop at some little estancia in the absolute dead center of nowhere and they'd take you in like you was kin. You could see that the revolution hadn't done them no good. A lot of em had lost boys out of the family. Fathers or sons or both. Nearly all of em, I expect. They didn't have no reason to be hospitable to anybody. Least of all a gringo kid. That plateful of beans they set in front of you was hard come by. But I was never turned away. Not a time.

For Grady, Mexico has retained a certain vitality lost in the United States. "Don't you think if there's anything left of this life it's down there?" he asks Billy at one point. His obsession with the Mexican woman might be seen as a way to come to terms with, even to embrace, the "other." The presence of Americans south of the border is not welcome by all, as shown in Eduardo's remarks to John Grady during their knife fight: "They drift down out of your leprous paradise seeking a thing now extinct among them. A thing for which perhaps they no longer even have a name." The story's outcome underscores how difficult it is to surmount a history of hostility, distrust, and misunderstanding.

The novel's epilogue, transcending the tragic story, features a seventy-eight-year-old Billy, at "the second year of the new millennium" and his encounter with a Mexican fellow-traveler. In their exchange, in the mutual listening and telling of dreams and stories, readers are urged to consider the metaphysical import of dreams, stories, death, the relationship between life and representations of it, and the contingent forces that conspire to make a particular life what it is, and not something else. "Every man's death is a standing in for every other," the Mexican pronounces toward the end, as a kind of moral. "And since death comes to all there is no way to abate the fear of it except to live for that man who stands for us."

Harold Branam
Updated by William Hoffman and Allen Hibbard

Other major works

PLAY: *The Stonemason*, pb. 1994.
SCREENPLAY: *The Gardener's Son*, 1996.
TELEPLAY: *The Gardener's Son*, 1977.

Bibliography

Arnold, Edwin T., and Dianne C. Luce, eds. *A Cormac McCarthy Companion: "The Border Trilogy."* Jackson: University Press of Mississippi, 2001. A collection of essays providing a critical overview of McCarthy's trilogy.
_____. *Perspectives on Cormac McCarthy*. Oxford: University Press of Mississippi, 1993. This collection of ten essays examining the works of McCarthy serves as an excellent introduction to his novels. A thorough bibliography is included.
Bell, Vereen M. *The Achievement of Cormac McCarthy*. Baton Rouge: Louisiana State University Press, 1988. The first thorough critical study of McCarthy, in which Bell

explains McCarthy's unconventional methods and his emphasis on language as responses to the fact that the real world is tainted by evil. Contains a good bibliography and a full index.

Bloom, Harold, ed. *Cormac McCarthy.* Philadelphia: Chelsea House, 2002. A collection of the best critical work on McCarthy intended as an introduction for students.

Bowers, James. *Reading Cormac McCarthy's "Blood Meridian."* Boise, Idaho: Boise State University Press, 1999. Examines the historical context of McCarthy's macabre brand of western expansion.

Jarrett, Robert L. *Cormac McCarthy.* New York: Twayne, 1997. Contains the most information on McCarthy. Includes bibliography and index.

Lilley, James D., ed. *Cormac McCarthy: New Directions.* Albuquerque: University of New Mexico Press, 2002. A collection of essays focusing on the mythic aspects of McCarthy's writing.

McCarthy, Cormac. "Cormac McCarthy's Venomous Fiction." Interviewed by Richard B. Woodward. *The New York Times Magazine,* April 19, 1992, 28-31. In one of his rare interviews, McCarthy discusses his views on the nature of evil and the allure of violence. His belief is that an independent life and a life of harmony are incompatible.

Owens, Barley. *McCarthy's Western Novels.* Tucson: University of Arizona Press, 2000. Study of McCarthy's fiction set in the American West.

Rebein, Robert. *Hicks, Tribes, and Dirty Realists: American Fiction After Postmodernism.* Lexington: University Press of Kentucky, 2001. An assertion that gritty realism has gained ascendency over metafiction in American writing. Examines the works of McCarthy, Dorothy Allison, Annie Proulx, Thomas McGuane, Larry McMurtry, and Louise Erdrich.

Wallach, Rick, ed. *Myth, Legend, Dust: Critical Responses to Cormac McCarthy.* New York: Manchester University Press, 2000. Collection of reprinted reviews and essays on McCarthy.

Mary McCarthy

Born: Seattle, Washington; June 21, 1912
Died: New York, New York; October 25, 1989

Principal long fiction • *The Oasis*, 1949; *The Groves of Academe*, 1952; *A Charmed Life*, 1955; *The Group*, 1963; *Birds of America*, 1971; *Cannibals and Missionaries*, 1979.

Other literary forms • First known as a book reviewer, drama critic, and essayist, Mary McCarthy also wrote short stories, collected in *The Company She Keeps* (1942), *Cast a Cold Eye* (1950), and *The Hounds of Summer, and Other Stories* (1981). Her drama criticism is collected in *Sights and Spectacles, 1937-1956* (1956) and in *Mary McCarthy's Theatre Chronicles, 1937-1962* (1963). *Venice Observed* (1956) and *The Stones of Florence* (1959) are books of travel and art history. *The Writing on the Wall, and Other Literary Essays* (1970) and *Ideas and the Novel* (1980) are literary essays and lectures. *On the Contrary: Articles of Belief* (1961) contains autobiographical essays and literary criticism. *Memories of a Catholic Girlhood* (1957) and *How I Grew* (1987) are memoirs of her childhood and youth. Her books *Vietnam* (1967) and *Hanoi* (1968) oppose United States involvement in the Vietnam War, an interest that she continued in *Medina* (1972) and in *The Seventeenth Degree* (1974). *The Mask of State* (1974) presents impressions of the Watergate affair hearings.

Achievements • From the appearance of her first book reviews, when she was just out of college, to the time of her death, Mary McCarthy was one of the leading figures on the American literary scene. In her novels as much as in her essays and reviews, she was above all a critic, a sharp observer of contemporary society. For students of twentieth century American culture her work is indispensable.

Biography • Born into an affluent family of mixed Irish and Jewish heritage on June 21, 1912, in Seattle, Washington, Mary Therese McCarthy had a segmented childhood. After six years of what she called a "fairy-tale" existence of happiness, both parents died of influenza in 1918 during a move to Minneapolis. Mary and her three younger brothers, placed with their grandaunt and uncle, then entered a bleak phase of intense, strict Roman Catholicism, which McCarthy described in *Memories of a Catholic Girlhood*. In 1923, McCarthy's grandparents moved her to a convent school in Seattle for the seventh and eighth grades; she spent her ninth grade year in a public school and then her remaining high school years at the Annie Wright Seminary in Tacoma, from which she graduated in 1929 at the top of her class. In the same year of her graduation as a Phi Beta Kappa from Vassar College in 1933, she married Harold Johnsrud; the marriage lasted three years. She reviewed novels and biographies for *The New Republic* and *The Nation*, worked for the left-wing publishers Covici Friede, and, in 1937, involved herself in Trotskyite politics. In 1937, she became drama editor for the *Partisan Review*.

The next year, McCarthy married Edmund Wilson and gave birth to a son, Reuel Wilson; also, at Wilson's urging, she wrote her first fiction, a short story. Thereafter, the stories she wrote for *Southern Review*, *Partisan Review*, and *Harper's Bazaar* were collected in 1942 in the book *The Company She Keeps*. She separated from Edmund Wilson in 1945, the same year that she was teaching literature at Bard College, and in 1946, she married Bowden Broadwater. In 1948, she taught one semester at Sarah Lawrence College and, in 1949, was a Guggenheim Fellow, an award that was repeated in 1959. Also in 1949, she received the *Horizon* literary prize from the publishers of her novel *The Oasis*. In 1961, she was divorced from Broadwater, married James Raymond West—a State Department official assigned to Paris—and went to live with him in France.

Two events dominated the 1960's for McCarthy. The first was the enormous popular success of her novel *The Group*, which became a number-one best-seller. The second was the Vietnam War; she was an outspoken critic of United States policy in Vietnam. During the 1970's she published two novels with social and political themes: *Birds of America* in 1971 and *Cannibals and Missionaries* in 1979; the latter, she said, would be her last novel.

In 1980, an offhand remark on *The Dick Cavett Show* embroiled McCarthy in a prolonged legal battle that became a cause célèbre in the literary community. McCarthy said of dramatist Lillian Hellman that "every word she writes is a lie, including 'and' and 'the.'" Hellman sued. The resulting legal maneuvering was costly for McCarthy (in contrast, the wealthy Hellman did not count the cost), ending only in 1984, when, after Hellman's death, the suit was dropped before going to trial. Meanwhile, legal issues aside, the controversy brought several of Hellman's autobiographical works under close scrutiny, and the consensus was that McCarthy's judgment, clearly stated in hyperbolic terms, was vindicated.

In 1987, McCarthy published *How I Grew*, the first installment in what was projected to be a multivolume intellectual autobiography. In general, critics found it inferior to *Memoirs of a Catholic Girlhood*, which had covered some of the same territory from a different perspective. McCarthy died in New York on October 25, 1989.

Analysis • Mary McCarthy's novels often feature herself, with an assumed name, as protagonist; she also exploited her husbands and other people close to her for fictional purposes. Her characters generally have a superior education or intellect so that citations and quotations from learned sources—mainly classical or artistic— spring into their conversations. This heightened discourse promotes compact paragraphs of dialogue, in which several persons speak to the same topic, in contrast with the usual fictional technique of a separate paragraph for each speaker. Yet, in the close conceptual unity of McCarthy's novels, lengthy paragraphs of extensive character analyses frequently fill several pages without interruption. As a result, the technique of several speakers in one paragraph seems to support the general schema. It supports, also, the paradigm of the group.

Structurally, the three novels preceding *The Group* develop around separate chapters, each presenting the viewpoints and the consciousness of the different characters; their point of unity is the common awareness of the social group. A protagonist, often a reflection of the author, generally emerges from among these peripheral persons, but the effect of each chapter remains that of the portrait or sketch.

Several factors of McCarthy's work can be inferred from this structure. As an orphan and a Roman Catholic among Protestants, she no doubt had an early sensitivity to the significance of the group and the outsider. Furthermore, the intensely autobiographical nature of her work blurs the lines of genre, so that her essays read like short stories and her short stories like essays. Genre distinction, then, becomes a problem in any analysis of her work. An example is *The Company She Keeps*, short stories that are pulled into book form and revolve around a central theme—the quest—and parallel the structure of her novels. Furthermore, McCarthy did not term *The Oasis* a "novel" but called it a *conte philosophique*. Also, several chapters of her novels were published individually as short stories before being incorporated in the novels. The effect of this technique raises the question of whether she pushed the boundaries of the traditional novel outward or merely retreated to its earliest phases of development. She lamented the loss of a "sense of character" in modern novels, saying it began to fade with D. H. Lawrence. She admired Leo Tolstoy, Gustave Flaubert, George Eliot, Charles Dickens, and "all the Elizabethans."

The dominant quality of McCarthy's work is satire, and much of it is achieved by exaggeration and generalization. The dominant organization is the pairing of a separate character with each chapter, infused with an occasional chorus of viewpoints. McCarthy compared the technique to ventriloquism: The author throws her voice into various characters who speak for her. The long paragraphs of explication or character analysis tend to minimize plot; the concentration is on the psychological effects of what are frequently trivial incidents—as in *The Oasis*, when a couple illegally picking berries on the group's farm destroys the group.

The themes of McCarthy's novels generally concern the social failures of a group—of utopian communities in *The Oasis*, of progressive education in *The Groves of Academe*, or of cultural progress in *The Group*. The interest in group attitudes can be best observed in the political content of McCarthy's novels, many of which feature a person who had some affiliation with the Communist Party and defected or failed to become a member. Her work also shows a persistent aversion to the efforts of Senator Joseph McCarthy to eradicate communists in the United States.

The Oasis • McCarthy's first novel, *The Oasis*, was published in *Horizon* under the title *A Source of Embarrassment* and puts into practice the theories of Arthur Koestler about "oases," small libertarian groups that would try, as McCarthy said, "to change the world on a small scale." Set at Pawlet, Vermont, at an abandoned hotel on an isolated mountain in 1946 or 1947, the novel brings together a group of about fifty people of varying backgrounds and motives. The characters seek to revive the concept of utopian communities and welcome defectors from Europe. Their efforts, however, remain confined to the daily problems of food gathering and management and fall short of the larger goals.

First, the group fails to agree on its purpose. The purists aspire to a millennium but the realists seek only a vacation or a retreat from atomic warfare. They disagree, also, about who should be permitted to join the group, and some oppose the admission of businessman Joe Lockman. Next, they find that intellect, good intentions, and the simple life without electricity do not bring about moral reform: Personal relationships and property ownership intrude. Joe Lockman leaves oil in the kitchen stove that singes the eyebrows of Katy Norell, and then, as a prank, he frightens Will Taub by pointing a gun at him. Later, when intruders pick their wild strawberries (the stolen fruit in their Eden), Katy is highly offended at the theft of *her* property, and Joe is indignant about the other colonists' attempts to drive away the berry pickers, until he realizes that it was his property, the gun, they used in the assault.

The first to defect from the community is Will Taub, in whom many readers recognized Philip Rahv, and Katy, who resembles Mary McCarthy, dreams of the dissolution of the community at the book's end. With Joe Lockman cast in the role of the outsider, with little plot and with incident minimized, and with much explication of philosophical theory and discussion of ideals and goals, the book sets the style for McCarthy's other novels.

The Groves of Academe • Suspense is greatly improved in McCarthy's next novel, *The Groves of Academe*, set in a small Pennsylvania college called Jocelyn and resembling Bard College. Directing its satire at progressive education, this novel pits the progressive against the classical, satirizes the small college in general, and exposes the evils of McCarthyism, focused in Senator Joseph McCarthy's House Committee on Un-American Activities. The group here is the English department faculty, from which Professor Henry Mulcahy finds himself dismissed. He rallies the faculty to his support, although he is a poor academician and deserves dismissal, and gains it through an appeal for sympathy for his wife and children. McCarthyism brought him to the position—the president hired him because he had been unjustly accused of being a communist sympathizer—and, finally, it accounts for his retention. Mulcahy loses his chief faculty supporter when she discovers that he lied about his wife's illness, but he gains another weapon through a visiting poet who recognizes him from Communist Party meetings. At the climax of the novel, the McCarthy scare is shown at its most evil: Protecting the college, the well-meaning president conducts an interview into Mulcahy's past, which results in Mulcahy's being charged with libel. The unstable Mulcahy triumphs and secures his position at Jocelyn—certain to continue bullying students and colleagues alike—and the president resigns.

A Charmed Life • In *A Charmed Life*, Martha Sinnott returns to a group of artistic people at New Leeds, a small New England village based on Wellfleet, Cape Cod, where she had lived with her former husband (much like McCarthy had lived at Wellfleet and returned with a second husband). Martha returns determined to be different from and independent of the New Leedsians who live a charmed life of many accidents, none of which kills them. Here, time, which signifies the mortal, is askew and awry, as indicated by the many problems with clocks and calendars. Part of Martha's anxiety about her return to New Leeds is the possibility of meeting her former husband (based on Edmund Wilson) with his new wife and child and the fear that he will reestablish domination over her. When he seduces her and she later finds herself pregnant, she cannot remember the date well enough to determine whether her former or present husband is the father. Her moral decision to have an abortion because she cannot live a lie results in her death; returning from borrowing money for the abortion, she drives on the right side of the road, contrary to New Leeds custom, and meets another car head-on. The charmed life of New Leeds goes on, but Martha lives and dies an outsider.

McCarthy called this novel a fairy tale. Loosely analogous to "Sleeping Beauty," Martha Sinnott pricks her hand at the beginning of the novel, lives in self-doubt on the fringes of the immortality of New Leeds (the timelessness of a century of sleep), and is awakened to the new existence of pregnancy and decision. The prince who wakens her with a kiss (the seduction), however, is an evil prince.

The Group • With a theme of the failure of modern progress, *The Group* was published in November, 1963. At that time, Betty Friedan's *The Feminine Mystique* (1962) and other feminist writings had focused on the problems of women, and the public was responsive to works focused on the problems of the emancipated woman. Although the novel is set in the seven years from 1933 to 1940, the progressiveness of the eight *cum* nine young Vassar women seemed to be the progress that was engulfing women of the 1960's. Like gleanings from an alumnae bulletin, the random appearances, different voices, and loose ends are not expected to be resolved. The undistinguished occupations of the group, also, confirm the alumnae magazine reports of most women graduates, but somehow more is expected of Vassar women. Not only the money but also increased competition for admission meant that, by 1963, most women could not get into Vassar College. For the general public, there is some comfort in the failure of the culturally advantaged.

The novel begins with the wedding of Kay Strong in 1933 and ends with her death seven years later at the age of twenty-nine. Of the eight members of the group who had lived in the same dormitory, plus one outsider, Kay seemed to be most forward-looking and progressive. Like McCarthy, she comes from the West and, immediately upon graduation, she marries her lover of some time, a mostly unemployed playwright named Harald Petersen who resembles Harold Johnsrud. Part of McCarthy's personality is dispersed among the other characters, especially Libby MacAusland, a woman of formidable intellect who writes book reviews and becomes a literary agent.

The elegant, beautiful, and wealthy Elinor Eastlake disappears into Europe and reemerges a lesbian prior to Kay's death. Polly Andrews becomes attached to a married man who is obviously well adjusted except that he pays twenty-five dollars a week for psychiatric counseling. Working in a hospital, Polly becomes engaged to another man, a psychiatrist who has defected from the profession and thus augments the satiric attack on psychiatry. Helena Davison, in Cleveland, remains the stable rich girl, highly intelligent and analytic. Priss Hartshorn marries a pediatrician, and, attempting to breast-feed her son and train him by modern theories, provides the satire on this aspect of progressivism. Pokey Prothero, from a household organized and represented by an invaluable butler, plans to become a veterinarian.

Kay, during a fight with Harald, gets a black eye and finds herself committed to a mental hospital. Despite Harald's admission that she does not belong there, she decides to stay for a rest and then disappears from the story until she reemerges after a divorce and a year in the West. Back East, ready to start a career again, she falls to her death while spotting planes from her window and becomes the first casualty of the war.

Representing a culmination of the group philosophy and the disjointed voices of the earlier novels, *The Group* with its timely feminist content earned for McCarthy a great deal of money and many appearances on talk shows and in magazines. Some Vassar alumnae were recognizable in it, and the film version did not name the college. This novel established McCarthy as a popular writer, but she did not attempt to capitalize on it with a follow-up novel. Instead, eight years later, she brought out a novel of a different sort altogether.

Birds of America • Departing from the group structure, McCarthy's next novel, *Birds of America*, begins in 1964 with Peter Levi's return at the age of nineteen to Rocky Port, Maine, after an absence of five years. During his absence, his favorite horned owl died. With his divorced and remarried mother, Rosamund, he searches for a waterfall that they cannot find—the victim of a highway project. In their respective ways, the village and the mother cling to fashions of the past but rapidly succumb to modernity.

Peter goes to the Sorbonne for his junior year in college but finds his ideals of French culture in conflict with the realities. His friends are American; he has a painful Thanksgiving dinner at an American general's home discussing vegetarianism and the war in Vietnam; he runs afoul of the French police while watching a demonstration; and he spends Christmas vacation in Rome where the masses of tourists interfere with his appreciation of the Sistine Chapel. Returned to Paris, he attempts in his Kantian way—"Behave as if thy maxim could be a universal law"—to help the street drunkards. Everywhere he goes, he tangles with human refuse, which is best revealed in a long letter home about the filth of Parisian toilets. Clinging to his preferences for nature, however, he grows vegetables and other plants in his apartment and joins a bird study group. At a zoo at the close of the novel, he is attacked by a swan while attempting to feed it from his hand. He wakens, later, in a hospital recovering from a reaction to a penicillin shot. At this point, philosopher Immanuel Kant speaks to him, saying that "nature is dead, my child."

Peter (obviously modeled on Reuel Wilson) calls his father "babbo," is familiar with Italy, speaks both French and Italian, and is an intellectual like his mother. This novel, much different from the other seven, is the only one with a clear and unmistakable protagonist. The group Peter satirizes are tourists as a group; but the group does not make up the novel's characters.

Cannibals and Missionaries • The group of *Cannibals and Missionaries*, originally formed as a committee of six to fly by Air France to Iran to investigate reports of the Shah's torturing of prisoners, expands, by the time the plane is hijacked to Holland, to twenty-four hostages and eight terrorists. Set during the administration of President Gerald Ford, the novel takes its title from the puzzle in which three cannibals and three missionaries must cross a river in a boat that will hold only two people, and if the cannibals outnumber the missionaries, they might eat the missionaries. In the novel, however, there is no clear indication as to which group represents the cannibals and which the missionaries.

In one passage of explication, McCarthy points out that the terrorists' demands accomplish nothing but the reabsorption into the dominant society of whatever they demanded; prisoners released, for example, are eventually returned to prison. Confined in a Dutch farmhouse, hostages learn of their terrorists' demands from television: $1.25 million, Holland's withdrawal from the North Atlantic Treaty Organization (NATO), the breaking of relations with Israel, and the release of "class war" prisoners from Dutch jails. Like the other groups in McCarthy's fiction, the members of this group are pulled together in a common cause; even though divided between hostages and terrorists, the hostages willingly aid the terrorists in some efforts and feel triumphant in the successful completion of a task, such as hiding the helicopter that brought them to the farmhouse. At the novel's conclusion, however, all but four are killed, one of whom claims that she has not been changed by the experience.

The European settings of the last two novels reflect McCarthy's travel experiences and utilize her interest in art. In *Cannibals and Missionaries*, McCarthy returned to her early interest in communism and to the group structure with separate narrative voices.

Although *The Groves of Academe* is still highly esteemed as an example of the academic novel, and *The Group* is read by students of popular fiction and women's issues, McCarthy's novels considered by themselves do not make up a lasting body of work. Rather, they derive their lasting significance from their place in the life and work of an exemplary woman of letters.

Grace Eckley

Other major works

SHORT FICTION: *The Company She Keeps*, 1942; *Cast a Cold Eye*, 1950; *The Hounds of Summer, and Other Stories*, 1981.

NONFICTION: *Sights and Spectacles, 1937-1956*, 1956; *Venice Observed*, 1956; *Memories of a Catholic Girlhood*, 1957; *The Stones of Florence*, 1959; *On the Contrary: Articles of Belief,* 1961; *Mary McCarthy's Theatre Chronicles, 1937-1962*, 1963; *Vietnam*, 1967; *Hanoi,* 1968; *The Writing on the Wall, and Other Literary Essays*, 1970; *Medina*, 1972; *The Mask of State*, 1974; *The Seventeenth Degree*, 1974; *Ideas and the Novel*, 1980; *Occasional Prose,* 1985; *How I Grew*, 1987; *Intellectual Memoirs: New York, 1936-1938*, 1992; *Between Friends: The Correspondence of Hannah Arrendt and Mary McCarthy, 1949-1975*, 1995 (Carol Brightman, editor); *A Bolt from the Blue, and Other Essays*, 2002 (A. O. Scott, editor).

Bibliography

Abrams, Sabrina Fuchs. *Mary McCarthy: Gender, Politics, and the Postwar Intellectual.* New York: Peter Lang, 2004. Study of gender and political issues in McCarthy's late writings.

Brightman, Carol. *Writing Dangerously: Mary McCarthy and Her World*. New York: Clarkson Potter, 1992. Supplements but does not supersede Carol W. Gelderman's earlier biography. Like Gelderman, Brightman was able to interview her subject, and her book reflects not only inside knowledge but also (as its subtitle suggests) a strong grasp of the period in which McCarthy published. Includes a biographical glossary and notes.

Epstein, Joseph. "Mary McCarthy in Retrospect." *Commentary* 95 (May, 1993): 41-47. Provides a summary of McCarthy's work; comments on her role in intellectual life in America; discusses the relationship of her life to her fiction.

Gelderman, Carol W. *Mary McCarthy: A Life*. New York: St. Martin's Press, 1988. Gelderman offers an objective biography of McCarthy. Although much of the narrative is familiar, the book is well written and amply documented. The photographs provide important perspective on McCarthy's childhood and a satisfying glimpse into her adult life. This biography makes good reading for a general audience as well as for a student of McCarthy.

Goldman, Sherli Evens. *Mary McCarthy: A Bibliography.* New York: Harcourt, Brace and World, 1968. Goldman explains that Mary McCarthy was "more collaborator than subject" in this work. The book is divided into five categories: books, contributions to books, contributions to periodicals, translations into foreign languages, and appendix of miscellanea. The appendix lists interviews, McCarthy's translations of French works, and Braille and recorded editions of books by McCarthy.

Kiernan, Frances. *Seeing Mary Plain: A Life of Mary McCarthy.* New York: W. W. Norton, 2000. A comprehensive biography full of vivid details and anecdotes but marred by a lack of focus on certain essential aspects of McCarthy's life and work.

Kufrin, Joan. *Uncommon Women.* Piscataway, N.J.: New Century, 1981. In a book that examines women who have succeeded within several different fields, McCarthy is "The Novelist" for the chapter so named. The portrayal of the writer is friendly and informal, largely the transcription of an interview in McCarthy's home in Maine. McCarthy comments on her writing process of extensive revision. The two photographs capture a sense of fun and humor in McCarthy. A light and readable piece.

McCarthy, Mary. *Conversations with Mary McCarthy.* Edited by Carol W. Gelderman. Jackson: University Press of Mississippi, 1991. A series of interviews with the author, dating from 1962 to 1989.

Pierpont, Claudia Roth. *Passionate Minds: Women Rewriting the World.* New York: Alfred A. Knopf, 2000. Evocative, interpretive essays on the life paths and works of twelve women, including McCarthy, connecting the circumstances of their lives with the shapes, styles, subjects, and situations of their art.

Stock, Irvin. *Mary McCarthy.* Minneapolis: University of Minnesota Press, 1968. Stock's forty-seven-page essay includes an overall critical comment on McCarthy's work, noting the moral concerns evident in her fiction. Stock also provides a brief biography. He summarizes and then provides analysis of *The Company She Keeps, Cast a Cold Eye, The Oasis, The Groves of Academe,* and *The Group.* Stock's character studies are particularly good.

Stwertka, Eve, and Margo Viscusi, eds. *Twenty-four Ways of Looking at Mary McCarthy: The Writer and Her Work.* Westport, Conn.: Greenwood Press, 1996. Part of the Contributions to the Study of World Literature series, this volume is based on essays presented at a conference on the author at Bard College in 1993.

Carson McCullers

Born: Columbus, Georgia; February 19, 1917
Died: Nyack, New York; September 29, 1967

Principal long fiction • *The Heart Is a Lonely Hunter,* 1940; *Reflections in a Golden Eye,* 1941; *The Ballad of the Sad Café,* 1943, serial (1951, book); *The Member of the Wedding,* 1946; *Clock Without Hands,* 1961.

Other literary forms • Carson McCullers published a number of short stories, some of which are included in the volume containing *The Ballad of the Sad Café* and some in a collection of short works, *The Mortgaged Heart* (1971), edited by her sister, Margarita G. Smith. The latter also contains some magazine articles and notes of her writing. McCullers adapted *The Member of the Wedding* for the stage in 1950 (a film version appeared in 1952). She wrote two plays, including *The Square Root of Wonderful* (1957). McCullers's poetry is published in *The Mortgaged Heart* and in a children's book, *Sweet as a Pickle and Clean as a Pig* (1964).

Achievements • Like William Faulkner, McCullers has literary kinship with those older, midnight-haunted writers—Edgar Allan Poe, Nathaniel Hawthorne, and Herman Melville among them—who projected in fable and with symbol the story of America's unquiet mind. Against her southern background she created a world of symbolic violence and tragic reality, indirectly lighted by the cool Flaubertian purity of her style. Of the writers of her generation, none was more consistent or thorough in achieving a sustained body of work.

Several of McCullers's works received critical acclaim. "A Tree, a Rock, a Cloud," a short story sometimes compared in theme to Samuel Taylor Coleridge's "The Rime of the Ancient Mariner" (1798), was chosen for the O. Henry Memorial Prize in 1942. The dramatic version of *The Member of the Wedding* was extremely successful, running on Broadway continuously for nearly fifteen months, and it was named for both the Donaldson Award and the New York Drama Critics Circle Award in 1950. In addition, McCullers was a Guggenheim fellow in 1942 and 1946, and she received an award from the American Academy of Arts and Letters in 1943.

Biography • Carson McCullers was born Lula Carson Smith on February 19, 1917, in Columbus, Georgia. Marguarite Smith, McCullers's mother, was very early convinced that her daughter was an artistic genius and sacrificed herself and, to some extent, McCullers's father, brother, and sister, to the welfare of her gifted child. McCullers grew up, therefore, with a peculiar kind of shyness and emotional dependence on her mother, combined with supreme self-confidence about her ability. McCullers announced early in life that she was going to be a concert pianist, and she indeed displayed a precocious talent in that direction. Smith placed her daughter under the tutelage of Mary Tucker, a concert musician, who agreed that McCullers was talented.

McCullers came to love Mrs. Tucker and her family with an all-consuming passion, a pattern she was to follow with a number of other close friends during her life. Dr. Mary Mercer, a psychiatrist friend of McCullers's during her later years, suggested that the emotional devastation of the adolescent girl in *The Member of the Wedding*, when she was not allowed to accompany her beloved brother and his bride on their honeymoon, was an expression of McCullers's despair when the Tuckers moved away from her hometown. She seemed to experience every break in human contact as personal betrayal or tragedy.

Writing was also an early enthusiasm of McCullers. As a child, she created shows to be acted by herself and her siblings in the sitting room. Her mother would gather in neighbors or relatives for an appreciative audience. In an article titled "How I Began to Write" (*Mademoiselle*, September, 1948), McCullers said that these shows, which she described as anything from "hashed-over movies to Shakespeare," stopped when she discovered Eugene O'Neill. She was soon writing a three-act play "about revenge and incest" calling for a cast of a "blind man, several idiots and a mean old woman of one hundred

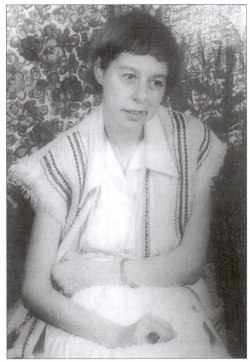

Library of Congress

years." Her next opus was a play in rhymed verse called *The Fire of Life*, starring Jesus Christ and Friedrich Nietzsche. Soon after, she became enthralled by the great Russian writers Fyodor Dostoevski, Anton Chekhov, and Leo Tolstoy—a fascination she never outgrew. Years later, she was to suggest, with considerable cogency, that modern southern writing is most indebted to the Russian realists.

The Smith household, while never wealthy, was not so hard-pressed for money as McCullers sometimes later pretended. Lamar Smith, her father, was a respected jeweler in Columbus, Georgia, and a skilled repairer of clocks and watches. There was enough money, at least, to send the seventeen-year-old McCullers to New York City to attend the famous Juilliard School of Music. There was not enough, however, to replace the tuition money she lost in the subway. Perhaps she was too moritified to ask for help, foreseeing that her father would simply send her a ticket to return home.

Whether through carelessness or naïveté, McCullers found herself almost penniless in New York. Having already paid her tuition for night classes at Columbia University, however, she intended to survive as best she could with whatever odd jobs she could find. Her inexperience and ineptness led to her being fired repeatedly. One way or another, McCullers managed to support herself through the school term. By the time she came home in the summer, she had begun to write in earnest, and the dream of being a concert pianist was entirely displaced by the vision of becoming a great writer. She had launched her publishing career by selling two short stories to *Story* magazine: "Wunderkind" and "Like That." Her first novel, *The Heart Is a Lonely Hunter*, was in its formative stages.

Back home, McCullers met a handsome young soldier, Reeves McCullers, who shared both her ambitions of living in New York and of becoming a writer. In 1936, Reeves left the army and traveled to New York to attend Columbia University, as McCullers was doing. His college career lasted only a few weeks, however, before he withdrew entirely to escort McCullers back home to Georgia to recover from one of her many serious illnesses.

In 1937, Carson and Reeves were married, although Reeves was financially in no condition to support a wife. Though idyllically happy at first, their marriage became increasingly troubled. Although McCullers's first novel, published when she was twenty-two, brought her immediate recognition in the literary world of New York, her husband met with continual frustration in his own ambitions. Their problems did not derive simply from the professional dominance of McCullers. Both she and her husband were sexually ambivalent. The repressed homosexuality and odd love triangles that are so characteristic of McCullers's fiction had some correlation to real-life situations. McCullers had a disconcerting tendency to fall in love with either men or women, and to suffer inordinately when such attentions were repulsed. As her fiction suggests, she believed that one of the central problems of living was to love and be loved in equal measure.

McCullers often left Reeves to his own devices when professional opportunities or invitations came her way. She was offered a fellowship, for example, in the prestigious Bread Loaf Writers' Conference, where she consorted with such persons as Robert Frost, Louis Untermeyer, John Marquand, and Wallace Stegner. During that same summer, she also met Erika and Klaus Mann, Thomas Mann's children, and Annemarie Clarac-Schwartzenbach, a prominent Swiss journalist and travel writer. McCullers fell deeply in love with the stunning Annemarie. When Annemarie left the country, it was another terrible "desertion" for McCullers. *Reflections in a Golden Eye*, McCullers's second novel, was dedicated to Annemarie.

In 1940, McCullers and her husband separated, and McCullers moved into a two-room apartment in a large Victorian house in Brooklyn Heights, owned by George Davis, editor of *Harper's Bazaar*. The old house became the temporary home for a stimulating group of artists, including poets W. H. Auden and Louis MacNeice, composer Benjamin Britten, tenor Peter Pears, fan dancer and writer Gypsy Rose Lee, and novelist Richard Wright. These were only the earlier residents. A group of musicians and composers, including Aaron Copland, Leonard Bernstein, and David Diamond, joined the ranks at one time or another. Diamond was to become another of those fateful friends who was emotionally involved with both McCullers and Reeves. Also temporarily in residence were Salvador Dali and his wife Gala, as well as other prominent Surrealist painters.

A new and terrifying illness drove McCullers back to the South to her mother's care. She was afraid this time that she was going blind. Years later, doctors declared that this episode, when she was barely twenty-four years old, was her first cerebral stroke. There was no paralysis, but her recovery was slow.

McCullers and Reeves tried again to live together in New York and for a time took comfort in a new intimacy with their friend David Diamond. McCullers was invited to Yaddo, a retreat for resident artists situated a few miles from Saratoga Springs, New York. The motherly overseer of the colony, Elizabeth Ames, became almost a second mother to McCullers, who returned again and again to this peaceful setting and considered it the place most conducive to writing.

McCullers eventually divorced Reeves; he went back into the service, became a much-decorated war hero, was wounded several times in action, and finally returned as an officer beloved by his men. McCullers was so admiring of his new role that they were remarried. As a civilian husband, however, Reeves could not maintain the independence and pride he had won as a soldier. He turned increasingly to drink and eventually expressed the desire to commit suicide. When, in Europe, he seemed determined that they should both hang themselves, McCullers fled from him in terror and returned home alone. Shortly thereafter, Reeves was found dead in a Paris hotel.

After McCullers finished *The Member of the Wedding*, which proved immensely popular, her friendship with dramatist Tennessee Williams encouraged her to attempt a stage adaptation of the work. After many trials in deciding on an agreeable version for the stage, the play finally was produced, starring Ethel Waters and Julie Harris. McCullers wrote one other play, *The Square Root of Wonderful*, which was not nearly so successful. *The Member of the Wedding* was eventually adapted into a motion picture with the original cast. John Huston produced a film version of another of McCullers's works, *Reflections in a Golden Eye*, shortly before her death.

McCullers's last years were a nightmare of pain, though she continued to maintain a fairly cheerful social life while partially paralyzed and often bedridden. She had two strokes; underwent several operations on her paralyzed left arm, leg, and hand; had a cancerous breast removed; broke her hip and elbow in a fall; and finally died after another massive stroke. She was fifty years old.

Analysis • Carson McCullers's fiction has a childlike directness, a disconcerting exposure of unconscious impulses in conjunction with realistic detail. She is like the candid child who announces that the emperor in his new clothes is really naked. She sees the truth, or at least a partial truth of the human psyche, then inflates or distorts that truth into a somewhat grotesque fable that is sometimes funny but always sad.

Such a tragicomic effect derives, apparently, from an unusual openness to subconscious direction, combined with conscious cultivation of a style that best exploits such material, weaving into it just enough objectively observed reality to achieve plausibility. McCullers herself explained the technique by which she achieved the fusion of objective reality with symbolic, psychic experience. In "The Russian Realists and Southern Literature," first published in *Decision*, July, 1941 (now available in *The Mortgaged Heart*), she speaks of the charge of cruelty that was brought against both Russian writers (particularly Fyodor Dostoevski) and southern writers such as William Faulkner and herself, though she does not refer to her own works.

> No single instance of "cruelty" in Russian or Southern writing could not be matched or outdone by the Greeks, the Elizabethans, or, for that matter, the creators of the Old Testament. Therefore it is not the specific "cruelty" itself that is shocking, but the manner in which it is presented. And it is in this approach to life and suffering that the southerners are so indebted to the Russians. The technique briefly is this: a bold and outwardly callous juxtaposition of the tragic with the humorous, the immense with the trivial, the sacred with the bawdy, the whole soul of a man with a materialistic detail.

What is peculiar to the Russians and the southerners is not the inclusion of farce and tragedy in the same work, but the fusion of the two so that they are experienced simultaneously. McCullers uses Faulkner's *As I Lay Dying* (1930) as an example of this technique. She could as effectively have demonstrated it with her own *Ballad of the Sad Café*, which is a masterpiece of tragicomedy. The relative lack of success of the earlier *Reflections in a Golden Eye* results partly, perhaps, from her inability to balance the sadomasochistic elements with elements of satire or farce. She reportedly claimed that incidents such as the rejected wife cutting off her nipples with garden shears were "hilariously funny." This may demonstrate an oddly warped sense of humor, a failure of craft, or simply ignorance about her own creative processes, or it may simply be a way of shunting off rational explanations of a work of art, a red herring to confuse critics. As a novelist, McCullers operates like a poet or perhaps like a Surrealist painter, who tells the truth but "tells it slant."

The thematic content of McCullers's works is consistent: All her stories deal with the metaphysical isolation of individuals and their desperate need to transcend this isolation through love. Love is the key to a magnificent transformation of leaden existence into gold, but the exalted state is doomed because love is so seldom reciprocated. Though this feeling (and it is more feeling than thought) may stem from McCullers's early fears and dependence on her mother, it strikes a universal chord. The fact that McCullers projects this terrible sense of unrequited love into all kinds of human relationships except that between mother and daughter may be suggestive in itself. In an interview with Virginia Spencer Carr, Lamar Smith, Jr., said that his sister did not depict a meaningful mother-daughter relationship in her fiction because she did not want to strip herself bare and show the utter dependency that she felt for her mother.

The Heart Is a Lonely Hunter • Nevertheless, McCullers successfully universalizes the state of metaphysical isolation as a perennial human condition, not merely a neurotic regression to childhood. Her first novel, *The Heart Is a Lonely Hunter,* has Mick Kelly as its child character, who clings to John Singer, the deaf-mute, who, she fancies, understands and sympathizes with her problems. McCullers's own definition of the character in "Author's Outline of 'The Mute'" (*The Mortgaged Heart*) reveals an almost transparent self-dramatization: "Her story is that of the violent struggle of a gifted child to get what she needs from an unyielding environment." Only metaphorically is Mick's struggle "violent," but even when McCullers presents physical violence in fiction it often seems to function as the objective correlative to mental anguish.

McCullers casts Jake Blount, the ineffectual social agitator, as a would-be Marxist revolutionary, but he may seem more like an overgrown frustrated child. Her outline says, "His deepest motive is to do all that he can to change the predatory, unnatural social conditions existing today. . . . He is fettered by abstractions and conflicting ideas. . . . His attitude vacillates between hate and the most unselfish love."

Dr. Benedict Copeland is the more believable character, representing the peculiar plight of the educated African American in the South, who has internalized white society's condemnation of black cultural traits. His daughter's black dialect and careless posture embarrass him, and he frowns on what he considers the irresponsible fecundity and emotionality of the black youth. What McCullers calls his "passionate asceticism" has driven away even his own family.

Biff Brannon, the proprietor of the local restaurant, is the dispassionate observer of people, sympathetic, in a distant way, with all human oddities. Like Mick, he seems almost a part of McCullers, a grown-up version of the child who sat silently in the corners of stores watching people, who loved to listen to the voices of African Americans, and who paid her dimes repeatedly to see the freaks in the side shows. Brannon is also sexually impotent, with homosexual leanings. He is cold and withdrawn with his wife and has a repressed attraction for Mick in her tomboyish prepuberty—an impulse that fades as soon as she shows sexual development.

All of these characters pivot around the deaf-mute, John Singer, who is the central symbol of humankind's metaphysical isolation. They take his silence as wisdom and pour out their hearts to his patient but unreceptive ears. He does lip-read, so he knows what they are saying, but he has no way to communicate with them in reply. Moreover, the experiences they confide to him seem so alien to his own that he does not really understand. Mick talks about music, which he has never heard; Jake Blount rants about the downtrodden working classes; Dr. Copeland speaks of his frustrations as a racial leader without any followers; and Biff Brannon simply looks on with no project of his own.

John Singer shares their universal need to love and communicate with a kindred soul. The object of his adoration is another mute, a sloppy, mentally disabled Greek named Antonopoulus, who loves nothing but the childish pleasure of a full stomach. When the Greek dies in an institution, Singer commits suicide. The whole pyramid of illusion collapses.

This bleak tale suggests that the beloved is created in the lover's mind out of the extremity of his need and projected upon whomever is available. Singer drew the love of these desperate souls on account of his polite tolerance of their advances coupled with an essential blankness. They looked into his eyes and saw their own dreams reflected there, just as Singer himself read a secret sympathy and understanding in the blank round face of Antonopoulus, who was actually incapable of such sentiments.

The haunting quality of this story may derive partly from the impression of getting an inside look at a multiple personality. McCullers displays a curious ability to divide her ambivalent psyche to create new, somewhat lopsided beings. McCullers had never seen a deaf-mute, for example, and when Reeves wanted to take her to a convention of deaf-mutes, she declined, saying she already knew John Singer. Marxist political agitators may have been just as foreign to her actual experience, but she could create one from the jumble of liberal sentiment she acquired through educated friends and through reading. If the issues were not clear in her own mind, it did not really matter, because Jake was a confused and drunken loser. McCullers has been praised by black writers for her sensitive portrayal of African Americans, yet the peculiar warmth of the relationship between Dr. Copeland's daughter Portia, her husband, and her brother suggests the triangular love affairs McCullers sometimes acted out in her own life and dramatized several times in other fiction.

Reflections in a Golden Eye • McCullers wrote *Reflections in a Golden Eye* in a short period of time, "for fun," she said, after the long session with *The Heart Is a Lonely Hunter.* The idea for the story germinated when, as an adolescent, she first went to Fort Benning, but she also drew on her experience of Fayetteville, where she and Reeves lived for a while, and nearby Fort Bragg. The story caused considerable shock in conservative southern communities. Americans generally were not prepared for a fictional treatment of homosexuality. A perceptive reader might suspect the latent homosexuality in Biff Brannon, but there is no doubt about Captain Penderton's sexual preferences. Moreover, the sadomasochism, the weird voyeurism, and the Freudian implications of horses and guns are unmistakable. If *The Heart Is a Lonely Hunter* is about love, *Reflections in a Golden Eye* is about sex and its various distortions. These characters are lonely, isolated people, driven by subconscious impulses. The story concerns two army couples, a houseboy, a rather primitive young man, all of them somewhat abnormal, and a horse. One suspects the horse is akin to a dream symbol for the ungovernable libido.

Captain Penderton is impotent with his beautiful wife, Leonora, but is drawn to her lover, Major Langdon. The major's wife is sickly and painfully aware of her husband's affair with Leonora. Mrs. Langdon is solicitously attended by a Filipino houseboy, who is also maladjusted. The other character is Private Williams, an inarticulate young man who seems to be a fugitive from somebody's unconscious (probably Captain Penderton's). He has a mystical affinity for nature, and he is the only person who can handle Leonora's high-spirited stallion, Firebird. Captain Penderton is afraid of the horse, and he both loves and hates Private Williams. D. H. Lawrence's *The Prussian Officer* (1914) may have provided a model for Penderton's relationship to Private Williams, since McCullers was an admirer of Lawrence. Private Williams is quite different, however, from the perfectly normal, healthy orderly who is the innocent victim of the Prussian officer's obsession. The silent Private Williams enacts a psychodrama that repeats, in different terms, the sexual impotence of Penderton. Having seen Leonora naked through an open door, he creeps into the Penderton house each night to crouch silently by her bedside, watching her sleep. When Penderton discovers him there, he shoots him. The scene in the dark bedroom beside the sleeping woman is loaded with psychological overtones. Not a word is spoken by either man. In one sense, the phallic gun expresses the captain's love-hate attraction to the private; in another sense, Penderton is killing his impotent shadow-self.

Technically speaking, *Reflections in a Golden Eye* is superior to McCullers's first novel; at least, it has an admirable artistic unity. Its four-part structure has the precision of a tightly constructed musical composition. In content, the story line seems as gothic as Edgar Allan Poe's "The Fall of the House of Usher" (1839), yet the style is objective and nonjudgmental—like the impersonal eye of nature in which it is reflected. McCullers was perfecting the kind of perception and style she spoke of in her essay on the Russian realists, presenting human action starkly without editorial comment.

The Ballad of the Sad Café • McCullers's next work, *The Ballad of the Sad Café*, was a more successful treatment of archetypal myth, with its psychodramatic overtones tempered this time by humor. Like the true folk ballad, it is a melancholy tale of love. The setting is an isolated southern village—little more than a trading post with a few dreary, unpainted buildings. The most prominent citizen is known as Miss Amelia, a strong, mannish, cross-eyed woman with a sharp business sense. She runs the general store and operates a still that produces the best corn liquor for miles around. There is nothing to do for entertainment in town except drink her brew, follow the odd career of this sexless female, and listen to the melancholy singing of the chain gang, which suggests a universal entrapment in the dreary reality of one's life.

The story concerns a temporary hiatus from boredom when Miss Amelia and the observing townspeople become a real community. Love provides the means for a temporary transcendence of Miss Amelia's metaphysical isolation and, through her, sheds a reflected radiance on all. Like John Singer, Miss Amelia chooses an odd person to love, a homeless dwarf who straggles into town, claiming to be her cousin and hoping for a handout. Although Miss Amelia had thrown out her husband, the only man who had ever loved her, because he expected sexual favors when they were married, she unaccountably falls in love with this pathetic wanderer. She takes Cousin

Lymon in and, because he likes company, begins a restaurant, which becomes the social center of the entire community. All goes well until the despised husband, Marvin Macy, is released from the penitentiary and returns to his hometown, bent on revenge for the monstrous humiliation Miss Amelia had visited upon him.

Another unusual threesome develops when Cousin Lymon becomes infatuated with Marvin Macy. The competition between Macy and Miss Amelia for the attention of Cousin Lymon comes to a tragicomic climax in a fistfight between the rivals. Miss Amelia, who has been working out with a punching bag, is actually winning when the treacherous Cousin Lymon leaps on her back, and the two men give her a terrible drubbing. Macy and Cousin Lymon flee after they vandalize Miss Amelia's store and her still in the woods. Miss Amelia is left in a more desolate isolation than she has ever known and becomes a solitary recluse thereafter. The coda at the end recalls again the mournful song of the chain gang.

There is no more somber image of spiritual isolation than the glimpse of the reclusive Miss Amelia at the window of her boarded-up café: "It is a face like the terrible, dim faces known in dreams—sexless and white, with two gray crossed eyes that are turned inward so sharply that they seem to be exchanging with each other one long and secret gaze of grief." This story, written in a style that precludes sentimentality, is surely McCullers's most successful treatment of unrequited love and betrayal. The fight scene is a satire of all traditionally masculine brawls for the love of a woman, witnessed by the entire community as a battle larger than life, for a prize both morally and physically smaller than life. Besides the satire on all crude American substitutes for the duel of honor, this story may also call to mind Faulkner's famous gothic tale "A Rose for Emily," about the genteel aristocratic lady who murdered her lover to keep him in her bed. Miss Emelia is certainly the absolute opposite to all conventions about the beautiful but fragile southern lady, who is entirely useless.

The Member of the Wedding • *The Member of the Wedding* is possibly the most popular of McCullers's novels, partly because it was converted into a successful Broadway play—in defiance of one critic's judgment that the novel is entirely static, totally lacking in drama. In fact, the story has a quality somewhat akin to closet drama, such as George Bernard Shaw's "Don Juan in Hell," which is performed by readers with no attempt at action. The endless conversation occurs in one spot, the kitchen of a lower-middle-class home in the South. There are occasional forays into the outer world, but always the principals return to the kitchen, where real experience and visionary ideals blend in an endless consideration of human possibilities.

The protagonist, a motherless adolescent girl named Frankie Addams, is the central quester for human happiness, foredoomed to disappointment. She is similar to Mick in *The Heart Is a Lonely Hunter.* It is no accident that both their names reflect the genderless state of prepuberty; moreover, neither has been indoctrinated into the attitudes and conventional expectations of little girls. In the isolation and boredom of Frankie's life, the only exciting event is the upcoming marriage of her older brother. Frankie conceives of the dream that will sustain her in the empty weeks of the long, hot summer: She will become a member of the wedding and join her brother and his bride on their honeymoon and new idyllic life of love and communion.

This impossible dream is the central issue of those long conversations in the kitchen where the girl is flanked by a younger cousin, John Henry, who represents the childhood from which Frankie is emerging, and the black maid, Berenice, who tries to reason with Frankie without stripping her of all solace. Ignorant as she is of the dynamics of sexual love, what Frankie aspires to is not a love so self-seeking as eros, nor quite so all-encompassing as agape. She envisions an ideal love that establishes a permanent and free-flowing communication among the members of a small, select group. This imagined communion seems to express an unvoiced dream of many, sometimes situated in a visionary future or an equally visionary past. Berenice, for all her gentle earthiness, shows that her vision of a golden age is in the past, when she was married to her first husband. She admits that after that man died, her other two marriages were vain attempts to recapture the rapport she had known with her first husband.

A curious irony of the story is that Frankie, with her persistent goal of escaping her isolated personal identity in what she calls the "we of me," actually comes closest to that ideal in the course of these endless conversations with the child and the motherly black woman. This real communion also passes away, as surely as the imagined communion with the wedded pair never materializes. John Henry dies before the end of the story, symbolic perhaps of the passing of Frankie's childhood. Reality and banality seem to have conquered in a world unsuited to the dreams of sensitive human beings.

Clock Without Hands • McCullers's last novel, *Clock Without Hands*, written during a period of suffering and ill health, moves beyond the not quite adult problems of adolescence at the cost of much of her lyricism. Perhaps the novel is a somewhat feeble attempt to emulate the moral power of Leo Tolstoy's *The Death of Ivan Ilyich* (1886). It concerns a very ordinary man who faces death from leukemia and suspects that he has never lived on his own terms. The theme is still loneliness and spiritual isolation, but it has taken on existential overtones. The protagonist, J. T. Malone, like Tolstoy's Ivan, discovers too late that moral dignity requires some kind of commitment to action. In his new and painful awareness of his own moral vacuity, there are few decisions left to make. He does make one small gesture, however, to redeem an otherwise meaningless life. He refuses to accept the community's order to bomb the home of an African American who had dared to move into a white neighborhood. McCullers's description of Judge Clane, Malone's aging friend, reveals with precision the peculiar combination of sentimentality and cruelty that characterizes conventional white racism of the old southern variety.

Although Carson McCullers will probably endure as a writer with a very special talent for describing the in-between world before a child becomes an adult, the no-man's-land of repressed homosexuality, and the irrational demands of love in the absence of any suitable recipient of love, the range of her fiction is quite limited. Somehow, the "child genius" never quite achieved maturity. Nevertheless, all people are immature or maimed in some secret way; in that sense, every reader must admit kinship to McCullers's warped and melancholy characters.

Katherine Snipes

Other major works

SHORT FICTION: *The Ballad of the Sad Café: The Novels and Stories of Carson McCullers*, 1951; *The Ballad of the Sad Café and Collected Short Stories*, 1952, 1955; *The Shorter Novels and Stories of Carson McCullers*, 1972.

PLAYS: *The Member of the Wedding*, pr. 1950, pb. 1951 (adaptation of her novel); *The Square Root of Wonderful*, pr. 1957, pb. 1958.

NONFICTION: *Illumination and Night Glare: The Unfinished Autobiography of Carson McCullers*, 1999 (Carlos L. Dews, editor).

CHILDREN'S LITERATURE: *Sweet as a Pickle and Clean as a Pig*, 1964.

MISCELLANEOUS: *The Mortgaged Heart*, 1971 (short fiction, poetry, and essays; Margarita G. Smith, editor).

Bibliography

Bloom, Harold, ed. *Carson McCullers*. New York: Chelsea House, 1986. Essays on McCullers's novels and major short stories. Includes introduction, chronology, and bibliography.

Carr, Virginia Spencer. *The Lonely Hunter: A Biography of Carson McCullers*. Garden City, N.J.: Anchor Press, 2003. First published in 1975, this nearly definitive biography offers an interesting read and provides significant biographical elements that are related to McCullers's works. The complexity, pain, and loneliness of McCullers's characters are matched by their creator's. Includes an extensive chronology of McCullers's life, a primary bibliography, and many endnotes.

_____. *Understanding Carson McCullers*. Columbia: University of South Carolina Press, 1990. A thoughtful guide to McCullers's works. Includes bibliographical references.

Clark, Beverly Lyon, and Melvin J. Friedman, eds. *Critical Essays on Carson McCullers*. New York: G. K. Hall, 1996. A collection of essays ranging from reviews of McCullers's major works to tributes by such writers as Tennessee Williams and Kay Boyle to critical analyses from a variety of perspectives.

Cook, Richard M. *Carson McCullers*. New York: Frederick Ungar, 1975. A good general introduction to McCullers's novels, short stories, and plays. Cook's analyses of the short stories and *The Ballad of the Sad Café* are especially good, though the book includes chapters on each of the novels, McCullers's life, and her achievements as well. Cook, while admiring McCullers, recognizes her limitations but nevertheless praises her success with portraying human suffering and isolation and enabling readers to relate to the most grotesque of characters. The book's endnotes and primary and secondary bibliographies may be useful in finding other sources.

Gleeson-White, Sarah. *Strange Bodies: Gender and Identity in the Novels of Carson McCullers*. Tuscaloosa: University of Alabama Press, 2003. Exploration of the gender and identity themes that permeate McCullers's novels.

James, Judith Giblin. *Wunderkind: The Reputation of Carson McCullers, 1940-1990*. Columbia, S.C.: Camden House, 1995. Examines McCullers's place in literature as a southern female author. Bibliographical references and an index are provided.

McDowell, Margaret B. *Carson McCullers*. Boston: Twayne, 1980. A good general introduction to McCullers's fiction, with a chapter on each of the novels, the short stories, and *The Ballad of the Sad Café*. Also included are a chronology, endnotes, and a select bibliography. Stressing McCullers's versatility, McDowell emphasizes the lyricism, the musicality, and the rich symbolism of McCullers's fiction as well as McCullers's sympathy for lonely individuals.

Rich, Nancy B. *The Flowering Dream: The Historical Saga of Carson McCullers*. Chapel

Hill, N.C.: Chapel Hill Press, 1999. An examination of McCullers's work, including her dramas. Bibliography.

Savigneau, Josyane. *Carson McCullers: A Life.* Translated by Joan E. Howard. Boston: Houghton Mifflin, 2001. The McCullers estate granted Savigneau access to McCullers's unpublished papers, which enables her to deepen the portrait painted by previous biographers.

Whitt, Margaret. "From Eros to Agape: Reconsidering the Chain Gang's Song in McCullers's *Ballad of the Sad Café.*" *Studies in Short Fiction* 33 (Winter, 1996): 119-122. Argues that the chain gang was a rare visual example of integration in an otherwise segregated South; notes the irony suggested through the song—that the men must be chained together to find harmony.

Ross Macdonald

Born: Los Gatos, California; December 13, 1915
Died: Santa Barbara, California; July 11, 1983

Principal long fiction • *The Dark Tunnel*, 1944 (as Kenneth Millar; pb. in England as *I Die Slowly*, 1955); *Trouble Follows Me*, 1946 (as Millar; pb. in England as *Night Train*, 1955); *Blue City*, 1947 (as Millar); *The Three Roads*, 1948 (as Millar); *The Moving Target*, 1949 (as John Macdonald; reissued as *Harper*, 1966); *The Drowning Pool*, 1950 (as John Ross Macdonald); *The Way Some People Die*, 1951 (as John Ross Macdonald); *The Ivory Grin*, 1952 (as John Ross Macdonald; reissued as *Marked for Murder*, 1953); *Meet Me at the Morgue*, 1953 (as John Ross Macdonald; pb. in England as *Experience with Evil*, 1954); *Find a Victim*, 1954 (as John Ross Macdonald); *The Barbarous Coast*, 1956; *The Doomsters*, 1958; *The Galton Case*, 1959; *The Ferguson Affair*, 1960; *The Wycherly Woman*, 1961; *The Zebra-Striped Hearse*, 1962; *The Chill*, 1964; *The Far Side of the Dollar*, 1965; *Black Money*, 1966; *The Instant Enemy*, 1968; *The Goodbye Look*, 1969; *The Underground Man*, 1971; *Sleeping Beauty*, 1973; *The Blue Hammer*, 1976.

Other literary forms • Ross Macdonald's reputation is based primarily on his twenty-four published novels, particularly on the eighteen that feature private detective Lew Archer. He also published a collection of short stories, *Lew Archer, Private Investigator* (1977), which includes all the stories from an earlier collection, *The Name Is Archer* (1955). *Self-Portrait: Ceaselessly into the Past* (1981) gathers a selection of his essays, interviews, and lectures about his own work and about other writers, including two essays first published in his *On Crime Writing* (1973). Macdonald wrote dozens of book reviews and several articles on conservation and politics.

Achievements • Macdonald was recognized early in his career as the successor to Dashiell Hammett and Raymond Chandler in the field of realistic crime fiction, and his detective, Lew Archer, was recognized as the successor to Sam Spade and Philip Marlowe. Macdonald's advance over his predecessors was in the greater emphasis he placed on psychology and character, creating a more humane and complex detective and more intricate plotting. He is generally credited with raising the detective novel to the level of serious literature. The Mystery Writers of America awarded him Edgar Allan Poe scrolls in 1962 and 1963. In 1964, *The Chill* was awarded the Silver Dagger by the Crime Writers' Association of Great Britain. The same organization gave his next novel, *The Far Side of the Dollar*, the Golden Dagger as the best crime novel of the year. Macdonald served as president of the Mystery Writers of America in 1965 and was made a Grand Master of that organization in 1974. In a review of *The Goodbye Look* in *The New York Times Book Review*, William Goldman called the Lew Archer books "the finest series of detective novels ever written by an American." His work has gained popular as well as critical acclaim: *The Goodbye Look*, *The Underground Man*, *Sleeping Beauty*, and *The Blue Hammer* were all national best-sellers. Three of his books have been made into successful motion pictures, two starring Paul Newman as Lew Archer: *The Moving Target* was made into the film *Harper* (1966), and *The Drowning Pool* was filmed in 1975. *The Three Roads* was filmed as *Double Negative* in 1979.

Hal Boucher

Biography • Ross Macdonald, whose real name is Kenneth Millar, was born in Los Gatos, California, on December 13, 1915. He published his early novels as Kenneth Millar or as John (or John Ross) Macdonald, but settled on the pseudonym Ross Macdonald by the time he wrote *The Barbarous Coast*, in order to avoid being confused with two other famous mystery writers: his wife, Margaret Millar, whom he had married in 1938, and John D. Macdonald. His family moved to Vancouver, British Columbia, soon after he was born, and he was reared and educated in Canada. After he graduated with honors from the University of Western Ontario in 1938, he taught English and history at a high school in Toronto and began graduate work at the University of Michigan in Ann Arbor during the summers. He returned to the United States permanently in 1941, when he began full-time graduate studies at Ann Arbor, receiving his master's degree in English in 1943. During World War II, he served as communications officer aboard an escort carrier in the Pacific and participated in the battle for Okinawa. In 1951, he was awarded a doctoral degree in English from the University of Michigan, writing his dissertation on the psychological criticism of Samuel Taylor Coleridge. Macdonald belonged to the American Civil Liberties Union and, a dedicated conservationist, was a member of the Sierra Club and helped found the Santa Barbara chapter of the National Audubon Society. He lived in Santa Barbara, California, from 1946 until his death from Alzheimer's disease on July 11, 1983.

Analysis • Ross Macdonald's twenty-four novels fall fairly neatly into three groups: Those in which Lew Archer does not appear form a distinct group, and the Archer series itself, which may be separated into two periods. His first four books, *The Dark Tunnel, Trouble Follows Me, Blue City*, and *The Three Roads*, together with two later works, *Meet Me at the Morgue* and *The Ferguson Affair*, do not feature Lew Archer. These six novels, especially the first three, are rather typical treatments of wartime espionage or political corruption and are primarily of interest to the extent that they prefigure the concerns of later works: *The Three Roads*, for example, contains Macdonald's first explicit use of the Oedipus myth as a plot structure and of California as a setting.

The first six Archer books, *The Moving Target, The Drowning Pool, The Way Some People Die, The Ivory Grin, Find a Victim*, and *The Barbarous Coast*, introduce and refine the character of Archer, build the society and geography of California into important thematic elements, and feature increasingly complex plots, with multiple murders and plot lines. Archer still shows traces of the influence of the hard-boiled detectives of Hammett and Chandler (he is named after Miles Archer, Sam Spade's partner in Hammett's *The Maltese Falcon*, 1930, but closely patterned after Philip Marlowe), but he also shows marks of the sensitivity and patience, the reliance on understanding and analysis, that separate him from his models. Even in these early books, Archer is more often a questioner than a doer.

The Doomsters • The next twelve Archer novels constitute Macdonald's major achievement. Crimes in these books are not usually committed by professional criminals but rather by middle-class people going through emotional crises. They followed a period of personal crisis in Macdonald's own life, during which he underwent psychotherapy; all these novels deal more or less explicitly with psychological issues. *The Doomsters*, although begun before his psychoanalysis, presents his first extended treatment of the plot of intrafamilial relations that dominates all the later books. Carl Hallman, a psychologically disturbed young man, appears at Archer's door after escaping from the state mental hospital. He has been confined there as a murder suspect in the mysterious death of his father. Although he knows himself to be legally innocent, he feels guilty for having quarreled violently with his father on the night of his death. This Oedipal tension between father and son, following the pattern of Sigmund Freud's famous interpretation, often serves as the mainspring of the plot in Macdonald's later novels. After hiring Archer to investigate the death, Carl panics and escapes again as Archer is returning him to the hospital. Carl's brother, Jerry, and sister-in-law, Zinnie, are subsequently murdered under circumstances that appear to incriminate Carl.

As it turns out, the case really began three years earlier, with the apparently accidental drowning of Carl's mother, Alicia. She had forced Carl's wife, Mildred, to undergo an abortion at gunpoint at the hands of Dr. Grantland. Mildred hit Alicia over the head with a bottle when she came out of anesthesia and assumed that she had killed her. Dr. Grantland actually killed Alicia and made it look like drowning, but he conceals this fact and uses his power over Mildred, who is becoming psychologically unstable, to persuade her to kill Carl's father. He has designs on the family's money, and Mildred is greedy herself. She is also influenced, however, by her hatred of her own father, who deserted her mother, and by her desire to possess Carl entirely, to gain his love for herself by eliminating conflicting familial claims to it. She murders his brother and sister-in-law, his only remaining family, as she increasingly loses touch with sanity. Women are frequently the murderers in Macdonald's books, and he analyzed the reasons behind this in an interview. He considered that people who have been victims tend to victimize others in turn, and he regarded American society as one that systematically victimizes women. Mildred's difficult childhood and gunpoint abortion provide a clear illustration of this theme.

The Galton Case • Although the focus on family psychology constituted a clean break with the Hammett and Chandler school as well as with most of his own early work, the next Archer novel, *The Galton Case*, was of even greater importance for Macdonald's career. In *The Doomsters*, the case is rooted in a crime committed three years earlier; in *The Galton Case*, as in most of the novels to follow, the present crime is rooted deeper in the past, in the preceding generation. This gives Macdonald the means to show the long-term effects of the influence of the family upon each of its members. The elderly Maria Galton hires Archer to trace her son Anthony, who had stolen money from his father after a quarrel (reminiscent of that between Carl Hallman and his father) and run off to the San Francisco area with his pregnant wife, Teddy, twenty-three years before. Archer discovers that Anthony, calling himself John Brown, was murdered not long after his disappearance. He also finds a young man calling himself John Brown, Jr., who claims to be searching for his long-lost father. Events lead Archer to Canada, where he learns that the young man is Theo Fredericks, the son of Nelson Fredericks and his wife. Mrs. Galton's lawyer, Gordon Sable, has planned Theo's masquerade as her grandson to acquire her money when she dies. However, a further plot twist reveals that Theo really is Anthony Galton's son. Fred Nelson had murdered Anthony twenty-three years before for the money he had stolen from his father and had taken Anthony's wife and son as his own under the name Fredericks.

This summary does not reflect the true complexity of the novel, which ties together a number of other elements, but does bring out the major theme of the son searching for his father, a theme that will recur in later works such as *The Far Side of the Dollar, The Instant Enemy, The Goodbye Look, The Underground Man,* and *The Blue Hammer.* As Macdonald explains in his essay "Writing *The Galton Case*" (1973), this plot is roughly shaped on his own life. His own father left him and his mother when he was three years old. Like Macdonald, John Brown, Jr., was born in California, grew up in Canada, and attended the University of Michigan before returning to California. It is interesting that each man assumed his lost father's name: Macdonald was Kenneth Millar's father's middle name. This transformation of personal family history into fiction seems to have facilitated the breakthrough that led him to write the rest of his novels about varying permutations of the relations between parents and children.

The Zebra-Striped Hearse • The exploration of the relations among three generations of fathers and sons in *The Galton Case* was followed by examinations of father and daughter relationships in *The Wycherly Woman* and *The Zebra-Striped Hearse.* Macdonald always counted the latter among his favorites for its intensity and range. In *The Zebra-Striped Hearse,* Archer is hired by Mark Blackwell to investigate his daughter Harriet's fiancé, Burke Damis, with a view to preventing their marriage. The implication is made that Mark sees Damis as a rival for his daughter's love. Archer discovers that Damis is really Bruce Campion and is suspected of having murdered his wife, Dolly, and another man, Quincy Ralph Simpson. Suspicion shifts to Mark when it is revealed that he is the father of Dolly's baby and then to Mark's wife, Isobel, who knew Dolly as a child. Harriet disappears, and Mark confesses to murdering her, Dolly, and Simpson before committing suicide. However, Archer believes that Harriet is still alive and tracks her down in Mexico. She had killed Dolly to clear the way for her marriage to Bruce and had also killed Simpson when he discovered her crime. Underlying her motive for Dolly's murder, however, is another Freudian pattern. The child of Mark and Dolly is Harriet's half brother, making Dolly a sort of mother figure and, by extension, making her husband, Bruce, a sort of father figure. Harriet thus symbolically kills her mother and marries her father.

The Chill • *The Chill* features one of Macdonald's most complex plots, but at its center is another basic family relationship, this time between a mother and son. Archer is brought into the case by Alex Kincaid, who hires him to find his wife, Dolly, who has disappeared the day after their wedding after a visit from an unknown man. The visitor turns out to have been her father, Thomas McGee, who has just been released from prison after serving a ten-year sentence for the murder of his wife and Dolly's mother, Constance. Later it is revealed that he had convinced her of his innocence and told her that Constance was having an affair with Roy Bradshaw. To learn more about Roy, Dolly has left Alex to go to work for Roy's mother, Mrs. Bradshaw, as a driver and companion. Shortly thereafter, she is found, hysterical, at the Bradshaws', talking about the murder of her college counselor, Helen Haggerty. Helen is soon discovered murdered and the weapon used is found under Dolly's mattress, though under circumstances that suggest that it may have been planted there. Archer learns from Helen's mother that she had been deeply affected by a death that occurred twenty years before. Luke Deloney had been killed in a shooting that was ruled accidental on the basis of an investigation that was conducted by Helen's father, but Helen was convinced that the facts had been covered up. Luke's widow admits to Archer that there had been a cover-up, that her husband committed suicide. Archer later discovers another connection between the recent death and those of ten and twenty years ago: Roy Bradshaw was the elevator boy at the building in which Luke died.

An investigation of Roy reveals that he has secretly married Laura Sutherland, having recently obtained a divorce from a woman named Letitia Macready. Archer confronts Mrs. Bradshaw with the latter fact (though not the former), and after an initial denial she confirms that twenty years ago Roy had briefly been married to a much older woman. Letitia turns out to have been the sister of Luke's wife, and it was rumored that she was having an affair with her sister's husband. Letitia apparently died in Europe during World War II, shortly after Luke's death.

Archer eventually draws a fuller story out of Roy: Luke, who was indeed Letitia's lover, found her in bed with Roy. There had been a violent struggle, during which Letitia accidentally shot and killed Luke. Roy married her and took her to Europe, later returning with her to America. He had been leading a secret double life ever since, concealing Letitia, now quite old and sick, from all of his friends as well as from the police and, especially, from his possessive mother. During this confession, Archer answers a telephone call and hears Laura, who believes that she is speaking to Roy, tell him that "she" has discovered their secret marriage. Roy attacks Archer at this news and escapes in his car to attempt to intercept the other woman, who had vowed to kill Laura. Roy is killed when Mrs. Bradshaw's car crashes into his. Archer knows by now that Mrs. Bradshaw is not Roy's mother, but his first wife: She is Letitia Macready. Roy has acted out the Oedipal drama of the death of a father figure, Letitia's lover Luke, and the marriage to a mother figure, the older woman who posed as his real mother. (Macdonald develops the obverse of this plot in *Black Money*, which pairs a young woman with a much older man.) Letitia murdered Constance McGee because Roy had been having an affair with her and murdered Helen Haggerty in the belief that it was she rather than Laura Sutherland whom Roy was currently seeing.

This unraveling of the plot has come a long way from Alex Kincaid's request that Archer find his wife, but one of the characteristics of Macdonald's later novels is the way in which seemingly unrelated events and characters come together. The deeper Archer goes into a set of circumstances involving people who know one another, the more connectedness he finds. These novels all have large casts of characters and a series of crimes, often occurring decades apart. After the proper connections are made, however, there is usually only one murderer and one fundamental relationship at the center of the plot. All the disparate elements, past and present, hang together in one piece.

Although Freudian themes continued to dominate Macdonald's work, he often combined them with elements adapted from other stories from classical mythology or the Bible. *The Far Side of the Dollar* has been seen as a modern, inverted version of the story of Ulysses and Penelope. Jasper Blevins, the fratricidal murderer of *The Instant Enemy*, explicitly draws the analogy between his story and that of Cain and Abel. He has also murdered one of his stepfathers, adding the Oedipal masterplot to the biblical plot, and murdered his own wife in one of the series' most violent books, perhaps reflecting the violence of the wartime period during which the book was written. The complex events of *The Goodbye Look* are catalyzed by the search for a gold box that is specifically compared to Pandora's box. Again the myth is combined with the primal story of the parricide, this time committed by a child. All three of these books also repeat the quintessential Macdonald plot of a young man's search for his missing father.

The Underground Man • The search for the absent father also sets in motion the events of *The Underground Man*, probably the most admired of Macdonald's works. This novel, together with his next, *Sleeping Beauty*, also reflects its author's abiding concern with conservation. Each novel examines an ecological crime as well as a series of crimes committed against individuals. In *Sleeping Beauty*, Macdonald uses an offshore oil spill, inspired by the 1967 spill near his home in Santa Barbara, as a symbol of the moral life of the society responsible for it, in particular that of the Lennox family, which runs the oil corporation and is also the locus of the series of murders in the book. In *The Underground Man*, the disaster of a human-made forest fire serves similar ends. The story begins unexceptionally: Archer is taking a day off at home, feeding the birds in his yard. He strikes up an acquaintance with young Ronny Broadhurst and Ronny's mother, Jean, who are staying at the home of Archer's neighbors. The boy's father, Stanley, disrupts the meeting when he drives up with a young girl, later identified as Sue Crandall, and takes his son to visit Stanley's mother, Elizabeth Broadhurst. They never pay the planned visit, and when Jean hears that a fire has broken out in that area, she enlists Archer to help her look for them. On the way there, Jean explains that her husband has gradually become obsessed by his search for his father, Leo, who apparently ran away with Ellen Kilpatrick, the wife of a neighbor, Brian, some fifteen years ago. It turns out that Stanley, accompanied by Ronny and Sue, obtained a key from Elizabeth's gardener, Fritz Snow, and had gone up to her cabin on a mountain nearby. There, Archer finds Stanley, murdered and half-buried. The fire originated from a cigarillo Stanley dropped when he was killed, creating a causal as well as symbolic link between the personal and ecological disasters.

After an investigation that is complex even by Macdonald's standards, Archer is able to reconstruct the past events that explain those of the present. The seeds of the present crimes are found in the previous generation. Eighteen years ago, Leo Broadhurst impregnated Martha Nickerson, an underage girl. She ran away with Fritz Snow and Al Sweetner in a car they stole from Lester Crandall. The incident was planned by Leo and Martha to provide a scapegoat to assume the paternity of her coming child. When they were tracked down, Al went to jail for three years, Fritz was sentenced to work in a forestry camp for six months, and Martha married Lester Crandall. Three years later, Leo was having an affair with Ellen Kilpatrick. She went to Reno to obtain a divorce from her husband, Brian, and waited there for Leo to join her.

While Ellen was gone, Leo went up to the cabin with Martha and their child, Sue. Brian, who knew about his wife's affair with Leo and wanted revenge, discovered the renewal of this earlier affair and informed Leo's wife, Elizabeth. She went up to the mountain cabin and shot her husband, believing that she killed him. Stanley, who had followed his mother that night, was an aural witness to the shooting of his father, as was Susan, also Leo's child. However, Leo had not been killed by the bullet. He was stabbed to death, as he lay unconscious, by Edna Snow, Fritz's mother, in revenge for the trouble that Leo and Martha's affair had caused her son and also as a self-appointed agent of judgment on Leo's adulteries. She forced Fritz and Al to bury Leo near the cabin. Fifteen years later, on almost the same spot, she murders Stanley, who is on the verge of discovering his father's body and Edna's crime. Life moves in a circle as Ronny witnesses Stanley's death in the same place that Stanley witnessed Leo's shooting. The connection is reinforced by Sue's presence at both events.

The Blue Hammer • The last novel Macdonald wrote is *The Blue Hammer,* and whether he consciously intended it to be the last, it provides in certain ways an appropriate conclusion to the series. It is the first time, apart from a brief interlude in *The Goodbye Look,* that Archer has a romantic interest. The effects of a lack of love preoccupy all the Archer novels, and Archer recognizes in this book that the same lack has had its effects on him. He has been single since his divorce from his wife, Sue, which took place before the first book begins. In the last book, he meets and soon falls in love with Betty Jo Siddon, a young newspaper reporter.

Macdonald knew that Raymond Chandler was unable to continue the Philip Marlowe novels after marrying off his detective, and perhaps he intended to end his own series similarly. It seems that the genre requires a detective who is himself without personal ties, who is able to and perhaps driven to move freely into and then out of the lives of others. Indeed, the involvement of Betty in the case does create a tension between Archer's personal and professional interests. Another suggestion that *The Blue Hammer* may have been intended to be the last of the Archer novels lies in its symmetry with the first, *The Moving Target.* In the earlier book, Archer kills a man in a struggle in the ocean, the only such occurrence in the eighteen books and an indication of the extent to which the compassionate Archer differs from his more violent predecessors. In the last book, he finds himself in a similar struggle, but this time manages to save his adversary. Archer specifically parallels the two events and feels that he has balanced out his earlier sin, somehow completing a pattern.

The plot of *The Blue Hammer* is built around the Dostoevskian theme of the double, a theme that Macdonald treated before in *The Wycherly Woman,* in which Phoebe Wycherly assumes the identity of her murdered mother, and in *The Instant Enemy,* in which Jasper Blevins takes on the role of his murdered half brother. The motif is developed here in its most elaborate form and combined with the familiar themes of the crimes of the past shaping those of the present and of the son's search for his true father, forming an appropriate summation of the major themes of MacDonald's entire Archer series.

Thirty-two years ago, Richard Chantry stole the paintings of his supposed half brother, William Mead, then serving in the Army, and married William's girlfriend Francine. William murdered Richard when he returned and assumed his identity as Francine's husband, though he had already married a woman named Sarah and had a son, Fred, by her. Seven years later, Gerard Johnson, a friend of William from the Army, appears at William's door with Sarah and Fred, threatening to blackmail him.

William kills Gerard and then takes his name, in a doubling of the theme of doubleness. He returns to live with Sarah and Fred and remains a recluse for twenty-five years to hide his crimes.

The case begins for Archer when he is called in to locate a painting that has been stolen from Jack Biemeyer. He learns that it was taken by Fred Johnson, who wanted to study it to determine whether it was a recent work by the famous artist Richard Chantry, who had mysteriously vanished twenty-five years before. If genuine, it would establish that the painter was still alive. Fred had seen similar pictures in the Johnson home and had formed the idea that Chantry might be his real father. William steals the painting, which is one of his own works, in a doubling of his earlier theft of his own paintings from Richard. The painting had been sold by Sarah to an art dealer, and William is forced to kill again to prevent the discovery of his true identity and his earlier murders. By the book's guardedly positive resolution, three generations of men—Fred Johnson; his father, William Mead; and Jack Biemeyer, who turns out to be William's father—have all come to the admission or recognition of their previously concealed identities and have come to a kind of redemption through their suffering.

Macdonald's work, in terms of quantity as well as quality, constitutes an unparalleled achievement in the detective genre. The twenty-four novels, particularly the eighteen that feature Lew Archer, form a remarkably coherent body of work both stylistically and thematically. The last twelve Archer books have received especially high critical as well as popular acclaim and have secured Macdonald's standing as the author of the finest series of detective novels ever written, perhaps the only such series to have bridged the gap between popular and serious literature.

William Nelles

Other major works

SHORT FICTION: *The Name Is Archer,* 1955 (as John Ross Macdonald); *Lew Archer, Private Investigator,* 1977; *Strangers in Town: Three Newly Discovered Mysteries,* 2001 (Tom Nolan, editor).

NONFICTION: *On Crime Writing,* 1973; *Self-Portrait: Ceaselessly into the Past,* 1981.

Bibliography

Bruccoli, Matthew J. *Ross Macdonald.* San Diego: Harcourt Brace Jovanovich, 1984. Describes the development of Macdonald's popular reputation as a prolific author of detective fiction and his critical reputation as a writer of literary merit. Includes illustrations, an appendix with an abstract of his doctoral thesis, notes, a bibliography, and an index.

Bruccoli, Matthew J., and Richard Layman. *Hardboiled Mystery Writers: Raymond Chandler, Dashiell Hammett, Ross Macdonald.* New York: Carroll and Graf, 2002. A handy supplemental reference that includes interviews, letters, and previously published studies. Illustrated.

Gale, Robert. *A Ross Macdonald Companion.* Westport, Conn.: Greenwood Press, 2002. A Macdonald reference work, including listings of works, characters, family members, and professional acquaintances, as well as a select bibliography.

Kreyling, Michael. *The Novels of Ross Macdonald.* Columbia: University of South Carolina Press, 2005. A penetrating examination of Macdonald's eighteen detective novels.

Mahan, Jeffrey H. *A Long Way from Solving That One: Psycho/Social and Ethical Implications of Ross Macdonald's Lew Archer Tales.* Lanham, Md.: University Press of America, 1990. Explores the Archer stories and their importance in the detective-fiction canon. Includes bibliographical references.

Nolan, Tom. *Ross Macdonald: A Biography.* New York: Charles Scribner's Sons, 1999. The first full-length biography of Macdonald. Discusses the origins of the novels and critical responses to them.

Schopen, Bernard A. *Ross Macdonald.* Boston: Twayne, 1990. A sound introductory study, with a chapter on Macdonald's biography ("The Myth of One's Life"), on his handling of genre, his development of the Lew Archer character, his mastery of the form of the detective novel, and the maturation of his art culminating in *The Underground Man.* Provides detailed notes and an annotated bibliography.

Sipper, Ralph B., ed. *Ross Macdonald: Inward Journey.* Santa Barbara, Calif.: Cordelia Editions, 1984. This collection of twenty-seven articles includes two by Macdonald, one a transcription of a speech about mystery fiction and the other a letter to a publisher that discusses Raymond Chandler's work in relation to his own. Contains photographs and notes on contributors.

Skinner, Robert E. *The Hard-Boiled Explicator: A Guide to the Study of Dashiell Hammett, Raymond Chandler, and Ross Macdonald.* Metuchen, N.J.: Scarecrow Press, 1985. An indispensable volume for the scholar interested in tracking down unpublished dissertations as well as mainstream criticism. Includes brief introductions to each author, followed by annotated bibliographies of books, articles, and reviews.

South Dakota Review 24 (Spring, 1986). This special issue devoted to Macdonald, including eight articles, an editor's note, photographs, and notes, is a valuable source of criticism.

Speir, Jerry. *Ross Macdonald.* New York: Frederick Ungar, 1978. Serves as a good introduction to Macdonald's work, with a brief biography and a discussion of the individual novels. Includes chapters on his character Lew Archer, on alienation and other themes, on Macdonald's style, and on the scholarly criticism available at the time. Contains a bibliography, notes, and an index.

Wolfe, Peter. *Dreamers Who Live Their Dreams: The World of Ross Macdonald's Novels.* Bowling Green, Ohio: Bowling Green State University Press, 1976. This detailed study contains extensive discussions of the novels and a consideration of the ways in which Macdonald's life influenced his writing. Includes notes.

Thomas McGuane

Born: Wyandotte, Michigan; December 11, 1939

Principal long fiction • *The Sporting Club*, 1969; *The Bushwhacked Piano*, 1971; *Ninety-two in the Shade*, 1973; *Panama*, 1978; *Nobody's Angel*, 1982; *Something to Be Desired*, 1984; *Keep the Change*, 1989; *Nothing but Blue Skies*, 1992; *The Cadence of Grass*, 2002.

Other literary forms • In addition to writing novels, Thomas McGuane produced work for motion pictures and for popular magazines. He wrote the screenplay and directed the film version of *Ninety-two in the Shade* (1975), wrote the scripts for *Rancho De-Luxe* (1973) and *The Missouri Breaks* (1975), and shared credit with Bud Shrake for *Tom Horn* (1980) and with Jim Harrison for *Cold Feet* (1989). *An Outside Chance: Essays on Sport* (1980) contains many of his magazine pieces, and *To Skin a Cat* (1986) is a collection of short fiction.

Achievements • Early in his career, McGuane was heralded as one of the most promising writers of his generation, one with a good chance to become a major American writer. He appeared on the cover of *The New York Times Book Review* and was compared favorably with Ernest Hemingway, William Faulkner, and Saul Bellow. *The Bushwhacked Piano* won the Rosenthal Award, and *Ninety-two in the Shade* was nominated for a National Book Award. During the mid-1970's, however, when he began to devote the majority of his energies to writing for films, McGuane was dismissed as a sellout. During the late 1970's, his film career seemingly over, McGuane returned to publishing novels. Although Hollywood would continue to option screenplays written during the 1970's, McGuane maintained that novels were his true calling and that his goal was to be "a true man of literature, . . . a professional." *Something to Be Desired* and *Keep the Change* reaffirmed his position as a contender for inclusion in the American canon. His offbeat 2002 novel, *The Cadence of Grass*, about a dysfunctional Montana family, helped sustain that position. In 1989, Thomas McGuane received the Montana Centennial Award for Literature.

Biography • Thomas McGuane was born in Wyandotte, Michigan, on December 11, 1939. He graduated with honors from Michigan State University in 1962, took an M.F.A. from the Yale Drama School in 1965, and spent 1966-1967 at Stanford on a Wallace Stegner Fellowship. His parents were New England Irish who migrated to the Midwest, where his father became an auto-parts tycoon. McGuane once stated that he inherited his storytelling impulse from his mother's family, who loved verbal sparring and yarn spinning. Newspaper and magazine articles on McGuane often comment on the manic behavior, heavy drinking, and drug use that marked his film years, as well as on his eventual return to sobriety, family life, and hard work. McGuane chose to pursue a career as a writer apart from life in the academic world, believing that his chances of writing interesting novels would be diminished were he to confine himself to life in English departments.

McGuane developed an interest in raising and training cutting horses. He became a champion horse cutter, competing regularly in rodeos, and an accomplished sailor and fisherman, spending a part of every year at fishing haunts in Florida and Georgia. He also began to direct his energies toward conservation, working as director of American Rivers and of the Craighead Wildlife-Wildlands Institute.

Analysis • Thomas McGuane's fictional universe is a "man's world." His protagonists appear to do whatever they do for sport and to escape ordinary reality. They seek a world where they can, without restraint, be whomever they choose to be. This goal puts them at odds with prevailing social customs and middle-class ideas of morality and achievement. However, most of these quests end in frustration. Finding themselves quite apart from the normal flow of society, McGuane's protagonists must try all the harder to fulfill themselves. As a result, they easily become self-absorbed and further jeopardize whatever ties they might once have had to conventional life. Usually such a tie is to a woman,

© Kurt Markus

who, for her own self-fulfillment, must forsake the protagonist in the end.

The Sporting Club • McGuane's first novel, *The Sporting Club*, concerns the adventures of well-to-do Michiganders who maintain the exclusive and grand Centennial Club, to which they repair to fish and hunt. The story is limited to the point of view of James Quinn, who has emerged from a protracted adolescence to take over the family's auto-parts factory. Quinn's friend Vernor Stanton, however, refuses to take up the ordinary life and spends his time in the pursuit of games. Stanton is bored by the elitist pretensions of the club members and the pride they take in its noble heritage, and he is frustrated with Quinn for outgrowing the need for freedom and frolic. Stanton engineers a series of adventures that ultimately result in the collapse of the club. The noble pretensions of the membership are exploded when Stanton unearths a photograph that shows their ancestors engaged in an outlandish "sexual circus at full progress." After the current members see the photograph, the pretense upon which they build their lives collapses, and they run rampant with, as Quinn puts it, "moral dubiousness," emulating the sexual circus of the forefathers. In this way, McGuane manages to show that the established social order is rotten at its foundation, and the only sensible thing to do is to quest for a life in which one determines one's own values. Exposing this truth does nothing, however, for the survival of the McGuane protagonists. By the end of the aftermath occasioned by the photograph, Stanton is living under the surveillance of mental health workers at what is left of the club, and Quinn returns to the family business. They are no longer freewheeling protagonists able to make "the world tense."

The Bushwhacked Piano • In *The Bushwhacked Piano*, Nicholas Payne is more fortunate. Even though his father has the finest law practice in Detroit, Payne has no intention of doing anything respectable. He wants no part of his father's "declining snivelization" and "the pismire futilities of moguls." Payne does, however, want Ann Fitzgerald, an aspiring poet and photographer, whom he sees as almost a goddess.

Ann's parents do not approve of Payne; appearances, hard work, and achievement mean everything to them. They take Ann from Michigan to their ranch in Montana, but Payne follows because movement appeals to him, as well as the romantic idea of an almost unworldly mate. Ann is also sleeping with an establishment boyfriend whom she will not give up completely because she knows that someday she will have to behave like a conventional adult. For now, however, camera in hand, she joins Payne on an expedition to Florida to sell fraudulent bat towers. She goes more for the experience than simply to be with Payne, and ultimately she leaves him.

Payne not only loses Ann but also is arrested for selling a useless bat tower. Nevertheless, breaking the law is not as serious as breaking conventions. Payne goes free when he agrees to reenact his trial for a television program. Life, McGuane seems to say, is indeed a bewildering proposition, and the only way to emerge victorious is to determine one's goals and always keep them uppermost in mind. Indeed, neither the loss of Ann nor the scrape with the law has a lasting effect on Payne. Those who live the conventional life will never understand Payne, but he will not relent. The novel ends with Payne proclaiming, "I am at large," which is the same language used to describe an outlaw on the loose. Payne's movement outside conventional spheres will not stop. He is, for better or for worse, in charge of his own life, the artist of his own destiny.

Ninety-two in the Shade • In *Ninety-two in the Shade*, Thomas Skelton attempts to engineer his own fate when he tries to become a fishing guide with his own skiff off Key West. Nicole Dance, an established guide and murderer, forbids him to do so. When Dance plays a joke on Skelton, the young man burns Dance's skiff in retaliation. Dance vows to kill Skelton if he guides, but Skelton guides anyway, his fulfillment depending on it. The situation here is much the same as in earlier McGuane fiction. The protagonist must assert himself against the normal flow of life. With his life in danger, Skelton ought not to guide, but he knows that "when what you ought to do [has] become less than a kind of absentee ballot you [are] always in danger of lending yourself to the deadly farce that surrounds us." Couched in McGuane's wisecracking language is the idea that the deadly farce occurs when one absents oneself from vital energies and capitulates to the flow of ordinary life. Skelton must stand up for the self he desires to be and attempt the life he wants.

Ninety-two in the Shade could be considered McGuane's most optimistic book if it were not for the fact that when Skelton becomes a fishing guide, Dance kills him. Until the very end, Tom seems to have everything going his way. He has determined his own values and his own fulfillment. He has the support of family and a fulfilling love relationship with Miranda, a local schoolteacher. However, he also has his feud with Nicole Dance, who shoots him "through the heart." In spite of the protagonist's courage to pursue goals and the conviction to stand up to adversity, life does not come equipped with happy endings.

Panama • McGuane's fourth novel, *Panama*, more clearly points up the frustrations of the unconventional life. Protagonist Chester Hunnicutt (Chet) Pomeroy has become an overnight sensation, performing all the loathsome acts of the imagination for audiences. He has, for example, crawled out of the anus of a frozen elephant and fought a duel in his underwear with a baseball batting practice machine. He also vomited on the mayor of New York, which ended his career. As the novel opens, Chet has returned to Key West, Florida, in the hope of putting his life back together by reconciling with his wife, Catherine, who stuck by him until he became a national disgrace.

Even though she still loves him, Catherine wants nothing to do with him because his behavior is still bizarre. At one point, he nails his hand to her door; at another, he snorts cocaine off the sidewalk. He has lost his memory and given up all hope. Catherine accepts the fact that she cannot change him and leaves him for good to the emptiness he calls home.

Chet combats this emptiness by evoking a transcendent presence of Jesse James, who has the power to inhabit his loved ones. He prefers that James inhabit his father, a snack-foods tycoon. A typical McGuane protagonist, Chet is bothered by the security and ordinariness of his background. He insists that his father is dead and claims James as an ancestor, suggesting that Chester Hunnicutt Pomeroy really wishes he were someone else. Because the glories of the Old West are not available to him, he creates the myth of himself through bizarre behavior.

Chet's outlaw myth leads him nowhere. At the novel's conclusion, his father forces a reconciliation. Chet knows that all his father wants is for Chet to say hello, to acknowledge him as his father. To admit that his father lives will be to agree that Jesse James is dead. Chet will have to accept himself for who he is: the son of an obscure packager of snack foods, the perfect symbol of conventional modern life.

Nobody's Angel • *Nobody's Angel* is McGuane's first novel to be set entirely in the West, a West that McGuane characterizes as "wrecked." In Deadrock, Montana, farmers abuse the land, cowboys are lazy, and American Indians are nowhere to be found. Returning to this damaged world is thirty-six-year-old Patrick Fitzpatrick. Patrick is as unconventional as earlier McGuane protagonists. As a whiskey addict and a professional soldier, he has been a tank captain in the Army for all of his adult life, most recently in Europe, and the only place he feels secure is inside his womblike tank. Suffering from "sadness for no reason," he has returned to the family ranch, which he will someday own. He feels stranded on the ranch because becoming a property owner is not a meaningful achievement for him. Patrick appears to be in the worst shape of any McGuane protagonist. He is not only without goals but also without any sense of himself, conventional or unconventional.

The effect of the wrecked West is seen in the character of Patrick's grandfather. The old man has been a cowboy all of his life, has known real gunfighters, and has run the ranch like an old-time outfit. The West has changed, however, and everything from sonic booms to valleys cluttered with yard lights has got the old man down. The only things he feels good about are Australia, which he has heard is open country like Montana once was, and Western films. His one fit of excitement comes when he signs on to be an extra in a Western about to be filmed locally. Even that, however, is accompanied by overtones of sadness and ends in disappointment. The film is *Hondo's Last Move*, evocative of a legendary but nonexistent West popularized by actor John Wayne and writer Louis L'Amour. Even then, the "last move" refers to the dying of the West and perhaps Hondo himself. To make matters worse, the project folds when the distributor forsakes Westerns for science fiction. In the end, the old man moves into town and takes an apartment from which he can see the local film theater, which plays old Westerns, and a little bar in which hangs the head of the best elk he ever shot. The open West has been reduced to one-bedroom apartments, yesterday's films, and mounted animals, which serve only to remind him of a glorious past.

In *Nobody's Angel*, McGuane continued to work the theme of unfulfilled love. Patrick hopes to bring purpose into his life by means of a love affair with Claire Burnett. Claire and her husband, Tio, are second-generation nouveau-riche Oklahomans summering in Montana. Not a genuine stockman like Patrick's grandfather, Tio is mainly interested in oil, cattle futures, row crops, and running horses. Because Tio's main hobby is pretending to be a good old boy, Patrick sees him as a personification of the substanceless modern West.

Patrick believes that "Claire could change it all" and wishes theirs could be a sentimental love story, the kind found in romantic books. Claire, however, will not become a part of Patrick's dream. Her commitment to Tio goes beyond Patrick's understanding. Her family provided the money to support their lifestyle. Tio's people are poor Okies, and this discrepancy in their backgrounds has driven him to incurable delusions of grandeur, to the point that Claire has promised that she will not abandon him. Even though she tells Patrick that she loves him, she never stops loving Tio, and Patrick's dream of a storybook romance crumbles. Even when Tio dies, Claire will not marry Patrick. She makes has sex with him one last time, explaining that love is "nothing you can do anything with." Patrick is not able to cope with Claire's pragmatic attitude about love and their relationship. She gives him a picture of herself, but he does not keep it with him, because it reminds him of the frustrations of his romantic hopes.

In the end, Patrick survives, but not in the West. When he was a teenager, Patrick invented an imaginary girlfriend named Marion Easterly. Even though he was eventually discovered, the fantasy has remained a part of his consciousness. He had hoped that Claire would replace Marion, but a living woman will never become the woman of a man's imagination, and when Claire dismisses him, Patrick rejoins the Army and finds fulfillment in his fantasy. Word filters back that he is now a blackout drinker in Madrid and that he is living with a woman named Marion Easterly. Patrick Fitzpatrick remains "at large"—in the sense that his heavy drinking and fantasy lover keep him outside the normal boundaries of life—but without the hope and energy of Nicholas Payne. The McGuane protagonist seemingly must find a way to accommodate himself, at least partially, to the concerns of conventional life.

Something to Be Desired • In *Something to Be Desired*, the McGuane protagonist combines both unconventional and conventional goals. Lucien Taylor grows tired of normality and destroys his perfectly fine marriage with self-absorbed erratic behavior. After his single life becomes empty, he, like Chet, tries to put it back together again by reuniting with his former wife, Suzanne, and their son, James. Lucien's plight is not entirely the result of his disenchantment with conformity; he is victimized by his capricious lust.

Lucien's sense of sexual discipline was broken in college by Emily, who slept with him on their first meeting. Emily was engaged to a medical student and continued to sleep with both young men at the same time. Ultimately, she is abused by her surgeon husband and becomes totally self-absorbed and manipulating. Emily is a woman as selfish as Claire, and she continues her self-absorbed actions throughout the novel, exploiting everyone, including Lucien. Lucien, however, married Suzanne, who "took the position that this was a decent world for an honest player." This basic decency is what Lucien eventually comes to value, but when he hears that Emily is free of her marriage, he thinks nothing of destroying his own and returning to Montana in quest of her. Lucien is troubled by the lack of romance in his life, an element that Suzanne and James cannot provide. Suzanne sums up Emily by calling her the queen of the whores, an assertion which is borne out when, on her penultimate appearance in the novel, she is seen sleeping naked next to her purse.

Such a portrayal of women who do not measure up to male ideals or fantasies is not rare in McGuane's fiction: Ann (*The Bushwhacked Piano*) and Claire (*Nobody's Angel*) are two other disappointing women. Lucien has dreamed of Emily since their first encounter. Not until he finally decides that he wants nothing more to do with her does she tell him that she regards his concern for her an infantile gesture, a thing she holds in contempt. Indeed, she does not even think enough of him to shoot him, which she has done to her husband and, by this time, another lover. Lucien, however, like Nicholas Payne in *The Bushwhacked Piano*, does not lose momentum. He pulls off a crackpot piece of venture capitalism. Through a series of exchanges, he comes to own Emily's ranch and develops its sulfur spring into a thriving health spa. In short, he becomes rich. In this way Lucien remains unconventional, at the same time—new for a McGuane protagonist—gaining that which is admired by conventional society. Even though McGuane still maneuvers his protagonist through some outlandish paces because of his peripatetic penis, McGuane at the same time imbues Lucien with a sense of purpose higher than sport or making the world tense. Lucien, once his new wealth requires him to bring a semblance of order into his life, begins to want to think of himself as a working man with a family to support.

When Suzanne and James come for a visit, Lucien first attempts to reach James from the security of his own masculine interests. He takes him out to band some hawks. He baits the trap with a live pigeon. When the hawk strikes the pigeon, James screams and crawls off. As Lucien bands the hawk, James shakes. While Lucien admires the hawk, James's natural inclination is to cradle the dead pigeon; he manifests a sense of compassion that his father lacks. The violent world of nature is awful to him. Lucien actually finds himself liking the fact that his son is timid and made of more delicate and sensitive stuff than his father. McGuane is, nevertheless, not becoming sentimental. Later, when he understands how nature works, James explains that killing pigeons is how hawks have to live, but the fact remains that James was terrified by the killing. His explanation is not so much an emulation of his father's more hard-boiled ways as it is an acceptance of them as his father's ways. James is actually reaching toward a relationship with his father.

What is important here is that Lucien is attempting to reestablish his family because such a reestablishment would be better for all of them, not only for him alone. Lucien's is one of the few nonselfish acts committed by a McGuane protagonist. He would like not to see the child become a "hostage to oblivion." He wonders how he could leave him unguarded. His reward is that James begins not to fear his father.

Winning back Suzanne, however, is not as easy. She is too skeptical to welcome the sadder-but-wiser protagonist back into her arms. She tells him the truth about himself: He is self-absorbed, insensitive to those who love him, and not worth the effort of reconciliation. Lucien is going to have to recognize her as an independent and worthy person. Before the novel's end, she works through her sense of him as a totally selfish person, but even though she admits to loving Lucien, she is not sure if she is ready to trust him. As she and James drive away from the ranch, she does not look back. She is charting her own course, which may or may not include Lucien.

What is important here is that the McGuane protagonist has progressed through the state of self-absorption with adventure and sport. He has begun to understand that what matters about life is not being "at large" to commit glorious exploits, but being a part of a larger whole that includes the other people in the world. The full life is not lived in furious battle with the forces of conventionality but in achieving deep and lasting relationships with human beings.

Keep the Change • In *Keep the Change*, Joe Starling, Jr., an artist of limited talent, must come to understand this same truth. Chained by the ghost of his father, an overachiever who ultimately dies a failure, the young Starling's life is empty for no reason. He is not satisfied with his various successes as an artist, craftsperson, cowboy, or lover, because everything pales in comparison with his expectations for himself. He ricochets among Montana, Florida, and New York City without fully realizing that individual human meaning is something created rather than found.

Two of McGuane's most fully realized female characters offer Starling the possibility of a fully actualized life, but he is too full of himself to seize the opportunity. Ellen Overstreet, a rancher's daughter as wholesome as the new frontier, presents him with the vulnerability of awkward young love. The dynamic Cuban Astrid, whom Starling loves for her outlandishness, sticks by him until he is hopelessly lost in pointlessness. After she leaves him, Starling seems to be beginning to understand that sharing the routine concerns of daily life with Astrid may be the source of true meaning.

Keep the Change signals a new development in McGuane's perception of male competition. Games are no longer seen as means to make sport of conventionality. Joe Starling's rival here is Billy Kelton, an honest and simple, if luckless, cowboy, who marries Ellen Overstreet. Kelton is Starling's physical superior and twice humiliates him with beatings. Violence here is real, not comic, and because it is real, it is bewildering and confusing. Kelton understands that his physical prowess is dehumanizing, and, in facing the struggles of life with his wife and daughter, he shows Starling the importance of a deeper, if simpler, emotional life.

The key to the novel is found in a painting of Montana mountains, the white hills, which hangs in a decaying mansion that once belonged to the most powerful man in the territory. The work itself is indistinguishable: "It had seemed an unblemished canvas until the perplexity of shadows across its surface was seen to be part of the painting." Ultimately, Starling discovers that the shadows are in fact its only real feature. There is no painting; there never has been a painting. However, "somewhere in the abyss something shone." That "something" is the meaning Starling seeks. He is the one who determined meaning in the painting and, by extension, in the hills themselves. He must then act to create a life for himself; he must determine his own meaning.

Nothing but Blue Skies • *Nothing but Blue Skies*, McGuane's eighth novel, continues the progression from self-absorption to maturity begun in *Something to Be Desired* and *Keep the Change*. Perhaps his most expansive work, it follows the breakdown and recovery of Frank Copenhaver after his separation from his wife, Gracie. An ex-hippie turned real estate speculator and cattle trader, Frank gradually loses control of his minor empire of rental properties, turning his scattered attention instead to awkward sexual encounters with the local travel agent and episodes of drunken self-destructiveness. Only a visit by his college-age daughter, Holly, can keep him momentarily in balance. Her brief stay includes an idyllic afternoon of fishing that buoys Frank's spirits, only to intensify the sense of loneliness and loss when she leaves again.

It is Holly who manages to suspend Frank's downward spin by creating a family crisis. She summons her estranged parents to Missoula to meet her new "boyfriend," Lane Lawlor, a gray-haired archconservative campaigning to "impound" the streams and rivers in Montana in order to retain the water that flows out of the state. Frank and Gracie meet to discuss the situation, but at each of the meetings Frank makes a fool of himself by failing to control his temper. The couple is finally brought together at a political rally where Lane Lawlor is the speaker and Holly his piano-playing assistant. The rally ends when Gracie, like Frank, secretly in attendance, attacks Lane and Frank joins the melee. In the aftermath they realize that Holly has engineered their reunion by pretending to fall for Lane. Frank also understands that Gracie has "nearly ruined" him in an attempt to break down his self-involvement and force him to see her and himself in a new way.

Nothing but Blue Skies is clearly McGuane's most optimistic and fully developed novel. In Frank Copenhaver, McGuane gives his typical protagonist a complexity and vulnerability that many of his earlier versions lack. Perhaps more notable, the novel's women show a richness of characterization often missing from earlier works. Gracie, Holly, and Lucy Dyer, the travel agent, all transcend easy generalities and stand firmly as independent, fully formed characters.

The core of *Nothing but Blue Skies* is Frank's bewilderment in the face of losing Gracie and his rehabilitation through public humiliation. McGuane's strength in creating such a character lies in his understanding of how life can be renewed through the comic downfall of the protagonist, his fall into public degradation a necessary starting point for rebuilding the life he has sold away through the soul-shrinking manipulations of business. Stripped of all attainments and pride, Frank Copenhaver can only start over. After all, as Gracie tells him, "There's nothing crazier than picking up exactly where you left off."

In Thomas McGuane's modern West, life is what you make it, nothing more, nothing less. His protagonists must work to fulfill hopes not by going against the grain of the conventional life, but by partaking of its normal flow and by building useful foundations on its undramatic but real joys.

Dexter Westrum
Updated by Clark Davis

Other major works

SHORT FICTION: *To Skin a Cat*, 1986; *Gallatin Canyon*, 2006.

SCREENPLAYS: *Rancho DeLuxe*, 1973; *Ninety-two in the Shade*, 1975 (adaptation of his novel); *The Missouri Breaks*, 1975; *Tom Horn*, 1980 (with Bud Shrake).

NONFICTION: *An Outside Chance: Essays on Sport*, 1980; *Some Horses*, 1999; *The Longest Silence: A Life in Fishing*, 1999.

Bibliography

Carter, Albert Howard, III. "Thomas McGuane's First Three Novels: Games, Fun,

Nemesis." *Critique* 17 (August, 1975): 91-104. Although McGuane's use of the pathos and humor inherent in competition has become decidedly more sophisticated as he has matured, this article is essential for understanding the early novels.

Ingram, David. "Thomas McGuane: Nature, Environmentalism, and the American West." *Journal of American Studies* 29 (December, 1995): 423-459. Analyzes environmental and outdoors themes in McGuane's work.

Klinkowitz, Jerome. *The New American Novel of Manners: The Fiction of Richard Yates, Dan Wakefield, Thomas McGuane.* Athens: University of Georgia Press, 1986. Examines the twentieth century novel of manners and customs. Includes index.

McClintock, James I. "'Unextended Selves' and 'Unformed Visions': Roman Catholicism in Thomas McGuane's Novels." *Renascence* 49 (Winter, 1997): 139-151. Focuses on McGuane's works from *The Sporting Life* through *Nothing but Blue Skies*, comparing him with a host of writers including, particularly, Flannery O'Connor.

McGuane, Thomas. "Thomas McGuane." Interview by Kay Bonetti. In *Conversations with American Novelists: The Best Interviews from the "Missouri Review" and the American Audio Prose Library,* edited by Kay Bonetti et al. Columbia: University of Missouri Press, 1997. Extended interview with McGuane.

Masinton, Charles G. "*Nobody's Angel:* Thomas McGuane's Vision of the Contemporary West." *New Mexico Humanities Review* 6 (Fall, 1983): 49-55. This article analyzes *Rancho DeLuxe* and *Nobody's Angel* and insightfully concludes that McGuane finds the contemporary West absurd and without hope.

Morris, Gregory L. "Thomas McGuane." In *Talking up a Storm: Voices of the New West.* Lincoln: University of Nebraska Press, 1994. A 1989 interview with the novelist, in which he discusses his relationship to the West, his working methods, and the state of the American novel.

Rebein, Robert. *Hicks, Tribes, and Dirty Realists: American Fiction After Postmodernism.* Lexington: University Press of Kentucky, 2001. An assertion that gritty realism has gained ascendency over metafiction in American writing. Examines the works of McGuane, Dorothy Allison, Annie Proulx, Cormac McCarthy, Larry McMurtry, and Louise Erdrich.

Wallace, Jon. *The Politics of Style: Language as Theme in the Fiction of Berger, McGuane, and McPherson.* Durango, Colo.: Hollowbrook, 1992. Examines McGuane's use of language. Contains a bibliography.

Westrum, Dexter. *Thomas McGuane.* Boston: Twayne, 1991. The first book-length study of McGuane's fiction. It provides a basic biography and a detailed overview of the author's work through *Keep the Change.*

Hugh MacLennan

Born: Glace Bay, Nova Scotia, Canada; March 20, 1907
Died: Montreal, Quebec, Canada; November 7, 1990

Principal long fiction • *Barometer Rising*, 1941; *Two Solitudes*, 1945; *The Precipice*, 1948; *Each Man's Son*, 1951; *The Watch That Ends the Night*, 1959; *Return of the Sphinx*, 1967; *Voices in Time*, 1980.

Other literary forms • Throughout his career, Hugh MacLennan was a prolific writer of nonfiction. Following his youthful attempts at poetry and the publication of his dissertation on a Roman colonial settlement in Egypt, *Oxyrhynchus: An Economic and Social Study* (1935, 1968), MacLennan began writing articles, reviews, autobiographical pieces, travel notes, and essays, publishing in a variety of magazines, including *The Montrealer*, *Maclean's*, and *Holiday*. Journalism sometimes served as a necessary supplement to his income and occasionally was used to try out material later incorporated into his novels. It has been claimed that his talent finds truer expression in his essays than in his novels; while this may be a questionable judgment, there is no denying the excellence of much of his nonfiction. Selections from the more than four hundred essays that he wrote have been collected in four books, the first two of which won Canada's Governor-General's Award: *Cross-Country* (1948), *Thirty and Three* (1954), *Scotchman's Return, and Other Essays* (1960), and *The Other Side of Hugh MacLennan: Selected Essays Old and New* (1978, Elspeth Cameron, editor). Additionally, his concern for Canada's history and geography has found expression in his *Seven Rivers of Canada* (1961, revised as *Rivers of Canada*, 1974) and *The Colour of Canada* (1967). *Rivers of Canada*, in which MacLennan provided the text to accompany the beautiful photography of John DeVisser, contains some of his best writing.

Achievements • MacLennan, as his biographer Elspeth Cameron has observed, "set out to be a writer, not a 'Canadian' writer," yet it was as a Canadian "nationalist" that he was first recognized, and in spite of his intermittent attempts to renounce this label, it was as a distinctively Canadian writer that his career and his reputation developed. He held a solid place as something like the dean of Canadian letters; for many years he was a public figure in Canada, appearing on radio and television, frequently being asked to comment not only on Canadian writing but also on culture generally and politics. He made continual attempts to tap the American market (with some success, especially with *The Watch That Ends the Night*); his works have been translated into many languages; his last novel, *Voices in Time*, is international in setting, yet MacLennan was thought of both in his own country and elsewhere as a, perhaps *the*, Canadian novelist.

Having written two unpublished novels with international settings, MacLennan turned to his own Halifax, Nova Scotia, when writing *Barometer Rising*. This first published novel was immediately successful and was praised for its Canadian nationalism. His next novel, *Two Solitudes*, treated the divisions between the English and French cultures in Quebec; the book's title, taken from Rainer Maria Rilke, entered popular usage as a convenient phrase to sum up this cultural schism. MacLennan continued to be hailed for his contributions to defining a Canadian identity. When his third novel, *The Precipice*, attempted to develop an international theme, presenting the love between a Canadian woman and an American man, he met with less critical acceptance. He returned to writing about Nova Scotia in *Each Man's Son* and followed this with a novel set primarily in Montreal, *The Watch That Ends the Night*. This work was both a critical success and a best-seller, not only in Canada but also throughout the English-speaking world; it also sold well in translation. MacLennan's reputation as a major novelist was assured; it was bolstered by Edmund Wilson's lavish praise in *O Canada* (1965). Even the many unfavorable reviews of MacLennan's subsequent novel, *Return of the Sphinx*, which treated the Quebec independence movement, did not call into question his importance in Canadian writing. Those who thought this importance was only historical and that his novelistic powers had passed their peak were proven wrong by his subsequent and last novel, *Voices in Time*, which was well received even though it clearly transcended Canadian national issues.

As *Voices in Time* suggests, seeing MacLennan in the narrow focus of Canadian nationalism is too limiting. It is certainly true that his work was informed by his nationality and that younger Canadian writers owe a debt to his pioneering treatment of Canadian themes. It is also true that his achievement must be primarily judged thematically. Although he was competent in plotting and occasionally excellent in characterization, these were not his strong points. He was a conservative novelist in craft, contributing no new forms to the genre, although his own technique did develop, especially in his use of point of view and manipulation of time.

Granting that MacLennan emphasized theme and wrote out of his Canadian experience, his relationship to Canada can be best understood, however, if he is seen not as a nationalist or a local colorist, but rather as a writer who used his Canadian background to put into perspective his political, social, and psychological ideas and to reinforce his sense of history. It is essentially as a creator of novels of ideas that MacLennan bids fair to appeal to future generations of readers around the world.

Biography • John Hugh MacLennan was born in Glace Bay, Cape Breton, Nova Scotia, on March 20, 1907. He drew on his memories of this birthplace, a coal-mining company town set at the edge of the Atlantic, explicitly in *Each Man's Son*, but his impressions of the seagirt land, a topography appropriate to the Scottish Highland character that was his heritage, entered, less directly, into much of his work. In this setting, his father practiced medicine among the miners. A dominating figure, "the Doctor" was to become the prototype of a number of characters in his son's novels.

In 1915, when MacLennan was eight, the family moved to Halifax, a venerable but lively port that fascinated the boy. The small city, with its sense of community, became a lifelong ideal for MacLennan, as did the contrasting beauty of the Cape Breton countryside where the family spent time in the summer, prefiguring the thematic retreat to the woods of many of MacLennan's fictional characters. As recounted in *Barometer Rising*, much of Halifax was destroyed by an explosion in 1917, but the city was rebuilt, and MacLennan was reared there, doing well in both studies and sports, and graduated from Dalhousie University in 1928.

Later in that year, a Rhodes Scholarship allowed him to attend Oxford. While there he played rugby and tennis; an excellent athlete, MacLennan, as a novelist, frequently used sports to reveal character. At Oxford, he also wrote poetry and traveled extensively, during vacations, on the Continent. These holidays, especially those to Germany, were drawn upon in his first two, unpublished, novels and returned to in

Voices in Time, and some of his own experiences from this time were used in creating those of his character, Paul, in *Two Solitudes*.

MacLennan also studied at Oxford, quite diligently in fact, and graduated in 1932, proceeding to graduate studies at Princeton. Returning to England, he met, on the ship, an American, Dorothy Duncan, who was to become his first wife. His developing love and his new devotion to becoming a novelist absorbed more of his attention than did his studies. While he did not find Princeton congenial, he completed his doctorate in history, with a dissertation discussing the Roman colonial settlement at Oxyrhynchus in Egypt.

In 1935, in the midst of the Great Depression, MacLennan's degree was not able to secure for him the university teaching position he desired; he accepted a job teaching at Lower Canada College, a boys' school in Montreal. (He was to give a fictionalized satiric portrait of the school in *The Watch That Ends the Night*.) After a year at the school, he married Duncan and settled into a life of working as a schoolmaster during the day and writing at night, sinking in roots as a Montrealer, which he was to remain.

MacLennan's first novel, *So All Their Praises*, had been completed while MacLennan was at Princeton; it was accepted by a publisher that ceased operation before the book was published. His second novel, *A Man Should Rejoice*, suffered a similar fate in 1938; its publication was postponed and finally dropped. These novels, the first owing a debt to Ernest Hemingway, the second to John Dos Passos, although never published, have their virtues. They both present comments on the political situation preceding World War II and employ international settings.

For his next novel, MacLennan turned, upon his wife's suggestion, to Canada. *Barometer Rising* is set in Halifax in 1917. It was an immediate success. MacLennan continued his teaching and writing career in Montreal; an ear problem kept him out of the war. After the success of his second published novel, *Two Solitudes*, and the establishment, additionally, of his wife's successful career as a writer (Dorothy Duncan published nonfiction; one of her books, *Partner in Three Worlds*, 1944, won the Governor-General's Award for nonfiction), he resigned from Lower Canada College in 1945. Following a period of journalism and broadcasting and the publication of *The Precipice*, in 1951 he took a part-time position teaching in the English department at McGill University; he assumed a full-time post in 1964, becoming professor emeritus in 1979.

During the years in which he was establishing himself as a writer in Montreal, publishing *Cross-Country*, *Each Man's Son*, and *Thirty and Three* (a period described in *The Watch That Ends the Night*), his wife's declining health—she suffered a series of embolisms—added greatly to the pressures he experienced. Duncan died in 1957. MacLennan dedicated *The Watch That Ends the Night* to her; the novel, originally titled *Requiem*, has as its heroine a figure whose characterization owes much to Duncan. MacLennan married Frances Walker in 1959 and after a period of producing nonfiction—*Scotchman's Return, and Other Essays, Seven Rivers of Canada*—wrote *Return of the Sphinx*. This novel was unfavorably reviewed by a number of Canadian critics, but MacLennan continued to receive numerous honorary degrees and public recognition. He began consideration of another novel but interrupted work on it to write *Rivers of Canada*. His last novel, *Voices in Time*, appeared to favorable reviews in 1980. In 1982, MacLennan retired from McGill, after more than thirty years of teaching there. He died in Montreal on November 7, 1990, at the age of eighty-three.

Analysis • Hugh MacLennan began as a historian, and, in a sense, he remained one throughout his long writing career. His doctoral dissertation, *Oxyrhynchus*, discussing the history of an area in Egypt during the seven hundred years that it was subject to the Roman Empire, foreshadowed such major themes in his novels as colonialism, the wanderer, the town-country antithesis, and geographical determinism. Underlying both the dissertation and the novels is a view of historical causality.

As Erich Auerbach has remarked, "Basically, the way in which we view human life and society is the same whether we are concerned with things of the past or things of the present"; a corollary of this may be that when a writer is, like MacLennan, both a historian and a novelist, his or her narratives of individual human lives will be shaped by larger forces that transcend the concerns of the psychological novelist. In MacLennan's fiction, geography is preeminently such a force.

In both his fiction and his nonfiction, MacLennan had a continual concern for the impact of geography upon character, and thus, as people make history, upon action, fictive or historical. The fact that a Canadian, living in a frequently harsh terrain and climate, would appreciate the significance of geography is hardly surprising, but MacLennan went further, adopting a geographical theory of history. His sense of geography's interaction with psychology and history provides the ideological framework that, more than any other single factor, gives his work its distinctive character. This framework is especially useful to MacLennan as a way of putting into perspective his personal experience, for he drew less upon "pure" invention than do many novelists. His method, in both his essays and his novels, was to use personal experience to support general and philosophical concepts.

This means that, fundamentally, MacLennan wrote novels of ideas; it does not mean, however, that his ideas were necessarily free from self-contradiction or that they remained entirely consistent throughout his career. His ideology, complex but ultimately growing from a sense of the fundamental importance of geography, is most explicit in his first three published novels, in which he worked toward a definition of Canadian identity by first contrasting Canada to England (*Barometer Rising*), then dealing with the potentials of Canadian unity (*Two Solitudes*), and finally differentiating Canada from the United States (*The Precipice*). The next novel, *Each Man's Son*, is transitional in that it conveys a strong sense of the land, Cape Breton in this case, while anticipating the greater interest in psychology that characterized his subsequent novels. Even in these later novels, however, history as geography remains a basic concept. Although psychological concepts became more important to MacLennan, he employed topographical images to express this interest.

Character, then, in a MacLennan novel is closely related to theme, as is plot, and the theme is tied to setting. Although he created a fairly wide range of characters, including some minor figures that are presented with Dickensian humor, the central focus in his characterization was either on the "love interest" or on a conflict of generations. Both of these recurring motifs are normally subservient to theme in that the characters, whether they come together in love, as, for example, Paul and Heather in *Two Solitudes*, or stand apart in years, as do Alan Ainslie and his son in *Return of the Sphinx*, represent different value systems or cultures. Their psychology, which motivates their interactions, is seen in terms of their conditioning by history and, ultimately, by geography.

Admittedly, this emphasis is modified, especially in the later novels, by Mac-Lennan's concern with various ideological factors, such as Calvinism in *Each Man's Son*, and by his interest in psychological theories, especially Freudianism, particularly notable in *Return of the Sphinx*. Nevertheless, similar imagery and recurring motifs, reflecting a sense of historical causation, run through both his earlier and later works. One finds, for example, the antithesis between the city and the country; the retreat into the woods; the theme of the wanderer, exiled from his or her roots; frequent references to weather; and imagery of trees, gardens, and water, in all of his novels.

MacLennan's novelistic techniques did change, however, as he developed his craft, as can be seen in his plotting, use of point of view, and style. In plotting, as in many aspects of his craft, MacLennan was old-fashioned; he kept the reader interested in how the story will come out. MacLennan was by nature given to relatively happy endings, but after the upbeat conclusions characterizing his first three novels, his optimism became tempered, appearing more as a coda following climactic elements of tragedy in *Each Man's Son, The Watch That Ends the Night*, and *Return of the Sphinx. Voices in Time* has a series of climaxes occurring at different points in the novel and producing different effects on the reader. The fact that MacLennan was able to unify the various narratives included in this, the most complex of his works in its plotting, is an indication of the development of his craftsmanship.

MacLennan's ability to manipulate increasingly complex narrative patterns is closely related to his mastery of point of view. Although none of MacLennan's novels approaches a Jamesian concern for this aspect of the art of fiction, with *The Watch That Ends the Night*, as he moved away from straightforward chronological sequences, he slipped skillfully between first- and third-person narration. *Return of the Sphinx* uses third-person narration but with a shifting between the viewpoints of different characters. This novel, however, lacks what Henry James called "a fine central intelligence." Alan Ainslie does not provide this unifying quality as effectively as does John Wellfleet in *Voices in Time*; Wellfleet's perspective gives coherence to the novel's varied narrative strands.

As MacLennan's ability to structure his novels developed, slowly and within a fairly conventional framework, yet with increasing skill in his craft, so did his style mature. His earlier novels exhibited some tendency toward overwriting. *Barometer Rising* has "set-pieces" that skirt the borders of sentimentality; *Two Solitudes* is sometimes verbose; *The Precipice* is not free from clichéd expression. In *Each Man's Son*, the style, reflecting the dramatic structure, is tightened. *The Watch That Ends the Night* contains superior passages of description, although the dialogue (never one of MacLennan's strengths) occasionally shows some of the stilted qualities of the earlier novels. *Return of the Sphinx* is notable for its economy of style and in this respect prepares for *Voices in Time*, in which MacLennan's style is the most fully unselfconscious and "organic."

MacLennan, then, is a novelist whose works may be read for the pleasure to be found in an interesting story well told, but he remains a writer less likely to be remembered as a storyteller or fictional craftsperson than as a man of ideas, a dramatizer of history.

Barometer Rising • When, following his wife's advice to write of that which he knew best, MacLennan turned to his hometown, Halifax, he used it not only as the novel's setting but also as its subject. In *Barometer Rising*, he was also writing of Canada; Halifax, with its colonial attitudes overlaying social and ideological divisions, is a microcosm of a new Canada. The book's title is in large part explained in a subsequent essay, in which MacLennan describes Halifax as a barometer for the whole country.

What goes up must have been down; if the barometer rises, if, by implication, Canada faces a halcyon future, it does so only after a great storm and a particularly violent stroke of lightning. The action of *Barometer Rising* is centered on an actual historical event, the blast that occurred when a munitions ship exploded in Halifax harbor on December 6, 1917. The largest single human-made explosion before Hiroshima, it destroyed a major portion of the town and killed some two thousand people.

A result of Halifax's role in World War I, the explosion is also symbolically related to Canada's involvement in that bloody conflict. Although the concurrent destruction of life, property, and outworn colonial beliefs—the old world dying with a monstrous bang—constitutes the core of the book, a number of other motifs are woven into its thematic patterns. The conflict of generations, the return of the wanderer and the Odysseus theme, the psychological aspects of technological change—these are all important elements of the novel that continued to reverberate in MacLennan's subsequent work. Underlying all the thematic strands is the author's view of historical process, a view that puts a strong emphasis upon the conditioning significance of physical geography.

It is Halifax's geographical situation that underlies the book's basic contrast, that between old and new Canada, colony and country. The harbor gives the town its meaning; facing away from the rest of Canada, Halifax looks toward Great Britain and the Continent, both in a literal and a figurative sense. From the topographical facts, carefully elaborated at the beginning of the novel, derive the prevailing attitudes of the Haligonians: It is the preservation of England that motivates all of what happens in Halifax; the colonial mentality prevails. Had the geography been different, the town's development and activity would have been different, and, consequently, its people would have been different.

If geography is destiny, there is no rigid determinism in MacLennan's view of that destiny. Halifax, although pointed toward Britain physically and thus psychologically as well, is part of the New World and has, therefore, the potential for a different orientation. This reorientation follows from the book's central event, the explosion, an event that, while the result of accident, is influenced by topography in both cause and effect. The explosion is a result of the collision, in Halifax harbor, of a munitions ship with a Norwegian freighter; the crash occurs because the physical nature of the harbor limits visibility. As a result of the destruction, new values arise from the rubble of the old; Halifax is no longer dominated by the rigid ideas of its old colonial aristocracy.

Although the story has this allegorical quality, with a message made explicit in a concluding passage on what might be termed Canada's "manifest destiny," its allegory is fleshed out with particular, three-dimensional characters, conditioned by geography and history, but living out their private lives within the interstices of that conditioning framework.

Neil Macrae, the book's hero, is, like Odysseus, a soldier returned from the war, bearing an assumed identity acquired after he was falsely accused of disobeying an order during an attack in which he was thought to have been killed. His accuser is the novel's villain, Colonel Wain, representative of the old order, and father of Penelope—whose Homeric name is intentional—the heroine with whom Neil is in love. The cast is completed by a number of skillfully drawn secondary characters derived from MacLennan's memories, including Penny's younger brother Roddie, modeled on MacLennan himself, and Angus Murray, also in love with Penny, the first in a series of heroic doctors who appear in MacLennan's novels.

Following the explosion and the vindication of Neil's conduct during the attack in France (the outcome of the battle depending, just as does the collision in the harbor, on terrain), Neil and Penelope are finally united; the storm is over, and the future is bright. Although the novel is marred by this rather facile happy ending and by its general didacticism, the basic interest in both action and character, reinforced with symbolism, makes *Barometer Rising* artistically satisfying. Although MacLennan was to write more subtly in future novels, *Barometer Rising*, representing clearly his basic approach, fiction as dramatized history, remains one of his best achievements.

Two Solitudes* and *The Precipice • MacLennan's next two novels also used a love story to express theme and continued to demonstrate his interest in the impact of geography upon the character of a people. *Two Solitudes*, centered upon the romance between Paul Tallard and Heather Methuen, begins with a description of the landscape of Quebec; throughout, the symbolism of the river, the forest, and the town reinforces the theme of the relationship of the English and French in Quebec. *The Precipice*, with its love affair between a Canadian woman and an American man, contrasts Canada and the United States by relating the character of the peoples to their respective terrains. Set primarily in Ontario, the novel uses Lake Ontario as a dominant symbol, reinforced by references to weather, gardens, the city, and other prevalent MacLennan imagery.

Each Man's Son • Similar imagery informs *Each Man's Son*; thematic conflicts are drawn between two sides of the Scottish Highlands character, between religion as a sense of sin and religion as inspiration, and between science and superstition, particularly focused through the contrast between the mines and the sea of Cape Breton. A major turning point in the plot occurs when Dr. Ainslie (whose name is taken from a Cape Breton place-name) gives his to-be-adopted son, Alan, a lesson in history, followed by one in geography.

The Watch That Ends the Night • Arguably MacLennan's best novel, *The Watch That Ends the Night* demonstrates a significant advance in his technique. The didactic quality of his earlier novels is reduced; the imagery becomes more involved, as does the handling of time; characters take on more interest, not as symbols but in their own right. Concurrently, the sense of the formative power of geography upon character is moved more to the background, as though Canada, having been conditioned by geography, is able to go beyond this conditioning. Nevertheless, in this, as in all his novels, MacLennan writes from essentially the same perspective on history and employs many of the same patterns in fictional construction.

Again, just as in the earlier novels, the book is based on a strong sense of place, in this case Montreal, described in memorable, often loving detail. Again, the plot centers upon a love interest, a triangle involving George Stewart, who has autobiographical connections with MacLennan; Jerome Martell, a doctor with mythic qualities; and Catherine Carey, a remarkable woman (who takes on, for Canada, some of the symbolism Kathleen ni Houlihan did for Ireland) whose portrait owes something to MacLennan's wife Dorothy. George loves Catherine, but she marries Martell. After Martell is thought to have been killed by the Nazis, Catherine and George eventually marry, but, much later, Martell reappears. (The story begins at this point, and is told primarily through flashbacks.) Although Catherine stays with George, suffering a heart condition, she has little time left to live.

Within this framework, MacLennan presents a rich picture, with numerous well-realized minor characters, of Montreal during the Great Depression and during the time of the Korean War. For all his interest in psychology in this work, it is, as are all his novels, less a "novel of character" than a working out, through characters, of ideas, and a dramatization of social-historical processes. Although the plot (except in the New Brunswick section) does not hinge on terrain, the imagery does. Images derived from nature control much of the book's tone, with references to rivers and oceans particularly important. In *The Watch That Ends the Night*, MacLennan moved beyond any mechanical application of historical theory to the novel; he did not, however, change his fundamental view of the forces underlying human events.

Return of the Sphinx • MacLennan's next novel, *Return of the Sphinx*, reintroduced Alan, from *Each Man's Son*, now a grown man with his own son. Dealing, on the surface, with events of the Quebec liberation movement during the 1960's, it is set mainly in Montreal and Ottawa but contains a "retreat to the woods" section and begins with an explicit statement of the impact of geography and weather upon culture; it ends with images of the land. Beneath the political action lies a deeper psychological theme, in essence that of the Oedipus complex, as MacLennan extends in this novel his interest in psychological theory, begun in *Each Man's Son* and continued in *The Watch That Ends the Night*; he also extends his use of imagery derived from nature and geography to express psychological states.

Voices in Time • In MacLennan's final novel, *Voices in Time*, his lifelong interest in the perspective provided by history is obvious and central to the book's structure. Indeed, the direct, albeit complicated manner in which this interest informs the novel may be a key to its success. MacLennan's focus on history was always essentially pragmatic—to use the past to understand the present and anticipate the future; this is what *Voices in Time* undertakes.

The book intertwines the stories of three men from three different generations: Conrad Dehmel, born in Germany in 1910, a concentration-camp survivor; Timothy Wellfleet, a Canadian born in 1938 who becomes a television interviewer; and John Wellfleet, another Canadian, born in 1964. John Wellfleet is the central narrator. He is one of the few humans who has lived through the "destructions" of atomic explosions, and when the novel opens in 2039, he is approached by the young André Gervais, who has found materials related to Wellfleet's family and wants the old man to use them to reconstruct the past that has, in effect, been destroyed for Gervais and his friends. Wellfleet works out Dehmel's story, involving opposition to Hitler and love for a Jewish woman, and finds it subsequently connecting to Dehmel's stepson Timothy, who interviews Dehmel on television in 1970. As a result of the interview, during which Timothy accuses Dehmel of having been a Nazi, Dehmel is assassinated.

Obviously, the presentation of this material, these voices from different times, calls for a complicated structure: Timothy's story is told by John Wellfleet; Dehmel's by both Wellfleet and, through diaries, by himself; and Wellfleet's own story is concluded by Gervais. The time scheme moves from 2039, to the late 1960's, to 1909, to 1918-1919, to 1932-1945, to a climax in 1970, and finally to 2044.

Like the time scheme, MacLennan's view of causation that underlies this historical presentation is intricate, especially as compared to *Barometer Rising* and his earlier novels. Nevertheless, his belief in the significance of geography, nature, and landscape in motivating character can still be seen, even though the landscape has become primarily urban, and character may be formed, or deformed, by *separation* from fundamental geography. Nature continues to provide MacLennan with a thematic contrast to the urban, technological environment and to be a source of much of his imagery. Timothy is cut off, in his technological world, from natural geography; at nineteen thousand feet, he flies over the woods his father's generation had known intimately. Dehmel finds a temporary salvation, in both the world wars, in Germany's Black Forest. John Wellfleet lives on the outskirts of what was once Montreal, with trees, flowers, and birds. Drawing upon Walt Whitman, MacLennan uses lilacs and a star to make a contrast with urban technology and its sense of time; he has Wellfleet think of the "time-clocks" of plants and birds. In one key passage, civilization is compared to a garden. Most significant, perhaps, when compared to the thoughts about civilization, its rise and fall, and time, which MacLennan presents in *Rivers of Canada*, is the mentioning of rivers, as when, for example, the cautious optimism that tempers the tragic events narrated in *Voices in Time* is symbolized by the return of salmon to the St. Lawrence River.

Voices in Time was MacLennan's final novel and was a fitting climax to a successful career. It indicated that although he assuredly has a major position in the history of Canadian letters, he was one of those novelists who, although solidly rooted in time and place, transcended both. His ability to dramatize his geographical sense of history suggests that MacLennan is a writer who will continue to speak to future generations, to be, himself, a voice not stilled by time.

William B. Stone

Other major works

NONFICTION: *Oxyrhynchus: An Economic and Social Study*, 1935, 1968; *Cross-Country*, 1948; *Thirty and Three*, 1954; *Scotchman's Return, and Other Essays*, 1960; *Seven Rivers of Canada*, 1961 (revised as *Rivers of Canada*, 1974); *The Colour of Canada*, 1967; *The Other Side of Hugh MacLennan: Selected Essays Old and New*, 1978 (Elspeth Cameron, editor); *On Being a Maritime Writer*, 1984; *Dear Marian, Dear Hugh: The MacLennan-Engel Correspondence*, 1995 (Christl Verduyn, editor).

EDITED TEXTS: *McGill: The Story of a University*, 1960.

MISCELLANEOUS: *Hugh MacLennan's Best*, 1991 (Douglas M. Gibson, editor).

Bibliography

Buitenhuis, Peter. *Hugh MacLennan*. Edited by William French. Toronto: Forum House, 1969. A biography of MacLennan, critical analyses of his six novels and his nonfiction, and a bibliography. Buitenhuis supports MacLennan's preoccupation with Canadian nationhood. The assessment of MacLennan's strengths and weaknesses is evenhanded but somewhat academic.

Hochbruck, Wolfgang, and James O. Taylor, eds. *Down East: Critical Essays on Contemporary Maritime Canadian Literature*. Trier, Germany: Wissenschaftlicher, 1996. Contains Susanne Bach's useful study "The Geography of Perception in Hugh MacLennan's Maritime Novels."

Leith, Linda. *Introducing Hugh MacLennan's "Two Solitudes": A Reader's Guide*. Toronto: ECW Press, 1990. An excellent source for students of the novel. Includes bibliographical references and an index.

Lucas, Alec. *Hugh MacLennan.* Toronto: McClelland and Stewart, 1970. Each chapter addresses a different component of MacLennan's vision in general and social morality in particular. The introduction, conclusion, and a bibliography constitute the rest of this clear assessment of MacLennan's fiction and essays.

Tierney, Frank M., ed. *Hugh MacLennan.* Ottawa, Ont.: University of Ottawa Press, 1994. A good critical study of MacLennan. Provides bibliographical references.

Twigg, Alan. "Hugh MacLennan." In *Strong Voices: Conversations with Fifty Canadian Authors.* Madeira Park, B.C.: Harbour, 1988. This absorbing 1979 interview focuses mainly on MacLennan's lifelong interest in Canadian nationhood and the influence of that interest on his writing.

Woodcock, George. *Introducing Hugh MacLennan's "Barometer Rising": A Reader's Guide.* Toronto: ECW Press, 1989. This careful, instructive methodology for reading the novel also includes a chronology of MacLennan's life and publications, biographical details, an assessment of MacLennan's place in Canadian literature, and a partially annotated "Works Cited."

_____. "Surrogate Fathers and Orphan Sons: The Novels of Hugh MacLennan." In *Northern Spring: The Flowering of Canadian Literature.* Vancouver, B.C.: Douglas and McIntyre, 1987. In this essay from his two-part book on Canadian prose writers and poets, Woodcock examines what he perceives in MacLennan's writing as a central metaphor for the definition of "Canadian" nation: a generational theme. Also discusses the strongly didactic element that pervades MacLennan's works.

Larry McMurtry

Born: Wichita Falls, Texas; June 3, 1936

Principal long fiction • *Horseman, Pass By*, 1961; *Leaving Cheyenne*, 1963; *The Last Picture Show*, 1966; *Moving On*, 1970; *All My Friends Are Going to Be Strangers*, 1972; *Terms of Endearment*, 1975; *Somebody's Darling*, 1978; *Cadillac Jack*, 1982; *The Desert Rose*, 1983; *Lonesome Dove*, 1985; *Texasville*, 1987; *Anything for Billy*, 1988; *Some Can Whistle*, 1989; *Buffalo Girls*, 1990; *The Evening Star*, 1992; *Streets of Laredo*, 1993; *Pretty Boy Floyd*, 1994 (with Diana Ossana); *Dead Man's Walk*, 1995; *The Late Child*, 1995; *Comanche Moon*, 1997; *Zeke and Ned*, 1997 (with Ossana); *Duane's Depressed*, 1999; *Boone's Lick*, 2000; *Sin Killer*, 2002; *By Sorrow's River*, 2003; *The Wandering Hill*, 2003; *Folly and Glory*, 2004; *Loop Group*, 2004; *Telegraph Days*, 2006.

Other literary forms • *In a Narrow Grave* (1968) is a collection of nine essays Larry McMurtry wrote for various periodicals, mostly concerning Texas. He collaborated on the script for the 1971 motion picture adaptation of his novel *The Last Picture Show* and wrote other scripts. In 1975-1976 he wrote monthly articles for *American Film* magazine, some of which were collected in *Film Flam: Essays on Hollywood* (1987).

 Crazy Horse (1999), the story of the great Sioux leader, was McMurtry's first foray into biography. He followed that book with *Sacagawea's Nickname: Essays on the American West* (2001); and *The Colonel and Little Missie: Buffalo Bill, Annie Oakley, and the Beginnings of Superstardom in America* (2005). He also wrote books on his travels, *Roads: Driving America's Great Highways* (2000) and *Paradise* (2001).

Achievements • McMurtry's early reputation was based on his depiction of hard modern times in North Texas. *Horseman, Pass By, Leaving Cheyenne,* and *The Last Picture Show* are all located in that area, where the frontier and the old ranching way of life were disappearing while McMurtry was growing up. The second group of three novels, *Moving On, All My Friends Are Going to Be Strangers,* and *Terms of Endearment,* concerns an interrelated group of characters in the Houston area and focuses primarily on failed marriages. McMurtry's Pulitzer Prize and his greatest public success, however, came with his first venture into the traditional Western, his novel of the frontier past, *Lonesome Dove,* considered by many critics to be his finest achievement and the finest novel ever written in that form. During his later years, McMurtry returned to the ranch country of *Lonesome Dove* in *Anything for Billy, Some Can Whistle,* and *Boone's Lick.* He rounded out the story of *Lonesome Dove*'s Gus McCrae and Woodrow Call in *Streets of Laredo, Dead Man's Walk,* and *Comanche Moon.*

 McMurtry did not struggle in obscurity. Several of his books were made into Academy Award-winning films: *Horseman, Pass By,* made into the 1963 film *Hud; The Last Picture Show* in 1971; and *Terms of Endearment* in 1983. He himself won an Academy Award for the screenplay to *Brokeback Mountain* (2005), written with Diana Ossana and adapted from a story by Annie Proulx. *Lonesome Dove* brought McMurtry a Pulitzer Prize and was made into an outstanding television miniseries. His books have routinely become best-sellers.

Biography • Larry Jeff McMurtry was born in Wichita Falls, Texas, in 1936, grandson of a pioneer cattleman in North Texas and one of four children of a ranching family. McMurtry grew up on the ranch, graduated from high school in Archer City, Texas, the locale of much of his early fiction, in 1954, and after one semester at Rice University attended North Texas State University, from which he graduated in 1958. He married Josephine Ballard in 1959; the marriage, which produced one son, ended in divorce in 1966.

McMurtry went back to Rice as a graduate student in English in 1958, beginning work on his first two novels. *Horseman, Pass By* was accepted for publication while he was at Rice and was published while he was a writing student at Stanford University in 1961. Between 1961 and 1969 he taught off and on at Texas Christian University and at Rice, while two more novels were published and he worked on his first long novel, *Moving On*. He had worked occasionally as a book scout for California bookstores while at Stanford, and in 1969 McMurtry left Houston and moved to Washington, D.C., where he became a partner in a bookstore. Thereafter, he divided his time between the store and his writing.

Many of McMurtry's books have been made into motion pictures, most notably *Hud* (1963; the screen name of *Horseman, Pass By*), *The Last Picture Show*, which was filmed by Peter Bogdanovich in Archer City, and *Terms of Endearment* (1983). Actors in all these films (Patricia Neal, Cloris Leachman, Shirley MacLaine, and Jack Nicholson) won Oscars for their performances. *Lonesome Dove* was made into a miniseries for television, with Robert Duvall and Tommy Lee Jones in the major roles. A film version of *Texasville* was released in 1990. McMurtry chose to lead a quiet life, devoted mostly to his two professions, and avoided talk shows and gossip columns.

Analysis • Larry McMurtry's best fiction has used the Southwest as its location and the characters typical of that area for its subjects. In the early years of his career, he dealt with life in the dying towns and decaying ranches of North and West Texas, often using boys on the brink of manhood to provide perspective on a way of life that had reached a stage of corruption and betrayal. His trilogy, following these early novels, dealt with the tangled relationships among somewhat older characters and reflected McMurtry's own move from Archer City to Houston. Later, he invested the Western novel with new vigor in two novels, his classic *Lonesome Dove* and the satiric *Anything for Billy*, which holds the legend of Billy the Kid up to ridicule.

McMurtry has shown the ability to change his locales and his subject matter when he feels the need for novelty, and he has been willing to revive characters from earlier novels to suit new purposes. He has been most successful in exploring the past and present of his native Texas, a state and a state of mind that provide seemingly inexhaustible material for his special blend of satire, romance, and tragedy.

McMurtry has used a variety of styles, from the elegiac to the rapid narrative, from the hilarious to the mournful. He has shown an unusual ability to depict interesting and sometimes outrageous characters, especially women. Although his fictional locales moved away from Texas for a time, in his later works he has gone back to the settings and sometimes the characters of his earlier works. A regional writer, he has transcended the usual limitations of regional writers and attracted a broad audience.

Horseman, Pass By • McMurtry himself eventually said that *Horseman, Pass By*, published when he was only twenty-two, was an immature work. This first novel, a story of ranch life, narrated by a seventeen-year-old boy whose grandfather's livelihood and life are ended when his herd of cattle must be destroyed, sets many of McMurtry's themes: the ease with which people learn to betray others, in this case the old man's betrayal by Hud, his stepson; the mental and physical wear inflicted by the harsh Texas land; and the importance of the affection an older woman (in this case the Bannon family's black cook, Halmea) can give to a young man. This novel and McMurtry's next, *Leaving Cheyenne*, are clearly preparations for the success of *The Last Picture Show.*

The Last Picture Show • McMurtry's third novel is set in the small, dying North Texas town of Thalia (there is a town with that name in Texas, but its geography does not fit the fictional town, which is clearly modeled on Archer City). Its central characters are Sonny Crawford and Duane Moore, two boys in their last year of high school. Neither is in fact an orphan, but neither lives with his surviving parent; they rent rooms in the town's rooming house, support themselves working in the oil fields, and hang out at the town's pool hall, run by their aging friend and mentor Sam the Lion. In the course of about six months, Duane and Sonny learn hard lessons about life and love.

Sonny is the more sensitive of the two. He falls into a passionate affair with Ruth Popper, the frustrated and lonely wife of the high school athletic coach—a stock figure whose latent homosexuality is masked by an aggressive masculinity in the presence of his athletes. Ruth begins the affair in desperation and is startled by the depth of her feeling for Sonny, while the boy is surprised and gratified by the experience. Both realize that the affair cannot last, but Ruth is devastated when Sonny leaves her at the invitation of the town's reigning beauty, Jacy Farrow.

Jacy has been Duane's girlfriend, a monster of selfishness who plays games with both Sonny and Duane, almost destroying their friendship. She keeps putting off Duane's demands that she marry him and insists on seeing another young man and going with him to wild parties in Wichita Falls. When Duane leaves town to work in the oil fields, Jacy decides to take Sonny away from Ruth Popper. Duane finds out, fights with Sonny, and blinds his friend in one eye by hitting him with a beer bottle. Jacy persuades Sonny to elope with her as an adventure, arranging matters so that her father will stop them before they are actually married. Jacy's wise and experienced mother, Lois, offers Sonny brief consolation and shows him that he must make peace with Ruth Popper.

878 *Notable American Novelists*

The boys' adventures have been made possible by the wise counsel and care of Sam the Lion. He has taught them about life, given them parental refuge, and shown them the limits of behavior by closing them out when they are involved in the mistreatment of his mentally disabled ward, Billy. The safety of their world is shattered when Sam dies suddenly, leaving his pool hall and restaurant in the care of Sonny. The young man is forced to face the cruelty of the world when Billy, sweeping the streets of Thalia in his customary way, is hit and killed by a passing truck. The boys are reconciled when Duane leaves to join the Army and fight in Korea.

The Last Picture Show, named for the film theater that is forced to close, symbolizing the decay of Thalia, is a compound of nostalgia, harsh realism, and tragedy. It deals with the almost inevitable loss of innocence of its central characters and with the hard realities of injury, loss, and death. It is frank about sex (Australian authorities banned the novel at one time), but it makes clear the price Sonny and Ruth Popper pay for their affair. At the same time, its depiction of adolescence is often amusing and colorful; the boys take off on a wild adventure south through Texas and into Mexico, they enjoy playing bad basketball for an increasingly frustrated Coach Popper, they enjoy earning their own livings. With the exception of the incident involving the joke played on Billy, they do harm only to themselves.

The Last Picture Show shows the meanness of the people in a small town: Ruth Popper is scorned for loving a boy much younger than herself; the sheriff and other observers are callously indifferent when Billy is killed; Sam the Lion has had to live without the love of his life, Lois Farrow, because of the mores of the town; the coach, despite his poor teams and his general ignorance and stupidity, is looked up to and admired by most of the town. Duane, the more conventional of the two central figures, is sometimes a bully and sometimes a fool.

There is a kind of soft quality to the novel, nevertheless. Most of those the boys encounter are sympathetic to them, including the waitress in Sam's café, the woman who is forced to close the theater, Ruth Popper, and Sam himself. They have no parents, but there are plenty of surrogates to guide and care for them, and they seem always to be forgiven by those they have hurt. Billy carries no grudge against either of them, Sam eventually shows that Sonny has done his penance, and even Ruth forgives Sonny for leaving her. Duane is hard enough not to need forgiveness.

Texasville • McMurtry revived Thalia, Sonny, and Duane in *Texasville*, a comic look at Thalia after it has experienced the boom of high oil prices and then been hit by the oil depression of the early 1980's. In *Texasville* Sonny recedes into the background, a forgetful and lonely middle-aged man who seems to suffer from something like premature Alzheimer's disease. The focus is on Duane, whose oil business has gone to pot, whose marriage to Karla (a new character) is in deep trouble, and whose love life and civic responsibilities provide material for comedy. His life is further complicated by the return to Thalia of Jacy, thrice-married film starlet, mother of three children, saddened and made more human by the death of her young son. *Texasville* is longer, more comic, and more complicated than *The Last Picture Show*, but it is less affecting. Only the episode in which Sonny wanders off and is found sitting in the wreckage of the old theater recalls the tone of the earlier novel.

The Last Picture Show was McMurtry's sometimes bitter, sometimes nostalgic farewell to the North Texas setting of his early work. The next stage in his career focused on young people in the Houston area, beginning with *Moving On*, a long depiction of the damage wrought by a marriage that is falling apart, and a sad picture of university life and the lives of traveling rodeo performers. This second phase of McMurtry's career ended with *Terms of Endearment*, the story of a lively widow and her troubled daughter, who eventually dies of cancer.

All My Friends Are Going to Be Strangers • Typifying this second stage is *All My Friends Are Going to Be Strangers*, a novel held together only by the central character and narrator, Danny Deck, who was introduced in *Moving On*. Danny's experience is to some extent based on that of his creator. Early in the book, while he is a graduate student at Rice, Danny's first novel is accepted for publication. In the euphoric mood that follows, he leaves Rice and marries Sally, a beautiful and sexy young woman who holds no other interest for Danny and who proves to be a monster. Her former lover accompanies them part of the way to California, leaving after they survive a flash flood in West Texas. After the couple moves to San Francisco and Sally becomes pregnant, she relieves her boredom by engaging in an affair with a blind musician and pushes Danny out of her life. Danny goes downhill, lives in a rundown hotel, and finds himself unable to do satisfactory work on his second novel.

Jill, a brilliant film cartoonist he meets on a brief excursion to Hollywood, pulls Danny out of his slump and lives with him for a while, setting his life in order. Temporarily he thinks that he has found the love of his life, and his writing is stimulated by an idea she has provided. Jill, however, has lost interest in sex (which seems to be Danny's chief interest), and their relationship deteriorates until she leaves him to return to Hollywood and Danny sets out for Texas.

The episodic nature of *All My Friends Are Going to Be Strangers* continues when Danny returns to Texas. He pays a visit to his Uncle L, providing a satiric picture of an old-time cowboy gone eccentric; he returns to Houston and makes love to various women, including Emma, the wife of his best friend, and Jenny, who had been his landlady; he goes through a nightmarish experience signing copies of his book at a bookstore; he has a horrible, violent encounter with Sally's parents, who prevent him from seeing his newborn daughter; he is harassed and cruelly beaten by two Texas Rangers who take a dislike to his long hair. He goes for several days without any real sleep. In the end he walks into the Rio Grande, pushing the manuscript pages of his new novel under the water and possibly intending to commit suicide by drowning; that is never clear.

Danny's experiences are intended to show the dislocating effects of early success on a young man who has cut himself off from his roots and has become unable to establish real connections with any other human beings. He falls in love easily enough, but neither Sally nor Jill can return his love in the way he needs, and he has no way to extend his brief affair with Jenny. His encounter with Emma can lead only to guilty feelings for both of them.

Danny is just as much at sea in the other kinds of life he experiences. The editor of his publishing house takes him briefly into a world of authors and sophisticates in which he feels himself to be totally out of place. His brief experience in Hollywood exposes him to people who mystify and amaze him, but for whom he has no respect. He twice pays brief visits to the Stanford campus where McMurtry spent two years, but what he gets from those experiences is the knowledge that he enjoys taking drugs and that he is no scholar. Uncle L shows him that there is nothing for him in ranching life, and the professor from whom he took Sally in the beginning makes it clear that the professorial life is dull and unrewarding.

All My Friends Are Going to Be Strangers is a depressing book. Danny Deck is neither admirable nor particularly amusing. The book is saved by two things. One is McMurtry's undoubted skill as a writer, which enables him to describe scenes as disparate as the flash flood, Uncle L's encounter with his wife, and a literary party in a posh San Francisco suburb vividly and entertainingly. The other is the presence of several interesting minor characters, from Wu, the exiled Chinese writer who admires Danny's work and plays table tennis with him, to Mr. Stay, the former-communist bookstore owner and sonnet writer who hosts the book-signing party. Several of the women, including Jill, Emma, and Jenny, are memorable and distinctive. The novel suggests, however, that McMurtry's Houston years did not provide the material or the inspiration for his best fiction.

Some Can Whistle • In a much later work, Danny Deck proves not to have killed himself: McMurtry brings him back in *Some Can Whistle* as a successful middle-aged writer who has chosen to live in relative isolation. He finds the daughter he has never known, T. R., and brings her and her two children to live with him. She is lively, engaging, and interesting; for a while she seems to be able to revive Danny's wish to be in closer touch with other human beings, but in the end, when T. R. is suddenly killed, the habits of his lifetime are too strong. He has not changed enough from his earlier self.

McMurtry, in the group of novels that followed *All My Friends Are Going to Be Strangers*, seemed to be trying to demonstrate that he could write successful novels that had nothing to do with Texas or with the life of a writer. The brief satiric glimpse of Hollywood given in *All My Friends Are Going to Be Strangers* was expanded in *Somebody's Darling*, whose central character is a film director trying to cope with her early success and the demands of two men she loves. The world McMurtry entered as a bookstore owner is reflected obliquely in *Cadillac Jack*, whose protagonist is an itinerant antique dealer and whose chief setting is Washington, D.C. The entertainment industry comes under further examination in *The Desert Rose*, which has as its heroine an aging topless dancer in Las Vegas. Each of these novels is entertaining and well written, but none did much to enhance McMurtry's reputation.

Lonesome Dove • That enhancement had to wait until McMurtry decided to write a novel in one of the oldest and most persistently popular of American fictional traditions, the Western. With rare exceptions, Western novels have not been treated by critics as serious literature, since they have tended to follow hackneyed patterns of characterization and action. Patterns established by such writers as Ned Buntline in the nineteenth century were passed on almost intact to more recent writers such as Zane Grey and Louis L'Amour. What McMurtry did in *Lonesome Dove* was to reinvent the Western novel by taking its basic elements and elevating them to the level of epic. *Lonesome Dove* has attained the status of a classic of Western fiction.

The characters in *Lonesome Dove* are familiar to readers of Western fiction, here given new names: the silent hero, Woodrow Call, who cares more for horses than for women and who leads other men by example and by courage; the other hero, Gus McCrae, talkative and easygoing, always ready for emergencies; the prostitute with a heart of gold, Lorena (Lorie) Wood; the evil renegade half-breed, Blue Duck; the naïve but courageous boy, Newt; the strong almost-widow, Clara Allen; the handsome but weak gambler, destined to come to a bad end eventually, Jake Spoon; the unimaginative but dependable sheriff, July Johnson; the comic deputy, July's aide Roscoe; and a cast of thousands.

McMurtry's achievement in *Lonesome Dove* is twofold. First, he puts his huge cast of characters into motion. Beginning with a run-down livery stable and cattle-trading business in a tiny Texas town south of San Antonio called Lonesome Dove, the former Texas Rangers Call and Gus put together a herd by rustling from Mexican ranches across the Rio Grande, hire enough cowboys to run the drive, and set out for Montana, where Jake Spoon has told them there is a world of grass unclaimed by white men. Their journey is difficult and tragic, lightened at times by comedy, but it is never dull or ordinary. Lorie, whose beauty has been the only relief to the boredom of Lonesome Dove, makes Jake take her along, to the great disgust of Call, the former Ranger captain who can see no use for women anywhere, much less on a cattle drive. She and Jake are not part of the drive, but they stay close to it; many of the cowboys, in love with Lorie, are kept in a state of agitation—especially the top hand, Dish, who desperately wants to marry her.

McMurtry's approach to his material is leisurely. More than two hundred pages at the beginning, exceeding one-fourth of the long novel, are devoted to preliminary events in Lonesome Dove and the first stages of the drive: the arrival of Jake, a former Ranger on the run from a murder charge, with his news of Montana; Call's sudden and uncharacteristic decision to go, after ten years of relative inactivity; the raids into Mexico to steal horses and cattle; the gathering of an outfit to supplement Newt, Pea Eye, and Deets, the Hat Creek crew; Lorie's instant love for Jake, even though she quickly sees his weakness. Most of this material is humorous, largely because Gus is a man who refuses to take life seriously. The raid into Mexico is exciting and potentially dangerous, but even this adventure turns to comedy when the Hat Creek cowboys encounter two lost Irish brothers who left Ireland headed for Galveston and wound up missing their target by several hundred miles. The Irish brothers, despite their unfamiliarity with horses and cattle, are hired on.

The second major factor in McMurtry's success in *Lonesome Dove* is his ability to take stock characters and humanize them by making them recognizable and distinctive human beings while at the same time elevating them to mythic proportions. Call is a projection of the strong but silent type of frontiersman, quiet, self-contained, but restless and capable of angry outbursts. Despite his abilities, he is emotionally strangled. Gus McCrae is almost superhuman. When necessary, he can fight more effectively than other men, but he is also warm and sympathetic to women and to young boys in trouble, such as Call's unacknowledged bastard son, Newt. He brings Lorie out of her catatonic state and wins her love, but he is human enough to wish that he could have Clara instead. Newt Dobbs is the typical young man; subjected again and again to grief and strain, he grows and matures. The black scout, Deets, is everything a scout should be.

The pace of the novel accelerates once the herd is on the trail. As soon as the drive begins, disaster strikes. Two days out, the herd is hit by a storm, and the riders must stay up all night to keep the cattle from dispersing. The next day, crossing a stream roiled by the storm, the younger and sadder of the Irish brothers stirs up a nest of cottonmouth snakes and is horribly killed. It is the first of several deaths the men will encounter on their long odyssey.

Only late in this initial section does McMurtry introduce another set of characters: July Johnson, the sheriff of Fort Smith, Arkansas; his unhappy pregnant wife, Elmira, a former prostitute; her son, Joe; and the deputy Roscoe. In Fort Smith, July's brother, the town mayor, has been accidentally killed by a shot fired by Jake Spoon, and the mayor's widow is urging July to track down Jake and bring him back to hang.

July, recovering from jaundice and convinced that the shooting was an accident, is reluctant to go, but eventually he sets out, at Elmira's insistence taking Joe along. Shortly thereafter, Elmira, pregnant with July's child, leaves town on a riverboat to seek out her former lover, the gambler Dee Boot, and July's sister-in-law insists that Roscoe track down July to tell him that his wife is gone.

All these characters, and others, eventually meet on the plains. Jake leaves Lorie to go to town to gamble, and while he is gone the Comanchero Blue Duck, a bitter, crafty, and resourceful renegade, kidnaps the terrified Lorie, takes her north to the plains, and keeps her barely alive only to sell her body to Kiowas and buffalo hunters, an experience that robs her of speech and very nearly of her sanity. She is rescued by Gus, but the cost of the rescue is high: July Johnson, still looking for Elmira, insists on helping Gus, and while they are dispatching the six Kiowas and two buffalo hunters who hold Lorie, Blue Duck sneaks into their small camp and murders Roscoe, July's stepson Joe, and a young girl who has been traveling with Roscoe.

Jake, in the meantime, has become entangled with the three Suggs brothers, hard cases who are getting harder. Jake accidentally kills another man and goes along with the Suggses, who kill several more, including the rancher Wilbarger, who has earlier befriended Gus. Call and Gus track down the Suggses and hang all three brothers; reluctantly, they also hang Jake.

Many of the elements of the plot resolve themselves in the Nebraska frontier town of Ogallala. Clara Allen, the only woman Gus has loved and lost, lives there with her comatose husband and two daughters. Elmira arrives first, has her baby, and departs with her buffalo-hunter escort, both soon to be killed by Sioux. Her lover, Dee Boot, is hanged. July Johnson comes next, sees his son, whom Clara has kept, and stays on as a hand at Clara's ranch. Gus and Call arrive with the herd, and Clara and Gus have a happy reunion, but she makes it clear that she will never marry him, even when her husband dies. Lorie finds herself welcomed by Clara, and she stays on when the herd moves north to Montana. Newt and the other young cowboys go to Ogallala and have their first experience with whores, and Newt decides to become a ladies' man like Gus.

In the final section, the herd moves north to Montana and to encounters with still-violent American Indians. Deets is killed by a desperate young warrior who fails to comprehend that Deets is not hostile. Gus and the cowboy Pea Eye, scouting ahead for a ranch site, are cut off by a roving band and attacked. Pea Eye gets away, but Gus is wounded. He escapes from the Native Americans but dies in Miles City after refusing to allow the doctor to amputate both of his gangrenous legs.

Call finds a spot for a ranch, and the men build a ranch house and corrals and spend a hard winter there. When spring comes, Call leaves Newt in charge of the remaining men and the cattle, tacitly acknowledging that he is Newt's father, but he cannot bring himself to call the boy his son. He fulfills his promise to take Gus's body and bury it in a Texas glen where Gus and Clara had picnicked years earlier. On his long and difficult journey, Call passes through Ogallala, where Clara's husband has died and she and Lorie are mourning for Gus. Later, he pauses long enough to witness Blue Duck's death. Call is shot and goes through numerous other trials, but he manages to bury Gus; as the end, he makes his way back to the deserted town of Lonesome Dove.

In *Lonesome Dove* McMurtry is at the height of his powers. The disparate strands of the plot are handled skillfully, as the story moves easily from the herd to July Johnson to Jake Spoon to Elmira and then back to the herd. McMurtry's ability to depict action comes into play often, in the violent scenes of the young Irishman's death, Gus's explosion into the Kiowa camp where Lorie is held, the sudden thunderstorms that batter the cowboys and scatter the herd, the sudden descent of a plague of grasshoppers, and many other scenes. He is equally skilled at depicting character, not only the major figures such as Call, Gus, Clara, and Lorie, but also young Newt and such minor characters as the cook Po Campo, Roscoe, Wilbarger, and Elmira. There is a leavening of humor, some of it hilarious, not only in the early sections of the novel but also throughout. At the same time, there is no attempt to downplay the violence and hardship of the lives of these men and women; the long journey is marked by one violent death after another. The hard life of the frontier is represented not only by Lorie's terrible experience in the hands of Blue Duck and the sudden deaths among the cowboys, but also by Clara's loss of three sons and a husband to the harsh conditions of life on the prairie.

It is entirely fitting that the ending is grim. The most powerful scene in the final section is Clara's condemnation of Call when he returns to Ogallala with Gus's body, bringing the final notes the dying Gus wrote to Clara and Lorie. Her scathing denunciation of his single-mindedness and the human sacrifice and misery the trip caused raises disturbing questions about the meaning of the heroic journey the men have accomplished. The surviving hands are left on the isolated ranch in Montana. Clara and Lorie remain on the ranch outside Ogallala, with July hoping to marry Clara and Dish hopelessly in love with Lorie. Call has no idea where to go after the trip back to Lonesome Dove is ended.

Anything for Billy • The tone of McMurtry's next novel about the frontier, *Anything for Billy*, is very different. This book is a satiric retelling of the story of Billy the Kid, seen from the perspective of an easterner who has been addicted to dime novels of the West. The combination of humor and violent action that marked *Lonesome Dove* is present in the later novel but without the tragic undertone that gives *Lonesome Dove* its special power.

Streets of Laredo, Dead Man's Walk, **and** ***Comanche Moon*** • McMurtry's besetting weakness has clearly been his penchant for reviving characters and using them in sequels to novels that seem to have been sufficient in themselves. Most of his novels can be classified as parts of trilogies, sometimes widely separated in their dates of publication. For example, *Duane's Depressed*, published in 1999, returns to the setting and characters introduced in *The Last Picture Show* and updated in *Texasville*. The pattern is stretched even further in the Lonesome Dove cycle. That very long novel, which fittingly concludes in tragedy and pathos, has since become the basis for a virtual library of sequels and prequels. In *Streets of Laredo, Dead Man's Walk,* and *Comanche Moon*, the leading *Lonesome Dove* characters of Augustus McCrae and Woodrow Call, as well as lesser figures, are revived.

Adding to the confusion, the order of publication of the three later novels in the cycle does not follow the chronological stages in the characters' lives. *Streets of Laredo* is a true sequel, following the career of Woodrow Call after he has returned Augustus McCrae's body to the nearly deserted village of Lonesome Dove. It ends with a crippled Call, minus an arm and a leg, dependent on Pea Eye and his wife Lorena and their many children. *Dead Man's Walk* jumps back in time to the years between the Mexican War and the Civil War when McCrae and Call are about twenty years old and are new recruits to the Texas Rangers. It takes its title from the Spanish phrase (*jornada del muerto*) describing a barren stretch of land in what is now central New

Mexico, where much of the action of the novel takes place. *Comanche Moon* takes the heroes through the years of the Civil War to their decision to leave the Rangers and settle in the village of Lonesome Dove.

As is the case with the earlier cycles, the first book in the series is the most successful. One reason for this is that most of the salient facts are known. It is clear from *Lonesome Dove* that Gus never marries Clara Allen. The manner of his and Deets's deaths is presented in the earlier book, as are many other references to events earlier in time. Almost inevitably, this causes an absence of suspense. More important, however, there is in the later books of the series a sense of strain and a feeling that the author is adding incidents and plot lines simply to provide excitement. This is especially true of *Comanche Moon*, in which there is no clear, dominant plot line. Instead there are several plots interwoven in brief chapters, and much of the information is superfluous. It is enough to know that Blue Duck is a brutal savage, for example; the details of his early life add very little to the character.

The strain is more evident in the invention of two major new characters, Inish Scull and his wife, Inez. Scull is a Boston millionaire and Harvard graduate who is the captain of the company of Texas Rangers in which McCrae and Call are enrolled. His relentless search for adventure leads him to enter Mexico on foot with only a Kickapoo scout for company. He finds his enemy, Ahumado, known as the Black Vaquero, but is taken prisoner. Subjected to a variety of tortures, climaxing with the removal of his eyelids, he manages to survive, although he temporarily goes crazy. Inez, while Inish is so engaged, is indulging her proclivities for young men and for spending Inish's and her own money. Their role in the story ends in farce, back in Boston. Inez continues to beat her husband with a bullwhip, and Inish turns down an invitation from Generals Sherman and Sheridan to take command of the Western regiments that are crushing any remaining American Indian resistance. These exaggerated characters do not fit well into a realistic novel.

Duane's Depressed • After McMurtry's relative lack of success with the five historical novels that followed *Lonesome Dove*, he returned to a contemporary setting in *Duane's Depressed*, which completes the trilogy begun with *The Last Picture Show* and continued in *Texasville*. Duane Moore, now on the brink of old age, is the mayor of Thalia. To the astonishment of the rest of the town, he abandons his pickup truck one day and begins to walk wherever he needs to go. His marriage in trouble again, he also breaks with convention by going for help to a young woman psychiatrist. *Duane's Depressed* is not McMurtry's finest novel, but it is fresher and less strained than the books that preceded it and is a clear improvement over its predecessor, *Texasville*.

John M. Muste

Other major works

NONFICTION: *In a Narrow Grave: Essays on Texas*, 1968; *It's Always We Rambled: An Essay on Rodeo*, 1974; *Film Flam: Essays on Hollywood*, 1987; *Crazy Horse*, 1999; *Walter Benjamin at the Dairy Queen: Reflections at Sixty and Beyond*, 1999; *Roads: Driving America's Great Highways*, 2000; *Paradise*, 2001; *Sacagawea's Nickname: Essays on the American West*, 2001; *The Colonel and Little Missie: Buffalo Bill, Annie Oakley, and the Beginnings of Superstardom in America*, 2005; *Oh What a Slaughter: Massacres in the American West, 1846-1890*, 2006.

EDITED TEXTS: *Still Wild: Short Fiction of the American West*, 2000.

Bibliography

Busby, Mark. *Larry McMurtry and the West: An Ambivalent Relationship.* Denton: University of North Texas Press, 1995. Examines McMurtry's treatment of the West in his works. Includes bibliographical references and an index.

Jones, Malcolm. "The Poet Lariat." *Newsweek,* January 11, 1999, 62-63. This review of Duane's Depressed contains a great deal of useful factual information about McMurtry's life and career.

Jones, Roger Walton. *Larry McMurtry and the Victorian Novel.* College Station: Texas A&M University Press, 1994. A brief study of one of McMurtry's models, the long and complex novel with easily recognizable heroes and villains.

Nelson, Jane. "Larry McMurtry." In *A Literary History of the American West,* edited by Max Westbrook and James H. Maguire. Fort Worth: Texas Christian University Press, 1987. A brief study placing McMurtry in the context of the modern Western novel and showing some of the ways in which he has reinvented the form and given it more tragic shadings.

Rebein, Robert. *Hicks, Tribes, and Dirty Realists: American Fiction After Postmodernism.* Lexington: University Press of Kentucky, 2001. An assertion that gritty realism has gained ascendency over metafiction in American writing. Examines the works of McMurtry, Dorothy Allison, Annie Proulx, Thomas McGuane, Cormac McCarthy, and Louise Erdrich.

Reilly, John M. *Larry McMurtry: A Critical Companion.* Westport, Conn.: Greenwood Press, 2000. An overview of McMurtry's work, supplemented by a biographical chapter. Looks at McMurtry's use of history, his uses of the conventions of the Western genre, and the relationships between his novels and their sequels.

Reynolds, Clay, ed. *Taking Stock: A Larry McMurtry Casebook.* Dallas: Southern Methodist University Press, 1989. A valuable collection of essays, containing a bibliography edited by Charles Williams and important essays by Louise Erdrich and Ernestine P. Sewell.

Woodward, David. "Larry McMurtry's *Texasville:* A Comic Pastoral of the Oil Patch." *Huntington Library Quarterly* (Spring, 1993): 167-180. A study of the author's use of an old traditional form in a modern setting.

Norman Mailer

Born: Long Branch, New Jersey; January 31, 1923

Principal long fiction • *The Naked and the Dead,* 1948; *Barbary Shore,* 1951; *The Deer Park,* 1955; *An American Dream,* 1965; *Why Are We in Vietnam?,* 1967; *The Armies of the Night: History as a Novel, the Novel as History,* 1968; *Marilyn,* 1973; *The Executioner's Song,* 1979; *Of Women and Their Elegance,* 1980; *Ancient Evenings,* 1983; *Tough Guys Don't Dance,* 1984; *Harlot's Ghost,* 1991; *Oswald's Tale: An American Mystery,* 1995; *The Gospel According to the Son,* 1997.

Other literary forms • Beginning with *The Armies of the Night,* Norman Mailer published several works that cross the conventional boundaries of fiction and nonfiction: a "novel biography," *Marilyn;* a "true life novel," *The Executioner's Song;* and an "imaginary memoir," *Of Women and Their Elegance.* Because of his sophisticated handling of style, structure, point of view, and characterization, much of Mailer's journalism and reportage approaches the novel's complexity of language and form: *Miami and the Siege of Chicago: An Informal History of the Republican and Democratic Conventions of 1968* (1969), *Of a Fire on the Moon* (1970), *The Prisoner of Sex* (1971), *St. George and the Godfather* (1972), and *The Fight* (1975). His essays, interviews, short stories, and poems have been collected in *Advertisements for Myself* (1959), *Deaths for the Ladies and Other Disasters* (1962), *The Presidential Papers* (1963), *Cannibals and Christians* (1966), *The Short Fiction of Norman Mailer* (1967), *The Idol and the Octopus: Political Writings on the Kennedy and Johnson Administrations* (1968), *Existential Errands* (1972), and *Pieces and Pontifications* (1982). His work in drama and literary criticism appears in *The Deer Park: A Play* (1967) and *Genius and Lust: A Journey Through the Major Writings of Henry Miller* (1976).

Achievements • With the appearance of *The Naked and the Dead* in 1948, Mailer was hailed by many critics as one of the most promising writers of the postwar generation. Since his early acclaim, Mailer's reputation has risen and fallen repeatedly—in part because of the unevenness of his writing and in part because of his intense participation in the causes and quarrels of his age. More important, however, his work has often been misunderstood because of its remarkably changing character and its innovative procedures, for Mailer relentlessly searches for the style and structure that can most effectively express his ambition to make "a revolution in the consciousness of our time."

By whatever standard Mailer is judged, it is clear that several of his books have a secure place not only in postwar literary history, but also in the canon of significant American literary achievements. *The Naked and the Dead* and *The Armies of the Night* continue to receive attention as masterpieces, and his other novels have begun to benefit from the serious exploration accorded to the finest works of fiction. *The Executioner's Song*—very favorably reviewed when it first appeared—may eventually rank with Mailer's greatest writing because it contains a complexity of point of view and characterization rivaled only by *The Naked and the Dead, An American Dream,* and *Why Are We in Vietnam?*

In addition to receiving several literary honors and distinctions—including the National Book Award, the Pulitzer Prize, and election to the National Institute of Arts and Letters—Mailer has been the subject of more than a dozen book-length studies and hundreds of articles. His work is an essential part of college syllabi in contemporary literature, not only because he has addressed crucial events, concerns, and institutions such as World War II, the Cold War, Hollywood, Vietnam, the Pentagon, and capital punishment, but also because he has treated all of his important themes in the light of a deeply imaginative conception of literary form. As Robert Merrill notes, far too many critics have treated Mailer's writing as simply a record of his opinions. They have taken his musings for assertions, and they have failed to see that he aims at conveying the "meaning" of characters and

Library of Congress

events with the fluidity of metaphor. What Mailer *imagines* rather than what he *believes* is important in assessing all of his prose—and what he imagines consists of entertaining several possible selves, and several sides of issues and events, simultaneously. In other words, he rejects fixity of thought in favor of the play of prose, which in turn parallels the complex play of characters and events.

Biography • Norman Mailer grew up in Brooklyn, New York, and attended Harvard University (1939-1943), where he studied aeronautical engineering and became interested in writing. After he graduated from Harvard, he married Beatrice Silverman and was inducted into the U.S. Army, serving with the 112th Cavalry out of San Antonio, Texas. He was overseas for eighteen months in Leyte, Luzon, and with occupation forces in Japan. His varied experience as a field artillery surveyor, clerk, interpreter of aerial photographs, rifleman, and cook undoubtedly contributed to the comprehensive portrayal of the military in *The Naked and the Dead*.

After his discharge from the army in May, 1946, Mailer immediately began work on *The Naked and the Dead* and completed it within fifteen months. In the next two years (1948-1950), he traveled in Europe, studied at the Sorbonne, wrote articles and delivered speeches, campaigned for the election of Henry Wallace, worked briefly as a screenwriter in Hollywood, and finished his second novel, *Barbary Shore*, which was poorly received—in part because of his sympathetic engagement with Marxist ideas and his aggressive exploration of shifting political attitudes in the postwar years.

For the next ten years, Mailer was beset by various personal and professional traumas. He divorced his first wife—they had one daughter—in 1952. He married Adele Morales in 1954; he stabbed her with a penknife on November 19, 1960, after a party organized to launch his New York City mayoral campaign. The couple was divorced in 1962. During this period, Mailer had difficulty getting his third novel, *The Deer Park*, published, while he simultaneously struggled to complete another novel. After the births of his second and third daughters, Mailer married Lady Jeanne Campbell, who gave birth to his fourth daughter in 1962. With the publication of *Advertisements for Myself*, he began to find a way of rescuing the fragments and dead ends of his career, and with his essay "Superman Comes to the Supermarket" (1960), he evolved a supple way of dramatizing and musing on social and political issues that freed him from the constraints of his not entirely successful first-person narrators in *Barbary Shore* and *The Deer Park*.

In many ways, the 1960's were Mailer's most productive years. Not only did he publish his two most sophisticated novels, *An American Dream* and *Why Are We in Vietnam?*, and adapt *The Deer Park* for the stage, but also he directed and acted in three films—*Wild 90* (January, 1968), *Beyond the Law* (October, 1968), and *Maidstone* (1971)—which provoked him to write important essays on the nature of film and prepared him for his innovative "novel biography," *Marilyn*. He was an active journalist during this period, covering political conventions and the moon shot, and out of his reportage he created a book, *The Armies of the Night*, that transcends the immediate occasion of its conception—a protest march on the Pentagon—in order to probe the shaping processes of history and fiction and their mutuality as human constructs. In 1963, Mailer divorced Lady Jeanne Campbell and married the actor Beverly Bentley, with whom he had two sons. He campaigned unsuccessfully for mayor of New York City in 1969 and fathered a fifth daughter by Carol Stevens in 1971. He subsequently married and divorced her, taking Norris Church as his sixth wife.

During the 1970's and 1980's, Mailer continued to write nonfiction while working on his Egyptian novel, *Ancient Evenings*. Although he began in the mid-1970's to withdraw from public attention, his appearance in the film *Ragtime* (1981) and his defense of Jack Abbott, a writer-convict who committed a murder shortly after his release from prison, revived the image of a controversial, embattled author. As several reviewers pointed out, both *Ancient Evenings* and *Tough Guys Don't Dance* have first-person narrators who bear considerable resemblance to Mailer. His controversial tenure as president of the U.S. chapter of PEN (Association of Poets, Playwrights, Editors, Essayists, and Novelists), along with the film adaptation of *Tough Guys Don't Dance*, which Mailer wrote and directed, once again focused public attention on him.

During the 1990's, Mailer produced three very different books, none of which seemed to enhance his reputation. *Harlot's Ghost*, a very long novel, is a compendium of his fictional themes—particularly Mailer's obsession with the Central Intelligence Agency (CIA) and with conspiracy theories. Nevertheless, his novel is a provocative reading of Cold War history, which may be reevaluated favorably if his promised sequel (*Harlot's Ghost* finishes with the words "to be continued") materializes.

Oswald's Tale again crosses the line between fact and fiction. It resembles *The Executioner's Song*, for once more Mailer worked with tape-recorded interviews, and he visited the former Soviet Union to collect material on his subject. Although *Oswald's Tale*, a very thorough investigation of Lee Harvey Oswald's period in the Soviet Union, received many good reviews, it seemed to have been lost in the flood of books on President John F. Kennedy's assassination.

Finally, Mailer's nonfiction *Portrait of Picasso as a Young Man* (1995) received largely negative reviews, mainly because he was faulted for projecting too many of his own views onto the artist's life and because he did little primary research—borrowing instead from works such as John Richardson's acclaimed multivolume biography. Yet, as with *Marilyn*, Mailer's *Picasso* deserves more careful reading precisely because of the commonalities Mailer establishes between himself and his subjects.

In his later years, Mailer settled into an active, yet rather sober, literary life, continuing to devote himself to writing but shying away from the feuds and controversies that marked so much of his career.

Analysis • Some of Mailer's earliest writing, including "The Greatest Thing in the World," a prizewinner in a 1941 *Story* magazine contest, reveals that even at a very early age he could write accomplished, imitative apprentice fiction in the modes of Ernest Hemingway and John Dos Passos. Before his own service, Mailer was exploring the experience of war in "A Calculus at Heaven" (1942), which suggests his ambition to portray the sweep of his time, to show the psychological and sociological preconditions of war and the existential choices it demands.

The Naked and the Dead • Mailer advanced with astonishing rapidity from his first attempts at fiction, to his own war experience, to the writing of *The Naked and the Dead*. Although it is a very long novel, its coverage of so many diverse elements in remarkably fluid prose and in a compact four-part structure conveys a sense of a single complex concert of human motives and the vagaries of existence. *The Naked and the Dead* is far more than a war novel, more than a political novel, for it examines the way human experience is shaped and interpreted, and it establishes the ground out of which human character and belief arise.

Part 1, "Wave," concerns preparations for the invasion of Anopopei, an island held by the Japanese. The first wave of troops will assault the beaches by riding through the surf and charging ashore. One wave against another, humanity against the nature of its own enterprise, is one of the dominant themes of the novel, as its second paragraph indicates by describing an anonymous soldier who "lies flat on his bunk, closes his eyes, and remains wide-awake. All about him, like the soughing of surf, he hears the murmurs of men dozing fitfully." The poker game the soldiers play, like the war itself, has its meaning in "the margin of chance," in the calculation and skill that is nevertheless vulnerable to luck, good or bad. Much of what makes the novel fascinating is its persistent aligning of the interface between planning and probability; each soldier tries to gauge what his chances are of surviving, or—in Sergeant Croft's and General Cummings's cases—dominating the war, although almost every man, like Martinez, has at least one moment of fear, of total vulnerability, when he feels "naked" and almost certainly dead under fire.

Part 2, "Argil and Mold," shifts from the reactions of the combat soldiers to war to the grand strategy of General Cummings, who plans on shaping his army to fit his master design. For Cummings, the war—like history itself—must have a pattern, one that he can follow and channel in his direction. He disclaims the operations of chance; seeming accidents, he contends, are actually a result of a person's failure to capitalize on the opportunities life affords. If Cummings does not yet know the precise trajectory of history, he is confident that he will be percipient enough to discover it eventually. His game is not cards; it is chess. "The trick is to make yourself an instrument of your own policy," Cummings advises his resistant subordinate, Lieutenant Hearn, who refuses to credit the General's command not only over the forces of history but also over Hearn himself.

In the course of his conflict with Hearn, Cummings reveals his disdain for the liberal's "exaggerated idea of the rights due" to persons as individuals. In the General's reading of history, it is not the development of individuality but of power concentrations that counts in evaluating the causes of the war. As a result, he violates the integrity of much of the experience that is portrayed in the novel, for each character—including the General—is given a unique biography, a singularity of purpose that defies the notion that individuals can be permanently fashioned as part of a power bloc. After the initial success of his landing on Anopopei, Cummings is thwarted: "The campaign had gone sour. . . . [H]is tactics were as well conceived as they had ever been, his staff performances as thorough, his patrols as carefully planned, but nothing happened. . . . A deep unshakable lethargy settled over the front-line troops." Like Hearn, Cummings finds he cannot argue his army into action for an indefinite period of time.

Each of the principal characters in the novel behaves not only in terms of his background (the "Time Machine" sections delineate prewar experiences) and his participation in a platoon (the "Chorus" sections suggest the extent to which individual experience can be collectivized), but also in terms of the power argument between Cummings and Hearn. That is why it is almost inevitable that Hearn will ultimately be placed at the head of Sergeant Croft's platoon, for Croft has often kept his men together by the force of his own will, by an invincible belief in the rightness of his position that is virtually identical to Cummings's self-assurance.

Like Cummings, Croft contends with a geographical and ethnic cross section of soldiers: Red Valsen, "the wandering minstrel" from Montana, who distrusts all permanent relationships; Gallagher, "the revolutionary reversed," an Irish Catholic from Boston who seems perpetually angry at the way the more privileged or the more conniving have deprived people of their dignity but who is also profoundly prejudiced against other groups, especially the Jews; Julio Martinez, the Mexican American, who desperately asserts his loyalty, his integrity, by taking pride in courageously executing Croft's dangerous orders; Joey Goldstein, who from his "cove in Brooklyn" tries to ingratiate himself in a world inhospitable to Jews; and Wilson, the affable southerner who traffics easily with women and the world, and who is without much sense of life's disparities and of how he has hurt as well as charmed others with his "fun." These characters and others are meant to convey the multiplicity of experience that Croft crushes in disciplining his platoon.

In one of the most telling scenes in the novel, Croft allows a captured Japanese soldier time to recover his composure, to express his humanity, to plead for his life, and to sense that he is in the presence of other compassionate human beings, before brutally shooting him in the very moment of his happiness. Croft's cruelty is the most extreme extension of Cummings's declaration that individuals do not count, that single lives are valued too highly. Ultimately, this kind of merciless wiping out of opposition does not make Croft a better soldier; his attempt to scale Mount Anaka has been futile from the beginning, and the Japanese are defeated without the imposition of either Croft's or Cummings's will. Just as Croft's men accidently blunder into the hornets that drive them back down the mountain, so in part 3, Major Dalleson, a mediocre, timid officer, blunders into easy and rapid victory over the Japanese while Cummings is away from the campaign seeking naval support for an elaborate plan that in the end proves superfluous in the defeat of a Japanese army almost disintegrating by itself for lack of food and military supplies.

Part 3, "Plant and Phantom," prepares for the novel's abrupt denouement by exploring Friedrich Nietzsche's troubling premise that "even the wisest among you is only a disharmony and hybrid of plant and phantom. But do I bid you become phantoms or plants?" The question of human nature is unanswerable; human beings are divided creatures, both body and mind, and neither side of that nature can entirely suppress the other even in the shrewdest of individuals. In the novel, people live and die as plants and phantoms, as thinking and feeling beings who are bound by the conditions of nature and by the consequences of their own actions, over which they often have surprisingly little control. People are truncated, their lives are suddenly cut off, even as their thoughts appear to extend their hold over events. Thus, Hearn drives his men to the other side of the island, so that they can reconnoiter the possibility of an invasion behind Japanese battle lines. He suffers from weariness, from the men's resistance, from his own self-doubt, but he reasserts himself:

> As they moved along out of the hollow he felt good; it was a new morning, and it was impossible not to feel hopeful. The dejection, the decisions of the previous night seemed unimportant. He was enjoying this, but if he was, so much the better.

> A half hour later, Lieutenant Hearn was killed by a machine gun bullet which passed through his chest.

Hearn dies as swiftly as the Japanese defense crumbles, and in both cases the dissolution is all the more devastating when one considers their determination to survive.

Part 4, "Wake," is retrospective, a brief review of the invasion wave of part 1. The reality of the invasion has not conformed to expectations. Even after the fact, Major Dalleson deludes himself about the significance of the campaign, supposing that the forces Cummings finally deployed with naval support behind Japanese lines were decisive. Dalleson's self-deception is just like Martinez's delusion that Hearn did not heed reports of Japanese in the pass where he died. Martinez forgets that Croft had cautioned him not to mention the Japanese to Hearn. In taking a superior attitude to Brown, Stanley forgets, or never actually realizes, his former sycophancy that ensured, with Brown's help, his promotion to corporal. Wilson muddles his trickery of his buddies—getting them to pay more for their liquor so he can have an extra bottle—into a belief in his generous provision for them.

Even more self-conscious characters such as Hearn and Cummings catch themselves in self-deceptions. Hearn believes that he is rebelling against Cummings by crushing a cigarette on the General's immaculate floor when in fact he is playing his superior officer's game, getting himself into a position where Cummings is able to employ Hearn as just another pawn in his military strategy. Cummings, in turn, bitterly admits to himself that Hearn has a way of depriving him of his sense of command, for Hearn (who is something like a wayward son) represents the intractability of the fighting force Cummings wants to regard as an extension of himself. Mailer brilliantly reveals the ironies of Cummings's command in the General's discovery of the cigarette butt "mashed into the duckboards in a tangled ugly excrement of black ash, soiled paper, and brown tobacco." Cummings has been having bouts of diarrhea; what he sees on the floor is a manifestation of his lack of control, his inability to make his body, like his men, obey his rigorous schedule. In this encyclopedic novel—Mailer's attempt to write the equivalent of Leo Tolstoy's *War and Peace* (1865-1869) in his generation, to show that, like Napoleon, Cummings fails to reduce history to the curve of his desire—no character can claim mastery over himself or the world, for the interplay between individuals and events is too complex, too contingent, to be predictable, even though characters such as Cummings and Croft pursue their careers with the monomania of Herman Melville's Ahab in *Moby Dick* (1851).

The *Naked and the Dead* almost seemed to write itself, Mailer comments in *Advertisements for Myself*. In retrospect, Mailer felt he could not go on repeating a best-seller formula based on a skillful melding of Hemingway and Dos Passos. Given Mailer's ambition to be a great writer, it is not surprising that his obsession with style prompted him to devalue his first novel. If *The Naked and the Dead* is derived from the styles of other writers, it also conveys a sense of history that is almost entirely lacking in Hemingway and is diminished in Dos Passos by rather crude melodrama and determinism. In Mailer, there is no clear division of historical villains and heroes; on the contrary, he develops a dramatic dialogue of ideas that arise persuasively out of carefully delineated personalities. He did not equal this achievement for some time, perhaps because he had to go through various attempts at finding a style, a singular—even quirky—manner that is as individual as Dos Passos's "Camera Eye" sections in *U.S.A.* (1937) or the radically charged prose of William Faulkner's best work.

Barbary Shore • Mailer's next novel, *Barbary Shore*, was a disappointment to critics and to Mailer himself, even though he suggests in *Advertisements for Myself* that the novel helped to prepare him for becoming the kind of writer he would remain for the rest of his career. *Barbary Shore* seems detached from many of the basic assumptions of *The Naked and the Dead*, which has a naïve confidence when viewed from the perspective of its successor. Although history is not controllable in *The Naked and the Dead*, it is not even certain that history is knowable in *Barbary Shore*, where several characters and events have a phantasmagoric quality. Characters often speak in an allegorical dialogue, so that the Soviet Union, for example, is referred to as "the land beyond the sea." One of the main characters, McLeod, has had a variety of identities, and it is never entirely clear what the truth of his life has been—not even to himself. The first-person narrator, Mike Lovett, is an amnesiac who vaguely recalls fragments of his past—most of them are memories of war—but is not sure that they are, in fact, his own.

At one time a foreign agent for the Communist Party, McLeod is pursued by Hollingsworth, who is some kind of government operative, an agent of the American status quo, on a mission to recover a "little object" (which is never identified) that McLeod is presumed to have stolen while working for what was probably a government agency—perhaps the same agency for which Hollingsworth works. The novel is further complicated by the presence of Guinevere, an apolitical sexual provocateur, who is discovered to be McLeod's wife. She attracts the amorous attentions not only of Lovett, Hollingsworth, and McLeod but also of Lannie, a bizarre, troubled woman who aligns herself first with Lovett, who befriends McLeod, and then with Hollingsworth. Hollingsworth alternately disputes and accedes to McLeod's hold over Lovett, for Lovett, with his lack of a past, represents the pure present over which conflicting personalities and ideologies contend.

Presumably, Mailer abandoned the realistic mode and third-person narration of *The Naked and the Dead* in favor of the ambiguities of *Barbary Shore* in order not only to suggest the Cold War period of shifting loyalties and competing ideologies but also to probe the divisions within his characters who suffer from crises of conviction. McLeod, for example, has tried but failed to follow the course of history, to remake the world into the fulfillment of revolutionary socialism. *Barbary Shore,* however, is unable to take the measure of McLeod in the way *The Naked and the Dead* judges Cummings, for McLeod's dialogue with others, in which the weaknesses of his position are diagnosed, becomes a monologue that upsets the balance of the novel and makes it seem as if McLeod has somehow rescued himself from his defeat. Lovett is unwilling to abandon him even though he is fairly sure that McLeod has murderously attempted to enforce his revolutionary purpose on others. It is true that his passing on of "the little object" to Lovett represents his final refusal to capitulate to the status quo, to the "two different exploitative systems," but his gesture to ameliorate "mankind in barbary," in a world where there is "war and preparation for new war," must be balanced by the novel's first historical parable.

Lovett describes his fantasy of a plump, complacent, middle-aged traveler who is anxious to get home. He is tired and "unaccountably depressed" after a long trip and suddenly shocked to find that while he recognizes the city in which he travels as his home, "the architecture is strange, and the people are dressed in unfamiliar clothing," and he cannot read the alphabet on the street sign. He tries to calm himself in the belief that he is dreaming, but Lovett shouts, "this city is the real city, the material city, and your vehicle is history." The fantasy aptly conveys the novel's contention that people think they know the course of their life, think that they can read the signs of history, when in fact what they have taken to be so familiar, so easily apprehended, is elusive, strange, and terrifying.

The Deer Park • It is not difficult to regard Mailer's third novel, *The Deer Park,* as a mature rewriting of *Barbary Shore.* Once again, there is a first-person narrator, Sergius O'Shaugnessy, who, like Lovett, is a writer. Although Sergius knows his past, he is an orphan who shares Lovett's sense of uncertainty: "I was never sure of myself. I never felt as if I came from any particular place, or that I was like other people." His feeling of being like a "spy or a fake" recalls Lovett's adamant refusal to become a spy for Guinevere. Sergius, however, is more self-aware, more active as a writer in this novel than Lovett is in *Barbary Shore,* where his writing is a given but is not really explored. *The Deer Park,* on the other hand, is the product of Sergius's imagination; it represents his coming to terms with himself and the world. Although his friendship with Charles Eitel, a blacklisted Hollywood scriptwriter and director, is reminiscent of Lovett's friendship with McLeod, Eitel's story is framed in Sergius's words; Sergius contrasts Eitel's defeat with his victory.

Cold War politics play just as important a part in *The Deer Park* as in *Barbary Shore,* but the former eschews the strained allegorical rhetoric of the latter. Some of *The Deer Park*'s finest passages are the dialogues of Hollywood studio executives and politicians, in which the exploitative aspects of capitalist culture and government become apparent in the language, even in the physical gestures and tones of voice the characters employ, so that Mailer avoids merely talking *about* political issues by demonstrating how they arise in careers such as Eitel's. He has been a communist sympathizer, a fellow traveler, whose presence embarrasses his motion-picture bosses. He then alienates them by refusing to cooperate with a congressional committee investigating subversives. Eitel turns from Hollywood with the hope that he can recover his talent honestly as an artist but finds that the great film he had always dreamed of creating has been corrupted by his absorption of the cheap techniques of commercial filmmaking. Eventually, he capitulates by agreeing to testify about his communist past and to construct his film according to Hollywood conventions.

At the same time, Sergius's own life story—from orphan to war hero—draws Hollywood interest, and he is sorely tempted to sell his biography—sell himself, in effect—to the studio, where he may also become a film star. What prevents him from doing so is Eitel's example, or rather Sergius's interpretation of Eitel's biography, for at the end of the novel it is Sergius who has made some meaning out of Eitel's career:

> "For you see," [Eitel] confessed in his mind, "I have lost the final desire of the artist, the desire which tells us that when all else is lost, when love is lost and adventure, pride of self, and pity, there still remains that world we may create, more real to us, more real to others, then the mummery of what happens, passes, and is gone."

Sergius goes on to imagine that Eitel equates the creative act with Sergius's rebellion, with "the small trumpet of your defiance."

Sergius invents an Eitel from whom he can learn, and his lessons are facilitated by his relationships with many of Eitel's friends and lovers. Lulu Meyers, for example, has been married to Eitel but now is free to engage in an affair with Sergius, which she eventually terminates, much to his despair. Sergius, however, avoids the extremes of self-pity and self-aggrandizement by reconstructing the affair between Elena Esposito and Eitel that is taking place during his pursuit of Lulu. Eitel's coldness, arrogance, and self-deceptiveness come through in Sergius's version of the affair, but, like McLeod, Eitel is essentially a sympathetic figure and more believably so than McLeod, since Eitel's tragic realization of his limitations is not muffled by the slightest self-justification at the end of the novel.

If the novel's Hollywood milieu is like Louis XV's Deer Park, that gorge in which innocents like Sergius are engulfed, Sergius barely escapes the gorge by imagining for himself the lives of its victims, of its pimps and prostitutes, of its sultans and sycophants. If *Barbary Shore* begins to put the first-person narrator, the writer as actor, in a paramount position, then *The Deer Park* examines the drama of that position, which Mailer directly comments on in *Advertisements for Myself*, where he acknowledges the increasingly autobiographical nature of his narrators. Not that Sergius is in any simple way Mailer—in fact, he is far less self-conscious about his style than Mailer usually is—but Sergius's quest as a writer who needs to find his words, his style, through direct involvement that tests him against his characters' actions, provided Mailer with the conception of himself and the process of literary creation that has become central to nearly all of his work. Indeed, the process of literary creation itself becomes his theme. In other words, the writer himself becomes his subject.

An American Dream • *An American Dream*, by its very title, points to Mailer's fascination with the notion that America is a complex fiction, a drama of reality that is captured in the dynamic language of its narrator, Stephen Rojack, Mailer's hipster hero par excellence, a war hero, a college chum of John Kennedy, a congressman, college professor, psychologist, television personality, and actor resembling the Sergius O'Shaugnessy who was supposed to be the major figure in Mailer's uncompleted novel, delivered in the form of "Advertisement for Myself on the Way Out" at the conclusion of *Advertisements for Myself*.

Rojack is also the first Mailer narrator to have an intellect, a vocabulary, and a multiplicity of roles that are commensurate with his author's own activities as soldier, writer, politician, film director, actor, and television personality. As a result, Rojack, like Mailer, registers and revalues his experience. Like his creator, he is never content with a single formulation of reality; on the contrary, he is a complex of shifting moods in response to the modulations of his environment. As Jennifer Bailey phrases it, in Mailer's mature work "identity is always a fiction insofar as it depends upon a constantly changing milieu for its definition."

All of Rojack's actions have to be viewed within the existential requirements of reality in the novel rather than within rigid moral codes applied by readers who want to keep "concepts firmly in category." For some readers, the novel's sense of absolute relativity, of moral fluidity, is repugnant, and *An American Dream* has been rejected out of hand as Mailer's most disturbing work, since Rojack as hipster does not merely live close to violence: He purges and cleanses himself through murdering his wife, Deborah.

In conventional fiction, Rojack's act of murder might be taken as the surest sign that he has lost control of himself. Yet, quite the contrary is true in Mailer's daring fiction, for Rojack regains possession of himself in committing his crime. In some of his most sharply driven, economical prose, Mailer has Rojack explain in the first chapter that he doubts his perception of the world in terms of a rational paradigm. He notes that "the real difference between the President and myself may be that I ended with too large an appreciation of the moon, for I looked down the abyss of the first night I killed: four men, four very separate Germans, dead under a full moon—whereas Jack, for all I know, never saw the abyss." In other words, Rojack senses the occult nature of reality, of forces that terrorize him until he has the courage to act in harmony with them.

Until he reached a point of self-identification, Rojack "remained an actor. My personality was built upon a void." He quit politics "before I was separated from myself forever by the distance between my public appearance that had become vital on television, indeed nearly robust, and my secret frightened romance with the phases of the moon." Virtually the entire novel is written in a style that dramatizes Rojack's search for a new basis on which to live. After considering suicide, after literally expelling from his system the rotting, half-digested food and drink that signify a life he cannot ingest, he confronts his estranged wife, "an artist with the needle," a woman from an influential family who has represented his "leverage" on life. Doing away with Deborah means confronting his case by himself, and he has never had "the strength to stand alone."

Rojack begins to stand alone by following the hipster's course set out in *The White Negro* (1957). He recognizes, in the words of that essay, that "one must grow or else pay more for remaining the same (pay in sickness, or depression, or anguish for the lost opportunity), but pay or grow. . . . What he must do . . . is find his courage at the moment of violence, or equally make it in the act of love." Rojack finds his lover, Cherry, a blond with various qualities that remind him of Grace Kelly and Marilyn Monroe. More than that, however, is his sense that Cherry has "studied blondes," as if she has absorbed all of their styles. The multiplicity of her appeal is like the manifold manifestations of life that he intuits rather than grasps logically. Cherry, and many of the other characters in the novel, are viewed in a world of heightened senses, particularly the sense of smell. Rojack is constantly getting whiffs of things, of moods, of symbolic correspondences between people and ideas: "One kiss of flesh, one whiff of sweet was loose, sending life to the charnel house of my balls." The incredible number of smells that assault him prevent the novel from becoming mystical and abstract. Rather, the intangible linkages are permeated with the corporeality of bodies and beings. In this way, the world becomes an integral function in his psychic economy, and he is even able to face his wife's formidable father, Oswald Kelly, who would just as soon push Rojack to his death as to make him observe the proprieties of the funeral ceremony, where he expects Rojack's presence will help to subdue Kelly's embarrassment over the suspicious circumstances of Deborah's death.

Rojack's tie to Kelly becomes stronger when he discovers that Cherry has been Kelly's mistress—just one of those "coincidences" that rule Rojack's uncanny sense of the connections between lives. As he tries to save his integrity by confronting Kelly, he loses Cherry, who is murdered. He has been divided between returning to her and once again challenging the abyss, the drop from Kelly's high-rise apartment to the street, which represents the void Rojack must fill with his self-definition. At the end of the novel, in Las Vegas, he realizes that he has gambled for his life, that life is a gamble. If he has not been "good enough" to get it all, to have Cherry, he becomes "something like sane again," and departs for a "long trip to Guatemala and Yucatan," just two places, perhaps, on the itinerary of his voyage to selfhood.

Why Are We in Vietnam? • If the examples of Hemingway and Dos Passos prevail over *The Naked and the Dead* and Mailer's other early fiction, and if F. Scott Fitzgerald figures prominently in the composition of *The Deer Park*, then the measure of Mailer's progress as a writer can be taken in *Why Are We in Vietnam?*, a novel that invites deliberate comparison with Faulkner. Mailer deftly describes a bear hunt, as does Faulkner in "The Bear," that explores the fundamental meanings of American identity inherent in the conquest of animals and environment. People must prove themselves no matter how much they override the intimate connections between humankind and nature. Rusty, the narrator D. J.'s father, "is f——ed unless he gets that bear, for if he don't, white men are f——ed more and they can take no more." This kind of reasoning leads to Vietnam, Mailer implies, just as the hunting of bear leads to slavery and other forms of subjugation in Faulkner. Both D. J. and Faulkner's Ike McCaslin come to identify with the animals whose lives they take and with the nature they usurp, so that they must also commune with their feeling of solidarity with life itself, as D. J. does in his remembrance of the mountain goat he has killed:

> It hit D. J. with a second blow on his heart from the exploding heart of the goat and he sat up in bed, in the bunk, listening to the snores, stole out to the night, got one breath of the sense of that *force* up in the North, of land North above him and dived back to the bed, his sixteen-year-old heart racing through the first spooks of an encounter with Herr Dread.

However close Mailer comes to Faulkner in terms of style and theme, *Why Are We in Vietnam?* is still an insistently original novel. In the passage quoted above, for example, the point of view is wholly that of D. J., of the Texan teenager who has never encountered the raw elements of life, who is a disc jockey in his ventriloquizing of many voices in the manner of a radio rock-music personality. Although the prose has Faulkner's relentless flow, its flippant and frenetic beat suggests the repetitive rhythms of technology that heat up D. J.'s talk.

Even more striking is Mailer's playful sport with his narrator's identity. Is D. J. "a Texas youth for sure or is he a genius of a crippled Spade up in Harlem making all this s—— up?" Or is D. J. imitating a "high I.Q. Harlem Nigger"? "There is no security in this consciousness," he maintains, since much of what one takes to be reality is an American dream, or rather a "dream field," a "part of a circuit" with "you swinging on the inside of the deep mystery." Almost inevitably, one is reminded of Ralph Ellison's *Invisible Man* (1952), narrated by a shifting persona, a man of many guises who impersonates others, who like D. J. follows many channels, as if he is broadcasting to the world at large, a world he has somehow subsumed in his supple prose. D. J. brashly appropriates and transforms the styles of others; whereas Ellison's narrator mellowly hints that on the "lower frequencies" he speaks for "you," D. J. commands: "Goose your frequency"—in other words, rev up your sensibility, your reception of the totality D. J. imagines.

As in *An American Dream,* the tendency for the language to turn mystical is checked, even substantiated, by scatological images and metaphors. Some readers find the style offensive, but it is absolutely at the heart of Mailer's vision, since he wants to show on a visceral level how the ideology of consumption works. Because he believes that "the secrets of existence, or some of them anyway, are to be found in the constructions of language" ("The Metaphysics of the Belly"), his style must go to the scatological site of those secrets. To extend D. J.'s remark, the world is "s—" made up by human beings, and in America such "s—" prevails because of the incredible amount of resources that are used, turned into waste products, into refuse that Americans refuse to see.

As Mailer sums it up in "The Metaphysics of the Belly": "Ambitious societies loathe scatological themes and are obsessed with them." The last words of the novel, "Vietnam, hot dam," reflect D. J.'s anticipation; here is still another frontier on which to test himself, another territory for him to explore like Huckleberry Finn, to whom he compares himself at the beginning of the novel. D. J., "disc jockey to America," echoes the country's heated urge to dominate, to damn itself. Or is the minority voice mimicking the majority's will? "Which D. J. white or black would possibly be worse of a genius if Harlem or Dallas is guiding the other, and who knows which?" All the jive talk keeps the channels of possibility open at the end of *Why Are We in Vietnam?*, so that the question of the title has been answered in some ways but is still open-ended, like the identity of the narrator. The reader is left perfectly pitched between alternative readings, once again in the grip of the existential reality that Mailer has faultlessly articulated.

The Armies of the Night: History as a Novel, the Novel as History • *The Armies of the Night* climaxed a period of impressive creativity for Mailer in the mid-1960's. A culmination of the self-review he began in *Advertisements for Myself* and *Cannibals and Christians,* it is a definitive portrait of himself as writer and actor, a discovery of his nonfiction aesthetic, and a subtle amalgam of documentary notation and novelistic interpretation that convincingly captures the complexity and ambiguity of the march on the Pentagon. The book's authority is established by its point of view: Mailer's assessment of himself in the third person, sticking close to his own consciousness in the same way that Henry James sidles along Strether in *The Ambassadors* (1903). Thus, Mailer is able to preserve the spontaneity of historic moments in which he is free to act like a fool or a philosopher while reserving the right as an aloof narrator to judge himself and others with the benefit of hindsight and later research. Futhermore, as Richard Poirier observes, Mailer "manages to be a witness of the present as if it were already the past. He experiences it from the perspective of his future talk and writing about it." The Mailer of the march is at various times "the Beast," "the Historian,"

898 Notable American Novelists

"the Participant," "the Novelist," and "the Ruminant," all of which emphasize the many different guises he assumes depending upon the evolving context of his actions.

As rich as a novel in its use of dialogue and characterization, *The Armies of the Night* humorously pursues the contentions of competing personalities—of the poet Robert Lowell and Mailer himself in this example:

> "I don't know, Cal, your speech really had a most amazing impact on me." Mailer drawled the last few words to drain any excessive sentimental infection, but Lowell seemed hardly to mind.
>
> "Well, Norman, I'm delighted," he said, taking Mailer's arm for a moment as if, God and kingdom willing, Mailer had finally become a Harvard dean and could be addressed by the appropriate limb. "I'm delighted because I liked *your* speech so much."

By using circular dialogue, the search for an agreeable exchange between very different personalities—Lowell, "at once virile and patrician," and Mailer, "the younger, presumptive, and self-elected prince"—they have made a story of their relationship that they can share and repeat. The fictive quality of real events—one of Mailer's major points—is ably demonstrated by his own style. As Mailer says before this dialogue, "the clue to discovery was not in the substance of one's idea, but in what was learned from the style of one's attack."

The book shuttles from such intimate dialogue and precise character delineation to panoramic sweeps of the crowds of the Pentagon march. Book 1, "History as a Novel," portrays Mailer as actor in order to show that history is understood only through a deep appreciation of the intersection of very personal feelings and public affairs. No episode, no idea, no impression remains unqualified by the circumstances out of which it arises, and chapter titles constantly emphasize the way in which the literary imagination shapes historical experience.

Book 2, "The Novel as History," goes even further than book 1 in suggesting that history as a whole can make sense only when the interpreter employs all the "instincts of the novelist," for the record of the march is contradictory, fragmentary, and skewed by various viewpoints. Only an act of profound imagination, a reading of the significance of the event itself, can possibly make its constituent parts coalesce, and Mailer convincingly shows that he has studied the record and found it wanting. History is essentially interior and intuitive, he avers. He then proceeds to elaborate a complex re-creation of events that concretely exposes the factitiousness of newspaper accounts.

Beyond the immediate causes and consequences of the march on the Pentagon, Mailer sees the event as a rite of passage for the young marchers, especially the ones who refuse to flee when their fellows are brutally beaten into submission in one of the most riveting and frightening pages in all of Mailer's writing. The coming of knowledge, of a historical fatalism, creeps into both Mailer's prose and his characters' weary postures as he recites events from America's past that reveal that it was founded on a rite of passage. It is as if these young people are suddenly imbued with historical consciousness, although Mailer's ruminations and their agony are kept separate on the page. Nevertheless, in his coda he suggests that if the march's end took place in the "isolation in which these last pacifists suffered naked in freezing cells, and gave up prayers for penance, then who was to say they were not saints? And who to say that the sins of America were not by their witness a tithe remitted?" His final words balance an earlier passage where he describes the marchers' opponents, "the gang of Marshals" who in their "collective spirit" emit "little which was good," and one of whom "paid tithe to ten parallel deep lines rising in ridges above his eye brows." Mailer achieves a harmony of form and an equilibrium of language that make the novel's ending seem as complex as the history it imagines, and as moving in its depiction of ignorance and confusion as the Matthew Arnold poem, "Dover Beach," from which Mailer's title is taken.

Marilyn • Although they are satisfactory in sections, *Of a Fire on the Moon*, *The Fight*, and Mailer's other writings from the late 1960's to the mid-1970's do not equal *Marilyn*, his follow-up study of the ambiguities of fiction and history so magnificently explored in *The Armies of the Night*. *Marilyn* has a twofold purpose: to measure faithfully and evaluate the obstacles that bar the biographer's way to a full understanding of his subject's life, and to suggest tentatively a biographical method that will aim at recreating the whole person even though conceding that the search for wholeness is elusive and problematical.

Furthermore, Monroe ranks with Mailer's other major characters, such as General Cummings. Just as Cummings works to make himself an instrument of his own policy, so Monroe paints herself into the camera lens as an instrument of her own will. She is Napoleonic and yet divided against herself, a Dreiserian character who traverses the continent in quest of her true self in much the same way as Lovett, O'Shaugnessy, and Rojack do, detecting voids in themselves and voyaging to find their genuine identities. Much of Mailer's work in film, and his discussions of film in "Some Dirt in the Talk" and "A Course in Film-Making" (both collected in *Existential Errands*), lead directly to his perception of Monroe's disrupted sense of self. Although his later "imaginary memoir," *Of Women and Their Elegance*, in which Monroe recalls her last years, seems less substantial than *Marilyn*, he carries his concern with "twin personalities" a step further by integrating his narrative with Milton Greene's provocative photographs, which are studies in the doubling of personality in a divided world.

The Executioner's Song • Set against the background of his reflexive writing of the 1960's and 1970's, *The Executioner's Song*, Mailer's next major work of fiction, is a startling book. Its sentences are simple and clear, with an occasionally striking but not elaborate metaphor. Absent from the narrative is Mailer's characteristic sentence or paragraph, which is long and comprehensive—an encyclopedic attempt to gather all of reality in one magnificent statement. There is no intrusive voice to sum up the life of Gary Gilmore, a convicted and executed murderer, and the age in which Gilmore grows to kill. Mailer does not explicitly explore a theory of biography and does not comment, except in his afterword, on his interaction with the life he has written. His book seems keyed to a new aesthetic.

In spite of its 1,056 pages, *The Executioner's Song* is not a garrulous work; it is a quiet book punctuated by myriad silences. There is a double space following nearly every paragraph of the book, indicating the gap between events, the momentary pause that intervenes even in events that seemingly follow one another swiftly and smoothly. Reality is defined by these frequent intervals of silence, periods of stillness that intimate how much is left unsaid and how many characters fail to connect with one another. Gilmore is the most solitary character of all, cut off in large part from humanity and therefore able to murder.

A great deal of the book is dialogue or paraphrase of dialogue, which enhances the dramatic clash of details and conflicting points of view. Even the long descriptive passages and the evocations of characters' thoughts consist only of the results of the reporter who has interviewed these characters for their thoughts and who conveys what he has heard and observed. Hence, there is no privileged retrospective narrator to unify the book's disparate materials.

Mailer has called *The Executioner's Song* a "true life novel." By "novel" he seems to mean something somewhat different from his use of the term in *The Armies of the Night* and *Marilyn*, in which he employs a novelistic narrator to probe the unspoken motivations of his characters and to organize reality in creative metaphors. Of his unusual departure from past practice he remarks in *The New York Times Magazine* (September 9, 1979):

> I was convinced from the start that the materials were exceptional; it had the structure of a novel. Whenever I needed a character for esthetic balance—a new character of imposing dimensions—one just appeared out of nowhere. If I had conceived *The Executioner's Song* as a novel entirely drawn from my own imagination, I doubt I could have improved on those characters.

Mailer conceives of the characters as revealing themselves to him, so that he does not have to serve as a mediating voice. Instead, he orchestrates their disclosures by surrounding them with a quiet space and spare style that preserves their individual integrity.

Reading such sparely created scenes, one is tempted to comb through the details over and over again in order to search for the pertinent clue that will point to the meaning of Gilmore's story, but as Joan Didion points out in her review in *The New York Times Book Review* (October 7, 1979),

> the very subject of *The Executioner's Song* is that vast emptiness at the center of the Western experience, a nihilism antithetical not only to literature but to most other forms of human endeavor, a dread so close to zero that human voices fade out, trail off, like skywriting.

Mailer has chosen, this time, to make a literature that is articulately mute, almost muzzled in its restrained revelations of actions that remain voiceless, dumb, and frighteningly uncommunicative:

> "Why'd you do it, Gary?" Nielsen asked again quietly.
> "I don't know," Gary said.
> "Are you sure?"
> "I'm not going to talk about that," Gilmore said. He shook his head delicately, and looked at Nielsen, and said, "I can't keep up with life."

For Mailer, *The Executioner's Song* is biography in a new key, since he attends to the integrity of individual lives without quickly elevating those lives into symbolic significance. At the same time, the continuity of his concerns is apparent in his ambitious desire to show that true life must be mediated through the imaginative power of a singular intelligence. He understood that *The Executioner's Song* required a voice, flexible and comprehensive, in order to embody the myriad voices that make up reality. There are patterns that can be perceived on rereading the book, yet no single pattern is definitive. Gilmore seems to reach some genuine self-understanding and consistency, but his behavior is still sometimes contradictory and enigmatic. He approaches his execution wanting to die, and yet he searches for every possible means of escape. *The Executioner's Song* remains faithful to the elusiveness of self, to both the revelation and the inscrutability of identity.

Ancient Evenings • Beginning with the opening sentence—"Crude thoughts and fierce forces are my state"—*Ancient Evenings* embarks on a style that is new to Mailer and to his readers who have been accustomed to an active voice transforming everything it articulates. Something very strange is happening to the passive voice of the novel's first narrator-protagonist, the ka (spiritual emanation) of Menenhetet II, who is undergoing the process of rebirth. The first book of the novel is awesome and quite wonderful in its depiction of a consciousness trying to differentiate itself from all that surrounds it.

After the first book, much of the novel is narrated by Menenhetet I, the great-grandfather of Menenhetet II. Menenhetet I is the great ancestor who has been able to live four lives (1290-1100 B.C.E.) by learning how to ejaculate into a woman at the very moment of his death, thereby conceiving himself anew in a lover who becomes his mother. Menenhetet I aspires in his first life to supplant his Pharaoh as ruler of Egypt and dies in the act of sexual intercourse with the Pharaoh's queen. Menenhetet I carries Mailer's conception of himself and of the hero in his fiction to the farthest extreme: He is a man of many ages, the self-invented avatar of Menenhetet II's quest for distinction. Menenhetet I has been a warrior and high priest, a scholar and man of action, a great lover of queens and yet a farmer of peasant origin. In his fourth life, Menenhetet I would like to be the vizier of Ramses IX (Ptahnem-hotep). In the very act of telling his four life histories to Ramses IX, however, Menenhetet I reveals an overweening ambition and fatal attraction to magical practices (including the repulsive eating of bat dung) that disqualify him for the role of Pharaonic confidant.

Ancient Evenings is embedded in the lush details of ancient Egypt, in the rhythms of an alien time. Even sympathetic readers have noted a numbing sameness in the prose that suggests that the author has striven too hard for unity, for the merging of the opposites that create so much exciting tension in *The Naked and the Dead*, *The Armies of the Night*, and *The Executioner's Song*. *Ancient Evenings* is Norman Mailer at his neatest, with the loose ends of his philosophy and his prose knit together rather impressively. Nevertheless, it seems static and too thoroughly thought-out; absent from it is the rough-edged stimulation of a writer on the make, who is best when he is suggestive rather than explicit, when he is promising to complete the circle and join the halves without ever quite doing so.

Tough Guys Don't Dance • Like Mike Lovett in *Barbary Shore*, Tim Madden in *Tough Guys Don't Dance* is an amnesiac: He cannot remember what happened the night before, and he cannot account for the large amount of blood on his car seat. He is clearly kin to Stephen Rojack. More or less kept by his prized wife, the wealthy Patty Lareine, Madden, a writer, finds that he cannot work when she deserts him.

As her name suggests, Lareine has been Madden's imperious queen, and he seems at a loss when he is not in the service of his "medieval lady." At the same time, he has clearly chafed under her rule, for he regrets having broken his code of male self-sufficiency. As a result, the couple's marriage has been turbulent, and in its later stages, husband and wife seem most alike in their murderous inclinations. The novel

begins with Madden wondering whether the severed head he discovers in his marijuana hideaway is the result of a drunken evening's debauchery with another
woman, which turned violent when Patty Lareine returned home.

The characters in *Tough Guys Don't Dance* relate to one another as in an Arthurian
romance. Madden discovers that his wife has had another lover, the deputy police
chief, Alvin Luther Regency, a powerfully built, maniacal rival, who is part of the plot
to set up Madden (who has already served a short term for possession of cocaine).
Complicating matters further for Madden is the lurking presence of his envious former schoolmate, Meeks Wardly Hilby III, who was once married to Patty Lareine and
from whom Madden stole her. If Madden can make sense of the two murders, he can
also begin to put his life back together—including his failed relationship with Mad-
eleine Falco, his witty, tough counterpart, who left him when he took up with Patty
Lareine and who now finds herself mired in a bad marriage to the dangerous Regency.

Readers who prefer murder mysteries with taut, spare plots and prose may bristle
at the complications of Mailer's syntax and philosophizing. The heads and bodies
buried in different locations are indicative of the splits in the human psyche that
Mailer has pursued in much of his writing. Usually Mailer is able to finesse the shifts
between the novel's ideas and events, and his delineation of characters through
clipped dialogue is convincing. At a few points, his narrative flags, perhaps because
he has tried to do too much, to integrate characters, ideas, and plot simultaneously
in a single narrative voice.

Harlot's Ghost • *Harlot's Ghost* is a mammoth and intermittently gripping novel of
the CIA, charting the career of Harry Hubbard, protégé of the legendary Hugh Tre-
mont Montague ("Harlot"), and a key participant in CIA operations in Berlin, Uruguay, Washington, D.C., Miami, and Cuba. The novel is based on a close reading of
nearly one hundred books about the organization and on Mailer's vivid imagination,
which often calls upon themes and characters he has rehearsed in several works of
fiction and nonfiction, including speculations on the murder of Marilyn Monroe, Ernest Hemingway's suicide, and the nature of Cuban leader Fidel Castro's heroism.

Mailer's thesis is that a CIA operative is by definition a deceiver, a person who is always playing more than one role, an actor whose sense of reality is constantly shifting,
making it difficult to maintain loyalties and friendships, never sure of his or her own
ground. Harry Hubbard, the son of a fabled CIA agent, worries that he is not "tough
enough" and takes on risky ventures such as the Bay of Pigs fiasco. As a matter of survival within the agency, he finds himself acting as a double agent—at one point reporting to both his mentor, Harlot, and to his father, Cal.

Through Harry's letters, diaries, and first-person narrative, Mailer manages to
cover most of the dramatic events involving the CIA from 1955 to 1963. This very
long novel (near thirteen hundred pages) is burdened with too much learning and
too little plot—no detail is too trivial to include as long as it impinges on Harry's consciousness. There are some wonderfully realized characters (E. Howard Hunt and
William King Harvey), but they do not quite redeem Mailer's turgid prose.

The Gospel According to the Son • By contrast, *The Gospel According to the Son* is a restrained retelling of the Christ story from Christ's point of view. Mailer successfully
finds a voice quite different from his own for the first-person narrator. Christ is portrayed as very much of a man—driven by his divine mission but also doubting his abil-

ity to carry it out. Christ often compares himself to Moses, another reluctant prophet who feared he was not worthy of the Lord's trust.

Mailer's Christ gently but firmly takes issue with certain aspects of the Gospels. He is a miracle worker, yet he notes how often accounts of his powers have been exaggerated—the projections of those who fervently believe in him. Mailer ingeniously accounts for many of Christ's most famous sayings, such as "Render unto Caesar the things that are Caesar's." Such statements show a Jesus with a tactical and political sense—challenging the status quo, to be sure, but also adopting a diplomatic stance when it serves his purposes.

If Mailer can be faulted, it may be (surprisingly) for not being daring enough. His Jesus seems a little dull and not at all the charismatic figure that surely attracted Mailer in the first place. In Mailer's obvious desire to respect the Christ story while humanizing it, he has perhaps not risked quite enough in making Christ a believable character.

Carl Rollyson

Other major works

SHORT FICTION: *New Short Novels 2,* 1956; *The Short Fiction of Norman Mailer,* 1967.

PLAY: *The Deer Park: A Play,* pb. 1967.

SCREENPLAY: *Tough Guys Don't Dance,* 1987.

POETRY: *Deaths for the Ladies and Other Disasters,* 1962.

NONFICTION: *The White Negro,* 1957; *The Presidential Papers,* 1963; *Cannibals and Christians,* 1966; *The Bullfight,* 1967; *The Idol and the Octopus: Political Writings on the Kennedy and Johnson Administrations,* 1968; *Miami and the Siege of Chicago: An Informal History of the Republican and Democratic Conventions of 1968,* 1969; *Of a Fire on the Moon,* 1970; *The Long Patrol: Twenty-five Years of Writing from the Work of Norman Mailer,* 1971 (Robert Lucid, editor); *The Prisoner of Sex,* 1971; *Existential Errands,* 1972; *St. George and the Godfather,* 1972; *The Faith of Graffiti,* 1974 (with Mervyn Kurlansky and Jon Naar); *Some Honorable Men: Political Conventions, 1960-1972,* 1975; *The Fight,* 1975; *Genius and Lust: A Journey Through the Major Writings of Henry Miller,* 1976; *Pieces and Pontifications,* 1982; *Portrait of Picasso as a Young Man,* 1995 (also known as *Pablo and Fernande: Portrait of Picasso as a Young Man,* 1994); *The Spooky Art: Thoughts on Writing,* 2003; *Why Are We at War?,* 2003.

MISCELLANEOUS: *Advertisements for Myself,* 1959; *The Time of Our Time,* 1998; *Modest Gifts: Poems and Drawings,* 2003.

Bibliography

Bloom, Harold, ed. *Norman Mailer.* Philadelphia: Chelsea House, 2003. Collection of critical essays about Mailer that have been assembled for student use.

Castronovo, David. "Norman Mailer as Midcentury Advertisement." *New England Review: Middlebury Series* 24 (2003): 179-194. Review of Mailer's literary heritage at the time he published *Why Are We at War?*

Glenday, Michael K. *Norman Mailer.* New York: St. Martin's Press, 1995. A good critical survey of important themes and strategies in Mailer's writings.

Gordon, Andrew. *An American Dreamer: A Psychoanalytic Study of the Fiction of Norman Mailer.* Madison, N.J.: Fairleigh Dickinson University Press, 1980. One of the most penetrating studies of Mailer's fiction and nonfiction, which shows how deeply rooted in his work are aspects of his biography.

Leeds, Barry H. *The Enduring Vision of Norman Mailer.* Bainbridge Island, Wash.: Pleasure Boat Studio, 2002. An analysis of Mailer's works that includes Leeds's 1987 interview with his subject. A good introduction to Mailer.

Leigh, Nigel. *Radical Fictions and the Novels of Norman Mailer.* New York: St. Martin's Press, 1990. Explores the political and social views of Mailer and how they come across in his fiction. With an index and bibliography.

Lennon, J. Michael, ed. *Conversations with Norman Mailer.* Jackson: University Press of Mississippi, 1988. A collection of the most important interviews with Mailer, which reveals his developing and changing attitudes toward his work.

_____. *Critical Essays on Norman Mailer.* Boston: G. K. Hall, 1986. A collection of criticism on Mailer's work, important reviews, and an extremely valuable overview by Lennon of Mailer's reputation as it evolved.

Mailer, Adele. *The Last Party: Scenes from My Life with Norman Mailer.* New York: Barricade, 1997. Although this memoir focuses on a short (about eight years) period of Mailer's life, it is the most detailed book about him.

Manso, Peter, ed. *Mailer, His Life and Times.* New York: Simon & Schuster, 1986. Provides an excellent narrative survey of Mailer's career in its cultural and political contexts.

Merrill, Robert. *Norman Mailer Revisited.* New York: Twayne, 1992. A revised version of one of the best introductory studies. It includes a chapter on Mailer's novels of the 1980's, a chapter on his biography and his legend, and a concluding assessment of his career. The chronology, notes, and annotated bibliography make this a very useful volume.

Rollyson, Carl. *The Lives of Norman Mailer: A Biography.* New York: Paragon House, 1991. Contains much more discussion of Mailer's writing than does Mills or Manso, including a chapter on *Harlot's Ghost.* Detailed notes and comprehensive bibliography.

Wenke, Joseph. *Mailer's America.* Hanover, N.H.: University Press of New England, 1987. Concentrates on Mailer's attitudes toward America in his major fiction and nonfiction, including *Ancient Evenings* and *Tough Guys Don't Dance.*

Bernard Malamud

Born: Brooklyn, New York; April 26, 1914
Died: New York, New York; March 18, 1986

Principal long fiction • *The Natural,* 1952; *The Assistant,* 1957; *A New Life,* 1961; *The Fixer,* 1966; *The Tenants,* 1971; *Dubin's Lives,* 1979; *God's Grace,* 1982; *The People,* 1989.

Other literary forms • Although acknowledging his significant achievements as a novelist, many critics believe that Bernard Malamud's most distinctive and enduring contributions to American fiction are to be found in his short stories, particularly those collected in *The Magic Barrel* (1958) and *Idiots First* (1963). Malamud published three more volumes of short fiction in his lifetime: *Pictures of Fidelman: An Exhibition* (1969), a collection of six linked stories featuring the same protagonist; *Rembrandt's Hat* (1973); and *The Stories of Bernard Malamud* (1983), twenty-five stories largely drawn from previously published volumes. The posthumously published volume *The People, and Uncollected Stories* (1989) gathers a number of previously uncollected stories, most of them early pieces from the 1940's but also including two from the 1980's.

Achievements • Along with novelists such as Saul Bellow and Philip Roth, Malamud is among the most distinguished of a number of Jewish writers who did much to set the tone of postwar American fiction. Malamud's singular achievement is to have captured the experience of Jews in America at a point of transition between cultures. His characters—not only the Jews but also their Gentile counterparts—are not yet quite a part of American culture, nor have they fully abandoned the old culture of which they are no longer members. Out of this sense of dislocation and the struggle to create a new life, Malamud created most of his early stories and novels. Although not all the novels have Jewish protagonists—the first two in fact do not—the dilemma is constant; the Gentile characters are as displaced and alienated as the Jewish ones. He received numerous awards for his fiction, including two National Book Awards and a Pulitzer Prize.

Biography • Bernard Malamud was born in Brooklyn to Russian immigrant parents. His father, like Morris Bober in *The Assistant,* was a small grocer, and the family moved around Brooklyn as business dictated. When Malamud was nine years old, he had pneumonia and began a period of intensive reading. Later, encouraged by his teachers, he also began writing short stories.

From 1932 to 1936, Malamud was a student at the City College of New York. He later began work on a master's degree at Columbia University, and, while teaching night school at Erasmus Hall, his own alma mater, he started writing in earnest. He married Ann de Chiara in 1945, and four years later, he and his family moved to Corvallis, Oregon, where for twelve years Malamud taught English at Oregon State. A son was born before he left for Corvallis, a daughter after he arrived. While there, he published his first three books; after leaving, he wrote his satire of academic life in an English department, *A New Life.* Returning to the East in 1961, Malamud taught for many years at Bennington College in Vermont. He died in New York on March 18, 1986.

© Jerry Bauer

Analysis • In *The Natural,* Iris Lemon tells the protagonist that all people have two lives, "the life we learn with and the life we live with after that. Suffering is what brings us toward happiness." Although her statement requires qualification, it is a suggestive summary of the major theme of Malamud's work: the journey toward a new life, a journey marked by suffering, which may or may not be redemptive. In fact, however, Malamud's characters usually have three lives: one from which they have not learned and that they are attempting to leave behind, a life the reader sees in flashbacks and confessions as well as in brief opening scenes; a middle life, the learning life, which is the substance of the books; and the new life promised to successful characters at the end. Malamud's novels, then, are in the tradition of the *Bildungsroman,* but they have older protagonists than do most American novels of education. What Malamud depicts in each of his novels is a renewed attempt to find new life and to convert suffering to meaning, a second journey toward knowledge.

Of the old life, Malamud usually shows his readers little. *The Natural* opens with a brief pregame sketch that quickly shows Roy Hobbs's past. In *The Assistant,* the reader sees the robbery for which Frankie Alpine will try to atone, and in *The Fixer,* there is a short portrait of Yakov Bok's past in his village. Malamud's characters are trying to forget the past, so even when it enters their minds, they try to shove it away. Moreover, Malamud's novels usually begin with a journey away from a past life. Whether European Jews coming to America or moving from their shtetl to Kiev, or whether American Jews traveling from New York to Oregon or baseball players leaving the country for the big city, Malamud's protagonists are always travelers, uneasy with their past, uncertain of their future. In fact, they often try to conceal their past: Alpine and Hobbs work conscientiously to obliterate the stories of their earlier lives. Yakov Bok drops his prayer things, a reminder of his old life and its ways, into a river. One of Malamud's most frequent devices is to have characters change their names in an attempt to escape their past identity. Bok, trying to pass as a Gentile, becomes Yakov Ivanovitch Dologushev, his initials ironically spelling "yid."

What all of Malamud's characters must learn, however, is that they have to accept responsibility for their past actions. Paradoxically, while the evil that his characters have done remains with them and so must be acknowledged, the good can be erased. At the end of *The Natural,* Roy Hobbs, a failure in his quest for a new life, discovers that for his part in throwing the league playoffs, all of his baseball records will be expunged from the record books.

The journey is always a quest, as the mythological base of *The Natural,* Malamud's first and prototypal novel, makes clear. The public part of the quest takes place in the world of men, and its lesson is that of law, of the inner check, of renunciation. Hobbs is a natural hitter, but he lacks good judgment, both on the field and off. Frankie Alpine in *The Assistant* continually steals from Morris Bober. Saving Bober's daughter Helen from being raped, he is unable to control his own sexual appetite and rapes her himself. "Why do Jews suffer so much?" he asks Morris Bober, and after replying that to live is to suffer, Morris adds, "I think if a Jew don't suffer for the Law, he will suffer for nothing." Although Alpine is not yet a Jew, he does suffer for nothing.

Acceptance of the law, curbing one's appetite, is the first lesson. As Levin thinks in *A New Life*, "Renunciation was what he was now engaged in. It was a beginning that created a beginning." However, law alone is not enough, and Malamud's questers must pass a second test as well for their journeys to be successful: the test of love, of dream, of acceptance of life in its fullness and ambiguity. Helen Bober could marry Nat Pearl, studying to be a lawyer but lacking dreams, or she could choose Louis Karp, pure appetite, lacking law. She chooses neither, and at the novel's conclusion a chance remains for Frankie Alpine, who is learning what W. H. Auden calls a "law like love." In *A New Life*, Levin first picks up Henry James's *The American* (1876-1877), a book that makes a case for renunciation, but Pauline Gilley, another man's wife whom Levin first renounces but later accepts, moves the discussion to William Dean Howells, who, like Malamud, prefers the economy of pain.

Another qualification to Iris Lemon's statement is necessary: Suffering is what *may* bring one toward happiness. The quest is not successful for all of Malamud's characters. Many of them, already displaced from their European homelands, refuse to undertake another journey. Others learn the wrong lesson from their old life. "*Rachmones*, we say in Hebrew," says Yakov Bok. "Mercy, one oughtn't to forget it." Many, particularly women (there are no Jewish mothers in Malamud), do forget it and harden their hearts. Still others, having undertaken the journey, are, like Roy Hobbs, too selfish ever to move beyond themselves.

Not only do Malamud's novels tell and retell the same story, but they do so with similar casts and with the same images. The protagonist is typically without a close family, sometimes orphaned. He is often a schlemiel or a schlemazl, always wanting to escape his past, but unlucky and clumsy in the attempt. He is likely to be self-deceived. Early in *The Assistant*, while still stealing, Alpine tells himself that he is "an honest guy." Later he says, "Even when I am bad I am good," inaccurately viewing himself as a man of stern morality.

Especially in the early novels and short stories, there is a father figure, and the learning relationship is dramatized in terms of an apprenticeship. These figures become less important in the later novels. By *A New Life*, a transitional book, both would-be father figures, the inane Fairchild and the more scholarly but weak Fabrikant, are failures. After *A New Life*, the questers are orphaned even in this middle life.

Malamud also makes frequent use of the double, figures both actual and dreamed. Roy and Bump Baily, the player he replaces, are identified with each other: They share the same girl and the same fault. Frankie Alpine enacts in his dreams the crimes Ward Minogue, his darker opposite, actually commits. In *The Tenants*, Harry Lesser and Willie Spearmint (born Bill Spear—black people also change names in Malamud) act out the common racial stereotypes, reverse them, and then destroy each other's work and life. An image from William Shakespeare's *King Lear* (pr. c. 1605-1606), each as the other's shadow, dominates the book.

Women in Malamud's work are of two types: the dark ladies (Memo Paris, who betrays Roy Hobbs, and Harriet Bird, who shoots him; Avis Fliss, who spies on Levin; and Zenaida, who gives false testimony against Bok) and the potentially redemptive ladies of the lake (Iris Lemon, Helen Bober, Pauline Gilley, Fanny Bick in *Dubin's Lives*). The function of the good women is in part to hear the hero's confession, enabling him to acknowledge his past, but the women confess too, and, as in Nathaniel Hawthorne, an earlier fabulist, the protagonists have the obligation to accept the women's ambiguous moral nature, a test they often fail. Roy, for example, who wants Iris's sympathy, is disquieted when she tells him that at the age of thirty-three she is a grandmother.

Malamud is also consistent in his metaphors. The journey is often from a prison to freedom. Stores are identified as prisons; Alpine feels both imprisoned and entombed in Bober's grocery. Bok exchanges a shtetl for a prison but learns the meaning of freedom while he is confined. Levin says that if you make the wrong basis for your life, "you spend your whole life in jail," though he later realizes that the prison is himself.

Another metaphor involves moving from a mirror to a window—and beyond. Characters must not reject the mirror, refuse to see themselves as they truly are, as Irene Bell, née Belinsky, does when she refuses to look into a dropped mirror in *The Tenants*. However, after they know themselves, the characters sometimes become so fascinated with their own image that they cannot move on. *The Natural* opens with Roy Hobbs on a train, striking a match to look out the window but seeing only his own reflection; throughout the novel, he never achieves any higher values than those centered on himself.

Progress, the attempt to make contact with another, is often symbolized by gazing through a window—transparent, but still dividing, the attempt finally a failure. A common example of this failure is voyeurism; Levin eyes Pauline Gilley's house and watches her through binoculars at a basketball game, while Gerald, her husband, watches several characters through the viewfinder of his camera. Lesser in *The Tenants* is watched through a keyhole. Frankie Alpine climbs an airshaft to watch through a window as Helen Bober showers, and William Dubin in *Dubin's Lives* sneaks to Fanny Bick's house to spy on her and her boyfriend through a window.

Consistent images are linked in Malamud's novels. They must have about them a touch of red or black, a reminder of their human imperfection. They are associated, often by their names, with flowers (Iris, though with Lemon), with birds (Harriet Bird, Avis Fliss), and with trees. The bad women have sore breasts (Memo, Avis) and are like trapped birds and twisted trees.

If there is a conversion—an acceptance of the old life and a promise of a new—it takes place in an isolated, natural spot, such as the park in the urban world of *The Assistant*, where Alpine tells Helen that the best part of Leo Tolstoy's *Anna Karenina* is Levin's conversion in the woods; the lake in *The Natural* (Memo, the bad woman, is, however, associated with polluted waters); the woods in *A New Life*, where Malamud's Levin is converted; and the artificial jungle of *The Tenants*, where the meeting of Lesser and Spearmint ends in death. In *Dubin's Lives*, Dubin is running through the countryside when he first meets Fanny, and it is there that they finally make love.

Despite this consistency of theme, character, and image, Malamud's fiction changed during his career. The early works, with their blend of romance and realism, represent Malamud's best writing. About midway through his career, however, he seemed to have tired of his form; his novels became more discursive, his protagonists more articulate. On one hand, he moved toward experimentalism, but on the other hand, toward the novel of ideas. Quoting Herman Melville that to have a mighty novel, one needs a mighty theme, suggesting that "the purpose of a writer is to keep civilization from destroying itself," Malamud in his later novels reached obtrusively for significance. The protagonists of these later works are frequently blocked artists: the writers in *The Tenants*, the biographer in *Dubin's Lives*.

The Natural • Malamud's first novel, *The Natural*, is a fanciful combination of American baseball lore with the myth of the wasteland. Here, the wasteland is a New York baseball team, the Knights, whose coach, Pop Fisher, is the fisher king of the legend. The quester and protagonist of the novel is Roy Hobbs, his name meaning rustic king. Roy undergoes a double-edged test to see if he can bring life to the baseball team, but the center of the novel is what Roy himself does—or does not—learn from the tests, the chance of a new life for the quester. Though *The Natural* is in many ways the least Jewish of Malamud's novels, it is the prototype for the rest of his fiction; the story it tells and the patterns it uses are those that persist through Malamud's work.

The pregame section of the novel, the brief history of the past life in which Hobbs does not learn and that he will attempt to leave behind, opens with the image of Hobbs staring at his own reflection in the train window. This inability to look beyond himself, his egocentric view of the world, is Hobbs's undoing. Both parts of Roy's testing are also prefigured in this section, which is a microcosm of the novel as a whole. In the public test, Roy, a pitcher, is challenged by an established batting king, whom Roy strikes out as Malamud draws the mythic parallels. The cost of that success is that Roy slays his first father figure, his mentor who catches the pitches without adequate chest protection, is injured, and dies.

If Roy is at least partially successful in his physical challenge, he is not at all so in the world of moral choice. In the pregame section, he is questioned by the first of the women in the novel, Harriet Bird. The episode is based on the real-life shooting of a ballplayer. Harriet invites Roy up to her hotel room. She tests him with a series of questions about the value of his ambitions, but when Roy's self-centered answers reveal the limits of his aspirations—he plays only for his own glory—his unalloyed confidence is rewarded with a bullet. The section ends with a fantastic tableau: Harriet Bird doing a grisly nude dance around the fallen body of Roy Hobbs.

The nine inninglike sections of the novel that follow repeat more spaciously the double test the quester has to undertake to revitalize the team and prove himself worthy of a new life. When Roy arrives, everything is dismal: The Knights are losing, the players are dispirited, Pop Fisher is ailing. Even the drinking fountain produces only rusty water. After Roy begins to play, however, the team's luck changes. Armed with his mythic bat, Wonder Boy, Roy hits five home runs and energizes the team. Rain falls, and the process of restoring life-giving water to the land begins. Roy, however, gets his chance to play only when another player, Bump Baily, is injured. Again, Roy's success depends on the suffering of another, suffering on which Roy is too willing to capitalize. Roy and Bump are doubles, Bump a darker projection of many of Roy's faults. As the fans and team members point out, they share a common limitation: They play for themselves rather than for the team. The high point of Roy's career is Roy Hobbs Day, an event that occurs in the middle of this symmetrical novel. He is given a white Mercedes, a symbolic lancer on which he proudly rides around the stadium.

Roy's acceptance speech has only one theme, his own greatness, and from this triumph, Roy's downward path, indicated by his batting slump, begins. Although there are short times of solid hitting, as when Roy agrees to play for another, the on-field slump is accompanied by Roy's involvement with the illegal off-the-field dealings of the team's owner, who is setting up the throwing of the league playoffs, a fictive event modeled on the notorious "Black Sox" scandal of the 1919 World Series. Roy is in a world beyond his experience. Baffled by the owner's oily, cliché-ridden speeches, Roy participates in the fix. Although at the end of the playoff game Roy tries to play well to reverse the evil he has already done, it is too late; he can no longer free himself and strikes out. The story that begins with Roy striking out an aging star comes full circle with a new young pitcher striking out Roy.

In the private half of the test, Roy once again fails. As he has earlier made the wrong choice with Harriet Bird, he once again makes the wrong moral choices in this section of the novel. He becomes involved with the dark lady, Memo Paris, and they drive off together to a beach, even though the sign cautions danger, warning them of polluted water. There can be no symbolic cleansing here. Memo tries to explain the values she has learned from the suffering in her past, but what she has learned is solely to look out for herself. Roy wants to say something comparable about his own life, but he can think of nothing except more boasting about his future. When he returns to the ballfield after this episode, his grim future is apparent and his lack of control is magnified. The mystic meal is transformed into a large banquet where Roy eats so much he becomes too sick to play.

Memo's counterpart, the redemptive lady of the lake, is Iris Lemon. Like Memo and Harriet, she is associated with birds, flowers, and water, and as with Memo, the key scene involves a journey to the lake; Iris's role, however, is as potential savior of Roy. They drive together to a lake sheltered from the outside world, and it is there that Iris, too, questions Roy about his values, but she tries to lead him beyond boasting. She begins a confession of her own life. Although she is a grandmother at the age of thirty-three, she has learned from her suffering, has transformed it into meaning. Roy is thirty-four, but something about Iris's confession repels him. They make love, and Iris becomes pregnant—she is the only fruitful woman in the novel—but Roy finally rejects her. In the last game of the playoffs, he sees her in the stands, but he is intent on trying to hit a dwarf who habitually heckles him from the bleachers. The ball instead hits Iris, who has stood to cheer for Roy. In the final scene between them, Iris tells Roy that she is pregnant, that he has created a new life for another at least, and she asks Roy to hit one for their child. It is too late, and Roy strikes out. He thinks of all the wrong choices he has made and wants to undo them, but he cannot.

In addition to the myth of the wasteland and the quest for new life, a central image of the novel occurs in a dream Roy frequently has. It involves Roy and his dog in a forest, a secluded place where he can follow his innermost thoughts without shame. Driving once with Memo, Roy thinks he sees a boy and a dog emerging from the woods, a boy whom Memo seems to hit. Whether she has or not, Memo speeds on—leaving behind her destruction of Roy's innocence and his illusions. In the forest he thinks he will lose his directions in order to find himself, lose his life in order to save it, but for Roy, whose middle life is marked with nothing but wrong choices, there is no salvation, no learning. The boy and his dog have vanished along with Roy's innocence, and he has rejected Iris, who could have saved him.

The Assistant • In Malamud's second novel, *The Assistant*, the surface of the myth is quite different. The pastoral world of baseball gives way to an urban business setting. The rustic king gives way to the petty thief, and the myth of heroic action on which the fate of many depends is replaced by the legend of a saint. Spaciousness is super-seded by narrowness, movement by confinement. *The Natural* is often humorous and always marked by energy; even evil is active. In *The Assistant*, gloom and lethargy hand over every scene, and the despair is oppressive. The mythic parallels in *The Natural* are elaborate and schematic; in *The Assistant*, implicit and suggestive.

These differences sketched, however, *The Assistant* remains another telling of Malamud's basic myth. For most critics, it is his most successful; the fusion of ro-mance and realism, of surface accuracy with poetic evocation, is seamless and com-pelling. Like Roy Hobbs, Frankie Alpine, the protagonist of *The Assistant*, is without parents. Both find older men from whom to learn, and both are partially responsible for their deaths. When the lessons they encounter involve renunciation, a check on their passions, they refuse to heed the wisdom. Both learn the wrong lessons from their suffering, at least for a time, and both cheat for financial gain. The two novels are stories of their protagonists' education, and they both open with a glimpse of the old life: Frankie Alpine and a friend rob Morris Bober, the Jewish shopkeeper to whom Alpine apprentices himself. That old life indicated, Malamud settles into the central concern of his books: the middle life, the learning life, where suffering may promise the characters a new and better future.

Frankie returns to the scene of his robbery and begins to help Morris Bober in the grocery store. The relationship between the two is one of father and son, typically cast as master-assistant, an educational apprenticeship. There are three pairs of natu-ral fathers and sons in the novel, and they contrast with Frankie and Morris in their inadequacy. The most promising of these is that of Nat Pearl, one of Frankie's rivals for Helen Bober's affection, with his father. Nat becomes a lawyer, but although he rises financially, he is shallow compared to Alpine, and his treatment of Helen is un-kind. Less successful is the relationship of the loutish Louis Karp with his father, who is trying to arrange a marriage between Louis and Helen. The worst is that between Detective Minogue, who investigates the burglary, and his son Ward, who, with Frankie, has perpetrated it.

What Frankie must learn from his surrogate father is stated in a crucial scene in which Frankie asks Morris why Jews suffer so much. Morris first answers that suffer-ing is a part of human existence: "If you live, you suffer." He goes on, though, to indi-cate that suffering can be meaningful if one suffers not only *from*, but also *for.* Frankie's question is ironically self-directed, for it is Alpine himself, the non-Jew, who is suffering more than he has to: He is suffering not only the existential guilt that comes with living but also the contingent guilt that comes from his own stealing. Like Roy Hobbs, Alpine cannot check his appetite, and he continues to steal from Morris even while trying to atone for the earlier robbery. Though he steals only small amounts, though he promises himself he will repay Bober, and though he assures himself that he is really a good man, Alpine continues to violate the law, and he suf-fers unnecessarily for this violation. At the end of the novel, Alpine becomes a Jew and replaces Bober in the store. This action is not, as some critics have suggested, the pessimistic acceptance of a Jew's suffering or a masochistic embracing of Morris's de-spair; it is rather an acknowledgment of guilt for the suffering Alpine has imposed on others and on himself and the resolve to be like a Jew in suffering *for* something, in making suffering meaningful.

Alpine must learn more than just law, however, for human needs are more com-plex than that. When Helen Bober meets Nat Pearl on the subway, he is carrying a thick law book; her own book seems to her protection, and when he asks what it is, she replies, Miguel de Cervantes' *Don Quixote de la Mancha* (1605, 1616). Like Quixote, she is a dreamer, unsatisfied with her life as it is, and it is this quality that she will share with Frankie and that draws them together. The dialectic that informs Malamud's work is represented here: the law book, from a discipline that recognizes human limitations and demands attention to the responsibilities of this world, and *Don Quixote*, the book that allows one to look beyond these limits and provides a model for noble action. Helen rejects Nat Pearl because the law is insufficient by itself. Her action is not a rejection of the law, for she rejects Alpine too, when he lives in a world of dreams, unbound by law, for his dreams lead him into actions the law forbids. The generative force is a synthesis of the two.

Helen is, then, the other person from whom Frankie will learn. The fact that he has the capacity for knowledge and for gentle action—as well as for the lawlessness that has marked his life—is shown by his constant identification with St. Francis. He is from San Francisco, and his name resembles that of the saint. He looks at pictures of and dreams about St. Francis, striving for his quality of goodness. With Helen, too, though, Frankie must learn to moderate his passions; with her, too, he violates the law. A voyeur, like so many Malamud characters, he climbs an airshaft to watch her showering. The mirror having been replaced by a glass, the glass remains itself a partition, separating the dreamer from the object of his desires. More serious is his rape of Helen in the park. It is the low point of the novel: Morris fires Frankie; his business is failing, and Morris tries to commit suicide. Frankie looks at himself in the mirror, finds himself trapped inside a prisonlike circle, and hates himself for always having done the wrong thing. He returns to the store and resolves to bring it back to life for the hospitalized Morris. Although Helen and her mother do not like Frankie's return, they have little choice but to accept him, and although Frankie occasionally backslides, he makes firmer progress at controlling his passions.

Helen never fully accepts Frankie in the course of the novel, but she does reject her other suitors, and in a series of dreams, the reader discovers a tentative acceptance of Frankie: In his dreams, Frankie, like St. Francis, performs a miracle, turning a wooden rose he has carved and given to Helen into a real flower. In life, she has thrown the present away, but in the dream she accepts it. Helen, too, dreams of Frankie, out in the snow, making "a wife out of snowy moonlight."

Unlike *The Natural*, with its unambiguously pessimistic ending, *The Assistant* ends on a note of hope. Morris has died and Frankie has taken his place, and there is a suggestion that Frankie may be entrapped by the small grocery and the poverty of the Bobers' life, but there is also, in his conversion to Judaism and in his gradual winning of Helen's trust, a more powerful suggestion that he has learned the lessons of love and law, of dream and check, and that this middle life, for all its suffering, may indeed bring him toward happiness and offer him the promise of new life.

The Fixer • *The Fixer* is Malamud's most ambitious novel, both because the reality he creates to embody his myth—the historical trial of a Russian Jew accused of murdering a Christian boy—is the most distant from his own experience and because the purposes of the tale, its philosophic underpinnings, are the most explicit and have the most scope.

As usual the novel opens with a journey. The main character, Yakov Bok, sees his travels, the leaving of his shtetl for a new life in Kiev, as an escape from his past. Bok attempts to strip away his Jewishness: He shaves his beard and cuts his earlocks. On the ferry across the river to his new hell, he drops his prayer things into the water.

Like many of Malamud's characters, Bok is first adopted by an older man as an employee/foster son. This father figure, whom Yakov finds lying drunk in the snow, is without wisdom; indeed, he is a member of a militantly anti-Semitic organization. His daughter is the first woman with whom Bok becomes involved, but she also turns against Bok, accusing him of raping her. Because, however, she has written him letters avowing her love, even those who want to cannot believe her.

There are other dark women. On leaving the village, Bok is given a ride by a Jew-cursing Christian; he dreams of Lilith. The most powerful of these women is a member of a gang; she has killed her own son and accuses Bok of the deed and of a sexual assault on the boy. In this version of Malamud's story, not only does the father figure fail but there is also no redemptive counterpart of these betraying women to offer Bok hope or love.

Most of the novel takes place after the discovery of the murdered child's body and the imprisonment of Bok. The prison is a consistent metaphor in Malamud for the confined lives of his characters; Bok has left a figurative prison for a literal one. Malamud allows Bok escape through the agency of his mind, especially in his dreams. Like those of most of Malamud's characters, however, Yakov's dreams are full of bitterness and terror. If they provide him with a vision and a remembrance of life beyond the prison, they also remind him of the limits of his existence.

A second relief for Bok is that one of the Russian prosecutors, Bibikov, knows of Bok's innocence, and they share a philosophical discussion, its base in Baruch Spinoza, throughout the novel. Bok emphasizes that Spinoza, although he is a philosopher who asserts humanity's freedom, recognizes that people are limited; his name for that restrictive force is Necessity. The accumulated suffering in *The Fixer* is a powerful documentation of Necessity, and forces outside human control play a more significant role in this novel than in any other of Malamud's works.

If Necessity is so powerful, asks Bibikov, where does freedom enter? Bok replies that freedom lies within the mind: One rises to God when one can think oneself into nature. Bok also learns from one sympathetic guard, who quotes to him from the Bible that those who endure to the end will be saved. Yakov learns to endure, and he does so through the freedom his mind creates. He learns also that thoughtful endurance is not enough, for neither Bibikov nor that guard, Kogin, is allowed even to survive: Bibikov takes his own life, and Kogin is murdered.

Bibikov has explained to Bok that there is in Spinoza something Bok has missed, another kind of freedom, more limited but nonetheless real: "a certain freedom of political choice, similar to the freedom of electing to think." It is this freedom that Bok finally affirms. He has undergone the extreme suffering that Necessity entails. For most of the novel there is hope that in his mind he is at least free and can create new worlds, and there is hope that he will endure. The novel ends with a more political hope. Bok, at least in his dreams, elects to shoot the czar. He has created political freedom by electing to think of himself as free. Again he cites Spinoza that if "the state acts in ways that are abhorrent to human nature, it's the lesser evil to destroy it."

Much of *The Fixer* is a moving dramatization of these ideas, and much of it as well conforms to the basic pattern of Malamud's myth, which he has developed so often and so well. However, *The Fixer* is marred, and its faults suggest those that damage many of Malamud's later works. The philosophy seems too often grafted onto a rather static tale, the story itself an excuse for the ideas rather than the ideas a product of the story. The historical events have been distorted to fit the ideas. There is no reason Malamud should be bound by fidelity to historical truth, but all of his revisions seem to be in the direction of simplicity—not the simplicity that allows the novelist focus, but a simplicity that reduces moral complexity to schematism. All the intellectual weight of *The Fixer* is given to one set of people who hold one set of values; it is not simply that the novel presents good versus evil, but that it presents eloquent and intelligent good versus inarticulate and stupid evil.

In the novels that followed *The Fixer*, Malamud's problems with form and with integrating form and meaning became more noticeable. *The Tenants* suffers from inadequately worked-out ideas. *Dubin's Lives* is marred by structural redundancy and by a facile ending, although it features an articulate and convincing hero, a failed artist's search to find himself. Dubin's own life is finally one of promise, and that is the story Malamud knew to tell.

God's Grace • *God's Grace* is the story of Calvin Cohn, the only surviving human after humankind has destroyed itself in a nuclear war. The novel opens with Cohn aboard a ship, where he discovers another survivor, a chimpanzee. Most of the book is set on an island where they discover other chimps, a reclusive gorilla, and some baboons. Unlike *Dubin's Lives*, *God's Grace* returns to the playfully fantastic style of Malamud's early stories, but like all of his work, it is another accounting of the middle life. For Cohn, the old life is completely dead; this is his new chance to re-create a life for himself—and for all the world. In part resembling Robinson Crusoe and his story of survival, *God's Grace* is more centrally a fable about Cohn's attempt to maintain his faith in a God who has allowed this destruction and his faith that humankind can develop order among the creatures that remain. He plays a record of his father singing, "They that sow in tears shall reap in joy," and that becomes Cohn's rationalistic credo.

When the chimpanzees begin talking, Cohn has a chance to verbalize his thoughts, but though this development would seem promising, Cohn's thoughts are insistently didactic. He is intent on teaching the animals to act morally, but his attempt fails: The tone darkens and the animals begin destroying each other and finally Cohn himself. His faith in the efficacy of reason to tame nature's cruelty is naïve, and just as he underestimates the darker passions, he omits love entirely from his list of virtues. In an ending reminiscent of the close of "The Magic Barrel," another story about the relationship of law and love, the gorilla George, who has remained outside the group, attracted only when Cohn is playing records of his cantor father's chanting, begins a Kaddish for the dead Cohn and his vanished dreams. Malamud asks perhaps too much of this work: The realism of survivorship does not always blend with the fantasy of animal speech; the playful beginning gives way too abruptly to the brutal ending, yet much that is sustained recalls Malamud's work at its best.

The People • At the time of his death, Malamud was working on a novel titled *The People*, having completed the first draft of sixteen of a projected twenty-one chapters. This unfinished work, published posthumously, is the story of a Jewish refugee who, like Levin in *A New Life*, is an anomalous figure set down in the American West. In *The People*, however, the time frame is the late nineteenth century, not the 1950's, and Malamud's protagonist is captured by a group of Native Americans whose chief and advocate he eventually becomes. Like *God's Grace*, *The People* is a fable, a darkly comic tale marked by the bleakness faintly laced with hope that characterizes Malamud's last works.

Howard Faulkner

Other major works

SHORT FICTION: *The Magic Barrel*, 1958; *Idiots First*, 1963; *Pictures of Fidelman: An Exhibition*, 1969; *Rembrandt's Hat*, 1973; *The Stories of Bernard Malamud*, 1983; *The People, and Uncollected Stories*, 1989; *The Complete Stories*, 1997 (Robert Giroux, editor).

NONFICTION: *Talking Horse: Bernard Malamud on Life and Work*, 1996 (Alan Cheuse and Nicholas Delbanco, editors).

Bibliography

Avery, Evelyn, ed. *The Magic Worlds of Bernard Malamud.* Albany: State University of New York Press, 2001. A wide-ranging collection of essays on Malamud and his writings, including personal memoirs by members of his family and friends.

Bloom, Harold, ed. *Bernard Malamud.* New York: Chelsea House, 2000. Part of the Modern Critical Views series, this collection of essays assesses the whole spectrum of Malamud's writings. Includes a chronology of his life and a bibliography.

Davis, Philip. *Experimental Essays on the Novels of Bernard Malamud: Malamud's People.* Lewiston, N.Y.: Edwin Mellen Press, 1995. A selection of essays examining the long fiction.

Giroux, Robert. "On Bernard Malamud." *Partisan Review* 64 (Summer, 1997): 409-413. A brief general discussion of the life and work of Malamud, commenting on his major novels and short-story collections, his reception of the Pulitzer Prize, and the National Book Award.

Malamud, Bernard. Introduction to *The Stories of Bernard Malamud.* New York: Farrar, Straus and Giroux, 1983. This untitled introduction by Malamud offers an invaluable insight into the mind and theories of the writer himself. After a short literary autobiography, Malamud details his belief in form, his assessment of creative writing classes, and the reasons he loves the short story.

_____. "Reflections of a Writer: Long Work, Short Life." *The New York Times Book Review* 93, no. 20 (March, 1988): 15-16. This essay, originally a lecture at Bennington College, offers numerous anecdotes and details about Malamud's life as a writer. He elaborates upon his influences, his various professions, his friends, and some of his theories.

Nisly, L. Lamar. *Impossible to Say: Representing Religious Mystery in Fiction by Malamud, Percy, Ozick, and O'Connor.* Westport, Conn.: Greenwood Press, 2002. Comparative study of religious mystery motifs in the writings of Bernard Malamud, Walker Percy, Cynthia Ozick, and Flannery O'Connor.

Ochshorn, Kathleen. *The Heart's Essential Landscape: Bernard Malamud's Hero.* New York: Peter Lang, 1990. Chapters on each of Malamud's novels and his short-story collections. Seeks to continue a trend in Malamud criticism that views his heroes as tending toward the mensch and away from the schlemiel. Includes a bibliography but no notes.

Smith, Janna Malamud. *My Father Is a Book: A Memoir of Bernard Malamud.* Boston: Houghton Mifflin, 2006. An intimate and extensive biography of Bernard Malamud, depicting his personal life and writing career.

Watts, Eileen H. "Jewish Self-Hatred in Malamud's 'The Jewbird.'" *MELUS* 21 (Summer, 1996): 157-163. Argues that the interaction of assimilated Jew and the Jewbird in the story reveals the political, social, and psychological fallout of assimilated Jew as good tenant, unassimilated Jew as bad, and Gentile as landlord.

Herman Melville

Born: New York, New York; August 1, 1819
Died: New York, New York; September 28, 1891

Principal long fiction • *Typee: A Peep at Polynesian Life*, 1846; *Omoo: A Narrative of Adventures in the South Seas*, 1847; *Mardi, and a Voyage Thither*, 1849; *Redburn: His First Voyage*, 1849; *White-Jacket: Or, The World in a Man-of-War*, 1850; *Moby Dick: Or, The Whale*, 1851; *Pierre: Or, The Ambiguities*, 1852; *Israel Potter: His Fifty Years of Exile*, 1855; *The Confidence Man: His Masquerade*, 1857; *Billy Budd, Foretopman*, 1924.

Other literary forms • After the financial failures of *Moby Dick* and *Pierre*, Herman Melville, as if turning a new corner in his literary career, began a series of short stories. Published between 1853 and 1856, either in a collection (*The Piazza Tales*, 1856) or individually in journals such as *Putnam's Monthly Magazine* and *Harper's Monthly* magazine, the tales present an enigmatic addition to Melville's artistry. Melville had difficulty with the short forms, and he seemed unable to work out the plot and characters in the space required. His best stories are novella length: "Benito Cereno," "The Encantadas," and "Bartleby the Scrivener." With the publication of *The Apple-Tree Table, and Other Sketches* (1922), all of Melville's stories became available in collection.

Melville also wrote poetry, which suffers from the same unevenness that plagues his short fiction. A handful of poems, gathered selectively from *Battle-Pieces and Aspects of the War* (1866), *John Marr, and Other Sailors* (1888), and *Timoleon* (1891), are worthy of being anthologized with the best poetry of the nineteenth century. His worst poem, *Clarel: A Poem and Pilgrimage in the Holy Land* (1876), a long, flawed reflection on Melville's travels in the Holy Land, continues to be of interest only for its revealing autobiographical and philosophical content. "Hawthorne and His Mosses," Melville's only serious attempt at criticism and analysis, is important as an assessment of Nathaniel Hawthorne's first important sketches.

Achievements • Melville's achievements, before the discovery of *Billy Budd, Foretopman* and the subsequent revival of Melville studies, were viewed simply as writings from "a man who lived among the cannibals." He was remembered only for *Typee* and *Omoo*, his slight but extremely popular South Seas adventures. Although important as the beginnings of the popular tradition of exotic romances, *Typee* and *Omoo* are not classics. Only with the publication of *Billy Budd, Foretopman*, and the critical scrutiny that its publication encouraged, were *Moby Dick, Pierre*, and the rest reassessed, and Melville's reputation as a leader among giants affirmed.

Apart from introducing the South Seas tale to the American public, *Pierre* is arguably the first important work of psychological realism, and *Moby Dick* is a masterpiece of metaphysics, allegory, philosophy, and literature. The assessment of Melville's work was not realized until years after his death and almost seventy years after Melville had given up the novel form for the quick money of short stories, the personal introspection of poetry, and the security of a government post in the New York customs office. Melville was never psychologically or ideologically attuned to the demands of his public, and, thus, popularity eluded him in his lifetime.

Biography • Herman Melville was born in New York City, August 1, 1819, the third child of a modestly wealthy family. His father, a successful merchant, traced his lineage back to Major Thomas Melville, one of the "Indians" at the Boston Tea Party. His mother, Maria Gansevoort Melville, was the only daughter of General Peter Gansevoort, also a revolutionary war hero. Melville had a happy childhood in a home where there was affluence and love. He had access to the arts and books, and he was educated in some of the city's finest private institutions. His father, however, considered young Melville to be somewhat backward, despite his early penchant for public speaking, and marked him for a trade rather than law or a similar professional pursuit.

Library of Congress

The prosperity that the Melvilles enjoyed from before Herman's birth came to an end in the economic panic of 1830. Unable to meet creditors' demands, despite the financial aid of his family, Melville's father lost his business and was forced into bankruptcy. After attempts to save the business, he moved the family to Albany and assumed the management of a fur company's branch office. The move seemed to settle the Melvilles' financial problems until the cycle repeated itself in 1831. Melville's father again suffered a financial reversal, went into physical and mental decline, and died on January 28, 1832.

After his father's death, Melville became, successively, a bank clerk and accountant, a farm worker, a schoolteacher, and, after another economic failure—this time his brother Gansevoort's fur business—an unemployed, but genteel, young man seeking a job in New York City. With the aid of his brothers, Melville secured a berth on a Liverpool packet and thus launched his sea career, and indirectly, his literary fortunes. After one cruise, however, Melville returned to schoolteaching. When the school closed for lack of funds, he and a friend determined to go West to visit Melville's uncle in Illinois, hoping to find some type of financially satisfying arrangement there. Failing to find work, Melville returned to New York City and signed aboard the *Acushnet*, a new whaler making her maiden voyage. From 1841 to 1844, Melville was to participate in seafaring adventures that would change American literature.

On his return to New York in 1844, he found his family's fortunes somewhat improved. He also found that the stories he had to tell of his travels were enthusiastically received by his friends and relatives. Finally persuaded to write them, he produced *Typee* and published it in 1846. The immediate success and acclaim that followed the publication assured Melville that he had finally found his place in life. He followed *Typee* with its sequel, *Omoo*, which achieved a similar success, and resolutely set out to make his living by his pen. He found the financial return of two popular novels was not sufficient to support him, however, and he applied for a government position and was rejected. Melville married Elizabeth Shaw, moved to New York City with most of his family, and started a third novel that became *Mardi, and a Voyage Thither.*

The visionary and allegorical structure of *Mardi, and a Voyage Thither* did not appeal to the readers of his previous successes, and its failure frustrated Melville. In need of ready funds, he began two "potboilers" in order to produce those funds. After the publication and success of *Redburn* and *White-Jacket*, Melville moved his family to a farm in the Berkshires, which he dubbed "Arrowhead" because of Indian artifacts he found there, and assumed the life of a country gentleman and a member of the loosely knit literary society that included Oliver Wendell Holmes, Nathaniel Hawthorne, and others living in the vicinity of Pittsfield, Massachusetts.

How Hawthorne and Melville met is not known, but that they met is witnessed by the production of *Moby Dick*. It was likely that Hawthorne encouraged Melville to write as he saw fit, not as the public demanded. Their correspondence reveals an intense, cordial friendship that was of immense value to Melville during this time of his greatest personal, emotional, and artistic development. Hawthorne was one of the first, not to mention the few, to praise Melville's whaling story. Despite Hawthorne's praise, *Moby Dick* was a financial and critical failure. *Pierre*, the "rural bowl of milk" that followed *Moby Dick*, defied Melville's predictions for its success and was also a failure. The dual failure caused Melville considerable pain and bitterness. As a result of the failures and the debt to his publishers, Melville turned away from the novel to the short-story form.

Melville was to publish two more novels in his lifetime, but neither was commercially successful. Melville began writing poetry in addition to the short story, but his poetry was even more introspective than his fiction, and by the time he was appointed to the customs office of New York City in 1866 he had virtually stopped publishing for public consumption.

The security of the customs office eliminated Melville's need for the slim financial return of publication, and he no longer felt compelled to write for an unwilling public. Yet, he continued to write. At his death, he left a box full of manuscripts of his unpublished work during the years from 1866 to his death (he had published some poetry). When the box was opened, it was found to contain one more novel. *Billy Budd, Foretopman*, published in 1924, was the final piece of Melville's frustration. He never finished it and never attempted to publish it, but since its discovery and publication it has been recognized as one of Melville's masterpieces. When Melville died in 1891, his obituaries recalled him not only as a man who wrote novels of adventure but also one who had "fallen into a literary decline." It was left for another generation to appreciate and revere him.

Analysis • Herman Melville's career as a novelist breaks down, somewhat too neatly, into a three-part voyage of frustration and disappointment. The first part of his career is characterized by the heady successes of *Typee* and *Omoo*, the second by the frustrating failure of, among others, *Moby Dick*, and the third by his increasing withdrawal from publication and the final discovery of and acclaim for *Billy Budd, Foretopman*, thirty-two years after Melville's death. After the initial successes of *Typee* and *Omoo*, Melville never again achieved anything approaching popular success, but it was the acclaim over those two novels that assured Melville that he should attempt to make his way as a novelist. It probably did not occur to Melville at the time, but he was introducing a new genre into American literature.

Typee struck the American public like a ray of sunshine falling into a darkened room. The fresh descriptions and intriguing narrative of an American sailor trapped among the Rousseauesque natives of the Marquesas Islands were hailed on both sides of the Atlantic Ocean, and its sequel, *Omoo*, was received even more enthusiastically. The problems inherent in Melville's harsh treatment of missionaries and imperialism and the general disbelief of the veracity in the author's tale aside, the works satiated a public thirst for exotic places. The fact that *Typee* and *Omoo* have survived in the estimation of critics is testimony to Melville's art even in those early stages of his development.

Typee • Whether it is the simple narrative or the dramatic suspense of impending doom that holds the reader, *Typee* offers a flowing romantic atmosphere of timeless days, pointless endeavor, and mindless existence. The Happy Valley in which Melville's Tommo finds himself trapped is an idyllic setting for the lovely Fayaway and Tommo to live and love. In *Typee* there is none of the agonizing speculation on life, humanity, philosophy, or the cosmos, which readers later came to expect of Melville. With only slight exaggeration and minimal research, Melville created the picture of a world beyond the ken of his readers but that would never die in his memories.

Omoo • *Omoo*, a sequel to *Typee*, is only an extension of that idyll. There is a basic difference between *Typee* and *Omoo*, however; *Typee* is a tightly woven dramatic narrative, incorporating the day-to-day suspense of whether Tommo would be the Marquesan cannibals' next meal; *Omoo* is a more picaresque representation of the events, the charm in *Omoo* depending solely on the loosely tied chain of events encountered by the narrator and his companion, Dr. Long Ghost, among the people of Tahiti. There is no threat hanging over them, as in *Typee*, and there is no necessity for escape. *Omoo* also differs in that it takes place in a tainted paradise. Tahiti has been, in *Omoo*, Christianized and settled and, thus, the Tahitians are familiar with the white sailor and his games. This reduction of innocence colors *Omoo* in a way not reflected in *Typee*.

There is an inescapable glow of romance throughout Melville's two Polynesian novels. The record of missionary abuse and the encroachment of civilization does not make an overbearing appearance, but it does lay the groundwork for the reflections of Melville's despair and convoluted indictments of man and his world in later, more mature works.

Mardi, *Redburn*, and *White-Jacket* rapidly followed Melville's early successes. *Mardi*, opening like a continuation of *Typee* and *Omoo*, shocked readers when it lapsed into philosophical allegory. *Mardi*'s subsequent failure prompted Melville, in search of fame and funds, to return to sea narrative in *Redburn* and *White-Jacket*, but despite their modest successes, Melville reviled them as hackwork.

Moby Dick • In *Moby Dick*, there is evidence that Melville intended it to be little more than a factual account of the whale fisheries in the South Pacific detailed with first-hand tales of adventures on a whaler. When completed two years after its beginning, it was a puzzling, intricately devised literary work in which a white whale is the central character. Around this central figure, Melville weaves symbolism, speculation, philosophy, and allegory on life, God, man, and the human condition. In short, Melville had created an epic romance that stood at the brink of becoming mythology.

The plot of *Moby Dick*, when not interrupted by authorial asides and digressions, is relatively direct. A young man, Ishmael, comes to the sea seeking a berth on a whaling ship. He finds the *Pequod*; falls into a friendship with the cannibal harpooner Queequeg; discovers that the ship is captained by a madman, Ahab, who is driven to wreak vengeance on the white whale that took off his leg on a previous voyage; finds himself in a crew that is a microcosm of the world's peoples; watches as Ahab drives the ship and crew in pursuit of Moby Dick; and is the sole survivor when Ahab is killed in a direct confrontation with the whale. By itself, the plot is thrilling but does not have the ingredients of greatness. The layers of fiction—the levels that the reader must traverse in order to rend the novel for all of its substance—make the work magnificent. To the surface adventure, Melville adds gleanings from volumes of cetological and marine lore, his own observations on the psychology of man, and, finally, his ultimate speculations on good and evil—the basic morality of man and of humankind's place in the universe.

Melville's frequent displays of marine erudition are often cursed as flaws in an otherwise closely woven fabric. They seem to do little for the on-rushing spectacle of Ahab and his monomania, and they almost function as literary irritants designed to interrupt the reader's chain of thought. They are not intended to enhance the characterization of Ahab or his crew, nor are they an integral part of the narrative; they are, however, the essence of the novel's central character, the whale. Without Melville's lore, there is no reality to the ominously ethereal presence of Moby Dick. The periodic chapters of information and background are the author's reminders to the reader of the whale's presence and that the whale drives the story forward. The lore is also the foundation of belief in the whale. It promotes and maintains the physical presence of the whale by the sheer weight of scientific or pseudoscientific data. When the whale finally appears, the reader has been sufficiently educated and prepared. Melville creates the whale, vicariously, with his lore and trivia and sets the stage for its appearance.

In describing Ahab, his ship, and the crew, Melville employs a nonnarrative form of characterization, where each individual is the subject of an inquiry or is an example of a human type. Of the major characters, Ahab is the most complex, but the others form a society in which that complexity can best be displayed. Starbuck, the first mate, Stubb, the second mate, and Flask, the third mate, are only the closest of several layers of the crew around Ahab. Queequeg, Tashtego, and Daggoo, the harpooners, form the next layer, and the rest of the crew fill out Ahab's world. Like Fleece, the ship's cook, and Pip, the mad cabin boy, they all perform vignettes that enlarge and enhance the magnitude of Ahab and his quest. For example, Ahab feels compelled to explain the real reasons behind his insane search for the white whale only to Starbuck, the conscientious, scrupulous first mate. Rather than simple revenge, as Starbuck supposes it to be, Ahab proposes to strike through the "pasteboard masks" of reality by striking at the whale. In his reasoning with Starbuck, Ahab demonstrates a side of himself that is otherwise hidden; there is purpose, calculation, and preparation in his madness. Ahab's insanity, thereby, becomes a divine sort of madness, and he transcends mere earthly logic to become an epic madman jousting with creation. It is through Starbuck and the others that the reader learns most about Ahab, and it is in such relationships that one sees the mastery of Melville's artistry.

Ahab becomes more than a simple villain when viewed against the backdrop of Starbuck and the other characters. He becomes a monolithic character testing a universe that he sees as perverse and unkind toward human existence. He dares to confront nature itself and to challenge it to single combat. It is Queequeg who unwittingly provides the clues to the venture's outcome. He has a coffin built when he fears he will die of a fever, and when Moby Dick rams the *Pequod*, it is the coffin that supports Ishmael, the only survivor. The coffin becomes the symbolic remainder of Ahab's world. Humans and their science cannot stand against nature and hope to survive. It is Ahab's hamartia to believe that he can survive, and his belief is the final sign of his ultimately evil nature.

Ahab would, he tells Starbuck, "strike the sun if it offended me," and he considers himself as the equal of any other force in nature. He forgets that he is limited by human frailty—or he believes he is no longer subject to the laws of temporal existence or his own physical shortcomings. He is, in one sense, a blighted Prometheus who can offer nothing but his vision to his fellow men, and they blindly accept it. Ahab's greatest evil is the corruption of his relatively innocent world, and its ultimate destruction is his sole responsibility.

Melville used many symbols and devices in *Moby Dick*, and they are important strands by which the story is held together. The names alone are important enough to demand attention. The biblical significance of Ishmael and Ahab, and of Jereboam and Rachel, needs no explanation. Starbuck, Stubb, and Flask all have significance when examined symbolically. The mythical ramifications of a voyage beginning on Christmas night enlarge as the story unfolds. The ultimate device is Ishmael himself. Ostensibly the story's narrator, he only appears in about every fourth chapter after the first twenty-five. When he does appear, it is difficult to keep track of whether the narrator or author is speaking. Ishmael, however, is never used in an omnipotent, obtrusive manner that would belie his place on the *Pequod*, and, thus, the point of view remains clear. Ishmael opens the novel and announces "and I only am escaped alone to tell thee," but he is there primarily to provide a frame for the story. This very flexible point of view is an adroit device by which the author can distance himself from the story while still involving himself in a story as few authors have or will. When Melville finds Ishmael to be an encumbrance, he sheds him and speaks for himself. It remains an open question whether the story is Ishmael's, Ahab's, the whale's, or Melville's. It is not necessary, however, that the dilemma be resolved in order to appreciate and acknowledge the massive achievement in *Moby Dick*.

Billy Budd, Foretopman • After the failure of *Moby Dick* to be a commercial success, Melville's increasingly sour approach to novel-writing produced *Pierre*, perhaps the first psychological novel in American literature but also a miserable failure; *Israel Potter*, a rewriting and fictionalizing of a Revolutionary War diary; *The Confidence Man*, a sardonic, rambling, loosely constructed allegory on American society; and *Billy Budd, Foretopman*. The last of Melville's attempts in the novel form, *Billy Budd, Foretopman* was never offered for publication by the author and was discovered and published in the mid-1920's. Despite its checkered publication history (it has appeared in any number of flawed or badly edited forms), *Billy Budd, Foretopman* has come to be recognized as Melville's final word on the great problems with which he first grappled in *Moby Dick*. Its form and simplicity make it the perfect companion for the epic proportions of *Moby Dick*. Its message is such that it seems Melville created it as a catharsis for the unanswered questions in the greater work.

Billy Budd, Foretopman is a masterful twisting of historical event into fiction in order to maintain the tension of a gripping story. While so doing, Melville explores the stirring, but somewhat less exciting, problems of the conflict between man, good and evil, and the law. Melville uses a blend of the historically significant British mutinies of the *Nore* and at Spithead in 1797 and the 1842 execution of three alleged mutineers of the United States ship *Somers*, in which his cousin Guert Gansevoort played a significant part, to mold the setting and motive for his story leading to the trial and execution of the "handsome sailor." The events leading to the trial are relatively unadorned, and there is little question prior to the trial where the reader's sympathies should be and which characters embody which attributes of human nature.

There is a slightly melodramatic air about the principal characters in *Billy Budd, Foretopman.* Claggart, by shrewd characterization and description, is the evil master-at-arms who is in direct conflict with the innocent, pure, guileless Billy Budd. Melville never makes clear why Claggart develops his seemingly perverse prejudice against Billy, but a definite line of good and evil is drawn between the two men. The evil is magnified by the mysterious impetus for Claggart's antipathy toward Billy; the good is intensified by Billy's naïve ignorance of Claggart's malice, even though the entire crew seems to know of it and understand the reasons for it, and by his cheerful mien not only in the face of Claggart's bullying but also in spite of the circumstances that brought him to the *Indomitable.*

Billy is wronged from the beginning, when he is impressed from the American *Rights of Man* to the British *Indomitable* (the names of the ships being a sly piece of Melville commentary on Great Britain's Royal Navy, the War of 1812, and Billy Budd's predicament, among other things). He is instantly recognized and accepted by his new mates on board the *Indomitable* and becomes a full and useful member of the crew and a good shipmate. Claggart, who has the unenviable job of policing a British man-of-war and administering the Queen's maritime justice, seems to extend himself to bring charges against the new man. When Billy is implicated in a mutiny rumor, Claggart seizes the opportunity to bring him before a drumhead court-martial. At the hearing, Claggart concentrates all of his inexplicable venom against Billy Budd in false charges, innuendo, and lies calculated to ensure a guilty verdict for which Billy will be hanged.

The wonder of Billy Budd and Claggart is that Melville, while portraying the two extremes of human morality in human forms, avoids creating flat caricatures. Billy and Claggart seemingly are real people operating in a real world, and they develop in very believable ways, even given Claggart's behavior toward Billy. At the climax of the trial, perhaps the most fantastic moment in the novel, there is no appreciable relaxation of the verisimilitude Melville creates, even though Billy strikes Claggart dead with one crashing blow of his fist. The other major character of the novel fills the momentary gap in the credibility of the story after Claggart's death. Captain Vere commands not only the *Indomitable* but also the trial, and it is he who pushes the novel through its climactic scene and who, in essence, takes the message of the novel from Billy Budd and develops it to its fruition.

Edward Fairfax ("Starry") Vere appears at length only from the trial to the end of the novel, but, despite the title character and his antagonist, Vere is the heart of the novel. He is everything Billy and Claggart are not. He is a complex character—a philosophical ship's captain—and a man who is caught between many pressures as he decides the fate of a man whom he evidently likes. Faced with the precedent of the historical mutinies that Melville introduces into the novel's background, Vere feels the necessity of creating Billy Budd as an example to other prospective mutineers. Seeing Billy's innocence, and understanding at least part of Claggart's fulsome character, Vere is loathe to condemn a man who probably was within his moral right to strike his superior. Even so, the need for order and the maritime sense of justice force Vere to send Billy to the yardarm. Vere, more than anyone, recognizes that he is sacrificing an innocent man for the good of his ship, its crew, and, ultimately, his society. He sentences Billy under the prescription of law, but he begs his forgiveness as a moral human being.

The sacrifice of the innocent is a theme that pervades Western literature, but in *Billy Budd, Foretopman*, Melville confronts the struggle between chaos and order, law and morality, and humankind and society. There is no clear decision as Vere dies in battle; Billy haunts him to his end. However, the society, the system for which Billy was sacrificed, survives and prevails. Vere remains incomprehensible except to the man he condemns. Billy Budd understands but does not have the capacity or the will to exert himself in order to save himself. He is reminiscent, in some respects, of the Christ-figure he has universally been called. In the final analysis, Vere, Claggart, and Billy are all sacrificed, and the initial skirmishes between good and evil become almost trivial when compared to the moral and philosophical riddles Melville poses.

From *Omoo* and *Typee* to *Moby Dick* and *Billy Budd, Foretopman*, Melville traverses the paths to maturity and complexity not only in prose fiction but also in philosophical and spiritual understanding. Nevertheless, there is little difference between Tommo and Billy Budd, the two innocents of civilization. Ahab and "Starry" Vere are similar enough to be recognized as brothers of the quarterdeck and of humankind. While facing different problems and decisions, they both meet them and deal with them similarly—and both die for their causes. The thread of the sea is unmistakable in Melville, but he recognized the function of the ship at sea as a symbol or as an experimental station, isolated and representative of the world he examined. Melville had his causes and injected them into his stories, but he is primarily interested in the human condition. He inspects all facets of each character ruthlessly and meticulously, without judgment and without prejudice, and he allows the results of his inspection to speak for themselves without gratuitous commentary. Since the revival of Melville studies with the discovery of *Billy Budd, Foretopman*, Melville's reputation as one of America's most significant authors is secure.

Clarence O. Johnson

Other major works

SHORT FICTION: *The Piazza Tales*, 1856; *The Apple-Tree Table, and Other Sketches*, 1922.

POETRY: *Battle-Pieces and Aspects of the War*, 1866; *Clarel: A Poem and Pilgrimage in the Holy Land*, 1876; *John Marr, and Other Sailors*, 1888; *Timoleon*, 1891; *The Works of Herman Melville*, 1922-1924 (volumes 15 and 16); *The Poems of Herman Melville*, 1976 (revised, 2000).

NONFICTION: *Journal up the Straits*, 1935; *Journal of a Visit to London and the Continent*, 1948; *The Letters of Herman Melville*, 1960 (Merrill R. Davis and William H. Gilman, editors).

MISCELLANEOUS: *Tales, Poems, and Other Writings*, 2001 (John Bryant, editor).

Bibliography

Bloom, Harold, ed. *Herman Melville*. Philadelphia: Chelsea House, 2003. Collection of critical essays about Melville that have been assembled for student use.

Burkholder, Robert B., ed. *Critical Essays on Herman Melville's "Benito Cereno."* New York: G. K. Hall, 1992. Includes a few early reviews and sixteen previously published articles on Melville's novella, as well as three new articles written especially for this volume. Essays range from Newton Arvin's claim that the work is an artistic failure to more contemporary historicist critiques debating whether the work presents African Americans in a positive or a negative light.

Davey, Michael J., ed. *A Routledge Literary Sourcebook on Herman Melville's "Moby Dick."* New York: Routledge, 2004. Useful handbook to *Moby Dick* designed for students.

Delbanco, Andrew. *Melville: His World and Work.* New York: Alfred A. Knopf, 2005. This biography places Melville in his time and discusses the significance of his works, then and now.

Dryden, Edgar A. *Monumental Melville: The Formation of a Literary Career.* Stanford, Calif.: Stanford University Press, 2004. Ambitious biography of Melville focusing on the relationship between his writing and his life.

Hardwick, Elizabeth. *Herman Melville.* New York: Viking Press, 2000. A short biographical study that hits all the high points and some low ones in Melville's life, from his early seagoing expeditions to his settling down in middle age and finally his languishing in his job as a New York customs inspector.

Heflin, Wilson L. *Herman Melville's Whaling Years.* Edited by Mary K. Bercaw Edwards and Thomas Farel Heffernan. Nashville: Vanderbilt University Press, 2004. Meticulously researched and endlessly fascinating study of the years that Melville spent whaling—the experience on which he would later draw for *Moby Dick* and other works.

Higgins, Brian, and Hershel Parker, eds. *Critical Essays on Herman Melville's "Moby Dick."* New York: G. K. Hall, 1992. A comprehensive selection of contemporary reviews, later essays on individual works, Melville's themes and techniques, discussions of literary influences and affinities, specific studies of Ahab and Ishmael, and new essays exploring Melville in the context of antebellum culture and of his learning.

Levine, Robert S., ed. *The Cambridge Companion to Herman Melville.* Cambridge, England: Cambridge University Press, 1998. An indispensable tool for the student of Melville. With bibliographical references and an index.

Parker, Hershel. *Herman Melville: A Biography.* Vol. 1, 1819-1851, Vol. 2, 1851-1891. Baltimore: Johns Hopkins University Press, 1997-2002. This two-volume biography of Melville by the most distinguished authority on his life and art covers his life from birth in 1819, to the publication of *Moby Dick* in 1851, to his death in 1891. Especially helpful on the early life of Melville and the controversies that arose from his early novel's being labeled obscene and blasphemous.

Renker, Elizabeth. *Strike Through the Mask: Herman Melville and the Scene of Writing.* Baltimore: Johns Hopkins University Press, 1996. Argues that Melville was obsessed with the difficulties of the material act of writing, as reflected in his repeated themes and leitmotifs, such as the face or mask. States that Melville's depression, violent nature, and wife abuse are reflected in his writing. Notes, list of works cited, index.

Rollyson, Carl E., and Lisa Paddock. *Herman Melville A to Z: The Essential Reference to His Life and Work.* New York: Checkmark Books, 2001. A comprehensive and encyclopedic coverage of Melville's life, works, and times in 675 detailed entries.

James A. Michener

Born: New York, New York(?); February 3, 1907(?)
Died: Austin, Texas; October 16, 1997

Principal long fiction • *Tales of the South Pacific*, 1947; *The Fires of Spring*, 1949; *The Bridges at Toko-Ri*, 1953; *Sayonara*, 1954; *The Bridge at Andau*, 1954; *Hawaii*, 1959; *Caravans*, 1963; *The Source*, 1965; *The Drifters*, 1971; *Centennial*, 1974; *Chesapeake*, 1978; *The Covenant*, 1980; *Space*, 1982; *Poland*, 1983; *Texas*, 1985; *Legacy*, 1987; *Alaska*, 1988; *Journey*, 1988; *Caribbean*, 1989; *The Eagle and the Raven*, 1990; *The Novel*, 1991; *Mexico*, 1992; *Recessional*, 1994; *Miracle in Seville*, 1995.

Other literary forms • Although James A. Michener considered himself primarily a novelist, he was also an accomplished short-story writer, esssayist, art historian, and editor. Major themes in his nonfiction are travel and American politics. *The Voice of Asia* (1951) is also in that tradition. *The Floating World* (1954) is a philosophical essay on Japanese art, a theme he treats in four other works, most notably in *Japanese Prints from the Early Masters to the Modern* (1959).

Achievements • During the early 1950's, Michener was heralded as the new voice in American fiction. Still basking in the considerable praise that followed his first book, *Tales of the South Pacific*, and the Pulitzer Prize that accompanied it, he shared the reflected glow of Richard Rodgers and Oscar Hammerstein's musical adaptation, *South Pacific* (1949). Although critics objected to the romantic cast of his early novels, they also found much to praise. Critical reaction to his later novels has also been mixed: Although some critics consider the books brilliant for their sweeping panoramic scopes, others have condemned the novels for their masses of superfluous information, undeveloped characters, and lack of depth. Despite the doubts of literary critics as to the merits of Michener's novels, an eager public has responded to them enthusiastically.

In addition to the Pulitzer Prize, Michener's writing earned for him a number of honorary degrees and awards, including the appointment to several government committees. His work on two of these committees—the Centennial Commission and the National Aeronautics and Space Administration (NASA) Advisory Council—contributed to research for his fiction. In 1977, President Gerald Ford awarded Michener the Medal of Honor, America's highest civilian award.

Biography • Although standard references state that James Albert Michener was born on February 3, 1907, in New York City to Edwin and Mabel Michener, the actual facts of his birth are unknown; he was a foundling whom Mabel Michener reared from shortly after his birth, moving at times to the county poorhouse to help the family through poverty and illness. On a scholarship, Michener attended Swarthmore College, from which he graduated summa cum laude in 1929. For ten years, he taught at a variety of schools and universities, including the School of Education at Harvard, and during the early 1940's he became an editor at Macmillan. Although as a practicing member of the Society of Friends (Quakers) he might have been exempted from combat, in 1942 he volunteered for active duty in the U.S. Navy and was sent to the Pacific.

© John Kings

After the war, royalties and a small percentage of ownership in the musical *South Pacific*, which opened in April, 1949, assured him financial freedom to travel and write. Michener thus became an independent writer and scholar, publishing more than forty books, and an even greater number of articles, from his home base in Bucks County, Pennsylvania. He also wrote shortened versions of many of his novels for inclusion in the *Reader's Digest* series of condensed books.

Overcoming serious heart problems during the 1980's, Michener remained active until his death, writing and traveling. In addition, he generously supported literature and the arts, endowing a fellowship for young writers and contributing in many other ways to the benefit of individual artists and arts institutions. In particular, Michener donated more than one million dollars to the Bucks County, Pennsylvania, Free Library, more than three million dollars to the James A. Michener Art Museum in Doylestown, and more than seven million dollars to his alma mater, Swarthmore College. Part of the latter donation was used to teach students discipline-specific ways of writing. For his numerous contributions to benefit humanity, Michener was named Outstanding Philanthropist in 1996 by the National Society of Fund-raising Executives.

Michener built a legacy as a storytelling phenomenon. He was a world traveler who was at home on virtually every continent, having reportedly lived in 121 different states and countries, in which he gathered background for his novels. His secrets to success were determination, hard work, self-reliance, and an incredible memory. Unlike many other novelists who write by pulling plots and characters out of their heads, Michener was a meticulous researcher, a craftsman who would not begin to write until he had absorbed the details of the culture, the history, the geography, and the people of the country he had chosen for his next work.

In his books, Michener emphasized the importance of harmonious relationships among people and the continuing need to overcome ignorance and prejudice. Although the critics were often unkind to Michener, he was adored by the public, who have bought an estimated seventy-five million copies of his books. Plagued by numerous health problems during the 1990's, Michener died on October 16, 1997, after declining to continue receiving dialysis treatments for kidney failure. Up until his end, Michener remained productive, completing *This Noble Land* in 1996 and *A Century of Sonnets* in 1997.

Analysis • In almost all of James A. Michener's novels, the story line is a loosely woven thread, a framework, a context in which to tell tales and provide geographic and historic detail. Although in his notes on *Centennial* Michener explains four different narrative devices he developed in the course of his writing career, each is still a framing device for a series of related events or information. Throughout all of his work Michener is the social science editor and teacher, using quantities of well-researched data and imaginative incidents to explain issues from his particular point of view. In many of his writings, it is apparent that Michener is not only a very competent writer, historian, and geographer, but also a competent psychologist and geologist. Although each of his novels has a historical basis that covers hundreds or thousands of years, each is rooted in its own time as well.

Much of Michener's writing, both fiction and nonfiction, is journalistic in style, but his staccato rhythms are interrupted from time to time by florid descriptions and precise diversions, such as recipes and statistical contrasts. All of his writing is permeated by an unmistakable creed that affirms human values and a deep concern for America. The harsh facts of his early life shaped Michener's career, and his writing is that of a grateful man driven to repay society for the chances he was given in life. There is more to his writing, however, than a need to express gratitude: His broad panoramas are peopled with Dickensian characters from every part of society, although his sympathies remain with the sad and the unfortunate—even rogues such as Oliver Wendell in *Centennial* and Jake Turlock in *Chesapeake*—who can get by on their wits. Underscoring all of Michener's work is a strong statement of human courage and human tolerance, coupled with a driving concern for humanity's relationship with its environment. Many of his novels focus on racial discrimination of some kind, and each teaches the value of hard work and the necessity for change. As in his nonfiction, Michener does not hesitate to portray society's weaknesses. Although critics have frequently panned both his style and the values it embodies, particularly in his later work, these same late novels have consistently been best sellers.

Tales of the South Pacific • Ironically, *Tales of the South Pacific* was not a best seller, even though of all Michener's works it is perhaps the most familiar. Although it continues to sell as many copies today as when it was originally published and has won the Pulitzer Prize, the book was first printed on the cheapest paper with the poorest binding available—so little did the publisher think of its chances—and new chapters did not even begin at the tops of new pages. Even after its award, the novel would have continued to die a slow death were it not for the musical comedy based on it. Few successful writers have had a less auspicious beginning.

Tales of the South Pacific is a framing story that sets up many of Michener's themes; with it the author began a literary romance with the Pacific islands that would last for more than fifteen years and characterize much of his work. In this work, nineteen related episodes tell the story of America's commitment to the Pacific theater during World War II. The treatment of character as well as setting is significant to the body of Michener's work. No one character can be called the protagonist, although Tony Fry (a navy lieutenant) and the narrator are most central to the plot. By not having a protagonist, Michener implies that this is not the story of one man but rather the shared experience of all those who were in the Pacific during the war years. The narrator makes no moral judgments: Men and women are presented at their finest and their weakest moments; some die in war, but life somehow goes on.

The Bridges at Toko-Ri • With the exception of *The Fires of Spring*, a semiautobiographical novel that develops much of Michener's personal life through 1929, both the fiction and nonfiction which followed *Tales of the South Pacific* are steeped in Pacific history and his own war experience. All are connected as part of a cumulative statement; the collection *Return to Paradise* (1951), for example, with its alternating essays and stories, begins with the description of islands emerging from the sea, the same technique Michener employs in the first of his "blockbuster" novels, *Hawaii*. Of these early works, *The Bridges at Toko-Ri* is particularly significant. The novel exemplifies Michener's typical blend of fact and fiction, as he exposes his reader to the Asian world and the Korean War experience. With the publication of the novel, the author observed that it was the "purest writing" he had done so far.

Although *The Bridges at Toko-Ri* is a short novel and neatly divided into sections—"Sea," "Land," and "Sky"—in it, Michener provides his strongest development of character. The protagonist is Harry Brubaker, a twenty-nine-year-old veteran of World War II and promising Denver lawyer, who resents fighting in Korea. In the first section, Brubaker is rescued from the frozen sea by another three-dimensional character, Mike Forney, a cocky Irishman from Chicago. Michener included an expanded version of both these characters in his later novel *Space*. The "Land" interlude takes place in Japan, a liberty stop, where Brubaker must rescue Forney and his friend from jail before he can visit with his family, who has come to see him there. In a human brotherhood scene typical of Michener, the Brubakers meet a Japanese family in a private pool at their hotel; paddling naked, the families intermingle and converse, resolving any conflict left over from the days before. At this point, the major conflict of the novel begins, however, as the carrier crew starts to plan its assault on four bridges across the canyon of the enemy center at Toko-Ri. Connected to the questions about the attack are more rhetorical ones, addressed to the reader: Will the flyers knock out the bridges? Will this make the communists stop the war? Have Americans lost the strength to make this sacrifice? Where will America's last stand against the communists come—in California, or Colorado, on the banks of the Mississippi?

The climax of the novel comes in "Sky," when the heroic Brubaker and Forney destroy the bridges but are killed in the aftermath of the attack. The action reaffirms that America has produced men who will always fly against bridges. The energy of this short section is powerful, deeply rooted in Michener's own naval air experience and the passion of his convictions.

Caravans • *Caravans* is a transitional novel for Michener; while the setting is still Asia, it marks a western movement in both action and thought. Precursor to *The Drifters*, *The Source*, and to a lesser extent *Poland*, *Caravans* begins in 1946, in the aftermath of World War II. Here, the journalistic style that marks much of Michener's fiction is handled through a first-person narrator, Mark Miller, a junior-grade State Department officer stationed in Afghanistan. During the opening pages of the novel, Miller is sent on a mission to locate Ellen Jaspar, a high-spirited college girl from Dorset, Pennsylvania, who left Bryn Mawr College to marry an Afghan exchange student named Nazrullah. The plot is a series of adventures laced with romance, even after Ellen is found with a nomad caravan in the desert. The connecting link for the related incidents is the ancient route of the Kochis, whom Miller joins in the hope of convincing Ellen Jaspar to return to her parents. Again, in usual Michener fashion, the plot provides a context within which to describe geographic and historic detail and argue thematic questions.

In his excellent discussion of Michener's major works, George J. Becker points out that for more than twenty years the author was concerned with the "stresses and false values that beset American youth"; Becker applies his insight to *The Drifters*, but it is equally true of *Caravans*. Although the time of the story is 1946, Ellen Jaspar is almost a stereotype of college youth during the early 1960's, when the novel was written, in her dress, ideas, and lifestyle. For the last third of the book, she and Miller articulate the fiery rhetoric of campuses across America.

The thematic substance of *Caravans* goes further than any of Michener's previous work in its discussion of racial and religious prejudice. The dark-skinned Nazrullah explains his educational experience in Germany and America, infuriating Miller by comparing the American treatment of black people to the German treatment of Jews. Although the reader's sympathy is with Miller, Nazrullah's point is well made. It is underscored in the climactic moment of the novel, when Miller—a Yale man, perhaps the most civilized member of the cast—announces that he is Jewish and nearly kills Dr. Stiglitz for his wartime Nazi efforts.

The majority of characters in the novel are Muslim, and a few are Christian. Repeatedly, however, the novel turns on a Jewish element, directly anticipating Michener's next major novel, *The Source*. Even Kabul, the Afghan capital, is used to show "what Palestine was like at the time of Jesus."

Chesapeake • *Chesapeake* was the first of Michener's highly popular novels to deal with an indigenously American subject (one might take exception here with *Hawaii*, but that work seems clearly to belong to his earlier preoccupation with the Pacific). As in *Centennial* and later in *Texas*, Michener hoped to chronicle the making of America and to celebrate the courage of those who took part in that achievement. Spanning nearly four hundred years, the novel moves from the first Native Americans who settled the land to the funeral, in 1978, of one of the Quaker descendants of the earliest Caucasians. In part, it is an instructive, political book, dealing with governments in Great Britain and France as well as the United States, culminating with Pusey Paxmore's suicide over his involvement in the Watergate scandal. For the most part, the focus is narrow—the eastern shore of Chesapeake Bay—despite the long roster of historical characters, from John Smith and George Washington to Daniel Webster and Henry Clay.

Here the episodes are organized in a fairly straightforward pattern—allowing for slight digression with a chapter devoted to a family of geese and another to a batch of crabs—and the third-person omniscient point of view does not shift. Four fictional families provide the substance of the book: the Roman Catholic family of Edmund Steed who flees religious persecution in England and joins John Smith in exploring the land in 1607; the family of London thief and indentured servant Timothy Turlock, who arrives a generation later; the Quaker family of Edward Paxmore, who comes in search of religious freedom by way of Barbados and ironically receives the first slaves in the area; and the Caters, a family of former slaves, who build their contribution to the novel from the time just before the Civil War. Although there is great discussion of loyalties, each of the first three families fares well in the Revolution: Steed is an interpreter for the French, Turlock a sharpshooter, Paxmore a builder of fine ships. The War of 1812 continues the tension that creates the climax of the novel, with the Emancipation Proclamation and the War Between the States. Certain characters are given focus—Rosalind Steed, for example—but Michener does not slow down to develop any of them fully; many are types used to maintain the human element while the narrative sweeps over succeeding generations. This large movement does not, however, mitigate the value of the novel.

From the outset, Michener's emphasis is on human courage and tolerance and humanity's relationship with its environment. Ample descriptions build a love for the land and for the watermen who work it; later chapters deal with ecological concerns—erosion, litter, and landfill. Early chapters ennoble the Native American and lament his passing. Perhaps the greatest weight throughout is given to the issues of racial and religious freedom. The suffering of both the Steeds and the Paxmores offers compelling insight into the theocracy of Puritan New England and those who came to America seeking religious freedom. In ironic contrast, both the Steeds and the Paxmores own slaves. The final struggle for black freedom comes at the start of the twentieth century, with an amendment to the Maryland constitution intended to disenfranchise African Americans. Although the Steed and Turlock clans support it, Emily Paxmore champions the defeat of the bill by arguing that it can be applied equally to all European immigrants after 1869, and the campaign becomes her own personal Armageddon.

Chesapeake is a big novel (it includes even a recipe for oyster stew). The fragments that fill the end are the unresolved conflicts of modern time—except for an account of the passing of Devon Island. As the scene of much of the action slips into the sea, Michener affirms that it will come again and again until at last the "great world-ocean" reclaims it.

Space • Although his other novels touch on the twentieth century, *Space* and *Recessional* are Michener's two pieces of fiction that concentrate solely on life in twentieth century America. In *Space*, he chronicles the space program from its inception in 1944 to an ebb in 1982 through a series of incidents that connect neatly to his work before and after it. The novel begins on October 24, 1944, with scenes that introduce four major characters. The first is Stanley Mott, an American engineer, in London at the request of the American president, whose job it is to see that the German installation at Peenemunde is not bombed before three of the chief scientists can be captured alive. The second is Norman Grant, drawn much like Harry Brubaker, in the climactic naval battle of Leyte Gulf. The third is John Pope, a seventeen-year-old football hero from Grant's hometown of Clay. Finally, there is Dieter Kolff, one of the scientists whom Mott must rescue, who survives the bombing because he is with his girlfriend.

The next part of the novel introduces the women who are loved by these men and advances the story through them. Because of the ingenuity of a Nazi officer who later becomes a leader of the American aerospace industry, Dieter Kolff and Leisl come to the United States, shepherded by Mott and his wife, Rachel. Pope gets appointed to Annapolis, on the recommendation of Grant, who has become senator from the state of Fremont; Pope's wife, Penny, earns a law degree and goes to work for Grant when he is appointed to the space committee; Grant's wife, Elinor, preoccupied with little green men, becomes the principal supporter of Leopold Strabismus and the Universal Space Associates.

These characters, and those who flesh out their stories, create the substance of the novel. Although Michener's focus is on the space program, these people are among the most fully developed in all of his work. Systematically moving through the various stages of America's efforts in outer space, he keeps the weight of his research in careful balance with the stories of human lives. This is particularly true in the second half of the novel, which centers on six fictional astronauts (Pope among them). Although the reader is drawn into the explorations (particularly the Gemini flight, which Pope shares with his likable opposite, Randy Claggett, and their adventures on the dark side of the moon), one's interest is held by the characters at least as much as by the technology. This is particularly true of the capable con man Strabismus.

At first Strabismus seems an unnecessary diversion—similar to the recipes Michener offers for Polish sausage or oyster stew—but as the story builds, he becomes an integral part of the work. Playing off the initials U.S.A., Strabismus moves through a series of lucrative rackets until he sets himself up as a preacher with the United Salvation Alliance. As he panders to the fears of the uneducated, he crusades against "atheistic humanism" and advocates a return to fundamentalism that will prohibit the teaching of evolution and forbid national park rangers from describing the geological history of their areas. He launches impassioned attacks on homosexuals and fosters a virulent anti-Semitism. Michener clarifies his point of view in the final confrontation between Strabismus and the "heroes" of his novel. Finally, Michener suggests, the conflict is part of the long march of history and will continue thousands of years hence.

Poland • Two massive novels are representative of Michener's later works: *Poland* and *Texas*. The first is a well-researched chronicle of Polish history that moves backward and forward, connecting the communist country of modern time to the thirteenth century raids of Genghis Khan through the development of three fictional families. In the acknowledgments, in which the author explains his reasons for choosing this particular subject, he sounds very much as he did three decades before, when clarifying his interest in Asia. In both instances, the geographical and ideological positions of the areas indicate that they will become political focal points. Again, Michener is using his fiction to educate readers of his time, moving through history to explain the present.

Texas • *Texas* is perhaps Michener's largest novel: More than two hundred characters are involved in its story, a number of whom are historical figures, and dialogue is the primary vehicle through which their story is told. Michener tracks the major events in Texas history, including the struggle for independence from Mexico. The battles of the Alamo, Goliad, and San Jacinto form the backdrop for fictional characters who illustrate the migrations of the Spanish, Europeans, and Americans to Texas. With its narrative framework and blending of fact and fiction, the novel compares neatly with many of its predecessors. Despite its scope, however, one would be hard-pressed to claim that *Texas* is among the finest of Michener's works.

Mexico • *Mexico* traces the history of Mexico from fictional pre-Columbian Indians to modern Mexico through the eyes of an American reporter. Begun by Michener during the 1950's, *Mexico* was set aside because of negative comments by the publisher, eventually was lost, and then was rediscovered and completed by Michener in 1992. The narrative's structure differs from Michener's previous novels, with more concentration on the present than the past. Norman Clay, the central character, is a Princeton-educated Virginian whose family roots have been in Mexico since the 1840's. Clay is sent to Mexico as a Spanish-speaking journalist to cover a series of bullfights between two celebrated matadors, Victoriano Leal and Juan Gomez. Through Clay's eyes, the readers discover Mexico, its turbulent history, and the part that Clay's family played in it. A variety of conflicts are portrayed, including Spaniard versus Indian, Catholic versus pagan, the quest for the exploitation of gold and silver, war, civil war, and revolution in the twentieth century.

A gripping story unfolds that becomes a vivid portrait of a fascinating country. The cultural conflicts of a class-torn society are epitomized through the tale of the sad, bitter, dirty, sometimes lucrative business of being a matador. In Mexico, bullfighting is not only a sport, but it is also an art form, big business, and festival, mirroring the sordid, grisly, and violent aspects of the Mexican culture. *Mexico* shows that Michener had not lost any of his ability to tell a great story while providing his readers with interesting information about how different cultures live, think, and interact.

Miracle in Seville • As in *Mexico*, Michener uses a journalist as the narrator and participant in *Miracle in Seville*. The narrator, Shenstone, is sent by his editor to Seville, Spain, to write the story of Don Cayetano Mota, owner of a famous ranch where fighting bulls have been raised for decades. However, Shenstone never writes the story, because he believes that he will lose his credibility as a journalist if he reports the unbelievable events that he witnessed while in Seville.

By using a journalist as the narrator, Michener provides a realistic framework for detailing the classical Spanish bullfight with its four distinct parts, as well as the context for describing the appearance, personalities, and techniques of four matadors who will fight in Seville after Easter. Michener places the reader in Seville, seeing, smelling, hearing, and experiencing the bullfights, the processions, and the parade. Character development becomes secondary in the narrative, as Michener is much more interested in telling the story of Don Cayetano, who is seeking to restore the lost honor and glory of his ranch with the help of the Virgin Mary. Through Shenstone, Michener paints a portrait of Spain as a country where bullfighting is an art form, where religious faith is sincere and often dramatic in its expression, and where constant effort is required to sustain personal and family honor.

Miracle in Seville stands apart from Michener's other novels. Although it resembles his previous novels in its focus on the culture of a particular place, it is his only novel that presents events that cannot be rationally explained, creating a strong aura of fantasy. However, even though it is an adult fairy tale, this novel exhibits a well-developed story and a vivid sense of location.

Whatever the critical verdict on Michener the novelist may be, it is clear that Michener the educator-through-fiction has been a great success. To a popular audience numbering in the millions, he has communicated the uniquely modern sense of the long view of history.

Joan Corey Semonella
Updated by Alvin K. Benson

Other major works

SHORT FICTION: *Return to Paradise*, 1951; *Creatures of the Kingdom: Stories of Animals*, 1993.

NONFICTION: *Proposals for an Experimental Future of the Social Sciences: Proposals for an Experimental Social Studies Curriculum*, 1939 (with Harold Long); *The Unit in the Social Studies*, 1940; *The Voice of Asia*, 1951; *The Floating World*, 1954; *Rascals in Paradise*, 1957 (with A. Grove Day); *Selected Writings*, 1957; *Japanese Prints from the Early Masters to the Modern*, 1959; *Report of the County Chairman*, 1961; *The Modern Japanese Print: An Appreciation*, 1962; *Iberia: Spanish Travels and Reflections*, 1968; *Presidential Lottery: The Reckless Gamble in Our Electoral System*, 1969; *Facing East: The Art of Jack Levine*, 1970; *The*

Quality of Life, 1970; *Kent State: What Happened and Why,* 1971; *A Michener Miscellany, 1950-1970,* 1973; *About "Centennial": Some Notes on the Novel,* 1974; *Sports in America,* 1976; *In Search of Centennial: A Journey,* 1978; *Collectors, Forgers, and a Writer: A Memoir,* 1983; *Testimony,* 1983; *Six Days in Havana,* 1989; *Pilgrimage: A Memoir of Poland and Rome,* 1990; *My Lost Mexico,* 1992; *The World Is My Home: A Memoir,* 1992; *Literary Reflections: Michener on Michener, Hemingway, Capote, and Others,* 1993; *William Penn,* 1994; *This Noble Land,* 1996; *A Century of Sonnets,* 1997; *Talking with Michener,* 1999 (interviews; with Lawrence Grobel).

EDITED TEXTS: *The Hokusai Sketchbooks: Selections from the Manga,* 1958.

Bibliography

Becker, George Joseph. *James A. Michener.* New York: Ungar, 1983. Survey of Michener's early writings in the publisher's Literature and Life series

Day, A. Grove. *James A. Michener.* 2d ed. New York: Twayne, 1977. Written from the point of view of one who knew and worked with Michener. Its excellent bibliography is limited, naturally, to materials published before 1977.

Grobel, Lawrence. *Talking with Michener.* Jackson: University Press of Mississippi, 1999. Collection of interviews with Michener by a friend of seventeen years.

Groseclose, Karen, and David A. Groseclose. *James A. Michener: A Bibliography.* Austin, Tex.: State House Press, 1996. A detailed chronology of Michener's life, including the most important events, his publications, honors, awards, and his contributions to society, education, and politics. Contains a comprehensive bibliography about Michener and presents an informative synopsis of each of Michener's novels, as well as a compilation of Michener's works.

Hayes, John P. *James A. Michener.* Indianapolis: Bobbs-Merrill, 1987. A helpful biography.

May, Stephen J. *Michener: A Writer's Journey.* Norman: University of Oklahoma Press, 2005. Michener's own writing is used to paint a portrait of him as a journalist and popular writer who never achieved the literary acclaim that he craved. Includes 19 black and white photos.

Michener, James A. *The World Is My Home.* New York: Random House, 1992. A memoir of Michener's life and writing.

Roberts, F. X., and C. D. Rhine, comps. *James A. Michener: A Checklist of His Works.* Westport, Conn.: Greenwood Press, 1995. As part of the series on Bibliographies and Indexes in American Literature, Roberts and Rhine have compiled a comprehensive list of Michener's writings. Excellent reference work that contains a selected, annotated bibliography.

Severson, Marilyn S. *James A. Michener.* Westport, Conn.: Greenwood Press, 1996. Severson's book, part of the series of Critical Companions to Popular Contemporary Writers, presents a complete overview of Michener's life, including his writing style, themes, ideas, and concerns. Also provides an excellent, detailed analysis of nine of Michener's forty-eight books. Includes a partial bibliography of works by Michener, of information and criticism about Michener, and of reviews of some of Michener's books.

Shaddinger, Anne E. *The Micheners in America.* Rutland, Vt.: Charles Tuttle, 1958. Information on Michener's parentage.

Silverman, Herman. *Michener and Me: A Memoir.* Philadelphia: Running Press, 1999. Silverman, who first met Michener before the latter's literary success, recounts his memories of over fifty years of friendship.

Henry Miller

Born: New York, New York; December 26, 1891
Died: Pacific Palisades, California; June 7, 1980

Principal long fiction • *Tropic of Cancer*, 1934; *Black Spring*, 1936; *Tropic of Capricorn*, 1939; *The Rosy Crucifixion*, 1949-1960, 1963 (includes *Sexus*, 1949, 2 volumes; *Plexus*, 1953, 2 volumes; *Nexus*, 1960); *Quiet Days in Clichy*, 1956.

Other literary forms • In an interview, Henry Miller once described himself as one part a writer of tales and one part a man electrified by ideas. This simple dichotomy provides a way to classify Miller's work, but, in truth, his whole canon is autobiographical. The many collections of his shorter pieces—portraits, essays, stories, travel sketches, reviews, letters—are all of value in ascertaining the truth of his life, his admitted literary goal. For example, *The Colossus of Maroussi: Or, The Spirit of Greece* (1941), Miller's first book about Greece, is ostensibly about George Katsimbalis, a leading figure in modern Greek letters. Katsimbalis, however, turns out to be Miller's alter ego, a fascinating monologuist, and the book becomes the record of Miller's attaining peace of heart through the elemental beauty of Greece. *The Time of the Assassins: A Study of Rimbaud* (1956) is less about Arthur Rimbaud than about the romantic affinities between Miller's and Rimbaud's lives. In Miller's books, all things become translated into images of his own mental landscape.

Achievements • When Miller repatriated in 1940, only *The Cosmological Eye* (1939), a collection of short pieces drawn from *Max and the White Phagocytes* (1938), had been published in the United States; all of his fiction was deemed too obscene for publication. In France, *Tropic of Cancer* and *Tropic of Capricorn* had been seized in 1946, and Miller was convicted as a pornographer. After an outcry of French writers, this conviction was reversed, but in 1950, *Sexus* was banned in France, and in 1957, it was condemned as obscene in Norway. When *Tropic of Cancer* was finally published in the United States, in 1961, by Barney Rosset of Grove Press, more than sixty suits were instituted against Miller and the book. Miller became the most litigated-against author in history, and the book was only allowed to circulate after a Supreme Court decision in 1965. The furor over his books' alleged obscenity prevented dispassionate evaluation of his literary merit for many years, and Miller feared that he would be dismissed as the "King of Smut." He was, however, inducted into the National Institute of Arts and Letters in 1957, and he received a citation from the Formentor Prize Committee, in France, in 1961 and the French Legion of Honor in 1975.

These memberships and citations, however, do not mark Miller's true achievement. His true quest and calling was to narrow the gap between art and life. The fact that he—or his public persona of Paris expatriate, Big Sur prophet, desperado, clown, artist-hero, satyr—was the focus of critical attention throughout his life, rather than his books, testifies to the measure of success he achieved. Miller wanted to become free, as free as the young boy of the streets he had been in his childhood, in the face of a culture he saw as sterile, mechanical, and death-driven. He also wanted to discover and embody the truth of his life in art, in his "autobiographical romances." His defiant spit in the face of art in his first book, *Tropic of Cancer*, prompted critics to label his works as "antiliterature." Rather than deprecating literature, however, Miller saw art as a means to life more abundant. He conceived of his work as enlightening, as offering his vision of reality. Often described as a *roman-fleuve* of the life of Henry Miller, his fiction is neither strictly autobiographical nor realistic in method. As an artist, he notes in *The Wisdom of the Heart* (1941), he must give his reader "a vital, singing universe, alive in all its parts"; to accomplish this, he relied on the verbal pyrotechnics of Surrealism and the temporal discontinuities of stream of consciousness. The result was a series of works full of contradictions, repetitions, incongruities, and rhetorical flights, all documenting his growth as a man and as an artist.

Larry Colwell

Biography • Henry Valentine Miller was born on December 26, 1891, in the Yorkville section of New York City. Both of his parents were of German stock: His father, a gentleman's tailor, came from jovial people; his mother and her family typified the austere, industrious, respectable bourgeois life against which Miller was to rebel so vehemently. For the first nine years of his life, the family lived in the Williamsburg section of Brooklyn, the Fourteenth Ward. For Miller, this was a child's paradise. When he was ten, his family moved to Decatur Street, the "Street of Early Sorrows," in Brooklyn's Bushwick section. His teenage experiences there helped form his attitudes on life, literature, and women. Miller was an affable young man; his special friends at this time were members of the Xerxes Society, a musical crowd. Male conviviality would be important to Miller throughout his life.

Miller was a model student and graduated as salutatorian from high school, but his formal education ended after a few months at the City College of New York. Always an avid reader—he had read through the Harvard Classics as well as many romantic and adventure tales—Miller became an autodidact. By the time he was twenty, he had devoured such diverse authors as Joseph Conrad, Madame Blavatsky, and François Rabelais and had decided that he wanted to be a writer—about what, he did not know. Besides frequenting theaters in New York and Brooklyn, Miller was often seen at burlesque shows and in brothels. If his mother seemed cold and difficult to please, these women were open for sexual pleasure. Despite these experiences, Miller developed an intense idealism about love and the perfect woman, centering his longing on a school classmate, Cora Seward. At the same time, though, he began in 1910 an affair with a widow, Pauline Chouteau, closer to his mother's age.

In an effort to escape this passionate entanglement, Miller went to California in 1913, winding up miserable as a ranch hand near Chula Vista. Only hearing Emma

Goldman in San Diego, extolling anarchism, redeemed the trip. The next year Miller was back in New York, working in his father's tailor shop (described in *Black Spring*) and reading omnivorously. He was attracted to universalizing ideas and grander interpretations of the meaning of life than those of his Brooklyn milieu. During the years 1914-1915, Miller began to study piano seriously; through this enthusiasm, he met Beatrice Sylvas Wickens, whom he married in 1917. Their stormy courtship and marriage is depicted graphically in *The World of Sex* (1940, 1957), *Tropic of Capricorn*, and *Sexus*. Drifting through many jobs, Miller found his way to the bottom—Western Union. His experience as a messenger employment manager opened his eyes to the underlying misery in America. His sympathy with these victims, adrift in a dehumanized urban landscape, was responsible for his unpublished first novel, *Clipped Wings*, dedicated to Horatio Alger. Miller's disillusionment with the American Dream came at a time when his marriage was also foundering. His response, rather than despair or self-pity, was to begin keeping a journal and extensive files of material for later use. He was beginning to become a writer, establishing an aesthetic distance from life and from himself.

Miller's delivery as a full-fledged artist was through the agency of June Edith Smith, the Mona, Mara, "She," or "Her" of his fiction, his second wife, whom he met at a Broadway dance hall in 1923 and married the next year. June was a creative artist—of herself and her life story—who showed Miller the bridge between life and the imagination. Convinced that he was a great writer, she made him quit his job and devote his life to his work. This metamorphosis is recorded in *Tropic of Capricorn* and *Plexus*. To relieve their desperate poverty, June began peddling a series of brief prose sketches Miller had written called "Mezzotints," signed "June E. Mansfield." Miller might have freed himself from a conventional American life, but June—her schemes, her stories, her lovers, herself—held him completely in thrall. When June eloped with her lover Jean Kronski to Paris in 1927, Miller began to record notes of his obsessional attachment to her. His life with June was to be the book he tried to write throughout his life, culminating in *The Rosy Crucifixion*. His second unpublished novel, *Moloch*, the story of Miller's experiences during the year 1923, was written under unique pressure: One of June's admirers promised her a year in Europe if she completed a book. *Moloch* was their ticket to Paris.

Miller's trip to Paris with June in 1928-1929 was unproductive; he painted watercolors instead of writing books. Only when he returned alone to Paris in 1930 and ran out of resources did he begin to live and write truly. Living a marginal life, he not only completed his novel about June and Jean, *Crazy Cock*, but he also discovered "Henry Miller," the voice and main character of his "autobiographical romances." Alfred Perlès, "Joey," contributed his bohemian lifestyle and epicurism to Miller's new persona. The French Surrealists gave artistic form to Miller's sense of incongruity.

The photographer Brassai helped Miller see the poetry of the sordid side of Paris. Walter Lowenfels and Michael Fraenkel converted him to the "death school"—although Miller knew that he, for one, remained very much alive. Anaïs Nin became his ministering angel. Her love restored his faith in both himself and womankind. Her own journals confirmed him in the belief that his true subject was himself. Through her, he met the psychoanalyst Otto Rank: Miller's interest in psychology (and Nin) brought him back to New York for a brief period in 1936 to work as an analyst, but more important, it helped him understand his past and himself, which were to become the central concerns of his life. He kept a "dreambook" in this period, some of which reappears in his fiction. *Tropic of Cancer* and *Quiet Days in Clichy* draw on Miller's first two years in France. By 1936, Miller's apartment in Villa Seurat had become the center of an industrious artistic circle, which was joined in 1937 by Lawrence Durrell, Miller's first disciple. Far from Wambly Bald's Paris *Tribune* picture of the great American hobo artist, Miller in his Paris years worked with Germanic regularity and thoroughness on his fiction and essays.

By 1939, Miller was able to finish *Tropic of Capricorn*. With its completion, Miller's furious literary activity abated. He began to lose interest in the narrative of his life and became engrossed in spiritual literature—astrology, Zen, Theosophy, Krishnamurti, the I Ching. When he left Paris in 1939, at the advent of World War II, to visit Durrell in Corfu, Greece, the stage was set for his third metamorphosis. He records in *The Colossus of Maroussi* that in Greece he discovered a new goal in life: not to be a writer, but simply to be. Images of simplicity—the land, sea, and silences of Greece—awakened in Miller, the city man, a response to the allure of nature.

Back in America in 1940, Miller continued his autobiographical saga, but his only major fictional endeavor in the next forty years was to be *The Rosy Crucifixion*, written between 1942 and 1959, in which he tried to capture the elusive truth of his relationship with June. Most of his writing during this period was nonfiction. On an advance from Doubleday, Miller and the painter Abraham Rattner went on a tour of the United States from 1940 to 1941. The resulting book, *The Air-Conditioned Nightmare* (1945), turned out to be a jeremiad rather than a travelogue.

In 1942, Miller moved to California, settling into a cabin at Big Sur in 1944. There, amid its natural splendor, he found his Walden. Miller was again the center of a circle of painters and writers, a group that came to national attention through a 1947 *Harper's* magazine article, "Sex and Anarchy in Big Sur." Life, however, was not an orgy for Miller. He still remained in poverty, supporting himself by selling his watercolors and begging from his friends. In 1944, he married his third wife, Janina M. Lepska, who attempted to introduce domestic order into his life, but by 1948, she had left him. She and Conrad Moricand, an astrologer friend from his Paris days, were castigated as "devils" in his account of his life at Big Sur, *Big Sur and the Oranges of Hieronymus Bosch* (1957). In 1953, he married Eve McClure; their marriage was dissolved in 1962. In 1967, he married Hiroko "Hoki" Tokuda, a twenty-nine-year-old cabaret singer from Tokyo; that marriage ended in divorce in 1978. His later travails in love are described in *Insomnia: Or, The Devil at Large* (1970). Indeed, his later works seem to have been written to cleanse himself of the demons that possessed him. His final days were spent in Pacific Palisades, California. The acclaimed founder of the sexual revolution of the 1960's died on June 7, 1980. He was eighty-eight years old.

Analysis • Miller's books, in their frank sexual description, pushed back the last frontier of American literary realism. Sex was, for Miller, a means by which to study the cosmos: He noted in *The World of Sex* that

> to enter life by way of the vagina is as good a way as any. If you enter deep enough, remain long enough, you will find what you seek. But you've got to enter with your heart and soul—and check your belongings outside.

Whatever he sought, women became his connection to the universal. Although women are often depicted as sexual objects in his fiction, sex, he insisted, is "an elemental force. It's just as mysterious and magical as talking about God or the nature of the universe." The way in which Miller used obscenity against the bourgeoisie is telling: that sex was considered "dirty" reflected the puritanical nature of the culture he was attacking.

Because of his use of the obscene, the world of Miller's books is often repulsive and degrading, filled with grotesque characters living on the margin of society. The harsh reality of life must be accepted, he felt, before it could be transcended. In *My Life and Times* (1971), he explained, "The only way you can prove you are not of it is by entering into it fully. . . . When you fully accept something, you are no longer victimized by it." Savoring the dregs of civilization, Miller castigated its pretensions with anarchic glee. Indeed, Miller's value lies not in a depiction of some salvific vision (reality always remains a bit hazy in his fiction), but in his searing indictment of the modern world's impoverishment of "soul life." Miller shared D. H. Lawrence's horror of the mechanical modern world and endorsed Lawrence's response—the instinctual life—yet for all his apocalyptic prophecies, Miller was no Lawrentian messiah. Indeed, the "Henry Miller" of the novels is a *flâneur*, an American picaro.

Tropic of Cancer • Ernest Hemingway's *The Sun Also Rises* (1926), Miller admitted in an interview at the age of eighty-four, was the impetus for his journey to Paris, the artists' mecca. What Miller found there during the 1930's forms the basis of his first and best novel, *Tropic of Cancer*. Paris provided both the impetus and the substance of his disjointed narrative. Paris, Miller writes, is like a whore, "ravishing" from a distance, but "five minutes later you feel empty, disgusted with yourself. You feel tricked." Whores—Germaine, Claude, Llona, and others—and their hangouts dominate Miller's Paris, suggesting the debunking of romantic ideals, which was necessary for Miller before he could write. This is apparent in the evolving nature of his relationship to his wife Mona in the book. It begins with his anticipation of their reunion, which proves blissful but short-lived. Although he claims that "for seven years I went about, day and night, with only one thing in my mind—*her*," after she returns to America, her image—like all the rest of his old life—"seems to have fallen into the sea," until he can only wonder "in a vague way" at the novel's conclusion whatever happened to her. Paris has replaced her as the center of his attention, and Paris makes far fewer demands on his inner self. Like his superficial relationships with whores, his stay in Paris is a fruitful form of self-destruction out of which a new self emerges.

The predominant metaphor in *Tropic of Cancer* is that of the river, of all that flows, in contrast to the stultifying conceptions and conventions of modern civilization. Early in the book, the sight of the Seine, and the great unconscious life that it represents, is inspirational. He later learns to see the world without "boundaries" or preconceived notions and recognizes it "for the mad slaughterhouse it is." His two trips outside Paris demonstrate his acclimatization and the death of his illusions. Returning from Le Havre, he recognizes the essential attraction of Paris for him, and he demonstrates in his outwitting of a whore his adjustment to the scene. Returning from Dijon, that bastion of medievalism that reminds him of the North (a bad place in Miller's geography, redolent of the coldness and sterility of his German ancestors), where everybody is constipated and even the toilet pipes freeze, he recognizes his previous dependency upon women, "a fear of living separate, of staying born." This realization enables him to free Fillmore from the clutches of the rapacious Ginette and himself from Mona. The climax of the episode, and of the book as well, takes him again to the River Seine. He has already announced his love for everything that flows—"rivers, sewers, lava, semen, blood, bile, words, sentences"—and in this climax, he surrenders himself with religious intensity to the flux of time and space: "I feel this river flowing through me—its past, its ancient soul, the changing climate."

While a parade of other displaced persons in Paris passes through the book, they are all, like Moldorf, a "sieve through which my anarchy strains, resolves itself into words." Unlike the Jews Boris and Moldorf, the reborn Miller enjoys his suffering, because it confirms his sense of this world as a "putrid sink." Van Norden exists as a foil to Miller, both in relation to women and to himself. Van Norden is a neurotic egotist who uses women to try to forget himself, personifying the lovelessness of the modern world, where passion is removed from sex. As he watches Van Norden and his fifteen-franc whore grinding away, Miller compares him to a runaway machine or a maimed war hero: The human reality that gives meaning to the act is missing. Fillmore is another foil to Miller; like the typical American expatriate, he has come to France for wine, women, and song. Miller helps him escape Ginette and a marriage into the French bourgeoisie, and he returns to America disillusioned. Miller stays behind, his illusions gone, replaced by an appetite for life. The women characters of the book are negligible—with Mona's disappearance from his world, the woman has been replaced by her pudendum.

Tropic of Cancer is Miller's gleeful song over the corpse of the twentieth century: "I will sing while you croak." The comedy, sexual and otherwise, is at the expense of everyone, himself included. The novel played a decisive role in Miller's career: In it, he found the distinctive voice that he never thereafter abandoned. Miller describes the realization of the insufficiency of all ideas and the justification for the abandonment of conventional beliefs: "I am only spiritually dead. Physically I am alive. Morally I am free. . . . The dawn is breaking on a new world." The book ends on this note of openness to a better life.

Tropic of Capricorn • *Tropic of Capricorn* is Miller's *Künstlerroman*, depicting his own development as an artist. It records his struggle to achieve detachment from America and from his past life and become an angel, "pure and inhuman," in possession of his spiritual core. It is written from the perspective of one who has awakened from the "nightmare" of history, an achievement at first inspired by his friend Ulric and by the works of D. H. Lawrence and Fyodor Dostoevski, and later catalyzed by "Her," Mara.

The book opens "on the ovarian trolly," when the persona of Miller is still unclear, mired in the chaos of his surroundings. America is a "cesspool of the spirit," and its statistical wealth and happiness is a sham: Everywhere, there is testimony to man's inhumanity to man. This inferno is revealed to him through his job as employment manager at a branch of the Cosmodemonic (or Cosmococcic) Telegraphic Company of North America. His own persona might still be gestating, but those of the messengers, Carnahan, Guptal, Dave Olinski, Clausen, Schuldig—with clipped wings all—are surely in focus. Their stories, as well as those of Miller's "merry crew," reveal the underside of America and constitute Miller's anti-Horatio Alger story. Determined to escape being a "failure or ridiculous," Miller sees art as a way out.

At the beginning of the second part, Miller's friend Kronski advises him that good writers must first really suffer. Miller scoffs at this "Jewish" advice, preferring the "terrific animal sense of adjustment" of his German milieu, but the experience with Mara that is to come—in this book only intimated surrealistically—will leave him a marked man. For the moment, eating is all, and his reminiscences of good food take him back to his "wonderful past" when his Aunt Caroline gave him a thick slice of sour rye bread. The bread, through the lenses of Miller's nostalgia, becomes transformed into the "communion loaf." Adulthood can only be a diminished realm: "The taste goes out of bread as it goes out of life. Getting the bread becomes more important than the eating of it."

The next section of the book, "An Interlude," depicts "general sexual confusion." It is clear that, in some sense, sex is the agent for Miller's regeneration—at least it provides him with an escape from the workaday world that is death in life. Sex is ultimately disappointing to Miller, however, and his thinking "via the penis" leads absolutely nowhere. It only helps him to establish his first mask—that of Capricorn or the Goat—to deal with his life: "In this strange Capricornian condition of embryosis God the he-goat ruminates in stolid bliss among the mountain peaks." Moreover, sex puts Miller in touch with natural vitality.

What Miller really wants is love, the "Real Thing." From a wistful description of Una, his first love, Miller proceeds to the Amarillo Dance Hall: His encounter there with Mara is volcanic. Henceforth, he will be "Gottlieb Leberecht Müller," a man who has lost his identity. Mara, a fabulous creature whose life is a web of illusion, resembles a figure of mythology, a Juno or a Circe, or an archetype, a Terrible Mother.

Together with Mara in their black hole of Calcutta, Miller hibernates, "a blazing seed hidden in the heart of death." She is fascinating but terrible—"a dead black sun without aspect," a "great plunder-bird." In the coda, reflecting on this book as "a tomb in which to bury her—and the me which had belonged to her," Miller makes another attempt to explain how she became the Beatrice who led him to the paradise of the imagination. The language he uses reveals that she might actually represent his unconscious life, the life whose very existence America denied. United with Mara, "the inner and the outer ego are in equilibrium. . . . Henceforth I take on two sexes. . . . I shall seek the end in myself."

As an artist, Miller achieves personal harmony and, more important, power. He feels a kinship with Knut Hamsun's Herr Nagel, the artist as unacknowledged saint, driven to art "because the world refuses to recognize his proper leadership." Like Peter Abelard, like Christ, Miller sees his life as instructive, an object lesson in self-fulfillment: "All my Calvaries were rosy crucifixions, pseudotragedies to keep the fires of hell burning brightly for the real sinners who are in danger of being forgotten."

The value of Miller's work transcends the expression of his personality, however vital and unique that was. In the "Defense of the Freedom to Read" (1957), Miller notes, "Whatever I may say about my own life which is only a life, is merely a means of talking about life itself." Like Walt Whitman, Miller extended the literary terrain of American literature, democratizing it as well. Besides his direct influence on Lawrence Durrell and the Beat generation of the 1950's—Jack Kerouac, Allen Ginsberg, Lawrence Ferlinghetti, and Gregory Corso—Miller's influence can be detected in much postwar American fiction, with its blending of colloquial, surreal, obscene, fantastic, and desperate rhetoric. Miller's confessions provided a voice for the alienated individual who, against all odds, remains sure of his own humanity.

Honora Rankine Galloway

Other major works

PLAY: *Just Wild About Harry: A Melo-Melo in Seven Scenes*, pb. 1963.

NONFICTION: *Aller Retour New York*, 1935; *What Are You Going to Do About Alf?*, 1935; *Max and the White Phagocytes*, 1938; *Money and How It Gets That Way*, 1938; *Hamlet*, 1939,

1941 (2 volumes; with Michael Fraenkel); *The Cosmological Eye*, 1939; *The World of Sex*, 1940, 1957; *The Colossus of Maroussi: Or, The Spirit of Greece*, 1941; *The Wisdom of the Heart*, 1941; *Murder the Murderer*, 1944; *Semblance of a Devoted Past*, 1944; *The Angel Is My Watermark*, 1944 (originally published in *Black Spring*); *The Plight of the Creative Artist in the United States of America*, 1944; *Echolalis: Reproductions of Water Colors by Henry Miller*, 1945; *Henry Miller Miscellanea*, 1945; *Maurizius Forever*, 1945; *Obscenity and the Law of Reflection*, 1945; *The Air-Conditioned Nightmare*, 1945; *The Amazing and Invariable Beauford Delaney*, 1945; *Why Abstract?*, 1945 (with Hilaire Hiler and William Saroyan); *Patchen: Man of Anger and Light, with a Letter to God by Kenneth Patchen*, 1946; *Of, by and About Henry Miller: A Collection of Pieces by Miller, Herbert Read, and Others*, 1947; *Portrait of General Grant*, 1947; *Remember to Remember*, 1947; *Varda: The Master Builder*, 1947; *The Smile at the Foot of the Ladder*, 1948; *The Waters Reglitterized*, 1950; *The Books in My Life*, 1952; *Nights of Love and Laughter*, 1955 (Kenneth Rexroth, editor); *A Devil in Paradise: The Story of Conrad Mourand, Born Paris, 7 or 7:15 p.m., January 17, 1887, Died Paris, 10:30 p.m., August 31, 1954*, 1956; *Argument About Astrology*, 1956; *The Time of the Assassins: A Story of Rimbaud*, 1956; *Big Sur and the Oranges of Hieronymus Bosch*, 1957; *The Red Notebook*, 1958; *Reunion in Barcelona: A Letter to Alfred Perlès*, 1959; *The Henry Miller Reader*, 1959 (Lawrence Durrell, editor); *The Intimate Henry Miller*, 1959 (Lawrence Clark Powell, editor); *To Paint Is to Love Again*, 1960; *Stand Still Like the Hummingbird*, 1962; *The Michael Fraenkel-Henry Miller Correspondence, Called Hamlet*, 1962 (2 volumes); *Watercolors, Drawings, and His Essay "The Angel Is My Watermark,"* 1962; *Books Tangent to Circle: Reviews*, 1963; *Lawrence Durrell and Henry Miller: A Private Correspondence*, 1963 (George Wickes, editor); *Greece*, 1964; *Henry Miller on Writing*, 1964 (Thomas H. Moore, editor); *Letters to Anaïs Nin*, 1965; *Selected Prose*, 1965 (2 volumes); *Order and Chaos chez Hans Reichel*, 1966; *Collector's Quest: The Correspondence of Henry Miller and J. Rivers Childs, 1947-1965*, 1968; *Writer and Critic: A Correspondence*, 1968 (with W. A. Gordon); *Insomnia: Or, The Devil at Large*, 1970; *My Life and Times*, 1971 (Bradley Smith, editor); *Henry Miller in Conversation with Georges Belmont*, 1972; *Journey to an Unknown Land*, 1972; *On Turning Eighty*, 1972; *Reflections on the Death of Mishima*, 1972; *First Impressions of Greece*, 1973; *Reflections on the Maurizius Case*, 1974; *Letters of Henry Miller and Wallace Fowlie, 1943-1972*, 1975; *The Nightmare Notebook*, 1975; *Books of Friends: A Tribute to Friends of Long Ago*, 1976; *Four Visions of America*, 1977 (with others); *Gliding into the Everglades, and Other Essays*, 1977; *Sextet*, 1977; *An Open Letter to Stroker!*, 1978 (Irving Stetner, editor); *Henry Miller: Years of Trial and Triumph*, 1978; *My Bike and Other Friends*, 1978; *Some Friends*, 1978; *Joey: A Loving Portrait of Alfred Perlès Together with Some Bizarre Episodes Relating to the Other Sex*, 1979; *Notes on "Aaron's Rod" and Other Notes on Lawrence from the Paris Notebooks of Henry Miller*, 1980 (Seamus Cooney, editor); *The World of Lawrence: A Passionate Appreciation*, 1980 (Evelyn J. Hinz and John J. Teunissen, editors); *Reflections*, 1981; *The Paintings of Henry Miller*, 1982; *From Your Capricorn Friend: Henry Miller and the "Stroker," 1978-1980*, 1984; *Dear, Dear Brenda*, 1986; *Letters from Henry Miller to Hoki Tokuda Miller*, 1986 (Joyce Howard, editor); *A Literate Passion: Letters of Anaïs Nin and Henry Miller*, 1987; *Henry Miller's Hamlet Letters*, 1988; *The Durrell-Miller Letters, 1935-1980*, 1988; *Henry Miller and James Laughlin: Selected Letters*, 1996 (George Wickes, editor).

Bibliography

Brown, J. D. *Henry Miller*. New York: Frederick Ungar, 1986. A concise assessment of Miller's work in relation to the events of his life, with a particularly good summary chapter titled "Autobiography in America." Brown writes with clarity and knows the material well. Includes a chronology of the events of Miller's life, a bibliography of his writing through 1980, and useful sections listing interviews, bibliographical collections, biographies, and selected criticism.

Dearborn, Mary V. *The Happiest Man Alive: A Biography of Henry Miller.* New York: Simon & Schuster, 1991. Admiring biography of Miller.

Ferguson, Robert. *Henry Miller: A Life.* New York: W. W. Norton, 1991. A full and sensitive treatment of Miller's life and work. See especially the first chapter for the problems involved in interpreting Miller, the response of feminist critics, and the difficulties of evaluating Miller's memoirs. Includes notes and bibliography.

Gottesman, Ronald, ed. *Critical Essays on Henry Miller.* New York: G. K. Hall, 1992. Divided into sections on the "early" Miller (includes biographical material and book reviews); the "phallic" Miller (including conflicting interpretations by Norman Mailer and Kate Millett); the "orphic" Miller; the "American" Miller; and various retrospectives of his life and career, including memoirs. Includes introduction and bibliography.

Jahshan, Paul. *Henry Miller and the Surrealist Discourse of Excess: A Poststructuralist Reading.* New York: P. Lang, 2001. Arguing that descriptions of Miller's literary style as "Surrealist" evade a serious analysis of the work, Jahshan shows that Miller's texts share with those of the French Surrealists an imagery of excess, but one that is economically and masterfully geared toward a reader whose response(s) help in constructing a peculiarly Millerian version of stylistic deviation.

Lewis, Leon. *Henry Miller: The Major Writings.* New York: Schocken Books/Random House, 1986. Concentrates on the seven books regarded as the heart of Miller's achievement as a writer, offering detailed critical analysis of each book as well as a comprehensive estimate of Miller's entire life as an artist. Relates Miller to the American writers he admired and to Albert Camus and the Surrealists of the 1920's to locate him within literary and cultural traditions. Includes a bibliography and related criticism.

Mathieu, Bertrand. *Orpheus in Brooklyn: Orphism, Rimbaud, and Henry Miller.* Paris: Mouton, 1976. Mathieu is an expert on the work of Arthur Rimbaud, and his study focuses on the parallels between Miller and the French poet, particularly in regard to Miller's *The Colossus of Maroussi* (1941). Mathieu is very knowledgeable, writes with energy and insight, and offers the useful thesis that Miller's work is constructed on a plan similar to Dante's *The Divine Comedy.*

Mitchel, Edward, ed. *Henry Miller: Three Decades of Criticism.* New York: New York University Press, 1971. A representative compilation which indicates just how much controversy and personal response Miller's work elicited during the first three decades after *Tropic of Cancer* was published.

Widmer, Kingsley. *Henry Miller.* Rev. ed. Boston: Twayne, 1990. Updates Widmer's 1962 work, taking into account the final years of Miller's career and the criticism that appeared after Widmer's study. A succinct yet comprehensive introduction. Includes chronology, notes, and annotated bibliography.

Wright Morris

Born: Central City, Nebraska; January 6, 1910
Died: Mill Valley, California; April 26, 1998

Principal long fiction • *My Uncle Dudley*, 1942; *The Man Who Was There*, 1945; *The Home Place*, 1948; *The World in the Attic*, 1949; *Man and Boy*, 1951; *The Works of Love*, 1952; *The Deep Sleep*, 1953; *The Huge Season*, 1954; *The Field of Vision*, 1956; *Love Among the Cannibals*, 1957; *Ceremony in Lone Tree*, 1960; *What a Way to Go*, 1962; *Cause for Wonder*, 1963; *One Day*, 1965; *In Orbit*, 1967; *Fire Sermon*, 1971; *War Games*, 1972; *A Life*, 1973; *The Fork River Space Project*, 1977; *Plains Song, for Female Voices*, 1980.

Other literary forms • Several of Wright Morris's books, including *The Inhabitants* (1946), *God's Country and My People* (1968), and *Love Affair: A Venetian Journal* (1972), are "photo-texts." They feature photographs accompanied by brief prose passages. In the first of these, Morris describes the "inhabitants" of America from coast to coast through photographs of their structures—buildings that have affected the "indwellers." Pictures of porch fronts in the West, for example, reveal New England influences, as do the inhabitants of the dwellings. The photographs, although not synchronized with the text, appear on facing pages and combine with it to make a larger statement than would be possible from either medium used alone—a statement about America and its people and their place in the changing world. Fences, privies, and churches are among the other artifacts pictured on unnumbered pages and bearing a poetic relationship to the human characters described in the text; it is up to the reader to determine the truths thereby conveyed.

God's Country and My People, more autobiographical yet less nostalgic than its predecessors, suggests present-day values and their usefulness to a later generation. *Love Affair*, utilizing color photographs taken in Venice in 1969, presents the problem of "shouting" that everything is of interest, while the black and white pictures of the photo-texts of the plains are more selective in their emphasis. Morris also published several collections of photographs: *Wright Morris: Structures and Artifacts, Photographs, 1933-1954* (1975), *Photographs and Words* (1982), and *Picture America* (1982). A meditation on photography and writing, *Time Pieces: Photographs, Writings, and Memory*, appeared in 1989.

Morris's books of essays include *The Territory Ahead* (1958, 1963), a work of criticism expressing his admiration for the artistry of Henry James and the vitality of D. H. Lawrence, and his concern about the misuse of the past by sentimental illustrators or writers. *A Bill of Rites, a Bill of Wrongs, a Bill of Goods* (1968) contains more critical essays deploring the practices of professional reviewers, of speed readers, and of symbol hunters, and the passing of the reader who simply wants to establish a dialogue with the writer. The writer's duty, Morris says, is to bring the real world into a field of vision that will give it meaning and to stir the readers' imagination. In this sometimes angry book, Morris also denounces advertising, which has created the consumer culture with its longing for possessions, and technological expertise, which allows humankind to explore space without at all improving life on Earth.

Morris's third book of essays, *About Fiction* (1975), describes the ideal reader,

Jo Morris

discusses point of view, and compares realism with "fabulation"—a more artistic, shapely, idea-filled narrative, exemplified by the works of John Barth, Thomas Pynchon, and Vladimir Nabokov. *Earthly Delights, Unearthly Adornments* (1978) surveys Morris's own career and the course of American writing through quotations, recollections, and pictures. Perhaps the best summation of these books of essays is to be found in the subtitle of *About Fiction, Reverent Reflections on the Nature of Fiction with Irreverent Observations on Writers, Readers, and Other Abuses.*

Morris's other works include an anthology, *Wright Morris: A Reader* (1970), which contains two short novels, *The Works of Love* and *The Field of Vision,* two short stories, and selections from eight other novels. *Real Losses, Imaginary Gains* (1976) is a collection of thirteen short stories; another volume of Morris's short fiction appeared in 1986, *Collected Stories: 1948-1986.* The memoir *Will's Boy* (1981) was followed by two other autobiographical works: *Solo: An American Dreamer in Europe, 1933-1934* (1983) and *A Cloak of Light: Writing My Life* (1985).

Achievements • Although a few of Morris's books have European settings, he is most effective when writing about his native Nebraska and characters returning home to try to recapture memories or relive the past. The fact that Morris was unusually concerned with his craft is evidenced by his several books of essays on the writing of fiction and the readers thereof. A prolific writer, Morris was primarily a delineator of character, rather than a constructor of intricate plots. He pays considerable attention to the "artifacts" of his characters' worlds and to the workings of their minds, most particularly to the kinds of thoughts that are never expressed aloud.

Morris is almost inevitably compared to both James Agee and Walker Evans because of his poetic, reflective prose about the dignity of rural life and because his photography is reminiscent of Evans's in *Let Us Now Praise Famous Men* (1960). Morris combines the talents of both men in his photo-texts, conducting a search for the meaning of America through word and picture.

Although Morris always received critical acclaim, he did not enjoy a popular success. Robert Knoll suggested that the reason may be Morris's failure to involve the reader in the exciting events of his fiction. He rather invites the reader casually, as did Robert Frost, to come along and clear the leaves away. His poetic style is as far removed as prose can be from the popular journalistic narrative mode. Although Morris knew that readers do not want fictive distance, he created novels that question rather than confess, that disturb rather than reassure.

Morris received three Guggenheim awards, two of them for photography and the third for fiction (*The Deep Sleep*), the National Book Award for *The Field of Vision* and *Plains Song, for Female Voices*, and the National Institute for Arts and Letters Award for *Ceremony in Lone Tree*. He received a National Institute Grant in 1960 and was fiction judge for the National Book Award in 1969.

Biography • Wright Marion Morris's mother died six days after he was born in Central City, Nebraska. He then lived with his father in Schuyler, Kearney, and other small Nebraska towns along the Platte River before moving to Omaha. He worked for two summers on his uncle Harry's farm in Norfolk, Nebraska, but the move to Chicago in 1924 brought him a different kind of employment at the YMCA. He attended college in California for five weeks, then worked for several months on the Texas ranch of his uncle Dwight Osborn. He entered Pomona College in Claremont, California, but withdrew to spend a year in Austria, Italy, Germany, and France. He had written some brief prose sketches while at Pomona, and he returned to California to begin his first novel.

Morris married Mary Ellen Finfrock of Cleveland, Ohio, in 1934. Between 1935 and 1938, he wrote two novels and the sketches for *The Inhabitants* and developed the interest in photography that flourished during two summers at Wellfleet, Massachusetts. In 1940-1941, he toured the United States, taking pictures to be used in *The Inhabitants*. He lived in California two more years before moving to Haverford, Pennsylvania, in 1944. In 1954, he began spending more time in Venice, Italy, Mexico, and Greece, returning intermittently to California. He lectured at the University of Southern California and at Amherst College and taught at California State University, Los Angeles. He was a professor of English at San Francisco State University from 1962 until his retirement in 1975.

In 1961, Morris divorced his first wife and married Josephine Kantor. In 1983, he was selected to occupy the Visiting Writers' Chair at the University of Alabama. In 1992, an exhibit of Morris's photography was held in San Francisco. Morris died of unreported causes in Mill Valley, California, where he had lived since the early 1960's, on April 26, 1998. In the obituary in *The New York Times*, Ralph Blumenthal noted that Morris is "often called one of the nation's most unrecognized recognized writers."

Analysis • A novelist who has been read more—and surely appreciated more—in Europe than in his own country, Morris explored the legacies of heroism and nostalgia, the dreams and delusions examined by earlier twentieth century American writers. Another concern of Morris, whose novels seldom display violence, is the rise of violence in America. His narratives often take place within a twenty-four-hour time period, suggesting the capture of a finite period of time as the photographer captures a finite space with his camera. This limitation of time unifies Morris's novels, which are more intimately related by the device of recurring characters. Indeed, David Madden and other critics have suggested that one must read Morris's entire canon in order to understand any one novel.

The spirit of place, whether it be the central plains, a California beach, a Philadelphia suburb, or an Alpine chateau, is central to Morris's novels, and the impingement of objects or places upon humanity a major facet of Morris's imagination, as they had been to Henry James, who believed that places gave out a "mystic meaning." Admittedly influenced by James and by D. H. Lawrence, Morris was his own man for five prolific decades. Fortunate to have as his birthplace the "navel of the universe," the central United States, from that vantage point he "salvaged" meaningful artifacts that represent an earlier American life and, concomitantly, the values of that life.

Accused by Alfed Kazin of overloading his fiction with symbols, Morris disavowed any conscious symbolic creation, noting that symbols may appear without the author's deliberate intent in any good work of fiction. Obsessed by the cliché, which he considers a dead repository for something once alive, he peoples his fiction with stereotypes and challenges himself to bring them back to life. Wayne Booth described Morris's transformation of clichés as "toying" with them. Madden saw the characters' coming to terms with clichés as absolutely essential to their knowledge of the enjoyment of love, sex, their bodies—even of travel. He added that after Morris, clichés are never the same, because they are killed and resurrected in the same moment, reappearing in an improved form.

It is not easy to generalize about an oeuvre as varied as Morris's, but he does frequently disregard chronology, an attempt to possess time and understand it being one of his obsessions. A recurring relationship, as Madden pointed out, is that of the hero and his "witnesses"—the characters who are transformed because their lives have intersected his. The contact, strangely enough, is often more meaningful after the death of the hero. Booth noted that the novels of Morris begin with a problem or a misunderstanding and conclude with a solution or a clarification. Although this statement could be made about most plots, it is not the beginnings and the endings that occupy Morris's inventive mind, but what is in between. The resolutions that he works toward require especially appropriate intervening incidents that require "a lot of doing." Morris, added Booth, thinks of his introductions not as promises to the reader, but as problems to be solved by the author himself. What is important in this kind of plot progression is the quality of the middle, and here Morris excels.

Believing that the fiction writer must do more than reproduce facts, Morris transmutes his raw material, particularly his experience of the Midwest, through his imagination into something that he sees as more real than life itself.

My Uncle Dudley • *My Uncle Dudley*, Morris's somewhat autobiographical first novel, concerns an odyssey in an old Marmon touring car from California to the banks of the Mississippi. The central character, Uncle Dudley, a cross between a modern-day Odysseus and Don Quixote, describes himself as a "horseless knight." His impossible dream of committing one single audacious act is realized when he spits a stream of brown tobacco juice accurately into the eye of a sadistic, perverted policeman.

What is experimental about this novel is the use of the unnamed adolescent narrator, known only as the Kid, who records no emotion at all, thereby enabling the author himself to remain detached. As Madden noted, the heroic act requires a witness. The Kid is Uncle Dudley's witness, through whose imagination the reader recognizes heroism and an unexpressed affection.

Morris acknowledges a debt to Mark Twain's *Adventures of Huckleberry Finn* (1884), although he had not then read the Twain work "as a writer." The Kid is the Huck figure, Uncle Dudley the Jim-father, and the journey in the Marmon a flight from repressive civilization similar to the downriver trip of the raft. The unifying element in Morris's narrative is not the river or the road, however, but Uncle Dudley himself, whose final foolhardy act qualifies him as the first in a long line of heroes.

The Man Who Was There • Agee Ward, the "protagonist" of *The Man Who Was There*, has gone to war and has been reported missing in action; he makes his presence felt through his absence, and is a hero not of action, as was Uncle Dudley, but of imagination. In the novel's first section, he is remembered at Grandmother Herkimer's funeral by Private Reagan, a boyhood friend, whose stare causes the minister to change his sermon subject to the desire for immortality. The middle section of the book, titled "The Three Agee Wards," re-presents the hero through the media of family photographs, sketches, and letters, through knowledge about his ancestors, and through the mind of the village barber, who has seen him in the eyes of his now deceased mother. Her gravestone inscription announces, "She died that he might live."

The unity of the novel results from the hero's power to transform others. Agee has become a painter and a writer, whose notebooks contain drawings of such artifacts as a pump and a privy; his perspective is faulty because his memory fails and because he cannot reconcile the real and the imaginary in his own mind.

The last witness to be transformed is his spinster landlady Gussie Newcomb, who becomes Agee's symbolic next of kin when she is notified by the War Department that he is missing. She barely remembers her lodger, but when the people who do remember him want to look at his belongings, Gussie moves into the apartment herself. Peter Spavic, who has kept up Agee's album, and who is obviously a witness, enables Gussie to absorb Agee's personality, the transformation assisted by her communion with the missing man's personal artifacts. Gussie begins to drink, to tell Agee jokes, to dress in some of his costumes, and to take the initiative in her relationship with her suitor, Mr. Bloom. She sits in the dark, as Agee had sat, and she agrees with Peter to name his first son Ward while she will name her first child Agee.

The book explores an idea that was then a cliché: the effect of a dead or missing-in-action soldier on those left at home. Agee, a hero in the literal sense because he actually wants to combat fascism, transforms his witnesses by his very absence, at the same time suggesting the problems of an artist who tries to filter reality through his imagination.

Man and Boy • The first few chapters of Morris's novel *Man and Boy* have been widely anthologized, with slight changes, as the short story "The Ram in the Thicket." The first of Morris's novels to depart from the plains tradition, *Man and Boy* takes place in Philadelphia and New York and describes a single day in the life of the remnants of a family. The Navy is to name a destroyer in honor of the Boy, who has died a hero. His father Warren recollects the day he gave the Boy an air rifle, a gift that caused his mother to abolish Christmas henceforth and the Boy to become a hunter, who perhaps wanted to die. Recalling the diverse impressions of Agee Ward in *The Man Who Was There*, the Boy Virgil appears to his parents in different ways, transforming them both, but not improving their relationship.

Warren Ormsby, the Man, is a westerner who boasts that his pioneer grandfather used to eat three rabbits as a meal. He soon learns, however, that his wife Violet is not very "feminine." She has, in fact, appropriated to herself the virtues once attributed to pioneer men. Warren has to call her "Mother" and allows her to dominate the household. She rids the house of germs and bathroom sounds, and even of conversation. Although Ormsby cares for the birds in a way that is to him a form of worship, a "Eucharist," Mother insists on calling them by their Latin names. After the Boy is dead, he appears to his father in a dream, wearing "bright, exotic plumage" and accompanied by a flock of birds. When the father tries to join the birds, they attack him.

Even in his dream, he recognizes the Mother's effort to destroy the Boy's love for his father, who has been systematically unmanned by Mother.

Indirectly responsible for her son's death, Mother is selected to christen the boat named for her son; thus ironically ensuring the continuation of killing, to which she has been so opposed. The Boy lives on in the imagination of the Man, but Mother's power may extend over that realm eventually; it has embodied the sanitized house and defeated the United States Navy on the day of the ceremony.

The Works of Love • Morris has admitted that he gave an inordinate amount of time to writing *The Works of Love*. In his first novel, he had set out to make a hero of a nonheroic figure, in the second to allow a man who was not present to dominate the action, and in the third, to allow a man to be dominated by a ruthless female, who finally won his grudging respect, if not admiration. In *The Works of Love*, the protagonist, Will Brady, learns to love in a prodigious, self-conscious, almost methodical manner, even though he has not himself been loved or found suitable recipients for his own works of love. The self-centered women in his life have not appreciated his fumbling, inarticulate efforts at communication. Two of them have been prostitutes, one of whom laughed when he proposed marriage; the other ran away and mailed him another man's baby son to adopt. After his marriage to the widow Ethel Bassett, who sleeps like a mummy tightly wrapped in a sheet, he lies beside her listing in his incipiently loving mind her reasons for doing so. The last woman to whom he tries to become a father-husband is a cigar-counter girl turned alcoholic streetwalker. In an effort to understand and grow closer to his adopted son Willy, Will searches the pages of Booth Tarkington's *Penrod* (1914) and Mark Twain's *The Adventures of Tom Sawyer* (1876) for enlightenment. His final role, that of a department store Santa Claus, allows him to touch and love little children, at the same time distributing some of the works of his abundant love.

Will handles the eggs that he sells with the same gentle touch that he reserves for women, sensing perhaps that both species contain the miracle of life. He is more at home, however, with the eggs than with the women, always a stranger in his own house. In his pursuit of love, he finally cuts himself off from all midwestern, rural roots and heads for Chicago on a quest to fill his emotional void. His incapacity to receive love, his failure to understand himself, and especially his inability to communicate his feelings have set up an almost insurmountable barrier between Will and his love-objects. Significantly more at home in a hotel than in his house, he has, for most of his life, failed to connect with the rest of humankind.

The Deep Sleep • In *The Deep Sleep*, Morris again presents a hero who has died, this time Judge Howard Porter. Porter's "witnesses" include the hired man Parson, who has worked for the Porter family for thirty years and loves the almost unlovable Mrs. Porter; the Judge's son-in-law Paul Webb, who gets to know him well just before the funeral, and the Judge's mother, who communicates by tapping her cane and never became acquainted with her son at all. Mrs. Porter had known her husband twice— once in the biblical sense, when their first child was conceived, and a second time just before the funeral, when she told their daughter Katherine that she missed him.

Paul Webb discovers that Mrs. Porter had not ruled her husband as iron-handedly as she had thought. Like Violet Ormsby's husband, the Judge had found a basement-toilet retreat where he stashed his whiskey. In addition, Paul discovers, Judge Porter had an attic hideout where he smoked cigars and admired his expensive Swiss watch, while he carried a cheap, loud, dollar watch in public. The artist Webb is objective enough to get a balanced picture of the Porter family as he studies the house, room by room. Although his wife Katherine fears that he cannot show her mother the sympathy she deserves, the fact that the two finally arrive at the same conclusion about Judge and Mrs. Porter suggests that both are fair in their appraisal.

Like Gussie in *The Man Who Was There*, Webb takes on an additional characteristic of the dead man every time he gains a new insight. As Webb becomes the Judge's spiritual son, he reaches a better understanding of Mrs. Porter. The two watches become the artifacts that connect Webb and his mother-in-law, whose sense of order ("Never go to bed with dirty dishes in the house") leads to an understanding with daughter Katherine. Webb finds satisfaction in a compassionate act: He places the gold watch in the cabinet, where Mrs. Porter will have the pleasure of finding it herself.

David Madden explains that the novel's title refers to the deep sleep into which American men of the twentieth century have allowed themselves to fall. Like the sleep induced in Adam before God created Eve from his rib, it is so deep that the man never awakens. Woman is born; she dominates, and man sleeps on. The fact that this is a twentieth century phenomenon is demonstrated in Morris's 1980 novel *Plains Song, for Female Voices*, whose character Cora carries out her wifely duties with such distaste that she bites herself on her wedding night. Her husband Emerson feels obliged to explain to the frontier doctor that Cora suffers from the bite of a horse; the uncomplaining Cora finds most of her life as a Nebraska farmwife distasteful, but rebellion never occurs to her.

The Huge Season • Another novel with a dead hero, *The Huge Season* is different because it is told from the single viewpoint of Peter Foley, a professor of classics in a small Pennsylvania college and himself a fully developed character. Foley attempts to escape the bondage of two experiences from the past. The first took place at Colton College in California: Foley shared a suite with several other young men, among them Charles Lawrence, a would-be great tennis player who has since committed suicide. The second experience was a single day spent in New York after one of his other suitemates, Jesse Proctor, testified before a congressimal committee on unamerican activities.

Lawrence, the hero who affects all the other men, is another midwesterner with an audacious grandfather. Lawrence himself tries to be audacious, both in the bullring and on the tennis court. He succeeds at tennis, not because he plays well, but because he wills himself to win. As is to be expected, the hero strongly influences the lives of his witnesses—three of them actually write books about him.

Foley finally frees himself from captivity by re-creating the past in his mind while wearing his hero's jacket around the house. As he achieves his own freedom, Foley at the same time understands more about America. The title of the novel refers to the past—the youth—that Foley realizes is over when he is released into the present. Lawrence, however, continues to live in the imagination of his witness, who has also acquired the tennis player's audacity.

Love Among the Cannibals • The past, so important in *The Huge Season*, is missing in *Love Among the Cannibals*. Macgregor and Horter, two middle-aged Hollywood songwriters, take two girls to Acapulco, one a Memphis "chick" who reads Norman Vincent Peale, the other Eva the Greek. The story is about people who live to the tune of "What Next?," a song in progress when Horter and Eva meet. Their car, a fire-engine-red convertible with green leather upholstery, has a built-in record player. Macgregor, a true Hollywood cliché and composer of sentimental popular music, insists that what he is looking for in a woman is "the real thing." Horter, who writes clichéd lyrics because that is what Hollywood demands, persuades Billie, Eva, and Mac that they can write a Mexican musical if they have the proper setting. Mac and Billie find romance in Acapulco and swear to be true to each other, but Eva leaves with a ladybug-shaped biologist, Dr. Leggett.

The Hollywood beach with its suntan oil and portable radios symbolizes the artificial present with no traditions or values, the Mexican beach the real present, unspoiled, honest, and authentic. The two "artists" deal in clichés of the kind demanded by mass culture, but Horter recognizes that even clichés can be powerful. He is transformed in Mexico by the natural, physical powers of the Greek, who is unabashedly tanned all over. As he appreciates her vitality and audacity, he even considers returning to the life of a serious poet. He has been stripped to essentials and returned to a wholeness and a recognition of his past that bring with them a hope for the future.

The Field of Vision • Morris's critics generally agree that *The Field of Vision* and *Ceremony in Lone Tree*, both dealing with the same central characters, are his most successful novels. Both employ several narrators viewing the same events and interpreting them differently. The actions of the main character, Gordon Boyd, are witnessed by his best friend, Walter McKee. The two are in love with the same woman, but Lois chooses the more stable Walter.

In *The Field of Vision*, Nebraskans Gordon and Walter recall their experiences while attending a bullfight in Mexico. More than any Morris character, Gordon, a failed writer, is a prisoner of his past, formed by three pivotal events. As a boy, Gordon tries to walk on water but ends by trying to drag himself out in a feeble effort at convincing Walter he can at least swim. The second is Gordon's ripping the back pocket off Ty Cobb's pants during an exhibition baseball game in Omaha, yet another incident witnessed by Walter. When Walter introduces Lois, Gordon kisses her. They fall in love, but she marries Walter anyway, feeling constant guilt afterward. The passive, ineffectual Walter realizes how she feels but is unable to help her.

These events are repeated from several points of view until they take on almost mythic dimensions. The walk represents Gordon's penchant for audacity and accompanying failure. The pocket, which Gordon always carries with him, becomes a tattered emblem of his unattained dreams. The kiss suggests the characters' lack of romantic fulfillment, the kind of emotional austerity all too typical of the residents of Morris's Midwest. Gordon attempts an exorcism of sorts by tossing the imitation coonskin cap of McKee's young grandson into the bullring and lowering the boy, named Gordon, down to retrieve it.

Ceremony in Lone Tree • *Ceremony in Lone Tree* gathers four generations in a small Nebraska town, their birthday celebration for Lois's elderly father contrasting with a backdrop of contemporary violence. While an atomic bomb fails to go off at a Nevada testing site the day before, two other bombs have exploded: The nephew of one character runs down three bullies with his hot rod, killing two of them, and Charlie Munger murders ten people during a shooting spree in nearby Lincoln because he wants to be somebody. Morris's America seems capable of only two extremes of behavior: violence or enervating nostalgia. The protagonists have sunk into a stultifying slumber from which even irrational murder and the threat of nuclear annihilation cannot arouse them.

Gordon, accompanied by a tawdry young woman he calls Daughter, arrives to seek a final break with his past through dying a symbolic death. Walter, on the other hand, finally awakens from his deep sleep to stand up to his friend for the first time. Stirred to action by a subconscious recognition of her emotional paralysis, Lois fires her father's ancient six-shooter, the shot ironically causing the old man to drop dead on the morning of his ninetieth birthday. These acts seem to free the McKees from the past somewhat, though the novel, as is typical of Morris, ends ambiguously. *Ceremony in Lone Tree* is the most detailed of Morris's many explorations of the American need to free itself both from the tenacious hold of the past and the banality of the present so that the future can unfold without encumbrance.

Plains Song, for Female Voices • After several decades of novels about women who dominated their men, lured them into sex, and left them, or married them and honeymooned shrouded in a sheet, Morris's *Plains Song, for Female Voices* should perhaps have redressed some grievances. Madge, however, the only happy wife in the novel, is content with being a bearer of children and smelling Fels-Naptha soap. Cora, a plain Ohio girl, who marries Emerson to move to Nebraska, becomes Madge's mother. Cora's world is Emerson's farm, and although she finds enjoyment only with her chickens and her garden, she never considers widening her horizon. Sharon Rose, Madge's cousin, is the modern woman and artist who shuns men altogether, finding her happiness in fleeing Nebraska for Chicago and music study. Sharon cannot understand her past and cannot understand why her relatives are content with their bleak lives, but she does attain a certain amount of self-knowledge.

Like so many of Morris's protagonists, Sharon tries to go home again. What startles her memory is not the paint scaling off Emerson's house but the absence of people. The dipper (a marvelous artifact) floats in a bucket of water, and Sharon smells scorched ironing. Displeased that Madge's husband Ned refers to his car as a "good girl," Sharon becomes ill when Avery, who plans to be a veterinarian, chips tartar off the teeth of a Maltese cat with his thumbnail while she is at the dinner table. On the train on the way back to Chicago, however, Sharon is ashamed of disliking these friendly, decent people. She writes Madge's daughter to suggest that Blanche attend a private school for girls in Waukegan and spend her weekends in Chicago, because Sharon cannot bear the "thought of Blanche thick with child by some loutish youth."

When the pretty girl arrives, Sharon deliberately dresses her in a way to "emphasize her adolescence" so that the "idling males" will not be tempted to molest her. When she finds Blanche with a "beardless, oafish" young man, his arm about the girl's waist, she knows that her efforts to "citify" Blanche—actually to make her independent—have been in vain, and she allows her to return home to her daddy, whom she has missed a great deal.

Sharon finally teaches at Wellesley, more respected than liked by her students. On her last trip home for Cora's funeral, Madge's daughter Caroline assures Sharon that because of her example, the girls "don't get married anymore unless [they] want to." All that is left of her parents' farm is a pitted field of stumps. "There was nothing worth saving," says Caroline, who adds that she would never forgive Cora for her failure to complain about the hard farm life.

Funerals and eggs—an unlikely combination—continue to recur in Morris's fiction. Unlikely, until one realizes that, in a Morris novel, the dying will "connect" with and transform many characters, perhaps even achieving resurrection through them, and that eggs, important to Morris since his father sold them, represent not only a new and ongoing life but also the rural Midwest to which he returns again and again for his fictional world.

The wasteland motif, actually verbalized in some of the novels, is to be found in a society without imagination, as on the Los Angeles beach where women wear bathing caps that look like fake hair. The one who can deliver others from such a wasteland is a man or woman with a creative heart—an audacious artist who dares to transform the clichés of the past into the wonders of the present and future, who can convert the raw material of America into values that enable humanity to endure.

Sue L. Kimball
Updated by Michael Adams

Other major works

SHORT FICTION: *Green Grass, Blue Sky, White House,* 1970; *Here Is Einbaum,* 1973; *The Cat's Meow,* 1975; *Real Losses, Imaginary Gains,* 1976; *Collected Stories, 1948-1986,* 1986.

NONFICTION: *The Inhabitants,* 1946; *The Territory Ahead,* 1958, 1963; *A Bill of Rites, a Bill of Wrongs, a Bill of Goods,* 1968; *God's Country and My People,* 1968; *Love Affair: A Venetian Journal,* 1972; *About Fiction: Reverent Reflections on the Nature of Fiction with Irreverent Observations on Writers, Readers, and Other Abuses,* 1975; *Wright Morris: Structures and Artifacts, Photographs, 1933-1954,* 1975; *Earthly Delights, Unearthly Adornments: American Writers as Image-Makers,* 1978; *Will's Boy,* 1981; *Photographs and Words,* 1982; *Picture America,* 1982; *Solo: An American Dreamer in Europe, 1933-1934,* 1983; *A Cloak of Light: Writing My Life,* 1985; *Time Pieces: Photographs, Writing, and Memory,* 1989.

MISCELLANEOUS: *Wright Morris: A Reader,* 1970.

Bibliography

Bird, Roy K. *Wright Morris: Memory and Imagination.* New York: Peter Lang, 1985. An excellent appraisal of self-consciousness in Morris's fiction. Bird moves from a discussion of Morris's use of the past, namely the author's ambivalence toward it, to an analysis of his linguistic technique. The final chapter contains a detailed analysis of *The Fork River Space Project* and *Plains Song, for Female Voices.* Contains a bibliography.

Booth, Wayne C. "The Shaping of Prophecy: Craft and Idea in the Novels of Wright Morris." *American Scholar* 31 (1962): 608-626. An excellent reappraisal of Morris's work, focusing on *Love Among the Cannibals, The Territory Ahead,* and *Ceremony in Lone Tree.* Booth argues that Morris's fiction is structured around a distinction between the everyday time-bound world of "reality" and a more timeless world of platonic reality.

Crump, G. B. *The Novels of Wright Morris: A Critical Interpretation.* Lincoln: University of Nebraska Press, 1978. In an effort to demonstrate Morris's importance and clarify his contribution to modern fiction, Crump begins his study by addressing the major critical positions toward Morris's writing, thus isolating significant features of the author's work. Then he offers a new theoretical groundwork for criticizing the author's fiction: a major dualism between the real and the ideal.

Hamilton, James. "Wright Morris and the American Century." *Poets and Writers* 25 (November/December, 1997): 23-31. In this extended interview, Morris discusses his decision to stop writing, his feelings about America, and his family.

Hollander, John. "The Figure on the Page: Words and Images in Wright Morris's *The Home Place*." *Yale Journal of Criticism* 9 (Spring, 1996): 93-108. Discusses how Morris's *The Home Place* mixes text and photographs; examines the work's original way of presenting word and image in a mode that appears to mix ekphrasis and illustration.

Howard, Leon. *Wright Morris.* Minneapolis: University of Minnesota Press, 1968. In this brief but insightful pamphlet surveying Morris's novels, Howard asserts that no other American novelist has approached Morris in the variety and shaping of the raw materials. According to Howard, the novelist's unique medium is the high seriousness of brilliant comedy in which the absurd is laid bare with neither bitterness nor hope.

Knoll, Robert E., ed. *Conversations with Wright Morris: Critical Views and Responses.* Lincoln: University of Nebraska Press, 1977. This collection of lectures, interviews, critical essays, and photographs is one of the best sources of information about Morris and his work for the general reader. Much is illuminated in the discussions of Morris the novelist and Morris the photographer. Extensive bibliography.

Madden, David. *Wright Morris.* New York: Twayne, 1964. This work assumes little or no prior knowledge of Morris's writing. Its main purpose is to examine each of Morris's novels (ending with *Cause for Wonder*) in quasi-chronological order so that the reader might see how the author's themes and methods develop from novel to novel. Madden also discusses characterization and the influence of setting (the Midwest) on Morris's work. Bibliography of primary and secondary sources.

Morris, Wright. *A Cloak of Light: Writing My Life.* New York: Harper and Row, 1985. In this extremely informative and insightful autobiography, Morris not only explores the formation of his character but also his writing. Among other things, Morris discusses his faculty of image-making or what he calls time retrieval—a faculty that has served him well both as a photographer and as a writer.

Trachtenberg, Alan. *Distinctly American: The Photography of Wright Morris.* London: Merrell, 2002. Analyzes Morris's documentation of vernacular America in photography.

_____. "Images and Icons: The Fiction and Photography of Wright Morris." In *Under the Sun: Myth and Realism in Western American Literature*, edited by Barbara Howard Meldrum. Troy, N.Y.: Whitston, 1985. This lengthy essay is the best examination of the relation between Morris's photography and his fiction.

_____. "Wright Morris's 'Photo-Texts.'" *Yale Journal of Criticism* 9 (Spring, 1996): 109-119. Discusses Morris's mixing of words and photographs in three works of fiction in which image and text stand beside each other in quite unexpected ways; shows how each work addresses similar questions about the role of images in the making of fiction.

Wydeven, Joseph J. *Wright Morris Revisited.* New York: Twayne, 1998. A scholar who has written often about Morris updates Madden's study.

Toni Morrison

Born: Lorain, Ohio; February 18, 1931

Principal long fiction • *The Bluest Eye*, 1970; *Sula*, 1973; *Song of Solomon*, 1977; *Tar Baby*, 1981; *Beloved*, 1987; *Jazz*, 1992; *Paradise*, 1998; *Love*, 2003.

Other literary forms • Toni Morrison, primarily a novelist, edited *The Black Book* (1974), a collection of documents and articles on African American history compiled by Middleton Harris, and published a short story, "Big Box," in *Ms.* magazine (1980). Morrison's first play, *Dreaming Emmett* (1986), was commissioned by the New York State Writers Institute of the State University of New York. Morrison has written many essays, some of the most notable of which are "The Site of Memory" in *Inventing the Truth: The Art and Craft of Memoir*, edited by William Zinsser (1987), and "Unspeakable Things Unspoken: The Afro-American Presence in American Literature" (*Michigan Quarterly Review* 28 [Winter, 1989]: 1-34). "Honey and Rue," with lyrics by Toni Morrison and music by André Previn, was commissioned by Carnegie Hall for soprano Kathleen Battle and premiered in January, 1992. Morrison published another collection of essays, *Birth of a Nation 'hood: Gaze, Script, and Spectacle in the O. J. Simpson Case*, in 1997 and *Remember: The Journey to School Integration* in 2004.

Achievements • Morrison is widely regarded as one of the most significant black American novelists to have emerged during the 1970's. Her novel *Sula* was nominated for the National Book Award in 1975. In 1977, *Song of Solomon* won the National Book Critics Circle Award. The former was a Book-of-the-Month Club alternate and the latter, a main selection. In 1988, *Beloved* was awarded the Pulitzer Prize, and in 1993, Morrison earned the Nobel Prize in Literature.

Morrison's fiction, especially *Song of Solomon*, has been compared to Ralph Ellison's *Invisible Man* (1952) for its mixture of the literal and the fantastic, the real and the surreal. Morrison has been praised for her use of language and for the sense of voice that emerges not only in her dialogue but also in the movement of her narratives. Morrison's novels are also remarkable for their sense of place, for the detailed, coherent physical worlds she creates. Finally, her fiction is noteworthy for its depiction of the deep psychic realities of women's experience.

Biography • Toni Morrison was the first black woman to receive the Nobel Prize in Literature. Morrison, whose father was a shipyard welder, was born the second of four children. In the first grade, she was the only black student and the only child able to read in her class. Her early literary influences included Leo Tolstoy, Gustave Flaubert, and Jane Austen. At Howard University, Morrison toured the South with the Howard University Players. She married in 1958 and divorced in 1964. She has two children, Harold Ford and Slade Kevin.

Morrison received her bachelor's degree in English and minored in classics. She taught at the State University of New York at Purchase as a professor of English from 1971 to 1972 and was the Albert Schweitzer Chair in the Humanities at the State University of New York at Albany from 1984 to 1989. Beginning in 1989, Morrison held the position of Robert F. Goheen Professor in the Council of the Humanities at Princeton University. Other positions include trustee of the National Humanities Center, cochair of the Schomberg Commission for the Preservation of Black Culture, and member of the American Academy and Institute of Arts, the American Academy of Arts and Sciences, the National Council on the Arts, the Authors Guild, and the Authors League of America. Morrison became a popular public lecturer, focusing on African American literature.

Analysis • In all of her fiction, Morrison explores the conflict between society and the individual. She shows how the individual who defies social pressures can forge a self by drawing on the resources of the natural world, on a sense of continuity within the family and within the history of a people, and on dreams and other unaccountable sources of psychic power.

Lynda Koolish/Courtesy, University Press of Mississippi

The Bluest Eye • In *The Bluest Eye*, Morrison shows how society inflicts on its members an inappropriate standard of beauty and worth, a standard that mandates that to be loved one must meet the absolute "white" standard of blond hair and blue eyes. Morrison's narrator says that two of the most destructive ideas in history are the idea of romantic love (canceling both lust and caring) and the idea of an absolute, univocal standard of beauty.

In the novel, the most extreme victim of these destructive ideas is Pecola, who finds refuge in madness after she has been thoroughly convinced of her own ugliness (confirmed when she is raped by her own father, Cholly). Mrs. Breedlove, Pecola's mother, is another victim who gets her idea of an unvarying standard of beauty from romantic motion pictures that glorify white film stars. When she realizes the impassible gap between that ideal and her physical self (she has a deformed foot and two missing teeth), she also gives up any hope of maintaining a relationship with Cholly, her husband, except one of complete antagonism and opposition. Mrs. Breedlove even comes to prefer the little white girl she takes care of at work to her own daughter, Pecola, whom she has always perceived as ugly.

The ideal of unattainable physical beauty is reinforced by the sugary, unattainable world of the family depicted in the school readers—of Mother and Father and Dick and Jane and their middle-class, suburban existence. The contrast between that false standard of life and the reality lived by the children makes them ashamed of their reality, of the physical intimacy of families in which the children have seen their fathers naked.

Although Pecola is thoroughly victimized, Freida and Claudia MacTeer, school-mates of Pecola, do survive with some integrity and richness. Freida seems to accept Shirley Temple as the ideal of cuteness, but her sister Claudia, a center of conscious-ness in the novel, responds with anger and defiance, dismembering the hard, cold, smirking baby dolls she receives at Christmas. What Claudia really desires at Christ-mas is simply an experience of family closeness in the kitchen, an experience of flow-ers, fruit, and music, of security.

Claudia's anger at the white baby dolls springs from a conviction of her own reality and her own worth. In defense of her own individuality, Claudia rejects Shirley Tem-ple and "Meringue Pie," the high yellow princess, Maureen Peal. It is that defense of her own reality that makes Claudia sympathize with Pecola and try to defend her, even to the point of sacrificing Freida's money and her own.

Claudia is especially puzzled and regretful that nobody says "poor baby" to the raped Pecola, that nobody wants to welcome her unborn baby into the world. It would be only natural, "human nature," it seems, for people to sympathize with a vic-tim and rejoice at the creation of a human life. Instead, the springs of human sympa-thy have been dammed up by social disapproval. Suffering from the self-hatred they have absorbed from the society around them, the black community maintains inflexi-ble social standards and achieves respectability by looking down on Pecola. The two MacTeer sisters appeal to nature to help Pecola and her unborn baby, but nature fails them just as prayer did: No marigolds sprout and grow that year. The earth is unyield-ing. The baby is stillborn. Eventually, even the two girls become distanced from Pecola, whose only friend is an imaginary one, a part of herself who can see the blue eyes she was promised. Pecola functions as a scapegoat for the society around her, and Claudia's sympathy later grows into an understanding of how the community used Pecola to protect themselves from scorn and insult. What finally flowers in Claudia is insight and a more conscious respect for her own reality.

Sula • *Sula* also explores the oppressive nature of white society, evident in the very name of the "Bottom," a hillside community that had its origin in the duplicitous white treatment of an emancipated black slave who was promised fertile "bottom land" along with his freedom. In a bitterly ironic twist, the whites take over the hill-side again when they want suburban houses that will catch the breeze. In taking back the Bottom, they destroy a place, a community with its own identity. In turn, the black community, corrupted by white society, rejects Sula for her experimenting with her life, for trying to live free like a man instead of accepting the restrictions of the tradi-tional female role.

Sula provokes the reader to question socially accepted concepts of good and evil. As Sula is dying, she asks her girlhood friend Nel, "How do you know that you were the good one?" Although considered morally loose and a witch by the townspeople, the unconventional Sula cannot believe herself to be an inferior individual. Con-trasting the traditional role of mother and church woman that Nel has embraced, Sula's individuality is refreshing and intriguing. Despite her death, Sula maintains an independence that ultimately stands in proud opposition to the established network of relationships that exist within conventional society.

The novel shows that the Bottom society encompasses both good and evil. The people are accustomed to suffering and enduring evil. In varying degrees, they ac-cept Eva's murder of her drug-addict son, Plum, and Hannah's seduction of their husbands, one after another. The community, nevertheless, cannot encompass Sula, a woman who thinks for herself without conforming to their sensibilities. They have to turn her into a witch, so that they can mobilize themselves against her "evil" and cherish their goodness. Without the witch, their goodness grows faint again. Like Pecola, Sula is made a scapegoat.

Growing up in the Bottom, Sula creates an identity for herself, first from the reality of physical experience. When she sees her mother Hannah burning up in front of her eyes, she feels curiosity. Her curiosity is as honest as Hannah's admission that she loves her daughter Sula the way any mother would, but that she does not like her. Hearing her mother reject her individuality, Sula concludes that there is no one to count on except herself.

In forging a self, Sula also draws on sexual experience as a means of joy, as a means of feeling sadness, and as a means of feeling her own power. Sula does not substitute a romantic dream for the reality of that physical experience. She does finally desire a widening of that sexual experience into a continuing relationship with Ajax, but the role of nurturing and possession is fatal to her. Ajax leaves, and Sula sickens and dies.

A closeness to the elemental processes of nature gives a depth to the lives of the Bottom-dwellers, although nature does not act with benevolence or even with consistency. Plum and Hannah, two of Eva's children, die by fire, one sacrificed by Eva and one ignited by capricious accident. Chicken Little and several of those who follow Shadrack on National Suicide Day drown because acts of play go wrong and inexplicably lead to their destruction. Sula's supposed identity as a witch is connected to the plague of robins that coincides with her return to the Bottom. The people of the Bottom live within Nature and try to make some sense of it, even though their constructions are strained and self-serving.

On one level, Sula refuses any connection with history and family continuity. Her grandmother Eva says that Sula should get a man and make babies, but Sula says that she would rather make herself. On the other hand, Sula is a descendant of the independent women Eva and Hannah, both of whom did what they had to do. It is at least rumored that Eva let her leg be cut off by a train so that she could get insurance money to take care of her three children when BoyBoy, her husband, abandoned her. When her husband died, Hannah needed "manlove," and she got it from her neighbors' husbands, despite community disapproval. In their mold, Sula is independent enough to threaten Eva with fire and to assert her own right to live, even if her grandmother does not like Sula's way of living.

To flourish, Morrison suggests, conventional society needs an opposite pole. A richness comes from the opposition and the balance—from the difference—and an acceptance of that difference would make scapegoats unnecessary. The world of the Bottom is poorer with Sula dead and out of it.

Song of Solomon • In *Song of Solomon*, Morrison again traces the making of a self. The novel is a departure for Morrison in that the protagonist is not female, but a young man, Milkman Dead. Milkman grows up in a comfortable, insulated, middle-class family, the grandson of a doctor on his mother's side and the son of a businessman, whose father owned his own farm. Son of a doting mother, Milkman is nursed a long time, the reason for his nickname, and is sent to school in velvet knickers. Guitar Baines, a Southside black, becomes Milkman's friend and an ally against the other children's teasing.

As the novel progresses, though, and as Milkman discovers the reality of his family and friends as separate people with their own griefs and torments, Milkman comes to feel that everyone wants him dead. Ironically, Milkman's last name actually is "Dead," the result of a drunken clerk's error when Milkman's grandfather was registering with the Freedmen's Bureau.

Milkman learns that his mere existence is extraordinary, since even before his birth, his father tried to kill him. Milkman survived that threat through the intercession of his mother and, especially, of his aunt, Pilate, a woman with no navel. After having been conjured by Pilate into making love to his wife again, years after he had turned against her, Macon Dead wanted the resulting baby aborted. Ruth, the baby's mother, out of fear of her husband, took measures to bring about an abortion, but Pilate intervened again and helped Ruth to find the courage to save the child and bear him.

In the present action of the novel, Hagar, Milkman's cousin, his first love and his first lover, pursues him month after month with whatever weapon she can find to kill him. Hagar wants Milkman's living life, not his dead life, but Milkman has rejected her, out of boredom and fear that he will be maneuvered into marrying her. At this point, he does not want to be tied down: He wants freedom and escape.

Hagar, like Pecola of *The Bluest Eye*, feels unlovely and unloved, rejected because Milkman does not like her black, curly hair. Pilate says that Milkman cannot *not* love her hair without *not* loving himself because it is the same hair that grows from his own body. Hagar is another victim of an absolutely univocal standard of beauty, and she is a character who needs a supporting society, a chorus of aunts and cousins and sisters to surround her with advice and protection. Instead, she has only Pilate and Reba, grandmother and mother, two women so strong and independent that they do not understand her weakness. Unhinged by Milkman's rejection of her, Hagar chases Milkman with various weapons, is repeatedly disarmed, and finally dies in total discouragement.

Trying to find out about his family's past, Milkman travels to Virginia, to Shalimar, a black town, where the men in the general store challenge him to fight, and one attacks him with a knife. Milkman does not understand why these people want his life, but they think he has insulted and denied their masculinity with his powerful northern money and his brusque treatment of them, by not asking their names and not offering his own.

The most serious threat to Milkman's life, however, turns out to be Guitar, Milkman's friend and spiritual brother. When Guitar tries to kill Milkman, he is betraying the reality of their friendship for the idea of revenge against whites and compensation for the personal deprivation he has suffered. Guitar thinks that Milkman has a cache of gold that he is not sharing with him, so he decides to kill him. Guitar rationalizes his decision by saying that the money is for the cause, for the work of the Seven Days, a group of seven black men sworn to avenge the deaths of innocent black people at the hands of the whites.

Milkman's being alive at all, then, is a triumph, a victory that he slowly comes to appreciate after coming out of his comfortable shell of self-involvement. Unwillingly, Milkman comes to know the suffering and griefs of his mother and father and even his sisters Magdelene and Corinthians. The decisive experience in his self-making, however, is the quest for Pilate's gold on which his father sets him. In the first stage, the men are convinced that Pilate's gold hangs in a green sack from the ceiling of her house, and Guitar and Milkman attempt to steal it. The two friends succeed in taking the sack because the women in the house are simply puzzled, wondering why the men want a sack that is really full of old bones. In leaving the house, though, the two men are arrested, and Pilate must rescue them and the bones by doing an Aunt Jemima act for the white policemen. Milkman's father, Macon, is convinced that the gold still exists somewhere, and Milkman sets out to find it by going back to Pennsylvania, where Macon and Pilate grew up, and later to Virginia, where the previous generation lived.

Milkman's making of a self includes many of the archetypal adventures of the heroes of legend and myth. Like other heroes of legend, Milkman limps, with one leg shorter than the other, a mark of his specialness. Like Oedipus's parents, his parents try to kill him early in his life. There is a wise old lady who gives him help and advice. He goes on a quest for a treasure, and he hopes for gold and the hand of a beautiful princess. He solves a puzzle or riddle to achieve his quest and confirm his identity. He has a transcendent experience and reaches heights of prowess (he can fly). When his people turn against him, he gives his life for them.

Like *Sula*, too, Milkman creates a self from the reality of physical experience, the processes of nature, a connection to history and family continuity, and springs of human possibility through myth, dreams, legends, and other sources of psychic power. Milkman reaches an understanding of physical experience and the processes of nature in a struggle against the physical environment. As a rich city boy, Milkman was insulated from nature, but in his trip south to try to get the gold, he overcomes a series of physical obstacles to reach the cave where Macon and Pilate in their youth encountered white people and gold. Milkman gets there only after falling into the river and climbing up twenty feet of rock, splitting his shoes and the clothes that mark him as a city man. During the trip, Milkman loses his possessions—trunk, clothes, and whiskey—and he makes it on his own, in a place where his father's name and father's money do not protect him. Milkman succeeds in finding Circe, who years ago sheltered Pilate and Macon when their father was killed, and he reaches the cave where there is no longer any gold.

Milkman also encounters nature as an obstacle to be overcome when, after the knife fight in Shalimar, he is invited to go on a coon hunt into the woods with the older men of Shalimar. Again, Milkman undergoes a test, having to move through the woods in the dark, having to show the courage and physical endurance necessary to be one of the hunters. Milkman also experiences the music of the hunt, the communication between the men and the dogs, the language before language, of a time when people were so close to their physical reality that they were in harmony with all creatures.

Milkman also creates himself in searching for his origins. In searching for his fathers, he discovers himself; like the Telemachus of Greek mythology and James Joyce's Stephen Dedalus, Milkman must find the reality of his fathers to know his own potential. Milkman's original pursuit of the gold seems to be an impulse he gets from his father, the man of business, and even from his father's father, who was a lover of property. The quest, however, changes as Milkman pursues it, finding the thread of his family's history. Stopping in Pennsylvania, Milkman hears the stories of the men who knew his father and grandfather and who rejoice in their successes. The story of the Dead family dramatizes the dream and the failure of that dream for black people in America. When the older Macon Dead was killed by white men for his flourishing farm, the possibilities of his neighbors were narrowed and their lives scarred. Seeing his father and grandfather through their former neighbor's eyes helps Milkman to understand better the pride that Macon had when he said that his father had let Macon work side by side with him and trusted him to share in his achievements.

In Shalimar, Milkman also learns about his great-grandfather by piecing together the memories of people there and by deciphering the children's game and song, a song about Solomon and Rynah that seems to be interspersed with nonsense words. Milkman matches this song to a song that he had heard Pilate sing about Sugarman. He solves the riddle of the song, and he even figures out what the ghost of Pilate's father meant when he said, "Sing," and when he told Pilate to go get the bones. Finally, he discovers that his grandmother was an American Indian, Singing Bird, and that his great-grandfather, Solomon, was one of the legendary flying Africans, the father of twenty-one sons, a slave who one day flew back to Africa. His grandfather Jake had fallen through the branches of a tree when Solomon dropped him, trying to take his last baby son back with him. Learning about that magic enables Milkman himself to fly when he surrenders to the air and lets himself be upheld.

Milkman creates a self so that he can share it and even sacrifice it for a friend. With Pilate, Milkman buries the bones of Jake, his grandfather, on Solomon's Leap. Guitar, who has continued to stalk Milkman, shoots and kills Pilate, but Milkman, saying to Guitar, "Do you want my life? Take it if it is any good to you," leaps into the air and flies. Guitar is free to kill his friend, but Milkman soars.

The ending of the novel shows the transcendence of the spirit, as the hero achieves his destiny. The satisfaction of the ending, which also soars into legend, comes from the triumph of the human spirit, the triumph that even death cannot destroy. *Song of Solomon* is a beautiful, serious, funny novel that moves beyond the social to the mythic.

Tar Baby • *Tar Baby* explores three kinds of relationships: the relationship between black and white people; the relationships within families, especially between parents and children; and the relationship between the American black man and black woman. In the epigraph to the novel, Saint Paul reproaches the Corinthians for allowing contentions to exist among their ranks; the quote serves to foreshadow the discord that abounds in the novel's relationships.

In *Tar Baby*, Morrison depicts not a self-contained black society, but an onstage interaction between black and white people. The novel juxtaposes two families, a white family of masters and a black family of servants. The white family includes a retired candy-maker, Valerian Street, and his wife Margaret, once the "Principal Beauty of Maine," who is now in her fifties. The couple's only son Michael lives abroad; his arrival for Christmas is expected and denied by various characters.

The black family consists of the husband, Sydney Childs, who is Valerian's valet and butler, and the wife, Ondine, who serves as cook and housekeeper. They are childless, but their orphan niece Jadine plays the role of their daughter. (Valerian has acted as Jadine's patron, paying for her education at the Sorbonne.)

The pivotal character, however, who enters and changes the balance of power and the habitual responses of the families, is a black man who rises out of the sea. His true name is Son, although he has gone by other aliases. The veneer of politeness and familiarity between the characters is shaken by Son's abrupt appearance. Uncomfortable racial and personal assumptions are put into words and cannot be retracted. The Principal Beauty is convinced that Son has come to rape her: What else would a black man want? (Jadine is convinced that if Son wants to rape anyone, it is she, not Margaret.) Sidney finds Son a threat to his respectability as a Philadelphia black because when Son appears, the white people lump all black people together. Ondine seems less threatened, but most of her energy goes into her running battle with the

Principal Beauty. Jadine is apprehensive at Son's wild appearance, and later she is affronted by his direct sexual approach. Only Valerian welcomes Son. He sees him as a vision of his absent son Michael, and he invites him to sit down at the dining table and be a guest.

Son's coming is the catalyst that causes time-worn relationships to explode when Michael does not come for Christmas. His failure to appear leads to the revelation that the Principal Beauty abused her son as a child, pricking him with pins and burning him with cigarettes. Ondine, the black woman, finally hurls this accusation at Margaret, the white, and makes explicit what the two women have known mutually since the beginning. Valerian, who has been haunted by the memory of Michael as a lonely child who would hide under the sink and sing to himself, is hit with a reality much harsher than he has known or admitted.

Structured as it is in terms of families, the whole novel revolves around family responsibilities, especially between parents and children. Michael Street does not come home for Christmas, but the abuse he suffered as a child seems to justify his absence. Thus, the undutiful mother Margaret has thrown the whole family off balance. In the black family, later in the novel, attention is drawn to the undutiful daughter Jadine, although it seems implied that she has learned this undutifulness, partly at least, from whites, wanting her individual success to be separate from family ties and responsibilities.

This undutifulness also springs from a question of identity. In Paris, even before she comes to Valerian's island, Jadine feels affronted by a beautiful, proud, contemptuous African woman in yellow, who buys three eggs and carries them on her head. She is herself and embodies her tradition consummately, exhibiting balance and physical grace that symbolize spiritual poise. Jadine feels diminished and threatened by the African woman, who spits at her. The scorn sends Jadine back to her family, Sydney and Ondine.

Jadine is similarly disturbed by her dream of the women with breasts, the mothers, who reproach her for not joining that chain of mothers and daughters who become mothers with daughters. Although Jadine herself is an orphan, reared by Ondine and Sydney and owing much to their care, she refuses to take the self-sacrificing role of the woman who cares for her family. Jadine wants money and the power it brings in the white world. After a little more modeling, she wants to run her own business, perhaps a boutique. Also, she may choose a white husband, like the man who bought her a seductive sealskin coat.

Jadine is the Tar Baby of the novel, and Son is Brer Rabbit from the Uncle Remus stories. As the Tar Baby, Jadine acts as a possible trap for Son set by his enemies, white society. Jadine, who has absorbed many white values, wants money and success. Son wants something purer, something associated with nature (he is associated with the sea and the beauty of the savannahs) and with family tradition. Nature, direct physical experience, and family traditions that are integral to personal identity are all important values in Son's existence. Son has a home—the completely black town of Eloe—and there he abides by the ideas of respectability held by his father and his Aunt Rosa. (He asks Jadine to sleep at Aunt Rosa's, apart from him, and he comes to her secretly only when she threatens to leave if he does not.) To amuse herself in the traditional town, in which she is uncomfortable, Jadine takes photographs of the people and steals their souls, stealing their individual beauty and grace. In the photographs, they seem graceless, poor, and stupid, even to Son, who usually sees them with loving eyes.

Individually, Son and Jadine love each other, but they seem unable to find a world in which they can both thrive. However, Son is an undaunted lover, unwilling to let Jadine go, even when she flees from him. Son tries to return to Isle de Chevaliers, Valerian's island, to get news of Jadine, but the only way he can get there seems to be through the help of Thérèse, the half-blind, fifty-year-old black woman who says that her breasts still give milk. Thérèse takes him by boat to the island of the horsemen. Son has said that he cannot give up Jadine, but Thérèse tells him to join the fabled black horsemen who see with the mind. At the end of the novel, Son is running toward his destiny, whether that be Jadine and some way to make her part of his world or the black horsemen who ride free through the hills. Readers do not know what Son's fate is to be; they only know that Son is running toward it, just as Brer Rabbit ran from his enemy Brer Fox and from the Tar Baby. Like Milkman Dead at the end of *Song of Solomon*, Son leaps into mythic possibility; like Brer Rabbit, Son, the black man, is a figure with the power to survive.

Beloved • In editing *The Black Book*, a collection of African American historical memorabilia, Morrison discovered an article that would serve as the foundation of her fifth novel. *Beloved* is based on a true account of a runaway slave mother who, rather than allowing her children to be taken back into slavery, murders three of the four. As the novel begins, Sethe's sons, Buglar and Howard, have already run away, while Denver, the youngest child, survived the murder attempt and still lives with her mother in a house beset by her murdered sister Beloved's spirit. Morrison deliberately disorients the reader as she delves into the "interior life" of slavery, creating an experience similar to that of slavery, as the narrative breaks apart, shifts, and confounds. The author personifies 124 Bluestone Road as a tormented being when Beloved returns, emerging from a lake, fully clothed, the same age she would have been had she survived the infanticide. What the spirit wants initially is unclear. Morrison uses metaphorical imagery with tremendous skill, for example when describing Sethe's back, a relief map of scars from savage beatings, as resembling the branches of a chokecherry tree. When Paul D, a former slave whom Sethe once knew, moves in, Beloved wreaks havoc. The spirit behaves like an enraged toddler, but the damage she does is that of a full-grown woman. As the ghost continues to threaten her mother and sister, the characters' thoughts intertwine until one cannot be certain which character is which.

Jazz • Morrison intended *Jazz*, another novel inspired by a news article, to follow *Beloved* as the second of a trilogy, although the narrative does not pick up where *Beloved* ends. Joe Trace, a married man and cosmetics salesman, shoots his teen lover, Dorcas, at a party. She dies refusing to reveal his name. At her funeral, Violet, Joe's wife, a hairdresser, defaces the girl's corpse. Set in 1926, *Jazz* begins after Violet has cut the dead girl's face, twenty years after she and Joe arrived in Harlem from the South, where they scraped out a living as sharecroppers. After Dorcas's funeral, Violet returns home and releases her caged parrot, the only creature in her life who says "I love you" anymore. The deep, unrealized passion for human contact in *Beloved* takes root in *Jazz*, but it too becomes messy, dangerous, and out of control. Violet's mind unravels, and, strangely, she turns to Alice Manfred, Dorcas's aunt, for comfort. *Beloved*'s theme of mother loss, profound and frustrated, continues in *Jazz*: Dorcas's mother burns to death in an intentionally set fire; Violet's mother throws herself down a well from despair over not providing for her children. Years later, Violet longs so achingly for a child she considers stealing one. It is only at the end of *Jazz*, when Violet and Joe reconcile and Violet buys a sick parrot that she nurses back to health by playing jazz for it, that there is some hope of a lasting human connection.

Paradise • *Paradise*, Morrison's seventh novel, like her previous two, was inspired by a little-known event in African American history, this time the 1970's westward migration of former slaves set on establishing their own all-black utopia, known in the book as Ruby. Shifting back and forth across a century of time, *Paradise* begins in 1976, when a group of the settlers' male descendants attack a mansion-turned-convent of women, convinced it is the women's eschewing of male companionship and their questionable pasts that threaten the town's survival. Ruby is founded as a response not only to white racism but also to other African Americans who turned away settlers for having skin that was "too black." Twin brothers Deacon and Steward, the town's elders, are deeply committed to keeping Ruby as pristine and trouble-free as possible. Together, they symbolize Ruby's twin identity and conscience.

Initially, the town has no crime and therefore needs no police. There is no hunger; everyone assists those in need. However, such total isolation from the outside world proves to be the town's undoing, as the rebellion of the 1960's youth movement seeps into Ruby. A ragtag group of women, most escaping either abusive relationships or responsibilities of motherhood, settle outside Ruby. Among others, there is Consolata, the maternal leader; Seneca, abandoned as a child by her teen mother; and Pallas, a white woman fleeing from her wealthy but negligent parents. The violent confrontation between the men of Ruby and the self-exiled women is, in part, brought on by the black men's anger at women who have willfully chosen a life without them. *Paradise* is a significant addition to Morrison's body of work.

Kate Begnal
Updated by Nika Hoffman

Other major works

PLAY: *Dreaming Emmett*, pr. 1986.

NONFICTION: *Playing in the Dark: Whiteness and the Literary Imagination*, 1992; *Conversations with Toni Morrison*, 1994 (Danille Taylor-Guthrie, editor); *Birth of a Nation'hood: Gaze, Script, and Spectacle in the O.J. Simpson Case*, 1997; *Remember: The Journey to School Integration*, 2004.

CHILDREN'S LITERATURE: *The Big Box*, 1999 (with Slade Morrison and Giselle Potter); *The Book of Mean People*, 2002 (with Slade Morrison); *The Ant or the Grasshopper?*, 2003 (with Slade Morrison); *The Lion or the Mouse?*, 2003 (with Slade Morrison).

EDITED TEXTS: *To Die for the People: The Writings of Huey P. Newton*, 1972; *The Black Book: Three Hundred Years of African American Life*, 1974; *Race-ing Justice, En-gendering Power: Essays on Anita Hill, Clarence Thomas, and the Construction of Social Reality*, 1992; *Deep Sightings and Rescue Missions: Fiction, Essays, and Conversations*, 1996 (of Toni Cade Bambara).

Bibliography

Conner, Marc C., ed. *The Aesthetics of Toni Morrison: Speaking the Unspeakable*. Jackson: University Press of Mississippi, 2000. A collection of essays concentrating on the imagery and stylistics of Morrison's writings and her ability to convey the "unspeakable" aspects of African American experience.

Fultz, Lucille P. *Toni Morrison: Playing with Difference.* Urbana: University of Illinois Press, 2003. An examination of Morrison's approach to differences (for example, black and white, male and female, wealth and poverty) in her intricate narratives.

Furman, Jan. *Toni Morrison's Fiction.* Columbia: University of South Carolina Press, 1996. Part of the Understanding Contemporary American Literature series, this book addresses such topics as black womanhood, male consciousness, and community and cultural identity in Morrison's novels. Includes bibliography and index.

_____, ed. *Toni Morrison's "Song of Solomon."* New York: Oxford University Press, 2003. The essays collected in this volume represent the major critical responses to Morrison's novel; intended as a starting point for students first encountering the book.

Harris, Trudier. *Fiction and Folklore: The Novels of Toni Morrison.* Knoxville: University of Tennessee Press, 1991. A collection of essays that examine Morrison's novels from an African and African American mythological and folkloric perspective and examine the archetypes and antiheroes that pervade her stories. An important scholarly guide to understanding the subtext of Morrison's work.

Kubitschek, Missy Dehn. *Toni Morrison: A Critical Companion.* Westport, Conn.: Greenwood Press, 1998. An excellent source of literary criticism. Contains bibliography and index.

McKay, Nellie, and William Andrews, eds. *"Beloved": A Casebook.* New York: Oxford University Press, 1998. Student-friendly collection of critical essays on Morrison's novel *Beloved.*

Middleton, David L. *Toni Morrison: An Annotated Bibliography.* New York: Garland, 1987. The articles and essays by Morrison and the interviews with her listed here are arranged chronologically to present clearly the evolution of her ideas. Includes critical reviews of her fiction and a listing of honors and awards. Subject index provided. An indispensable guide.

Otten, Terry. *The Crime of Innocence in the Fiction of Toni Morrison.* Columbia: University of Missouri Press, 1989. In this groundbreaking study of Morrison's first five novels, Otten explores the mythic substance in her writings by tracing the motif of the biblical fall. Insightful readings and unflagging attention to the historical and literary backdrop. A valuable guide to the increasing scholarship on Morrison.

Peach, Linden, ed. *Toni Morrison.* New York: St. Martin's Press, 1998. Focuses on interpretation and criticism of Morrison's works and examines African American women in literature. Provides bibliography and index.

Samuels, Wilfred D., and Clenora Hudson-Weems. *Toni Morrison.* Boston: Twayne, 1990. This study analyzes five of Morrison's novels, including *Beloved.* The authors explore common themes such as black folklore and mysticism in Morrison's writings. Contains excerpts from interviews.

Tate, Claudia, ed. *Black Women Writers at Work.* New York: Continuum, 1983. This book is made up of interviews with Morrison and other black women writers. The Morrison interview contains some of her most cogent and forthright expressions of her commitment to politics in writing and a black or Afrocentric aesthetic.

Vladimir Nabokov

Born: St. Petersburg, Russia; April 23, 1899
Died: Montreux, Switzerland; July 2, 1977

Principal long fiction • *Mashenka*, 1926 (*Mary*, 1970); *Korol', dama, valet*, 1928 (*King, Queen, Knave*, 1968); *Zashchita Luzhina*, 1929 (serial), 1930 (book; *The Defense*, 1964); *Kamera obskura*, 1932 (*Camera Obscura*, 1936; revised as *Laughter in the Dark*, 1938); *Podvig*, 1932 (*Glory*, 1971); *Otchayanie*, 1934 (serial), 1936 (book; *Despair*, 1937; revised 1966); *Priglashenie na kazn'*, 1935-1936 (serial), 1938 (book; *Invitation to a Beheading*, 1959); *Dar*, 1937-1938 (serial), 1952 (book; *The Gift*, 1963); *The Real Life of Sebastian Knight*, 1941; *Bend Sinister*, 1947; *Lolita*, 1955; *Pnin*, 1957; *Pale Fire*, 1962; *Ada or Ardor: A Family Chronicle*, 1969; *Transparent Things*, 1972; *Look at the Harlequins!*, 1974.

Other literary forms • Vladimir Nabokov began, as many novelists do, as a poet. As a youth, he published privately what now would be called a chapbook and a full book of poetry before emigrating from Russia. Throughout his life, he continued to publish poetry in periodicals and several book-length collections, including *Stikhotvorenia, 1929-1951* (1952), *Poems* (1959), and *Poems and Problems* (1970). Some critics even consider the long poem "Pale Fire" (an integral part of the novel *Pale Fire*) a worthy neo-Romantic poem in itself. Nabokov also published a good deal of short fiction, first in a variety of short-lived émigré publications such as *Rul'*, *Sovremennye Zapiski*, and *Russkoe ekho*, and later in such prominent magazines as *The New Yorker*, *The Atlantic Monthly*, *Playboy*, *Harper's Bazaar*, and *Tri-Quarterly*. His stories were collected in *Vozrashchenie Chorba* (1930; the return of Chorb, which also included twenty-four poems), *Soglyadatay* (1938; the eye), *Nine Stories* (1947), and *Nabokov's Dozen* (1958), among others. His plays include: *Smert'* (1923; death); *Tragediya gospodina Morna* (1924; the tragedy of Mister Morn); *Chelovek iz SSSR* (1927; the man from the USSR); *Sobytiye* (1938; the event); and *Izobretenie Val'sa* (1938; *The Waltz Invention*, 1966).

Nabokov also worked on a screenplay for the film version of *Lolita* (1962). Besides translating his own works from Russian to English (and vice versa, as well as occasionally from French to Russian to English), he often translated the works of other writers, including Lewis Carroll's 1865 *Alice's Adventures in Wonderland*, and poetry of Rupert Brooke, Alexander Pushkin, Arthur Rimbaud, William Shakespeare, and Alfred de Musset. In nonfiction prose, Nabokov's fascinating life is recalled in three volumes of memoirs, *Conclusive Evidence* (1951), *Drugie Berega* (1954; other shores), and *Speak, Memory* (1966, a revision and expansion of the earlier works). Throughout his life, his often idiosyncratic criticism was widely published, and the publication after his death of several volumes of his lectures on world literature provoked much discussion among literary scholars. As a lepidopterist, Nabokov published a number of scholarly articles in such journals as *The Entomologist, Journal of the New York Entomological Society, Psyche*, and *The Lepidopterists' News*.

Achievements • An extraordinary individual, Nabokov's strength as a writer lay in his control and mastery of style. Writers are sometimes successful in a language other

Library of Congress

than their native language, but only a select few are capable of writing equally well in two languages, and Nabokov may be alone in his ability to master the insinuations of two extraordinarily different and subtle languages such as Russian and English. Under the pen name "V. Sirin," Nabokov was recognized as a noteworthy émigré novelist and poet in Berlin and Paris. After fleeing the rise of Nazism and settling in the United States, he became recognized as a major English-language author with the publication of *Lolita* in 1955. As was the case with Gustave Flaubert, James Joyce, and D. H. Lawrence, all of whose international sales were aided by the controversies surrounding their works, Nabokov received worldwide attention as critics debated the morality of *Lolita*, prompting the republication and translation of many of his earlier works. Few writers with such an uncompromising style achieve such popularity. Nabokov was often in financial difficulty before *Lolita*, yet he always remained the consummate craftsman. He has come to be regarded as one of the literary giants of his generation.

Biography • Vladimir Vladimirovich Nabokov was born to Vladimir Dmitrievich and Elena Rukavishnikov Nabokov in St. Petersburg, Russia, the eldest of five children. He grew up in comfortable circumstances, tracing his ancestry back to a Tartar prince of the 1380's and through a number of military men, statesmen, Siberian merchants, and the first president of the Russian Imperial Academy of Medicine. His father was a noted liberal who had helped found the Constitutional Democratic Party, was elected to the first Duma, and coedited the sole liberal newspaper in St. Petersburg. In his childhood, the young Nabokov was taken on trips to France, Italy, and Spain, and he summered on the country estate of Vyra, accumulating memories that would become woven into his later writings. His father, an Anglophile, provided governesses who taught the boy English at a very early age. He once remarked that he had learned to read English even before he had learned Russian. He was also taught French.

Entering puberty, Nabokov attended the liberal Prince Tenishev School, where he first developed a hatred of coercion but played soccer and chess, started collecting butterflies, and showed some artistic talent. He began writing poetry, and a now lost brochure of a single poem "in a violet paper cover" was privately published in 1914. In 1916, he privately published a recollection that provoked his cousin to beg him to "never, never be a writer," and in 1918, he collaborated on a collection with Andrei Balashov. Nabokov inherited an estate and the equivalent of two million dollars when his Uncle Ruka died, and he seemed to be on his way to the comfortable life of a Russian bourgeois when history intervened. His father became part of the provisional government in the March Revolution of 1917, but in October, when the Bolsheviks displaced the Alexander Kerensky government, the Nabokov family fled, first to the Crimea and then, in 1919, into permanent exile in the West on an old Greek ship ironically named *Nadezhda* ("Hope").

Nabokov studied at Trinity College, Cambridge University, paying little attention to anything but soccer, tennis, and girls. He did, however, do many translations (of Rupert Brooke, Seumas O'Sullivan, William Butler Yeats, George Gordon, Lord Byron, and others) and came under the influence of English poetry. He also read and was influenced by James Joyce. Despite his claim that he never once visited the library, he graduated with honors in French and Russian literature in 1923. This was shortly following his father's assassination in Berlin in March, 1922, as two reactionaries shot the elder Nabokov in error as he was introducing their intended victim. After Cambridge, the twenty-five-year-old Nabokov moved to Berlin, where, in 1925, he married Vera Evseevna Slonim, and a year later he published his first novel, *Mary*, under a pseudonym. He believed that his father had prior claim to the name "Vladimir Nabokov," and he wrote all of his early Russian works as "V. Sirin."

With very little money, Nabokov published poems, stories, and essays in Berlin's émigré newspapers, and later, as the Nazis grew in power (his wife was Jewish), in similar Parisian publications. He survived by teaching tennis, devising crossword puzzles in Russian, making up chess problems, teaching Russian, and translating. He sold the Russian translation of *Alice's Adventures in Wonderland* (*Anya v strane chudes*, 1923), for example, for the equivalent of five dollars. In 1934, his only son, Dmitri, was born, and four years later, Nabokov fled to Paris. As early as 1935, he decided to immigrate to the United States, probably recognizing that Europe was no longer safe. He was invited by the Soviet government during the 1930's to return to Russia several times, but he refused.

Nabokov's novels in Berlin and Paris had been relatively successful, and several had been translated into English with and without his assistance. He made the remarkable and difficult decision to abandon the language in which he had written so well. "My private tragedy," he later wrote, "which cannot, indeed should not, be anybody's concern, is that I had to abandon my natural idiom, my untrammeled, rich, and infinitely docile Russian tongue for a second-rate brand of English." Stanford University invited him to teach in the summer of 1940, and he set sail for America on the liner *Champlain* in May, just ahead of the German invasion. He had already begun writing his first English novel, *The Real Life of Sebastian Knight*, while in Paris, and, in 1941, it was published in the United States after several friends helped him edit it. He taught Russian grammar and literature at Wellesley College from 1941 to 1948, also serving as a research fellow at the Museum of Comparative Zoology at Harvard University. He became a prominent lepidopterist, publishing many monographs, articles, and reviews. He spent summers roaming America searching for butterflies and discovered several species and subspecies, including "Nabokov's wood nymph." After seeing praise for his work on the Lycaeides genus in a field guide, Nabokov is said to have remarked, "That's real fame. That means more than anything a literary critic could say."

In 1944, Nabokov published a critical book on Nikolai Gogol, and in 1947, his first novel written in the United States, *Bend Sinister*, appeared. From 1948 to 1959, he taught at Cornell University, carefully writing out his lectures, combining his attacks on such intellectual touchstones as Karl Marx, Charles Darwin, and especially Sigmund Freud with dramatic classroom readings. Well before the publication of *Lolita*, he was recognized as a remarkable talent in certain quarters, as is indicated by his receipt of grants from the Guggenheim Foundation in 1943 and 1953 and by an award from the American Academy of Arts and Letters in 1953; students in his classes at Cornell, however, were often unaware that their teacher was also a writer, although he published stories and articles in *The New Yorker, The Atlantic Monthly, Hudson Review*, and others. *Lolita* changed all that. Rejected by several American publishers, it was brought out by publisher Maurice Girodias's Olympia Press in Paris in 1955. As one of the most controversial books ever published—banned for a while in France, debated in the British parliament, and forbidden in many American libraries—it swept the best-seller lists and freed Nabokov from teaching. Besides the royalties, he received $150,000 and a percentage on the film rights and wrote a screenplay (which was later substantially changed) for Stanley Kubrick's 1962 film.

In 1960, Nabokov moved to Montreux, Switzerland, where he and his wife lived in a sixth-floor apartment in the Palace Hotel overlooking Lake Geneva, in order to be near their son Dmitri, who was having some success as an opera singer. In the wake of *Lolita*, Nabokov and his son translated many of his earlier novels into English and introduced several collections of his short stories to American readers. His novels *Pale Fire, Ada or Ardor, Transparent Things*, and *Look at the Harlequins!* were all published during this period. He was regularly discussed as a possible recipient of the Nobel Prize until his death of a viral infection in 1977.

Analysis • In 1937, Vladeslav Khodasevich, an émigré poet and champion of "V. Sirin's" work, wrote, "Sirin [Nabokov] proves for the most part to be an artist of form, of the writer's device, and not only in that . . . sense of which . . . his writing is distinguished by exceptional diversity, complexity, brilliance, and novelty." Khodasevich went on to say that the key to all Sirin's work was his ability to put all his literary devices on display, with little or no attempt to conceal them, thus entertaining his readers more with the revelation of how the magician performs his tricks, than with the trick itself. "The life of the artist and the life of a device in the consciousness of an artist—this is Sirin's theme." Khodasevich, although he had not yet read *The Gift*—purported to be Vladimir Nabokov's greatest Russian novel—had discovered the most important element of Nabokov's fiction.

Throughout his entire life, although Nabokov underwent great changes in his circumstances, he was consistent, whether writing in Russian or English, in his unflagging delight in literary devices of all sorts, art for its own sake, and a contempt for mimetic conventions, simplistic psychological motivation, ordinary plot structure, and anything that inhibits the literary imagination. He can, in many respects, be called an aesthete, but his rejection of most schools of thought makes him difficult to classify. He strove for and achieved a uniqueness that runs as a thread throughout his oeuvre. Clarence Brown once commented in a critical essay that "for well over a quarter of a century now . . . [Nabokov] has been writing in book after book about the same thing," and Nabokov is said to have admitted that Brown was probably correct.

Mary **and** *King, Queen, Knave* • Nabokov's first novel, *Mary*, is rather sentimental and probably based on Nabokov's regret for a lost love, but it already contains two elements he would use repeatedly—the love triangle and uncertain identity. *King, Queen, Knave*, however, is an even more obvious reflection of the Nabokov canon. In it, a character named Franz Bubendorf, a country bumpkin on his way to the city, apparently to be corrupted by the bourgeois life, is, in fact, already corrupted by his distaste for his own class, which distorts his perception. As if to emphasize this distortion of perception, Franz steps on his glasses and Berlin becomes a blur. Again, there is a love triangle, and each of the participants is, in his or her own way, unable to perceive reality. The melodrama of a love triangle and a planned murder is handled with the authorial detachment that is one of Nabokov's hallmarks. The novel becomes a parody of traditional forms, and the characters become obvious contrivances of the author. Derived from a Hans Christian Andersen work of the same title, the novel consists of thirteen chapters, as there are thirteen cards in each suit in a deck of cards. The card metaphor is carried throughout the work, even in the description of clothes.

Laughter in the Dark • *Laughter in the Dark* opens with a parody of the fairy tale revealing the entire plot, here a relatively conventional bourgeois love story that Nabokov typically manipulates. The main character, blinded by love, becomes literally blinded and trapped in a love triangle, which results in his murder (accomplished in a scene that is a parody of motion-picture melodrama). This type of parody, which partially represents Nabokov's delight in mocking inferior art, can also be seen as a parody of the reader's expectations. Nabokov constantly thwarts the reader who wants a nice, comfortable, conventional novel. The writer is always in control, always tugging the reader this way and that, never allowing a moment of certainty. Perceptions are distorted on all levels. The characters have distorted perceptions of one another. The reader's perception of events is teasingly distorted by the author. Nabokov operates a house of mirrors. If a reader expects realism, there will be no pleasure in the warped mirrors Nabokov presents. One must delight instead in the odd shapes and obvious deformities in the mirrors he has shaped.

Nabokov's Characters • Character types in the Russian novels also recur throughout Nabokov's career, so much so that some critics have attempted to pair earlier Russian novels with later English ones. Usually, the central figure is an outsider, an unusual person in his milieu. Bubendorf of *King, Queen, Knave* is a country boy in the city. In *The Defense*, the chess master Luzhin does not fit in with his family or his school and is sent into exile after the Revolution. Martin Edelweiss of *Glory* is in exile in London.

What is more important, however, is that these and many more of Nabokov's characters are isolated as much by their mental states as by their physical surroundings. Their fantasies, dreams, ambitions, and obsessions set them utterly apart from the ordinary world. Luzhin, for example, is so obsessed with chess that he cannot deal with the disorder of life. Cincinnatus in *Invitation to a Beheading* is thought peculiar by his fellow workers in the doll factory. In later English novels, immigrant Timofey Pnin is thought mad by his academic colleagues, Humbert Humbert and Adam Krug are seen as dangers to society, and Charles Kinbote intrudes and imposes on people. Generally, the main characters of Nabokov's novels are perceived as talented men, in some sense more valuable than the soulless people and society that persecute them. They are outsiders because they are extraordinary. They are free, imaginative, and capable of a kind of heroism that ordinary people lack: the ability to remake the world according to their own obsessions.

The Gift • *The Gift* is generally thought of as Nabokov's best Russian novel. Originally published serially in *Sovremennye Zapiski*, an émigré periodical, the fourth section was not included (for political reasons) in a complete edition until 1952. In *The Gift*, the central figure is Fyodor Godunov-Cherdyntsev, a brilliant émigré poet. As the book opens, he has just published a collection of poems, and much of the early part concerns his literary career. Later, his obsession with the memory of his father begins to dominate his everyday life, and he becomes caught in the typical confusions of the biographer: What is the truth and how can one see it? He feels an obligation to write a biography of his father but becomes trapped in assessing the various versions of his father's life. Later, he does succeed in writing a biography of Nikolai Gavrilovich Chernyshevski, a so-called "poetic history" based upon the idea that reconstructing the past is essentially a creative act—history only exists in the historian's imagination—and that the best biographies are literary creations.

The Gift has been seen as the summing up of Nabokov's experiences as an émigré writer, and similarities have been seen between the author's biography and the events and people in the novel. The book is heavy with allusions to Russian literature and has been called the Russian counterpart to *Ada or Ardor*, an extremely allusive and complex book that also focuses on the nature of the writer. In *The Gift*, many of Nabokov's favorite devices are employed: the love triangle, the ironic suicide, and the heightened perception of the hero, in which he imagines conversations with the dead.

The Real Life of Sebastian Knight • After his decision to begin writing in English, Nabokov produced two novels before the *succès de scandale* of *Lolita*. *The Real Life of Sebastian Knight* was begun in Paris and is ostensibly the biography of a fiction writer, Sebastian, narrated by his brother, "V." V. is shocked to discover upon his brother's death in 1936 that there was more to learn of Sebastian from his novels than he had learned in person. Once again, Nabokov introduces the theme that art surpasses reality. V. fights the various distortions of Sebastian's life yet, at the end of his biography, confesses that "Sebastian's mask clings to my face." V. created Sebastian, so Sebastian is V. (as both characters were created by Nabokov). Again, the novel is characterized by the use of parodistic techniques and distorted characters. One can easily recognize this novel as a Nabokov work, yet because of Nabokov's uncertainty at writing in the English language at this stage, the work is not completely satisfying. Nabokov admitted, for example, to having had native speakers help him with the editing, something he would never permit later.

Bend Sinister • Many resemblances have been noted between Nabokov and his brother Sergei, and V. and his brother Sebastian. Sergei, unlike Vladimir, stayed in Europe during the Nazi period and died of starvation in a concentration camp near Hamburg on January 10, 1945. These events perhaps explain the harsh allegorical tone of *Bend Sinister*, a novel that is, in some ways, better than its predecessor and perhaps one of the most accessible of Nabokov's novels. The hero, Adam Krug, is an intellectual whose ideas are largely responsible for the new regime in an Eastern European country. Krug, however, refuses to swear allegiance to the ruler of the regime, a fellow student from childhood named Paduk. "I am not interested in politics," he says. Inexorably, the ring of tyranny tightens around Krug, resulting in the arrest of friends, the death of his son, and Krug's death as he attempts to attack Paduk in a mad vision of schoolyard life.

The artist, the literary craftsman in Nabokov, was incapable, however, of writing a straightforward novel of outrage against fascists or communists. The country is not specified; numerous vague descriptions of setting give the work a Kafkaesque flavor. The regime is tyrannical—it wants the souls of its people as well as their cooperation (not unlike Big Brother in George Orwell's *Nineteen Eighty-Four*, 1949)—yet it is not a specific ideology that is being attacked. Any form of coercion that limits the imagination of the artist or the intellectual is the target. Although some critics have argued that Krug's flaw is that he refuses to become involved in politics, it is difficult to imagine *Bend Sinister*, in the light of other works, as being a call to commitment. Krug has made a commitment to his own intellectual life. He, like many Nabokov heroes, does not "fit in" and, like many Nabokov heroes, comes to a tragic end. The supremacy of the individual imagination is Nabokov's "message"; art is his morality. There is an abundant helping of satire and parody directed against the intellectual community and the "great" political leaders of the world. Paduk is shown as a sniveling, ugly weakling who craves Krug's approval, but the alternatives to his tyranny are shown to be equally preposterous. Even in reacting to the horrors of dictatorship, Nabokov remains the detached artist.

Lolita • *Lolita*, the novel that would provide a comfortable living for the author for the rest of his life, has been called everything from pornography to one of the greatest novels of the twentieth century. Today, when virtually every sexual predilection has been the subject of motion pictures and television, it is hard to appreciate the whirlwind of controversy that was stirred up by *Lolita*'s publication. Humbert Humbert, the central character and narrator, has an obsession for young girls that he has hidden by unhappy affairs with older women. He comes to the United States after inheriting a business and separating from his childish wife Valeria. Eventually, he becomes the boarder of Charlotte Haze and becomes sexually obsessed with her twelve-year-old daughter Lolita. He marries Mrs. Haze to be near Lolita, and when the mother is killed, he takes the girl on a trip across the United States. She is eventually stolen by Clare Quilty, who is, in many ways, Humbert's double, and Humbert goes on a two-year quest to rescue her. He finds the sad, pregnant Lolita married to a man named Richard Schiller and, in revenge, shoots Quilty. The novel is allegedly Humbert's manuscript, written as he awaits trial. According to the foreword, Humbert died in jail of a coronary thrombosis, and the manuscript was transmitted to one John Ray, Jr., Ph.D., who prepared it for publication.

As in all of Nabokov's works, however, a plot summary is absurdly inadequate in characterizing the book. *Lolita* is protean in its directions and effects. It has been seen as a satire on the United States (though Nabokov denied it), as a psychological study (although Nabokov called Freud a "medieval mind"), and as a parody of the romantic novel. Lionel Trilling argued that, since adultery was such a commonplace in the modern world, only a perverse love could cause the adequate passion mixed with suffering characteristic of great romantic loves: Tristan and Isolde, Abélard and Héloïse, Dante and Beatrice, Petrarch and Laura. Humbert often justifies his pedophilia by references to the courtly love tradition. There is also much reference to the story of Edgar Allan Poe's love for Virginia Clemm (Humbert's first teenage love was a girl named Annabel Leigh).

Although many critics attempted to justify *Lolita* as having an important moral message, Nabokov rebuked the notion by saying, "I am no messenger boy." His aesthetic philosophy would never have permitted him to subordinate his art to a moral. He once said that Lolita was about his love for the English language, but even that is an oversimplification of an immensely complex book. Among the various elements critics have noted are the doppelgänger relation of Quilty to Humbert, chess metaphors, puns on names, the question of the masks of the narrator (the probably unreliable Humbert through the clinical Ray through the mischievous Nabokov), and the supposed immortality of Humbert's love, a love that becomes timeless through a work of art. It has even been argued that Nabokov's description of Lolita very much resembles his description of a certain species of butterfly in his scientific studies. Although *Lolita*'s place in the canon of world literature is still debated, there is little doubt that it may be the finest example of the author's "game-playing" method of artistic creation.

Pale Fire • In *Pale Fire*, readers were once again amused, perplexed, or horrified with Nabokov's ironic wit. This experimental novel inspired extremes of praise— such as Mary McCarthy's judgment that "it is one of the great works of art of this century"—and mockery. The novel is presented in the form of a scholarly edition of a poem titled "Pale Fire" by John Shade, with commentary by Charles Kinbote. Both worked at Wordsmith University, where Kinbote seems to have believed that Shade was writing a poem about Kinbote's obsession with Charles Xavier Vseslav, "The Beloved," the King of Zembla who was forced to flee the revolution that replaced him. *Pale Fire* can be described as a series of Russian dolls, one enclosed within another. John Shade's poem (as edited by Kinbote) is explained by Kinbote, who intends to give life to the extraordinary personality of Shade. He writes in the foreword, "without my notes Shade's text simply has no human reality at all," but the reader soon recognizes that Kinbote is a madman who either is, or imagines himself to be, the displaced King of Zembla, and whatever human reality Shade may have exists only through his colleague's warped interpretation of events. On another level, the reader finds some of Shade's "reality" in the text of his poem and reads much into and between Kinbote's lines as the madman gradually exposes his own madness. Yet, Nabokov never wants his reader to forget that all this invention is entirely of his making. Much more is intended than a mere parody of scholarly editions, scholars, and neo-Romantic poetry. Once more, Nabokov wittily develops his lifelong theme that reality exists only in the eyes of its interpreter.

J. Madison Davis

Other major works

SHORT FICTION: *Vozrashchenie Chorba*, 1930; *Soglyadatay*, 1938; *Nine Stories*, 1947; *Vesna v Fialte i drugie rasskazy*, 1956; *Nabokov's Dozen: A Collection of Thirteen Stories*, 1958; *Nabokov's Quartet*, 1966; *A Russian Beauty, and Other Stories*, 1973; *Tyrants Destroyed, and Other Stories*, 1975; *Details of a Sunset, and Other Stories*, 1976.

PLAYS: *Dedushka*, pb. 1923; *Smert'*, pb. 1923; *Polius*, pb. 1924; *Tragediya gospodina Morna*, pb. 1924; *Chelovek iz SSSR*, pb. 1927; *Izobretenie Val'sa*, pb. 1938 (*The Waltz Invention*, 1966); *Sobytiye*, pr., pb. 1938.

SCREENPLAY: *Lolita*, 1962.

POETRY: *Stikhi*, 1916; *Dva puti*, 1918; *Gorny put*, 1923; *Grozd'*, 1923; *Stikhotvorenia, 1929-1951*, 1952; *Poems*, 1959; *Poems and Problems*, 1970.

NONFICTION: *Nikolai Gogol*, 1944; *Conclusive Evidence: A Memoir*, 1951; *Drugie Berega*, 1954; *Speak, Memory: An Autobiography Revisited*, 1966 (revision of *Conclusive Evidence* and *Drugie berega*); *Strong Opinions*, 1973; *The Nabokov-Wilson Letters, 1940-1971*, 1979; *Lectures on Literature: British, French, and German*, 1980; *Lectures on Russian Literature*, 1981; *Lectures on Don Quixote*, 1983; *Vladimir Nabokov: Selected Letters, 1940-1977*, 1989.

TRANSLATIONS: *Anya v strane chudes*, 1923 (of Lewis Carroll's novel *Alice's Adventures in Wonderland*); *Three Russian Poets: Translations of Pushkin, Lermontov, and*

Tiutchev, 1944 (with Dmitri Nabokov); *A Hero of Our Time,* 1958 (of Mikhail Lermontov's novel; with Dmitri Nabokov); *The Song of Igor's Campaign,* 1960 (of the twelfth century epic *Slovo o polki Igoreve*); *Eugene Onegin,* 1964 (of Alexander Pushkin's novel).

Bibliography

Bloom, Harold, ed. *Vladimir Nabokov.* New York: Chelsea House, 1987. Essays on Nabokov's handling of time, illusion and reality, and art. There are separate essays on each of his major novels, as well as an introduction, chronology, and bibliography.

Boyd, Brian. *Vladimir Nabokov: The Russian Years.* Princeton, N.J.: Princeton University Press, 1990. First part of an ambitious two-volume biography of Nabokov.

_____. *Vladimir Nabokov: The American Years.* Princeton, N.J.: Princeton University Press, 1991. In the course of the two volumes of this critical biography, Boyd discusses virtually all Nabokov's stories. Boyd generally provides a brief summary of each story, relating it to Nabokov's development as an artist and noting recurring themes. Each volume includes illustrations, extensive notes, and an exceptionally thorough index.

Connolly, Julian W. *The Cambridge Companion to Nabokov.* New York: Cambridge University Press, 2005. A concise introduction to Nabokov's life and his writing.

Foster, John Burt. *Nabokov's Art of Memory and European Modernism.* Princeton, N.J.: Princeton University Press, 1993. Burt divides his study into three parts: Nabokov's early years in Russia, his period in Europe, and his prolonged period in America. This is a more specialized study for advanced students.

Grayson, Jane. *Vladimir Nabokov.* Woodstock, N.Y.: Overlook Press, 2002. Richly illustrated biography of Nabokov.

Grayson, Jane, Arnold B. McMillin, and Priscilla Meyer, eds. *Nabokov's World: Reading Nabokov.* New York: Palgrave Macmillan, 2002. A collection of fifteen essays focusing on intertextuality in Nabokov's works and their literary reception.

Larmour, David. H. J., ed. *Discourse and Ideology in Nabokov's Prose.* New York: Routledge, 2002. Collection of critical essays on a wide variety of aspects of Nabokov's writing.

Parker, Stephen Jan. *Understanding Vladimir Nabokov.* Columbia: University of South Carolina Press, 1987. An introductory guide to Nabokov for students and non-academic readers. After an introductory chapter on the self-reflexive aspects of Nabokov's narrative technique, the book focuses on individual analyses of five Russian novels and four American novels. The section on the short stories provides brief summary analyses of "Spring in Fialta," "Cloud, Castle, Lake," "Signs and Symbols," and "The Vane Sisters."

Pifer, Ellen, ed. *Vladimir Nabokov's "Lolita": A Casebook.* New York: Oxford University Press, 2002. Nine essays and an interview with Nabokov are collected to provide a range of approaches to the reading of *Lolita.*

Schiff, Stacy. *Véra (Mrs. Vladimir Nabokov): Portrait of a Marriage.* New York: Random House, 1999. The story of a woman's fifty-five-year marriage to a brilliant but self-centered poet and novelist.

Wood, Michael. *The Magician's Doubts: Nabokov and the Risks of Fiction.* Princeton, N.J.: Princeton University Press, 1995. Wood's close reading of the Nabokovian texts shows the power and beauty of his language and the subtlety of his art, and it uncovers an ethical and moral foundation of his work that Nabokov denied existed.

Gloria Naylor

Born: New York, New York; January 25, 1950

Principal long fiction • *The Women of Brewster Place: A Novel in Seven Stories*, 1982; *Linden Hills*, 1985; *Mama Day*, 1988; *Bailey's Café*, 1992; *The Men of Brewster Place*, 1998; *1996*, 2004.

Other literary forms • In 1986, Gloria Naylor wrote a column, *Hers*, for *The New York Times*. She is also the writer of a number of screenplays, short stories, and articles for various periodicals. She is known primarily, however, for her novels.

Achievements • Enjoying both critical and popular acclaim, Naylor's work has reached a wide audience. *The Women of Brewster Place* won the 1983 American Book Award for best first novel and was later made into a television miniseries. Naylor's other awards include a National Endowment for the Arts Fellowship in 1985 and a Guggenheim Fellowship in 1988.

Surveying the range of black life in America, from poor ghetto to affluent suburb to southern offshore island, Naylor's work examines questions of black identity and, in particular, celebrates black women. In the face of enormous problems and frequent victimization, black women are shown coping through their sense of community and their special powers. Male readers might find less to cheer about in Naylor's early works, as she writes from a feminist perspective. Later works, however, recognize the plight of black men, acknowledging their struggles and celebrating their achievements. Though Naylor's focus is the black experience, her depictions of courage, community, and cultural identity have universal appeal.

Biography • The oldest child of parents who had migrated from Mississippi, Gloria Naylor was born and reared in New York City, her parents having left the South the year before her birth. An avid reader as a child, Naylor seemed to have inherited her passion for reading from her mother, a woman who would go to great lengths to purchase books to which she was denied access in Mississippi libraries since black people were not allowed inside. The year Naylor graduated from high school, Martin Luther King, Jr., was assassinated, and the shock of this event caused Naylor to delay her college education. She chose instead to become a missionary for the Jehovah's Witnesses in New York, North Carolina, and Florida. She eventually found missionary life too strict, but her zeal apparently carried over into her later feminism. Although her writings are not religious, a fundamentalist pattern of thinking pervades them. She tends to separate her characters into the sheep and the goats (the latter mostly men), the saved and the damned, with one whole book, *Linden Hills*, being modeled after Dante Alighieri's *Inferno* (c. 1320).

In high school Naylor read widely in the nineteenth century British novelists, but later in a creative writing course at Brooklyn College she came across the book that influenced her most—*The Bluest Eye* (1970), by the black American novelist Toni Morrison. The example of Morrison inspired Naylor to write fiction and to focus on the lives of black women, who Naylor believed were underrepresented (if

not ignored) in American literature. Naylor began work on *The
Women of Brewster Place*, which was
published the year after her graduation from Brooklyn College with a
bachelor's degree in English. By
that time, Naylor was studying on a
fellowship at Yale University, from
which she received a master's degree in African American studies in
1983.

Naylor's background and literary achievements won for her numerous invitations for lectureships
or other appointments in academia. She held visiting posts at
George Washington University, the
University of Pennsylvania, Princeton University, New York University, Boston University, Brandeis
University, and Cornell University.
Diverse in her pursuits, Naylor
wrote a stage adaptation of *Bailey's
Café*. She founded One Way Productions, an independent film com-
pany, and became involved in a literacy program in the Bronx. She settled in Brooklyn, New York. In 1996, she moved to St. Helena Island, off the coast of South Carolina, where a petty conflict with a neighbor whose brother was an agent of the
National Security Agency led to her being harassed by federal agents. In 2004, she returned to the novel form for the first time in six years by publishing *1996*, a fictionalized account of her experience.

Analysis • White people do not appear often and are not featured in the work of Gloria Naylor. However, their presence can be felt like a white background noise, or like
the boulevard traffic on the other side of the wall from Brewster Place. White culture
is simply another fact of life, like a nearby nuclear reactor or toxic waste dump, and
the effects of racism and discrimination are omnipresent in Naylor's work. Against
these stifling effects her characters live their lives and try to define their sense of black
identity, from the ghetto dwellers of Brewster Place to the social climbers of Linden
Hills to the denizens of Willow Springs, a pristine southern island relatively untouched by slavery and segregation.

Naylor writes about these settings and characters in a romantic mode that sometimes verges on the melodramatic or gothic. The influence of her earlier reading—
works by such authors as Charlotte Brontë and Emily Brontë, Charles Dickens,
William Faulkner, and Morrison—is apparent. The settings have heavy but obvious
symbolic meanings, some derived from literary references: Brewster Place is a dead-
end street, Linden Hills is a modern version of Dante's Hell, and Willow Springs recalls the magical isle of William Shakespeare's *The Tempest* (1611). The weather and
numerous details also carry symbolic freight, almost as much as they do for such an

emblematic writer as Nathaniel Hawthorne. In addition to literary influences, the symbolism seems to draw on Hollywood, particularly Hollywood's gothic genre, horror films; for example, in *Linden Hills* the character Norman Anderson suffers from attacks of "the pinks"—imaginary blobs of pink slime—while the rich undertaker Luther Nedeed locks his wife and child away in the basement.

These two examples also show, in an exaggerated fashion, how Naylor's characters fit into the Romantic mode. Her characters tend to go to extremes, to be emotional and obsessive, or to have a single trait or commit a single act that determines their whole life course. Although rather one-dimensional and melodramatic, they nevertheless linger in the memory. Such is the case with Luther Nedeed, who represents Satan in *Linden Hills*, and with the old conjure woman Miranda "Mama" Day, who represents Satan's usual opposition in the scheme of things.

In Naylor, this scheme of things illustrates how she has transferred her former missionary fervor, along with the framework of religious thought, to her feminism. Luther Nedeed's behavior is only the most sensational example of men's cruelty to women in Naylor's work; he has a large following. On the other hand, the mystical ability of Mama Day, the Prospero of women's liberation, to command the forces of nature and the spirit world is only the most sensational example of women's special powers in Naylor's thinking. Even the women of Brewster Place demonstrate these powers through their mutual love and support, enabling them to triumph over devastating personal tragedies and demeaning circumstances.

Naylor's men are another story: If not outright demons or headed that way, they seem to lack some vital force. Even the best men are fatally flawed—they are subject to "the pinks," are addicted to wine, or have weak hearts. Failing at key moments, they are useful only as sacrifices to the feminine mystique. A prime example is the engineer George Andrews of *Mama Day*, who, for all his masculine rationality and New York smarts, does not know how to handle (significantly) a brooding hen. A close reading of Naylor's works reveals the men's victimization, along with the women's; however, Naylor is concerned with the women in her earlier novels. Naylor's later works indicate that she has expanded her vision to include men.

The Women of Brewster Place • Naylor began fulfilling her commitment to make black women more prominent in American fiction with *The Women of Brewster Place*, subtitled *A Novel in Seven Stories*. The seven stories, featuring seven women, can be read separately, but they are connected by their setting of Brewster Place and by characters who appear, or are mentioned, in more than one story. The women arrive on the dead-end street by different routes that exhibit the variety of lives of black women, but on Brewster Place they unite into a community.

The middle-aged bastion of Brewster Place is Mattie Michael, who over the course of her life was betrayed by each of the three men she loved—her seducer, her father, and her son. She mothers Lucielia Louise Turner (whose grandmother once sheltered Mattie) when Ciel's abusive boyfriend destroys her life. In addition, Mattie welcomes her close friend Etta Mae Johnson, who also once gave Mattie refuge. Etta Mae is a fading beauty who has used men all of her life but is now herself used by a sleazy preacher for a one-night stand. The other women featured are the young unwed Cora Lee, a baby factory; Kiswana Browne, an aspiring social reformer who hails from the affluent suburb of Linden Hills; and Lorraine and Theresa, two lesbians seeking privacy for their love.

Few men are in evidence on Brewster Place, and these few inspire little confi-

dence. C. C. Baker and his youth gang lurk about the alleyway and, in the novel's brutal climax, rape Lorraine. The crazed Lorraine in turn kills the wino Ben, the old janitor who earlier had befriended her. However, Naylor acknowledges the plight of the
men. In her description of the gang members, she says,

> Born with the appendages of power, circumcised by a guillotine, and baptized with
> the steam of a million nonreflective mirrors, these young men wouldn't be called
> upon to thrust a bayonet into an Asian farmer, target a torpedo, scatter their iron
> seed from a B-52 into the wound of the earth, point a finger to move a nation, or
> stick a pole into the moon—and they knew it. They only had that three-hundred-
> foot alley to serve them as stateroom, armored tank, and executioner's chamber.

As these scenes suggest, Brewster Place is located in a ghetto plagued by social ills.
The women must face these on a daily basis in addition to their personal tragedies
and dislocations. Instead of being overcome by their sufferings, however, the women
find within themselves a common fate and a basis for community. They gain strength
and hope from their mutual caring and support. Besides their informal support system, they form a block association to address larger problems. The ability of women
to unite in such a community inspires admiration for their courage and their special
powers.

Linden Hills • The community feelings of Brewster Place, from which the women
gain a positive sense of identity, somehow make the ghetto's problems seem less awesome, paradoxically, than those of Linden Hills, an affluent suburb. If Brewster Place
is a ghetto, Linden Hills is a hell. Naylor underlines this metaphor by deliberately
modeling her novel *Linden Hills* after Dante's *Inferno*. Linden Hills is not a group of
hills, but only a V-shaped area on a hillside intersected by eight streets. As one travels
down the hill, the residents become richer but lower on the moral scale. Lester and
Willie, two young unemployed poets who perform odd jobs for Christmas money
(they are the modern counterparts of Vergil and Dante), take the reader on a guided
tour.

Lester's sister Roxanne deems black Africans in Zimbabwe unready for independence; one young executive, Maxwell Smyth, encourages another, Xavier Donnell,
no longer to consider Roxanne as a prospective corporate bride; and Dr. Daniel
Braithwaite has written the authorized twelve-volume history of Linden Hills without
making a single moral judgment. Other sellouts are more personal: The young lawyer Winston Alcott leaves his homosexual lover to marry respectably, and Chester
Parker is eager to bury his dead wife in order to remarry.

Significantly, Linden Hills is ruled by men. The archfiend is Luther Nedeed, the
local undertaker and real estate tycoon who occupies the lowest point in Linden
Hills. Speaking against a low-income housing project planned for an adjacent poor
black neighborhood, Nedeed urges outraged Linden Hills property owners to make
common cause with the racist Wayne County Citizens Alliance. Most damning of all,
however, is that Nedeed disowns his own wife and child and imprisons them in an old
basement morgue; the child starves, but the wife climbs up to confront the archfiend
on Christmas Eve.

Mama Day • It is clear that, while examining problems of middle-class black identity
in *Linden Hills*, Naylor has not overlooked the plight of black women. In *Mama Day*,
Naylor returns to a more celebratory mood on both subjects. The setting of *Mama*

Day is a unique black American culture presided over by a woman with even more unique powers.

The coastal island of Willow Springs, located off South Carolina and Georgia but belonging to no state, has been largely bypassed by the tides of American history, particularly racism. The island was originally owned by a white man, Bascombe Wade, who also owned slaves. Bascombe married Sapphira, one of his slaves, however, who bore their seven sons. In 1823 Bascombe freed his other slaves and deeded the island to them, his sons, and their respective descendants in perpetuity (the land cannot be sold, only inherited). Bascombe was more or less assimilated, and a black culture grew up on the island that was closely tied to the land, to the culture's beginnings, and to African roots. In other words, Willow Springs is definitely a mythical island—a tiny but free black state flourishing unnoticed under the nose of the Confederacy. Naylor underlines the island's mythic qualities by drawing parallels between it and the magical isle of *The Tempest*.

If Prospero presides over Shakespeare's island, then Prospero's daughter, Miranda "Mama" Day (actually a great-granddaughter of the Wades), presides over Willow Springs. Known and respected locally as an old conjure woman, Mama Day is a repository and embodiment of the culture's wisdom. In particular, she is versed in herbs and other natural phenomena, but she also speaks with the island's spirits. Mama Day uses her powers to heal and aid new life, but other island people who have similar powers are not so benevolent. One such person is Ruby, who stirs her knowledge with hoodoo to kill any woman who might take her man.

Unhappily, Mama Day's grandniece Cocoa, down from New York on a visit with her husband George, arouses Ruby's jealousy. By pretending to be friendly, Ruby is able to give Cocoa a deadly nightshade rinse, scalp massage, and hairdo. Just as a big hurricane hits the island, Cocoa begins to feel the effects of the poison. George, an engineer, native New Yorker, and football fan, works frantically to save Cocoa, but he is overmatched. With his urbanized, masculine rationality, he cannot conceive of what he is up against or how to oppose it. Suffering from exhaustion and a weak heart, he is eventually killed in an encounter with a brooding hen.

Meanwhile, Mama Day has been working her powers. She confronts Ruby in a conjuring match, good magic versus bad magic, just as in Mali's oral epic tradition of the thirteenth century ruler Sundjata and in other traditions of modern Africa. Ruby is destroyed by lightning strikes, and Cocoa is saved. It is too late for George the doubter, however, who learns about the mystical powers of women the hard way.

Bailey's Café • In each of Naylor's first three novels, clear links to the work that follow it are evident. The character Kiswana Browne in *The Women of Brewster Place* serves as the connection to *Linden Hills*, having moved from that bourgeois community to Brewster Place in order to stay in touch with the struggles of her people. Willa Prescott Nedeed, the imprisoned wife in *Linden Hills*, points the way to *Mama Day*, since she is grandniece to Mama Day and first cousin to Cocoa. It is George, Cocoa's husband, who provides the link to *Bailey's Café*, Naylor's fourth novel.

In perhaps her most ambitious work yet, Naylor moves her readers from the magical island of Willow Springs to an equally intriguing site, for Bailey's Café is both nowhere and everywhere. It is sitting at the edge of the world yet is found in every town. As the café's proprietor, Bailey (though that is not his real name), tells readers,

Even though this planet is round, there are just too many spots where you can find yourself hanging onto the edge . . . and unless there's some place, some space, to take a breather for a while, the edge of the world—frightening as it is—could be the end of the world.

His café offers that breather, though some who enter the front door decide not to take it, instead going right through the café out the back door and dropping off into the void.

Like the inhabitants of Brewster Place, the customers in Bailey's Café are marginalized people. Their lives have taken them beyond the poverty and hard times of their urban sisters and brothers to the very edge of despair. However, for the women who people this extraordinary novel, Bailey's is simply a place to get directions to Eve's boardinghouse. Sweet Esther, abused to the point that she will receive visitors only in the dark; Peaches, whose effect on men drives her to mutilate her face with a can opener; Jesse, whose loss of marriage, child, and good name lead her to female lovers and heroin; and the pregnant virgin Mariam, ostracized from her village and bearing the effects of female circumcision—all find at Eve's a haven for their battered souls.

Throughout the individual stories of these women, Naylor uses unifying imagery: flower imagery, since each woman is associated with a particular bloom; musical imagery, jazz mostly, though the chords of the broken lives suggest the blues; religious imagery, figuring heavily in Eve and her garden, but most noticeably in the virgin birth at the end of the novel. This birth is where the connection to *Mama Day* is made clear. Explaining the circumstances of his birth to Cocoa, George told of being left as an infant outside Bailey's Café by his mother, who was later found drowned. The last few pages of *Bailey's Café* reveal George as the drowned Mariam's child, recursively pointing back to *Mama Day*.

Similar to Naylor's other novels in its concentration on the diverse lives of black people, *Bailey's Café* nonetheless marks a shift for Naylor. This shift is evident in her inclusion of Mariam, from Ethiopia, who broadens the depiction of the black experience by encompassing an African one. Mariam is also Jewish, a fact that links her to the Jewish shopkeeper, Gabriel, in the novel. The coming together of the characters in celebration of the baby's birth—a celebration which intermixes different cultural and religious beliefs—brings a multicultural component to the novel absent in Naylor's other works.

Another notable change is Naylor's foregrounding of male characters. Bailey himself, the novel's narrator, is an example. His running commentary on the customers who find themselves in his establishment, his knowledge of the Negro Baseball Leagues, and his narration of his courtship of his wife Nadine make him a central and engaging figure throughout the book. Another example is Miss Maples, the cross-dressing male housekeeper at Eve's boardinghouse. His rather lengthy individual story is included with those of the women; it points to Naylor's intention to portray a different kind of male identity as well as her desire to cultivate a different relationship with her male characters. This shift links *Bailey's Café* to *The Men of Brewster Place*, Naylor's fifth novel.

The Men of Brewster Place • Naylor's return to Brewster Place gives readers the opportunity to revisit the male characters introduced in the first book (generally portrayed negatively) and see them in a different light. No longer assuming background roles, they are up front, giving an account of their actions in the first book. In *The Women of Brewster Place*, Mattie's son Basil skipped town while awaiting sentencing, causing his mother to lose the property she had put up for his bail. Here Basil does return, check in hand, to repay his mother for her loss; however, she is dead, and his unfulfilled desire to make amends leads him into a detrimental relationship and a prison sentence. Eugene, absent from his daughter's funeral in the first book, is in fact on site. His grief compels him to undergo a harsh punishment, one that has much to do with the fact that he could never tell Ciel that he is gay. C. C. Baker, responsible for the vicious gang rape of Lorraine, executes another heinous crime in this book but gives the reader insight into his tragic character. When he squeezes the trigger to kill his brother, he does so with eyes closed, thanking God "for giving him the courage to do it. The courage to be a man."

In *The Men of Brewster Place*, Naylor seems to be acknowledging that there is after all more than one side to a story and that she is ready to let the whole story be known. Passages from the first book provide continuity between the two works, as does the resurrected voice of Ben, the janitor killed by Lorraine. Reminiscent of the character Bailey in *Bailey's Café*, Ben is both character and narrator.

However, Naylor brings some new voices to Brewster Place when she introduces Brother Jerome and Greasy. These characters link together the lives of the men living in Brewster Place. Brother Jerome is a mentally disabled child with an ability to play the piano that speaks of genius. The blues that pour from his fingers speak to the lives of each man, rendering their conditions tangible. Greasy makes his brief but memorable appearance in the story called "The Barbershop," leaving the men to carry the burden of his self-inflicted demise. Naylor's portrayals of these two characters are perhaps the most moving of the book. These characterizations, along with the complexity of all the male characters, point to a Naylor who is taking a broader view. She had prefaced *The Women of Brewster Place* with a poem by Langston Hughes that asked the question, "What happens to a dream deferred?" In *The Men of Brewster Place*, she seems ready to acknowledge that deferred dreams are not only the province of women.

Harold Branam
Updated by Jacquelyn Benton

Other major works

NONFICTION: *Conversations with Gloria Naylor*, 2004 (Maxine Lavon Montgomery, editor).

EDITED TEXTS: *Children of the Night: The Best Short Stories by Black Writers, 1967 to the Present*, 1995.

Bibliography

Braxton, Joanne M., and Andrée Nicola McLaughlin, eds. *Wild Women in the Whirlwind: Afro-American Culture and the Contemporary Literary Renaissance*. New Brunswick, N.J.: Rutgers University Press, 1990. This wide-ranging collection of critical articles brings the cultural history of black women's writing up to the 1980's. Barbara Smith's article "The Truth That Never Hurts: Black Lesbians in Fiction during the 1980's" discusses the section of *The Women of Brewster Place* titled "The Two," but other articles also bear indirectly on important themes in Naylor.

Felton, Sharon, and Michelle C. Loris, eds. *The Critical Response to Gloria Naylor.* Westport, Conn.: Greenwood Press, 1997. Collection of critical essays on Naylor's writing.

Gates, Henry Louis, Jr., and K. A. Appiah, eds. *Gloria Naylor: Critical Perspectives Past and Present.* New York: Amistad, 1993. An excellent source for reviews and essays.

Kelley, Margot Anne, ed. *Gloria Naylor's Early Novels.* Gainesville: University Press of Florida, 1999. A good study of Naylor's early works. Includes bibliographical references and an index.

Montgomery, Maxine Lavon. "Authority, Multivocality, and the New World Order in Gloria Naylor's *Bailey's Café.*" *African American Review* 29, no. 1 (Spring, 1995): 27. Montgomery discusses *Bailey's Café* as a woman-centered work that draws on black art forms and biblical allusions. Though she fails to recognize the true identity of Mariam's child (George of *Mama Day*), Montgomery otherwise provides a valid reading of *Bailey's Café*, commenting on the "more mature voice" with which Naylor addresses the concerns of her earlier novels.

_____, ed. *Conversations with Gloria Naylor.* Jackson: University Press of Mississippi, 2004. Collection of extensive interviews with Naylor.

Naylor, Gloria, and Toni Morrison. "A Conversation." *The Southern Review* 21 (Summer, 1985): 567-593. Naylor visits Morrison, whose novel *The Bluest Eye* (1970) had the deepest influence on Naylor. Their conversation ranges over men, marriage, the inspiration for their various books, how they wrote them, and their characters. Naylor tried in *The Women of Brewster Place* not to depict men negatively and thinks that she succeeded.

Puhr, Kathleen M. "Healers in Gloria Naylor's Fiction." *Twentieth Century Literature* 40, no. 4 (Winter, 1994): 518. Puhr discusses the healing powers of Naylor's female characters, principally Mattie Michael (*The Women of Brewster Place*), Willa Nedeed (*Linden Hills*), and Miranda (*Mama Day*), as well as Naylor's healing places, particularly the café and Eve's garden in *Bailey's Café*. She also discusses Naylor's works in terms of African American ancestry, generational conflicts, and broken dreams.

Rowell, Charles H. "An Interview with Gloria Naylor." *Callaloo* 20, no. 1 (Winter, 1997): 179-192. Charles H. Rowell discusses a range of topics with Naylor, including her educational background, her feelings about writing, the genesis of *The Women of Brewster Place* and *Bailey's Café*, and her feelings about the novel she is intending to write, which turns out to be *The Men of Brewster Place*.

Stave, Shirley A., ed. *Gloria Naylor: Strategy and Technique, Magic and Myth.* Newark: University of Delaware Press, 2001. A collection of essays focusing on *Mama Day* and *Bailey's Café*. Stave argues for an elevation of Naylor in the American literary canon.

Whitt, Margaret Earley. *Understanding Gloria Naylor.* Columbia: University of South Carolina Press, 1998. A thoughtful book of criticism of Naylor's novels.

Wilson, Charles E. *Gloria Naylor: A Critical Companion.* Westport, Conn.: Greenwood Press, 2001. Part of the publisher's series of reference books for students on popular contemporary writers, this volume provides detailed plot summaries and analyses of Naylor's first five novels, along with character portraits, a biography of Naylor, and an extensive bibliography.

Frank Norris

Born: Chicago, Illinois; March 5, 1870
Died: San Francisco, California; October 25, 1902

Principal long fiction • *Moran of the Lady Letty*, 1898; *Blix*, 1899; *McTeague*, 1899; *A Man's Woman*, 1900; *The Octopus*, 1901; *The Pit*, 1903; *Vandover and the Brute*, 1914.

Other literary forms • Frank Norris's published work includes poems, short stories, essays, newspaper articles, novels, and literary criticism. Although he is best known today for his novels, Norris is also remembered for his popular short-story contributions to the San Francisco *Wave* and his insightful literary criticism, published in *The Responsibilities of the Novelist* (1903) and *The Literary Criticism of Frank Norris* (1964).

Norris's first published book, *Yvernelle: A Tale of Feudal France* (published in 1892 while Norris was still in college), was neither a short story nor a novel, but a medieval love poem written in the romantic verse style of Sir Walter Scott. Had it not been subsidized by Gertrude Norris (the author's mother), the book would probably never have been published. Today it is notable only for the high price it brings in the rare book trade.

Norris's success as a reporter was also minimal. His reports on the South African (Boer) War were published in the San Francisco *Chronicle*, but his later writings on the Spanish-American War were not published for some time afterward, and never by *McClure's Magazine*, which originally sent him there.

Norris was successful, however, as a short-story writer. Much of his early work first appeared in the San Francisco *Wave*, a weekly newspaper featuring mostly local literary talent. The stories he wrote for the newspaper were later collected in three volumes: *A Deal in Wheat, and Other Stories of the New and Old West* (1903), *The Third Circle* (1909), and *Frank Norris of "The Wave"* (1931).

The majority of Norris's writings were collected in a ten-volume *Complete Edition*, published by Doubleday, Doran and Company in 1928. During that same year, Doubleday also issued the Argonaut manuscript edition of Norris's works. Identical in content with the *Complete Edition*, the Argonaut manuscript edition was finely bound and included a manuscript page from *McTeague*. In the late twentieth century, more Norris pieces were unearthed, including his Harvard student theses. The record of his brief literary career is almost complete. His major works are still in print in both hardcover and inexpensive paperbound editions.

Achievements • Called by many (including himself) "the boy Zola" because his style was so reminiscent of that French author's writings, Norris spearheaded the naturalistic movement in American literature. Although Norris's contemporaries were, by and large, critical of his portrayal of the savage, seamy side of life, it is that very quality in his work that has helped to keep his fiction alive and readable. Even more than his challenge to the Victorian code of the turn of the century, Norris's capacity to portray corruption and its evil effects upon man and his ability to make scenes and characters seem vibrant and real, will rank him high among twentieth century writers.

Norris never achieved the immense popularity of some of the other writers of his day, such as Jack London. He did not even live to see his most successful novel, *The Pit*, become a best-seller. Indeed, it was not until publication of *The Octopus* that he was able to enjoy even a modest financial success. His readers were simply not able to accept his preoccupation with sordid realities, including his treatment of sex, which by Victorian standards was quite shocking. Because of his unsavory choice of subject matter, Norris was ignored by reviewers who understood only the elegant prose and fine writing of an earlier era. Today, Norris's pioneering work in American naturalism is universally acknowledged.

Biography • Frank Norris was the son of Benjamin Franklin Norris, a successful businessman specializing in wholesale jewelry, and Gertrude Doggett. Born in 1870, Norris's early years were spent in Chicago. Except for a trip to Europe when he was eight, Norris's childhood was rather uneventful.

At the age of fourteen, Norris moved with his family to California. They settled first in Oakland and then moved to a large house on Sacramento Street in San Francisco. Benjamin Norris began a real estate development business, building cheap houses for working-class people to rent, and enjoyed financial success. His son would later write about these houses in his first novel.

Frank Norris found San Francisco stimulating. The family home was located only a block from fashionable Van Ness Avenue with its ongoing series of parades and pageants, and only a few blocks from the business section of Polk Street with its rich variety of small shops—there was even a dental parlor with a grotesque golden tooth sign hanging from the building. The scenes and settings were memorable, and Norris captured many of them for later use as local color in his novels.

In 1885, Norris was enrolled in the Belmont Academy. This marked the beginning of a long, largely unsuccessful attempt at formal schooling. Norris had neither the temperament nor the talent in mathematics for scholarship, and, after breaking his arm playing football scarcely one year after enrolling, he quit the Academy for a convalescence at home. It was during this period that he made up his mind to pursue a career as an artist.

After a short stint at Boy's High School, Norris persuaded his parents to send him to the San Francisco Art Association School. His success there persuaded Benjamin Norris to send him to the finest art schools in Paris. Although Norris did not learn how to paint in Paris, he did learn the fundamentals and principles of art and also the discipline that would later serve him well as a writer.

Convinced that his son was not spending his time painting, Norris's father called him home in 1889. Norris returned from France with a new interest in writing and, more important, a solid foundation upon which to build his writing career.

In the fall of 1890, Norris entered the University of California, determined to become a writer. Almost at once he found himself at odds with the English Department faculty over proper methods of composition. His academic progress in mathematics was abysmal. Norris turned to a more social life and joined Phi Gamma Delta fraternity. There he found a perfect outlet for his frustrations and a wealth of amusements to occupy his time. Although his academic career at Berkeley was undistinguished, Norris's fraternity pranks were memorable.

While Norris was gaining a reputation as a prankster, his family was quickly breaking apart, and Benjamin Norris left, alone, for Europe; while on the trip, he fell in love with another woman. Upon his return, he divorced Gertrude, married his new love, and moved to Chicago; Norris never saw his father again.

984 Notable American Novelists

In 1894, Norris's marginal academic success caught up with him. Although he had done well in Joseph Le Conte's science classes, his failures in mathematics forced him to leave the university without a degree. Harvard appealed to him as the proper place to polish his writing talents, so he enrolled the following fall as a special student, taking courses in English and French. There he found success in the classes taught by Professor Lewis Gates. Under Gates's watchful eye, Norris began work on his first two novels: *Vandover and the Brute* and *McTeague*.

After a year at Harvard, Norris returned to San Francisco, taking a job with the *Chronicle* as a special correspondent. He persuaded the paper to send him to South Africa, where he covered the beginnings of the South African War. Norris's reports from the strife-torn land were not memorable, but the tropical fever he contracted would later contribute to his death.

Library of Congress

Norris next joined the staff of the San Francisco *Wave*, then under the editorship of John O'Hara Cosgrave. As an assistant editor, Norris wrote short stories, reviewed books and art exhibits, and composed feature stories to fill the pages of the weekly newspaper. He found it impossible to work for extended periods of time, however, and interrupted his employment at least twice: once to journey to the Big Dipper Mine near Colfax, California, where he finished *McTeague*; another time to begin work on his third novel, *Moran of the Lady Letty*. He found no trouble selling the first installments of this new novel to the magazines, and as it was running, the story caught the eye of S. S. McClure, who invited Norris to join the staff of Doubleday as a reader. The position paid poorly and offered little status, but Norris took it anyway, perhaps because it allowed him time to finish *Moran of the Lady Letty* and begin other projects as well. After a time, however, Norris began to hate his self-imposed poverty and, at the outbreak of the Spanish-American War, begged McClure to send him to Cuba to cover the conflict as a correspondent for *McClure's Magazine*. McClure agreed; Norris went to Cuba, met Stephen Crane, suffered another attack of fever, and was forced to return to New York. *McClure's Magazine* did not publish any of Norris's war reports.

Never sure of his status with McClure, Norris left the firm in 1899 to join the newly founded firm of Doubleday, Page and Company, again as a part-time, poorly paid reader. He wrote *Blix* and *A Man's Woman* and began *The Octopus* during this time, and he also married Jeannette Black. His major contribution to the firm came when

Theodore Dreiser's *Sister Carrie* (1900) was submitted; Norris read the novel in manuscript and insisted upon its publication. After a contract was signed, Doubleday raised objections to the novel and tried to cancel publication. Norris counseled Dreiser to stand firm and insist that his contract be upheld, whereupon Doubleday issued *Sister Carrie* in a limited edition and allowed it quickly to go out of print.

As Norris's royalties grew from the sale of his own novels, he found the financial independence to return to California, and he made plans to purchase a ranch in the southern range of the Santa Cruz mountains. He completed *The Pit*, the second book in his projected trilogy of wheat novels, and planned a journey to the tropics with his wife. That journey was interrupted, however, when Jeannette underwent surgery to remove an inflamed appendix. While she was recovering in the hospital, Norris, too, began suffering stomach pains. Thinking it only a minor ailment, he refused to go to a doctor until he became seriously ill. Suffering from peritonitis and weakened by fever, Norris entered Mt. Zion hospital in San Francisco and died there on October 25, 1902, at the age of thirty-two.

Analysis • Norris was one of a handful of writers at the turn of the century who applied the literary naturalism of Émile Zola to American subjects and themes. As a writer in this tradition, Norris treated his subject matter brutally but sincerely. His characters are but pawns, driven by outside forces over which they have no control. Devoid of souls, they are helpless creatures determined by their heredity and environment. In Norris's most successful novels, these naturalistic ideas are employed with great faithfulness, and his depiction of human beings following a slow but almost inevitable course toward destruction has an enduring power.

Norris's fiction underwent various stages of development. In *McTeague* and *Vandover and the Brute*, Norris focused his attentions on the naturalistic novel of character, where both McTeague and Vandover proceed slowly toward their almost inevitable destruction. In Norris's next three novels, *Moran of the Lady Letty*, *Blix*, and *A Man's Woman*, he bowed to social pressure: Moral values overwhelm deterministic forces in these inferior works. In Norris's last two novels, *The Octopus* and *The Pit*, he again returned to naturalistic themes, but in a broader, more worldly sense, showing greater compassion and involvement with his characters. The progression from *Vandover and the Brute*, a highly dispassionate view of one man's descent, to *The Pit*, which analyzes the social forces at work in the wheat industry, marks Norris's own maturation as both a writer and a man, and his increasingly complex worldview.

Vandover and the Brute • Written while Norris was still in college, *Vandover and the Brute* is concerned with moral weakness. It is the story of a wealthy man who, unable to sustain his ambition to become an artist, descends to a bestial level. As a study of moral and physical disintegration, the novel follows a characteristically didactic naturalistic course. Vandover's descent is governed by a series of chance events and hastened by his own flawed heredity. Because his position in society allows it, Vandover leads a life of pointless leisure. Unable to focus his desire to become an artist, he starts gambling, drinking, and leading a loose sexual life. A chance cut on his lip, followed by an unwanted kiss from Flossie (who by chance has contracted syphilis), passes a venereal disease to Vandover and eventually causes lycanthropy.

With the aid of Professor Le Conte's classes in science, Norris was able to research the disease that plagued Vandover. His careful analysis led to Vandover's realistic progression toward lycanthropy, which begins with the suicide of Ida Wade, one of the girls whom Vandover has seduced. Soon after Ida's death, Vandover's father dies, an event that seems to give Vandover direction, but the beast within him soon triumphs, the disease is allowed to run its course, and Vandover becomes a wretched, broken man. The novel concludes with Vandover cleaning the cheap houses Norris's father built for the San Francisco working class, although in the novel, the houses belonged to Vandover.

McTeague • *McTeague* was written soon after the completion of *Vandover and the Brute*; like Norris's first book, it emphasizes themes of chance, disintegration, and heredity. The novel is a study of the temperaments of two characters: McTeague, a scoundrel born in a California mining town, and Trina Sieppe, a working-class girl whose hoarding instincts eventually overcome her.

As the novel begins, McTeague is working with his father in the California mines. A traveling dentist arrives shortly after McTeague's father dies, and the young boy is apprenticed to the dentist so that he might learn a trade. McTeague is not bright enough to learn much—the result of his heredity—but he eventually learns enough to survive, and when his mother dies, he sets up dental parlors in San Francisco. The rich descriptive detail with which Norris renders McTeague's surroundings greatly contributes to the success of the novel.

McTeague is well satisfied with his existence: The earnings from his practice keep him supplied with a daily glass of steam beer and allow him enough leisure time to practice his concertina and socialize infrequently with his friends, among them Marcus Schouler, who lives in the flat above McTeague. Chance, however, intervenes in McTeague's ordered existence when Marcus's girlfriend, Trina, breaks a tooth, and Marcus brings her to McTeague for treatment. While they wait in the parlors, Trina buys a lottery ticket from the cleaning woman—a ticket that will later be worth five thousand dollars.

McTeague falls in love with Trina at first sight, and Marcus, rather than fighting for his girl, aids McTeague in courting her, even to the point of introducing him to Trina's parents. The path paved, McTeague asks Trina to marry him, and, on the day the announcement is made public, Trina wins the money through the lottery. It is this chance event that sparks Trina's inherited passion for hoarding, first evident on the day of the lottery payment when Trina, to McTeague's dismay, decides not to spend her winnings on a nice apartment, but rather to save the money. This first clash of temperaments leads to others as McTeague and Trina continue toward their eventual disintegration.

At first, Trina and McTeague are happy; they move into a flat across from the dental parlors and live comfortably. McTeague's ambitions to live in more spacious quarters, however, conflict with Trina's thrifty attitudes. Marcus reenters their lives; embittered by McTeague's good fortune, he attacks McTeague with a knife. This first conflict arouses physical violence in both men only briefly, but during their second encounter, which begins as a friendly wrestling match at the park, Marcus bites off McTeague's earlobe and McTeague retaliates by breaking Marcus's arm. After the incident, Marcus leaves the city, but not before first notifying the authorities that McTeague is practicing dentistry without proper credentials.

Stripped of his profession, McTeague loses his income, thus exacerbating his conflict with Trina over the management of their money. The animal within him brought to the surface, McTeague is no longer able to cope with his environment or with Trina's hoarding, which has become obsessive. He deserts Trina and then comes back and steals her money. After he has spent all the money, McTeague returns to Trina for more. This time, however, he beats her so mercilessly that she dies. Taking her entire lottery winnings, McTeague flees the city for the gold mines and his birthplace. He is followed, however, and forced to flee again, to Death Valley, where he again meets Marcus. This time, however, the struggle their encounter precipitates is fatal to both.

The parallels between *McTeague* and *Vandover and the Brute* are numerous. Both novels owe their genesis to the idea of human degeneracy: *Vandover and the Brute* is the story of one man's descent into the abyss; *McTeague* shows how the interaction of two characters hastens their descent. Chance also plays an important part in both novels. Vandover's cut lip becomes Trina's broken tooth; gambling for Vandover becomes the lottery for Trina. Life itself is a gigantic lottery; Norris is emphatic when he labels the agent of the lottery a "man of the world."

By separating himself from his characters in *McTeague*, Norris was able to deal objectively with the impact of instinct and chance upon them. McTeague becomes an animal—a brute from the mines. Trina, too, crippled by her hoarding instinct both physically (her fingers are amputated) and mentally, becomes little more than an animal, defending her gold as a wolf might defend its kill. *McTeague* is Norris's most powerful and successful novel; his rendering of the seamy, bestial side of human life is masterful.

Moran of the Lady Letty • *Moran of the Lady Letty* was Norris's third novel in manuscript, but his first in print. Unlike his first two books, *Moran of the Lady Letty* emphasizes the idyllic side of San Francisco: its festive life and colors and the invigorating wind from the Pacific. The story of a strong, primitive woman and an overcivilized man, the novel lacks the realistic intensity of *McTeague*; it is in many ways merely a popular romance.

Ross Wilbur is, like Vandover, a wealthy man. He spends every waking moment attending "functions": teas, cotillions, parties, and other festive gatherings of society. He also enjoys life at the docks and often spends time there gazing at the ships setting out to sea. One day, his shipwatching activities prove perilous, as Wilbur finds himself drugged and kidnaped aboard a filthy schooner piloted by a brutal captain and manned by an unsavory Chinese crew. Wilbur awakens to face the filth of the cabin and a new life aboard the *Bertha Milner*. Quickly, he shows his adaptive abilities as he adjusts to his new environment, hastened by a smashing blow to the chin by the half-civilized captain. As he adjusts to his new life, Wilbur also learns the intricacies of navigation (as Norris did when writing the novel) and the wonders of the sea, including the excitement of a sea-turtle chase. Life, it seems, is not so bad after all.

Soon after weighing anchor, the Chinese crew sights a ship at sea. The captain realizes that the bark they have sighted, the *Lady Letty*, is deserted save for its dead captain and his half-dead daughter, Moran. Consumed with greed, Captain Kitchell plots a salvage of the *Lady Letty* and her cargo, and Moran's murder, too, should she stand in his way. The greed that destroyed Trina in *McTeague* also kills Kitchell, however, when, while he is drunk aboard the *Lady Letty*, a sudden squall sinks the ship. Wilbur and Moran are suddenly left to fend for themselves aboard the *Bertha Milner* with her Chinese crew.

The strange adventures that follow serve to further Wilbur's advancement to manhood. Encountering a Chinese junk, Wilbur and Moran become embroiled in a battle with its crew over a piece of ambergris. In the heat of the battle, Moran mistakes

Wilbur for the enemy, and he is forced to subdue her physically. She melts at his physical prowess and surrenders to him. Ross Wilbur, at last, through the vigorous life of the sea, has become a man. In keeping with the theme of the novel—that civilization and social convention are corrupting—Wilbur's softness, brought on by society's overcivilization, is defeated. He has overcome Moran, who knows only the law of the strongest, and has vanquished her according to her own rules.

Except for the naturalistic details of sheer strength and primitive passions and a few realistic descriptive passages, *Moran of the Lady Letty* is little more than "a corking good story," as Norris described it. He followed similar popular conventions in his next two novels, *Blix* and *A Man's Woman*, before returning in a more ambitious fashion to the naturalistic formulas he so ably employed in *McTeague*.

The Octopus and The Pit • The third stage of Norris's development as a novelist came about with his projected trilogy on the wheat industry. In the first novel of the trilogy, *The Octopus*, Norris returned to naturalistic formulas. In *The Octopus*, the wheat is planted, grown, and harvested. In *The Pit*, the wheat is traded and taken to market. In *The Wolf*, the planned but never written conclusion to the trilogy, the wheat would be consumed by the hungry masses of Europe. Norris did not live to complete this third book. When he died in 1902, the second volume was only then being serialized.

The Octopus and *The Pit* both deal with the problems of society as a whole rather than with the individual. Although Norris was successful in remaining true to his theme in *The Octopus*, the theme and naturalistic treatment is blurred somewhat in *The Pit* by a dual story: the trading of wheat in the Chicago Board of Trade and the love story featuring the protagonists of the novel, Curtis Jadwin and Laura Dearborn.

Jadwin, a weak, irresolute man, is a famous capitalist speculator. A taker of chances, he manages for a time to corner the wheat market and enjoy financial prosperity. His fortunes are wiped out, however, when the wheat crops of the West are harvested. Helpless in the face of vast economic forces that he cannot control—and helpless too in the face of his own heredity, which has forced upon him an uncontrollable urge to gamble—Jadwin is destroyed.

There is another story in *The Pit*, however, which runs concurrent to the story of Jadwin's business: the story of the love between Jadwin and Laura, his wife. Laura feels alone and deserted when Jadwin occupies himself in the pit, completely absorbed in the business of trading wheat, and so has an affair with Sheldon Corthell, a superficial artist. The collapse of Jadwin's fortune in wheat breaks him completely, and, with nowhere else to turn, he reasserts his love for Laura. The novel ends, anticlimactically, with Laura and Jadwin facing west, ready to begin life anew. Thus, although powerful in its conception, Norris's last novel is not equal to his best work. He largely neglects his theme (the wheat is rarely physically present in the novel), abandoning naturalistic forces in favor of a love story with autobiographical overtones.

At his best when objectively and dispassionately analyzing his characters and allowing them to be subjected, like pawns, to the naturalistic forces of the universe, Norris faltered when he became too closely involved with his subject. When as in *Blix*, *Moran of the Lady Letty*, and *The Pit*, romantic themes are allowed to gain paramount importance, Norris's naturalistic intentions and power are subverted. Norris was more, however, than a didactic sociologist in the guise of a novelist. His best work is characterized by a faithful reproduction of setting, by creative exuberance. Thus, one does not merely read about Polk Street in *McTeague*, or the San Joaquin Valley in *The Octopus*, or the Board of Trade in *The Pit*, but one also breathes the air of these places, smells their pungent smells. It is this fundamental sense of reality that gives Norris's fiction a lasting appeal.

David Mike Hamilton

Other major works

SHORT FICTION: *A Deal in Wheat, and Other Stories of the New and Old West*, 1903; *The Joyous Miracle*, 1906; *The Third Circle*, 1909; *Frank Norris of "The Wave,"* 1931 (Oscar Lewis, editor).

POETRY: *Yvernelle: A Tale of Feudal France*, 1892; *Two Poems and "Kim" Reviewed*, 1930.

NONFICTION: *The Responsibilities of the Novelist*, 1903; *The Surrender of Santiago*, 1917; *The Letters of Frank Norris*, 1956; *The Literary Criticism of Frank Norris*, 1964.

MISCELLANEOUS: *The Complete Edition of Frank Norris*, 1928.

Bibliography

Boyd, Jennifer. *Frank Norris Spatial Form and Narrative Time*. New York: Peter Lang, 1993. Chapters on all of Norris's novels, with discussions of his pictorialism, his relationship to Émile Zola and naturalism, and the structures of his longer fictional works. Includes notes and bibliography.

Dillingham, William. *Frank Norris: Instinct and Art*. Lincoln: University of Nebraska Press, 1969. This study comprises a biographical sketch and a survey of Norris's work. Dillingham argues that certain attitudes of the academicians, such as hard work and close observation, influenced Norris's conception of painting and writing. Stresses naturalism. Includes an annotated bibliography.

Graham, Don. *The Fiction of Frank Norris: The Aesthetic Context*. Columbia: University of Missouri Press, 1978. This volume is one of the few studies concerning itself with the aesthetics of Norris's work. Much attention is given to his four most literary novels—*Vandover and the Brute*, *McTeague*, *The Octopus*, and *The Pit*. Includes an excellent bibliography.

_____, comp. *Critical Essays on Frank Norris*. Boston: G. K. Hall, 1980. A collection of reviews and essays aimed at presenting Norris as a vital and still undefined writer. Among the contributors are Norris's contemporaries William Dean Howells, Willa Cather, and Hamlin Garland. Literary critics include Donald Pizer and William Dillingham.

McElrath, Joseph R., Jr. "Beyond San Francisco: Frank Norris's Invention of Northern California." In *San Francisco in Fiction: Essays in a Regional Literature*, edited by David Fine and Paul Skenazy. Albuquerque: University of New Mexico Press, 1995. A discussion of the romantic transformation of the San Joaquin Valley in Norris's local-color sketches, as well as his treatment of San Francisco in some of his novels.

_____. *Frank Norris: A Descriptive Bibliography*. Pittsburgh: University of Pittsburgh Press, 1992. Very useful and full guide to published sources on Norris.

_____. *Frank Norris Revisited*. New York: Twayne, 1992. An updating and rewriting of a volume that first appeared in 1962 under the authorship of Warren French. This introductory study includes a chapter on the "novelist in the making," followed by subsequent chapters that discuss each of Norris's novels. Includes a chronology, notes, and an annotated bibliography.

McElrath, Joseph R., Jr., and Jesse S. Crisler. *Frank Norris: A Life*. Urbana: University of Illinois Press, 2006. A rarely seen glimpse into the life of Frank Norris and his writings on nineteenth century America.

Marchand, Ernest. *Frank Norris: A Study*. Stanford, Calif.: Stanford University Press, 1942. The first full-length critical study of Norris, this overview situates Norris's work against a social and intellectual, as well as a literary, background. Considers a wide variety of critical opinions about Norris's fiction. Excellent bibliography.

Walker, Franklin. *Frank Norris: A Biography*. New York: Russell and Russell, 1932. The first full-length biography of Norris, this study is uncritical of its subject. Extraordinarily detailed. Contains personal interviews with Norris's family and friends.

Joyce Carol Oates

Born: Lockport, New York; June 16, 1938

Principal long fiction • *With Shuddering Fall*, 1964; *A Garden of Earthly Delights*, 1967, revised 2003; *Expensive People*, 1968; *them*, 1969; *Wonderland*, 1971; *Do with Me What You Will*, 1973; *The Assassins: A Book of Hours*, 1975; *Childwold*, 1976; *The Triumph of the Spider Monkey*, 1976; *Son of the Morning*, 1978; *Cybele*, 1979; *Unholy Loves*, 1979; *Bellefleur*, 1980; *Angel of Light*, 1981; *A Bloodsmoor Romance*, 1982; *Mysteries of Winterthurn*, 1984; *Solstice*, 1985; *Marya: A Life*, 1986; *Lives of the Twins*, 1987 (as Rosamond Smith); *You Must Remember This*, 1987; *American Appetites*, 1989; *Soul/Mate*, 1989 (as Smith); *Because It Is Bitter, and Because It Is My Heart*, 1990; *I Lock My Door upon Myself*, 1990; *Nemesis*, 1990 (as Smith); *The Rise of Life on Earth*, 1991; *Black Water*, 1992; *Snake Eyes*, 1992 (as Smith); *Foxfire: Confessions of a Girl Gang*, 1993; *What I Lived For*, 1994; *You Can't Catch Me*, 1995 (as Smith); *Zombie*, 1995; *First Love*, 1996; *We Were the Mulvaneys*, 1996; *Man Crazy*, 1997; *My Heart Laid Bare*, 1998; *Broke Heart Blues*, 1999; *Starr Bright Will Be with You Soon*, 1999 (as Smith); *Blonde*, 2000; *Middle Age: A Romance*, 2001; *The Barrens*, 2001 (as Smith); *Beasts*, 2002; *I'll Take You There*, 2002; *Rape: A Love Story*, 2003; *The Tattooed Girl*, 2003; *The Falls*, 2004; *Missing Mom*, 2005; *Black Girl/White Girl*, 2006.

Other literary forms • Joyce Carol Oates's first play, *Miracle Play*, appeared in 1974, and others opened later to appreciative audiences. In addition, her short-story anthologies were published with regularity. They include *By the North Gate* (1963), which predated her first novel; *Upon the Sweeping Flood* (1966); *The Wheel of Love* (1970); *Marriages and Infidelities* (1972); *The Goddess and Other Women* (1974); *The Hungry Ghosts* (1974); *Where Are You Going, Where Have You Been?* (1974); *The Poisoned Kiss* (1975); *The Seduction* (1975); *Crossing the Border* (1976); *Night-Side* (1977); *All the Good People I've Left Behind* (1978); *A Sentimental Education* (1980); *Last Days* (1984); *Raven's Wing* (1986); *The Assignation* (1988); *Where Is Here?* (1992); and many others. Her poems have also been anthologized, and in 1974 Oates and her husband founded *The Windsor Review*. Although Oates is often recognized as one of America's primary writers of imaginative literature, she also is a highly respected reviewer and critic.

Some of Oates's best literary criticism is collected in *New Heaven, New Earth: The Visionary Experience in Literature* (1974) and *(Woman) Writer: Occasions and Opportunities* (1988). Oates is the editor of several anthologies, including *Night Walks* (1982) and *First Person Singular* (1983). She has also produced books on subjects as diverse as art and boxing, and has written widely on modern literature, collecting thirty-eight pieces from *The New York Review of Books*, *The Times Literary Supplement*, and *The New York Times Book Review* into *Uncensored: Views and (Re)views* (2005). Her extensive expression as a writer, thinker, and teacher have ensured her role as a respected and vigorous participant in American intellectual and literary life.

Achievements • As a prolific writer and as a teacher, Oates has collected numerous and varied prizes. Among them are the 1967, 1969, and 1973 O. Henry Prize Awards, the Richard and Hinda Rosenthal Award of the National Institute of Arts and Letters (1968), the National Book Award for 1970, and the Lotos Club Award of Merit (1975).

© Norman Seeff

In 1990 she received the Rea Award for the short story and the Alan Swallow award for her 1988 short-story collection *The Assignation.* She continued her prolific writing output into the twenty-first century, with novels such as *Blonde,* for which she won her National Book Award in 2001; *I'll Take You There,* and *The Falls,* as well as the short-story collections *Faithless: Tales of Transgression* (2001) and *I Am No One You Know* (2004). In 2003, she received the Common Wealth Award for Distinguished Service in Literature.

Biography • Joyce Carol Oates was born on June 16, 1938, in Lockport, New York. She received a modest education in a one-room schoolhouse and, as a child, had very little exposure to literature. This, however, did not quell her desire to write, and she spent much of her time as a child writing stories and short books. Even with all the writing and composing experience from her childhood, she would not publish her first story until 1959. While studying at Syracuse University, she won the *Mademoiselle* college fiction award for her short story "In the Old World." This would be her first in a series of public recognitions for her writing.

After receiving her bachelor's degree from Syracuse in 1960, where she was valedictorian, she went on to receive her master's degree from the University of Wisconsin. During her term at Syracuse, she had met her future husband, Raymond J. Smith, and they married in 1961. The Smiths then moved to Beaumont, Texas, and Oates began to work on her doctoral degree at Rice University. She would never accomplish this task; she and her husband moved to Michigan in 1962. While in Michigan, she taught English at the University of Detroit until 1967, when she and her husband began teaching at the University of Windsor in Ontario. During their tenure at the university, Smith and Oates cofounded *The Windsor Review.* After leaving the university in 1978, she went on to join the Princeton University Creative Writing Program. While a member of this program, she wrote not only fiction but also some brilliant essays on writers ranging from William Shakespeare to Norman Mailer.

Oates's teaching career proved rich and rewarding. In 1987 she was appointed Roger S. Berlin Distinguished Professor in the Humanities at Princeton. In addition to serving on the faculty at Princeton, Oates traveled extensively, often undertaking her journeys to bring attention to her most recently published novels and short-story collections. Throughout the years she gave public readings of her works and appeared as the keynote speaker at various national and international conferences. After joining the Princeton faculty she also toured Eastern Europe under the auspices of the U.S. Information Agency.

Analysis • There have been few writers to match Oates for sheer numbers—her novels, plays, short stories, and poems appear to multiply by themselves on library shelves. However, even though the curse of quantity is normally mediocrity, Oates consistently supplies a product of the highest quality, dense with meaning and filled with beautiful words and full-blown characters.

Oates's poor, unimaginative characters typically ply their swords through a fogged-in existence inflicted upon them by a fatalistic creator. They cannot escape from the miasma they must breathe, and so they are poisoned by it, confused by muddled thoughts in an unkind world. The characters finally become enraged by their situation and so do bloody battle to extricate themselves from it.

With Shuddering Fall • In her first novel, *With Shuddering Fall*, Oates introduces a theme that would pervade almost all the rest of her fiction works: the awful responsibility of freedom. Her characters struggle to divest themselves of their little lives in order to achieve personal freedom, but they are unable to cope with the consequences of their release from their former lives. They learn that they have abandoned not only their pasts but also their identities. Then they must struggle either to reclaim their selves or to forge new ones.

With Shuddering Fall is one character's reconciliation with her life, and this treaty gains for her a new appreciation of her history and that of her family. Karen must endure a sort of familiar ritual under the hands of her father, Hert, and her lover, Shar. At first Karen rejects her father's values. He is a legendary figure who wields great power and enjoys a close relationship with Karen; however, this is destroyed by the arrival of the violent, virile Shar who deposes Hert. Shar is not a new ruler, however, but an anarchist who wishes only to topple kings, not replace them. He leaves, and Karen follows, not because she believes in him but because she seeks to escape Hert and "a life dominated by fathers." After being free from her father, Karen begins to feel uprooted, aimless and nameless. Without Hert, she has "nothing of herself but a face, a body, a set of emotions." She discovers that she needs her familial history to add meaning to her identity and so finally refuses the history-less Shar and his attempts at nihilism.

One of these trials is Shar's proclivity for race-car driving in the lowland town of Cherry River. Cherry River is a town that seems to exist for the edification of the summer tourists and little else. It offers appreciation of self-gratification but not of history. The high point of the summer seems to be when Shar commits suicide on the race track. Oates shows that in a community with no shared history, the only communal ties that exist are with shared acts of violence.

The spokesperson for the novel is Max, a self-centered businessman, who is the only one intelligent enough to share Oates's philosophy with the reader. He appears in many other novels as the maniacal oracle who tries to make fate subservient to his will. He tries to cheat Karen of her birthright by confounding her with questions, but she eludes him and is, thus, saved. She returns to herself, her family.

Expensive People • *Expensive People* opens with the fictional narrator explaining to the reader that he is telling the truth. Richard Everett begins by setting up a paradox because nothing he "tells" can ever be the truth since everything in the book is imagined. He goes on to explain he is—or was—a child murderer in the sense that when he was young, he killed someone. *Expensive People* is written as a memoir, a memoir of someone who does not exist. In fact, Everett confesses that "it's possible that I'm lying without knowing it."

If *Expensive People* appears to be a parody of comic nihilism, of the nothingness of suburban life, it is. From Ernest Hemingway to John Barth, Oates pokes fun at those serious authors who proclaim the world to be formless and empty. Everett's mother, ironically nicknamed Nada, writes in her journal: "[I]n any first-person narration there can be a lot of freedom. Certain central events—what the hell can they be?— leading up to the death," certainly no less a self-criticism of the very novel she is in as well as those she despises for their negativism.

If Nada consoles herself with her own writing, poor Richard has little with which to comfort himself, unless it is the thought of his mother's death. He is convinced that she hates him, despite his near genius I.Q., and wishes to stave off his affections with a series of unwanted puppies. Finally, Richard's fantasies of matricide become confused with reality. In the end, the newspapers show nothing of Nada, only of their house. Richard fades into closure of the book.

Wonderland • It is not chance that Lewis Carroll's child adventure and Oates's novel *Wonderland* bear the same word in the title. Oates considers the work of this nine-teenth century English mathematician to ask the pertinent questions of life: Can all of life be just a game, and am I the only one who is not cheating? Both protagonists in the novels—Alice and Jesse Harte—run and jump from square to square on a large, mostly unseen chessboard. Along the way they are both transmogrified into oddly sized versions of their original selves. Finally, in order to survive, Jesse and Alice regain their normal proportions and become resolved with their communities.

In the beginning of the novel, the newly orphaned Jesse travels from his grandfather's farm to an orphanage and finally to the home of Dr. Pedersen, a brilliant but unbalanced surrogate father. He is the first of a triumvirate of adoptive fathers whom Jesse must survive. His biological father's initial attack has given Jesse the strength to deal with these surrogates. His father has slaughtered his wife and their unborn child and wounded Jesse before killing himself. Jesse escapes to his grandfather's farm where he recuperates until he must start his strange odyssey. In the Pedersen family, Jesse learns of things small and fantastic. He studies cell life and becomes involved in Dr. Pedersen's cancer research. The more he learns, the more he is confused by his father's view of life, which is overshadowed by death. At last, Pedersen grows impatient with Jesse and dismisses him from the family, saying, "You have no existence. You are nothing." Jesse must seek another, more receptive, lifestyle.

Jesse enters medical school, graduates, marries, and tries to forge a new family, a home, for himself. He keeps returning, however, to the site of his father's tragic demise in his dreams. His own children gradually start to shrink away like the Cheshire Cat. Michelle becomes Shelley and ultimately Shell, until Jesse can no longer grasp her—or the rest of his family—with any degree of certitude. Even Jesse's two father-figures, Cady and Perrault, become in turn distant and disdainful. Dr. Cady will not acknowledge anything but the ethereal, and Dr. Perrault will not admit that the mind is anything but actual. These two opposing views further succeed in alienating Jesse from a "real" life. To offset these unrealistic real people, Jesse creates an unreal friend, or series of friends, but she only promises disharmony and death, so he eventually rejects her, too.

In the end of the novel, the action quickens, racing toward the now of the narrative, 1971. Jesse returns to his father's psyche and discovers the final, perfect answer: "A clean, pure, empty being, a void." It is only through the total destruction of the universe that a peaceful existence (or nonexistence) can be enjoyed.

Childwold • The setting of *Childwold* is again Eden Valley, scene of the action in *With Shuddering Fall* and *Wonderland*. The novel is peopled by a variety of characters and is narrated by several of them in turn, as each becomes the lover of the central figure's mother, Arlene Bartlett. Arlene's daughter, Laney Bartlett, is the unconscious catalyst for much of the violence in the novel.

The primary reaction between Laney and another character occurs between her and Fitz John Kasch, a fiftyish hermit who lives among the debris of his large but deceased family. In Laney, Kasch sees not only his failed marriage but also his repressed desires. She becomes for him both an icon and a Tantalus, love and passion. Unable to avail himself of her, Kasch woos and wins Arlene and becomes another in a lengthy retinue of lovers.

Arlene is a figure of the sex goddess, but, unlike so many untouchable figures, she is the small statue in the back of the church, worn down by the grasp of many hands. This, however, does not dismay her; indeed, it invigorates her. Where many single women would not welcome pregnancy, Arlene revels in it; her children reaffirm her existence in a world of many people. Kasch, on the other hand, is unable to enjoy the company of others. He secrets himself in a small part of what was once the family manse, now a museum. He blames his self-imposed isolation on his divorce, brought on by his former wife's infidelity. Retiring into his hermitage, however, only amplifies his feelings of detachment from life. Although he seeks to redefine himself in various ways (as a voyeur, among others), he remains at one, in harmony with only himself. When he finally becomes reconciled to the Bartletts' violent way of life, he remains unfulfilled. He can satiate himself neither with the daughter nor with the mother.

Instead of an object of violence, of rape or murder, Laney becomes an object of Kasch's creation. It is at this point that *Childwold* most neatly resembles Vladimir Nabokov's *Lolita* (1955)—the story of a middle-aged man's obsession with a nubile, young teen. As did Humbert Humbert, of *Lolita*, Kasch casts a spell about Laney, using art as a medium, but she eventually escapes, moving though the two-dimensional world of Kasch's photographs to the world of nature outside his museum/prison. She frees herself from the world he is doomed to inhabit.

It is a world that is of his own design. After Arlene has joined Kasch, her former lover, Earl Tuller, returns to threaten and bully her. In a rage, Kasch kills him and seals his fate as a prisoner. He has dreamed of being a murderer, but now that his fantasy has been accidentally granted, he is unable to bear the results. He has been defeated by his own desires mixed with the mindless tide of the universe. The novel ends with Arlene musing over the turn their lives have taken. Laney returns to Kasch's mansion, but he will not answer the door. Imagining that she sees him behind a curtained window, she calls out. She feels she is strong enough, has changed enough from the girl that she was, to save him, and so in a flush of anticipation she waits for "a sign, a sign," but it never comes. Oates demonstrates in *Childwold* the tragic consequences of the conflict between humanity's ambitions and the machinations of the world.

Bellefleur • In *Bellefleur*, Oates combines the gothic grotesque and a sense of realism to create a novel that, incredibly, has believable unhuman creatures. If this type of book seems out of character for her, it may be she wishes to warn her audience that what seems extraordinary may, upon examination, be simply ordinary. In one episode, a huge rodent runs screaming into the house; the next morning, it is nothing but a cat. On the other hand, normality might suddenly become monstrous.

Bellefleur traces the history of the Bellefleur family through several generations and as many psychological aberrations. There are psychics in the family, the gnome who serves Leah Bellefleur, and several ghosts. Jedediah Bellefleur is the manifestation in this novel of the character who forces himself to exist against the will of nature. He is a recurring character in Oates's novels, and in *Bellefleur,* Jedediah is delightfully crazy. In the end, he is persuaded to continue the Bellefleur line despite his (and the reader's) misgivings.

The novel is difficult to read, because it jumps back and forth from past to present. Another difficulty stems from the fact that the main character of interest, the telepathic Germaine Bellefleur, ages only four years from her birth during the entire action of the novel, but her father ages two or three decades. The setting of the novel itself—the Adirondack mountain range—ages thousands of years. In addition, the mountains and the people shrink or grow spasmodically. The final chapters contain spiritual references that, at first, seem disjointed. After Gideon's transformation into the skeletal Angel of Death, however, a Native American appears to the ancestral Jedediah and tells him to embrace the world that he has abandoned. This is Oates's final message to the reader, that only in a full and relished life is there union with God's body. Thus, as in her first novel, Oates's characters do battle with their own existences, their own beings. They struggle, escape, and wander only to return to their initial resting places within themselves and within the confines of their destinies.

Mysteries of Winterthurn • The characters in *Mysteries of Winterthurn,* however, appear to have relinquished their resting places for ghostly—and ghastly—forays among the living. This gothic mystery novel has been hailed as a feminist dissertation, a charge that has not been denied by Oates. Although the main character is male and the action in the novel is seen through his eyes, most of the victims are women and children, and it is to their plight that the narrator and the reader grow sympathetic. In *Mysteries of Winterthurn,* Oates discusses the existence of women in a male-dominated society, and a pitiable existence it is.

Even though Oates owes much of her presentation of the situation of nineteenth century women and children to several other popular authors, her interpretation is uniquely her own. Her victims are disposable pawns in a society that is more than willing to sacrifice them for its own (male) devices. Oates inserts the supernatural into the novel to allow her women a modicum of revenge upon these perpetrators. If this seems to be impossible (the unreal attacking the real), Oates insists that once something is thought to be real, it becomes so whether it should be real or not. Thus, the view of women as passive, thoughtless beings is true for the men in her novel, even though it is a false concept. The women victims in the novel are freed by this misconception to react violently to those who misuse them because they (the women) cannot have acted in such a manner within the male scheme of things.

To drive this point home, Oates repeats it three times during the novel. The first story, "The Virgin in the Rose-Bower," deals with a sadistic husband and father, Erasmus Kilgarven, who has a hand in the brutal deaths of his two wives and commits incest for several years with his daughter, Georgina, causing her to become pregnant several times. Georgina kills her infants but claims that they have been destroyed by angels painted on the ceiling of her bedroom. The narrator, young Xavier Kilgarven, sees one painted angel bleed, and this leads to the discovery of several other infant corpses, silent witnesses to Erasmus Kilgarven's hideous habit. By claiming supernatural murder (and rape), Georgina is able to evade guilt and exact a small amount of revenge on her father.

In the persona of Iphigenia, her pen name, Georgina is also able to free her female family members by publishing her poetry. The money she receives from this enterprise, until her father forbids it as unseemly, is later used to finance even more unfeminine exploits by the young Perdita. Perdita needs no spectral avenger; she takes matters into her own hands, although she is never seen as a murderer by anyone but the reader. The only people who are capable of violent acts in *Mysteries of Winterthurn* are men; the women are those upon whom these acts are perpetrated. Thus, an invisible shield is created around Perdita, enabling her to murder several people in order to achieve her goal, union with young Xavier.

The third sister, Thérèse, is able to profit from her sisters' cloaked deeds, and, indeed, there are indications that she may be involved in Perdita's violent crimes in a peripheral manner. This is only hinted at, however; outwardly, Thérèse appears to be a happy, modern woman. It is here that Oates's use of paradox—the woman who is both angel and demon, visible and invisible—culminates. All the women in the novel have been so seduced by the theory of their own guilt that they must violently oppose it in order to free themselves.

Foxfire • Another brilliantly innovative work encompassing Oates's feminist vision is *Foxfire: Confessions of a Girl Gang*. This novel, set in upstate New York during the 1950's, centers on five high school girls who seek and get revenge on the men who exploit them. By chronicling the exploits of the Foxfire gang, which comprises Legs Sadovsky, Goldie, Lana, Rita, and Maddy Wirtz, Oates reveals how male exploitation of women and class conflict consistently reinforce each other. Unlike the female characters in *Mysteries of Winterthurn*, the girl gang members are not paralyzed by their fear, guilt, or insecurity. Finding strength in solidarity, the girls, all from low-income families who daily feel the sting of poverty and the humiliation of male chauvinism, resolve not to suffer at the hands of their exploiters, villains they cast as upper-class white men. The girls, in a wild experiment of role reversal, aggressively seek out their own victims, men who have hurt one or all of them. They subsequently put these men on "trial," and all their victims are "sentenced" to some punishment. By inflicting physical pain or by causing irreversible damage to the men's reputations, the girls see to it that the guilty suffer for the psychic wounds they have caused. Although Oates's sympathies clearly lie with the girls, she mitigates the gang's actions by providing them with an important insight. All the girls come to realize that evil is not strictly the province of men or the upper class; their own acts of violence clearly reveal to them that, tragically, the propensity for harming others exists in all human beings.

What I Lived For • In *What I Lived For,* Jerome "Corky" Corcoran, the main character, makes a discovery similar to that of the Foxfire gang. As Corky bounces from one volatile situation to another throughout the dense, highly intricate plot of the novel, he becomes the principal figure in a modern tragedy. The narrative, an account of the three most intense days of Corky's life, related by the protagonist himself, reveals his participation in situations and relationships that, as they disintegrate before his eyes, challenge all of Corky's beliefs in the innate goodness of humanity. They also force him to revise his opinion, not only of others, but also of himself. Finding himself entangled in these events, which are charged with class conflict, racial tension, political strife, and economic distress, Corky learns that the myths of success, the very myths that he has internalized and employed to sustain his dreams, are false and corrupt. This realization compels him to examine himself, body and soul. He concludes that he too is false and corrupt. He has worshiped the false gods of money and power and has neglected family, religion, and anything else that could have given real meaning and substance to his life. As the narrative proceeds to its tragic conclusion, Oates helps the reader perceive that Corky's flaws are particularly tragic because they are so universal.

My Heart Laid Bare • Like Nabokov's *Lolita*, *My Heart Laid Bare* presents a panorama of vast, gullible America, a jigsaw puzzle of independent states where people can change identities just by crossing a boundary line. The novel is a parodistic epic about a family of confidence artists in nineteenth and early twentieth century America whose careers are largely shaped by the political, financial, and sociological changes of that turbulent period. Oates's catchy (and somewhat misleading) title refers to a memoir her protagonist Abraham Licht intends to write someday but leaves unfinished at his death. Readers who expect to hear a famous woman author's personal confession may feel confused when they find themselves involved with a complicated semihistorical, semigothic, partially tongue-in-cheek story reminiscent of Oates's *Bellefleur*, *A Bloodsmoor Romance*, and *Mysteries of Winterthurn*. Oates called those popular books "parodistic," explaining that "they are not exactly parodies, because they take the forms they imitate quite seriously."

Abraham Licht is the quintessential laissez-faire social Darwinist of the late nineteenth century. He teaches his children that life is an endless struggle for survival, with every individual pitted against every other. Their only allegiance should be to the family, particularly to himself. Every outsider should be regarded as an enemy and potential victim.

Abraham's two oldest sons are temperamentally as different as Cain and Abel. Thurston is tall, handsome, and refined; Harwood is stocky, ugly, and vulgar. Harwood is the only member of the family who is vicious. When Thurston is scheming to make his fortune by marrying a wealthy society matron, the volatile Harwood creates a scene that exposes Thurston as a bounder and an imposter. When the deluded woman interposes between the quarreling brothers, Harwood inadvertently breaks her neck and flees. Thurston has no choice but to do the same—but in a different direction. Only Thurston is captured and, true to his family's code of honor, chooses to be hanged rather than point the finger at his brother. Ultimately, the wily Abraham saves his son by giving him a drug that makes the young man appear dead and spiriting him out of prison in a coffin.

Characters in the novel have a way of disappearing for years and reappearing under different names. Harwood comes back into the saga as Harmon Liges when he befriends Roland Shrikesdale III, a wealthy young tenderfoot vacationing in the Wild West. Harwood conceives a daring scheme based on the fact that he resembles his new friend so closely that they might be taken for twins. He lures his victim into the wilderness, commits a cold-blooded murder, then stumbles back into civilization wearing the dead man's clothing and pretending to be suffering from amnesia. The victim's mother unquestioningly accepts Harwood as her adored child. She has not long to live, and Harwood stands to inherit a large fortune; however, he overplays his hand by inviting Abraham to visit him so that he can show off his affluence and cleverness. The old woman's nephews, who would inherit the fortune if they could prove, as they suspect, that Harwood is an imposter and probably a murderer, investigate and discover the truth about the Lichts. Abraham finds it expedient to disappear when his son's dismembered body is delivered to him in a number of gift-wrapped containers.

In his old age, Abraham finally enters into his first legal marriage. His young bride Rosamund, as might be expected, belongs to a socially prominent family and inherits a fortune. They have a daughter and lead a peaceful life at Muirkirk. Abraham no longer needs to obtain money illegally. He invests all of his own and his wife's capital in corporate stocks. His whole career has been affected by the invisible hand of history, and it ends in disaster with the great Wall Street crash of 1929. During the subsequent Great Depression, he becomes dependent on his son Darian, who ekes out a living as a music teacher and part-time musician. Then Abraham discovers that Darian and Rosamund have fallen in love. This new blow to his inflated ego changes him into a violent psychopath, but he turns his rage against himself by committing suicide in the treacherous marsh after setting the family home afire in a grand old gothic finale.

Jennifer L. Wyatt
Updated by Traci S. Smrcka
and by Bill Delaney

Other major works

SHORT FICTION: *By the North Gate,* 1963; *Upon the Sweeping Flood,* 1966; *The Wheel of Love,* 1970; *Marriages and Infidelities,* 1972; *The Goddess and Other Women,* 1974; *The Hungry Ghosts,* 1974; *Where Are You Going, Where Have You Been?,* 1974; *The Poisoned Kiss,* 1975; *The Seduction,* 1975; *Crossing the Border,* 1976; *Night-Side,* 1977; *All the Good People I've Left Behind,* 1978; *The Lamb of Abyssalia,* 1979; *A Sentimental Education,* 1980; *Last Days,* 1984; *Raven's Wing,* 1986; *The Assignation,* 1988; *Heat, and Other Stories,* 1991; *Where Is Here?,* 1992; *Haunted: Tales of the Grotesque,* 1994; *Will You Always Love Me?,* 1994; *The Collector of Hearts,* 1998; *Faithless: Tales of Transgression,* 2001; *I Am No One You Know,* 2004; *The Female of the Species: Tales of Mystery and Suspense,* 2005; *High Lonesome: Stories, 1966-2006,* 2006.

PLAYS: *Miracle Play,* pr. 1974; *Three Plays,* pb. 1980; *I Stand Before You Naked,* pb. 1991; *In Darkest America: Two Plays,* pb. 1991; *Twelve Plays,* pb. 1991; *The Perfectionist, and Other Plays,* pb. 1995; *New Plays,* pb. 1998.

POETRY: *Women in Love,* 1968; *Anonymous Sins, and Other Poems,* 1969; *Love and Its Derangements,* 1970; *Angel Fire,* 1973; *The Fabulous Beasts,* 1975; *Women Whose Lives Are Food, Men Whose Lives Are Money,* 1978; *Invisible Woman: New and Selected Poems, 1970-1982,* 1982; *The Luxury of Sin,* 1984; *The Time Traveler,* 1989; *Tenderness,* 1996.

NONFICTION: *The Edge of Impossibility: Tragic Forms in Literature,* 1972; *The Hostile Sun: The Poetry of D. H. Lawrence,* 1973; *New Heaven, New Earth: The Visionary Experience in Literature,* 1974; *Contraries: Essays,* 1981; *The Profane Art: Essays and Reviews,* 1983; *On Boxing,* 1987; *(Woman) Writer: Occasions and Opportunities,* 1988; *George Bellows: American Artist,* 1995; *Where I've Been, and Where I'm Going: Essays, Reviews, and Prose,* 1999; *The Faith of a Writer: Life, Craft, Art,* 2003; *Uncensored: Views and (Re)views,* 2005.

CHILDREN'S LITERATURE: *Come Meet Muffin,* 1998; *Big Mouth and Ugly Girl,* 2002; *Freaky Green Eyes,* 2003; *Sexy,* 2005.

EDITED TEXTS: *Scenes from American Life: Contemporary Short Fiction,* 1972; *The Best American Short Stories 1979,* 1979 (with Shannon Ravenel); *Night Walks: A Bedside Companion,* 1982; *First Person Singular: Writers on Their Craft,* 1983; *The Best American Essays,*

1991; *The Oxford Book of American Short Stories,* 1992; *American Gothic Tales,* 1996; *Snapshots: Twentieth Century Mother-Daughter Fiction,* 2000 (with Janet Berliner); *The Best American Mystery Stories,* 2005 (with Otto Penzler).

Bibliography

Cologne-Brookes, Gavin. *Dark Eyes on America: The Novels of Joyce Carol Oates.* Baton Rouge: Louisiana State University Press, 2005. An analysis of selected, significant works wherein Cologne-Brookes attempts to expose Joyce Carol Oates's philosophical and cultural worldviews. Valuable addition to Oates's studies.

Creighton, Joanne V. *Joyce Carol Oates.* Boston: Twayne, 1979. A penetrating exploration of the themes that dominate Oates's work, such as self-definition, isolation, and violent liberation. Creighton devotes a chapter to the experimentalism of five short-story collections. Includes chronology, notes, and an annotated bibliography.

_____. *Joyce Carol Oates: Novels of the Middle Years.* New York: Twayne, 1992. Focusing on Oates's authorial voice and combining critical analysis of Oates's work with the author's own criticism of her work, this study serves as a companion to Creighton's earlier volume (above). Surveying fifteen novels written between 1977 and 1990, Creighton explores the autobiographical elements, feminist subtexts, and realistic dimensions of the novels. Select bibliography.

Johnson, Greg. *Invisible Writer: A Biography of Joyce Carol Oates.* New York: Dutton, 1998. Johnson provides a thorough analysis of Oates's work and life in this full-length authorized biography. Draws on a variety of sources, including Oates's private letters and journals.

_____. *Understanding Joyce Carol Oates.* Columbia: University of South Carolina Press, 1987. Geared to the general reader, this volume examines both Oates's major novels and some of her best-known stories. The focus is more on specific works than on Oates's overarching concerns. Easy to read, with a biography and bibliography.

Pearlman, Mickey, and Katherine Usher Henderson. *Inter/View: Talks with America's Writing Women.* Lexington: University Press of Kentucky, 1990. Numerous interviews with Oates have been published, but this one, conducted by Mickey Pearlman, reveals topics germane to the poetry: class relations, gender relations, and the vital role of memory in her creativity. Oates talks about the biographers (whom Oates labels "pathographers") who ascribe sickness and deviance to women writers, conflating personal and professional lives in a very damaging way.

Wagner, Linda, ed. *Critical Essays on Joyce Carol Oates.* Boston: G. K. Hall, 1979. A good collection of twenty-eight reviews and essays, some on particular works, others on general themes or stylistic considerations. The short stories receive less attention than the novels and even, surprisingly, the poetry. Extensive and evenhanded, with a chronology and bibliography, and a short but refreshing preface by Oates herself.

Wesley, Marilyn. *Refusal and Transgression in Joyce Carol Oates's Fiction.* Westport, Conn.: Greenwood Press, 1993. A feminist analysis, this work focuses on the family as portrayed in Oates's fiction. Wesley contends that the young protagonists of many of Oates's stories and novels commit acts of transgression that serve as critiques of the American family. Wesley maintains that the acts indict the society that produces and supports these unstable, dysfunctional, and often violent, families.

Tim O'Brien

Born: Austin, Minnesota; October 1, 1946

Principal long fiction • *Northern Lights*, 1975; *Going After Cacciato*, 1978, revised 1989; *The Nuclear Age*, 1981 (limited edition), 1985; *In the Lake of the Woods*, 1994; *Tomcat in Love*, 1998; *July, July*, 2002.

Other literary forms • Tim O'Brien wrote magazine and newspaper articles about the Vietnam War while he was a soldier. He published articles on American politics as a reporter for the *Washington Post* in the mid-1970's. Popular magazines and literary quarterlies also published his short stories and essays. *If I Die in a Combat Zone, Box Me Up and Ship Me Home* (1973, revised 1979) contains partially fictionalized memoirs, and *The Things They Carried* (1990) collects short stories that are also closely based upon his tour of duty in Vietnam. Some critics consider these books loosely organized, episodic novels.

Achievements • O'Brien won accolades from war veterans and literary critics for his fiction and memoirs concerning the Vietnam War. In 1976 and 1978 he received the O. Henry Memorial Award for chapters of *Going After Cacciato*, which also earned for him the National Book Award in 1979. He won the Vietnam Veterans of America Award in 1987 and, the same year, the National Magazine Award in Fiction for the short story "The Things They Carried." In 1990, he was awarded the Heartland Prize from the *Chicago Tribune*, and in 1991 he was nominated for both the National Book Critics Circle's Melcher Book Award and the Pulitzer Prize for *The Things They Carried*. He also received France's Prix du Meilleur Livre Étranger for that book and the James Fenimore Cooper Prize of the Society of American Historians for *In the Lake of the Woods*. O'Brien held fellowships from the National Academy of Arts, Breadloaf Writers' Conference, the American Academy of Arts and Letters, and the Guggenheim Foundation.

Biography • William Timothy O'Brien, Jr., was born in Austin, Minnesota, in 1946, placing him among the baby boom generation, which would become eligible for the draft during the Vietnam War (1964-1973). His father was an insurance salesman and a World War II combat veteran; his mother, Ava Schultz O'Brien, was an elementary school teacher. When O'Brien was nine years old, the family, which included a younger sister and brother, moved to Worthington, near the Minnesota-Iowa border, and he grew up there. His childhood, by his own account, was lonely. He played baseball and golf but occupied himself mainly with magic and reading.

After high school, O'Brien attended Macalester College and majored in political science. He participated in protests against the Vietnam War, wrote antiwar editorials for the college newspaper, and canvassed in support of Senator Eugene McCarthy's presidential campaign in 1968. He was elected student-body president his senior year. Immediately after graduating with a bachelor's degree, summa cum laude, he was drafted into the army. Despite his hatred for the war, he quelled the urge to flee to Canada and was trained as an infantryman.

In February, 1969, he arrived at an advanced firebase in Quang Ngai Province, Republic of Vietnam. Nearby was My Lai, a hamlet where troops from O'Brien's division had murdered as many as five hundred civilians in one day. O'Brien, like most Americans, did not learn about the massacre there until one year later. For most of every month his company patrolled a deadly combat zone, battling the Viet Cong and constantly terrified of land mines, disease, and the prospect of appearing cowardly. He saw many wounds and deaths. In fact, he was wounded by shrapnel from a grenade, and his best friend died in a skirmish, two events that deeply affected him. Even before leaving the country, he published accounts of his experience in Minnesota newspapers and *Playboy* magazine.

After his discharge in 1970, O'Brien studied at the Harvard School of Government. In 1973 he published *If I Die in a Combat Zone, Box Me Up and Ship Me Home*, and he joined the staff of the *Washington Post*, reporting on national affairs. He married Ann Elizabeth Weller, an editorial assistant; they divorced eighteen years later. After a year at the *Post*, he returned to his studies at Harvard but left before completing a degree, in order to become a writer. In the meantime he had published his first novel.

After finishing his fourth novel, *In the Lake of the Woods*, in 1994, O'Brien stopped writing, complaining that he was "burned out." With his girlfriend and a *New York Times* photographer, he returned to Vietnam. It was an emotional visit, during which he searched for the Quang Ngai firebase of his infantry company, spoke with Vietnamese veterans, and interviewed survivors of the My Lai massacre. In a famous *New York Times Magazine* article, "The Vietnam in Me" (1994), he told how the experience brought him close to suicide but finally helped him purge some of his anxious obsession with the war. Living in an apartment near Harvard, he resumed writing, in 1998 publishing *Tomcat in Love*. Although the Vietnam War influences the plot, it does so far less than in his previous fiction. O'Brien published his eighth book, *July, July*, in 2002. It follows the lives of the class of 1969 as they return for their thirty-year class reunion. Meanwhile, in 1999, O'Brien began teaching creative writing at Southwest Texas State University.

Analysis • O'Brien draws material for his novels from his own experience. He uses imagination and fiction to find meaning in these experiences, and because he was part of defining events of the post-World War II generation, the passions and ideas in his novels appeal to American readers with broad differences in political allegiance and social background. Having fought in Vietnam, O'Brien can create fictional soldiers so realistic in attitude, speech, and behavior that readers who are veterans of the war readily identify with them. An activist in the antiwar movement of the 1960's, O'Brien likewise draws faithful imitations of the political rebels of the times. A former graduate student in political science and a campaign worker, O'Brien offers fictional politicians convincingly lifelike enough to appeal to the American passion for political scandal. Moreover, coming from a small town in the Midwest, O'Brien (and some of his characters) appears to fulfill a particularly American literary convention: the small-town kid who does well for himself in the outside world. His characters include a university professor, a wealthy geologist, and a lieutenant governor.

Some critics complain that the distinction between historical or personal facts and fiction is blurred in O'Brien's work. Indeed, the "Tim O'Brien" who narrates his two volumes of memoirs is a fictionalized construct, as the author admitted. Similarly, he incorporates historical records, apparently quoted verbatim, in the novel *In the Lake of the Woods.* This mixing of fact and fiction, as well as of memory and fantasy, underlies O'Brien's thematic interests, all of which concern his characters' emotional struggle during events, more than the verisimilitude or logic of the events themselves. The novels are intimately personal, psychological, and exploratory. Among the major themes are the relation between storytelling and truth, father-son relationships, true courage, the psychological effect of war, loneliness, magic, and obsession.

To develop such themes, O'Brien uses narrative techniques that give readers access to the minds of characters, in order to portray their reactions to events in the plot. *Northern Lights, Going After Cacciato,* and *In the Lake of the Woods* are told from the third-person point of view either of an unnamed narrator or of a narrator whom readers are encouraged to identify with the author. This narrator recounts the thoughts and emotions of characters so that readers may empathize with their confusion and obsessions.

Marion Ettlinger/Library of Congress

The Nuclear Age and *Tomcat in Love* both employ the first-person point of view of the main character. Some episodes are told in the present tense and some in the past tense, as the characters reminisce. These techniques enable O'Brien to place the reader even more intimately in the minds of characters and display the tricky, often self-deluding action of memory. Moreover, rapid changes from past to present, changes from one story line to another within a novel's plot, intricate wordplay, and dreamlike sequences immerse readers in the mental states of the principal characters.

O'Brien told interviewers that he was obsessed with American writer Ernest Hemingway as a youth. Hemingway's influence is apparent. O'Brien writes in short, crisp sentences that often derive their power from vivid verbs. He relies on extensive dialogue and uses description more to reflect the impressions of his main characters than to construct a visually detailed setting. Unlike Hemingway, O'Brien frequently uses fragmentary sentences and questions to imitate the thought processes of characters, especially when they are under stress. Cumulatively, his style establishes an energetic narrative pace.

Going After Cacciato • *Going After Cacciato,* O'Brien's second published novel, was his first critical and popular success. A best seller, it quickly earned notice as one of the first serious literary treatments of the Vietnam War, winning the National Book Award in 1979, and it remained a classic statement of the war's bewildering effects on the young Americans drafted to fight there. Paul Berlin, the point-of-view character, is a member of an infantry platoon. With his platoon he chases one of their number who has deserted, Cacciato ("the hunted" in Italian). Cacciato has vowed to escape the war and walk all the way to Paris, a crazy idea that nevertheless earns him admiration among the other soldiers. They catch Cacciato near the Laotian border, and the literal plot is over. While on guard duty, however, Berlin fantasizes. He imagines that Cacciato constantly manages to evade them, and the platoon must pursue him to Paris. He dreams up grotesque adventures in countries along the route, some hilarious escapades, some adolescent sexual fantasies, and some chilling encounters. His fantasies interrupt and blend into the literal story of the chase, giving the narrative a nightmarish quality. Berlin and his fellow soldiers are innocents trapped in a corrupt, bizarre world, but the only character who seems truly courageous in the story is Cacciato. Even though his desertion is a nonsensical gesture, it frees him from the compromises to which the others cling: acceding to the draft, fighting a war that few believe in, conforming so as to not endure shame and disapproval.

In the Lake of the Woods • *In the Lake of the Woods* is O'Brien's most disturbing novel. It is an attempt, he contends, to understand evil. The story opens at the Lake of the Woods in northern Minnesota. John and Kathy Wade are on vacation, trying to knit together an unraveling marriage and lives in disarray. Lieutenant governor of the state, Wade has just lost the primary election for the U.S. Senate because news stories have revealed that he took part in the My Lai massacre in Vietnam. As a soldier, Wade was known as Wizard, a nickname he earned for his magic tricks, but the importance of deception and illusion is deep in his psyche, and he manages to erase most records of his involvement in the massacre, escape court-martial, and keep the secret even from his wife. As the story of his war experience, political career, and family life unfolds, the distinction between truth and the illusions he creates blur in his mind—and in the reader's. However, interrupting the narrative are sections called "Evidence," which contain transcripts of actual court-martial testimony and quotations from history books. These brief sections give the story historical perspective and keep it from turning completely into Wade's illusion.

The war haunts Wade; his failure to maintain protective illusions drives him toward madness. When his wife disappears from their cabin, Wade cooperates with the authorities in searching for her, but it becomes gradually apparent that Wade himself has murdered her. What is not clear, however, is whether he understands what he has done, so lost is he in self-delusions about his past. The end of the book is ambiguous. As the authorities increasingly suspect him of murder, Wade takes a speed boat out onto the lake, and his purpose seems to be to find his wife, escape the law, and commit suicide at the same time. Because this muddled behavior resulted from a lonely childhood and the My Lai massacre, Vietnam is cast as a pervasive, mysterious, malign burden on Wade and his generation.

Tomcat in Love • *Tomcat in Love* is a comic novel in texture but a serious work in intent; it reexamines the themes of love and disaster, storytelling and truth, and obsession. Thomas H. Chippering is a tenured professor of linguistics whose wife has divorced him. Told in flashbacks, the novel is a record of their relationship, beginning in childhood and continuing with marriage, her departure, and his desperate crusade to win her back and to punish her family for causing the divorce. Chippering is pompous, vindictive, pedantic, obsessed with words, and bent on trying to seduce every woman he encounters. He is also blind to his own faults and to the feelings of those around him, while constantly interpreting himself in a suave, heroic light. He has even fabricated a record as a hero in Vietnam to impress others. (Although the war does not dominate the story as it does in O'Brien's previous novel, it does figure in the plot.)

Much of the situational humor originates from Chippering's obvious self-delusions and the ridiculous mistakes he makes about others. His ex-wife spurns him, he loses his faculty position because of student complaints of sexual harassment, he becomes engaged to a woman whose first name he cannot bring himself to use, his ex-brother-in-law publicly humiliates him, and he eventually discovers that his ex-wife, contrary to what he had always believed, is even crazier than he is. Chippering has a few redeeming features that rescue the story from simple farce. His obsession is with the human heart, and he pursues the ambiguities of love with unflagging persistence, much as Miguel de Cervantes' Don Quixote pursued chivalry. In the end, he transcends his obsession and grows spiritually, learning to treat others, women especially, as human beings rather than as objects to manipulate or adore.

Roger Smith

Other major works

SHORT FICTION: *The Things They Carried*, 1990.

NONFICTION: *If I Die in a Combat Zone, Box Me Up and Ship Me Home*, 1973, revised 1979; "The Vietnam in Me," 1994.

Bibliography

Heberle, Mark A. *A Trauma Artist: Tim O'Brien and the Fiction of Vietnam*. Iowa City: University of Iowa Press, 2001. Examination of O'Brien's writings about the American experience in the Vietnam War.

Herzog, Tobey C. *Tim O'Brien*. Boston: Twayne, 1997. Critical biography addressed to informed readers from advanced high school students to university professors. Covers O'Brien's work from *If I Die in a Combat Zone, Box Me Up and Ship Me Home* through *In the Lake of the Woods*. Includes bibliography.

Kaplan, Steven. *Understanding Tim O'Brien*. Columbia: University of South Carolina Press, 1994. Kaplan stresses the importance of storytelling, memory, and imagination in O'Brien's life and fiction. Explicates O'Brien's first five books, particularly their theme of courage. Includes a generous bibliography. A concise, lucid introduction to O'Brien's work.

Lee, Don. "About Tim O'Brien." *Ploughshares* 21 (Winter, 1995/1996): 196-201. A concise and sensitive sketch of O'Brien's life and work through 1994, written on the occasion of O'Brien's guest editorship (with Mark Strand) of a volume of the literary review *Ploughshares*.

O'Brien, Tim. "The Vietnam in Me." *The New York Times Magazine*, October 2, 1994, 48-57. Revealing first-person account of the impact of the Vietnam War on O'Brien's life and prose.

_____. "You Can't Talk with People You Demonize." In *Patriots: The Vietnam War Remembered from All Sides*, edited by Christian G. Appy. New York: Viking, 2003. Another first-hand perspective on the Vietnam War in a broad collection of essays on the American experience in Vietnam.

Smith, Patrick. *Tim O'Brien: A Critical Companion.* Westport, Conn.: Greenwood Press, 2005. Part of the publisher's series of reference books on popular contemporary writers for students, this volume provides detailed plot summaries and analyses of O'Brien's novels, along with character portraits, a biography of O'Brien, and an extensive bibliography.

Tegmark, Mats. *In the Shoes of a Soldier: Communication in Tim O'Brien's Vietnam Narratives.* Uppsala: Ubsaliensis, 1998. A good study of problematic communication in O'Brien's writings on Vietnam. Includes a bibliography and index.

Vernon, Alex. *Soldiers Once and Still: Ernest Hemingway, James Salter, and Tim O'Brien.* Iowa City: University of Iowa Press, 2004. Comparative study of the war stories of representatives of three generations of American novelists.

Flannery O'Connor

Born: Savannah, Georgia; March 25, 1925
Died: Milledgeville, Georgia; August 3, 1964

Principal long fiction • *Wise Blood*, 1952; *The Violent Bear It Away*, 1960.

Other literary forms • Flannery O'Connor, most renowned as a writer of short fiction, published the short-story collection *A Good Man Is Hard to Find* in 1955; her canon also includes two posthumous collections, *Everything That Rises Must Converge* (1965) and *The Complete Stories* (1971). Three posthumous nonfiction works provide insight into her craft and thought: *Mystery and Manners* (1969), a collection of her occasional lectures and essays on literary art; *The Habit of Being: Letters* (1979), which consists of letters compiled by her literary executor, Sally Fitzgerald; and *The Presence of Grace* (1983), a collection of her book reviews.

Achievements • O'Connor's art was best suited to the medium of the short story, where her sharp, shocking, and grotesque characterizations could have full impact on the reader. Nevertheless, her depiction of the Christ-haunted Hazel Motes in *Wise Blood* ranks as the most memorable and piercing postmodern delineation of Western society's anxiety over God's absence. O'Connor's ability to create supernatural tension, to provoke the potentially hostile reader into considering the possibility of divine invasion of the human sphere, is unparalleled by any postwar writer. Seeing "by the light of Christian orthodoxy," O'Connor refused to chisel away or compromise her convictions to make them more congenial to her readers. She knew that it is difficult to place the Christian faith in front of the contemporary reader with any credibility, but her resolve was firm. She understood, in the words of the late John Gardner (*On Moral Fiction*, 1978), that "art which tries to tell the truth unretouched is difficult and often offensive," since it "violates our canons of politeness and humane compromise." O'Connor succeeded not in making Christianity more palatable but in making its claims unavoidable.

O'Connor was committed not only to telling the "truth unretouched" but also to telling a good story. This meant rejecting predetermined morals—homilies tacked onto stories and processed uncritically by her readers: "When you can state the theme of a story, when you can separate it from the story itself, then you can be sure the story is not a very good one." Instead of literary proselytizing, she offered a literature of evangelism, of incarnation, a fusing of literary form with authorial vision. Her evangelistic mode was not proselytizing, but *proclaiming*, the ancient and more honorable practice of declaring news, of heralding its goodness to a usually indifferent, sometimes hostile audience. O'Connor had a keen perception of her audience's mindset and cultural milieu; her proclamation was calculated to subvert the habitualization of faith and to make such notions as redemption, resurrection, and eternal life seem new and strange to a Western society that had reduced them to commonplaces empty of significance. Readers and critics continue to respond to O'Connor's clear spiritual vision and piercing narrative style, a style uncluttered by a false pluralism or sectarian debate. O'Connor, a devout Roman Catholic, neither

Courtesy, Georgia College & State University, Special Collections

preached nor compelled; she simply proclaimed.

O'Connor won a Kenyon Review fellowship in fiction in 1953, a National Institute of Arts and Letters grant in 1957, and an O. Henry first prize in short fiction in 1957. She also was granted honorary degrees from St. Mary's College (1962) and Smith College (1963). She spent the last months of her life completing the stories eventually published in her posthumous collection *Everything That Rises Must Converge*. *The Complete Stories* won the National Book Award for Fiction in 1971.

Biography • Mary Flannery O'Connor was born in Savannah, Georgia, in 1925 and moved with her mother to Milledgeville, Georgia, in 1938. She took her bachelor's degree from Women's College of Georgia in 1945 and received an M.F.A. degree from the State University of Iowa in 1947. She published her first short story, "The Geranium" (*Accent*, 1946), during her years in Iowa. In 1947, she won the Rinehart-Iowa fiction award for a first novel with a portion of *Wise Blood*.

On the strength of this award and her promise as a writer, O'Connor was offered a fellowship by the Yaddo Foundation. She accepted and spent several months at Saratoga Springs, New York, but eventually returned to Milledgeville. A few months later, O'Connor moved in with the Robert Fitzgerald family in Connecticut to complete *Wise Blood*. A serious illness, lupus erythematosus, redirected her life back to Milledgeville in 1951; there she would do the rest of her writing, and there she would die in 1964. From Milledgeville, she carried on a lively correspondence with friends, readers, critics, and her editors at Farrar and Giroux. When health permitted, she made trips to colleges and universities, many of them Roman Catholic schools, to discuss her work and literary art.

Analysis • Few postmodern writers have spoken as articulately and as compellingly about their craft and the relationship of their fiction to its perceived audience as did O'Connor. In her occasional prose, in her letters, and in her book reviews, O'Connor evinced an uncommonly perceptive grasp of her readers and the society in which they lived. Addressing the children of a demythologized and desacralized century, she confronted boldly the rancor and apathy with which modern culture meets the religious and the supernatural. To shake and sharpen the sensibilities of a culture made lethargic by the heritage of American civil religion, she turned to shock, to the literally awful and the grotesque, to proclaim her gospel: "To the hard of hearing you shout, and for the almost-blind you draw large and startling figures."

The underlying premise that informs all of O'Connor's fiction, and especially her two novels, *Wise Blood* and *The Violent Bear It Away*, is that men and women, as they are, are not *whole*. This "wholeness," lost in Eden, is now embodied and supplied to humans freely in the person of the incarnate Son of God. In order to make this now familiar theme "seeable" and creditable to her readers, O'Connor was led to herald a Christ who bore little resemblance to the "gentle Jesus, meek and mild" of childhood hymnody. Her Christ is a tiger who disturbs and terrorizes. One thinks especially of Hazel Motes, evangelist of the "Church of Christ without Christ" in *Wise Blood*, who fights ferociously to avoid that Jesus "in the back of his mind, a wild, ragged figure motioning to him to turn around and come off into the dark where he was not sure of his footing, where he might be walking on water and not know it and suddenly know it and drown."

Motes is a child of the fundamentalist South, but in O'Connor's economy, he is also Everyman; those who refuse Christ's offer to help them, force Him to haunt them. O'Connor used sudden death, disease, or trauma to depict the devastating encounter with Christ that must occur before one can be truly alive in this world. Worse things than mere death can befall a person made in God's image; her characters more often than not must be brought to the brink of crisis or death to see themselves as they are: in dire need of repentance and grace. In O'Connor's view, humankind did not accidentally stumble into rebellion against God; each man or woman deliberately chooses to do so. Consequently, she records with merciless precision the rationalizations of her protagonists, stripping them bare of their pretensions of goodness and innocence. She endeavored to confront her readers with the full scandal of Christianity. Those O'Connor characters who attempt to redeem themselves with arrant scientism or sheer intellectualism meet a savage Savior—manifested in a bull, a haunting prophecy, or a terrifying vision—who will not release them until they confess Him or utterly denounce Him.

For O'Connor, there was no middle ground, no neutral corner; all who are not with Him are against Him. Her narrative voice had little room for authorial compassion or tenderness. Relentlessly exposing human pride, avarice, and weakness, she agreed with writer C. S. Lewis that all things that are not eternal are eternally out of date. Western culture was already too sentimental, too complacent about Christ and Christianity; her mission was to pound on the table, to cast the moneychangers—sacred or secular—out of the literary temple.

One must ask how O'Connor avoided mere tractarianism, as her continuing popularity among critics and ubiquity in college literature anthologies attest she did. Part of the answer is that she frankly confronted the tenuous relationships that exist among audience, medium, story, and craft. It was her genius to lead her readers through and from the seemingly mundane and ordinary to a vision of reality as sacramental, as always pointing to a divine presence in human activity:

> When I write a novel in which the central action is baptism, I am aware that for a majority of my readers, baptism is a meaningless rite . . . so I have to see that this baptism carries enough awe and mystery to jar the reader into some kind of emotional recognition of its significance.

Her fiction strips away the jaded images of the faith, forcing a dynamic confrontation with the gospel as it is played out in the lives of professed believers and as it is rejected by the worldly wise. As the reader follows Hazel Motes or Francis Marion Tarwater on his journey to belief, he is confronted with grace—a grace that enlarges his perception of the world, enabling him to see both the natural and the supernatural anew, to both discover and retrieve deeper images of the *real*. As O'Connor states it, this journey frequently entails "an action in which the devil has been the unwilling instrument of grace. This is not a piece of knowledge that I consciously put into my stories; it is a discovery that I get out of them." It is this "awful rowing toward God" that is chronicled in O'Connor's two novels, *Wise Blood* and *The Violent Bear It Away.*

Wise Blood • Hazel Motes, the protagonist of *Wise Blood*, is, O'Connor says, a "Christian *malgré lui*," a believer in spite of himself, a harried wayfarer who has been displaced from Eastrod, Tennessee, and from the religious life of the South. That religious life is distinctively Protestant, the religion of a South of beleaguered prophets and street-corner preachers, a South haunted by Jesus and by a theological definition of humankind's identity and destiny. Motes is determined to escape salvation and anything that smacks of supernatural origin. Like Francis Marion Tarwater in *The Violent Bear It Away*, Motes's story is a reverse *Bildungsroman*, a novel of an antiquest in which the protagonist tries to *avoid*, rather than *seek*, his destiny.

O'Connor maintained that *Wise Blood* is a "comic novel," and nonetheless so because it deals with "matters of life and death." Though many readers try to locate the integrity of Motes in his vigorous struggle to escape that "ragged figure moving from tree to tree in the back of his mind," O'Connor avers: "His integrity lies in his not being able to [escape] it." His attempted flight from Jesus begins on the train to Taulkinham. Discharged from military service, Motes parries with a Mrs. Hitchcock, challenging her claim to redemption. "If you've been redeemed," Motes snaps, "I wouldn't want to be." Later, he exclaims to no one in particular, "Do you think I believe in Jesus? . . . Well, I wouldn't even if He existed. Even if He was on this train." Motes has determined that the way to avoid Jesus is to avoid sin; one who is not a sinner needs no redemption—he is already "clean"—if he is free from transgression. This "freedom," however, does not mean that Motes can avoid becoming a preacher. When he first reaches the city and decides to look up Miss Leora Watts—who owns the "Friendliest Bed in Town"—both she and the cabdriver who brings him there accuse him of being a preacher; he simply looks the part.

Very soon, Motes encounters some potential disciples: Enoch Emery, who wants to help him find a "new Jesus," and Sabbath Lily Hawks, the lustful daughter of a street preacher who feigns blindness. Following Sabbath and her father in order to ridicule their shallow evangelism, Motes declares that he will start a new church, a church *without* Christ. "I don't need Jesus," he tells the crowd gathering about him, "I got Leora Watts." Motes's obsession with the Hawks duo leads him to drive around the city in his beat-up Essex. His desperate flight from belief compels him to hound Asa Hawks, confronting him with the strange fact of his blindness—if Jesus is real, then why does He not heal His servants? Motes is tortured by his lack of a theodicy, a defense of God's absence; his only solace is to throw himself into his own "ministry": street-side preaching of the "Church of Christ without Christ" from the hood of his Essex.

Motes's nightly forays into sermonizing yield only one "convert," a would-be Aaron to Motes's Moses, Onnie Jay Holy—a slick packager of religion and faith who knows a money-making scam when he sees it. Crediting Motes-the-prophet with changing his life, Holy drowns out the frustrated antipreacher, who learns to speak the truth in spite of himself: "Listen!" Motes screams. "It don't cost you any money to know the truth!" It is at this point that O'Connor's protagonist has begun his inexorable trek toward recognizing his true state and the call of God. When Enoch Emery answers Motes's call for a "new Jesus" by stealing a mummified pygmy from a local museum and delivering it to the now domesticated Sabbath Lily Hawks, the reader is introduced to what Caroline Gordon called "the unholy family." Slinking into Motes's room, Sabbath introduces the mummy as their child. Sensing the blasphemy of the moment, Motes seizes the mummy and crushes it against the wall. The prophet must now leave this desecrated place and search for a new city in which he can begin his ministry afresh. Before he can leave, however, he must confront a false prophet— hired by Hoover Shoats, née Onnie Jay Holy—who has supplanted him on the streets of Taulkinham. Following him out onto a lonely road, Motes first knocks his car into the ditch and then runs over his counterpart, killing him and thus carrying out the Old Testament vengeance against false prophets.

From here, Motes almost inevitably heads for his own Calvary, his own "death unto life": The words of Jesus in Matthew 5:29, "And if thy right eye offend thee, pluck it out," are taken literally. Motes blinds himself so that he can see with a spiritual vision which bogus believers such as Asa Hawks and Hoover Shoats can never attain. He is fully focused now; there is no intent to escape or flee. His landlady, Mrs. Flood, represents the kind of "Christian" O'Connor loved to contrast with her dramatic, utterly committed antisaints such as Hazel Motes, the Misfit in "A Good Man Is Hard to Find," and Manley Pointer in "Good Country People." She cannot fathom Motes's sudden devotion—which extended to the bearing of the marks of Christ on his body: "I'm as good, Mr. Motes, not believing in Jesus as many a one that does," she boastfully proclaims. When she sees the barbed wire wrapped around his chest, she exclaims, "There's no reason for it. People have quit doing it." His reply, anthem and testimony for all latter-day believers, seals his fate: "They ain't quit doing it as long as I'm doing it." Motes's death is as anticlimactic as Christ's; the policemen who discover him in the drainage ditch, like the soldiers at the foot of the cross who bargain for Christ's robe, mouth inanities and treat Motes as a troublesome derelict, quite worthy of being put out of his misery.

The story of Hazel Motes is the tale of one of God's creatures and his struggle with the fundamental choice to serve God or deny Him. O'Connor's avowed purpose was to "deepen the mystery of free will," which is not the war between one will and another but of "many wills conflicting in one man." In *Wise Blood*, whose title comes from Enoch Emery's claim to "know things" because of his ancestral blood, O'Connor has created a parable of twentieth century man's inner debate over God's existence and presence in the modern world. It is ironic, although not too surprising, that O'Connor's Christian readers sometimes responded less enthusiastically to her achievement than did her nonreligious readers. Such a response was simply a corroboration of O'Connor's perceptions regarding the state of belief in postwar America.

The Violent Bear It Away • In her second novel, *The Violent Bear It Away*, written some ten years after she had originally begun *Wise Blood*, O'Connor once again returned to the theme of the antiquest, this time with a protagonist who tries to escape the daunting prophecy of his great-uncle. The title comes from an ambiguous passage found in Matthew 11:12: "From the days of John the Baptist until now, the kingdom of heaven suffereth violence and the violent bear it away." It is the dual message of this scripture that, in part, gives the novel its underlying power as still another O'Connor portrayal of the conflict of wills within man, a conflict of reason tempered with godly knowledge and an uncritical, gullible trust in the scientific method. The passage suggests, first, that with the coming of the promised Messiah, humankind can receive the kingdom of God; second, it suggests that there remain calloused and unprincipled unbelievers who will seek to bar the faithful from entering that hallowed ground. These two opposing forces are focused in the protagonist and antagonist of the novel: Francis Marion Tarwater and Rayber the schoolteacher.

Mason Tarwater had reared his nephew, Francis, to be "more than a Christian, a prophet." His prophetic task consisted of two matters: First, he was to make sure that the elder Tarwater had a proper burial, his gravesite marked by a cross; second, he was to baptize Bishop, the "dimwitted child" of Rayber. Mason had earlier tried to rear Rayber as a prophet, too, but he encountered a resistance that eventually turned into a vigorously antireligious posture. Mason had finally broken off all relations with Rayber after the latter wrote a psychoanalysis of Tarwater for a "schoolteacher's magazine" that mocked his beliefs. Francis Tarwater, also, does not come easily to his prophetic office. At his great-uncle's death, he abandons the old man and burns down his house, balking at his obsession with Jesus; the choice is not between "Jesus and the devil," he resolves—"it's Jesus or me." Francis, like Hazel Motes, is nevertheless haunted by the presence of Jesus: "Jesus? He felt a terrible disappointment in that conclusion, a dread that it was true." He can no more escape his destiny than Motes could; it is "hidden in the blood."

Rayber is a familiar O'Connor character type, the rationalist who attempts to explain away religion as illusion or delusion. He will have no part of the Tarwaters' prophetic ministry. Just as the sense of sight was a potent symbol in *Wise Blood*, O'Connor here uses the sense of hearing, Rayber's need for a hearing aid, to underscore his spiritual ignorance: "Do you think in the box," Francis Tarwater ridiculed, "or do you think in your head?" The religious people of Rayber's acquaintance—the Tarwaters, the Carmody family—have all been "exploited" people, bilked by the foolish rhetoric of insane cadgers and shysters. However, Rayber's will is not powerful enough to withstand the force of a prophet of God. True to his call, Francis must drown Bishop in baptism, the enduring Christian symbol of new life from death.

O'Connor organized the events of this novel into three distinct parts. Part 1 reveals the eccentric life of the prophet; as Elijah the Old Testament prophet gave his mantle to the younger Elisha, so Mason Tarwater passes his own "burden" to his charge. Part 2 depicts Francis Tarwater's struggle to free himself, like a latter-day Jonah, from the burden laid upon him; here the city is emblematic of all the distractions and temptations that might deter him from his task. Part 3 relates the purification and cleansing of the prophet who encounters his burning bush and receives his commission to "warn the children of God of the terrible speed of mercy" in the "dark city" beyond him.

The Violent Bear It Away more fully develops themes O'Connor explored in such short stories as "The Enduring Chill," "The Artificial Nigger," "Good Country People," and "The Lame Shall Enter First." Her consistent focus is placed upon the human will tortured by indecision, clouded by technology, and rendered impotent by its flight from knowledge of God. The only remedy offered is the laying down of weapons and the complete surrender of the soul. Francis Tarwater and Hazel Motes both discover that their only rest from this ordeal is acquiescence to the will of God.

Throughout her fiction, O'Connor defamiliarized the all-too-familiar concepts of conversion and discipleship and articulated the shallow view of Christ lurking behind modern faith. She wanted her readers to escape the jaundiced vision of their own time. In *Mystery and Manners*, she paralleled her task with that of St. Cyril of Jerusalem, who, in instructing catechumens, warned them of passing by the dragon on their way to the Father of Souls:

> No matter what form the dragon may take, it is of this mysterious passage past him, or into his jaws, that stories of any depth will always be concerned to tell, and this being the case, it requires considerable courage at any time, in any country, not to turn away from the storyteller.

O'Connor refused to turn away from the dragon or the storyteller, and she asked of her readers the same courage.

Bruce L. Edwards, Jr.

Other major works

SHORT FICTION: *A Good Man Is Hard to Find,* 1955; "Good Country People," 1955; "Revelation," 1964; *Everything That Rises Must Converge,* 1965; *The Complete Stories,* 1971.

NONFICTION: *Mystery and Manners,* 1969; *The Habit of Being: Letters,* 1979; *The Presence of Grace,* 1983; *The Correspondence of Flannery O'Connor and Brainard Cheneys,* 1986.

MISCELLANEOUS: *Collected Works,* 1988.

Bibliography

Caruso, Teresa, ed. *"On the Subject of the Feminist Business": Re-reading Flannery O'Connor.* New York: Peter Lang, 2004. Collection of critical essays exploring feminist themes in O'Connor's writings.

Cash, Jean W. *Flannery O'Connor: A Life.* University of Tennessee, 2002. A painstakingly researched portrait of O'Connor. Includes a bibliography and an index.

Desmond, John F. *Risen Sons: Flannery O'Connor's Vision of History.* Athens: University of Georgia Press, 1987. Desmond's argument is that O'Connor's fictions reenact Christian history and Roman Catholic theology through an art O'Connor herself saw as an "incarnational act." Discussing several major stories and the two novels, the book focuses on the metaphysical and the Christian historical vision as observed through reading O'Connor's fiction and emphasizes that *The Violent Bear It Away* represents the fullest development of her vision. Includes an extensive bibliography and useful endnotes.

Enjolras, Laurence. *Flannery O'Connor's Characters.* Lanham, Md.: University Press of America, 1998. Chapters on O'Connor's descriptions of the body, of wicked children, of "conceited, self-righteous Christians," of "intellectuals and would-be artists." Includes notes and bibliography.

Lake, Christina Bieber. *The Incarnational Art of Flannery O'Connor.* Macon, Ga.: Mercer University Press, 2005. Study of O'Connor's use of religious incarnation themes in her writings.

O'Gorman, Farrell. *Peculiar Crossroads: Flannery O'Connor, Walker Percy, and Catholic Vision in Postwar Southern Fiction.* Baton Rouge: Louisiana State University Press, 2004. Comparative study of O'Connor and Percy as southern writers who were devout Roman Catholics.

Orvell, Miles. *Flannery O'Connor: An Introduction.* Jackson: University Press of Mississippi, 1991. Chapters on the novels as well as explorations of O'Connor's treatment of the South, of belief, of art, of the American romance tradition, of prophets and failed prophets, and of comedy. Appendixes include a chronological list of the fiction, book reviews by Flannery O'Connor, notes, and bibliography.

Robillard, Douglas, Jr. *The Critical Response to Flannery O'Connor.* Westport, Conn.: Praeger, 2004. Includes contemporary reactions to O'Connor's works and scholarly and academic analyses of her work by various critics.

Seel, Cynthia L. *Ritual Performance in the Fiction of Flannery O'Connor.* Rochester, N.Y.: Camden House, 2001. A Jungian approach to the religious imagery and themes in the work of the novelist.

Spivey, Ted R. *Flannery O'Connor: The Woman, the Thinker, the Visionary.* Macon, Ga.: Mercer University Press, 1995. Attempts to understand O'Connor first as a southerner, then as a modernist intellect, and finally as a visionary thinker. Argues that O'Connor reflects the personal and social issues of the last decades of the twentieth century.

Walters, Dorothy. *Flannery O'Connor.* Boston: Twayne, 1973. This effective but early introduction to the works of O'Connor includes analyses of the short fiction and the novels. Walters argues perceptively and conventionally that O'Connor was predominantly a religious writer whose works can be classified as Christian tragicomedy. Walters also makes some useful observations about O'Connor's connections with earlier literary traditions. Includes a chronology of O'Connor's life, useful endnotes, and a select bibliography.

Westling, Louise Hutchings. *Sacred Groves and Ravaged Gardens: The Fiction of Eudora Welty, Carson McCullers, and Flannery O'Connor.* Athens: University of Georgia Press, 1985. A useful book for those interested in critical perspectives other than religious readings of O'Connor's fiction as well as for those curious about O'Connor's relationship with Eudora Welty and Carson McCullers, two of her rivals as masters of short fiction. This book is the first feminist study of O'Connor's fiction. Westling discusses the female characters and emphasizes that O'Connor often shows female protagonists as victims of male antagonists. Contains an extensive bibliography as well as useful endnotes.